$24.95

4-12-83

WESTERN FILMS

By Brian Garfield:

Nonfiction:
THE THOUSAND-MILE WAR: World War II in Alaska & the Aleutians
I, WITNESS: True Personal Encounters with Crime (Ed.)

Fiction:
CHECKPOINT CHARLIE
THE PALADIN
WILD TIMES
RECOIL
DEATH SENTENCE
HOPSCOTCH
THE ROMANOV SUCCESSION
KOLCHAK'S GOLD
THE THREEPERSONS HUNT
TRIPWIRE
GANGWAY! (with Donald E. Westlake)
DEATH WISH
LINE OF SUCCESSION
DEEP COVER
RELENTLESS
THE LAST HARD MEN
SWEENY'S HONOR
SLIPHAMMER
BUGLE AND SPUR
ARIZONA
THE VANQUISHED

Films based on stories or characters created by Brian Garfield:
DEATH WISH
THE LAST HARD MEN
RELENTLESS
WILD TIMES
SCRIMSHAW
HOPSCOTCH (also co-screenwriter and associate producer)
DEATH WISH II
FEAR IN A HANDFUL OF DUST

WESTERN FILMS

FILMS

A COMPLETE GUIDE

BRIAN GARFIELD

RAWSON ASSOCIATES
New York

Portions of Chapter 2 appeared, in somewhat different form, in the essay "The Western" in the May 1976 issue of *Fiction* magazine; copyright © 1976 by Brian Garfield, and reprinted herein by permission of the author. Portions of Chapter 5 appeared, in somewhat different form, in the essay " 'The Wild Bunch' Revisited" in the Spring 1980 issue of *The Armchair Detective;* copyright © 1980 by Brian Garfield, and reprinted herein by permission of the author.

Library of Congress Cataloging in Publication Data

Garfield, Brian, 1939–
    Western films.

    Bibliography: p.
    1. Western films—Dictionaries.   I. Title.
PN1995.9.W4G3   791.43′09′093278   81–48406
ISBN: 0-89256-218-8   AACR2

Composition by American–Stratford Graphic Services, Inc., Brattleboro, Vermont
Printed and bound by Halliday Lithograph Corporation, West Hanover, Massachusetts

Book design by Jacques Chazaud

10 9 8 7 6 5 4 3 2 1

First Edition

CONTENTS

TRIBUTE

Frederick D. Glidden. 1908–1975. Pseudonym: Luke Short.

Author of: **Ramrod, Blood on the Moon, Station West, Ambush, Dead Freight for Paiute, Vengeance Valley, Silver Rock, Coroner Creek, Ride the Man Down.**

All of them were filmed. Most of the films were superior; at least two were outstanding, because he was the consummate Western storyteller.

He was a man to whom good and evil were absolutes but men and women were not.

This book is dedicated to the memory of Fred Glidden: a good writer and a good man.

ACKNOWLEDGMENTS

Ace photographer Diana Bryant was this project's indispensable researcher; somehow she found many needed facts in hard-to-find sources. She deserves great thanks for her substantial contributions to this guide.

Critical assistance and specific facts regarding screenplays she wrote and filmmakers with whom she worked have been provided by the author's great friend Mary McCall, Jr., a former president of the Council of the Writers Guild of America, a fine writer, and a grand lady for whose gracious assistance I am deeply grateful.

*

Even before I visited my first movie set at the age of fourteen (Joel McCrea's **Lone Hand**, in 1953, on location in Colorado) I was enamored of Western movies and the people who made them. To all the moviemakers, writers and Westerners with whom I have worked, or kibitzed, or shared time and friendship, my profound admiration and thanks. Many of their names appear in this book.

I owe thanks to Warren Beatty and Cliff Robertson, both of whom contributed greatly to the movie of **Hopscotch**; I am only sorry their contributions were not acknowledged in the film itself, or its credits.

For varying reasons I should like especially to express my thanks and deep affection toward Abby Adams, Mort Abrahams, Henry Wilson Allen, Jim and Eileen Allen, Harry Atwood, Derek Ball, Lowyd and Debbie Ballantyne, Donald Balluck, Ned Beatty, Jonathan Bernstein, Miriam Biddelman, Lynn Biederstadt, Lawrence Block, Ian and Jean Botley, Harry Carey, Jr., Patrick Clayton, Daniel Coelho, Richard Compton, John Copeland, Oliver and Alyce Cox, Sidney Craig, William Creber, Harry and Dorothy Salisbury Davis, John and Greta Davis, Douglas Dirkson, Charles E. Drimal, Sr., Chuck Drimal, Sam Elliott, J. Donald Everitt, Jose and Stella Ferrer, Bryan Forbes, Michael Frank, Lucy Freeman, Monroe Friedman, Philip Friedman, George and Bette Garfield, Gwynne Glenn, Kendall Giler, Joe and Dori Gores, Bina Grossblat, James B. Harris, Bob Hartman, Charlton Heston, Pat Hingle, Arthur Ibbetson, John Jainchill, Ben Johnson, Dan and Hannah Johnson, Edward and Elaine Kemp, Harold and Elaine King, Edie and Ely

Landau, Hal Landers, Tony Lane, Carolyn Lefcourt, Alan MacLean, Walter Matthau, Bettye McCartt, Andrew V. McLaglen, Marcia Menter, David Morrell, Henry Morrison, Ronald Neame, Douglas Netter, Chet and Betty O'Brien, Frances O'Brien, John Paganelli, Otto and Carolyn Penzler, Otto Plaschkes, Pat Rees, Sam and Hilda Rolfe, Thomas V. Ruta, Timothy Scott, Sheridan Sellers, Walter Seltzer, Les Sheldon, Paul and Ruth Stern, Jeff and Jonathan Sweet, Russ Thacher, Ross and Rosalie Thomas, Thomas and Jane Thompson, Sharon Tipsword, George Valkenburgh, Ed Victor, Jim Wade, Jack Wallace, Jesse Wayne, Jay Werner, Donald E. Westlake, Shan Willson, and James and Gillian Wright.

Finally, very special thanks and love and admiration to that grand gent and fine writer William R. Cox—colleague, mentor and friend.

PREFACE

This guide to Western movies tries to provide in one volume a critical encyclopedia of all "A" Western features shown in the United States since the advent of talkies. The guide lists films alphabetically from **Abilene Town** to **Zandy's Bride**; each listing provides credits, information and commentary.

The scope of coverage is not limited strictly to traditional horse opera. There is no adequate definition of the term "Western"—the guidelines for inclusion in a book like this one must be arbitrary. Films like **Fort Ti** and **Seminole** are listed despite their Eastern settings because their themes mark their genre. There are American-made transplants and European-made oaters; gaucho movies, Westerns filmed in Spain by Italians or in Yugoslavia by Germans, outdoor Western-style adventures filmed or set in South Africa, Australia, Latin America and the Far North.

Additionally, and perhaps more tenuously, the guide lists certain films that are set in the West or flavored by Western trappings but are not Westerns in the usual sense: **The Misfits** and **The Grapes of Wrath** are included, for example; a note in the commentaries explains why. **Bus Stop** and **East of Eden**, however, were not sufficiently Western to merit inclusion. Nor does the book attempt to corral such subgenres as logging movies (**Come and Get It**) and oil wildcatting movies (**Boom Town**). These, though set in the American West, do not seem sufficiently Western in characterization or mythic flavor to warrant discussion here.

Westerns, however defined, are the subject of this guide. But its coverage is limited to "A" features. It gives little attention to the "B" oaters released prior to 1955 in the innumerable series identified with such Saturday matinee heroes as Ken Maynard, Gene Autry, Roy Rogers, Bob Steele or Lash LaRue. Chapter Four summarizes the history of the "B" Western (and the titles of John Wayne's 42 "B" Westerns, filmed in the 1930s and released by several Poverty Row studios, are listed therein) but the reader will find no Eddie Dew or Whip Wilson oaters in the main listings of this guide. Other books have covered those already.

In the movie industry's jargon a "B" film, or programmer, was a low-budget film designed for the lower ("B") half of a double-feature program or as the Saturday afternoon feature of a children's matinee. "B" films were rented to theatre chains by distributors at a flat rate. (By contrast, "A" features were distributed on the basis of a percentage of box-office income.) Most "B" pictures were churned out as segments of continuing series—eight or twelve a year—much like present day TV programs, employing assembly lines of writers, actors and crews. Often scenes for several movies in a series would be filmed simultaneously in order to make economical use of actors or sets.

Such programmers, along with the twelve- and sixteen-chapter serials, are outside the scope of this guide, although a few exceptional or notable examples have found their way into the listings.

Some students insist that the "B" Western died in 1953, its last product supposedly having been Allied Artists' **Two Guns and a Badge**, a dreary Wayne Morris vehicle. It may have been the last programmer filmed in that series but there is often a distinction between the time of a film's making and the time of its release. Another Wayne Morris oater, **The Desperado,** wasn't released until 1954, and in any case Allied Artists (formerly Monogram Pictures) continued releasing its William Elliott programmers into 1954; one of the last Elliott Westerns was **The Forty-Niners**. Quibbling aside, however, the fact remains that the "B" pictures, officially and technically, were dead by late 1954.

There is a terrible sameness about most "B" Western pictures. Enthusiasts and apologists insist that they not be dismissed out of hand, and it is true that the occasional programmer was artistically or technically superior to many "A" features, but the mass of "B" oaters is a trite trifle, of interest mainly to historians, stunt-action fans and nostalgic programmer-buffs.

Hundreds of cheap Westerns have been released in the years since the demise of the old "B" units. Small independent filmmakers for sixty years have specialized in Westerns for obvious reasons of economy. The spaghetti, sauerkraut and matzo-ball oaters of the 1960s and 1970s (Italian, German and Israeli Westerns), along with those made for U.S. television, took the place of the "B" films. Yet their quality varies a great deal and therefore this guide tries to give at least token coverage to as many such films as it can, although most of them appear in the appendices of abbreviated listings that follow the main guide.

Certain older films are not possible to track down today. Many prints and quite a few negatives have been destroyed, sometimes deliberately. And it just hasn't been possible to root out every ephemeral European or TV horse-opera ever filmed. Inevitably the guide must have missed quite a number of them. But such films lie on the periphery of the genre. The absence of a few of them should not void this book's claim to providing a virtually complete dossier on every significant "A" Western released since the talkies arrived in the late 1920s.

*

This volume discusses nearly two thousand films and it would be tedious and repetitive to preface each commentary with the phrase "in my opinion" but the reader must bear in mind the implicit pervasiveness of that phrase. This is a book of personal opinions; an opinionated book, if you prefer.

The guide tries to approach the Western on its own terms. Film criticism is an infant discipline, and there are few established criteria other than those that can be defined vaguely under the broad headings of taste and technical understanding and general experience of art. We are removed from early movies far enough to think of them in historical terms, and there has been a proliferation of overblown posturings by enthusiasts who attempt to bestow artistic importance on every sort of cinematic triviality from Abbott & Costello and Godzilla to Monogram Pictures and Zorro serials. Certainly it is useful to preserve such items—but the sensible archaeologist learns to treat yesterday's trash as yesterday's trash. Possibly a great deal can be learned from it but no amount of enthusiasm can convert it into art.

Therefore a forewarning may be necessary: although this guide often may treat honest little oaters with more respect than it tenders to pretentious cinematic dirigibles, that respect must be tempered by a realistic understanding of the distinction between the professionalism that entertains and the art that inspires. I enjoy good entertainments on their own terms. If I didn't, I would not have set out to write this book. But I can't pretend that a solid little movie like **Ramrod** is anything more than a momentary diversion. Not too many Westerns are indisputably important works of art. A fair number are good entertainments well crafted, happily diverting, keenly exciting, sometimes thoroughly satisfying and even provocative—but there's a limit to how seriously they should be taken.

Unhappily in the 1950s a number of self-important schools of film criticism emerged, led by the French magazine *Cahiers du Cinema,* in which old hack directors were lauded as "auteurs." The critic Benoit-Levy coined the term "auteur" in the 1940s but it didn't become the basis for an entire school of inflated critical attitudinizing until *Cahiers* came along a decade later; since then we have seen a relentless ramification of the *Cahiers* influence, to the point where Jerry Lewis is equated with Charlie Chaplin, and terms like "Hawksian"—presumably denoting qualities found solely in films directed by Howard Hawks—are flung recklessly about in disregard of the fact that nearly all Hollywood directors were hired hands on assembly-line productions and often had little control over scripts, casts or production aspects of "their" films. Pushing reality aside, the auteur theorists lionized the better directors as if they were artistic geniuses of great metaphysical significance, to be compared straight-facedly with the likes of Shakespeare, Michelangelo and Beethoven. In time these sophomoric *hommages* began to have a fatal effect on the one excellence the filmmakers had previously had: their splendid professional craftsmanship.

The *Cahiers* critics approached the cinema of mass entertainment in highflown artistic terms and their influence has been distressing at best: its result has been more or less what you would imagine might happen if a fast-food fry cook were told repeatedly that he was a culinary genius. Directors, writers, actors, cameramen and producers have been encouraged to think self-consciously of their reputations as creative artists rather than as artisans. The fry cooks of the movies are serving up McDonald's hamburgers disguised as chateaubriand. With a distressing number of movies, half-witted chaotic amateurism, and undisciplined self-expression, have become the norm. The movie industry has learned, to everyone's detriment, that it is much easier to fake art than it is to fake professionalism.

Such fakery will remain with us so long as critics are willing to be fooled by it, and critics frequently are eager to be taken in; film critics are especially gullible since their discipline is young and still lacks touchstones.

The problem is not so much that lousy movies are made. Lousy movies always will be with us. The problem begins when lousy movies are taken seriously. I confess a rash impatience whenever I encounter the sort of mind that holds **Little Big Man** to be anything more than a pretentious arty work of distasteful parody. Admittedly it's funny here and there, and well acted, but it is also anachronistic, dishonest and clumsily heavy-footed.

If you are accustomed to the pontifications of the popular schools of film criticism you may find this book iconoclastic; I hope you do; in any case you won't find it representative of other works.

*

I grew up in Arizona with movies that weren't yet "films" or "cinema." It was a rare week when a Rod Cameron or Randolph Scott oater wasn't playing at the Lyric or the State Theatre in Tucson. The Saturday matinee Western was a standard rite of male adolescence.

In my teens I devoted half a dozen years to futile attempts to sell Western stories to pulp magazines under the wing and tutelage of Fred ("Luke Short") Glidden and other yarnspinners. I did part of my growing up on Southwestern cattle ranches, and listened with great naive excitement to the tales of the old-timers. My first published novel was a highly derivative Western of the kind that an auteuriste critic might describe as "hommage" to Luke Short. Like many other Westerns I wrote in the 1960s it is long out of print and I mean it to stay that way. But it was a necessary and instructive step in a long professional apprenticeship that continues to this day.

My first film was produced in 1974; there have been several more since then—about one a year—and three of them have been Westerns, and I have worked on the sets of three films including two of the Westerns (**The Last Hard Men** and **Wild Times**), and I've moved into film production with my own company, partly in an effort to maintain some degree of control over the way my stories are filmed. **Hopscotch** (1980) was an Edie & Ely Landau production, but I was an associate producer and my company, Shan Productions, Inc., co-released the film with the Landaus and IFI. As this book goes to press we are preparing further films.

The point I wish to make is that while it may not be necessary that one be a Westerner and a writer-producer of films to criticize the Western movie genre, at least it may be helpful in providing one with a place to stand and a basis for knowledgeable criticism. Half the critics whose work I've read don't seem to understand the difference in function between a cinematographer and a camera operator. It is hardly surprising, therefore, when they attribute to directors all sorts of contributions that may have been made by writers, producers, actors, department heads or technicians.

Furthermore, even the cinematically knowledgeable books about Westerns—written by French "nouvelle vague" critics, British "cineastes" or American film buffs who appear never to have ventured west of the Hudson River—reflect a surprising ignorance of the American tradition of folk mythology that is the essence of the Western.

*

This book tries to bridge that gulf between "cinema" and the Western. As we'll learn in subsequent chapters, the Western did not originate as a cinematic form, although its roots are in performance rather than literature. One cannot treat the Western movie separately from its progenitors—especially the Wild West Shows—without distorting one's comprehension of the nature of the genre: it would be like trying to discuss the art of painting without knowing anything about the aesthetics of color or design.

The Western—together with jazz, the musical comedy and the detective story—may be classified as an art form native to the United States. Of these the Western is most deeply rooted in basic American cultural mythology: it is the essential folklore of the culture. It is an art form but not an elitist one; it has its roots in primitive populist folk tales and it has been characterized accurately as a body of morality plays. Because it is directed toward an entire population, it therefore defines and reflects the character and standards of that population: it is the collective dream of a culture and it reflects the fears and hopes of that culture.

The Western is not the creation of a unique artist; it is the creation of a nation. The character of the Westerner—a generic archetype rather than an idiosyncratic individual—personifies a moral attitude. One can see quite easily that this character has changed markedly over the years. In tracing such changes, we trace the changes in ourselves. The Western is the American mirror.

1
THE
WESTERN

This volume—a part-time labor of love—has been in preparation for nearly ten years, during which the production of Western films has waxed and then waned. Movie genres are cyclical. A popular hit of any genre will be followed by imitators until they become threadbare and the audience is sated and the fashion dies for a while. Later, sometimes, it is revived.

After the flurry of popularity of spaghetti-style Westerns in the mid-1960s the genre sagged until 1976 when, briefly, there was another enthusiastic Hollywood leap back into the saddle. That one was partly an exercise in sentimental nostalgia, partly a trendy follow-the-leader gambit. Its leaders were big-budget films: **Breakheart Pass, Buffalo Bill and the Indians, The Missouri Breaks, The Outlaw Josey Wales, The Shootist, The White Buffalo**. The fact that major producers were gambling big money on those films encouraged lower-budget filmmakers to follow suit with such Westerns as **The Duchess and the Dirtwater Fox, From Noon till Three, The Great Scout and Cathouse Thursday**, my own **The Last Hard Men, Mustang Country** and **The Return of a Man Called Horse**.

Trouble was, nearly all of them were turkeys. Either they were bad films or they lost money or both. Only a few of them—**The Shootist** and **Mustang Country** and (sorry) **The Last Hard Men**—attempted to honor the line of their descent; the rest were parodies, farces, polemics or eccentricities of one kind or another.

It wasn't a great surprise, therefore, when the rebirth of 1976 lasted but a few months. Hollywood shied, flinched and fled the genre; perhaps the industry realized that its filmmakers had lost touch with the West and the Western. In any case virtually no significant Westerns appeared thereafter until the 1978–79 season when a couple of tentative attempts to revive the genre were released: **Goin' South, Comes a Horseman**. But these were even more dreary than the losers of 1976. Then came another lacklustre flock in 1980–81, with the disappointing **Tom Horn**, the anemic **The Long Riders**, the dreadful **The Legend of the Lone Ranger**, the minor **Cattle Annie and Little Britches**, the polemical **The Electric Horseman**, the flawed **Bronco Billy**, the rancid **Comin' at Ya** and the despicable **Heaven's Gate**.

The decline of the Western in the 1960s–1980s seemed more than just cyclical; it had a deathly aura. It was a time in which the Western appeared truly to have lost touch with its roots. The trouble with the Westerns of the 1970s and 1980s was simply that they weren't Westerns at all.

In some ways, until the onset of that decline, the Western appeared to change surprisingly little over its seventy-year lifespan. If one compares **The Great Train Robbery** of 1903 with John Wayne's **The Train Robbers** of 1973 one finds that the train is still robbed, the good guys still shoot it out with the bad guys, and a semblance of the old moral underpinnings still supports the structure. But the heart and spirit seem to have gone out of it; **The Train Robbers** is listless junk. The Western may not have died but certainly, from the vantage point of the 1980s, it appeared moribund.

The decline evidently began at the end of the 1950s. Why?

*

The earliest Western movies were the one-reelers of E. S. Porter and Broncho Billy Anderson. They were filmed in New Jersey and they reflected an Eastern conception of the West. But production soon moved to California; and an authenticity of settings, costumes, attitudes and behavior arrived with the movies of William S. Hart and Tom Mix.

For many years thereafter, Westerns were made mainly by Westerners. Admittedly Mix and his followers sported showy costumes and emphasized athletic stunts and childish stories; but in their way they were as honestly Western as Hart, with his presumably gritty "realism" (about which I'll say more in a moment). Mix's films merely reflected a different aspect of the real West: the cowboy's Saturday penchant for duding himself up and showing off; the circus aura of rodeos and Wild West Shows.

Mix, Ken Maynard, Tim McCoy and many other early cowboy heroes were real Westerners, as were their successors like Gary Cooper, Rod Cameron, Tex Ritter, Rex Allen and others at every level of Western movie entertainment. Still others, not born to the saddle, westernized themselves so thoroughly that—like religious converts—they became more native than the natives themselves. These were such "Westerners" as John Wayne, Randolph Scott, William Elliott and director John Ford.

For fifty years the production of Westerns was mainly in the hands of such artisans. Possibly their view of Western history was as distorted as the view held by the revisionist debunkers who succeeded them, but at least they were intimate with the traits, the folkways, the language, the attitudes of real Westerners.

That is why their films tend to be more honest than the newer "researched" Westerns. The earlier generation didn't need to do research: it was born of the West.

One need only compare **Frontier Marshal** (1939) with **Doc** (1971) to exemplify the difference.

Both films ostensibly render the story of lawman Wyatt Earp and his curious friendship with the outlaw Doc Holliday. In terms of documented fact it's probably a toss-up as to which of the two films is more inaccurate. (Wyatt Earp was never the marshal of anything, in actuality.) Yet **Frontier Marshal** satisfies and entertains, even after forty years (it was filmed only ten years after Earp's death), while **Doc** already seems ersatz and badly dated. It's empty, uninspired, tedious. It's not simply a bad Western; it's not a Western at all. It's a revisionist polemic spiced up with Freudian anachronisms, kinky sex and dimestore symbolisms.

Doc was written, directed and performed by a group of New Yorkers whose knowledge of myths appears (on the evidence of the film) to be as abysmally wrongheaded as their nihilistic attitude toward history. A film like **Doc**—self-expressive excrescence—tells us nothing about the West or Westerns, while it tells us too much about its makers: it's a vanity showcase for the attitudinizing of its writer, director and cast. Such is the legacy of *Cahiers du Cinema*.

After 1960 or so, there were alarmingly few Westerns that reflected any genuine feeling for the West. The new filmmakers' emotional and spiritual ignorance blighted the genre. One cannot impose sophisticated cynicism from the urban East, or Italianate passions of lust and orgiastic viciousness, on a deep-rooted pastoral tradition of heroic morality.

*

It is worth pausing for a moment, before we go any farther, to examine the question of "authenticity" in movies.

When reviewers pontificate on the visual authenticity of a hokum flick like **The Culpepper Cattle Company** they are being conned by an illusion; such films are no more realistic than were those of the days when Hollywood's Indians rode in suicidal circles around parked wagon trains, or when Hollywood's 1866 cowboys shot it out with 1894 Winchesters. Such details are superficial; their realism, or lack of it, hasn't much to do with the dramatic quality of a film. The real personalities of Wyatt Earp (a frontier pimp) or Billy the Kid (a buck-toothed delinquent) have nothing to do with the merits of the films that have been made about them; the Western is folklore and to talk of it in terms of exact "authentic" realism is pointless. That kind of realism has never been required of any fantasy-folklore genre.

What ought to concern critics, however, and what did concern moviemakers of the Hart-Ford-Cooper generations, was an authenticity of frontier spirit: an attempt honestly to reflect the attitudes and dreams of the West itself, and of Americans toward their West. In respecting the Western myth, these filmmakers weren't purveying realism at all, but their visions of Western spirit, attitudes and dreams were powerful and, indeed, authentic.

*

The Western movie was crystallized and codified during the first two decades of the twentieth century.

It was a crucial time in the shaping of our national character—a period of great ebullience and the hearty bluff defensiveness of uncertainty; Teddy Roosevelt set the tone.

The nation had destroyed the Indian civilizations, survived a brutal civil war, quintupled its area and acquired overseas territorial possessions in a single century; now for the first time it was emerging as a world power. If one could personify the United States at the turn of the century, the most apt image might have been that of John Wayne: a swaggering crude giant, towering, sometimes clumsy and slow but clever and tough and filled with a stubborn righteous sense of purpose.

Beginning with Broncho Billy Anderson and William S. Hart, the Western hero on the screen typified America's wistful vision of itself as standard bearer of morality for the world. Our folk heroes reflected the agrarian dreams of a rural nation: the mythology of Manifest Destiny. The good people were the salt-of-the-earth types, modest men of property, and the bad guys invariably were those who tried to take property away from them; and the hero was the loner—the tough skilled professional or the stubborn, good-willed, ham-fisted innocent—who protected the little people from the bad guys.

It was an image that didn't disappear entirely until the end of the 1950s: the loner who came from nowhere, riding free across a spacious dramatic landscape, personifying dignity and honor, defending these virtues against the creeping compromises of modern society.

(A few later films tried to recapture the image—1980's **The Electric Horseman** for example—but by then it seemed more wistful than vital, and the propaganda was laid on thicker than the drama.)

The villains invariably were bankers, rustlers, land-grabbing saloonkeepers or big ranchers who tried to take homesteads away from little ranchers. In all cases the bad guys—including the stereotyped Indians—had the same thematic function: they posed a threat to property or livelihood. They tried to prevent pioneers from settling the land or they tried to take land or cattle away from the settlers.

The ultimate expression of this hundred-year cycle of mythology may be **Shane** (1953), in which one finds all the fundamental aspects of the old myth firmly rooted in place. The sovereignty of the little people's property rights, and the messianic protectorate created by the hero, are the keys to **Shane** and to most of the mainstream Westerns before it. Compare, for example, **The Westerner** and **The Virginian** and William S. Hart's **Hell's Hinges**.

The agrarian dream was opposed naturally to anything urban. Country people tend to distrust city people; the Western reflects that xenophobia. The villain often was an Eastern sort of dude, clad in a black business suit and located in an urban-style office in the bank or the saloon's back room.

Except in the Indian-fighting Westerns (and sometimes even there) the conflict usually was between virtuous rural Westerners and sneaky effete Easterners; these characters represented the moral positions in the Western parable.

(In the Indian-fighting Westerns the villain often was an army officer or Indian agent from "back East" who either didn't understand frontier ways or was trying to steal the Indians' land; the Indians themselves, more often than not, were dupes rather than the principal villains, even in those days when society tended to treat them as heathen savages.)

When the nation began to urbanize, the Western responded by beginning to change its pattern. But the change was slow. The dream itself went sour soon after the Crash of 1929, but the Western didn't reflect it until nearly a decade later when the Depression could no longer be ignored. Then the heroic wagon-train pioneers of an earlier era became the defeated flivver refugees of **The Grapes of Wrath**, following the same path West toward hope, but this time dispiritedly.

With a changing society we began to encounter the moral ambiguities and sophistications of **The Ox-Bow Incident**, and although that movie was at least a decade ahead of its time, it is useful to compare it with the previous generation's **The Virginian** in which the act of lynching is regarded as a heroic although unpleasant necessity, or with the succeeding generation's **The Missouri Breaks** in which the same kind of lynching is now regarded as an ambivalent issue that may be right or wrong depending on one's shifting loyalties. In **The Ox-Bow Incident** the lynching (the central event of the film) is treated quite clearly as an act of evil. The attitudes of the participants are ambiguous, but the film itself takes a clear moral stance, unlike the shabby **The Missouri Breaks** which takes no stance at all, or **The Virginian**, which takes its stance on the other side of the question.

It would seem therefore that in half a century we came full circle, and then some, in our moral attitudes. And the Western reflected those shifts vividly.

By the late 1940s and the 1950s we were still trying to cling to the simplicities of earlier attitudes. Randolph Scott and Gary Cooper were still fighting evildoers and varmints, but it wasn't working quite so well any more. In **Red River** and **Duel in the Sun** and **The Sea of Grass** and **The Furies** we began to see the dark aspect of agrarian freedom—the tyranny of economic power—and in **Rio Grande** we saw John Wayne fight Indians just as he'd fought them in scores of earlier movies but now he was beginning to realize that the fight was a bloody tragedy instead of a triumph because the Indians weren't villains; they were victims.

(The movie's director, John Ford, carried this realization much farther in his later film **Cheyenne Autumn**, which he admitted was produced in the nature of a penance.)

The Western inevitably kept changing to fit the new society it had to serve. By the early 1950s we saw the shift keyed by such films as **The Gunfighter**, in which the "hero" is no longer a messianic savior of threatened little people; now he's just an aging fighter in existentialist isolation, brooding through his last hours while he waits for a punk kid to find him and kill him. Anarchy, a loss of roots, cynicism began to creep into the Western.

The same brooding sense of isolation characterized many of the more important Westerns of the midcentury period. No longer were we obsessed with the grandiose ambitions of Manifest Destiny; urbanization had reduced us to an ignoble struggle for survival—a sense that we were clinging to the planet by our fingernails. The sweeping empire-building sagas—**Western Union, Cimarron, Union Pacific**—gave way to tough gritty survival yarns: **The Naked Spur, From Hell to Texas, High Noon**. In the Western environment, a sense of hostility replaced the old sense of opportunity.

Yet, right through to the middle of the 1950s, the character of the Western hero remained stubbornly intact for the most part.

Beset by the complexities and problems of new sophistications and new cynicisms, the hero himself resisted change. One can see this conservative determination clearly in the chronology of Gary Cooper's screen roles in Westerns. From **The Virginian** (1929) to **The Westerner** (1940) to **High Noon** (1951), Cooper played a fairly constant character. Admittedly the character grew darker and more somber with age: the Virginian is a lighthearted practical jokester; the Westerner is still comical but has more of a conscience; Will Kane of Hadleyville is quite grim and scared. But the values for which these three Cooper heroes stood were constant: all the old-fashioned virtues of an agrarian tradition of chivalry. Cooper, in person, was a farm boy.

But then in his last decade Cooper appeared in several Westerns in which we saw him struggle with ever-increasing difficulty to come to grips with the elusive shifts in values that were taking place in the real world.

In **Garden of Evil** he was forced to defend a pack of greedy prospectors who didn't deserve protection.

In **Vera Cruz** he was tempted to steal a gold shipment.

In **Man of the West** he was cast (unconvincingly) as an ex-member of a vicious outlaw gang, now reformed.

In **They Came to Cordura**—an inquiry into the nature of courage—he played a soldier who'd been disgraced after committing an act of cowardice and who tried to find redemption by discovering the real meaning of courage; in so doing, he proved himself more courageous than anybody.

Finally, in his last Western, **The Hanging Tree**, we find Cooper playing a washed-up drunk who's lost his faith in everything; it takes compassion for a blind girl to bring him struggling back to a reaffirmation of the heroic aspirations of his youth.

Yet in his last Westerns Cooper still prevailed: he reconfirmed the old values. He died without having to deny the morality he'd represented on the screen for more than thirty years. Cooper's Westerner is still a poignant reminder of dreams that once had validity and vitality.

As audiences we always knew better than to take the old melodramas with literal seriousness. It is silly to pretend we've outgrown them; our reality never was on that level in the first place.

But superficially we've become more sophisticated: we no longer can put up with the conventions that became cliches through repetition, and there's no point making a reactionary plea for a return to the formulas of yesterday's fashions. Still, the Western worked well and honestly in its own time, up through to the end of Gary Cooper's life. Our sense of pleasure was stimulated by the films—it still can be, by the best of them—and more importantly, perhaps, they reinforced standards of morality to which we wanted to aspire.

But very shortly after Cooper's death in 1961 the world and the Western underwent savage changes. Our belief in heroic possibilities died with John F. Kennedy and the soldiers of Vietnam.

The Man Who Shot Liberty Valance—the last of John Ford's "classic" Westerns, released just a few months after Cooper's death—seemed quaint and anachronistic even then. Very quickly it was supplanted by the ruthless amoral brutalities of **A Fistful of Dollars**, which was filmed only two years later, although the two movies seem to have been created in different centuries. **Valance** was the last fluttering gasp of a dying school; it was tired and tedious and overlong, while **Dollars**, with its whiplash violence and undeniable excitement, caught the enthusiasms of jaded audiences. Of the two, **A Fistful of Dollars** is by far the more important film, because it destroyed all the handholds by which the old Western had clung to survival.

Dollars was the progenitor of the new Western; Clint Eastwood replaced Gary Cooper as the reigning Western star. (There is something of a physical resemblance, and Eastwood even played a character named "Cooper" in **Hang 'Em High**.)

The morality-play Western was dead. Mindless, heartless, the new Western was born.

*

The old romanticism wasn't replaced by realism, although that was the word the new-wave people used. It was replaced by a debunking, demythologizing anti-romanticism that was as unrealistic as what it replaced.

It also seemed to be a lot less enjoyable.

The new filmmakers took the fun out of the adventure movie. The Westerns of the two decades after Cooper's death stank of sophistry; they rarely gave either pleasure or challenge; they were glib, vulgar, didactic, often boring; they were without taste and often without the minimal capacity to entertain.

Audiences respond best to that which moves the heart as well as the intellect. It isn't enough for a film to be technically and stylistically superb or to be filled with sly, cynical jokes. If that were all we needed, then Robert Altman's **Buffalo Bill and the Indians** would have been a good movie. If we cannot care about the characters in a drama—if we can't really give a damn what happens to them—then the work is a failure. In the end this is why most "art films" are not art at all; they only try to look like it.

Tantalizing ambiguity is no substitute for human drama. Eccentricities and "personal statements" are not substitutes for story structure. Actorish improvisations are not substitutes for good writing. And movies are more than mere photography.

In its scramble toward pomposity and "relevance" the film art lost much of its spirit. Fad filmmakers of the '60s and '70s mistook effects for effectiveness; they seemed to prefer style to substance; they confused violence with action; when they made Westerns they behaved like funeral directors—they were pumping formaldehyde into the corpse to give it a naturalistic surface in the hope that nobody would notice the smell of putrefaction.

The embalming job succeeded for a while, but was exposed with the abortive 1980 release of the first (four-hour) version of Michael Cimino's horrible Western **Heaven's Gate**—the movie that came more perilously close to breaking Hollywood's back than had anything since **Cleopatra** two decades earlier.

Heaven's Gate is a sitting duck. It is such an easy target that one feels almost embarrassed to take potshots at it. It was a nightmare extravagance, the ultimate exercise in undisciplined amateurish self-indulgence on the part of an obscenely irresponsible corporation and an enthusiastic but incompetent young writer-director who seemed to know nothing about drama, professionalism or the West. That such an inept filmmaker could exist is not surprising; what is astonishing is the extent (reportedly approaching $50 million) to which he was indulged by the executives of United Artists who refused to pull the plug on his production after it exceeded its initial budget limit of about $12 million.

The film (in both its original elephantine version and the later cut-shorter version that was released in the spring of 1981) is inexcusably bad in all respects except the technical; its production values and photography admittedly are splendid, and this testifies to the fact that Hollywood still has the world's finest aggregation of film technicians. But too much of the industry's management is in the hands of bankers, accountants, parking-lot tycoons, former actors' agents and other businessmen who know nothing of entertainment, let alone art.

Of the operating heads of all the major studios and film companies in 1980–81, virtually none had ever actually produced, written, directed or otherwise been involved in the actual making of a motion picture.

The studio moguls who dominated Hollywood years ago have been denigrated as nickelodeon pitchmen, glove salesmen and tasteless rubes. Yet the Goldwyns, Selznicks, Warners and Yateses (and, yes, even the Mayers and Cohns) had one thing the present generation lacks: they liked movies.

They had a sort of self-respect; they had confidence in their own taste and judgment, rather than in the computerized results of box-office surveys or the flip pontifications of newspaper reviewers, or the cocaine-stoned Great Ideas of the wild new generation of enfants terrible. The old mogul's attitude was a simple one: "If I like the movie then the public will like it." They were populists; they identified themselves with their audiences; they were fighters.

They appreciated disciplined professionalism. None of them, certainly, would have tolerated the excesses of a **Heaven's Gate** or the amateurism of a Cimino.

The industry executives of the early 1980s no longer had that self-confidence, and in any case most of them weren't autonomous; a studio head who knows he'll lose his job if he makes a wrong decision is not likely to make many decisions at all, and the result is that the only films that were produced easily were low-budget genre pictures—horror movies, inane drug-culture comedies—that were virtually guaranteed to make money because they were so predictably derivative.

The new film bosses understood nothing about movies; they understood only balance sheets, deal-making and trends. If **Superman** is a hit, let's make films about all sorts of comic-strip heroes. If **Heaven's Gate** is a flop, let's not make any more Westerns. Apparently it didn't occur to the new moguls that **Heaven's Gate** failed because it was a bad Western, and not simply because it was a Western.

In fact, what I really find surprising is that amid the Philistine ignorance of the new Hollywood there still seems room for good filmmakers. We still have good filmmakers— quite a few of them. Their survival is encouraging for the future of the art. Yet by the early 1980s it seemed unlikely that any of them ever could create a new Great American Western; the climate simply didn't seem to be there for it.

*

The old-fashioned Western died with Gary Cooper. Its eulogies were two warm cinematic paeans that appeared shortly after his death: **Lonely Are the Brave** and **Ride the High Country**, both released in 1962.

In the two decades after them, we had virtually no Westerns that weren't characterized by pretentious artiness or self-conscious editorializing or excessive bloody violence or smirking parody.

During the '60s and the '70s new Westerns still occasionally stirred the public interest, but when these were bearable it was only because of the paucity of good competition. A handful of entertaining oaters like **Butch Cassidy and the Sundance Kid**, and one controversial masterwork like **The Wild Bunch**, were the exceptions that only emphasized the genre's general weariness and poverty of spirit in those decades.

Mostly the period was characterized by a fragmentation of the Western into dwindling subgenres. One group of films seemed to reflect a blind groping return toward the old cliches: these were most of John Wayne's later films and the rash of low-budget wilderness movies, many of them produced by ultra-right-wing companies, like **The Adventures of Frontier Fremont**. These were as simpleminded as TV series dramas.

Another category merely sneered: it viciously debunked whatever weary stereotypes remained from the old oaters. One found this wild striking-about in Westerns like **Doc** and **Dirty Little Billy** and **Heaven's Gate**—a kind of enraged anarchy, a mania to insult and debunk.

And there were still a few plodding middle-of-the-road formula Westerns that trudged exhaustedly on, with Glenn Ford or Robert Mitchum or Dean Martin or James Stewart. This category dwindled away toward the late 1970s, as the stars of that generation faded into retirement. Most of those pictures seemed to have the tongue tentatively poked into the cheek. They had nothing to say and nothing to add; it was sad to watch them go through the same tired old motions without inspiration or enthusiasm.

Then there were the cop-out satires like **Blazing Saddles** and **Hearts of the West**—some were sidesplittingly funny and some were duds but they had in common their tendency to ridicule the audience more than they ridiculed the Western: they seemed to reflect an assumption that audiences used to believe the myths literally.

*

The difficulty is this: the Western is a matter of character, and that character is a matter of morality. Western films after 1962 (with a few signal exceptions like **The Wild Bunch**) displayed neither character nor morality. For that reason I offer this book not so much as a summation of the story till now, but mainly as a fond and impassioned obituary notice for the Western movie. For all practical purposes it is dead, although conceivably it may be revived.

While it lasted, it was great fun.

2

THE

GENRE

The Western is an American folklore: a mythology, depending on fantasy rather than history. There never was a quick-draw showdown in the real West, and most of the other familiar trappings of the genre are equally fictitious.

Yet for generations the old folklore has maintained its appeal to audiences everywhere; and it seems there will always be a popular fascination with Westerns from **Stagecoach** to **Shane**. Paperback Western novels by Zane Grey, Max Brand and Louis L'Amour are perennially popular. Revival festivals of old Western movies are among the most attended film programs at universities or specialty movie houses; dubbed or subtitled Westerns appear constantly in cinemas throughout Europe and the Orient; program managers of TV stations know that an old John Wayne oater is always a guarantee of high ratings for The Late Show.

The genre is alive in our memories; it is still with us.

*

It is not possible to single out any individual work as the first Western —certainly not the turn-of-the-century movies **Cripple Creek Bar Room** or **The Great Train Robbery**, since the Western genre predated the cinema by decades. The genre didn't spring to life fully grown. Its antecedents are numerous: Homeric tales, Arthurian legends, early romances. James Fenimore Cooper's frontier tales were not Westerns but they helped shape the genre. A principal contributor has been the sort of word-of-mouth history we call folklore.

In written form the first Westerns that are unarguably Westerns are the dime novels of the 1860s and thereafter.

These paperback-pulp thrillers set the patterns for the lower-class Westerns that have appeared ever since; there's little practical difference between an 1875 dime novel and a 1935 Max Brand novel, except that Brand was a bit more polished and less extravagant. Paperback-original Westerns are still being published today whose plots, characters and never-never-land settings are in clear direct line of descent from the yarns of the scribes who turned out dime novels more than a century ago.

*

Ned Buntline may not have been the most important of the dime novelists, or even the most popular, but he is the one who is remembered today, partly because his own boisterous life was as exciting as any of his pulp yarns. "Ned Buntline" was a pen-name, actually, the nom-de-plume of Edward Z. C. Judson, an American rogue who was acquainted personally with a number of "heroes" whose reputations he helped to create, like Wyatt Earp, Wild Bill Hickok, and especially Buffalo Bill Cody.

Buntline was a genuine creator, although some of his creations—like the Know-Nothing Party—were of dubious distinction. His most successful creation was Buffalo Bill. When Buntline met him, William Frederick "Buffalo Bill" Cody was a Nebraska buffalo skinner who liked to spin vivid campfire yarns, usually under the stimulation of whiskey in enormous quantities. Buntline, through the magic of fiction and publicity, turned this hard-drinking loudmouthed skinner into one of the greatest folk heroes the nation ever knew.

James Butler "Wild Bill" Hickok—who, with Cody, was among Buntline's first Western-hero creations—was a neurotic Kansas gambler-rake, ultimately fired from a law-enforcement job in Abilene when he shot a local citizen by mistake; and Wyatt Earp, when Buntline met him, was selling gold bricks in Dodge City.

These men were colorful and vivid. Cody was indeed a celebrated buffalo hunter; Hickok was, without exaggeration, a notorious gunman; Earp was a professional gambler and a strikingly handsome ladies' man. Still, Billy Dixon was as fabulous a hunter as Cody, and Bill Tilghman was a far more heroic and important lawman than Hickok or Earp ever became —yet nobody remembers Dixon or Tilghman, because they lacked an instinct for press-agentry and a willingness to be exploited. Cody, Hickok and Earp loved it when Buntline made celebrities of them. After a while, in his later years, Earp seemed convinced he really had been a hero. That's how persuasive Buntline could be.

I based the Bob Halburton character in **Wild Times** (portrayed in the film by Pat Hingle) on Buntline, and other representations of him have turned up here and there in films, but it sometimes surprises me how seldom the character has appeared; he was, after all, more responsible than any other individual for the birth of the Western as we know it—not so much with his novels as with his stage and arena performances.

For it wasn't the dime novels, or any other literary presentations, that really did the job of popularizing these Western characters to the point where they became our national legends. The Western myth, from the very beginning, was cemented in the American imagination by acting-out.

Buntline turned Cody and Hickok into theatrical stars. His lurid melodrama **Heroes of the Plains** opened in New York in 1871, toured the nation's theatres for several seasons, and was a sellout. At the same time, Doc Carver's Wild West Show was hitting the road, bringing fascinated Easterners to parks and fairgrounds to see wonderful feats of equestrian and ballistic expertise.

Buntline's first play was a ridiculously simpleminded vehicle in which Cody and Hickok, playing themselves, fought it out with endless waves of ferocious villains, both red and white. The subsequent popularity of the dime novels about Buffalo Bill resulted more from Cody's showmanship than from any merit in Buntline's floridly written books.

Quickly Cody's theatrical melodrama expanded in size and spectacle until no proscenium stage could contain it. For a while he went into partnership with Doc Carver, who had invented the arena show. Meanwhile Hickok, never comfortable as a play-actor, quit and went back to Dakota to die, but Cody went on to become the most popular star America had yet seen.

Sitting Bull and hordes of Indians and buffalo hunters joined his Wild West Show, which toured with its own prefabricated arena to entertain the multitudes with Texas Jack's hard-riding acrobatics, Annie Oakley's marksmanship and Cody's melodramatic "reenactments" of Indian battles, gunfights, hand-to-hand cliffhangers and stagecoach hold-ups.

Buffalo Bill's show was mainly just an elaboration of Doc Carver's, and Cody wasn't one-tenth the sharpshooter Carver was, but Cody soon eclipsed his sometime partner because of his flamboyant showmanship. Yet Carver went on, well past the turn of the century, and scores of imitators sprang up before the end of the era. Among the more popular was the 101 Ranch Show, whose star attractions included Bill Pickett—the black cowboy who invented the rodeo sport of bulldogging—and former spurious lawman, soldier and adventurer Tom Mix.

Most of the Wild West Shows had dwindled and disappeared by about 1915, although Tom Mix revived the institution in 1929 and toured his show for several years with some success; vestiges of the shows still appear in circuses, rodeos and touring fairs in which Western movie and TV stars appear; the 1980 Clint Eastwood film **Bronco Billy** gave a charming and wistful depiction of latter-day Wild West Shows, and that same year we released the TV miniseries **Wild Times**, the hero of which, Colonel Hugh Cardiff (portrayed by Sam Elliott), was loosely based on Doc Carver, with a dash of Cody thrown in.

Americans in the late twentieth century seem only dimly aware of how enormously influential the Wild West Shows were. They were the most spectacular arena entertainments since the Roman Circuses. In the late nineteenth century they drew crowds the equal in numbers of those of 1980's biggest rock concerts; they were smash hits not only in America but throughout Europe as well, often in royal command performances.

The Wild West Shows were overtaken by the novelty of motion pictures, but by then they had cemented all the ritual myths, and the movies simply perpetuated these.

Those myths were reinforced by the dime novels and, to a surprising extent, by the newspapers.

*

Sensationalism was what sold the papers of the day. Jesse James, the Daltons and their ilk became household names because of excessive yellow "news" coverage, and the journalistic hype was abetted by publicity-hungry individuals like Pat Garrett (the New Mexico sheriff who killed Billy the Kid and then wrote a lurid book about it) and organizations like the Pinkerton Detective Agency.

This brand of popularization endured well into the twentieth century: it takes no forcing to substitute Clyde Barrow or Dillinger for Jesse James or Cole Younger, and to substitute J. Edgar Hoover's FBI for the Pinkertons; the newspaper copy of the 1930s was eerily similar to that of the 1870s, trumpeting the exploits of the robbers, and the FBI was just as publicity-minded as the Pinkertons had been; the result was the folkloric glorification of generations of Western outlaws. (Had it not been for the strident and endless publicity, Jesse James might never have survived in folklore; the actual amount of money he stole was pitifully small.)

Between the Wild West Show/dime novel mythification of the pioneers and lawmen, and the yellow-press glorification of the outlaws, the West became America's greatest preoccupation in the 1880s. (In 1881 a New York reporter journeyed all the way to Tombstone to interview Doc Holliday. Holliday declined to be interviewed, but the reporter hung around and delivered some quotes attributed to Holliday during a drunken evening at a card game in a saloon. This shabby journalism was regarded as an important scoop.) Movies, which didn't come on the scene until twenty years later, not surprisingly began by pandering to that preoccupation.

*

Hardcover Western novels and romances began to appear in the 1880s, published by respectable houses like Lippincott. They were several cuts in quality above the dime novels and penny dreadfuls; they enjoyed fair sales —a few were best-sellers—and provided inspiration to later generations of Western storytellers.

Most prominent and significant of the early Western novelists was Charles King, whose work was a strong influence on the later writings of James Warner Bellah and Ernest Haycox. It can be said without much exaggeration that Charles King was the father of the Cavalry-Indian movie. (He later wrote one of the greatest of them.) King's novels have an enviable authenticity: he composed them while serving as a U. S. Cavalry officer under Generals Crook and Miles on the frontier, stationed in Indian-fighting army posts and riding in the campaigns against Cochise, Geronimo and the Sioux.

King's first novel, **The Colonel's Daughter**, was published in 1881 and has a strong claim to being the first true Western novel ever written.

King's stories are Victorian romances but they were written with surprising vigor and humor; they stand up today and are fascinating as curiosities, progenitors, and surprisingly well-crafted books. They prove that the Western had become an established genre of popular fiction long before Owen Wister published his novel **The Virginian** in 1902, and they put the lie to the scholarly claim that Wister's book was "the first Western."

Charles King's rank progressed from captain to general during his writing career; he wrote scores of books and was the scenarist and screenwriter of Buffalo Bill Cody's epic motion picture of 1913 about the Indian Wars—a film with several variant titles that has been lost for decades, although still-photographs from it exist, along with at least one reel in a private collection. (It is discussed in the next chapter.)

It is easy to attribute too much importance to obscure pioneers, but undoubtedly it is true that the great Cavalry movies of John Ford probably could not have been made had it not been for the signposts left along the trail by General Charles King.

*

Novelists like King and Wister helped shape the genre, but its real genesis was in performance (stage melodramas and Wild West Shows), which put the emphasis on visible action and visual spectacle. From the beginning the Western's most striking dramatic effects have been physical: the panoramic vistas of the scenic West, the graphic nobility of figures on horseback, the excitement of fast hard action. These attributes can be rendered only imperfectly in prose.

Only a handful of novelists—notably the late Ernest Haycox—really succeeded in rendering into narrative prose that intense pictorial vividness of the West which filmmakers have captured so mightily with their cameras. Haycox, a great stylist of the American West, was the literary counterpart of the painters Frederic Remington and Charles M. Russell.

It is doubtful that the Great American Novel will ever be written because almost by definition it must be a Western but it's nearly impossible for any novelist not to succumb to the natural expressiveness of the landscape: he's provided with an embarrassment of riches, and can't help being overwhelmed by the grandeur and innate conflicts of the setting and the mythology that already exist. Writers from Buntline, King and Wister to Frederic Manfred (**King of Spades**) and Douglas C. Jones (**Winding Stair**) have struggled heroically but none seems to have risen terribly far above his material and most likely none ever will.

There have been some very good Western novels. A checklist would include Wister's **The Virginian**, Willa Cather's **My Antonia**, Zane Grey's **Riders of the Purple Sage** (which, according to his detractors, is the only readable book Grey wrote), Eugene Manlove Rhodes's **Paso Por Aqui**, Walter Van Tilburg Clark's **The Ox-Bow Incident**, Ernest Haycox's **Bugles in the Afternoon**, A. B. Guthrie's **The Big Sky**, Jack Shaefer's **Shane**, Charles O. Locke's **Road to Socorro**, Alan LeMay's **The Searchers**, Paul I. Wellman's **Jubal Troop**, Tom Lea's **The Wonderful Country**, Charles Portis's **True Grit**, Elmore Leonard's **Valdez is Coming** and dozens, perhaps hundreds, of others; but none of them seems likely to be remembered as great literature.

No; the literature of the West is not suited to the novel. It is a genre of visual spectacle, and it found its medium—and its own highest expression—in the movies.

*

In the twentieth century the Western for practical purposes has been the Western movie, and that statement leads us to the question of authorship. Who creates a Western movie?

It is fashionable to identify film directors possessively with movies: "Howard Hawks's **Red River**." With that phrase the *Cahiers* school and its sycophants have created the implication of an authorship that seldom exists in fact, especially where the Western is concerned.

A fine director can make great contributions to a film, but usually it is not "his" film any more than it is the star's. Now and then a director is strong enough to impose his own style upon a film to the extent that a filmgoer can recognize it: Alfred Hitchcock, Orson Welles, John Ford. But in Hollywood more often it was the producer who imposed a style on his films. Goldwyn, Selznick, Warner, Thalberg—their pictures had distinctive attributes. When one studies the films of the 1930s and 1940s, often it is easier to distinguish the product of one studio from that of another than it is to distinguish between an adventure film directed by William A. Wellman, say, and one directed by Raoul Walsh. Wellman and Walsh directed many films splendidly; that is not the point. The industry in which they were employed seldom permitted its hired directors to be the authors of films; the system simply wasn't set up that way.

Directors did not write their movies. Normally they did not cast the principal roles. They did not determine the size of the budget or the schedule of shooting days. They did not decide on the picture's locations. They were constricted by the "studio look"—the staccato pace and cheap sets of Warner Brothers pictures, the lavish gloss of MGM's soundstages. They had to tailor films to the needs of the stars—camera angles for Garbo, lighting for Dietrich, an emphasis on hard swift action for verbally inept performers from Tom Mix to Guy Madison. And they rarely edited their own films.

The studios were assembly-line factories. The directors were section foremen: responsible for the manufacture, but not the design, of the products.

Therefore to take an auteuriste approach to the career of a Hollywood director is the equivalent of crediting an astronaut with having conceived, designed and built his spacecraft. One can conclude only that most of the critics who became spokesmen for the auteur theory were people who had never been on a movie set, never followed the development of a film from conception to release, never really known what a director does and what he doesn't do.

Ironically, one of the most vehement and vocal proponents of the auteur theory—French filmmaker Jean-Luc Godard—has admitted that he and his confreres promulgated the theory back in the 1950s "just to protect ourselves" against producers, distributors and other powerful forces. Speaking at the New York Film Festival in October 1980,

Godard confessed that the auteur theory was a hoax and a fraud, and expressed regret that it "has brought a lot of damage to some young boys' brains." Godard's belated change of heart seemed to coincide, oddly enough, with his decision to become a writer and producer as well as a director.

In the meantime, however, the theory affected filmmakers and critics alike, and caused considerable distortion in our perceptions of Western films.

Let's take an example: one of the better films of the genre—**Lonely Are the Brave** (1962). The men chiefly responsible for it were Edward Abbey, Kirk Douglas, Edward Lewis, Walter Matthau, David Miller and Dalton Trumbo.

How many of those names do most readers recognize? Whose film is **Lonely Are the Brave**? Without "inside" knowledge or a trivia-buff's wonderful memory, can the average reader even guess which of those six people is most responsible for the film's success—or even which of them is credited as its director?

One might begin by trying to rule out Matthau and Douglas because they're both well-known actors, but one must remember that each of them has directed feature films. (Matthau directed **Gangster Story**; Douglas directed **Scalawag** and **Posse**.) Can one be sure neither of them directed **Lonely Are the Brave**?

Edward Abbey wrote the small superb novel **The Brave Cowboy**, on which the film is based. Dalton Trumbo rendered it into a screenplay. Edward Lewis and Kirk Douglas jointly produced the film. Douglas and Walter Matthau starred in it. And David Miller directed this little gem. Miller has directed a large number of films during a long and productive career. They range in quality from good to terrible: **Love Happy**, **Back Street**, **The Opposite Sex**, **Captain Newman, M.D.**, **Hammerhead**, **Executive Action**, numerous others. Early in his career he directed the 1941 version of **Billy the Kid**, with Robert Taylor in the title role. On the evidence of his films he is a journeyman professional—as good or as weak as the material and the partners he works with. I've never met him, but I rather doubt he would claim to be the "auteur" of **Lonely Are the Brave**.

The story was created by Edward Abbey and no one else. The film version of it probably was conceived by Kirk Douglas and Edward Lewis, and then was rendered into a scenario by Dalton Trumbo. If this film was like most others, Trumbo's screenplay probably underwent a variety of revisions before filming began; contributing to the rewrite probably were the star, the producer, the director and perhaps a few others as well. The film itself is enhanced greatly by the engaging performances of Douglas and Matthau and, also, by those of Gena Rowlands and Carroll O'Connor in key supporting parts.

Despite all those facts, if one were to believe the auteuristes, then this movie is "David Miller's **Lonely Are the Brave**."

Is it really?

*

With a few exceptions like **The Wild Bunch**, no outstanding Western screen classics have been produced that were not based on previously published written material.

That statement includes, emphatically, John Ford's celebrated Westerns.

The quality of most Western films is in direct proportion to the quality of the published source on which the production was based. If one is as well versed in novelists and screenwriters as one is in directors, one may find that the names of the writers are a far more dependable index of film quality than are the names of the directors. Alan LeMay, Dudley Nichols, James Warner Bellah, Luke Short—there is a very long list of writers whose stories or screenplays were "bankable" guarantees of superior motion pictures. One simply cannot say the same thing about any American film director. Even John Ford directed pictures of remarkably uneven quality, and nearly all his best Westerns were written by LeMay, Nichols or Bellah. Those that weren't—like **Cheyenne Autumn**—were invariably of inferior quality.

It would be senseless to turn over the cart and insist that henceforth we describe every film as the writer's movie. Writers don't make movies. But any sensible analysis must lead to the conclusion that no director is any better than the story with which he begins. A great director will make a great film if he has a great screenplay; otherwise he will merely make a better film than a poor director would have made.

What a superior director can bring to his work is poetic vision, like that of John Ford.

Although he had written a few rudimentary screenplays in his silent-movie apprentice days, Ford was not really a writer and he was not at all a creator of stories. He adapted existing stories for the screen.

Ford's visual artistry—made possible on screen by his employment of superb cinema photographers like Archie J. Stout and Winton Hoch (Ford was famous for seldom, if ever, looking through the lens of a camera himself)—was influenced heavily by the pictorial compositions of Frederic Remington. Ford's use of lighting and atmospheric shadows was something he learned from Fritz Lang and other celebrated German directors of the 1920s UFA school. His sense of spectacle and action was acute and innate, but it should be pointed out that it sometimes was misdirected, as in **Stagecoach**, in which some of the action sequences were filmed all too obviously on sound stages with the scenery recreated by rear projection. And in the famous scene in which the stagecoach is pursued across sand flats by Indians, the rubber tire tracks of the camera truck are plainly visible. He *was* capable of mistakes.

Ford nonetheless was a poet in several ways. When he was directing his actors he would implore them, "Make it scan." No one can dispute that he made quite a few splendid movies: beautifully conceived, balanced, photographed, acted; marvelously entertaining and often deeply moving. Yet he was limited, as any director must be, by the nature and quality of the raw material—the stories—with which he had to work, and by the restrictions imposed by the producers or studios for whom he directed films. (Even after he formed his own production company, he still had to contend with budgets and other requirements inflicted on him by such studios as Republic, RKO or Warner Brothers.)

Because Ford did not create his film stories, he cannot be described as a total filmmaker. It is unfair to compare him with, say, a Charlie Chaplin or an Ingmar Bergman, who wrote, produced, directed and often photographed his own films. Ford's films, no matter how greatly they reflect the style and vision of John Ford, are never solely his creations. (And one notes that those with inferior stories, like **Two Rode Together**, are markedly inferior films.)

The saying has been attributed to Shaw that a camel is a greyhound designed by a committee. That definition fits the Hollywood film perfectly. It is nearly impossible to create a film that is as good as its initial conception was; it is nearly impossible to salvage a respectable film from the incursions of committee-thinking; it is nearly impossible to create anything one could call a work of art by group-collaboration; and yet, surprisingly often, the nearly-impossible is done, and a good film somehow emerges.

For those of us who are willing to take pleasure from that which is less than utterly perfect, there is a considerable body of very good Western films—and a much greater body of fair, mediocre, poor and irredeemably bad ones—to look at. It is through that massive body of work that this book attempts to guide the reader.

3
THE
SILENTS

The Great Train Robbery was not the first movie, or the first Western, but like Wister's novel it is the one we remember, partly because it is still around. For the record, it was produced by Thomas A. Edison in 1903 and it was conceived, directed and photographed by Edwin S. Porter, one of Edison's cameramen. Its cast included George Barnes, Marie Murray, the soon-to-be-ubiquitous Tom London and—in a bit part to which he was relegated because he couldn't ride a horse well enough—one Max Aronson, who was soon to change his name to G.M. "Broncho Billy" Anderson.

It was a ten-minute movie broken down into fourteen scenes, some of them intercut with one another. It contained the movies' first traveling matte shot (the train going past the telegrapher's window). It wasn't the first Western film; it was preceded by dozens, beginning in 1894, shot by the Edison Co. and later by American Mutoscope & Biograph Co.; these included such featurettes as **Indian War Council**, **Buffalo Dance**, an Annie Oakley movie, several Buffalo Bill vignettes and **Sioux Indian Ghost Dance**. Especially popular were two films of Buffalo Bill's Wild West Show —1894 and 1898—and Edison's **Cripple Creek Bar Room**. The first copyrighted Westerns, with plots, were released in 1903; they were **Kit Carson** and **The Pioneers**, the latter a 21-minute epic with a plot not altogether unlike that of **The Searchers** (1956). Nevertheless **The Great Train Robbery** (released a few months after those two) was one of the first American motion pictures to arrange a plotted dramatic story into edited, intercut consecutive scenes: the robbery, the chase, finally the fight on top of the moving train—all too soon to become cliches—and the denouement with the good guys overcoming the bad guys in that climactic shoot-out, based on the Wild West Show melodrama formula, which set the pattern for every oater that came after.

Porter's one-reeler spawned innumerable imitators. Within five or six years "the Western" had become a common staple of nickelodeon entertainments. It quickly developed many attributes, few of which offer any surprises to those of us armed with hindsight. But we may tend to forget the fact that those early silent Westerns weren't exercises in historic legends; they were depictions of current events.

Al Jennings was robbing trains in reality when **The Great Train Robbery** appeared; Butch and Sundance were robbing South American banks. Emmett Dalton was in prison; Wyatt Earp was prospecting along the Colorado River; Bat Masterson was sports editor of the New York *Telegraph*; the Oklahoma "Sooners," soon to be celebrated in Edna Ferber's novel **Cimarron**, were proving up homesteads; and up in Montana a judge moved to a new ranch with his family, including his two-year-old son, Frank James "Gary" Cooper. And out on the prairie the greatest of the old-time peace marshals, Bill Tilghman, was still pursuing miscreants —including the train-robber Al Jennings.

The real West did have real heroes. They were the men who did some of the things that Earp, Masterson, Hickok and the rest got credit for. But how many people today have heard of Tom Smith, Bill Tilghman or Burt Mossman? None of them had press agents; none of them had Ned Buntlines. They didn't want, or have time for, public-relations campaigns. It is only in recent times that scholars have dug into the back pages of Western history to find them. But it's too late for any of them to become household-word legends now. In any case, as John Ford was fond of pointing out, legends grow better when they are not constricted by facts.

Bill Tilghman, who had been a lawman as far back as Hanging Judge Isaac Parker's court in Fort Smith in the 1870s, was still packing a badge in 1903 (and, indeed, was still packing one nearly twenty years later when he was gunned down by a Prohibition-era bootlegger). Tilghman had chased Youngers, Daltons and Doolins. He caught most of them. Now he caught Al Jennings, who was the last of the well-known train robbers. The result of the arrest was curious, to say the least: Jennings, after serving a couple of years in prison, went into partnership with Tilghman, and together they produced a motion picture.

The Bank Robbery (1908) starred Jennings and was photographed by Tilghman. It was filmed on actual Oklahoma locations and purported to tell the story of one of Jennings' capers. It was released by the partners' Oklahoma Mutoscene Company but didn't catch on with audiences—partly because Tilghman's camera work cut everybody off at the neck and Jennings' face was visible only once or twice in the long shots.

But the fact that it was made at all is an interesting reminder of how contemporary the early Westerns were.

Like most of the "notorious" Western outlaws, Al Jennings wasn't really a very desperate character; he was more comical than menacing. A few years after the Oklahoma Mutoscene venture, he went out to Hollywood and starred in several low-budget Westerns; he was still kicking around the industry several decades later, living on his reputation and working occasionally as technical adviser on major Hollywood oaters.

Emmett Dalton did the same thing, working—along with his aged mother—as technical adviser on films like **When the Daltons Rode**. Frank James had played himself in theatrical melodramas about his and Jesse's career. Tom Mix was an ex-rodeo rider. The number of Western characters who appeared in, or contributed to, Westerns was quite considerable: Tim McCoy, for example, was a South Dakota rancher before becoming a star of "B" oaters. More recently, Rex Allen—the last "B" star groomed before the demise of the programmers—came to movies from an early career as an Arizona cowhand. Academy Award-winning actor Ben Johnson was a rodeo champion, hired by Howard Hughes as a horse-handler on his production of **The Outlaw**, then "discovered" by John Ford, who hired Johnson as an actor because of his good looks and equestrian excellence.

The early Westerns weren't mythologized histories; they were more like the gangster films of the 1930s—romanticizations of contemporary preoccupations. The frontier was still the most thrilling aspect of American fantasy life, and the film industry found a big audience for Westerns right from the beginning.

In the wake of the success of **The Great Train Robbery**, Max Aronson starred in **Life of an American Cowboy** (shot in Illinois, 1906), then went west and starred in the first

Western made in the West: Selig's **The Girl from Montana** (1907); then he opened an Essanay studio in California. There in 1910 he made **Broncho Billy and the Baby** (1910), the first of dozens. In creating his series character, "Broncho Billy" (based on a character in a short story by Peter B. Kyne), Aronson/Anderson managed to do what the major film producers of the day were trying desperately to avoid: he created audience demand for a single actor. (Indeed, he was the first person to receive screen credit of any kind.) He thereby instigated both the star system and the "B" movie. (Nearly all his films were cut from the same cloth and woven on the same looms.)

*

This is not the place to expound on the curious history of the Trust, the various corporate battles, the ferocious competitions for movie markets, the rise of the stars and the independents, or the myriad technical advances that were made during the formative 1903–1917 period in the movie industry. All those topics have been discussed at length in the motion picture histories.

But this does seem the proper place to try to restore some accuracy and perspective to our recollection of how the early Western developed.

The early Westerns, from Porter through the 1920s, were characterized by silly melodramatic plots, paper-thin characterizations, music-hall romantics and absurd emoting, not to mention the ridiculous heavy-breathing dialogue that appeared coyly on title cards. With few exceptions (and they are striking), it was not until the last few years of silent movies —the late 1920s—that any semblance of "adult" drama crept into the content of the Western. (The same can be said for the other movie genres with equal truth.)

Nevertheless, the costumes and physical backgrounds of many of the early oaters were quite authentic—far more so than those of later years. The reason is obvious and has already been stated: the early Western film was contemporary. Neither costume departments nor designers existed in the young industry; films used whatever settings and costumes were handy. Historical romances used musty rags from theatre-supply houses but those places didn't stock cowboy clothes; the players wore their own clothes, or outfits from ordinary haberdashers', and they performed against existing scenery. Therefore it wasn't surprising that the early oaters, preceding and including those of William S. Hart, were "realistic."

Certainly the most realistic of all, and probably the most striking, must have been Buffalo Bill's epic reconstruction, on film, of the entire history of the Plains Indian wars, from Powder River to Wounded Knee.

*

The epic had so many different titles at different times that it cannot properly be named; they included **Buffalo Bill's Indian Wars** and **From the Warpath to the Peace Pipe**.

This extraordinary film, briefly released in 1913, starred many of the original participants including Cody himself, General Nelson A. Miles (who captured Geronimo in Mexico, and later was in command of the sorry mess at Wounded Knee), General Frank Baldwin and Indian hero Dewey Beard, who had been the last to surrender at Wounded Knee.

The film was extremely expensive and long. Subsidized by the army's recruiting department, it was filmed on the actual locations of its episodes and in some sequences employed more than ten thousand extras, hundreds of whom were actual veterans, recreating their roles in history.

The screenwriter was General Charles King, the best-selling novelist and former aide to Generals Miles and Crook; director was Theodore Wharton; financing was provided mainly by the army, the Denver *Post* and the Sells-Floto Circus, which had employed Cody since the demise of his Wild West Show a few years earlier. (He died in 1915, broke.)

It wasn't Cody's first movie. Thomas Edison had filmed acts from his Wild West Show in 1894 for a moving-picture peep-show machine; several featurettes ensued, including one starring Annie Oakley. Later, in 1898, with an enormous piano-sized camera, Edison had photographed about twenty minutes of the Show in St. Louis, and released it as a special extravaganza in nickelodeons. That two-reel film still exists; we used it as a basis for staging the Wild West Show in **Wild Times**; at least two good prints of it are available—one in Texas, the other in Wyoming. Beginning in 1909, Cody appeared as himself in the Australian **Buffalo Bill**, then—in the United States—in **Buffalo Bill's Far West and Pawnee Bill's Far East** (1910), in **Sitting Bull—The Hostile Sioux Indian Chief** (1914) and finally in **Patsy of the Circus** (1915). (And he has been represented by actors in at least forty movies since then.)

Still photographs from the epic **Indian Wars** film exist, along with a partial reel of footage, but no one has found an intact print of the entire movie. It appeared briefly in theatres in Denver, where it had been produced, and in New York. But it was soon shelved, apparently for political reasons: it depicted the Plains Indians as heroic defenders, the white soldiers as interloping treaty-busting conquerors. Released at a time when the First World War was on the horizon, Black Jack Pershing was loping along the Mexican border and American boosterism was at a long-term high, Cody's film was an embarrassment both to its producers (Frederick Bonfils and Harry Tammen, publishers of the Denver *Post*) and to the government, which had supported the production. Under pressure from their own "consciences" as well as from Washington, the producers withdrew the film. It never went into general distribution, and therefore very few prints of it were made. No copies are known to survive.

The loss to film aficionados and historians alike is immense.

*

The making of such films as Cody's, along with the common use of real cowboy costumes and gear—and real towns as sets—gives one pause, in the face of many critics' tendencies to fawn over the supposed uniquely authentic realism of the films of William S. Hart.

Born in 1870 (in the East), raised in the West, Hart was a friend of Wyatt Earp and Al Jennings. It would have been astonishing if his films had been anything other than realistic in their costumes and settings.

Indeed, although not too many Westerns other than Hart's survive from the 1907–1917 decade, there is ample evidence to suggest that the Broncho Billy, Ince and Griffith Westerns—and even Tom Mix's earlier films—were no less "realistic" than Hart's.

But Hart went right on making similar movies into the mid-1920s while the rest of the Western world changed swiftly, as Tom Mix created his rodeo-costume flamboyance and Wild West Show acrobatics. Today Hart is remembered mainly for his later films—and those were outdated even in their own time. By stubbornly clinging to earlier conventions, Hart lost his stardom; by the 1930s he had become a pest in retirement, forever complaining about the anachronisms in movie costumes, guns, sets and historical depictions. To some extent he was right, and his services as technical adviser on films like **Billy**

the Kid (1930) were of great value in ensuring accuracy of detail. But, for a trained thespian, Hart displayed a curious compulsion to put realism of background ahead of pictorial excitement and dramatic values; to the last, in this odd way, he never became a cinematic man.

We shall return to Hart. But first let's catch up with the events that followed Max Aronson's creation of Broncho Billy.

*

Within a year or so after 1909, when Carl Laemmle produced the big-scale **Hiawatha** for the screen, Broncho Billy Anderson had become an outstanding celebrity. Even European filmmakers were producing "Broncho" Westerns in profusion now that Anderson had shown the way. Few of Anderson's films of that period would be of much intrinsic interest if they survived today; most of them relied on what later became Hart's and Wallace Beery's trademark—the plot about the outlaw reformed by a sentimental attachment to a helpless girl or an obnoxious child. But they did establish a big world market for Westerns.

Anderson, the first real movie star, dwindled into obscurity after the First World War; like Hart, he couldn't change. But he went on, alive but neglected, nearly forever—picking up scraps on the edge of the industry; his last screen appearance as an actor was in **The Bounty Killer** in 1965.

In the meantime the man who had started Anderson on his way, Edwin S. Porter, passed the baton in 1908 by directing a two-reel Western for Edison called **Rescued from an Eagle's Nest**. It introduced to the screen—as an actor—a man of intense visage named David Wark Griffith.

The movie was one of Porter's last, and it was D. W. Griffith's first. Aside from that historical significance the movie had few merits but it served to bring Griffith into the industry. Within months he had moved behind the cameras into a position from which, for years to come, his genius would dominate the development of the motion picture.

*

One of Griffith's first films was a Western: **Ramona**, from the novel by Helen Hunt Jackson—the story of the tragic Indian girl (Mary Pickford, the "Biograph Girl") and the white man she loves (Henry B. Walthall). Released in 1910, **Ramona** showed Griffith's mastery not only of the camera—wielded by the important pioneer cinematographer G. W. "Billy" Bitzer—but of signal dramatic techniques like cross-cutting and narrative close-ups. It also was the first movie based on a novel the copyright in which was paid for by the filmmakers: Biograph paid $100 for the movie rights to Jackson's 1884 romance.

Griffith's films were so much more exciting than their contemporaries that even the critics of the day were aware that cinema history was being made by the new director at Biograph. Then Griffith made **The Last Drop of Water** and **Fighting Blood** (both 1911), both of which were actionful wagon-train melodramas (the latter marking the first screen adaptation of a Zane Grey novel) and Griffith's commanding position was assured.

The techniques Griffith developed were quickly imitated and refined by others who began to produce Westerns far superior to Broncho Billy's or any others that had gone before. Chief among these directors was Thomas Ince, who created—once again with a Western, interestingly enough—yet another crucially important improvement in the art: the screenplay.

As soon as the plots of silent movies became too complex for improvisation on the spot it became necessary—just as it had with Homeric legends and medieval morality plays—to write down the stories so that the breakdown of scenes could be established. At first, plays and novels were used as scenarios, sometimes with key passages underlined. But Thomas Ince was the first filmmaker in America to employ the use of detailed written screenplays, which enabled him to make movies far longer and more complex than those that had preceded him.

Among Ince's earliest efforts were **Custer's Last Fight** (1912, a curiously conscientious depiction honoring both sides) and in the same year **The Indian Massacre**, again an amazingly sober and adult rendering of the problems and way of life of both settlers and Indians. The star was Francis Ford (John Ford's older brother), supported by a large cast headed by Ann Little and William Eagleshirt. Ince's photography for this very early silent feature was so good that it was still showing up as stock footage in movies made forty years later (including **Geronimo**, 1939).

Ince's next effort was the well-directed but hysterically overplotted **The Woman** (1913) but by then he had made his mark; his contribution of the well-wrought play, along with Griffith's mastery of narrative cinema, had brought the young motion picture to maturity—a point beyond which there were refinements but no further major evolutions before the advent of color and sound. (Actually the first Western in color had already been released—the British film **Fate**, 1911, with a plot similar to that of the later **A Man Called Horse**.)

The form, if not the content, of the movie was now established. The way had been opened for the spectacular arrival of the screen's first two giant Western heroes: William S. Hart and Tom Mix.

One thinks of Hart as the pioneer, Mix as the second generation. But actually Mix appeared on the screen before Hart did. In 1910 Mix appeared as a Wild West Show cowboy entertainer in **Ranch Life in the Great Southwest**, a documentary; in the next three or four years, before Hart appeared, Mix made several Westerns and became established as a stock-company leading man in oaters like Selig's **Chip of the Flying U**, 1914, directed by Colin Campbell from Peter B. Kyne's novel.

But Mix wasn't yet a towering celebrity and those early films were run-of-the-mill, not to be singled out from the great numbers of Westerns being produced at the time. Certainly his movies were eclipsed by such big-budget efforts as Selig's **The Spoilers** (1914, again directed by Campbell, the first of five film versions of this Rex Beach novel, starring William Farnum).

Tom Mix was hardly noticed at all, in fact, particularly by comparison with the tidal splash made on the moving-picture world by the arrival in Hollywood of Cecil B. De Mille.

Under the aegis of Jesse L. Lasky and Samuel Goldfish (soon to change his name to Samuel Goldwyn), De Mille went out to Hollywood in 1913 with the entire New York stage cast of the Edwin Milton Royle play **The Squaw Man**. On a budget of about $20,-000, in three weeks' filming, De Mille created a milestone in movie history.

No prints are known to have survived, but the six-reel film, from a screenplay by Beulah Marie Dix, earned more than $400,000 and became the very first blockbuster smash-hit movie.

(**The Squaw Man** was the second major full-length feature made entirely in Hollywood; the first—also in 1913 but a few months earlier, and also an oater—was **Arizona**, directed by Lawrence McGill, starring Cyril Scott and Gertrude Shipman; it was not a big hit. The first movie of any kind made in Hollywood had been Griffith's **In Old California** in 1910, a melodrama filmed in two days; it was not memorable but it was, again, a Western: over and over, one sees that the history of early American movies is largely the history of the Western.)

Amid its huge cast **The Squaw Man** introduced to the screen such luminaries as Dustin Farnum (thereafter a star for many years) and Raymond Hatton (who would appear in thousands of films in a fifty-four-year career, culminating in the poignant role of the bottle-collecting grandfather in **In Cold Blood**, 1967). Also in the cast were a number of stage actors many of whom soon would become the stock-company of Hollywood's early decades: Winifred Kingston, Monroe Salisbury, Billy Elmer, Red Wing, Al Reno, Joseph E. Singleton, Fred Montagne, Foster Knox, Baby DeRue, Dick Lestrange, and thousands of extras.

Spurred by success, Lasky's Paramount Pictures put De Mille in charge of one epic Western after another—five more in the next eighteen months. These included the first movie versions of Owen Wister's **The Virginian** (1914, with mainly the same cast as **The Squaw Man**) and David Belasco's play **Girl of the Golden West** (with Mabel Van Buren, House Peters, Billy Elmer, Theodore Roberts and again Raymond Hatton); the latter, remade umpteen times, is the chestnut about the road agent, the girl storekeeper who loves him, and the lawman who plays cards with her to settle the outlaw's fate.

De Mille also directed **Call of the North**, Stewart Edward White's lavish romance about fur-trading frontiersmen and Indians, and another David Belasco play, **Rose of the Rancho**; this was the weakest of the lot but it made a fortune. It has the kind of absurd plot that has been satirized for decades, complete with mustache-twisting land-grabber villain, demure heroine and stalwart hero, not to mention the cavalry riding to the rescue in the last reel.

Finally De Mille wrote and directed **Trail of the Lonesome Pine** (1915), from the novel by John W. Fox, Jr., and the play by Eugene Walter (in which William S. Hart had starred on the New York stage). The stars were Charlotte Walker, Earle Foxe, Thomas Meighan and Theodore Roberts and the story was the one about Virginia moonshiners, revenooers, and the still-owner's daughter who falls in love with a federal agent.

Against all that big-gun competition from De Mille and his imitators, it is no wonder that Tom Mix remained in obscurity. The surprise is that William S. Hart did not. Quietly, with his first starring part in an Ince film, **The Bargain**, Hart made a smash hit.

*

William Surrey Hart had been raised out West with a Sioux nurse but he trained as a stage actor and starred in Shakespearean plays in the theatrical companies of Belasco and Modjeska before settling into predominantly Western stage roles in New York productions of **The Squaw Man**, **The Virginian** and **Trail of the Lonesome Pine**.

Hart was not regarded in his day as an outstanding stage actor. His acting style was forceful but monotonous. Today it can be almost embarrassing to watch his archaic screen performances. Yet in spite of his stylized Victorian techniques—which, taken objectively, are no more distressing than those of the later Method performers—Hart did manage to imbue his gunslinger characters with remarkably subtle ranges of personality and emotion. Even today he can be a commanding giant on the screen, a figure of nobility and dignity.

That particular Western character Hart created on film—the noble bad man—was not original with him, and it was emulated with varying degrees of success by Harry Carey, Wallace Beery, Gary Cooper, Randolph Scott, William Elliott, John Wayne and Clint Eastwood, among others. But none of them, except Cooper, was able to add a great deal to what Hart did with the characterization of this archetypal protagonist. Today, in those examples of his work that survive, William S. Hart remains the essential Western hero. (It is an achievement all the more remarkable because of the dated cliches of all his films.)

In 1913 Hart appeared in a New York movie, **The Fugitive**, and a year later he went to Hollywood to work for Thomas Ince. His first Ince film was **On the Night Stage**, a five-reel feature in which Hart received third billing, below Robert Edeson and Rhea Mitchell. But his role actually was the starring part—that of the bandit reformed by love of a preacher's wife. The film survives and can be seen today, and in large measure it gives us the screen character from which Hart rarely deviated thereafter.

Hart's first top billing came in **The Bargain** (1914), which Hart himself directed from an Ince screenplay. Thenceforth Hart would direct many of his own pictures, although the best of them were directed by Lambert Hillyer or King Baggott; Hart was a heavy-handed director.

The Bargain was a hit, but after this triumph Hart inexplicably was confined to a string of two-reelers produced by Triangle (a company owned by Harry Aitken; the triangle was producer-directors Griffith, Ince and Mack Sennett). It is possible that Ince was jealous of Hart, since **The Bargain** proved more popular than the films Ince himself directed at the time. In any case none of Hart's early short oaters survives, but the public seems to have received them happily. Then in 1916 Hart made three full-length features that cemented his position as reigning Western star: **The Aryan**, **The Return of Draw Egan** and **Hell's Hinges**, the latter written by C. Gardner Sullivan and directed by Lambert Hillyer.

(It is interesting to note that in 1916 Sullivan, at $75 a week, was Hollywood's highest paid screenwriter. Ince employed him exclusively to write Hart's scenarios.)

Hell's Hinges co-starred Clara Williams, Alfred Hollingsworth, Louise Glaum and Jack Standing; the young John Gilbert appeared in a bit part, his film debut. Outlaw Hart rides into the town of Hell's Hinges to take a job as hired gunslinger for the bad guy; but love of the preacher's sister reforms him. He turns on his employer and wipes out not only the bad guys but the whole rotten town. It ends with a holocaust of fire, vividly shot.

The plot in essence is barely distinguishable from those of **On the Night Stage** and other Hart movies. But it was filmed with splendid enthusiasm and remains an outstanding movie of its time.

As a movie for today, **Hell's Hinges** is only a curiosity. It's made of oozing sentimentality and scenery-gnawing pantomime: all the furious grimaces and swooning passions of dreadful Edwardian extravagance. The movie pioneers were rudimentary dramatists and indifferent writers; their stories were childish. (The vaunted "realism" of these Hart films was in costumes and sets, not in characters or stories.) But this caveat applies to nearly all the pre-1924 silent features, not merely Westerns; the movies were influenced by popular theatre and literature and they reflected the unsophistication of Wild West Shows, slapstick farces and potboiler novels. With occasional exceptions the movies of that period are of interest mainly for historical reasons. One cannot expect to find a 1916 equivalent of **The Searchers**.

As drama **Hell's Hinges** is no worse than its contemporaries. As a well-made film it is professionally superior to nearly all other films produced that year. And it should be remarked that, as over-emoted and as juvenile as they may have been, Hart's plots often were those of real drama as opposed to those of melodrama—the distinction being that in one the conflict rises out of character, while in the other it rises out of contrived events.

Hart carried his brooding reformed-outlaw oaters on well into the 1920s. But by the late teens they had been supplanted in public favor by the showy escapist happy-ending adventures of Tom Mix.

Mix hit his stride when he signed with Fox in 1917, devised his colorfully overdressed persona and soon eclipsed everybody else at the box office. Within eight years, with Hart fading into retirement, Mix would be earning nearly a million dollars a year as one of the reigning members of Hollywood's royal family.

At the same time, people other than Ince, Hart and Mix were making Westerns (a fact that seems neglected by some film historians). In 1916 Hollywood produced dozens of them on all sorts of budgets and standards. Notable that year were **The Half Breed**, starring Douglas Fairbanks with a screenplay by Anita Loos, and a remake of **Ramona** with Monroe Salisbury and Adda Gleason, this version directed by the actor Donald Crisp. De Mille labored to bring forth **Romance of the Redwoods**, an overlong Mary Pickford vehicle—eight reels of syrupy sentimentality leading to an O.Henry-style trick ending that didn't suit so ambitious a film.

The year 1917 saw another milestone for the Western but it was not noticed as one at the time. The occasion was the release of the Universal production **Straight Shooting**, starring Harry Carey, Hoot Gibson and Molly Malone. It was a cattle baron versus nester range-war movie, with Carey a drifting outlaw who intervenes; it was a well-made silent picture, is still exciting today, and was the first full-length feature (and the only surviving early silent film) directed by John Ford.

Ford was to make hundreds of silent movies, most of them two- and three-reel oaters. (The length, in running time, of a "reel" can vary with several factors, but as a general rule one assumes ten minutes per reel. Most—but not all—"full length" silent features were five to eight reels long, which is to say forty-four to eighty minutes; they tended to be somewhat shorter than today's films.) Ford's early Westerns usually featured Tom Mix, Harry Carey or Hoot Gibson. In them, he refined and perfected his techniques, doing his apprenticeship.

He was not to make a strong impression on the industry until several years later; in the meantime the movie houses of the late teens satisfied their customers with Hart's **The Silent Man** (1917), Mix's **Durand of the Badlands** (1918), William Farnum in Zane Grey's **Last of the Duanes** (1918) and a 1918 Essanay production called **Shooting Mad**—typical of, and among the better films of, Broncho Billy Anderson. It is still kicking around; it was nearly the last movie in which Anderson starred. (His last, that same year, was **Son of a Gun**.)

De Mille's entry for 1918 was **The Squaw Man**—again. He grew fond of remaking his own films and was to do this one yet again a decade later. Among its players this time around were Noah Beery, Sr., and Jack Holt—two players who would continue to star in films well into the era of the talkies. De Mille's 1918 version ran ten minutes longer than the original but it used the same screenplay and was still the same weepy yarn about the black-sheep English aristocrat who marries an Indian girl and encounters great tribulations and a tragic ending. (On stage in 1905 Jack Holt's role of badman Cash Hawkins had been played by William S. Hart.)

For the moment we'll pass over the "B" Westerns, which by 1919 were well entrenched; they are covered in the next chapter. Among the important "A" Westerns of that year were a version of Bret Harte's **The Outcasts of Poker Flat** with Harry Carey, and one of **Valley of the Giants**, notable chiefly because its director, James Cruze, soon would come to prominence with a far more ambitious undertaking. There was Tom Mix's **The Daredevils**, a fast-action movie that Mix wrote, directed and starred in; and there was D. W. Griffith's only surviving full-length (eight-reel) Western, **Scarlet Days**, a Paramount release starring Richard Barthelmess; unfortunately it's a poor example of the master's art, characterized by pretentious acting and a thin plot; it hardly seems possible it was made by the same man who gave us **The Birth of a Nation** and **Intolerance**.

Finally 1919 saw the release of a German film, **Halbblut**—a Teutonic adaptation of **The Half Breed**. It was the first movie to be directed by UFA's Fritz Lang, who would bring important innovations—and some significant Westerns—to his later Hollywood career.

(If it sometimes appears that nearly everybody in the movies started with a Western, it's probably true.)

*

In 1920 Famous Players-Lasky gave us **The Roundup** with Roscoe "Fatty" Arbuckle. Spoofs had already begun, with Douglas Fairbanks and Mack Sennett poking fun at horse opera, burlesquing the formulas that had become cliches in theatrical and Wild West shows. In later years the attempts to satirize would continue but rarely with success, perhaps because the Western too often behaved as its own worst parody.

Hart's **The Toll Gate** (1920) was one of his best and it still commanded big ticket sales. There was a version of another oft-filmed yarn, **The Last of the Mohicans**, but the big Western of 1920 was **The Mark of Zorro**. Fred Niblo directed it from Johnston McCulley's novel *The Curse of Capistrano*. The film stands up nicely, a classic, possibly Douglas Fairbanks's best movie, a zesty, funny swashbuckler with dash and charm. Probably everybody, even youngsters, knows the plot: the masked rider Zorro, protector of the poor and avenger of injustice, proves when unmasked to be the gentle foolish fop Don Diego Vega. Fairbanks's supporting cast included Noah Beery, Sr., Noah Beery, Jr. (age seven), Marguerite de la Motte, Robert McKim and Charles Mailes. The photography by Tony Gaudio was splendid and it's still a must-see movie with a grand comic performance by Fairbanks and great buffoonery by Beery, Sr.

The next few years saw hundreds more oaters; both Mix and Hart remained strong at the box office. Mix came out with **Just Tony** (his horse was named Tony) in 1921 and then in 1922 his **Sky High** appeared; it survives and is engagingly circusy, filmed on location at the Grand Canyon and mixing airplane stunts with edge-of-the-cliff fisticuffs. Filled with vitality it was one of Mix's best purely escapist amusements.

Directors King Vidor and James Cruze shepherded Westerns to the screen—respectively **The Sky Pilot** (1921), about a dude preacher, and **Ruggles of Red Gap** (1921), the first film version of the English butler-out-West comedy, with Taylor Holmes in the title role. (There were numerous Westerns that year; 854 American feature films were released in 1921—that's still the record.)

In 1922 **The Spoilers** was remade with Noah Beery and in 1923 Fox remade **Trail of the Lonesome Pine**, photographed by James Wong Howe.

The year 1923 saw two Zane Grey stories filmed, both by Paramount and both starring Richard Dix and Lois Wilson: **To the Last Man** and **Call of the Canyon**. And it saw one of William S. Hart's most ambitious productions, **Wild Bill Hickok**, a poignant if sugar-coated biography in which Ethel Grey Terry co-starred as Calamity Jane. Hart wrote it and directed it, and starred as Wild Bill.

De Mille was there again in 1923 with another remake, **The Virginian**, with Dustin Farnum in the Owen Wister story about the nameless ranch foreman, the schoolteacher, the wayward happy-go-lucky pal and the villainous Trampas. But 1923 is remembered mainly by film historians as the year of the movie that William S. Hart turned down.

Hart refused the script because he said it wasn't realistic. A shame, really, because had he appeared in it, his career might have been given the boost it needed to keep him in films. Instead, he was to leave the screen within two years.

The film—**The Covered Wagon**—has been described as the first epic Western. It follows a wagon train from Missouri to Oregon with many Indian battles and corny conflicts amongst the pioneers. Today, aside from its magnificent Monument Valley and Death Valley location photography, its publicized excellences are elusive; it is still kicking around but unfortunately it's a bore because the characters don't ring true and the plot has great holes in it. Yet in its time it was a huge success. It was directed by James Cruze from a screenplay by Jack Cunningham based on the novel by Emerson Hough. The Hart role finally went to J.Warren Kerrigan; other roles were played, with uneven effectiveness, by Lois Wilson, Alan Hale, Tully Marshall and Ernest Torrence. The cameraman, to whom a great deal of the credit for the film's phenomenal popularity belongs, was Karl Brown. Montana rancher Tim McCoy provided the Sioux Indians for the filming, and accompanied them to California, and stayed on in Hollywood to become one of the best of the "B" Western stars.

To cash in on its runaway hit, Paramount released a sequel (of sorts) to **The Covered Wagon** barely a year later: **North of 36**, again based on an Emerson Hough novel and again featuring Ernest Torrence and Lois Wilson. The hero this time was played by Jack Holt and the director was Irvin Willat. In many ways it was superior to the original but it didn't capture the public's imagination. It told the story of a post-Civil War cattle drive—much like the one in **Red River**—and it was filled with virile action. At the same time, Famous Players-Lasky released Zane Grey's **Wanderer of the Wasteland**, directed by Irvin Willat, starring Jack Holt, Noah Beery and Billie Dove; it was a big hit because it was the first major mass-distributed movie in Technicolor. But this and numerous other 1924 Westerns (like the first-rate **The Border Legion**, a Zane Grey story directed by William K. Howard) were eclipsed by the release of the epic with which director John Ford at last came into his own: **The Iron Horse**.

*

It was Ford's fortieth Western. At nearly three hours it is the longest film Ford ever made, and his biggest as well, with a cast of six thousand people headed by George O'Brien, Fred Kohler, Madge Bellamy, Chief Big Tree, Iron Eyes Cody and J. Farrell MacDonald. A Fox release, **The Iron Horse** was based on a screenplay by Charles Kenyon and John Russell, and featured excellent Nevada location photography by George Schneiderman.

The film is still available for viewing, fortunately. In fanciful form it tells the story of the building of the Union Pacific railroad—part history lesson (although filled with inaccuracies and anachronisms), part slapstick comedy, part romance, part melodramatic hokum. Often mawkish, it remains enjoyable for its cinematic spectacle but certainly not for its naive, contrived story, which incorporates nearly all the stubborn cliches of ludicrous pulp fictions and childish stagy fads of the time. There's no subtlety and no sophistication in it, none of the grandeur that Ford found as he grew older in moral themes or the larger-than-life heroes of his later films. One can't expect to find in **The Iron Horse** a romantic masterpiece the equal of **She Wore a Yellow Ribbon** or a drama half so stirring as **The Searchers**; the story has more in common with the Tim Holt programmers of the 1940s.

Yet in its complexity and photography, action and production, the film was leagues ahead of **The Covered Wagon** and easily a match for any Western of the succeeding half-dozen years, up to **The Virginian** (1929), which lifted the Western onto a much higher artistic plane.

Ford had a broad sense of crude humor; and he had a conviction that comedy relief was essential; he carried that belief to his grave but the comedy relief worked only fitfully and in certain films. More often his slapstick jokes do not fit the grandiose schemes of his films—they seem out of place, as if they belong in some other and lesser movie. (This is true even as far into his maturity as **The Searchers**.)

THE WESTERNER (1940): Gary Cooper as the archetypal Western Hero. With Doris Davenport. United Artists

The costumes were contemporary outfits from ordinary haberdashers. William S. Hart, c. 1918. Author's collection

William S. Hart as technical adviser on the set of BILLY THE KID (1930); with star Johnny Mack Brown. MGM

Max Aronson, alias Broncho
Billy Anderson, c. 1908.
Author's collection

Tom Mix, perhaps the greatest action cowboy star of all. Author's
collection

ARIZONA BOUND (1927):
Gary Cooper comes to stardom.
Paramount Pictures

In sum, **The Iron Horse** was and is an entertaining film, a milestone; but one must approach it in the proper frame of mind.

(Footage from the film, and most of its plot as well, turned up again in 1939 in De Mille's **Union Pacific**.)

*

In 1925 James Cruze directed his first Western after **The Covered Wagon**; this was an obvious attempt to repeat its success—**The Pony Express**. It starred Ricardo Cortez, Betty Compson, Wallace Beery and Ernest Torrence. Contrived and molasses-slow, it died quickly but it was some years, yet, before the industry began to realize that in Cruze it had a turgid second-rate director; in the late 1920s he was still the highest-paid director in Hollywood, and his record stands as the highest-paid director in silent pictures.

Much better for 1925 was **The Great Divide**, an MGM Wallace Beery vehicle in which a Boston girl (Alice Terry) comes to a Western mining camp and is almost raped. A very daring movie for its time, much more explicit than the first film version (1915) had been, it stirred up quite a controversy.

Go West was Buster Keaton's 1925 comic attack on the Western, and it's still one of the best. Keaton unleashes a stampeding cattle herd on an unsuspecting Eastern city in this Hal Roach opus.

Douglas Fairbanks, directed by Donald Crisp from a Jack Cunningham screenplay, appeared in 1925 with Mary Astor, Warner Oland, Jean Hersholt and Donald Crisp (all four of whom would have successful careers in talkies) in a sort of sequel to his five-year-old classic, but **Don Q., Son of Zorro** did not measure up. Meanwhile Tom Mix kept churning them out—**The Best Bad Man**, with Clara Bow (the "It" girl) is perhaps his best-remembered film from 1925, although Mix also appeared as Lassiter in a Fox version of Zane Grey's **Riders of the Purple Sage**, the strong story about the drifter grimly bent on revenge. It has rarely been filmed very well and Mix was miscast as the grim, dour gunslinger; Hart would have been far better suited to it; but still, Mix's film was (and is) a good example of his work, and very much worth seeing.

Probably the second-best Western of 1925 was again a Zane Grey yarn, **The Thundering Herd**, a Famous Players-Lasky picture directed by William K. Howard. It starred Jack Holt, Noah Beery, Sr., Tim McCoy, Lois Wilson, Raymond Hatton and—in a bit part, his very first movie—Gary Cooper. This one had good action scenes, particularly a magnificent race of covered wagons across a frozen lake, and it was great fun despite the hackneyed plot.

But by far the outstanding Western of 1925 was William S. Hart's last and greatest movie: **Tumbleweeds**.

*

Hart lived on until 1946 but he felt that the audiences had deserted him in favor of flashy circus cowboys; he decided to retire gracefully rather than dwindle away into low-budget independent movies or character roles. Determined to go out in a blaze of glory, he conceived **Tumbleweeds** as his swan song. And because he knew it was his last shot, he put everything he had into it.

Hart co-directed with King Baggott from a C. Gardner Sullivan screenplay. His supporting cast included Lucien Littlefield and Barbara Bedford. **Tumbleweeds** is a gritty epic of the Oklahoma land rush, much more stirring—even today—than either of the later versions of **Cimarron**, which covers some of the same historical ground.

In 1939 United Artists re-released **Tumbleweeds** with the addition of soundtrack music, sound effects and a moving eight-minute prologue delivered poignantly on screen by Hart, then nearly seventy. That version still exists—in fact it is sold on commercially pre-recorded videotape cassettes—and it can be very rewarding. It's a fine example of how good silent movies could be, and a fine introduction to William S. Hart.

*

When Hart retired, his mantle passed not to Tom Mix (who represented the peak of "B" Westerndom) but to Gary Cooper, who worked his way up through supporting roles in several silent pictures to stardom in **Arizona Bound** (1927). Cooper wore the mantle nobly until his death in 1961, at which time I think the Western died. But Gary Cooper's is properly the story of talkies rather than silents, and he is best left to a later chapter.

In 1926, before reaching stardom, Cooper appeared in supporting roles in two Westerns. The first was Goldwyn's **The Winning of Barbara Worth**, a United Artists release directed by Henry King; Frances Marion's screenplay was based on Harold Bell Wright's best-selling novel. It starred Ronald Colman, and Cooper was fourth down the supporting-cast list. The movie is a romance about irrigation engineers making the Colorado River banks bloom, and it bears little resemblance to the novel. It was followed by **The Vanishing American**, from the Zane Grey yarn, directed for Paramount by George B. Seitz; Richard Dix and Lois Wilson headed the cast with Noah Beery, Sr., and Cooper in support. Some beautiful scenes were shot in Monument Valley and there was plenty of action, and Dix was believable as the tragic noble Indian hero, but the whole thing was pretty much reduced to the "B" level of plot and character.

The film's star, beefy square-jawed Richard Dix, went on to become a curious sort of footnote in Western movie stardom—his career as a top-billed leading man went on for decades, but he was lugubriously dependable rather than exciting and never was thought of among the major box-office stars. Still, he never played a part less than that of the hero and he starred in an amazingly large number of "A" features (mostly but not exclusively Westerns), many of them quite good, including the Academy Award-winning **Cimarron** (1931), straight into the 1940s before age, and changing fashions in leading men, relegated him to starring parts in "B" crime movies. Virtually forgotten now by all but dedicated movie buffs, Dix was a reliable and engaging workhorse of the movie industry—often unexciting but always very believable.

*

Nineteen twenty-six was the year of cartoonist Walt Disney's arrival in Hollywood and the year of Rudolph Valentino's death; it was also the year in which John Ford made his last silent Western, **Three Badmen**, a sentimental land-rush yarn with George O'Brien and Tom Santschi—no masterwork, but it was the last real Western that Ford would make before **Stagecoach** in 1939.

Nineteen twenty-seven was a big year for Hollywood. If there weren't any outstanding Westerns at least there were quite a few satisfying ones. Al Jolson was singing on the screen but sound didn't catch up with Westerns for another year or two and in the meantime there was MGM's **Winners of the Wilderness**, a Tim McCoy vehicle notable for Joan Crawford's presence in it; there was a pretty good version of **The Last of the Mohicans** with Wallace Beery; Hoot Gibson starred in a superior **Man in the Saddle**—with Boris Karloff as a baddy—while Gilbert Roland and Mary Astor co-starred in Warner Brothers' **Rose of the Golden West**, filmed handsomely on locations at Capistrano and Monterey; and prolific director William K. Howard surprised audiences with his gloomy Germanic psychological Western **White Gold**, a curiously ambiguous "mood" story with memorably eerie photography by Lucien Andriot. The Western, it seemed, was starting to grow up.

Scenarist Frances Marion wrote more than three hundred screen stories; in the 1930s she won two Oscars for her screenplays. In the 1920s she married an army chaplain named Fred Thomson and brought him into the movie industry, where he became one of the better "B" Western stars. Most of his movies were frank—but good—imitations of Tom Mix's films, but in 1927—shortly before his sudden accidental death—Thomson made a surprisingly successful **Jesse James**, short on fact but long on action and rather sophisticated motivations.

At the same time his fellow "B" star, the superbly athletic Ken Maynard, was showcased in **The Red Raiders**, a spectacular actioner; Maynard was even better at stunts and trick riding than Tom Mix was, and this big-budget picture gave him an opportunity to show off his best acrobatic routines. It was juvenile entertainment, not a serious film, but marvelously exciting for all that. Stunt action footage from these Ken Maynard silents was used in Westerns for decades thereafter.

By early 1928 the industry was in straits of uncertainty. Were talking pictures a revolution or a passing fad? In any case thousands of silent movie theatres still had to be fed with product, and although production in 1928 was far more tentative than it had been only a few months earlier, the studios did continue to produce action movies—mainly Westerns—because the confinement of talkies to microphone-equipped sound stages made the new talking pictures very static.

In 1928 Edwin Carewe directed a remake of **Ramona** for United Artists with Warner Baxter and the gorgeous Dolores Del Rio; Joan Crawford appeared in **Rose Marie** (a silent operetta!), directed by Lucien Hubbard from the stage hit by Rudolf Friml and Oscar Hammerstein II; Crawford also appeared in a Tim McCoy programmer, **Law of the Range**, directed by W. S. Van Dyke for MGM; and Dustin Farnum appeared as General Custer in **The Flaming Frontier**, a major Universal release featuring Hoot Gibson in support. There were numerous others—with Harry Carey, Tom Mix and others—but the really memorable Western of this last year of significant silents was **The Wind**.

*

Director of **The Wind** was the Swedish actor-director Victor Sjostrom, who sometimes in Hollywood spelled his name Seastrom. He had directed several silent Greta Garbo features and he was to remain in films for many years: he appeared as the starring actor in Ingmar Bergman's **Wild Strawberries** in 1957. But **The Wind** was his most acclaimed work.

Frances Marion wrote the screenplay from a novel by Dorothy Scarborough. Sjostrom hand-picked cinematographer Jack Arnold and actors Lillian Gish, Lars Hanson, Montagu Love and Dorothy Cumming. The MGM production ran only seventy-one minutes in length, but it was an uncompromising merciless drama of compelling power that left audiences of the day shuddering for hours afterward.

A fragile Virginia girl (Gish) arrives on a dusty Texas plain, is driven mad by loneliness on her desolate homestead, murders her would-be seducer and then watches with horror while a howling wind sweeps away the sand from the shallow grave where her victim lies buried. In the end her own hysteria merges with that of the demon wind.

Lillian Gish's performance in the film was stunningly intense, and **The Wind** may have been the most powerful of the "psychological" Westerns prior to the release in the

1940s of such movies as **Pursued** and **Treasure of the Sierra Madre**. But the implacable melodrama of the picture sets it perilously close, for modern audiences, to the verge of laughability; the director's Scandinavian fatalism infected the film with an implausible determinism. In that respect it is similar to a more recent Scandinavian Western—Jan Troell's double-tiered **The Emigrants/The New Land** (see the main body of the guide, under both titles). But **The Wind** was undeniably an important picture, and it was the last significant silent Western.

It was followed in 1929 by some relatively ordinary films: Richard Dix in **Redskin**, with some footage in color; a fair version of Zane Grey's **Stairs of Sand** with Wallace Beery and Jean Arthur; a Universal production of Peter B. Kyne's story **Hell's Heroes**, directed by William Wyler and starring Charles Bickford.

In 1929 for the first time since 1912 there were no Tom Mix films. Mix lost everything in the stock-market crash; simultaneously, Fox felt he'd been washed up in films by the arrival of sound. So Mix, who had been by far the most popular cowboy star of the silents, retired temporarily from the screen and went on the road with his Wild West Show.

He was getting on in years by then—well into his fifties—and the hard-drinking years of carousing had begun to catch up with him, but he gave audiences their money's worth; he still was a handsome figure on horseback and he knew how to entertain.

In 1931 he returned to the screen and made a few talkies but he never regained the sort of splendid stardom he'd had. He soon retired again but went on making rodeo and fairground appearances until his death in a car crash in Arizona in the mid-1930s.

*

When talkies took over, there was room to believe the Western was doomed by the confinement of microphones to potted plants on indoor stages. The Western lay dormant for a couple of years, it is true, but then the technicians learned how to move their mikes outdoors. Then the Western came back stronger than ever, bringing Gary Cooper, John Wayne and the rest of a new generation to stardom.

4
THE
PROGRAMMERS

Before discussing the "A" Westerns of the talking-picture era, we must take a quick look at that forty-year mainstay of Western film production: the "B" movie.

From any sophisticated viewpoint, virtually all the Westerns of the 1903–1924 period were "B" pictures, shot in a few days and characterized by stories that were trite even in their own day. But those are the evidences of the growing pains of the art form. Formally, the programmers began with Broncho Billy's die-stamped two-reelers, made from 1909 through 1918, and the hundreds of ten- and twenty-minute Western quickies cranked out by "B" units run by assistants of Edison, Griffith, Ince and the rest. Some of these units, particularly at Fox and Triangle, were set up deliberately to give apprenticeship training to upcoming young directors like Raoul Walsh and John Ford, and to featured players hoping for stardom—such actors as Franklyn Farnum, Tom Mix, Ken Maynard, Lillian and Dorothy Gish.

John Ford made about forty Western featurettes for Universal, starting in 1917, most of them starring Harry Carey, Hoot Gibson or both; a few starred Tom Mix. Full-length (five reels or more) low-budget "B" pictures began production in earnest at about that same time with the Western programmers of William Desmond, Ken Maynard, Franklyn Farnum and Roy Stewart.

As early as 1920 the formulas of the "B" Western had codified themselves to the point where moviemakers could do their work with their minds on something else entirely. The plots nearly always hinged on one of three devices: the clearing of the hero's name, the rescue of the distressed damsel, or the avenging of a murdered father or brother.

These three plots, or combinations of them, were the chief ingredients of all "B" Westerns and quite a few "A" ones for the next four decades. The watchword was always, "Cut to the chase!" and the simplified plots were merely excuses to provide continuity from one frantic acrobatic sequence to the next.

Oddly, there wasn't much gunplay in the typical programmer. Guns were carried by everyone but used very seldom, except in those scenes where mounted posses chased fugitives, doing a great deal of shooting but rarely hitting anyone. Occasionally a bad guy would shoot someone from ambush, but the only time a good guy used his gun was when he shot the revolver out of the bad guy's hand or displayed his marksmanship by using one bullet to part the rope that was about to lynch his buddy.

This was partly a matter of morality: the films were made knowingly for juvenile audiences and in those days it was not thought heroic to shoot people. "B" Western heroes rarely shot anybody until the 1940s or thereabouts.

It was also partly a matter of cinematic awareness: a chase in which the hero leaps from his galloping horse onto a runaway stagecoach or a fleeing villain on horseback is visually far more exciting than a simple gunshot.

Mainly, however, it was a matter of understanding the audiences for whom the pictures were made. The moviemakers wanted to entertain, not to disgust. A disgusted audience wouldn't come back next week and buy another ticket. And parents would not allow their children to go to "immoral" movies. ("Morality" had more to do with violence than with sex in the early days of movies; prior to the establishment of the Motion Picture Code and the Hays Office, sexually suggestive scenes were commonplace in silent melodramas; bared female breasts were not unknown, and bedroom scenes sometimes got quite steamy, but none of this took place in "B" Westerns, which were pure to the point of scrubbed shiny cleanliness.)

The difference between a good programmer and a bad one was not so much in the quality of its story—the plots were all about the same—as it was in the care and vehemence with which the action stunts were filmed. The real stars were the stunt men—daredevils whose work in the long shots often earned them higher salaries than the close-up actors received whose names appeared in star-billing.

The "camp" fascination with nostalgia that began in the 1960s caused a flood of interest in, revivals of, and ridiculously sober analyses of the old "B" Westerns, and it is true that a surprising number of the early ones—and some from later on—were filmed with great vigor, good production values and magnificent action sequences. Nevertheless one needs to have a fairly stunted sense of artistic values to enjoy much exposure to these films today. The predictability of the programmers led critics to dismiss *all* Westerns as trite foolishness, and it cannot be denied that the programmers often actually did rely on such simpleminded cliches as white hats on the good guys and black hats on the bad guys.

*

By the early 1920s the oater programmers had settled into their hackneyed formulas. The major stars—those who appeared in the better productions—were Tom Mix, Harry Carey, Hoot Gibson and (briefly) Art Acord (he died in 1931); newcomers were Ken Maynard, the ill-fated Fred Thomson and the marvelous Buck Jones; a few years later they were joined by Bob Steele and Tim McCoy.

Lesser "B" stars of the 1920s included the likes of Buffalo Bill Junior, Art Mix (Tom's cousin), Ruth Mix (Tom's daughter), Wally Wales (also called Hal Taliaferro), Tom Tyler, Buddy Roosevelt, Lane Chandler, Bob Custer, Francis Ford, Jack Perrin, Al Hoxie, Bob Reeves, Guinn "Big Boy" Williams, William Fairbanks, Leo Maloney, Buzz Barton, Pete Morrison and Yakima Canutt, who was far more famous in the industry as a stunt man and second-unit director, although he did star in his own "B" series in the 1920s and co-starred in several series, including John Wayne's, in the 1930s.

There was also Rin Tin Tin, who was a better actor than some of the others.

Many of the early "B" cowboy stars became character actors later on. Quite a few are listed in the supporting casts of movies covered by this book. Lane Chandler and Guinn "Big Boy" Williams played important supporting roles in major Westerns for thirty years; Bob Steele, one of the most popular "B" stars from 1927 through 1944, was still appearing in small roles in television programs and the occasional movie as recently as the late 1970s. Tom Tyler, Hal Taliaferro and Francis Ford played roles of varying importance in minor and major films for decades after their brief shots at stardom—particularly Ford, whose younger brother John put him somewhere in virtually every movie he directed.

Some of these actors were talented mainly as athletes. Ken Maynard was much more comfortable with a spinning rope or a jump off a high cliff than he was with a mouthful of words. One husky silent oater star was quite popular in the 1920s but had to quit when the talkies came in—not because his voice was poor but because, unable to read or write, he found it too difficult to learn his lines.

Wealthy Joseph P. Kennedy, father of the political Kennedys, built FBO studios in the late 1920s and made scores of "B" Westerns, some of them quite good, with such stars as Mix, Thomson, Steele and Tom Tyler. After sound came in, FBO became RKO Radio and kept right on cranking them out; and later the studio fell into the hands of yet another adventurous industrial tycoon—the mysterious Howard Hughes.

*

The advent of sound caused a temporary curtailment in production of the programmers for a curious reason. Once the talkies were established, movie houses dismissed their pianists, organists and (in the big palaces) orchestras. The result was that the early talking "B" Westerns were far more silent than their "silent" predecessors had been. The excitement-enhancing adjunct, music, was gone.

Its absence made low-budget films seem flat and dull (especially since their dialogue was usually banal) until background music was introduced to the soundtracks of movies early in the new decade; it was 1933 or so before it became an industry standard, and even so, some of the cheaper programmers—many of those with John Wayne, for example—continued to get along without music until well into the late 1930s.

*

Of the top ten box-office stars of 1928, three had been cowboy stars: Mix, Maynard and Hoot Gibson. (In fairness it must be pointed out that a chief reason for "B" stars' often making the box-office top-ten list was the fact that in the course of a year a "B" star could appear in as many as twenty-four movies while an "A" star rarely made more than three. Since the top-ten list was determined according to how many tickets a star's pictures sold in the course of a year, it is not surprising that a Ken Maynard—with sixteen movies in 1926—could make a stronger box-office showing than a Richard Barthelmess, with two. In the 1940s Gene Autry frequently appeared on the top-ten list.)

By 1931, when total weekly movie attendance in the United States had dropped from one hundred million to half that, there were no cowboys on the list at all, unless one counts Wallace Beery.

But by the end of 1932 there were still sixty million people going to the movies every week and that audience needed a steady flow of films.

Soundstage-bound talkies had begun to bore them. Action was needed. And so the Western came back.

*

The innovation of the soundtrack brought no immediate changes to the "B" Western. Plots, action sequences and even dialogue remained the same, although of course the latter was spoken rather than flashed on title cards. Still, for the first few years a good many movies—even major productions like **The Virginian**—continued to use title cards to explain transitions between scenes. Even the sillier conventions were held over from silent days: for example it had become mandatory for cowboy heroes to wear gloves at all times—a fashion that had been created inadvertently by Tom Mix, who had delicate sensitive hands despite his rugged background and had been wearing gloves all his life to protect them.

Even the stars remained the same as they had been in the silents, with only a few defections caused by unattractive high-pitched voices or speech defects. Those who continued to headline horseback programmers were Ken Maynard, Harry Carey (despite his heavy Long Island accent), Buck Jones, Hoot Gibson, Tim McCoy, Tom Tyler and Bob Steele; they all made the transition without visible difficulty. As Tom Mix slipped into retirement a group of newcomers arrived—Johnny Mack Brown, George O'Brien (both down from "A" pictures), Rex Bell and John Wayne—but they brought no real changes to the formula until a few years later when it was further debased by the introduction of the singing cowboys, one of whom, oddly, was (singing voice dubbed) John Wayne.

Bob Steele's plots invariably required him to avenge the murder of his father, usually by insinuating himself incognito into an outlaw gang. Steele was physically small, and always looked like somebody's son. Some of the John Wayne programmers used the same wheeze; in fact if there was a single plot common to the majority of "B" oaters of that period it was this one. At times it surfaced in more ambitious films as well—there is a version of it in **The Iron Horse**—and it continued to do solid service right up into the 1950s.

Moviemakers of the 1930s lifted more than mere plots from the silents. If John Wayne in his early Warner Brothers oaters seems to be wearing Ken Maynard's cast-off silent movie costumes it's because Warners used extensive action-stunt footage from the old Maynard pictures in order to bring in Wayne's films on shoestring budgets. (This also explains why the scripts and dialogue often seem to have a tough time matching the action. Absurdities abound.)

Most "B" Westerns of the 1930s, and even some from the 1940s, reused miles of action footage from silents, some dating back as far as 1913. Often the thefts are comically obvious even to the unschooled eye.

*

Marion Michael Morrison, a USC football hero, earned side money as a prop man and general gopher on Hollywood's movie lots in the late 1920s. His good looks and very tall physique and his rowdy sense of humor brought him to the attention of director John Ford, who gave him unbilled bit parts in **Mother Machree** and a few other movies before recommending to fellow director Raoul Walsh that young Morrison might be the fresh new leading man Walsh was seeking to star in his forthcoming covered-wagon epic **The Big Trail**.

Morrison's name was changed to John Wayne and he played the starring role in the expensive 1930 film but it laid an egg—partly, said some observers, because of Wayne's wooden performance—and Fox's executives then found they had an expensively contracted "star" on their hands who presumably could neither act nor draw crowds. Resignedly Fox put him into a couple of lesser movies (not Westerns) where Wayne did no better. Cutting their losses, the studio chiefs sold Wayne's contract to Columbia Pictures.

Wayne spent nearly ten years at Columbia, Warners, Monogram and Republic, where he appeared in about sixty movies. Of these, forty-two were "B" Westerns of a quality ranging from fair to abysmal. In some of them he was "Singin' Sandy" (singing voice dubbed by Smith Ballew); in others he was a lone hero or a typical "B" hero with a sidekick, often played by George "Gabby" Hayes; and in the last eight—the "Three Mesquiteers" series for Republic—he was a replacement for Bob Livingston as one of three range-riding heroes (the other two being Ray Corrigan and Max Terhune). These eight were a cut above the rest in quality.

In three of his first four oaters Wayne played supporting roles (to Buck Jones and Tim McCoy); these three are generally reputed to be better films than the ones in which Wayne starred. After that he starred in all his "B" movies—that is, his name came first in the credits—but except for the Three Mesquiteers series, the budgets on many of these films were unusually threadbare, even for Poverty Row actioners (Wayne was considered a minor star, even among "B" players); and yet some of these films made money. There always has been and evidently always will be an audience for a John Wayne movie, no matter how terrible it is. Independent TV syndicates in the 1970s and 1980s assembled some of these old pictures in a series some of them billed as "The Worst of John Wayne." The leathery integrity that the Duke projected on the screen was part of it, but Wayne served a long apprenticeship and was bright enough to learn from it, and in the best of his later films there is a surprisingly deep display of truly good acting (or, as Wayne would have had it, "reacting").

Those films came later, however. In the meantime, for the record, here is a quick checklist of John Wayne's "B" Western programmers of the 1930s:

> **Range Feud**—Columbia, 1931 (starring Buck Jones)
> **Haunted Gold**—Warner Brothers, 1932 (starring Wayne)
> **Texas Cyclone**—Columbia, 1932 (starring Tim McCoy)
> **Two-Fisted Law**—Columbia, 1932 (starring McCoy)
> **Ride Him, Cowboy**—Warner Brothers, 1932 (starring Wayne)
> **The Big Stampede**—Warner Brothers, 1932 (with Noah Beery, Sr.)
> **The Telegraph Trail**—Warner Brothers, 1933
> **Somewhere in Sonora**—Warner Brothers, 1933 (with Paul Fix)
> **The Man From Monterey**—Monogram, 1933 (with George "Gabby" Hayes)
> **Sagebrush Trail**—Monogram, 1933
> **West of the Divide**—Monogram, 1933 (with Hayes)
> **Lucky Texan**—Monogram, 1933 (with Hayes)
> **Blue Steel**—Monogram, 1934 (with Hayes)
> **The Man from Utah**—Monogram, 1934 (with Hayes)
> **Randy Rides Again**—Monogram, 1934 (with Hayes)
> **The Star Packer** — Monogram, 1934 (with Hayes)
> **The Trail Beyond**—Monogram, 1934 (with Noah Beery, Sr., and Noah Beery, Jr.)
> **'Neath Arizona Skies**—Monogram, 1934 (with Hayes)
> **Lawless Frontier**—Monogram, 1935 (with Hayes)
> **Texas Terror**—Monogram, 1935 (with Hayes)
> **Rainbow Valley**—Monogram, 1935 (with Hayes)
> **Paradise Canyon** — Monogram, 1935
> **The Dawn Rider**—Monogram, 1935
> **Westward Ho** — Republic, 1935
> **Desert Trail**—Monogram, 1935 (with Paul Fix and Henry Hull)
> **New Frontier**—Republic, 1935
> **Lawless Range**—Republic, 1935
> **The Lawless Nineties**—Republic, 1936 (with Hayes)

King of the Pecos—Republic, 1936
The Oregon Trail—Republic, 1936
Winds of the Wasteland—Republic, 1936
The Lonely Trail—Republic, 1936
Born to the West—Paramount, 1938 (with Johnny Mack Brown,
    Marsha Hunt, Monte Blue, James Craig and Alan Ladd)
Pals of the Saddle—Republic, 1938
Overland Stage Raiders—Republic, 1938 (with Louise Brooks)
Santa Fe Stampede—Republic, 1938
Red River Range—Republic, 1938
The Night Riders—Republic, 1939
Three Texas Steers—Republic, 1939
Wyoming Outlaw—Republic, 1939
New Frontier—Republic, 1939

*

The last eight were the "Three Mesquiteers" movies, and of these the last two were released after Wayne's success in **Stagecoach**. Actually he remained under contract to Republic for nearly a decade thereafter but thenceforth he became the studio's top "A" star.

Supporting casts of these 1930s programmers often included up-and-coming youngsters whose presence in these films is of note because of hindsight; note the cast of **Born to the West** shown above; it is listed simply as an example.

The behind-the-camera credits of such programmers may explain the sameness of the films. Most of Wayne's 1933–1935 Monogrammers were written and directed by Robert N. Bradbury, who—aside from being one of the old pro "B" directors—was well known in Hollywood as the father of Bob Steele. The cameraman on these pictures was Archie J. Stout, who later became one of John Ford's ace photographers (**Fort Apache**). After Monogram and Republic split apart into separate companies, Wayne went with Republic, where most of his 1935–1936 oaters were directed by Joseph Kane, who later in the early 1950s directed some superior small-budget "A" Westerns. The scripts at Republic in 1935–1936 were written by prolific pros like the McGowan brothers, Stuart and Dorrell.

From 1936 to 1938 Republic put Wayne in a succession of cheap non-Western action pics without notable success, and then he returned to the saddle for the Three Mesquiteers series. It was directed by George Sherman and written by Luci Ward, Jack Natteford, Betty Burbridge and Stanley Roberts—at least two of them to each movie, in just about every possible combination.

The Mesquiteer characters were based on a series of pulp novelettes written by William Colt MacDonald, who cranked out hundreds of novels and thousands of short stories under various pseudonyms. And this fact brings up the question of the relationship between pulp magazines and "B" movies.

It is a relationship that hardly seems to have been explored at all—possibly because "B" movie students and old-magazine aficionados are rarely the same people. But the two subgenres fed off each other to a great extent.

Their life-span was the same—from about 1910 to the early 1950s—and the notable writers in both fields often were the same people. Steve Fisher and Frederick Faust were among the best known, Faust under various noms-de-plume like "Evan Evans" and "Max Brand"; under the latter name he created such heroes of pulp and movie fiction as Destry and Dr. Kildare.

The pulps provided two generations of writers with an invaluable apprenticeship. (I came along just too late; when I started trying to peddle stories to the pulps in the late 1950s, it sometimes seemed that every time I'd send a story to a magazine, the magazine would die. I never did sell a single story to a pulp magazine, and got downright paranoid about it after a while.) Writers like Dashiell Hammett were alumni of the pulp training-ground just as John Ford was a graduate of "B" movies.

The pulps and the "Bs" shared plots, attitudes and devices; it wasn't merely that the movies got their stories from the magazines—it worked both ways, with pulp Western stories being heavily influenced by the movies. In the last days of the pulps, for example, there was a profusion of stories clearly imitative of **High Noon**. Originality was an infrequent phenomenon in either of them but occasionally the pulps produced a Hammett or a James M. Cain, and occasionally the "Bs" produced a Ford, a Robert Mitchum or a splendid little movie like the 1941 version of **Riders of the Purple Sage**.

The 1930s gave Hollywood a profusion of independent studios. Republic, Monogram and Tiffany were the high-class "B" studios; behind them were such quickly forgotten Poverty Row empires as Action Pictures, Allied Pictures, Chesterfield, Eagle-Lion, Invincible, Liberty, Lone Star (later amalgamated with Monogram), Majestic, Mayfair and World Wide. These, along with the "B" units of the major studios, usually specialized in Westerns because horse opera was popular, audiences undemanding, Westerns producible outdoors cheaply. And "B" Westerns rarely required good acting by anybody except horses and stunt men.

By the mid-1930s four out of five U.S. theatres were playing double features. Programmers had to be manufactured at a tremendous rate to keep them supplied. Columbia alone, under Harry Cohn, produced an average of one full-length movie every six days. It was the zenith of "B" production and the 1930s introduced a big new group of new cowboy stars: Gene Autry, Tex Ritter, Roy Rogers, Dick Foran (those four being the principal singing cowboys), Charles Starrett, Jack Randall, Gordon (William "Wild Bill") Elliott, Smith Ballew, Tom Keene, Bob Livingston, Duncan Renaldo, Kermit Maynard (Ken's brother), Donald "Red" Barry and others to the point of tedium.

Of these the worst, in the opinion of many observers, were the singing cowboys but the insatiable market had to be supplied and Hollywood poured out nearly three hundred "B" Westerns—tuneful and otherwise—each year throughout the Depression. Dozens of serials increased that output, including such ultra-popular serials as **The Lone Ranger** which in 1938 introduced George Montgomery to the screen, and **Riders of Death Valley** (1941) which starred Dick Foran, Buck Jones, Charles Bickford, Monte Blue, Leo Carrillo, Lon Chaney, Jr., Noah Beery, Jr., and Rod Cameron.

*

One "B" phenomenon of the 1930s is of interest if only because of the financial empire it created.

The Hopalong Cassidy series—more than one hundred movies filmed at Paramount beginning in 1935 and then at United Artists in the 1940s—offers little attraction to most adult filmgoers aside from historical tidbits: Rita Hayworth, as Margarita Cansino, appeared in some of them, as did John Garfield and Robert Mitchum (usually as a villain's henchman). The pictures were well filmed, sometimes on impressive, remote locations, but the plots were humdrum and the character of the hero unfortunately bore little resemblance to the original Cassidy character from Clarence E. Mulford's engaging novels—a happy-go-lucky cowpoke who livened some of the best early Western fiction. (Mulford came along immediately after Wister.) In the novels the character is a slightly roguish drifter who might well have been portrayed on screen by the young Kirk Douglas. Indeed, the first actor to whom Paramount offered the part was David Niven. He turned it down, and the offer went to wiry character-actor James Gleason. Only when Gleason declined it did the role go to former silent De Mille star William Boyd, who re-created the Cassidy character to suit his own sanctimonious ideas about what young audiences wanted in their movie heroes.

Boyd's version provoked a lucrative reaction; his intuition about audiences proved right. In the end it led to a financial bonanza when in 1950 Boyd hocked everything he owned to buy back all rights to his old movies. He then sold them to television for a fortune.

Boyd's corporate Hopalong Cassidy enterprises brought to new extremes the exploitation of subsidiary rights by licensing the manufacture of Hopalong Cassidy T-shirts, capguns, bandannas, hats, holsters and comic books. I was about twelve when the craze hit its height, and nearly every kid I knew had an all-black Hopalong cowboy outfit complete with hat and white-fringed holster belt. (Personally I resisted it. My cronies and I played cowboys-and-Indians with capguns and big hats, but we favored Wild Bill Elliott and Don "Red" Barry movies over Hopalong Cassidy flicks; Elliott and Barry tended to play hard-riding outlaws and their pictures seemed much more exciting than Boyd's.)

By the time the Hopalong Cassidy craze dwindled in the mid-1950s it had poured some $50 million into the old actor's pockets. And evidently there is still great residual value in Hoppy. As recently as 1981, a court case confirmed that the Clarence Mulford estate still had a copyright that covered the Hopalong Cassidy films—an important decision, since it affected sales of videodiscs, videocassette tapes and 16mm film versions of the old series, which distributors had tried to contend were in the public domain and therefore not susceptible to royalty payments.

Wistfully one wishes the series had been good enough to deserve all the attention and money it accreted. It wasn't, but clearly something in Hoppy's slow, stern, self-righteous father figure appealed to juvenile audiences, much as Pa Cartright appealed to them a generation later in television's **Bonanza**.

The same kind of mawkishly prissy heroics and piety were to be found in the screen characters of such cowboy actors as the ageless hymn-singing Roy Rogers and tubby Gene Autry with his Cub-Scoutish "Ten Commandments of the Cowboy." It was these tumbleweed troubadours—armed with guitars as well as sixguns—who brought the "B" Western to its aesthetic nadir with their fringed lollipop costumes, their interrupting the action every seven minutes with a treacly song (as clockwork-predictable as TV commercials), and their managing to contrive the creation of a West that not only hadn't existed in history but couldn't be believed as fantasy: a West in which heroes flew airplanes to radio stations, stepped out of them, climbed aboard their horses and rode away to fend off Indian attacks on wagon trains.

*

Of the singing cowboy stars Dick Foran was one of the first, one of the shortest-lived in stardom, and probably the best. Born Nicholas Foran, the New Jerseyite was a tall handsome man and a good actor possessed of an excellent tenor singing voice. He had a wickedly keen sense of humor and had the magnetism to have become a major star. But he was under contract to Warner Brothers.

Warners—the studio of Paul Muni biopix and Edward G. Robinson gangster movies—was the only major Hollywood studio that never learned how to make Westerns.

True, the studio released a few good Westerns during the 1940s and 1950s—**The Search-ers** is the outstanding example—but these were independently produced, and merely distributed by Warners. The studio's own in-house product was always wrong, somehow. Nearly the only Westerns it made in the thirties were the Foran movies. In the forties its major Westerns were the Errol Flynn oaters, only one of which—**They Died with Their Boots On**—was worth sitting up for. Usually when Warners attempted to make a Western with its usual stable of fast-talking gangster types and wisecracking musical-comedy people, it produced a laughingstock absurdity like **The Oklahoma Kid**, in which James Cagney and Humphrey Bogart tried—ludicrously—to look like cowboys. (In **Virginia City** the studio actually had the nerve to cast Bogart as a Mexican bandit. His accent was hilarious.)

It seemed obligatory in the mid-1930s for every studio to have a "B" Western unit, and Warner Brothers obliged by cranking out nine programmers with Dick Foran. Not surprisingly they weren't very good, although Foran himself was noteworthy, both as a singer (his voice was by far the best of any of the cowboy warblers) and as a plausible cowboy hero with both charm and masculinity. Afterward Warners let Foran dwindle away into supporting roles in "A" pictures, the occasional lead in a serial and periodic parts in which he was forced to burlesque himself, like the young stalwart in **My Little Chickadee** or the hilariously stupid cowboy star trying to make a comeback in **Boy Meets Girl**. He was nominated for an Academy Award for his supporting role in **The Petrified Forest** but even this didn't inspire Warners to give him a boost; after a while, in disgust, Foran went back East into the theatre. He starred on Broadway in **Connecticut Yankee**, among other shows. Later he returned to Hollywood to play character parts. Right up to his death in 1979 he remained an engaging raconteur and a charming screen personality. Had Foran been handled properly, the singing-cowboy subgenre might have taken a better turn.

*

By 1940 the "B" pictures had reached their peak and begun their slow decline. Some old-timers retired early in the new decade but still another group of new faces arrived: Tim Holt, Rod Cameron, Kirby Grant, Jim Bannon, Sunset Carson, Jimmie Wakely, Eddie Dean, Monte Hale, Lash LaRue, Whip Wilson, Allan "Rocky" Lane, Wayne Morris, Russell Hayden, James "Shamrock" Ellison. The numbers and energy of the programmers dwindled steadily; vitality drained out of the aging genre. By 1950, production was down to a fraction of the output of the heyday. After the midcentury point only one new star appeared: Rex Allen, "The Arizona Cowboy," who lasted about three years as a "B" movie star, then became a TV cowboy and more recently could be found doing voice-over narration for documentaries, dog-food commercials and Disney movies. (As a guitar-playing kid, age thirteen, I appeared with two pals on the Rex Allen Show in Wilcox, Arizona. It was one of the highlights of our youth.)

A few old-timers held on into the early 1950s: Johnny Mack Brown from the 1920s; Gene Autry, Charles Starrett and Roy Rogers from the 1930s; and Tim Holt, Bill Elliott, Monte Hale, Allan Lane and Wayne Morris from the 1940s. But one by one they dropped away until in 1954 the last programmer trickled out of the last series.

After that, there were independent one-shot poverty-row actioners and cheap major studio "A" movies with Audie Murphy, George Montgomery and the like, but "B" pictures were officially dead, having moved to television. Companies like Lippert continued briefly to turn out Westerns featuring John Ireland, Lloyd Bridges or John Agar, but these were not series entries and must be regarded as minor "A" Westerns.

*

Many blamed the programmers' demise on TV but a more likely cause was inflation. The "B" oaters of the 1950s had more or less the same stories as those of the 1930s; but the production values of the older films were much better than those of the later ones. By 1950 every "B" moviegoer worth his salt could sketch you a map showing the location of every phony rock and bush on Monogram's back lot; he knew every turning of the Republic cave set and every chip of weathered paint on Eagle-Lion's Western town set. The programmers were weary by then; many a matinee house preferred to screen the older "B" pictures because recently the old outlaw gangs of twenty thundering stunt riders had dwindled to three stubbled bit players on spavined horses racing in circles around that familiar back-lot countryside, and audiences could not be blamed if they preferred even so negligible an entertainment as a 1936 Hopalong Cassidy movie on TV because it had been filmed lavishly on Sierra Nevada locations and the bad guys were truly formidable because there were so many of them. Stunts were far better in the older films, because more time and manpower had been available for preparation and execution; and there was a lot less static conversation on cheap interior sets.

In any case the "B" studios folded. A television company now uses the old Republic lot. Monogram survived by changing its image: it became Allied Artists, purveyor of "A" movies, but it finally died in 1980. The rest disappeared or became television companies.

The directors, writers and actors either found their way into TV or graduated to "A" films or disappeared.

Some of the "B" movies still exist in film vaults, TV station libraries and 16mm or video showrooms and catalogues. They don't turn up any more in cinemas or on prime-time TV. They were no worse than current television fare; actually in many respects they were better—certainly they were more honest. But their cliches were different from today's; they seem quaint now. A few diehard buffs continue to mourn their disappearance, and it can be said, at least of many "B" Westerns, that they were good clean fun.

5
THE
TALKIES

Talking pictures existed quite early. In 1922 Lee De Forest produced a talking movie of **Casey at the Bat**. Both color and wide-screen processes had been devised even earlier (the CinemaScope lens having been invented in 1913).

But all these inventions languished unexploited until it began to look commercially desirable to incorporate them into the existing pattern of the motion picture. When **The Jazz Singer** (1927) succeeded at the box office where **Casey** had not, the conservative profit-motivated bosses of the film industry decided—in more panic than confidence—that sound was here to stay.

It was during that tentative period of fear and confusion that Gary Cooper arrived on the screen. After his initial supporting appearances in a few Westerns and the hit war film **Wings**, Cooper came to stardom in three silent Paramount Westerns made in 1927.

The first was **Arizona Bound**, directed by John Waters and written by John Stone, Paul Gangelin and Richard A. Gates. Supported by Betty Jewel, Jack Dougherty and Guinn "Big Boy" Williams, Cooper played a cowboy who drifted into a town and eventually corralled a gang of stagecoach robbers. It was ordinary horse-opera.

Nevada, released on the heels of it, was a bit more successful. Again directed by Waters, it was written by John Stone, L.G. Rigby and Jack Conway from the Zane Grey novel. This one featured William Powell, Thelma Todd and Philip Strange in support of Cooper and provided a William S. Hart sort of story about a young outlaw reformed by the love of a good woman. The young Cooper carried the role with engaging easygoing dignity except in the love scenes, which he handled like a bashful twelve-year-old.

His third 1927 oater, **The Last Outlaw**, was directed by Arthur Rosson, had essentially the same writers and cast as **Arizona Bound**, and was hardly more than a throwaway "B" picture, with a plot about cattle rustling and the unmasking of a crooked sheriff.

All three of these pictures were made at a time when the industry knew that silent pictures were doomed; they were cranked out quickly as throwaways, designed simply to fill time in backwater circulation until all the theatres in the country had a chance to equip themselves with sound-reproduction gear.

In his next quasi-Western, **Wolf Song** (1929, Paramount), Cooper—by now a matinee idol after several non-Western hits—played a gritty fur trapper who falls in love with a Latin spitfire (Lupe Velez) and, after being shooed off by her stern father (Louis Wol-heim), abducts her to the mountains, with romantic rather than criminal intentions. An unintentionally funny and dreadful movie, it was directed by Victor Fleming; assistant director was Henry Hathaway, who soon would become an important director of West-erns; and the writers, from the novel by Harvey Fergusson, were John Farrow (himself to become an important director—see **Hondo**), Keene Thompson and Julian Johnson.

Wolf Song was a transitional film: two duets were sung by Velez and Russ Columbo; other than those and a few lines of lead-in dialogue it was a non-talking picture but it was ballyhooed as a singing Western, its nude swimming scene got a lot of publicity, and Paramount's flacks worked busily to puff the "torrid" off-screen romance between the two stars.

With the exception of the blockbuster Academy Award winner **Wings**, in which he had only a bit part (albeit a standout cameo; everyone noticed him), Cooper arrived on the scene in a four-year string of mediocre movies: sixteen of them, including five West-erns. Yet he survived them all, and by 1929, without yet having had top billing in a major hit, he was regarded as one of the most important stars in Hollywood.

The leap to stardom seemed inevitable. It had nothing to do with the quality of his vehicles or with his acting abilities, which were negligible in those early days. Cooper made it to the top on sheer magnetism. The camera loved him.

But it took more than that to stay at the top for thirty years. Cooper studied, worked, learned, and became the consummate professional.

In the remainder of his career he was to appear in seventy-six talkies, of which per-haps twenty were box-office successes beyond the ordinary. Charitably it could be said that about twenty of his films were good movies; of course these are not the same twenty, although there is some overlap. And of the films Cooper made in his talking-picture career from 1929 through 1960, only about twenty were Westerns. (The number could be increased to a maximum of twenty-five if one were to include such marginally Western movies as **Saratoga Trunk**, **Bright Leaf**, **Friendly Persuasion** and the Bob Hope comedy **Alias Jesse James**, in which Cooper made an unbilled comic cameo appearance.)

Indeed, the number of excellent—or even important—Westerns in which Cooper ap-peared is amazingly small. There were three superb ones, generally acknowledged to be classics of one kind or another: **The Virginian**, **The Westerner** and **High Noon**. And there were a few of somewhat lesser but still satisfyingly high quality like **The Hanging Tree**, **They Came to Cordura** and the underrated **Garden of Evil**. The rest—including the lavish but mediocre De Mille dirigibles **The Plainsman**, **Northwest Mounted Police** and **Unconquered**, and the zesty but juvenile actioner **Vera Cruz**—ranged from routine to downright bad.

Yet Cooper became, and remained, the screen's supreme Western hero.

*

Cooper's parents were English, and he had a first-class Eastern education, but he grew up in Montana; later he liked to describe himself as a Westerner, "an average Joe from the middle of the country," but that was role playing; for his part in **The Virginian** he had to take diction lessons from Randolph Scott to get the Virginia accent right because Cooper's own Ivy League speech would have been dreadful for the part of the laconic drawling cowpoke.

He was an actor—there are critics who describe him as the greatest film star of all, and indeed John Barrymore, going even farther, called Cooper "the world's greatest actor" —a bit of hyperbole that didn't strike Cooper's admirers as being very far off the mark.

The role Cooper created for himself on the screen may have been fairly consistent from film to film, thereby giving rise to the popular and critical impression that all he did was play himself, but actually he played a wide variety of characters; and even in those roles that depicted him as "the regulation Gary Cooper hero," the screen persona was quite different from Cooper's real-life character. In person he was shy, to be sure, but he also could be loquacious, somewhat opinionated, inclined toward luxury and lavish spending, and often gentle nearly to the point of effeminacy; yet he was a "man's man"—he often hunted big game with his friend Ernest Hemingway, and where attractive women were concerned he was reputed to be an intercontinental swordsman without peer.

Like his contemporary Humphrey Bogart, Cooper developed mannerisms of speech and movement that were contrived specifically and deliberately for the camera. There were actors who at first didn't want to work with him because they felt he didn't give them enough; he directed his entire performance toward the camera, and quite often his movements or expressions were so understated that the other actors in the scene would think he was woodenly neglecting to react. Only later, when they saw the footage of the day's shoot, would they realize how expert his performance had been: what a wealth of expression there was in his face and the graceful little inclinations of his body.

Still, beneath the restraint and the mannerisms, the essence of Cooper's appeal was not much different in reality than it was on screen. Despite the actor's technique, it was the fundamental magnetism of the man that made Cooper a superstar. "Charisma" is an overabused word but it is what Cooper had, perhaps to a greater degree than any other screen performer, and it was so exactly suited to the motion-picture camera that it took only one talkie for Cooper's screen personality to be stamped on the consciousness of two generations of moviegoers. In 1929, in **The Virginian**, once or twice Cooper says "Yup" and "Nope." These catchwords of the laconic Western hero became so quickly and indelibly associated with Cooper that thenceforth he was forever characterized, his image solidified, by those two words, so that even serious critics for thirty years lambasted him mercilessly for his "Yup and Nope" performances, when in fact—so far as I have seen— he never used those expressions again, on the screen. Indeed, I've heard that he expressly refused to use those words in his movies. (In **Garden of Evil** he plays an exceedingly indrawn and laconic hero whose occasional response to a question is a noncommittal grunt; that's the closest I think he ever came to repeating the "Yup-Nope" pattern.)

On force of personality rather than quality of films, Cooper established himself as the Western hero of all time; the idealized image of American manhood on the screen. And with roles in just a handful of superior films, he established a mark for all other screen performers to measure themselves against. None ever reached it.

He was described, often enough, as a "natural" actor, but that wasn't it at all; it never is. Acting is a craft, a profession and at its highest level an art. Those who succeed are those who work and have talent.

Cooper was an intensely conscientious artist. Not a single blink of an eyelid on camera was not deliberated and intended. Every twitch of the expressive mouth was contrived for specific effect. The fact that he made it look natural was a measure of his success as an artist.

In **High Noon** the terror bleeds from Will Kane's eyes; yet there is not a single outward indication of that fear. This is not fortuitous casting, or the result of duodenal ulcers (which some critics have claimed); it is the supreme example of the actor's art: the ability to communicate character and feelings without the least hint of indicative emoting.

*

Cooper could not play a wisecracking cynic or a sadistic killer, and his sorties into the roles of sophisticated lounge lizards and conniving businessmen often were unconvincing.

His integrity could not be concealed from the camera, and this was one reason for the failure of such movies as **Man of the West** in which an audience is asked to believe that he used to be a member of Lee J. Cobb's vicious outlaw gang, or **Vera Cruz** in which the suspense fails because no one in the audience is likely to wonder whether Cooper is really going to steal that gold.

Cooper was a great character actor in the sense that he was able to project a particular character profoundly, albeit in a narrow range: the courageous soft-spoken man of honor. Sometimes he was a Westerner, sometimes an introspective compassionate Hemingway hero (**For Whom the Bell Tolls**), sometimes a befuddled small-town innocent (**Mr. Deeds Goes to Town**)—or a doctor, a soldier, a spy, a Foreign Legionnaire, an artist, an architect, so forth; he played them all as men of integrity, and his genius was in his ability to convince an audience beyond all doubt that this character he portrayed was absolutely real. When one saw him on the screen one never thought of him as an actor; one simply saw the character, and thought, "That is Gary Cooper."

*

Cooper played the part of a highly fanciful Wild Bill Hickok in De Mille's **The Plainsman**. The real Hickok, a complex man whose actual character was far more fascinating than most of the literary or screen versions have been thus far, gave up his acting career in Buffalo Bill's stage show in the 1870s because the ludicrous Ned Buntline scripts in which he was trapped were far beneath his dignity. He went back to Dakota, began to go blind, and was murdered. But during his brief career as a theatre star the untrained and thespically inept Hickok amazed a number of critics. He was a dreadful actor, they said, but he had a compelling and gigantic attraction—some sort of magnetism.

Perhaps, they said, it was simply that he was the real thing.

In a lesser way an air of reality enabled highly decorated war heroes like Audie Murphy and Neville Brand to achieve screen popularity despite (at least in Murphy's case) any evidence of acting ability: somehow the camera penetrated the clumsiness and found a core of reality.

With Gary Cooper we had both: an actor and the real thing.

*

Cooper may have been "the" Western hero but, for the most part, one views his movies in order to see Cooper, not to see the films. Few of his Westerns would be of special interest without him. No serious list of the genre's best films would be likely to include any more than three of Cooper's—the three already alluded to (**The Virginian**, **The Westerner**, **High Noon**). Tracing the development of the Western film, fortunately, is not as simple as that.

Critics of the genre tend to assess it historically, focusing attention on milestone films—the pace-setting works that influenced the maturation of the art. They emphasize seminal movies like **The Covered Wagon**, **The Iron Horse**, **Stagecoach** and **The Gunfighter**, each of which established new patterns for the genre to imitate.

But there is a difference between pioneer milestones and enduring entertainments. Today **The Covered Wagon** and even **The Iron Horse** strike many viewers as turgid bores—not nearly as much fun as, say, some of the Tom Mix films made at the same time—while **Stagecoach**, possibly the most famous Western of all, has become distressingly dated by its illogicalities, technical clumsinesses and innumerable cliches which have become painful through repetition in hundreds of imitative movies.

Although admittedly it's a period piece, the Gary Cooper version of **The Virginian** seems much fresher today than **Stagecoach**—even though it is a decade older. **The Gun-fighter**—more recent and thus less dated—nevertheless has suffered with time because its innovations were worn down in subsequent films to hackneyed predictabilities. This is less true of quite a few uncelebrated and half-forgotten films of the same period like **Canyon Passage** and **Four Faces West**, both of them made several years earlier than **The Gunfighter** but seemingly much fresher today. In historical terms it would be hard to deny their relative unimportance, but I must confess I like them better. I think they are artistically equal or superior to **The Gunfighter**, and they haven't been imitated to death.

Those who write about films seem obliged to nominate their "ten best" but rather than fall into that trap I prefer to submit a list of twenty-six movies as representative of the best that I think the various Western subgenres have to offer. That I make such a list at all is mainly an effort to show where my sympathies and prejudices lie, so that the reader may gain an impression of the kind of attitude with which I look at Westerns.

Critics are like religions in that no two are quite alike. Some appear to react to individual films out of visceral prejudice, for or against, after which they summon rationalizations to justify their opinions. Others come to films with consistent philosophical bias—like Andrew Sarris, whose pontifications are of the auteur school. Still others think of themselves as guardians of art against the Philistines—as if they, the critics, were the only men of taste; the most ridiculous of these has been John Simon, one of whose pronouncements—in the August 1978 *Saturday Evening Post*—was that there is no such thing, by definition, as a good Western. The Western, Simon says, is "an infantile genre." Wrong; Simon is an infantile critic. What he means is that he doesn't like Westerns, but he hasn't the grace to admit it in so simple a way.

The selective Bibliography at the end of this book provides a representative listing of books about, and critical opinions of, Westerns. The number of books about films threatens to surpass the number of films; this one tries to clear the air, render a one-volume source of information that would otherwise need to be looked up in dozens of separate sources, and apply common sense from the moviegoer's point of view to a subject that has been treated all too often by critics to whom sensibilities, facts and realities all seem to be negligible trivialities to be discarded in the lofty search for some systematic kind of metaphysical Truth.

My own feeling is that truth can be found in the films themselves, rather than in historical or systemic analyses of them. I selected the films listed here mainly for their aesthetic value today: these are the films I have, or in a few cases would like to have, in my own library.

One cannot pretend that any significant number of these movies can be counted among the cinema's great works of art. Some of them, in fact, are merely superior examples of minor subgenres. But all of them seem to add something on each reacquaintance. I seldom get bored with them; they stand the tests of time and repetition.

They are listed in chronological order:

The Virginian, 1929—still a fine interpretation of the classic myth, performed with zest and surprisingly up-to-date humor and subtlety.

Law and Order, 1932—Walter Huston in one of the best of the Wyatt Earp at the O K Corral movies. Prints of this one are hard to find.

Union Pacific, 1939—a bit quaint now, but it's enhanced by the unbeatable combination of its source material: Ford's **The Iron Horse** (some footage from which is reused here) and Ernest Haycox's good novel **Trouble Shooter**. One of the best of the epics.

The Westerner, 1940—a movie of giant legendary quality, with Cooper a stunning figure on horseback, and a towering performance by Walter Brennan as the venal, vital, childish and cunning Judge Roy Bean.

Western Union, 1941—the first successful spectacular Western in Technicolor, and still one of the most satisfying of all; some elements of the plot are dated, but Randolph Scott's tragic outlaw remains the best role of his career (with the possible exception of the one in **Ride the High Country**), and the action sequences are marvelous.

My Darling Clementine, 1946—lyrical, introspective, dreamlike; one of the most beautiful films directed by John Ford, with Henry Fonda fixing foursquarely the mythic image of Wyatt Earp.

Canyon Passage, 1946—a small, quiet, color movie that represents the best screen interpretation of the literary richness of an Ernest Haycox novel; long neglected, a true sleeper and a minor masterwork.

Ramrod, 1947—in some ways the most "classic" of all ranchland Westerns; a splendid little Luke Short film, consistently rewarding.

Pursued, 1947—rentlessly grim psychological Western with stirring performances by Robert Mitchum, Judith Anderson and Dean Jagger; a bit dated and hysterical, but the story still leaves one's hair standing on end, and its forcefulness is immense.

The Treasure of the Sierra Madre, 1948—the B. Traven-John Huston masterpiece about four prospectors and the madness of gold-greed: splendid in every way, with Bogart and Walter Huston simply astonishing.

Four Faces West, 1948—moving, touching, nearly forgotten gem about a man on the run and his compassionate pursuer; a Western in which not a single shot is fired.

Red River, 1948—John Wayne, Montgomery Clift and Walter Brennan directed by Howard Hawks in the cattle-drive movie against which all others must be measured.

Blood on the Moon, 1948—Mitchum again, and Luke Short again; directed by Robert Wise; a tough and complicated suspense movie with a disappointing plot but a wonderful flavor of the real West.

She Wore a Yellow Ribbon, 1949—John Wayne in his most touching role, in the only Technicolor film in John Ford's Cavalry trio.

Rio Grande, 1950—another John Ford-John Wayne cavalry movie, this one in black-and-white; I shall never decide which of these two is the better film; both are ageless and splendid.

The Gunfighter, 1950—a fine Gregory Peck performance as the doomed fighting man; for all its moody bitterness it is still capable of stirring the heart.

High Noon, 1952—a taut unified suspense thriller with the finest Gary Cooper performance of all: there are implausibilities in the plot, but if one accepts its premises, it is splendidly realized.

Ride the Man Down, 1952—a minor film but wonderfully representative of the little stock-company ranch-romance Westerns: beautifully performed and directed; the third Luke Short film on this list.

The Naked Spur, 1953—perhaps the tightest of the beleaguered-and-pursued suspense Westerns, magnificently acted by a wonderful ensemble.

Shane, 1953—a towering movie marred only by directorial self-consciousness and the miscasting of Alan Ladd; nevertheless it remains one of the supreme Westerns—the embodiment of the classic Western myth, and a grand entertainment.

Bad Day at Black Rock, 1954—a gripping tale of mystery and retribution; Spencer Tracy and Robert Ryan at their best.

Johnny Guitar, 1954—unique: an overwrought, overblown melodrama that borders on caricature and scenery-chewing absurdity; but it's powerful and towering, with mar-

John Wayne as a "B" oater star in the 1930s. Author's collection

Gordon Elliott, alias William "Wild Bill" Elliott. One of the best of the programmer stars. (THE PLAINSMAN AND THE LADY, 1946.) Republic pictures

Rex Allen, last of the "B" stars, relaxes between takes with fellow cowboy actor Slim Pickens, c. 1952. Republic Pictures

The transition from silents to talkies: Johnny Mack Brown and William S. Hart kid around on the set of BILLY THE KID (1930). MGM

The American Indian has been subjected to uneven treatment in Westerns. Iron Eyes Cody co-stars in SITTING BULL (1954). United Artists

THE WILD BUNCH (1969): Ernest Borgnine, William Holden, Warren Oates. A solemn, dignified procession, like holy warriors on a grand quest. Warner Brothers

THE WILD BUNCH
(1969): William Holden.
The end of the old ways.
Warner Brothers

RED RIVER (1948): John
Wayne, Montgomery Clift.
A great movie because a lot
of people were having good
days. United Artists

velous pictorial images and hearty performances and that haunting score. For buffs, it's a
"good bad movie."

The Searchers, 1956—called (by Roger Greenspun in *The New York Times*) the greatest American movie of all time; in any case it's a spectacularly fine one, the best of John
Ford and the best of John Wayne.

Lonely Are the Brave, 1962—a gemlike eulogy to the free West and an implicit farewell to the Western.

Ride the High Country, 1962—the sad and lovely tribute to the past with which Sam
Peckinpah succeeded John Ford as *doyen* of the Western.

The Wild Bunch, 1969—Peckinpah's masterpiece, and the only truly great Western
film of the post-Ford era; to be discussed later in this chapter.

*

It's very hard to leave it at that. Many films deserve a place on such a list. Among
those that nearly measure up are **Billy the Kid** (1930), **Broken Lance, Fort Apache,
Hondo, The Lusty Men, The Magnificent Seven, The Shootist**, Stagecoach (1939).

Among my personal favorites I would number **The Bravados, Colorado Territory,
The Far Country, From Hell to Texas, Garden of Evil, The Hanging Tree, J.W. Coop,
The Professionals, The Proud Ones, The Ride Back, The Rounders, The Sheepman,
Support Your Local Sheriff, They Came to Cordura, They Died with Their Boots On,
The Unforgiven, Valdez Is Coming, Yellow Sky** and possibly twenty others.

Many have serious faults, but none fails to reward its audience.

*

It is not my purpose in this book to re-cover all the ground that has been trampled in
other books, but it does seem that certain points need to be discussed because they have
been ignored or treated inaccurately in other publications.

A forbidding amount of scholarship remains to be done, for example, on the subject
of the black Western. When Sidney Poitier and Harry Belafonte announced with their
1972 production of **Buck and the Preacher** that theirs was the first black Western (that is,
made not only with black actors but by black producers and director), they were incor-
rect by at least fifty-six years and perhaps dozens of movies.

Students of the genre may trace it back still farther but at the moment the first black
Western appears to have been **Trooper K**, an independent production of 1916 about the
exploits of the (Negro) Tenth Cavalry Regiment in the wars against Geronimo's Apaches
in the 1870s and 1880s. The cast, writers, producers and director of this film were black
Americans.

It was followed by a number of independent black films like Oscar Micheaux's **The
Homesteader** (1919), until by the 1930s there is said to have been a steady little industry
in Westerns made by and for blacks—a kind of "black market" of cheaply produced indie
movies, often taken around in film cans by their producers and sold one by one out of a
car-trunk to movie houses in urban ghettos and the rural south.

Donald Bogle, in his book **Toms, Coons, Mulattoes, Mammies and Bucks**, points out
that a couple of these films were **Harlem on the Prairie** (1937) and **Bronze Buckaroo**
(1938), starring the black singer Herb Jeffrey; but Bogle lets it go at that. Actually, scores
of black oaters may have appeared and disappeared over the decades, most of them probably of sub-"B" quality and adding little to the existing plots, merely substituting black
casts for white ones, but now and then there may have been a movie of interest; it remains for dedicated students to discover them.

*

Racially the Western movie was never lily white. It was always concerned, for example, with American Indians and Spanish-Americans. But certainly until the 1960s it did not begin to reflect the extent of black participation in Western history. The real Deadwood Dick was black—a fact Hollywood ignored in its various depictions of him, most of which were in "B" films—and the virtual founder of the modern rodeo was the black cowboy Bill Pickett. The Ninth and Tenth Cavalry Regiments—manned by freed slaves—fought on the Plains and in the Southwest for twenty years, and "Black Jack" Pershing got his nickname as a result of having served as an officer with the Tenth. Settlement of the West after the Civil War was accomplished partly by ex-slaves, as is hinted at in **Buck and the Preacher**, and a number of prominent mountain men like Antoine Leroux were of at least partially Negro ancestry.

In the 1960s and thereafter, some of this neglect began to be rectified but sometimes the cure proved worse than the disease. The rash of "blaxploitation" Westerns in the 1970s, while reflecting an ethnic arrogance absent from earlier films, may have been no better in the long run than the movies that made fools of Stepin Fetchit, Willie Best and Mantan Morland. But then those critics who sniped hardest at the black adventure movies seemed to be complaining mainly about their lack of realism and I never saw the sense in that because **Buck and the Preacher** is no less realistic than its white counterparts. It is a second-rate movie, regardless of race, but quality and realism are two different things, and there are white Westerns that are a whole lot worse than **Buck and the Preacher**. The tendency in black movies to make stereotypes of all characters—good blacks, bad whites—is not a failing exclusive to black filmmakers; it happens whenever dimwitted movies are produced by cynical promoters whatever their race. Can anyone seriously contend that the admittedly dreadful **Soul Soldier** is any worse than the white spaghetti-sadism oaters like **A Stranger in Town**? It always struck me as curious that the same intellectual movie buffs who swooned over old Green Hornet serials could condemn black actors for appearing in black versions of the same sort of simpleminded adventure fantasies. After all the Mexicans that Clint Eastwood and Lee Van Cleef massacred on the screen in the spaghetti oaters of the 1960s and 1970s, it was hardly fair to complain about Nigger Charley's wiping out a few white bad guys.

*

In the 1960s, with a new awakening among minority groups, spokesmen for the American Indian movements began to complain that Hollywood had maligned and degraded the Native American on the screen—that movies had never been fair to the Indians. A public television series of half-hour documentaries in the early 1980s, hosted and narrated by Will Sampson, perpetuated this revisionist disparagement.

Actually the complaint was based on half-truths, but if you are trying to be heard you must be strident. The American Indian's case against Hollywood is only partly justified, but it probably needs to be stated strongly; otherwise it would be ignored.

Recognition of the dilemma of the Native American has appeared in numerous Western films in which both reality and conscience have been in ample evidence—contrary to the accusations of the Red Power activists.

As early as 1912, Thomas Ince attempted in **The Indian Massacre** to tell the red man's side of the story. (The massacre was of, not by, Indians.) Oft-filmed popular yarns like **The Squaw Man, Ramona** and **The Half Breed** showed varying degrees of sensitivity to the nature of prejudice on the part of both races. Buffalo Bill's multi-titled 1913 movie about the Indian wars, unfortunately suppressed, was a chronicle of white crimes and Indian sufferings. By 1934 Hollywood was mature enough to produce **Massacre**—a movie about Indians that was far more sincere, effective and original than the more recent **Tell Them Willie Boy Is Here**, which despite its favored position with urban critics was in fact a tiresome checklist of liberal stereotypes and cliches in which the characters were so thinly and implausibly drawn that one could not care much about any of them, red or white. The history of the Western is spotted with a fair, although not huge, number of Indian-oriented movies like **The Vanishing American**, **Broken Arrow**, **Apache**, **Flaming Star**, **Run of the Arrow**, my own **Relentless** and many more.

In thousands of movies Hollywood did treat the Indian shabbily. But it was not done with absolute consistency. And it is ridiculous to complain that the movies about Indians were not accurate in depicting the real life of Indians. They were just as accurate as were the movies about cowboys, gunfighters, lawmen, wagon-train pioneers or prospectors. Movies are not historical tracts; a mythic entertainment is not obliged to be a documentary. It is perfectly true that Apache Indians did not wear feathered warbonnets or live in teepees, and seldom rode horses (they more often ate them), but it is equally true that cowboys did not wear gloves and tied-down holsters or challenge one another to face-down gunfights on the street at high noon, and seldom rode along singing and strumming a guitar while an off-screen orchestra accompanied them.

Hollywood's record is neither worse nor better than that of the other media. Movies, like novels and magazines and broadcast programs, reflect the social attitudes of their times. When in the 1970s Marlon Brando and his colleagues condemned the movies of the 1930s because of their unfair attitude toward Indians, they were condemning the biases of the entire culture that existed at that time. I find obscene the fact that in the Southwest in the 1970s, some Chicano organizations tried to ban from TV such films as **The Treasure of the Sierra Madre**, **The Wild Bunch** and **Butch Cassidy and the Sundance Kid** because they maligned Mexicans. Such philistine efforts reveal mainly that the would-be censors are intellectually more offensive than any films they may want to ban.

The West's mythology reflected the agrarian white Victorian philosophy of Manifest Destiny. That attitude was created by and for the dominant class. The hindsight of today's concerns makes it ecologically and racially questionable; but it reflected the spirit of the time of its origin. To try to hide the old myth or rewrite it in our own image is an ambition doomed to failure: such efforts may destroy the old mythology (indeed, perhaps they already have done), but they will not replace it with anything that is worth a damn.

*

The best Westerns are movies that move. They move in terms of action; they move audiences emotionally.

Their heroes reflect the Hemingway aspect of courage ("grace under pressure") and their writers and directors always seemed to understand their obligations to seize, hold and satisfy audiences.

But after 1962 it appeared these precepts had been forgotten. Most of the Westerns of the post-Cooper years were flaccid bores—proving perhaps that one man's excitement is another's ennui, but making many of us nostalgic for the movies of the past (to the extent that we must guard diligently against "remembering" excellences that didn't really exist).

One reason for the passing of the Western has been a creeping paralysis of sensibilities in artists and audiences alike. The meaning of a drama of good and evil is lost when neither the dramatist nor the audience recognizes the distinctions between good and evil. The "good" guy, in many post-1960 Westerns, became merely the toughest guy; the most proficient killer became perforce the best man.

This syndrome can be traced back at least as far as 1950s movies like **The Fastest Gun Alive**. It denies the assertion of earlier folklore that the hero wins because he's on the side of the right. It turns that fantasy around: the hero is "right" simply because he kills his enemies before they can kill him. That, of course, is not heroism at all; it may be pragmatism, but it also reflects an attitude of nihilism—even fascism.

This inversion of the heroic fantasy led, at least for a while, to the veneration of filmmakers whose mindlessly sadistic movies debased the craft of film to a truly contemptible level.

The glorification of violence-for-its-own-sake found its most popular manifestations in the spaghetti Westerns of the middle and late 1960s, and its leadership in the films of Sergio Leone, from **A Fistful of Dollars** through **Once Upon a Time in the West** and his last (to date) Western, variously titled **A Fistful of Dynamite** and **Duck You Sucker**. While some of Leone's pictures have undeniable excellences—**Once Upon a Time** is curiously fascinating—nevertheless they finished the job of corrupting the Western genre, because they ceased to employ their violence in valid dramatic ways; they dispensed with the sturdy moral underpinnings of the true Western myth, and substituted for them a loathsome indifference to moral values which renders them not so much amoral as immoral. Their "heroes" kill people for a dollar or two, or to avenge a minor insult, or to prove how tough they are, or sometimes just for the hell of it.

A few simpleminded critics have blamed this moral collapse in films on the Viet Nam experience, but **A Fistful of Dollars** was filmed in 1964, before America or the world really became aware of Viet Nam at all. Viet Nam was, like the movies, a symptom rather than a cause.

The morality expressed in Leone's oaters, and in many of the American-made Westerns that succeeded them, is pretty much the morality of the crass characters who produce and distribute those kinds of movies: the pigsty morality of violent me-first greed. I acknowledge that these films have their apologists, and I hope I may be forgiven if I express a deep disgusted revulsion toward them.

The question of morality and violence in Westerns received growing attention after the release of **The Wild Bunch** in 1969. Director Sam Peckinpah's excesses of gore were displayed in other films after that one, but **The Wild Bunch** in its uncut version remains to date his bloodiest movie, and one of the goriest—and most beautiful—of all Westerns. Peckinpah's original release-print was 144 minutes in length but early reviews persuaded Warner Brothers to abridge it; the resultant 135-minute version still contained several off-putting sequences of blood geysering in slow motion: spurting from wounds, bubbling from lips, leaping from a slit throat, spattering walls and actors. (The version most commonly available in the early 1980s was cut down still farther, to a relatively tame 127 minutes, although Warner Brothers' subsidiaries were still distributing it fraudulently as the "original uncut" version. As for the version shown on commercial television, it was butchered to the point of incoherence.)

When the critical hullabaloo became strident, both Peckinpah and his star William Holden issued statements that the movie's gore had been deliberately designed to show how disgusting and painful real violence actually is, in contrast (presumably) to the painless violence of other Westerns in which actors get shot but never seem to get hurt. I would guess these defensive statements were dreamed up after the fact, since nothing in the story or the production of **The Wild Bunch** indicates that it was designed as an anti-violence movie. Its excessively lavish bloodbaths are in keeping with a line of Peckinpah's dialogue delivered in the movie by an old Mexican villager, speaking to Holden about a pair of drunkenly cavorting outlaws in the background: "We all dream of being a child. Even the worst of us. Perhaps most of all the worst of us." **The Wild Bunch** is like that: an acting-out of adolescent rage fantasies. While its effect on some audiences may be revulsion, I don't think that was Peckinpah's intention. Rather, I think he mistakenly expected audiences to come to a better understanding of the characters in the film because of their visible endurance of, and triumph over, the most painful of tests. (Most of the characters in the film do not survive, but they do prevail. Even in their deaths there are kinds of vindication, kinds of triumph. And certainly Peckinpah has found an extraordinary beauty in violence, in this film, as no other filmmaker has ever done.)

The excessive butchery in **The Wild Bunch** led most early critics and audiences to dismiss it as just another spaghetti-inspired ode to destruction. Actually it is quite the reverse. **The Wild Bunch** is the antithesis of the Leone films. Rather than being indifferent to morality, it is an agonized moral outcry. It is surely ironic that this most violent and bloody of all American Westerns is also, in its curious and contradictory way, the most stubbornly moral and moralistic of all the post-Cooper Westerns.

Writer-director Peckinpah garnered the reputation of a man without many inhibitions; his erratic personal behavior in the 1970s made occasional headlines, most of them having to do with drinking and fighting. Whether real or sham, the image he presented to the public was that of a crude primitive, of a roistering tough guy who chose the company of hardbitten villains, delighted in violence and epitomized all the worst qualities in the idea of "machismo." And certainly his unfortunate excesses in **The Wild Bunch**, no matter how well motivated, distracted audiences and obscured the fact that it is a towering movie, with a flavor of tragic grandeur hardly ever matched in the history of the Western film.

*

The Wild Bunch was released in the same season as **True Grit** and **Butch Cassidy and the Sundance Kid**. It stirred up controversy but didn't receive the critical accolades that the other two films inspired. Yet both **True Grit** and **Butch Cassidy** are really quite ordinary: excellently made but they added little to what already existed in the genre. If the John Wayne role of Rooster Cogburn in **True Grit** had been played instead by, say, Dean Martin, then the film probably would have attracted very little attention; it was markedly inferior to the novel on which it was based, and interest was stirred up partly because the book's title was well known (it was a best-seller) and partly because the cantankerous, hard-drinking, profane character was outside Wayne's usual range of stalwarts.

Both films attempted to approach the same theme as that of **The Wild Bunch**—it is, in a way, the theme of this book as well: the death of the old ways and values. Indeed, both **Butch Cassidy** and **The Wild Bunch** deal specifically with the death of the old outlaws (and Butch Cassidy's gang, in actuality, used to be called The Wild Bunch). But **True Grit** and **Butch Cassidy** approached their theme on a slick, glib level that left audiences with the feeling that all those shootings were good clean fun. **The Wild Bunch**, by contrast, is a serious drama that insists that death is not fun; that there is sad and terrible tragedy in the passing of the old ways; and that what has replaced the old values is much less than we had before. Edmond O'Brien, as the cackling old-timer, delivers the film's tag-line: "It ain't going to be like it was before, but it'll do." Meaning, it's all we've got left, so it'll *have* to do.

Peckinpah assumed leadership of the Western when John Ford retired, and a comparison of the two men is necessary to an understanding of the changes that took place in the Western during the 1960s.

*

The Westerns of the 1940s and 1950s had been dominated by Ford's romantic visions. His films virtually define the Western from 1939 to 1956: **Stagecoach, My Darling Clementine, Fort Apache, Rio Grande, She Wore a Yellow Ribbon, Three Godfathers, Wagonmaster, The Searchers**, and lesser films among them as well. There were other important Westerns in those days, of course, but hardly any of them failed to owe a great deal to Ford's influence; I doubt Howard Hawks could have directed **Red River** as he did if it had not been for Ford's having shown the way. (Hawks, his fans to the contrary, was never the artist Ford was.)

The Westerns of the 1960s and 1970s were dominated in a similar way by Sergio Leone and Sam Peckinpah. Leone's pictures were interesting but they were aberrations, like an evolutionary line taking a species to the cul-de-sac of extinction. (By 1980 the spaghetti Westerns were only a memory. A few of them were interesting but they did a great deal of harm. I am thankful they died. Unfortunately they left an indelible influence on the American Westerns that came after them.) Peckinpah, on the other hand, was a Westerner with authentic poetic visions, and these—like them or not—found their highest expression in **The Wild Bunch**.

What is amazing in any comparison of Ford and Peckinpah is not their differences but their similarities, which are numerous and striking. Both are primitives rather than sophisticates; this quality is in keeping with the nature of the Western. Both are hard-drinking advocates of the *macho* school of manliness, addicted to rough horseplay and crude practical jokes —Western characteristics traceable back to Tom Mix, Buffalo Bill and Wild Bill Hickok. Both directors epitomize the filmmaker as creator of pictorial images—in that sense both are important artists, and certainly no director since Ford has displayed the unerring painter's eye for cinematic composition that Peckinpah revealed in virtually all his movies up through **Pat Garrett and Billy the Kid**. (After that one, his work dwindled rapidly in quality; his later films, like **Convoy,** had no particular distinction and indeed could have been directed by anybody.) Ford learned from the painter Frederic Remington, and Peckinpah learned from Ford.

Both men are romantics: in a way, throwbacks to the simple agrarian idealism of our nineteenth-century dreams. But a striking philosophical difference manifests itself between the form that Ford's romanticism took and the form that Peckinpah's took. Ford affirmed traditional values without question. He was a storyteller who chose scripts that reinforced his visions: his reverence was almost painful toward old virtues and standards of good, right and heroism. Many of his cinematic heroes—in **Stagecoach**, the cavalry movies, **The Searchers**—are larger-than-life giants.

Peckinpah, by contrast, saw his romantic dreams infected by disillusion and cynicism. (Am I reading too much into his motivations, or could his disillusion have been caused by the fact that his early training as a writer-director was in commercial television? The TV networks are administered mostly by Neanderthals and baboons whose stupid insensitivity would make a cynic of anybody at all. You can't work in television and keep any sort of innocence.) Unable to ignore present-day realities as Ford was able to do, Peckinpah evidently concluded that the old values were matters of nostalgic wistfulness rather than contemporary reality.

The outlaw heroes of Peckinpah's films—Pike Bishop in **The Wild Bunch**, Billy in **Pat Garrett and Billy the Kid**—are honorable men but their honor dooms them because Peckinpah seems to believe it's inevitable that such heroes will be cut down by corrupt villains or petty assassins, just as the Kennedys and Martin Luther King—the last heroes of living American mythology—were cut down during the formative years of Peckinpah's experience as a feature-film director.

In Peckinpah's films we find the insistent theme of changing times: the message that those who wish to survive must knuckle under to the big corporate interests, the faceless holders of power who really run the world. There's no room left in Peckinpah's universe for the heroic loner, the iconoclast, the virtuous free individual, the hero who offers something grand and old-fashioned by way of aspiration and achievement. The real power—always in the background of Peckinpah's films—is seen to be masked by empty slogans, corruption and a sense of a remote manipulation (the equivalent of today's bureaucracy) that pays lip service to honor while crushing life blindly.

(By comparison the real power in the background of Ford's films was more often honorable and benevolent, and willing to bend the rules and throw the rule-book away when necessary: consider the clandestine but supportive backing that General Sheridan—J. Carrol Naish—provides to John Wayne in **Rio Grande**.)

It didn't really shock anyone when Peckinpah splashed the screen with gore in **The Wild Bunch**, just as it didn't really shock anyone when a President of the United States turned out to be a crook.

Peckinpah, at his zenith, was John Ford disillusioned. **The Wild Bunch** cannot be equated with the titillations of dreary, bloody opportunism that one finds in Leone's films and their imitators, in which we are left with bleak spectacles of puppet-like gunslingers wiping one another out in mechanical and unemotional massacres, to the accompaniment of Ennio Morricone's jangling but saccharine and falsely romantic music scores. There is no honest emotion at all in Leone's films; they are cartoons. Conversely, Peckinpah's movies are anything but unemotional. They are cries of raw pain.

They are, I suppose, warnings (from Peckinpah's point of view).

The Wild Bunch gives us the heroes of **The Magnificent Seven** a decade later: the world has changed under them; the old truths have died. Now the fighting men are soured, gone empty with disillusion and anger. "This was going to be my last one," says Pike Bishop (William Holden). "I'm not getting around so good any more. I was going to do this one and back off."

Dutch, his partner (Ernest Borgnine), replies flatly, "Back off to *what?*"—and Pike has no answer.

(It may be stretching a point, but **The Wild Bunch** was filmed at a time when Bishop James Pike, the iconoclastic clergyman, was much in the headlines decrying the war in Viet Nam. Bishop Pike becomes Pike Bishop in Peckinpah's film: a zealot, intending to lead his men to glory but actually leading them into disaster because he's not as bright as he thinks he is. If one assumes this to have been deliberate rather than coincidental, it reinforces the moral significance of the film.)

These are doomed men. First they were heroes, then they went bad; now they can go only to death; they've outlived their world. "They'll be waiting for us, Pike." And Pike replies, "I wouldn't have it any other way . . . We're finished, all of us." But they mean to go out in a blaze of valor; their indomitability has the magnificence of grand tragedy. They are determined to bring down Evil with them when they go. These are powerful characters in an extraordinarily powerful motion picture.

Deke Thornton (Robert Ryan), an ex-partner of Pike's, is being forced by a railroad boss (Albert Dekker) to track down his former friends. When two of them (Ben Johnson, Warren Oates) complain about this betrayal, Pike defends the man: "He gave them his word!" (The irony here is lost on most audiences because among the scenes the studio cut was a flashback showing how Pike's slow-witted betrayal sent Thornton to prison.)

Pike's current partner (Ernest Borgnine) shows the shift in values that has corrupted them all: "It ain't your word that counts. It's who you give it to." But Pike won't buy that. The contrast is between Pike's intractable dignity (the old ways) and what the film implies are the new ways: children torturing scorpions in a fire; Strother Martin and L.Q. Jones as killer-scavengers, stripping the dead of their gold teeth and boots; the railroad boss (Dekker) who salts a bank with sacks of steel washers to bait the outlaws into a trap; the inept U.S. Army, which can't even get mounted on its own horses; and the Mexican revolutionary "general" (Emilio Fernandez) who tortures prisoners for fun. ("General, hell," says Oates, "he's just a common bandit, just like us." But Borgnine corrects him: "No. Not like us. We don't *hang* nobody.")

In its currently accessible versions **The Wild Bunch** lacks some of its gore and several key scenes; all but one of those are flashbacks that serve to illuminate the characters and the thematic structure of the film. In one of them we see the death of Pike's girl friend—an event that embitters him. The one front-story sequence that was eliminated by the studio was a battle between Mexican rebels and government soldiers; this was intercut, contrapuntally, with the train-robbery sequence, and provided not only a balletic balance but also a graphic illustration of a plot point (the "general's" need for modern weapons, without which he loses this battle).

The Wild Bunch is a thematic reprise of Peckinpah's earlier **Ride the High Country**. His vision through these films is consistent—the death of valor and dignity, their replacement by flaccid denials of the value of courage and honor. Unfortunately his expression of that vision is flawed by the fact that he does not write well and the fact that he allows his exuberant penchant for gimmickry (all those blindingly quick intercuts; all those blood squibs gouting and geysering) to get in the way of his stories. He has been accused of misogyny—the women in his films usually are either villains or baggage or betrayers—and his views certainly are monolithic, stubborn, irascible and often childlike. As a writer he is not capable of creating whole characters who are not flawed by caricature or incompleteness; therefore he has to rely on his actors to bring them to life and usually his actors are not good enough to do it. Jason Robards lacked the range and the warmth to make us care enough about Cable Hogue; Kris Kristofferson was an overripe and inadequate Billy the Kid. But the cast of **The Wild Bunch** met the challenge.

The deep and moving honesty of **The Wild Bunch**—whether or not one can agree with its attitudes—is far beyond comparison with that of any of the pretentious, arty, pastoral Westerns that so captivated critics in the 1970s (**Bad Company**, **Days of Heaven**, so forth), or with the contemporaneous **True Grit** and **Butch Cassidy**, both of which are handsome entertainments but trivial works of art. **The Wild Bunch**, unlike the others, has moments of profound impact, as when the Bunch rides out of the Mexican village where it has licked its wounds and the villagers assemble to bid the outlaws farewell, watching the Bunch ride slowly out of the village to the strains of a tune sung softly by the villagers. In the hands of a lesser director it might have been hopelessly hokey and contrived, but it is wholly believable in its context; a solemn dignified procession, as if these are great holy warriors riding out on a grand quest.

The photography in these scenes (by Lucien Ballard) has great dramatic effect: it is a style of low-angle camera work we don't see very often any more. This scene is reprised in the film's closing shot to point up the statement of the movie—along with echoes of the bawdy laughter of the Wild Bunch: a free reckless laughter that will not be heard again.

Ballard's photography startled audiences in 1969; it contained a great many telephoto zoom shots, violent stunts shot in extreme slow-motion to create dreamlike balletic effects, and scenes shot at night or indoors that appeared to have been lit by natural sources. Subsequently filmgoers became accustomed to those techniques; by 1980 a viewer coming anew to **The Wild Bunch** would not notice anything unusual about its cinematography. It would be easy to forget how much of an effect the film had. Later Westerns like **The Long Riders** could not have been made had it not been for Peckinpah's movie.

It must be clear by now that I harbor a great and impassioned fondness for this ridiculously bloody movie. Of all the Westerns available to me, **The Wild Bunch** is the single film I screen most often. I have never tired of it; I have never failed to find new wonders in it; and yet I cheerfully accept the fact that there are perceptive people for whom the picture is loathsome and even tiresome. Some of them are people whose judgment and taste I respect. I can only say I love the film; I cannot condemn those who don't. Without such differences of opinion there would be no need for criticism or critics.

Suffice to say, then, that in my opinion (which is not engraved in tablets of stone) **The Wild Bunch** is the last great Western to have been filmed to date, and indeed one of the few great films of any kind.

*

The Wild Bunch is an entertainment (it is, just in passing, one of the most exciting "caper" movies ever made—better, in its own genre, than even the impressive **The Professionals**) and something more. In spite of its flaws, which should not be ignored, it is not only profound but also serious. (The two don't necessarily go together.) For example, at no time does Peckinpah descend to any of the standard Western devices; his story is too important for that. When the main character meets his end it is not in a stand-up duel with some awful villain; rather, he is done in by treachery—shot in the back by a small child. (The cruelty of children is a constant motif in this and other Peckinpah movies.) That is the true horror of the film, and its truth at the same time.

One didn't have to agree with Peckinpah's moral point of view but one had to concede that he had one. (It would be very hard for most people to agree with it wholeheartedly after seeing such dubiously valid movies as **Pat Garrett and Billy the Kid** and the misbegotten **Bring Me the Head of Alfredo Garcia**.) This moral sensibility, regardless how distorted, made Peckinpah all but unique among modern film writers and directors. Virtually everyone else in the industry after the early 1960s gave evidence of exactly that collapse of values that Peckinpah was attacking.

There was a cynical spirit among us; we no longer believed in much of anything at all. We elected dishonest men and fools to high public office, knowing as we voted that they were dishonest men and fools. Overwhelmed by outpourings of chicanery, agony and dilemma, we became the ultimate isolationists: we wanted merely to be left alone. We had no heroes left anymore. That was what Peckinpah said in his films. (In art, though, what matters is not what he said but how well he said it. In **The Wild Bunch** the statement is made with consummate artistry.)

In part it was technology that had rendered heroism anachronistic. It was not heroic but merely whimsical to cross the sea in an open boat when it could be done in a few hours in the comfort of a jetliner. After Viet Nam, courage was no longer honored; it was no longer acceptable to hate one's enemies; therefore we ended up hating the only available substitute: ourselves.

It was a world into which the virtuous hero on horseback did not fit.

6

THE

DIRECTORS

"Film is a director's medium."

That is the basis of the auteuriste argument. But it implies a syllogism based on fraudulent premises: that because the director is a creative force he therefore is the only creative force.

Auteurism is a feebleminded critical philosophy at best—nobody who has ever worked on a movie from inception to completion can possibly understand the theory, let alone accept it—but it has taken a strangler's grip since the 1950s, even to the point where most ordinary daily movie reviewers tend to credit directors with the sole praise or blame for "their" films.

As an illuminating example of reality as opposed to auteuriste fantasy, let us examine a director who has achieved a reputation among the self-styled Western movie *cineaste* experts second only to John Ford's; a director whose list of credits from 1926 to 1970 is both long and, in the aggregate, imposing; a director who in fact made only five out-and-out Westerns but who nevertheless has been called the second most important master of the genre: Howard Hawks.

Hawks is especially illustrative because after 1936 he produced as well as directed most of his pictures and therefore one can assume that his control over them was considerably greater than that of the average hired director.

Hawks made a large number of hit films. They included **The Dawn Patrol, Scarface, Sergeant York, To Have and Have Not, The Big Sleep** and **Gentlemen Prefer Blondes**, as well as a Western now regarded as a classic: **Red River**.

Then again, of course, Hawks directed such embarrassing turkeys as **Red Line 7000, Tiger Shark** and the elephantine **Land of the Pharaohs**.

When his five Westerns and the rest of his many films are listed together, one must have grave doubts whether the list can constitute an *oeuvre* with consistent elements beyond professional craftsmanship. What is there in common between **Red River** and the dull Rock Hudson comedy **Man's Favorite Sport**, or between **Scarface** and the abysmal **Rio Lobo**?

Among cinemaphiles, Hawks's greatest reputation was as an important "creator" of Westerns. Yet only one of his Westerns, **Red River**, is really an out-of-the-ordinary film.

Of his others, one is respectable if ponderous —**The Big Sky**—and one is competent but ordinary—**Rio Bravo**—and the last two—**El Dorado** and **Rio Lobo**—are dreary carbon copies of **Rio Bravo**, dwindling rapidly in quality; the last two, actually, are embarrassingly bad. (Hawks also directed parts of **Viva Villa** and **The Outlaw** but was not credited with either.)

Red River was a good movie because Russell Harlan photographed it, because Dimitri Tiomkin composed its score, because Christian Nyby edited it, because the actors were having good days and knew their jobs, because the crews were the best, because Borden Chase wrote it, *and* because Howard Hawks produced and directed it.

And actually Hawks all but ruined the film by spitefully editing most of John Ireland's scenes out (he was feuding with Ireland), and by changing the ending against the wishes of the author. The Hawks ending—Joanne Dru's speech—is admittedly a structural improvement but it's dreadfully written, so hard to swallow it risks losing the audience. Hawks was an excellent cinematic storyteller but a mediocre story creator; in many cases his meddling in screenplays did more harm than good to the films he directed. (For example, the novel on which **El Dorado** was based—Harry Brown's *The Stars in Their Courses*—has a much more interesting and less hackneyed story than Hawks's plodding film version.)

At the peak of his career (the late 1930s and the 1940s) Howard Hawks directed a large number of good films splendidly. It would be churlish and pointless to deny his virtues as a director; he was unquestionably an important and talented man. But he didn't create movies any more than a publisher's editor creates books. At best he participated in the creation.

But unfortunately there is nothing harder to kill than a bad idea whose time has come. Despite Godard's frank disclaimers, the auteur theory of film creation has reached the point where in too many quarters it is still treated as though it were the Eleventh Commandment.

The production system has nearly always imposed great limitations on everyone in moviemaking. Directors are not excepted. But given those limitations, a number of directors in the Western genre did outstanding work on occasion. Among them were Budd Boetticher (who in partnership with writer Burt Kennedy and actor Randolph Scott made several superior low-budget Westerns in the 1950s), Delmer Daves (**Broken Arrow, Cowboy, The Hanging Tree, Jubal, The Last Wagon, 3:10 to Yuma**), Henry Hathaway (**Rawhide, From Hell to Texas, Nevada Smith, Garden of Evil, True Grit**), Burt Kennedy (**Support Your Local Sheriff, The Rounders**), George Marshall (**The Sheepman, Pillars of the Sky, Texas, When the Daltons Rode, Destry Rides Again**), Nicholas Ray (**Run for Cover, The True Story of Jesse James, The Lusty Men, Johnny Guitar**), John Sturges (**Bad Day at Black Rock, Hour of the Gun, Last Train from Gun Hill, The Magnificent Seven**), Raoul Walsh (**The Big Trail, The Dark Command, Distant Drums**), William A. Wellman (**Buffalo Bill, The Ox-Bow Incident, Track of the Cat, Yellow Sky**) and William Wyler (**The Westerner, Friendly Persuasion, The Big Country**).

Others put a more specific mark on the Western. For instance Cecil B. De Mille gave us, if nothing else, consistency of size: it must be BIG. De Mille directed five Western talkies plus one version of the costume drama **The Buccaneer**, which half qualifies. Only one of his Westerns, **Union Pacific**, is really much good, but they all had the distinctive C.B. stamp: enormous spectacle, lavish sets and costumes, hordes of extras, low-cut bodices and heavy-breathing innuendo, vile villains, staunch heroes, an abhorrence of the real outdoors (he shot nearly everything indoors on vast sound stages with fake rear-projection scenery that was photographed by his second-unit assistant directors) and scripts that occasionally in vehemence made up for what they lacked in sophistication.

John Ford, the greatest of them all, won four Academy Awards for directing but, ironically, none was for a Western (unless you count **The Grapes of Wrath**). He was born Sean O'Fearna in 1895—in Maine, not in Ireland—and went to Hollywood in 1914 because his brother Francis had become a movie star there. Ford worked as an actor, then assistant cameraman, then prop man and finally stunt rider. He directed his first film in 1917—**The Tornado**, a two-reel oater that he wrote, starred and stunted in. He made a large number of silent features and of course **The Iron Horse**; after his 1939 success with **Stagecoach** he returned to the Western and in the 1940s made at least four splendid ones: **My Darling Clementine, Fort Apache, She Wore a Yellow Ribbon,** and **Rio Grande.** (The latter three are known commonly and collectively as "Ford's Cavalry Trilogy." All three feature John Wayne and Victor McLaglen, although Henry Fonda's villain steals **Fort Apache.**) Ford's lesser oaters of the period included **Three Godfathers, Wagonmaster** and **Drums Along the Mohawk**; he also directed **Young Mr. Lincoln** and **The Grapes of Wrath**, both of which have a strong flavor of Western Americana.

After 1950 his output dwindled; he went six years before making his next Western but when he did it was his masterwork, **The Searchers**. It was followed in the next eight years by **The Horse Soldiers, Sergeant Rutledge, Two Rode Together, The Man Who Shot Liberty Valance**, a segment of **How the West Was Won** and his last Western, **Cheyenne Autumn**, in 1964. Ford died in 1973. In all he had directed about a hundred and forty full-length movies and a large number of silent shorts.

Daring, sensitive and crochety, Ford reigned tyrannically over his stock-company of crews and actors. He maintained what amounted to a repertory company of Western performers: John Wayne, Ward Bond, Victor McLaglen, Ben Johnson, Harry Carey, Harry Carey, Jr., Francis Ford, Jane Darwell, George O'Brien, Mae Marsh, Grant Withers, Ken Curtis, John Agar, Hank Worden, Shirley Temple; sometimes it included Henry Fonda, Maureen O'Hara, Dick Foran and others. (It was a particular thrill for me when we were able to cast Ben Johnson and Harry Carey, Jr., in **Wild Times**; the two are among the last and best of the Western actors.)

Graphically Ford probably was the consummate American film artist. His work with the camera is less flashy than, say, Orson Welles's, but it is far more beautiful. He had a painter's eye for pictorial composition, even though he had very poor eyesight and relied on his cameramen to a greater extent than many directors do. Inevitably Ford made a few clunkers—**The Sun Shines Bright, Seven Women**—but his sound-era Westerns were nearly all good when they weren't superb. Without question he was the finest director ever to turn his hand regularly to the Western film.

Samuel Fuller is regarded by the *Cahiers du Cinema* critics as an important American film artist, "the intellectual's Peckinpah." God alone knows why. Fuller is a director whose excellences elude me. I don't think his films bear close scrutiny. His four Westerns are **The Baron of Arizona, Forty Guns, I Shot Jesse James** and **Run of the Arrow**. The first is unusual but dull; the third is routine; the others are rancid. (In 1980 Fuller came out of a lengthy retirement with a new film, the World War II movie **The Big Red One** with Lee Marvin. I thought it predictable and boring, but once again it found its supporters. I hope he doesn't make any more Westerns. **Forty Guns** is astonishingly obnoxious.)

John Huston easily could rest his reputation on one Western alone—**The Treasure of the Sierra Madre**. Always a maverick among American filmmakers, Huston had an erratic career but whenever he was counted out after some turkey he made a comeback with yet another fine movie. Among his Westerns **The Unforgiven** is good if a bit turgid, while **The Life and Times of Judge Roy Bean** is regrettable; he made two other films that border on the genre—**The Red Badge of Courage**, a minor masterwork, and **The Misfits**, a fascinating but flawed movie.

Anthony Mann died in 1967 and left behind him the nearest thing to an oeuvre of Westerns this side of John Ford. In the 1950s he teamed with scenarist Borden Chase and actor James Stewart to turn out a splendid series of action Westerns: **Winchester '73, The Naked Spur** (the only one not written by Chase), **Bend of the River, The Far Country** and (the least of them) **The Man from Laramie**. It is unquestionably a consistent and recognizable body of work; the films share a distinct flavor; but this oeuvre is the creation of the three-man team rather than Mann's alone. When he made Westerns without the other two, he often came a cropper, as with the unfortunate 1960 version of **Cimarron** or the disastrous **Man of the West**, which I think was the worst of Gary Cooper's later Westerns.

Sam Peckinpah came out of television and wrote screenplays for Westerns before he began directing films but his movie scripts were uniformly awful: **The Black Whip, The Glory Guys, Villa Rides**. It is an understatement to say he writes poorly. He directed many segments of Western TV series like **Wanted: Dead or Alive** and **Have Gun, Will Travel**; he created and helmed the short-lived but superb Brian Keith series **The Westerner**; and his first directorial outing on a feature was **The Deadly Companions** (1961), an interesting little actioner with unusual characters and bravura acting by Brian Keith, Maureen O'Hara and Chill Wills.

Peckinpah followed that debut a year later with the marvelous **Ride the High Country**, then spent three years making **Major Dundee**, a curious and ponderous Western that apparently was slashed by nearly an hour before its release. The movie is disjointed and sometimes hard to follow, but there is not much suggestion in it that another hour's footage would have saved it. Peckinpah then went into involuntary retirement for a while until he was able to make **The Wild Bunch**, after which he filmed **The Ballad of Cable Hogue, Junior Bonner, Pat Garrett and Billy the Kid,** and **Bring Me the Head of Alfredo Garcia**. Since then he hadn't done another Western at this book's press time; in 1980 he had been readying a picture called **The Texans** for Golden Harvest Productions but he left it, or was fired, and at last report there were lawsuits being filed.

Peckinpah is a man of oversized, sometimes frightening talent; even when his films are terrible they can be fascinating, and they rarely bore.

George Stevens made only three Westerns: **Annie Oakley, Giant**, and the one on which his reputation may rest, **Shane**. A meticulous and serious craftsman, Stevens planned every detail of his films carefully; he would spend weeks doing what another director might dismiss in a matter of hours. His talents, nevertheless, were limited. Still, when appropriately channeled they were imposing.

*

With the exceptions of Ford and Peckinpah, not one of the above-listed directors put his clear mark on the Western genre. The point of this cursory survey must be clear by now: the directors did not make the Western; the Western made the directors. Only Ford and Peckinpah had the excellence to rise above the material and make something new of it, and even their successes were only partial. Their oeuvres, like those distinctly lesser ones of Boetticher and Mann, were at least partly traceable to those who worked with them: actors, crews and writers. Most movies are made by families, not by soloists.

7

THE

WRITERS

In the first forty years of talking movies, thirty-six Westerns received Academy Award nominations for writing. The Oscar winners included Howard Estabrook for **Cimarron**, John Huston for **The Treasure of the Sierra Madre**, Philip Yordan for **Broken Lance**, William Goldman for **Butch Cassidy and the Sundance Kid** and "Robert Rich" for **The Brave One** in 1956. "Robert Rich" was a pen-name used by the blacklisted Dalton Trumbo. He didn't get to collect his award for years.

Trumbo wrote scripts for a few Westerns; they were mediocre except for **Lonely Are the Brave**, which was a reasonably faithful adaptation of the Abbey novel rather than a creative piece of work. He became a celebrity because of his courage in fighting the House Un-American Activities Committee witch-hunt, but his screenplays were wordy and often ponderous. One must look elsewhere to find the good oater writers.

Other celebrities have turned their hands to writing Western movies, often unexpectedly. A few examples of such curiosities are these:

*

Novelist, playwright, opinion monger and misanthropic wag Gore Vidal scripted **The Left-Handed Gun**.

Best-selling novelist Irving Wallace wrote several oaters like **The Burning Hills** and **Gun Fury**.

American institution John Steinbeck wrote the screenplay of **Viva Zapata**.

Best-selling novelist Leon Uris scripted **Gunfight at the OK Corral** (badly).

The late Pulitzer Prize novelist MacKinlay Kantor had screen-story credits that included **Hannah Lee, The Man from Dakota** and **Gun Crazy**.

Prolific novelist Stephen Longstreet has screen credits for **Stallion Road, Silver River** and others.

Rod Serling, science-fiction celebrity, scripted the Western **Saddle the Wind**.

As already noted, controversial director Sam Peckinpah wrote several Western screenplays for pictures he didn't direct, all bad.

Celebrated novelist-newspaperman-playwright Ben Hecht received writing credits on several Westerns of varying quality including **Viva Villa, The Indian Fighter** and **The Fiend Who Walked the West**.

Directors John Ford and
Henry Hathaway, c. 1962. MGM
(in conjunction with
How the West Was Won)

Sam Peckinpah. Warner Brothers

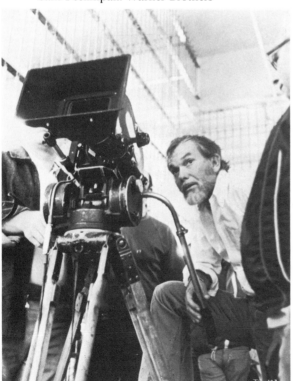

Director Joseph Kane on the set of
WYOMING (1947)—one of the
best of the mainstay "B" movie
directors. Republic Pictures

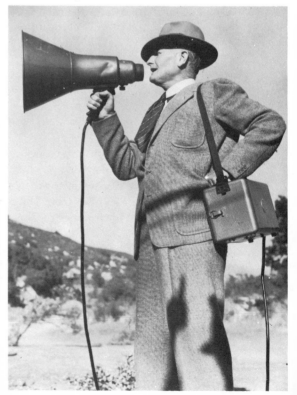

Novelist-screenwriter Niven Busch wrote, among others, DUEL IN THE SUN, PURSUED and THE FURIES. Paramount Pictures

Screenwriter William Bowers wrote THE GUNFIGHTER, THE SHEEPMAN and SUPPORT YOUR LOCAL SHERIFF. United Artists

It's still a record: 103 movies have been made from this writer's works, from RIDERS OF THE PURPLE SAGE (1918) to THE MAVERICK QUEEN (1956): novelist Zane Grey (1875–1939). Paramount Pictures (photo taken in 1936)

Novelist A.B. Guthrie, Jr. (**The Big Sky, The Way West**) wrote the screenplay of **Shane**, from Jack Schaefer's novel.

Novelist-playwright William Wister Haines (**Command Decision**) wrote a dozen screenplays including that of **The Texans**.

Playwright and best-selling popular anthropologist Robert Ardrey (**African Genesis**) wrote the screenplay for **The Wonderful Country**.

Playwright Frank D. Gilroy (**The Subject Was Roses**) scripted **The Fastest Gun Alive, Gunfight at Sandoval** and **From Noon till Three**; he also directed the latter film.

Director Frank Capra scripted **Westward the Women**.

Character actress Ellen Corby wrote "B" Westerns for the Hopalong Cassidy series.

Director Blake Edwards (the Pink Panther films, **"10,"** etc.) wrote the screenplays for **Stampede** and **Panhandle**, and appeared as an actor in several Westerns.

Craggy character actor Paul Fix co-scripted **Tall in the Saddle**.

Movie star Rory Calhoun wrote **Shotgun**.

Bad-guy actor Myron Healey scripted three "B" oaters.

Bad-guy actor Leo Gordon wrote more than a dozen feature films and countless Western TV shows; his movie credits, as writer, include **The Bounty Killer, Escort West** and **Black Patch**.

Actor Joseph Calleia scripted **Robin Hood of El Dorado**.

Actor-director John Huston began his Hollywood career as a screenwriter; his dozens of scripts include **Law and Order** and **The Treasure of the Sierra Madre**.

*

Critics of the Western have written a great deal about directors, actors, photographers and stunt men. Rarely have they discussed the writers who created the stories about which they pontificate. In this chapter we find ourselves treading virgin ground.

The issue is confused still further by the fact that there are two kinds of writing, where films are concerned. There is the story, and then there is the screenplay.

In recent years, stung by the needling of the Writers Guild of America and other groups, such review media as *Time* magazine have taken to listing the scriptwriters' names beneath those of the directors in their movie review columns. Often, frustratingly, that tells less than half the story. Writing a screenplay based on someone else's novel or story is a completely different endeavor from writing an original scenario for the screen. The former is an exercise in adaptation or interpretation, while the latter is an exercise in creation.

Novels, plays and short stories have always provided the lion's share of the source material for "A" movies. ("B" films, by contrast, normally were written directly for the screen by teams of writers who were employed in much the same way as television comedy writers are employed today.) Some "A" films are based on original screenplays but even in those cases quite a few are collaborations between the writer who contributed the story and the writer who actually wrote the shooting script.

Still more complication is introduced because various stages lead from novel or story to screen "treatment" (outline) to adaptation to first-draft screenplay to revised-first-draft screenplay to "polish" to shooting script; and these steps may employ the services of as many as half a dozen uncredited writers, including the producer, the director and the star, all of whom normally have a great deal—often far too much—to say about the screenplay. (Something gives actors the idea that in five minutes they can do better than the writer did in six months.) I've heard more than one bitter screenwriter complain that everybody on a movie, from the producer right down to the guy who sweeps out the studio, has script approval—everybody except the guy who wrote it in the first place. One reason why Hollywood seldom lives up to the promise of its unparalleled resources of talent and technicians is the adamant industry practice of empowering everybody in the company to fiddle with a film before its release. Hollywood grants total authority to no individual. Even if somehow a writer-producer-director keeps control over his film during the making of it, nevertheless the octopus organizations that finance, release and distribute movies retain the insidious privilege of re-editing films before distribution, and this privilege—coupled with the already crippled authority of writers and directors—guarantees in many cases that the movie you see will not be as good as it might have been.

Given such an archaic insensitive system, the amazing thing is that satisfactory films ever are made at all.

*

With apologies to his legion of fans I must point out that Zane Grey was not a very good writer, nor were most of the novelists and playwrights whose stories provided the material for the Westerns made in the thirty years of silent film: Harold Bell Wright, Peter B. Kyne, David Belasco, Edna Ferber, Rex Beach, Johnston McCulley and others. Owen Wister was better than those, but his talent was not a great one. The best Western novelists of that period were Willa Cather and Eugene Manlove Rhodes but no one ever put Cather on film (she didn't write shoot-'em-ups) and there was only one Rhodes story that worked well as a movie, much later and long after he died: **Four Faces West**, from Rhodes's short novel *Paso por Aqui.*

Probably the best slick-magazine writer to provide source material for pre-World War II Western movies was Clarence Mulford, but his Hopalong Cassidy novels were so cheapened and subverted by William Boyd's hack "B" operation that there was no way to tell, on the evidence of the films, that the books had been good ones.

From the late 1930s to the middle 1950s the best of the slick-magazine Western entertainments were written by James Warner Bellah, Luke Short and Ernest Haycox. Works by the first two were translated very successfully to the screen. But Haycox was too subtle a writer for the movies. Either his titles were bought and pasted onto inferior movies (**Sundown Jim** is a good novel but the "B" movie version was lousy) or his stories were revamped, bloated and twisted almost beyond recognition (**Union Pacific, Stagecoach**). In only one case was a movie faithful to a Haycox original, and that was with a minor novel and a relatively forgotten film (**Canyon Passage**); still, the power of the source material was great enough to elevate the film high above its contemporaries and it remains a beautifully stylized piece of work. By contrast, Haycox's masterpiece, the magnificent novel **Bugles in the Afternoon**, was degraded by Hollywood into a run-of-the-mill oater.

Among popular Western writers of the 1950–1980 period the most readable novelists were Henry Allen (writing under the pen-names Clay Fisher and Will Henry; his novels that were filmed included **The Tall Men** and **Pillars of the Sky**, but his best book—never filmed—probably was **From Where the Sun Now Stands**), Benjamin Capps (**The White Man's Road**), Frederic Manfred (**King of Spades**), Larry McMurtry (**Leaving Cheyenne, Hud, The Last Picture Show**), Glendon Swarthout (**They Came to Cordura, Bless the Beasts and Children, The Shootist**), Robert Flynn (**North to Yesterday**), Charles Portis (**True Grit**), Douglas Jones (**Winding Stair**) and Elmore Leonard (**Hombre, Valdez is Coming**). Generally, however, it is literary rather than cinematic qualities that set these writers above their colleagues. Many of their books have been transformed into movies, but seldom has it been done with much success.

It is a woeful shame that John Ford made no films from any of Ernest Haycox's stunning short stories about the cavalry, and that Willa Cather and Frederic Manfred have not had their novels adapted into movies; but it is a far greater shame that no overwhelming Western mythos has yet been created directly for the screen. Aside from **The Wild Bunch** (which wasn't created by Peckinpah; the original script was submitted to him by its authors, one of whom was actor Lee Marvin) there have been virtually no great original Western motion pictures.

Film is the real medium for the Western message; but as things stand, the Western movie has been both indebted to and hamstrung by the novel.

*

Among those who have written Western films a few stand out distinctively. James Warner Bellah, a regular contributor to the slick magazines, specialized in cavalry-Indian novels; films made from his stories include all three films in John Ford's "Cavalry Trilogy" plus Ford's **Sergeant Rutledge**.

Niven Busch wrote **Duel in the Sun, Pursued, The Capture** and **The Furies**. The latter three "psychological" Westerns had a great deal more in common than did the oeuvres of the men who directed them (respectively Raoul Walsh, John Sturges and Anthony Mann).

Borden Chase earned writing credits on more than thirty films including **Red River, Winchester '73, The Far Country, Man without a Star** and **Vera Cruz**. Chase's name on the credits was a virtual guarantee of superior entertainment.

Alan LeMay's name on a Western was a similar warrant of a good movie: **The Searchers**, of course, and **The Unforgiven, The Sundowners, High Lonesome, Cheyenne**, others.

Dudley Nichols was one of Hollywood's most respected adaptation screenwriters. His scripts—all based on other writers' published works—included **Stagecoach, The Tin Star** and **The Big Sky**.

Lamar Trotti's Westerns usually could be counted on to be large, slow-moving and ponderously heavy: **Brigham Young, Ramona, The Ox-Bow Incident, Hudson's Bay, Drums Along the Mohawk**.

Philip Yordan's list of credits is very long: more than fifty motion pictures, several novels and the play **Anna Lucasta**. His Westerns, all of high quality and with a consistency of flavor and characterization, include **Day of the Outlaw, The Bravados, Gun Glory, Johnny Guitar** and **Broken Lance**, for which he received an Oscar.

Even so brief a sampling as that above must confirm the notion that the name of the screenwriter often can be a better index to film flavor and quality than is the name of the director. There is a consistency to the work of many of these writers that is a far better guide than the erratic track records of most directors.

Your move, *cineaste*.

8

THE

CREWS

The essential septet of key figures in the making of a film consists of the producer, the director, the writer, the art director (production designer), the director of photography (cinematographer), the film editor and the composer of the soundtrack music score.

Every movie is a family, and most of these key people—plus the stars—become the clan chiefs of that family. (The composer and sometimes the editor often are left out of it because their jobs often don't start until the others have finished.) The clan chiefs' relationships with one another tend to set the tone for the entire company.

On the set itself, during actual filming, the director is boss. But usually it was the producer who put him there.

The producer decides what movie he wants to make. He creates, buys or chooses the story, assigns the writing of the screenplay, assembles the key people who will make the film, raises the money to finance it, and arranges for distribution of the film once it is made. Once he has done all that, he turns the job of making the movie over to the director. But most producers keep some degree of control over their directors, especially in the form of budgetary restrictions. (When they don't, disasters can happen; consider **Heaven's Gate**.) If the producer is a Philistine, then both the director and the movie are in trouble. If the producer is creative, and if he and the director have the same movie in mind, then he can provide a good deal of logistical and moral support that will make the job go better.

American films have given us a number of producers whose names on the credits of a movie indicate something about what sort of movie it will be. Samuel Goldwyn, David O. Selznick, Stanley Kramer, Darryl F. Zanuck—Hollywood's history is dominated by the names of the producers who shaped its movies. But most Westerns cannot be said to be primarily the children of their producers. For many years Westerns were made by studios in which each film's "supervisor" or "producer" was simply a studio employee whose job was to assemble the personnel, the budget and the physical properties necessary to make a movie whose production had been decreed by the head office. He might more accurately have been given the title of production manager. The studio itself was the producer, in reality.

Nearly all the important producers made Westerns at one time or another, but the Western is a genre on which individual producers left no real mark, with one or two distinct but minor exceptions: a case in point is A.C. Lyles, an independent producer of the 1960s and 1970s who created an odd sort of oeuvre of low-budget Westerns (**Apache Uprising, Black Spurs, Buckskin, Johnny Reno, Law of the Lawless, Town Tamer, Waco,** others) all of which were characterized by old-fashioned "B" scripts, abominable production values, abysmal directing, and the appearance in major roles of semi-retired old-time cowboy actors and former movie stars ranging from Dana Andrews and Howard Keel to Bob Steele, Johnny Mack Brown, Barry Sullivan, Richard Arlen, Bruce Cabot, Buster Crabbe, Rod Cameron and even Broncho Billy Anderson. Despite their mostly lousy quality, these films had a curiously fascinating flavor and, of course, an aura of warm nostalgia.

Robert L. Lippert, who owned a chain of West Coast movie theatres, set up his own production company in the late 1940s to feed his theatres with product—his audiences liked Westerns and the "B" studios were folding, so Lippert decided to step into the gap. For several years his company produced shoestring black-and-white oaters with surprisingly good scripts and gritty cinematic values; they stand up very well with time (**The Tall Texan, I Shot Billy the Kid, Little Big Horn,** so forth).

But these men were exceptions and their Westerns, while interesting, were outside the mainstream. No producer had as much influence on the Western as did Zane Grey, say, or John Ford.

*

Of all cinematic forms the Western seems the one most constantly dependent upon pictorial values. This puts the Western's cinematographer in a position of unusual importance. But one must remember that the job of a "director of photography" is determined by his relationship with the director and by the extent of the director's command of visual compositions. Many directors, including most of the best ones, are in fact their own directors of photography, and their cinematographers would more appropriately be defined by the old British title of "lighting cameramen"; they are in charge of lighting the scene rather than composing it.

Most movie directors position their own cameras. Some of them choose the lenses for each scene; others simply give the cinematographer an indication of what picture they want to appear on the screen, and leave the selection of lenses and openings to the cinematographer. In this heirarchy the "cameraman" is in fact the camera operator; he carries out the instructions of the cinematographer, and is the man who actually—physically—wields the camera. The cinematographer's chief job normally is to make sure that each shot is properly framed and lit, so that the director gets the photographic image he wants.

Obviously, however, the best cinematographers bring more than mere obedience to their jobs. They put their own brands on the lighting, composition and graphic coloration of films. Some of them have styles as distinctive as those of the directors.

Among the best and best known of the cinematographers who put their marks on the Western were Lucien Ballard (**Will Penny, True Grit, The Wild Bunch**), William Clothier (**Track of the Cat, The Horse Soldiers, Shenandoah**), Stanley Cortez (**Night of the Hunter, The Man from Del Rio**), Edward Cronjager (**Cimarron, Canyon Passage**), Floyd Crosby (**High Noon**), Tonino Delli Colli (the Sergio Leone spaghetti Westerns), Lee Garmes (**Duel in the Sun**), Bert Glennon (**Stagecoach, Wagonmaster, Rio Grande**), Loyal Griggs (**Shane**), Conrad Hall (**The Professionals, Butch Cassidy and the Sun-**

dance Kid), Russell Harlan (**The Big Sky**), Winton C. Hoch (**She Wore a Yellow Ribbon, The Searchers**), James Wong Howe (**Viva Villa, Hud, Hombre**), Milton Krasner (**Garden of Evil, Rawhide**), Charles Lang, Jr. (**Gunfight at the OK Corral, The Magnificent Seven**), Joseph MacDonald (**Broken Lance, My Darling Clementine, Viva Zapata, Yellow Sky**), Ted McCord (**The Treasure of the Sierra Madre**), William Mellor (**Bad Day at Black Rock, The Naked Spur**), Russell Metty (**Man without a Star, The Misfits**), Arthur Miller (**The Ox-Bow Incident, The Gunfighter**), Franz Planer (**The Unforgiven, The Big Country**), Ray Rennahan (**Whispering Smith, Unconquered, Arrowhead**), Harold Rosson (**The Red Badge of Courage**), Archie J. Stout (**Fort Apache, Hondo**), Robert L. Surtees (**Tribute to a Bad Man, The Hallelujah Trail**) and Gregg Toland (**The Grapes of Wrath, The Westerner, The Outlaw**).

*

The art director, or scenic designer, or set designer, or production designer—whatever you call him, his job is to supervise the appearance of everything that is photographed. He acts as the director's right-hand man in creating the "look" of the movie. He chooses or designs the locations, the sets, the furniture, the props; and he supervises costume selection or design.

Once a director becomes comfortable with a set designer he usually hires the same designer on film after film (if the producer allows him that choice); this is one reason why a director's films often have a similar "look" to them. It may be a combination of lighting techniques and production design—attributable to the employment of the same cinematographer and designer on film after film—more than a matter of a director's own individual style.

(I'm not insisting that directors don't have styles; many of them have highly distinctive styles; I am only pointing out that sometimes critics tend to give credit to the wrong people.)

The production designer often is the first department-head to be hired when a film is in pre-production; he must do a good deal of his work before filming begins. It is therefore commonplace for the production designer to be working on a film during its preliminary developmental stages, when the screenplay is still being polished. On one film I worked on, the director and the scenic designer and I shared an office while I wrote—in close working collaboration with the director—the final shooting-script draft of the screenplay, and the scenic designer (William Creber) contributed several excellent ideas and lines of dialogue to the script. It was an amiable and rewarding collaboration. When that kind of relationship works well, a kind of cross-pollinization takes place that enriches the film: each participant contributes ideas to the others. As a writer who spent nearly twenty years working in solitary seclusion making novels, and who came to film work relatively late, I found a great joy in the collaborative process: the people who actually make movies (as opposed, quite often, to those who finance them and otherwise dominate the industry) are mostly brainy and very enjoyable to work with—and they certainly are much better company than a typewriter.

*

Once filming is completed, the many hours of raw processed shots must be assembled into a coherent movie.

An expert film editor (cutter) has his counterpart in the kind of wartime ground-crew chief who could take mismatched parts from a dozen destroyed airplanes, cannibalize the hulks, fit the salvaged pieces together and create a new airplane from the wreckage —sometimes redesigning it in the process.

Many a poor film has been rescued by inspired editing. But then many a movie that might have been good has been ruined by lackluster editing, often at the insistence of studio bosses who think they know more about moviemaking than the moviemakers know. Nearly always they are wrong.

Editors like Daniel Mandell (**The Westerner**), Elmo Williams (**High Noon**), Barbara McLean (**Viva Zapata**), Jack Murray (**The Searchers**) and others too numerous to list have made raw footage into finished movies with extraordinary artistry. The degree to which a movie is actually *made* in the cutting room is astonishing to the uninitiated; one must watch an editor at work to realize how important his contribution is.

Books have been written about the many kinds of magic that can be performed on a Moviola editing machine, and there isn't space here to describe them in detail. It should be mentioned, however, that as with cinematographers and other department heads, the film editor's job is subordinate not only to the director's but also to the producer's. Many of the best movie directors are, in effect, their own editors; but an unfortunate number of producers or releasing-company executives have tended to second-guess their directors and editors, and re-edit pictures before their exhibition.

Ronald Neame, who is the finest director I have worked with, spends each Sunday during filming in the cutting room with the editor putting together rough assemblies of that week's footage; while some directors or editors may take as much as a year to edit a picture after it has been filmed, Ronnie usually has his director's cut finished within a few weeks after completion of photography, and he supervises every single scissor-cut and every single frame, first at the Moviola (which has a tiny screen) and then, approaching the final cut, in the big dubbing theatre with its enormous wide screen and its magnificent projection and audio equipment; he keeps total and direct control over scoring, soundtrack dubbing (both sound effects and dialogue tracks), film cutting and color processing. But Ronald Neame is an expert and dedicated director. I've also known a director who walked away from a movie when he'd finished shooting it, and only supervised the cutting (if at all) in the most cursory and general way. When that happens, the director is at the mercy of the cutter, who may either enhance or ruin his work, whether he's shot good footage or bad footage. The point is, footage is merely raw photography; it isn't a *movie* until it has been edited.

*

The film score—that "incidental" soundtrack music that first attracted attention by its absence from early talkies—began with the theatrical organists and orchestras of silent pictures. In the early days of sound it remained a sort of punctuation: scoring a film was a matter of providing music to match the mood or action of the visual scenes. Bad movies, and virtually all television films, still use music in that rudimentary fashion.

But screen composers learned to move beyond that notion. Over the years they developed the technique of composing scores that told us something about what did *not* show on the screen.

A dusty town street. Gary Cooper walking slowly across it. And this humdrum scene becomes a moment of tense suspense when Dimitri Tiomkin's **High Noon** score is added to it.

Bernard Hermann's heroic, almost Wagnerian music for **Garden of Evil** emphasizes the dwarfed loneliness of the travelers who crawl across its vast CinemaScope landscape, as does Max Steiner's sometimes wistful music for **The Searchers**. (By the same token an inappropriate or badly conceived film score, like that for **McCabe and Mrs. Miller**, can do severe damage to the effectiveness of an otherwise interesting movie.)

The Wild Bunch has many excellences. One of them is Jerry Fielding's magnificent score. It won an Academy Award. The movie would be much less without it.

*

The Western is a genre that owes a great deal to its second-unit directors and stunt coordinators. (Often the two functions are vested in one man.) Second-unit directors are employed either to speed up a production by heading a second separate crew that shoots on different locations from the first unit, or to fill in background shots in areas or climates where the stars and director prefer not to go. Cecil B. De Mille, for example, was notorious for his aversion to locations; he shot every foot of his own film on studio lots and sound stages; when it was necessary to go outdoors—for buffalo-hunting scenes in his plains epics, for instance—a second unit would take care of those annoying details, which usually turned out to be the best parts of his movies.

The Western requires specific and often peculiar kinds of stunt work. A whole breed of stunt men grew up in that sub-profession. Outstanding among them was Yakima Canutt, who invented the style of fist-fighting that was used for fifty years in oaters (it was more convincing than earlier styles). Canutt, over the years, devised ever more daring stunts for action-packed "B" Westerns—for example, outlaws jumping their horses off fast-moving trains. Canutt became the top stunt-coordinator and second-unit action director in Hollywood. (He also seems to have founded an entire dynasty. In charge of stunt and stunt-double work on our film **The Last Hard Men** were Joseph and Daniel Canutt. Joe doubled for Charlton Heston, and Danny for James Coburn.)

The exciting stunts in early Westerns—jumping on horseback across great chasms, or falling off cliffs—were done by live stunt men, not dummies. In recent years special-effects technicians have taken over some of these tasks. Dummies, cleverly rigged to look lifelike, are blown up in explosions. The strike of "bullets" against flesh is effected with plastic capsules of red ink triggered to burst open by a complex system of wires, pins and radio controls. The scene in **Shane** in which Jack Palance's bullet blows Elisha Cook off his feet was accomplished by harnessing Cook to a cable that was jerked from offstage. (The actor did the fall himself; it wasn't a stunt man.)

Still, stunt work is a proud profession and Hollywood's stunt people are as good today as they ever were; probably better, since many of them seem goaded by the constant challenge of outdoing their own previous stunts and everyone else's besides.

We had an exceptional aggregation of trick riders and other Western stunt specialists in the Wild West Show segments of **Wild Times**; it was a keen pleasure to watch them work. It only takes a short time around stunt people to learn that they are among the most carefully prepared professionals in the movie business. (They can't afford not to be. Today's careless stunt man is tomorrow's corpse.) Accidents do happen; a stunt woman in **Wild Times** had a nasty fall off the back of a galloping horse on which she'd been standing, and one stunt rider's shin was broken when he was kicked by a horse he was mounting from the rear, but they seem to take those risks in stride, so to speak.

Stunt men aren't the only people who lead rugged lives on movie locations. When we went into the Arizona mountains to film **The Last Hard Men**, we found that getting around in that beat-up terrain required athletic stamina and a good sense of humor on everybody's part. The film was the first to be shot in Pena Blanca Canyon—a location that had been rejected by previous movie companies because of difficult access and rocky, treacherous footing.

The Mitchell Panavision camera, though not as heavy as earlier machines, neverthe-less weighs about 135 pounds; a single man must carry each camera up and down the cliffs because footing in the rocky canyons permits neither trucking nor a two-man carry. In the cameraman's wake come streams of men on foot carrying heavy loads of arc light "brutes," tripods, film canisters and the endless impedimenta of moviemaking. Ankles were twisted and bruises were incurred and a good many oaths were heard; but at the same time the jokes became more frequent and the laughter became louder.

There was an *esprit* among them. There always is, to one extent or another, but on this movie there were special reasons for it. We were trying to make a throwback Western, an old fashioned good-versus-evil drama in which the hero (Charlton Heston) was heroic and the villain (James Coburn) was formidable. The crew was enthusiastic about this goal, and most of them—being sticklers for authenticity—were pleased with the atten-tion we all paid to historical detail, and pleased too that we were filming the picture where it was set, instead of acceding to the financial temptations of cheap Spanish labor or handy California facilities. The Tucson seen in the movie is actually Tucson (the standing set at Old Tucson, built in 1939 for the film **Arizona**). The Arizona deserts and mountains are in fact Arizona. Indeed, as far as we could determine, **The Last Hard Men** was the first major Western to have been both set and filmed entirely within the borders of Arizona. Even the original **Arizona** was shot partly on Hollywood sound stages. Over the years, Arizona locations have been used regularly by movie companies to represent Texas (**Giant**), Oklahoma (**Oklahoma!**), New Mexico (**Strange Lady in Town**), Ne-braska (**The Man Who Loved Cat Dancing**), Mexico (**Rio Conchos**) and others ad nau-seam; it was refreshing and unusual to have Arizona stand in for Arizona.

Another cause for unusual dedication on the part of the crew was simply the fact that Andy McLaglen was its director. Andrew V. McLaglen has a great many friends in the film business because he has made a great many films, ranging from forgettable half-hour TV segments to such successful big-budget movies as **McLintock**, **Shenandoah** and **The Wild Geese**. The son of actor Victor McLaglen, Andrew began his career as John Ford's assistant, and over the years has directed Westerns with virtually all the major action stars of the post-World War II era (Kirk Douglas, Rock Hudson, Dean Martin, Robert Mitchum, James Stewart, Richard Widmark, and of course John Wayne, several of whose films McLaglen directed). McLaglen sets an amiable open tone on the sets of his films. He's a professional; he knows what he wants, and knows how to get it without haranguing or pleading. Crews always like to work with a director who knows what he's doing.

It helps, of course, that he's six-foot-seven. Andy can dominate any set without ever having to raise his voice.

The Last Hard Men also was exceptional in that it was filmed in sequence. (That is, it was filmed in the same order in which we see it unfold on the screen.) This was done mainly because the structure of the story permitted it: the yarn is a pursuit tale, moving from place to place, and it would have been inconvenient and expensive to film it out of order because that would have required returning a hundred miles to some earlier loca-tion. Nevertheless in the inevitable course of things a fair amount of "matching" takes place—for example the outlaws' camp in the movie, ostensibly on top of a mountain, was filmed in a spot low on the mountainside because this afforded a great reduction in time and back-breaking effort; on screen one does not notice the difference—long shots of the mountain establish the setting and blend perfectly with closer shots filmed in the more accessible location. This matching of disparate settings did not interfere with the sequen-tial order of filming and the actors enjoyed the rare advantage of being able to develop their characters in coordination with the story's logical sequence of events, playing their parts straight through from beginning to end. A few retakes and close-ups, and the night-fire sequence, were shot out of order, but the rest of the film was made in the sequence in which we see it on the screen.

The title wasn't mine, incidentally. The novel was called *Gun Down* and the initial title of the movie was *Burgade* (the name of the hero); somebody at the studio tacked the new dreadful title on at the last minute, prompting complaints from Heston, Coburn and myself—none of us was happy to have our names on a movie the title of which made it look like a porn flick.

Whether **The Last Hard Men** succeeds as a movie is not for me to judge. But the weeks of filming were a demonstration that any film's excellences must be largely the work of inspired work on the part of everybody in the cast and crew. Movies don't just happen; they are made to happen.

9

THE

ACTORS

Westerns often caught actors on the way up and on the way down again. Entire careers were built on them (Randolph Scott) and flagging careers were rescued by them (James Stewart).

A surprising number of celebrated actors began their film careers with debuts in Westerns. A sampling: Dana Andrews, Gary Cooper, Irene Dunne, Henry Fonda, Glenn Ford, Clark Gable, Rita Hayworth, Rock Hudson, Walter Matthau, Robert Mitchum, James Stewart, John Wayne. (The late Lee J. Cobb debuted in **North of the Rio Grande**, a 1937 Hopalong Cassidy programmer, but that film is not listed in this guide.) Scores of other debuts are mentioned in the listings.

Western stars—true stars in Samuel Johnson's sense: those who dominate their medium—have been few. But the same is true in any genre. The Western had a handful of stars who were to the genre what Douglas Fairbanks and Errol Flynn were to swashbucklers, Doris Day to fluffy comedies or Astaire and Kelly to dance musicals. (Of course there were plenty of "B" luminaries—Anderson, Thomson, Maynard, Jones, McCoy, Boyd, Autry, Rogers: men who were identified exclusively with Westerns just as the Western was identified with them. But the serious Western, the movie for grown-ups, has found very few such dominant stars.) In strict terms there have been only seven such superluminaries in the history of the Western film: William S. Hart, Tom Mix, Gary Cooper, John Wayne, Joel McCrea, Randolph Scott and Clint Eastwood.

These were the stars who defined the "A" Western, shaped it to their own images and were identified with it—primarily, although not exclusively. Hart and Mix were the only ones among them who did not appear frequently in non-Western roles. Indeed, most of the others appeared in more non-Western films than Westerns. Both Scott and McCrea appeared as spies, soldiers and romantic or light-comedy leads in numerous films before they settled exclusively into cowboy parts in the 1950s; Wayne and Cooper made all sorts of movies, of course, as has Eastwood. But one thinks of them (Eastwood less than the others, perhaps) as predominantly Western stars.

Most of Hollywood's popular male stars appeared successfully in Westerns; some— James Stewart, Glenn Ford, Henry Fonda, Charles Bronson—specialized in Westerns during one or more intervals in their careers. Yul Brynner, Jeff Chandler, James Coburn,

Joseph Cotten, Joan Crawford, Clark Gable, Stewart Granger, Van Heflin, Charlton Heston, William Holden, Rock Hudson, Walter Huston, Alan Ladd, Burt Lancaster, Dean Martin, Steve McQueen, Ray Milland, Robert Mitchum, Paul Newman, Jack Palance, Gregory Peck, Anthony Quinn, Robert Redford, Burt Reynolds, Robert Ryan, Barbara Stanwyck, Spencer Tracy, Richard Widmark and Robert Young—these and others among the top film stars (even Leslie Howard!) were first-billed in the casts of expensive and sometimes worthwhile Westerns. Yet none of them is regarded as a Western star; they're not primarily cowboys.

Yet Glenn Ford is a better horseman than Randolph Scott; Richard Widmark sometimes looked more convincing in cavalry attire than did Joel McCrea; Robert Mitchum's prairie twang was just as believable as John Wayne's (although Wayne's was native-born); Charles Bronson was much more convincing in a fight than Gary Cooper was. Yet these qualities don't sum up a cinematic persona. In the end what remains is the imponderable: Glenn Ford is a horseman, but Joel McCrea is a Westerner.

To be sure, stars of lesser celebrity were identified closely with Westerns: Audie Murphy, Richard Dix, Rory Calhoun, Rod Cameron, so forth. But it would be silly to compare them in significance with Cooper, Wayne, McCrea, Scott or Eastwood. Those five, in talking pictures, are the supreme cowboy stars: the men who shaped our image of the Western hero.

*

Screen stardom requires photogenic charisma rather than acting skill. An actor need not be brilliant to be effective on screen. But in a Western he must look and talk like a Westerner, and unfortunately too many moviemakers have failed to understand that.

Quite a few producers and directors were Europeans or New Yorkers, foreign to the West, lacking the ear for distinctions in speech patterns or any sensitivity to Western mythology. As a result, the miscasting of dude actors in Western parts often was an annoying weakness in the genre. Woefully out of place in Western films, because their Eastern urban mannerisms and accents were dead giveaways, were actors like Lloyd Nolan, Arthur Kennedy, Edmond O'Brien, Scott Brady, Bill Williams and (in "B" pictures) Lash LaRue.

Most American screen actors, regardless of their thespic skills (Edmond O'Brien is a first-rate actor) have a poor ear for dialect; they are not trained in vocal mimicry. Among actors who have appeared frequently in Westerns there are surprisingly few who possess a good range of accents and speech patterns, and there is only one who excels: Robert Mitchum. Granted, the ability to mimic accents is a talent separate from acting, but it is important in a regional drama like the Western and one finds that the American stars who succeeded best in Westerns were those whose own natural speech patterns were Southern, Midwestern or Western. The fact that the population of the real West included substantial numbers of New Yorkers and New Englanders is beside the point; the mythic Western landscape is inhabited by Westerners and their accents are assumed to be different from those of Northeasterners.

*

Randolph Scott starred in a greater number of "A" Westerns than has any other leading man (well over fifty of them). John Wayne appeared in about forty, excluding his "B" pictures. Glenn Ford made about thirty-five Westerns, Joel McCrea about thirty. With other Western stars it becomes harder to fix numbers because the line between "A" and "B" can be hazy. Rod Cameron appeared in at least fifty Westerns but some of them—fifteen to thirty, depending on definitions—were "B" movies. Audie Murphy starred in thirty-odd Westerns, most of them conceded to be "A" pictures if minor ones, while William Elliott is represented in this guide by about a dozen films (he made more than sixty), all of which technically are programmers but they seem superior to Murphy's or Cameron's "A" pictures.

We often think of James Stewart as a Western star; we seldom think of Richard Widmark that way; yet both actors appeared in an equal number of oaters (about twenty).

Gary Cooper made barely twenty Western talkies, of which only a few are memorable; yet it would be difficult to dispute his reigning position among Western heroes of the screen.

One may draw one's own conclusions from those motley facts.

*

One strange canard has found its way into many books about Western films. They say Harry Carey, Sr., and Harry Carey, Jr., never appeared in the same film. Not true. Both actors are evident, in important roles, in **Red River.**

*

Movies after the 1950s began to call upon actors with less and less experience and ability to do work of more and more demanding precision. The new fashion, influenced by the *Cahiers* attitude and the techniques of television commercials, required the sketchiest of screenplays with the emphasis on very brief scenes and rapid jump-cuts. Dialogue was minimized. The revelation of character, which used to be a matter of screenwriting as interpreted by actor and director, became a matter of pure acting: the performer was expected to find the subtext between the sparse lines of the screenplay, and work out his own interpretation while the director was busy setting up tricky camera shots or devising splashy pictorial gimmicks of fast action and startling violence.

Characters in the best movies were, to use a hoary overworked phrase, well rounded. The audience had a sense of them as whole beings: we felt that if we met one of them we would know his past, his private demons, his quirks, how he would feel in given circumstances. We knew these things about him because we had seen his behavior and we had heard him talk about himself and we had seen him interreact with other characters in scenes that were long and complex enough to allow such development.

The old movies were made from "screenplays" in a literal way: they were an extension of theatre with the proscenium opened wide. Each play contained scenes in sequence; each scene was a playlet in itself with an introduction, a conflict or development of some kind and a climax. Theatrical tradition was followed: characters appear on stage, they notice one another and then very quickly one of them has to say or do something and the other has to react and reply.

But after a while it became fun for moviemakers to fiddle with devices that made it possible to avoid verbal confrontations. The cinema, after all, is a visual medium; it didn't even find its tongue until more than thirty years of silent movies had passed. (Television, by contrast, is an outgrowth of a purely aural medium, and even to this day TV is essentially radio with pictures—you can listen to it without watching it and still follow the story. That is not true with movies.)

The moviemaker discovered that he could cut quickly from one scene to the next without developing either. He could set up a startling chase sequence. He could cut to an extreme close-up to reveal a character's feelings from the squint of his left eye. (Unfortu-

nately a good many actors do not seem to have sufficiently expressive left ey
mind.) Dialogue becomes shorthand—a few isolated words here and there t
or "motivate" the action. No longer is it used to reveal character; film beco
dium of the meaningful silence, the pregnant pause, the "beat."

The jump-cut, devised by D.W. Griffith half a century earlier, reached
the result of its usage in television commercials. It speeds up the pace of a mo
penses with the old devices of storytelling continuity, the slow devices of dissolves and
fades that not only consumed time but also required considerable elongations of the
scenes they separated: one had to complete a scene—bring it to a climax and provide a
suitable curtain line—before one could dissolve to the next scene. The new filmmaker
found it easier to cut into the middle of a scene-in-progress, film the meat of it and
abruptly cut away to another scene, catching it too in mid-action.

On the face of it this advancement ought to enable the filmmaker to create far more
concentrated and complex motion pictures than he could before. After all, it allows for a
greater number of scenes, and therefore should encourage more depth and complexity in
films. Years ago we had to watch the cowboy walk out of the saloon, cross the boardwalk,
gather the reins, mount his horse, ride out of town, ride across country, arrive at the
ranch, dismount, walk up to the house, open the door, go inside, stare at the girl across
the room, meet her halfway and then take her into his arms. Now, by contrast, the cowboy turns away from the saloon bar and we cut instantly to the interior of the ranch
house where he's taking the girl into his arms (with or without clothes). We all can assume the mechanics of transportation that got him from one scene to the other; we don't
need to see them; we've just saved at least forty seconds of film and when we keep doing
that throughout the movie it ought to leave us with a great deal more time in which to
concentrate on the essentials of drama. Right?

No. It should work that way but in fact it seems to have had the opposite effect. There
is far less density in the newer films than there was in the older ones. They seem much
more distant from their characters. They give off an aura of superficiality; they leave an
impression that the story was too thin—that somehow the movie contrived to do in two
hours what could have been done in half an hour. As audiences we feel we've danced on
the surface of things and never gotten inside them. We never got to know the people; the
subsidiary characters were walk-ons and extras; we never had a chance to care about any
of them.

In the action-adventure film an essential factor is suspense. Suspense is clock-oriented;
time is a vital ingredient. The ticking of the clock in **High Noon** (clumsily satirized in
The Good Guys and the Bad Guys) is a device that creates enormous suspense, regardless
of how often we've seen it before. We are able to follow the linear sequence of events in
High Noon in terms of time: the passage of screen time and the passage of elapsed time
for the audience are virtually identical (about an hour and a half).

The jump-cut eliminated this function, and weakened movies as a result. The audience needs time to absorb effects, time to prepare itself for emotional climaxes. What
made the long ride from the saloon to the ranch house effective was the fact that we *knew*
the cowboy was riding to meet the girl and we prepared ourselves for the impact of that
moment when suddenly they were face to face. (A stunning example of such a moment is
the climax of **The Searchers** when at last John Wayne confronts Natalie Wood. Will he
kill her or kiss her? The suspense is magnificent and the catharsis exhausting.) When we
do away with the extended transition, we also do away with the emotional build-up.

Writers of vaudeville skits had a rule: "Plant it early, pay it off later." That rule applies to drama as well and it is as valid now as it ever was. But the jump-cut plants it now
and pays it off instantly. There is no time for reflection, development or suspense.

When a film is limited to brief truncated scenes, the underpinnings of character are sacrificed. It is impossible to develop most characters if their longest scenes give them three short lines of dialogue. Motion pictures need not be turgid with long speeches, but neither do they need to be exercises in pantomime punctuated by the occasional grunt. One finds that the John Ford films, for example, contained vastly more dialogue than the Westerns of the 1970s contained, yet we don't get bored by **She Wore a Yellow Ribbon**—quite the contrary; it is a very fast-paced film. The dialogue doesn't get in the way, slow things down or alienate the audience; it enables the audience to get involved in the people and the story. But that secret seems to have been lost somewhere around 1960.

A film that illustrates the distressing thinning-out of screenplays is **Hang 'Em High** (1968), a movie that had many of the ingredients necessary for a good movie. Its premise was a good fresh twist on the old vengeance plot. The cast was peopled by quite a few good character actors. The movie made a significant statement—in fact it was probably the only Clint Eastwood movie of the 1960s to face a moral question honestly. Photography, score and other production values were quite good.

Yet it didn't work. The intimations were there but the development was lacking. **Hang 'Em High** was defeated by the cinematic conventions of its era. Its weaknesses were the result of understatements throughout the film that placed impossible burdens on the cast. None of the actors had a chance to do anything with his role.

Ben Johnson had one short scene and died somewhere offstage. Bert Freed as the hangman did not have a single line of dialogue. Bruce Dern had to make himself believable as a villainous rat on about six scattered lines of dialogue. L.Q. Jones had to make himself into a complex man torn between his family and his loyalty to the hard-nosed range boss (Ed Begley), all on the strength of two scenes neither of which ran a minute in length. James MacArthur, as a sanctimonious preacher, read aloud from Scripture but hadn't a single word of dialogue of his own. Inger Stevens was given only one scene of consequence, and it was wholly a plot device contrived to explain a trauma in her background in order to motivate her actions. Ruth White had two or three sparse lines as a whorehouse madam. (Both actresses died soon after the film was released, unhappily.) Charles McGraw, as a sheriff afflicted with lumbago, was effective despite his paucity of lines—he always was—and other superior performers in the cast included Arlene Golonka, Alan Hale, Jr., James Westerfield, Ned Romero and Michael O'Sullivan, none of whom was noticeable at all. Bob Steele had one line. Ed Begley's display of arrogance diluted by terror was splendid but all too brief. Dennis Hopper was listed in the credits as a principal supporting actor but I couldn't even find him on the screen.

Clint Eastwood and Pat Hingle had the only roles of substance in the picture, and even these were aborted; one kept feeling there must be something there but it must have been left in the cutting room. We were given hints, essences, but no meat, no body, no sense of full real life going on.

Hingle attempted to develop his role, that of a judge clearly modeled on the real "Hanging Judge" Isaac C. Parker of Fort Smith, as that of a man of thoughtful but expedient morality. The script gave him only half a chance and Ted Post's TV-style directing did little to showcase the performance, but Hingle is an actor of awesome abilities and he came amazingly close to bringing it off in spite of the obstacles that were strewn in his path by screenwriters, director and the faddish stylized conventions of modern cinema.

Eastwood played Cooper, the hero. It was the sort of role that would have fit the real Cooper perfectly if the script had contained enough development to show us who the character was rather than simply what he did. Unhappily Eastwood isn't Cooper. Intriguing complexities were implied in the character of Jedediah Cooper but neither the writers, the director nor the star could bring these complexities to life. The end result is that the film **Hang 'Em High**, like Clint Eastwood's voice, was a thin expressionless whisper that left many audiences dissatisfied because of what it might have been. It failed to provoke any emotion. Several scenes potentially were quite moving but they passed by too quickly to register.

(Eastwood grew after that, of course. His story sense remained uncertain—his **The Gauntlet** was ridiculous trash—but he became a competent director and allowed his engaging sense of humor to emerge, and by the time he made **Bronco Billy** he had become a fairly good entertainer. It remains a thin movie by comparison with its obvious antecedents like **The Cowboy and the Lady**, but it has charm, warmth and humanity.)

Hang 'Em High started as a first-rate idea and ended as a superficial oater that went through the motions but left one with a feeling of having wasted two hours: we hadn't been stirred, we hadn't enjoyed it, we hadn't been given enough to think about, and we hadn't been entertained.

*

More than most film genres, the Western is identified by and with its stars. When one speaks of a Randolph Scott movie, a Joel McCrea movie, an Audie Murphy or Richard Dix movie, one describes instantly a flavor and a style. (By contrast one doesn't achieve nearly so exact an identification if one proposes "a Gregory Peck movie.") And the identity of the star can indicate the film's quality: a Jimmy Stewart or Henry Fonda or Joel McCrea Western is likely to be pretty much better than a George Montgomery or Jock Mahoney or James Craig oater.

In "B" Westerns as well, those stars who proved most durable and popular—Bill Elliott, Bob Steele, Johnny Mack Brown, Roy Rogers—had personalities of the kind that reflected on screen those traits traditionally taken to characterize the heroes of the accepted Western mythos: frankness, altruism, a suspicion of effete "Eastern" manners and yet a courtliness of their own, and the kind of courage that is kept sheathed until all peaceful means of achieving justice have been exhausted.

The Western hero exemplified a system of values; the actor who portrayed this hero was palatable only in proportion to the sincerity with which he portrayed those desired qualities.

The Western myth depends not on melodramatic devices or narrative hooks, but rather on the character of the Westerner. The best oaters are those in which a real dramatic conflict erupts from a juxtaposition of dissimilar characters. Those that fail, often enough, are those in which the characters are insufficiently defined or portrayed.

One clear example of these definitions is **Shane**, which ultimately fails to become the definitive Western movie largely because Alan Ladd does not project the specific kind of innate heroism that is required of the character. Gary Cooper in that role would have given the film a better chance at immortality (although it still might have failed, the result of director George Stevens's too-mannered pretentiousness).

By most accounts Ladd offscreen was an unhappy man filled with bitter anxieties. I don't mean to overstate this but there was an extent to which the small and petty nature of Ladd's personal problems affected not so much his performance as his persona.

In crime movies that didn't matter so much. The actor's personality usually could be subordinated to the requirements of the plot, and actors like Ladd and Bogart survived awful miscasting in comedies and Gothic melodramas, but when they appeared in Westerns it was as if they'd been stripped naked: Bogart wasn't plausible at all as the gunslinger of **The Oklahoma Kid** or the Mexican bandit of **Virginia City**, and Ladd in his various Westerns lacked the stature and dignity to bring off the roles that were given to him. In his way he wasn't a bad actor (although apparently his insecurities often made him underplay a part to the point of woodenness) and he portrays Shane with conviction; it's not a bad performance at all; it's just that it isn't the great performance, or the great characterization that the film would have needed in order to become the masterpiece it aspired to be.

From this we must conclude that our stereotyped conception of the Western, as a genre that can be defined in terms of standardized plots, is false.

The fact that most Westerns plod stolidly down the well-worn paths of a few hackneyed plots is no more significant than the plot similarities among war movies; it's more a matter of lazy writers' convenience than it is of any fundamental requirement of the genre itself. Westerns have been made that are bald retellings of innumerable classic tales. *The Brothers Karamazov* turns up in Western form as **Broken Lance**. *Hamlet* became **Johnny Hamlet**; *The Sea Wolf* was remade and Westernized as **Barricade**; *Mutiny on the Bounty* became **Red River**; the Arthurian legends inspired **The Virginian**; the Robin Hood mythology turns up in the Zorro stories; *The Asphalt Jungle* was remade as a Western called **The Badlanders**; a Western remake of *Gunga Din* was called **Sergeants Three**; *The Lost Patrol* was turned into a Western, **Badlands**, and even *Lysistrata* was made into a tuneful Western called **The Second Greatest Sex**. *Romeo and Juliet* in a Western setting becomes **Roseanna McCoy** and its plot also appears in innumerable other feud Westerns like Zane Grey's *To the Last Man*. And **Star in the Dust** is derived largely from the old English folk song "Sam Hall."

So much for plot; virtually any plot is adaptable to the all-encompassing Western. One finds echoes of Orpheus in **Inferno** and of the Light Brigade in **They Died with Their Boots On**. Perhaps the moral is that those who do not learn from the classics are doomed to repeat them.

The Western, then, is defined mainly in terms of its hero's character; and that is merely one more item on the list of things modern Western moviemakers seem to have forgotten. Short, sly, balding, shifty-eyed Jack Nicholson as a scruffy horse thief (**The Missouri Breaks**) is not exactly what Western mythology had in mind when it gave us Buffalo Bill and Gary Cooper.

*

Wyoming, site of **The Virginian**, was the first state to confer suffrage on its women citizens (an event celebrated in the film **The Lady from Cheyenne**). But the Western is a masculine genre.

Infrequently female stars have headed the casts of Westerns: Marlene Dietrich in **Destry Rides Again** and **Rancho Notorious**, Joan Crawford in **Johnny Guitar**, Raquel Welch in **Hannie Caulder**, Gene Tierney in **Belle Starr**, Barbara Stanwyck in **The Furies** and her various cattle-queen roles, Jane Russell and a few others in isolated movies. For a dozen years Yvonne DeCarlo was the queen of a small "A" Western subcategory, the dance-hall movie (**Salome Where She Danced**) but that was as close as any woman came to achieving stardom purely in oaters unless you count Marjorie Main in the Wallace Beery movies or Dale Evans in Roy Rogers's "B" oaters. The beautiful and good-humored Ella Raines graced a few low-budget "A" Westerns with feisty spirit (**Tall in the Saddle, Ride the Man Down**) and Veronica Lake was deliciously villainous in **Ramrod**; Jo Van Fleet chewed scenery amusingly in **Gunfight at the OK Corral** and **The King and Four Queens**; Maureen O'Hara acquitted herself splendidly in a few John Wayne pictures and in Peckinpah's **Deadly Companions**, and Greer Garson was a dedicated frontier doctor in **Strange Lady in Town**, but these were exceptions.

Other actresses—Marie Windsor, Barbara Britton, Julie Adams, Adrian Booth, Helena Carter, Patricia Morison—appeared often enough to be familiar to Western fans but none of them achieved major stardom by that route.

Mainly the Western was blithely indifferent to its ladies. The heroine usually suffered thanklessly, playing a peripheral role at best. Too many actresses were wasted in routine rancher's daughter roles throughout the eighty years of Western filmmaking (a span far longer than the duration of the actual Old West). Among these unfortunate ladies have been such actresses as Rita Hayworth, Patricia Neal, Jeanne Moreau, Dorothy Malone, Piper Laurie and Anne Bancroft.

The rate of attrition among actresses in Westerns was grim; the working life-span of a Western leading lady was traditionally only a fraction that of a hero, and male stars like Wayne, Fonda, McCrea, Scott and Stewart survived several successive generations of female co-stars.

The Western has been unkind to its women. The genre is to some extent descended, as Wister suggested, from the folk literature of medieval knighthood; it tends to shelve its women or put them on pedestals, off stage most of the time, the ranch becoming a counterpart of the medieval castle where the damsel awaited her lover's return from his adventures. (Either that or they're hookers with golden hearts.)

Wags have read all sorts of interpretations into this imbalance. The Western as homosexual; as male sexist mythology; as the fantasy of adolescent boys' minds. In the end, however, it simply reflects the dominant attitudes of the real West, in which men outnumbered women by about ten to one. The real West was damned hard on its women.

*

The Wild Bunch concerns fictitious characters. But there was a real Wild Bunch. It was also called the Hole-in-the-Wall Gang. Its leaders were Butch Cassidy and the Sundance Kid, whose story was told (with fair accuracy) in the William Goldman-George Roy Hill film of that title. Paul Newman's portrayal of Cassidy was by no means the first to appear on the screen; the turn-of-the-century bandit has been depicted many times, for example by Barton MacLane in **Best of the Badmen** (1948), by Neville Brand in **Badman's Country** (1958) and by Richard Boone in **Big Jake** (1971).

The archetypal Western hero is an amalgam. He has no name, although he has been epitomized in a few well-known characters like the Virginian (who, significantly, is nameless). Butch Cassidy, Wyatt Earp, Wild Bill Hickok and many others were real people but their realities disappeared, buried under coatings of calcifying legend, long before the advent of motion pictures. In some cases this has been a good thing. In others it has been unfortunate; for example Hickok, a superb marksman overcome in his thirties by neurotic anxieties and deteriorating eyesight, comes close to having been a Greek tragedian's hero in real life; beside this reality the Hollywood fictions about Hickok are sadly flaccid.

Hollywood has always chosen the easy course of capitalizing on ready-made heroes. The Lone Ranger was created on radio. Broncho Billy, the Virginian, Lassiter, Destry, Zorro, the Cisco Kid and Hopalong Cassidy were the heroes of popular stories and novels before they reached the screen. Dime novels and penny dreadfuls, Wild West Shows and yellow newspapers—these had made household names of Buffalo Bill, Billy the Kid, Jesse James, Bat Masterson, Wyatt Earp and the rest; the characters often had as much box-office appeal as the actors who played them.

In very few cases have the real characters been depicted accurately. There is no pressing reason why they should have been; movies are not obliged to render exact history. Hickok, Earp and Jesse James are handy names to assign to fictitious heroes in stories based on common myths. Wyatt Earp as portrayed by Richard Dix in **Tombstone** (1942) is interchangeable with Wild Bill Hickok as portrayed by the same actor in **Badlands of Dakota** (1941) or with Earp as portrayed by Joel McCrea in **Wichita** (1955) or with Bat

Masterson as portrayed by Albert Dekker in **The Woman of the Town** (1943) or by Richard Dix again in **The Kansan** (1943). All five give us an entertaining aura of history filtered through the skeins of legend and Hollywood formula.

(No one has made a movie about him but one of the most interesting Western characters, and one of the chief influences on Western films, has been Colonel Ranald Mackenzie, a cavalry officer who in the 1870s, disobeying orders and treaties, took his command across the border into Mexico to wipe out a band of Indians who had been raiding Texas and then taking refuge on rancherias in Mexico. Mackenzie's raid has provided the inspiration for the plots of innumerable Westerns, among them Ford's **Rio Grande** and Peckinpah's **Major Dundee**.)

With this warning—do not expect realism—let's have a brief look at some of these historical figures and the actors who have portrayed them.

(Please note that these listings are selective; they do not come near exhausting the number of actors or films portraying these characters.)

*

Billy the Kid died at the age of twenty-one, shot by Sheriff Pat Garrett, and in New Mexico he was indeed a figure of notoriety during the last two years of his life because of his involvement in the Tunstall-McSween feud and its eruption into the violent Lincoln County War; but most everything else in his legend is fabrication. Billy was a hapless delinquent of no great importance until Garrett killed him and forthwith produced a book, **The Authentic Life of Billy the Kid and How I Shot Him**; the book made Billy famous.

He wasn't a lone wolf; he was one of a group of low-lifes employed by both sides in a range war and it was the war itself, not Billy's exploits, that originally captured headlines. The real character might be found in a blend of the portrayals of Michael J. Pollard in the boring **Dirty Little Billy** (1972), Kris Kristofferson in Peckinpah's **Pat Garrett and Billy the Kid** (1973) and—romanticized to be sure—Johnny Mack Brown in what is still the best of the Kid pictures, **Billy the Kid** (1930). Others have been those of Audie Murphy in **The Kid from Texas** (1950, a whitewash but a fairly good actioner) and Paul Newman in **The Left-Handed Gun** (1958), a silly pretentious film the conscientiousness of which is symbolized in its title, inasmuch as the real Billy was right-handed. (The film's title is meant to imply homosexuality as well.) Jack Beutel played Billy in Howard Hughes's overwrought **The Outlaw** (1943), and Donald Barry played him in the creditable Lippert programmer **I Shot Billy the Kid** (1950). Chuck Courtney, Anthony Dexter, Nick Adams, Glenn Langan and Geoffrey Deuel portrayed Billy in various films, the latter in John Wayne's **Chisum**. One must mention finally Robert Taylor as **Billy the Kid** (1940), a film obviously designed to cash in on the contemporaneous popularity of Tyrone Power's **Jesse James**; the Taylor film was unconvincing, overblown and surprisingly poor, although for some reason it remains in some critics' minds the definitive biopic. (Pat Garrett doesn't even appear in it.)

Pat Garrett, Billy's nemesis, was a New Mexico politician of murky character—an amalgam of Old West gunslinger and modern well-greased politico, a crony of Theodore Roosevelt's; he was mysteriously shot to death on a dusty Southwest trail some years later. Peckinpah's version, portrayed by James Coburn (**Pat Garrett and Billy the Kid**, 1973), is compelling, well acted and closer than any other to the complexity of the original, but it still falls short because the character is more type than person. Wallace Beery (**Billy the Kid**, 1930) and Albert Dekker (**The Kid from Texas**, 1950) did standard characterizations. James Griffith in the low-budget **The Law vs. Billy the Kid** (1954) was more effective than he had any right to be. The only other Garrett of interest was the one played by John Dehner in **The Left-Handed Gun** (1958); it was a powerful performance but had no relationship to the real character. It should be mentioned, I suppose, that a character called Pat Garrett was played, fascinatingly, by Thomas Mitchell in **The Outlaw** (1943), but had nothing to do with history or even legend.

Jim Bowie, the man who invented the famous knife and died at the Alamo, has been portrayed heroically by Sterling Hayden in **The Last Command** (1955), stolidly by Alan Ladd in **The Iron Mistress** (1952) and hysterically by Richard Widmark in **The Alamo** (1960).

William F. "Buffalo Bill" Cody was an intricate character: hero, charlatan, showman, tycoon, drunk, yarnspinner, marksman, hero. He has been represented in more than forty films, few of which have portrayed him as other than a standard cowboy hero. Most Buffalo Bills on screen, like James Ellison in De Mille's **The Plainsman** (1936) or Forrest Tucker in **Pony Express** (1953), have been standard frontier heroes with little connection to the reality or even the myths of Cody. The character is depicted as a showman in **Annie Oakley** (1935, Melvyn Douglas), in **Annie Get Your Gun** (1950, Louis Calhern) and—dated and poor but still the best cinematic depiction of the legend—in **Buffalo Bill** (1944). In that film Joel McCrea is excellent, possibly the best acting of his career, but the movie is a period piece now, absurdly contrived and clichéd. In **Buffalo Bill and the Indians** (1976) Paul Newman's performance is interesting but the film itself is terrible, and no mention is made of the fact that Cody, while in some ways a fraud, was also a real-life plainsman hero. To make a thematic point, writer-director Robert Altman distorted the play on which the film had been based, and concentrated exclusively on the idea of Cody as image—the showman created entirely by press-agentry. In so doing, Altman trampled the truth of both history and legend: Cody was a real Westerner, a real hero, and that was the ultimate reason for his success and popularity. Like Gary Cooper, he was the real thing; he wasn't the cheap shabby sham Altman showed us.

Calamity Jane—whose last name was Canary—was big, loud, ugly, a hearty irascible frontier character. Many actresses have played persons called Calamity Jane on the screen—Doris Day, Yvonne DeCarlo, Jane Russell, Jean Arthur and other glamor girls—but the only thing they've had in common with the original was the name. (But Doris Day was delightful in the eponymous movie, all the same.) There is some doubt whether Canary ever really met Wild Bill Hickok at all, historically. It is highly unlikely the two characters had any sort of romance.

General George Armstrong Custer, the victim of the notorious self-inflicted hatchet job at the Little Big Horn river—an American hero or an American villain—has been portrayed numerous times. The definitive film whitewash remains Errol Flynn's, in **They Died with Their Boots On** (1941); it has little to do with history but it's a marvelously entertaining movie. Richard Mulligan, a good actor, played an oversimplified Custer in the message-larded **Little Big Man** (1970) and Robert Shaw played him ambitiously in **Custer of the West** (1967, a Western woefully lacking in any feeling for the West), but no actor really has come close to capturing the essence of this arrogant would-be presidential candidate to whom the bodies of dead Southerners and Indians were to be stepped on in the climb toward the lofty goal of his ambitions. In literature Ernest Haycox created a beautifully drawn portrait of Custer and his family in the novel **Bugles in the Afternoon**; but none of it came across in the film version (1952, Sheb Wooley). Ronald Reagan once played Custer (fittingly?) in **Santa Fe Trail** (1940).

Wyatt Earp, with his several brothers (Virgil, Morgan, Warren), traveled the gamblers' circuit of the West from Ellsworth to Dodge City to Fort Griffin to Tombstone. Adventurers of sorts, the Earps were hardly the altruistic upholders of law 'n' order that legend has made them. Their principal business was gambling; they bought into saloons and ran whorehouses on the side; Wyatt was a con man at times, selling phony gold bricks to tourists from a tripe and keister; the Earps were accused of horse and cattle theft and of stagecoach robberies, and warrants were sworn out for Wyatt's arrest in Arizona on several charges of murder, although none resulted in convictions. Wyatt Earp finally was run out of Arizona with a murder charge still hanging over his head; later he got it quashed through friendships with politicians.

Evidently in real life Wyatt carried a badge only once, as a federally appointed tax collector in Santa Cruz County, Arizona Territory; he took the job because the collector was allowed to keep half the money he collected. He got quite rich at it, although it is alleged he had to murder one or two stubborn individualists before he got his point across. Other than that, there is little evidence other than his own word that he ever served as a peace officer. He was never the marshal of Tombstone, in any case.

But in 1928 he collaborated with novelist-biographer Stuart N. Lake in authorizing the biography that was called **Frontier Marshal** and purported to be the true and authentic life and times of Wyatt Earp, peace officer, marshal of Ellsworth, Wichita, Dodge City and Tombstone. Lake's book served as the basis for most of the Earp movies that were made in the ensuing thirty-five years. It was largely fiction.

Nevertheless the Earps were handsome men, blond, splendidly costumed most of the time, usually described as "leonine"; physically both Henry Fonda (in **My Darling Clementine**, 1946) and James Garner (in one of the best acting jobs of his career, in **Hour of the Gun**, 1967) bear close resemblances to the mustachioed photos of Wyatt taken in Tombstone by the photographer C.S. Fly in 1880.

As to historical accuracy of incident, **Hour of the Gun** comes much closer than most others, but it's still pretty far off base.

The gunfight at the OK Corral did take place in fact, although there is dispute among scholars and old-timers as to which side, if either, was in the right. It is accepted by many historians that two of the men whom the Earps killed that day in 1881 were probably unarmed.

The Earp-Holliday crowd and the Clanton-McLowery crowd were feuding rival factions in the Tombstone area; each faction had its own political office—Virgil Earp was chief of police and John P. Clum, a friend of the Earps, was mayor of Tombstone, while Clanton crony John Behan was county sheriff—and most residents on the sidelines were hoping the two sides would wipe each other out. It was not altogether dissimilar to a mobsters' gang war. The Earps had one newspaper, *The Epitaph,* on their side (Mayor Clum owned it), while the Clantons had the other, *The Nugget,* on theirs, so it's a bit difficult to sort out the facts based on the wildly differing versions of events that were reported in the two newspapers. Trials followed the killings, but testimony by participants and eyewitnesses was totally contradictory, and nobody was convicted of anything.

All that is known for certain is that the gun battle took place. It lasted about half a minute. It was not a "gunfight" in the quick-draw showdown sense; weapons included rifles and a shotgun. About nine men took part. As many as six hundred shots seem to have been fired. Nearly everybody was injured, and four men died. Several more, including Morgan Earp, were killed in ambushes and shootings in the several weeks' aftermath of the battle.

When I was a kid in Arizona, old-timers around Tombstone still disputed the facts about the Earps with great heat and bitterness. There were families, even in the 1950s, who refused to talk to each other because of such arguments.

History aside, the Wyatt Earp legend entered the world's folklore and a number of good movies used it as their basis. One of the best, in addition to Ford's classic **My Darling Clementine** and the abovementioned underrated **Hour of the Gun**, is the surprisingly fresh and still entertaining Randolph Scott movie **Frontier Marshal** (1939). Joel

McCrea was a standard Earp in **Wichita** (1955) and Richard Dix in **Tombstone** (1942) also kept all the traditional cliches in place. Burt Lancaster played Wyatt in the overblown and overpraised **Gunfight at the OK Corral** (1957) and there have been innumerable other movie Earps, none of any particular distinction except for Harris Yulin in **Doc** (1971), which has the unhappy distinction of being undoubtedly the worst and most disgusting portrayal of Earp, who may have been hard and villainous but it's hard to buy a depiction of him as a slimy, vicious cretin. (Yulin is a good actor. It is the characterization, not the performance, that leaves a sour taste in one's mouth.)

Heroes clearly modeled on the Earp legends but bearing other names include those played by Robert Mitchum in the fitfully interesting **Young Billy Young** (1969), Barry Sullivan in the rancid **Forty Guns** (1957), Henry Fonda in the curious but often powerful **Warlock** (1959) and Walter Huston in the film that is still one of the best of the Earp subgenre, **Law and Order** (1932; Ronald Reagan reprised the part in lacklustre fashion in a 1953 remake with the same title).

James Butler "Wild Bill" Hickok has never been portrayed very well on the screen. Hunter, lawman, reluctant showman and partner of Buffalo Bill, gambler, ladies' man, and certainly the best marksman of his era with a .36 calibre Navy Colt revolver, celebrated drunk, sartorial dandy —Hickok died in his early thirties, shot in the back by a scruffy stable boy while playing cards in Deadwood. I recall a live television drama, sometime in the 1950s, in which Lloyd Bridges movingly played Hickok in his last days, eyesight fading, wits failing, driven by self-destructive demons; I've seen nothing else remotely like it. Otherwise the best performance, although a burlesque, probably was that of the superb and often neglected Jeff Corey in **Little Big Man** (1970). In a cameo appearance, L.Q. Jones played Hickok in my own **Wild Times** (1980). Gary Cooper, of course, played a fanciful Hickok in **The Plainsman** (1936) and it is a lovely job of acting and Cooper looked great in the part, but the movie is something of a bore.

There have been scores of other Wild Bills down through the years, including Charlton Heston in **Pony Express** (1953) and of course Gordon Elliott in the 1938 "B" serial **Wild Bill Hickok**, the result of which was that the actor changed his first name and became William "Wild Bill" Elliott.

John Henry "Doc" Holliday, an Atlanta dentist who went west for the climate on account of his tuberculosis, confounded medical experts by surviving some fifteen years past the year they'd given him; some credit his survival to strong drink and pure nastiness.

Holliday killed coolly and frequently; he was usually drunk; his customary weapon was the knife or the hide-out pocket derringer. Apologists for Wyatt Earp have contrived all manner of excuses to rationalize the close friendship between the two men. Holliday's physique was small, his personality rude and crude; he was miscast consistently in films, and generally (historically) misplayed, by robust actors who played him as a cultivated shotgun-toting aristocrat, polished but down on his luck.

I suppose the best remembered Holliday was that rendered by beefcake giant Victor Mature in Ford's **My Darling Clementine** (1946); it was an absurd but oddly touching performance, one of the best of the actor's career. I think the definitive movie Holliday to date was Jason Robards' in **Hour of the Gun** (1967); it was a wonderful job—caustic, sodden, bitter, yet human. Douglas V. Fowley in Hugh O'Brian's **Wyatt Earp** television series of the late 1950s was one of the more realistic impersonators; he played Holliday as an irascible meany. Kirk Douglas in **Gunfight at the OK Corral** (1957) played Holliday as one of his standard high-spirited intense cackling gunmen. Stacy Keach esoterically essayed the title role in **Doc** (1971), one of the worst Westerns of all time. Walter Huston played a character named Doc Holliday but not otherwise related to reality in **The Outlaw** (1943). In my own **Wild Times** (1980), Holliday is played by Dennis Hopper in a cameo appearance. I thought he was excellent but perhaps I was biased. Cesar Romero in **Frontier Marshal** (1939) and James Griffith in **Masterson of Kansas** (1954) were very interesting. There've been many others as well.

Jesse James, robber, had a criminal career that spanned nearly two decades. With his brother Frank, and various cousins and hangers-on, he led a campaign against banks and railroads in the Middle West that his apologists equated with that of Robin Hood. Actually their robberies netted very little money and what they did get had to be distributed among a large unwieldy number of gang members; they rarely had enough to eat, and therefore the legends about Jesse and Frank's giving money to the poor are of dubious accuracy. But they made great headline copy year after year; their legend, created by the yellow press and abetted by the Pinkertons, became an important part of America's folklore.

The definitive movie biography probably is still **Jesse James** (1939), with Tyrone Power as Jesse and Henry Fonda as Frank; the roles were reprised in the remake **The True Story of Jesse James** (1957, using essentially the same screenplay) by Robert Wagner and Jeffrey Hunter. Both films contain a conscientious rendition of the popular legend; both are well made and quite entertaining; neither has much claim to accuracy. In costumes, sets and the like, the remake is the more realistic, but the performances in the earlier version were somewhat better. Fonda reprised his role in **The Return of Frank James** (1940), a very popular sequel that had no basis in history or legend and was directed with curious leadenness by Fritz Lang. The James boys were portrayed by the Keach brothers, Stacy (as Frank) and James, in **The Long Riders** (1980), which was an interesting film unfortunately sliced too thin by excessive editing and anemic writing. The most spirited, if not hysterical, representation of Jesse was that of Robert Duvall in **The Great Northfield Minnesota Raid** (1972), a faddishly idiotic movie that suggested that the legendary highwayman was a raving psychopath driven by fundamentalist religious demons. There've been scores of Jesses and Franks throughout film history; in the early 1950s John Ireland seemingly kept turning up in one Jesse James movie after another, sometimes playing Frank, sometimes playing a bogus Jesse. But none of the others was of great note.

Tom Horn, Bat Masterson, Belle Starr, the Daltons, the Youngers, Cochise, Sitting Bull, Crazy Horse, Geronimo, Annie Oakley, Sam Bass, Ike Clanton, Jim Bridger, Jedediah Smith, Al Sieber, Kit Carson and innumerable other characters from actual history have been depicted with varying degrees of authenticity on the screen in Westerns of all types and sizes.

Mostly these celebrities were merely conveniences—box-office pegs on which to hang standard formula Western stories. Few films and few actors have been able to overcome the charismatic chemistry of the Western mythos in general or of the legendary characters as individuals. Even Gary Cooper was unable to do much out of the ordinary with the character of Wild Bill Hickok in **The Plainsman**: his interpretation was fascinating (see the review of the film in the main body of the guide) but the film itself would have hamstrung any actor. Producers and studio bosses mostly didn't care to fiddle with successful formulas, and writers mostly lacked the imagination to make more of the material at hand. There is still ample room for a hell of a movie about Hickok, Holliday or Cody.

*

The genre has been enhanced by the outstanding work of an established stock-company of supporting players who appeared exclusively or frequently in Westerns. Walter Brennan may be the best remembered—he won three Oscars—but Brennan was by no means the only, or most talented, of them.

THE LAST HARD MEN (1976):
Charlton Heston and Michael
Parks lead the posse. Hard riding
on difficult locations. Twentieth
Century-Fox

JOHNNY GUITAR (1954): Joan
Crawford, Sterling Hayden. Only
rarely did a woman head the cast
of a Western. Republic Pictures

RAWHIDE (1951): Tyrone Power, Susan Hayward, Hugh Marlowe. Hayward's determined strong woman was an unusual character in a Western. Twentieth Century-Fox

RIDE THE MAN DOWN (1952): J. Carrol Naish, Rod Cameron, Forrest Tucker—it always helps to have stalwarts in the cast. Republic Pictures

One consistently entertaining player was Henry Hull, seen here with director Raoul Walsh on the set of COLORADO TERRITORY (1949). Warner Brothers

Worth seeing in any movie: Ben Johnson (on the set of WILD TIMES, 1980, but out of costume—the hat, for Johnson, is standard wear). Author's collection

On a working set: John Wayne and director John Ford preparing a scene for THE HORSE SOLDIERS (1959). United Artists

It makes all the difference to a Western to have the presences of such stalwarts as Ben Johnson, Edgar Buchanan, Chill Wills, Slim Pickens, Arthur Hunnicutt, J. Carrol Naish, Victor Jory, Jim Davis, Forrest Tucker, Lee Van Cleef, Lee Marvin, Claude Akins, Roy Roberts, Michael Pate, Charles Bronson, Anthony Quinn, James Best, L.Q. Jones, Strother Martin, Harry Carey, Jr., Harry Dean Stanton, Bob Steele, Henry Brandon, R.G. Armstrong, John Anderson—these and many others, some of them on the way up to or down from stardom, are the supporting characters of countless oaters. Often their performances have been so alive with verve and force that they have made up for a good many inadequacies of scripts, stars and directors.

As an unabashed Western fan from childhood on, I arrived in the fall of 1979 on the set of **Wild Times** in a state of euphoria that only a fellow oater buff could truly understand: I had suggested, and gotten, the casting of Ben Johnson, Harry Carey, Jr., L.Q. Jones and Cameron Mitchell in key roles, and had asked for—and gotten—as the star of the picture Sam Elliott, who I felt had the best chance of any actor in the 1980s to assume the larger-than-life position in Western films last occupied by Gary Cooper. This will happen only if a miraculous renaissance of Westerns occurs, and I doubt the likelihood of that, but in any case I was very happy when Sam agreed to play Colonel Hugh Cardiff. And the additions of Pat Hingle, Gene Evans, Penny Peyser, Dennis Hopper and especially Timothy Scott—a wonderfully adept actor (he played News Carver in **Butch Cassidy and the Sundance Kid**)—didn't dampen my enthusiasms any.

The reminiscences of Ben Johnson and Harry Carey, Jr. (dubbed "Dobie" by his father when he was a kid because of the adobe brick color of his hair) fascinated me. They are gentlemen, in all the best senses of that word. They appeared together in dozens of movies including **Rio Grande, She Wore a Yellow Ribbon** and **Wagonmaster** (in which they starred, top-billed, for Ford); Carey appeared in **The Searchers**, while Johnson has graced such films as **Shane** and **The Wild Bunch**—in fact it sometimes seemed no classic Western since 1945 had been made without the participation of at least one of these two wonderful characters.

*

Many of the great ones are retired or dead. This may be yet another reason why the genre has wilted. Many of these fellows grew up in cow country uncluttered by plastic, neon or the contrails of jet planes. They were the last generation of frontiersmen. Ben Johnson threatens to retire, now and then; he has been riding the same black horse in movies for years and the horse, at this book's press time, is about twenty years old, and Ben allows as how he'll retire when the horse retires. Nobody takes that threat too seriously. But if it is true, the sad thought follows that no one can replace Ben Johnson. His boots cannot be filled by anyone else, any more than Gary Cooper's could.

*

One of the greatest pleasures of my life has been in working on, or even visiting, the working sets of Western movies, and collaborating in the making of them with the actors whose personalities on the screen have brought those movies to life. It's hard to get anybody to back the production of a Western with real money nowadays, but I keep hoping. I don't get tired of making Westerns. I still love them.

Maybe, as some of my erstwhile friends might say, I just want to keep doing it until I get it right.

10

THE

FILMS

The main section of this guide, immediately following this chapter, lists about fifteen hundred films, most of them "A" Western talkies released in the United States between 1928 and 1981. The listing for each film gives its principal credits: studio, year of first release, director, writers, cast, running time in minutes.

Cast lists often are incomplete because there isn't room to list every bit player. The length of the cast list depends on various factors: importance of the film, size of the cast, appearance of stock-company regulars, in some cases the appearance of an interesting actor in a small part, and in a few cases the limited availability of information, particularly with minor movies that have been lost.

At the end of the main guide are three appendices of foreshortened descriptions of approximately four hundred juveniles, documentaries, and made-for-television and foreign (spaghetti, sauerkraut) Westerns. If a film doesn't appear in the main guide, it may be listed in an appendix. Most of the Disney Westerns, for instance, appear in the appendix of juveniles.

Inevitably, among the films listed are a number I have not seen. In those cases—mainly ephemeral independent productions, made-for-TV movies, European imports, pre-1945 movies and lost minor films—the critique, if there is one, is based on the best available information.

Every class of entertainments has its aficionados. Even the lowly spaghetti Western has been the subject of high-flown learned essays in film journals. The majority of the Italian, Spanish and German Westerns are subjuvenile, however; apparently their writers' only exposure to the West has been to old "B" pictures and earlier European oaters. With many such films one can perceive that where they are not imbecilic they are rank plagiarisms. There is the occasional worthwhile European Western but it is the exception; for the most part the spaghetti-sauerkraut films are shot by international casts and crews who cannot communicate with one another, the dubbing is badly synchronized to the actors' lip movements, the writing is incompetent and the crafting of the films is far below an acceptable professional level. Many such films are covered in this guide, but few are of any value, and most of them are relegated to the appendix of abbreviated listings.

The critiques vary greatly in length. Their size is determined by the importance or interest—to me—of the film. A few celebrated Westerns have been treated quite briefly, precisely because they are so well known and I have very little to add to what everybody has already heard about them. Conversely, the occasional minor movie receives a lengthy appraisal because I found interesting quirks in it.

To conserve space the guide employs a system of abbreviations that I hope are obvious enough to prevent confusion. *D* means "directed by" and *W* means "written for the screen by" and includes adapters, story creators, outliners, screenwriters and polishers; when a film is based on a novel, play or other source, the source is identified. Numbers followed by *m* (**112m**) indicate the film's running time in minutes; this is given only in those cases where the precise running time is known.

(For a more precise breakdown of the writing credits, the serious student should consult *Who Wrote the Movie?*, a joint 1970 publication—with subsequent updates—of the Writers Guild of America, Inc., and the Academy of Motion Picture Arts and Sciences.)

Some commentaries mention "the Bob Steele plot." This is a shorthand device I've employed to describe the one about the young man who sets out to unmask the bad guys so as to avenge the murder of his parent, brother, wife, sister or child; it is such a ubiquitous formula that it would be wasteful to describe the plot each time this one appears.

*

Releasing studios are identified by these abbreviations:

AA—Allied Artists (formerly Monogram, now Lorimar)

AI—American International Pictures

BV—Buena Vista (Walt Disney releasing division)

CIN—Cinerama Releasing Corporation

COL—Columbia Pictures

EL—Eagle-Lion

EMB—Embassy Pictures, and Avco-Embassy Pictures

FOX—Fox Film Corp., and 20th Century-Fox

IND—Independent: released by an indie producer or distributor

LIP—Lippert (Robert L. Lippert Productions)

MGM—Metro-Goldwyn-Mayer and MGM Corp. (Sometimes distributed through United Artists)

MONO—Monogram (at times a division of Republic; later Allied Artists)

NGP—National General Pictures

PARA—Paramount Pictures

REP—Republic Pictures

RKO—RKO Radio Pictures, formerly FBO

SG—Screen Guild

UA—United Artists

UNIV—Universal Pictures, and Universal-International

WB—Warner Brothers

*

The above releasing credits are included not out of chauvinistic loyalty to industry companies but because it often is possible to obtain 16mm or Super-8 prints, or videodiscs or videotape cassettes, of films; and one must know which releasing organization can provide the films.

But it should be mentioned that a lamentably large number of the older films no longer exists.

More than half the films produced in the United States before 1950 are lost, apparently irretrievably. They were made with nitrocellulose film, which is highly flammable and self-destructive through the brittleness of age. Further, some films were destroyed deliberately, their negatives and prints reduced to powder so that the silver content of the old nitrate film could be sold.

Also it should be mentioned that color processes tend to fade with age, and that methods of color printing have cheapened with modern times, so that recent color movies tend to fade faster than old ones did. The result is that very few color movies with their colors intact, new or old, can be obtained.

The American Film Institute, established in 1967, is attempting to safeguard and restore old movies, but thousands are beyond recapturing.

*

The date provided with each film is the year in which the film was first released, usually in the United States. Normally that is the same as the copyright date but not always. Some films are held "in the can" for months, even years, after their filming. **A Talent for Loving** was filmed in 1969 but released (to television, never in theatres) in 1974. **The Outlaw** was filmed in 1940–1942 but its general release was delayed until 1950 because of its celebrated censorship difficulties; nevertheless this guide dates it at 1943 because that was the year of its first paid-ticket public exhibition in the United States.

The title under which each film is listed is the film's best-known title or the title under which it appears most frequently. (For example, the reader looking for **Desperate Siege** will be directed to see **Rawhide**, which was its original title; it was changed for a while in the 1960s so that its appearances on television would not be confused with episodes of the **Rawhide** TV series. The movie has nothing to do with that series.)

For the most part, foreign films are listed under the titles used in their U.S. releases. Only occasionally have British titles been included in the cross-reference listings. (Films often undergo transatlantic title changes: **Ride the High Country** was released in Britain as **Guns in the Afternoon**.)

Alphabetical order is absolute. For example the order of listings is **Fort Dobbs, For the Love of Mike, Fort Massacre**. Similarly **The Forty-Niners** comes ahead of **Fort Yuma**.

I could not bring myself to begin the alphabetical listing with **Aaron Slick from Punkin Crick**. You will find that movie listed under its alternate (TV) title, **Marshmallow Moon**. It seemed far more fitting to open the guide with the solid little **Abilene Town**.

*

It wasn't practicable to compile an index of names, although I realize this volume would be more useful if it provided a cross reference of actors, writers and directors. That would have added hundreds of pages to this already long book.

Perhaps someday, if the future provides enough Westerns and enough interest in them, a companion volume of updated entries may be assembled so as to include such an index. (The most recent films discussed in this edition are those released in the summer of 1981.)

*

Where it seems important to an appreciation of a particular film, the credits of cinematographers, composers and other contributors have been provided in the texts of the critiques, but these credits are omitted from the routine films.

In the cast credits I have not always adhered to the order of names in the official titles of the films. Sometimes an actor's contract enabled him to get top, or major, billing when in fact his role was minor; sometimes underpaid and underbilled actors actually played principal roles. Since I am under no obligation to honor the contracts between actors and filmmakers, I've tried to make the cast credits reflect the relative degree of each performer's actual participation, rather than the amount of clout his agent may have had in getting billing for him.

The guide assumes, arbitrarily, that Westerns made before 1950 were in black-and-white, and those made after 1950 were in color. Exceptions are noted. Where it seems noteworthy, such features as wide-screen, original 3-D release or the availability of alternate color and black-and-white prints have been mentioned.

Winners of the more significant Oscars (Academy Awards) are mentioned within the listings of the films that have won them; major Oscar nominees are mentioned as well. (Minor technical awards are disregarded, mostly. Space is too limited.)

Only one Western has won the Academy Award as "best picture": **Cimarron**, in 1932. But eleven others have been nominated for it: **In Old Arizona** (1929), **Viva Villa** (1934), **Stagecoach** (1939), **The Ox-Bow Incident** (1943), **High Noon** (1952), **Shane** (1953), **Seven Brides for Seven Brothers** (1954), **The Friendly Persuasion** (1956), **The Alamo** (1960), **How the West Was Won** (1963) and **Butch Cassidy and the Sundance Kid** (1969).

*

Not every entry is as complete as it might, or ought to, be. Sometimes it seemed not worth the trouble to search endlessly for elusive minutiae about pre-1935 "lost" films, foreign-made oaters, cheap indies or made-for-TV perishables. These last three are the "B" movies of our time. Many of them have never been put into general theatrical release in the United States. For example, the rock-bottom indies of Ferde Grofe, Jr. (like **The Proud and the Damned**) have appeared in this country only on independent television channels.

If a film seemed important enough to justify seeking out complete credits then I made every effort to get them. Otherwise I merely have told as much or as little as I know about it. Needless to say, errors—both factual and typographical (I set the book in type on a Xerox 860 word processor)—are nobody's fault but my own.

*

One final item. This book is not designed as a TV-table guide but I'm sure it will be used as one by some readers. The critiques are based on the original full-length uninterrupted theatrical showings, and one must keep in mind that a CinemaScope suspense film like **Bad Day at Black Rock** simply does not work on the tube. If I hadn't seen **Garden of Evil** on a big theatrical screen with a full-scale stereo sound system, I probably would have judged it a poor film on the evidence of its color-faded rendition on TV. Networks and stations often butcher a film in order to cram it into two forty-six-minute hours or a seventy-minute hour and a half. The interruptions of commercials will destroy the suspense of any taut film. And the TV screen not only reduces movies in grandeur but also cuts off both sides of a wide-screen movie.

In sum it is impossible to judge a film's quality by its exhibition on television, and the reader who keeps this guide near his TV set should bear that in mind. When you see a movie on TV you never know what has been cut out of it; often enough it's the heart.

Let's look at the movies.

ABILENE TOWN (1945, UA). D: Edwin L. Marin. W: Harold Shumate from Ernest Haycox's novel *Trail Town*. Cast: RANDOLPH SCOTT, ANN DVORAK, Rhonda FLEMING, Edgar BUCHANAN, Lloyd Bridges, Jack Lambert, Howard Freeman, Helen Boice, Eddy Waller, Dick Curtis. 88m.

Haycox was without peer among the slick-magazine Western serialists of the 1940s but his introspective writings seldom adapted well to the screen. In this film the characterizations and plot complications are more complex than in most routine oaters, thanks to Haycox; still, the screenplay reduces it to an imitation of the Wyatt Earp formula with the town marshal trying to maintain the peace in a Kansas railhead cow town by keeping antagonistic cattlemen and homesteaders from one another's throats. The ending is anticlimactic. Above average but minor.

ACES WILD (1936, IND). D: Harry Fraser. W: Monroe Talbot. Cast: HARRY CAREY, Gertrude MESSINGER, Edward Cassidy. 57m.

Gambler reforms. A sort of Wm. S. Hart yarn on a "B" budget.

ACROSS THE GREAT DIVIDE (1976, IND). DW: Stewart Rafill. Cast: Robert LOGAN, George "Buck" Flower, Heather Rattray, Mark Hall. 94m.

Brother and sister orphans are shepherded through the 1870s wilderness by a roguish young gambler (Logan), encountering comical tough guys, earnestly decent Indians and a variety of wild animals (including the inevitable grizzly bear). Pablum filmed on the cheap for the family trade, the movie's asset is excellent (uncredited) color photography of its British Columbia and Utah locations.

ACROSS THE WIDE MISSOURI (1951, MGM). D: William A. Wellman. W: Frank Cavett & Talbot Jennings from Bernard DeVoto's book. Cast: CLARK GABLE, RICARDO MONTALBAN, JOHN HODIAK, Adolphe MENJOU, Maria Elena Marques, J. Carrol Naish, Jack Holt, James Whitmore, Alan Napier, Douglas Fowley, Richard Anderson, Chief Nipo Strongheart. 78m.

Pioneer fur trappers in Blackfoot country, c. 1830. Gable preferred Westerns to anything else but unfortunately didn't make many. He enjoyed himself in this one; he and Montalban are most entertaining as a pair of ebullient mountain men. The movie renders a thoughtful treatment of Indian-white differences; plot is part romance, part history and all confusion, because MGM re-edited the movie to the point of mutilation before its release; the result is jerky and truncated. William Mellor's photography of high-country scenery is first-rate. Jack Holt's last movie. (He died in 1951.)

ADIOS, AMIGO (1976, IND). DW: Fred Williamson. Cast: FRED WILLIAMSON, RICHARD PRYOR, James BROWN, Thalamus Rasulala, Suhalia Farhat, Mike Henry, Victoria Lee, Robert Phillips, Lynne Jackson. 87m.

Flimsy, badly filmed but reasonably engaging con-man comedy follows the slapstick misadventures of two black swindlers in the old West. There's an unusual use of sketch drawings as partitions between scenes. It's cheap, ineptly filmed and unimaginatively written, but Pryor is amusing. For undemanding audiences.

ADVANCE TO THE REAR (1964, MGM). Also titled: COMPANY OF COWARDS. D: George Marshall. W: Jack Schaefer, Samuel Anthony Peeples & William Bowers, from William Chamberlain's novel *Company of Cowards*. Cast: GLENN FORD, STELLA STEVENS, MELVYN DOUGLAS, Joan BLONDELL, Jim BACKUS, Preston FOSTER, Andrew Prine, Alan Hale, Jr., Jesse Pearson, James Griffith. 97m.

Slapstick Civil War comedy. Yankee goldbricks are sent out West to tangle with Rebs and a pretty spy. It's a pratfall situation comedy. Melvyn Douglas and Joan Blondell liven up their few scenes, but despite all those good writers it's mostly an unfunny mess.

ADVENTURES IN SILVERADA (1949, COL). D: Phil Karlson. W: Kenneth Gamet, Tom Kilpatrick & Joe Pagano from a story by Robert Louis Stevenson. Cast: William BISHOP, Gloria HENRY, Forrest TUCKER, Edgar BUCHANAN, Edgar Barrier, Irving Bacon, Joseph Crehan.

Author-hero Robert Louis Stevenson travels out West, mixes it up with a masked stagecoach bandit and entertains us mildly for a while. Strange little movie is better made than it ought to be.

THE ADVENTURES OF FRONTIER FREMONT (1976, IND). D: Richard Friedenberg. W: Friedenberg, David O'Malley & Charles Sellier, Jr. Cast: DAN HAGGERTY, Denver PYLE, T. Miratti, Brian Frasier. 98m.

A young man in the Wyoming Rockies in 1835 befriends bears, wolves and a crusty mountain man (Pyle); cheerfully survives one catastrophe after another; and is indistinguishable from Grizzly Adams (also produced by the same Sunn-Schick people). Shifting from simpleminded charm to insincere bucolic sentimentality, this one leads to a hokey forest-fire climax, painful with coincidence. Emphasis is on rugged individualism and nostalgia for a clean, righteous, simple past that never really existed; this is in keeping with the conservative views of the companies that produce such films, sometimes with the aid of computers that analyze audience tastes. Scenery and animal photography (George A. Stapleford) are good.

THE ADVENTURES OF THE WILDERNESS FAMILY (1975, IND). DW: Stewart Raffill. Cast: Robert LOGAN, George "Buck" Flower, Susan Damante Shaw, Hollye Holmes, Ham Larsen. 100m.

Sister movie to, and almost indistinguishable from, *Across the Great Divide*, this is another wilderness family lollipop for the kiddie trade. Highlight as always is landscape and wildlife photography (Gerard Alcan) on Utah and British Columbia locations. Rudimentary entertainment.

AFRICA—TEXAS STYLE (1966, PARA). D: Andrew Marton. W: Andy White. Cast: HUGH O'BRIAN, JOHN MILLS, Tom NARDINI, Nigel GREEN, Adrienne CORRI, Ronald HOWARD, Charles Malinda. 106m.

An Ivan Tors production, made initially as a pilot for the *Daktari* television series; a cowboy goes to Africa to capture wild game by lassoing elands, zebras and the like. The animal footage is OK, the plot silly; O'Brian was never a convincing cowboy. John Wayne's version, *Hatari*, was several notches better than this one.

AGAINST A CROOKED SKY (1975, IND). D: Earl Bellamy. W: Douglas C. Stewart & Eleanor Lamb. Cast: RICHARD BOONE, Stewart PETERSEN, Henry Wilcoxon, Clint Ritchie, Jewel Blanch, Shannon Farnon. 90m.

Weary, cheap reprise of *The Searchers* has a crusty old-timer teamed with a teenager in an attempt to rescue the kid's sister who was kidnaped by Indians. Utah location photography (Joe Jackman) is palatable; the film itself is drivel: implausible and witless. A Doty-Dayton production.

THE ALAMO (1960, UA). D: John Wayne. W: James Edward Grant. Cast: JOHN WAYNE, RICHARD WIDMARK, LAURENCE HARVEY, Richard BOONE, Linda CRISTAL, Chill WILLS, Frankie AVALON, Patrick Wayne, Joan O'Brien, Veda Ann Borg, Joseph Calleia, Ken Curtis, Carlos Arruza, John Dierkes, Denver Pyle, Guinn "Big Boy" Williams, Hank Worden. 191m.

The story purports to be a salute to the heroes who fought for Texas's independence in 1836 and were wiped out at San Antonio's Alamo. Wayne portrays Davy Crockett, Widmark Jim Bowie, Laurence Harvey (miscast and mannered) Colonel Travis, and Richard Boone (blustery) Sam Houston. Any resemblance to historical persons is accidental; the script is true neither to history nor to drama. The first 130 minutes are childish and boring, with the actors chewing up the scenery; the drawn-out climactic battle (one hour) is amateurishly choreographed and oddly unexciting. *The Alamo* is a good example of Hollywood at its worst: nearly a classic for students of awful movies. A superior if flawed film version of this history is *The Last Command*, made only five years earlier. *The Alamo* won an Oscar for best sound (Gordon E. Sawyer, Fred Hynes) and was nominated for Oscars for best picture and for best supporting actor (Chill Wills).

John Wayne produced this soggy dirigible. Allegedly John Ford lent him a hand directing it but, it is said, the scenes Ford shot were not used in the final cut. It probably wouldn't have mattered; the movie is so doughy it absorbs its few excellences—like Dimitri Tiomkin's score and the vast photography (William Clothier) that only lights up its faults.

Reliable reports have it that Wayne spent nearly thirteen million 1960 dollars to make this interminable epic which is by turns adolescent, lusty, glutinous, ribald, simpering and flabbily actionful.

ALBUQUERQUE (1948, PARA). D: Ray Enright. W: Gene Lewis & Clarence Young from Luke Short's novel *Dead Freight for Paiute*. Cast: RANDOLPH SCOTT, BARBARA BRITTON, George "Gabby" HAYES, Lon CHANEY, Jr., Russell Hayden, Irving Bacon, George Cleveland. 89m.

A young Westerner (Hayden) challenges his stern, righteous uncle; and drifter Randolph Scott finds himself in the midst of a feud that threatens to become a range war. It's a good fast Luke Short yarn, well plotted with plenty of twists and fairly adult characters. Minor, but well done by all.

ALIAS JESSE JAMES (1959, UA). D: Norman McLeod. W: William Bowers, Daniel D. Beauchamp, Robert St. Aubrey & Bert Laurence. Cast: BOB HOPE, RHONDA FLEMING, WENDELL COREY, Jim DAVIS, Gloria TALBOTT, Will Wright, Mike Mazurki, Sid Melton, Jack Lambert, Glenn Strange, George E. Stone, Iron Eyes Cody, Harry Tyler, Nestor Paiva, I. Stanford Jolley. Guest stars: GARY COOPER, ROY ROGERS, GENE AUTRY, BING CROSBY, GAIL DAVIS, JAY SILVERHEELS, Hugh O'BRIAN, Ward BOND, James ARNESS, Fess PARKER. 92m.

This is an unacknowledged remake of a 1940 MGM comedy written by S.J. Perelman called *The Golden Fleecing* about a hapless insurance man (Lew Ayres, in that one) who sells a huge life policy to a notorious gangster (Lloyd Nolan). In the Western version Bob Hope is the idiot insurance salesman and Wendell Corey, as Jesse James, is the outlaw who buys $100,000 in life insurance from him. After that, of course, it is up to Hope to keep Jesse alive. It's a good premise but it worked better the first time; this version is flaccid, hardly worth much attention except to see the cameos by the guest stars. Cooper is very funny.

AL JENNINGS OF OKLAHOMA (1950, COL). D: Fred F. Sears. W: George Bricker from a book by Al Jennings & Will Irwin. Cast: DAN DURYEA, GALE STORM, Dick FORAN, Gloria HENRY, John DEHNER, Guinn "Big Boy" Williams, James Millican, Louis Jean Heydt, Harry Cording, Harry Shannon, George J. Lewis, Harry Tyler, Stanley Andrews. 79m.

The real Al Jennings was a runty inept train robber who got caught by Bill Tilghman, spent a while in prison and then made a movie with Tilghman; later Jennings appeared in a series of silent "B" oaters. Duryea here plays Jennings as an engaging rogue—a misunderstood outlaw who wants to go straight but has trouble because nobody trusts him, so he returns to crime. Duryea turns in a pleasant performance but it's routine.

ALLEGHENY UPRISING (1939, RKO). D: William Seiter. W: P.J. Wolfson & Neil H. Swanson. Cast: JOHN WAYNE, CLAIRE TREVOR, George SANDERS, Brian DONLEVY, Robert Barrat, Chill Wills, Moroni Olsen, John Hamilton, Eddy Waller, Wilfrid Lawson, Eddie Quillan, Ian Wolfe. 81m.

Wayne's first major vehicle after *Stagecoach* re-teamed him with Trevor in a Revolutionary War yarn with English villains (Sanders) and a snarling baddie (Donlevy) who plies Indians with booze and guns. Dated but there's lots of action.

ALL MINE TO GIVE (1957, UNIV). D: Allen Reisner. W: Dale & Katherine Eunson. Cast: CAMERON MITCHELL, GLYNIS JOHNS, Patty McCORMACK, Hope EMERSON, Rex Thompson. 102m.

Pastoral wilderness yarn shows Wisconsin pioneers facing frontier hardships. Not a hard-hitting movie but sometimes touching; not bad.

ALONG CAME JONES (1945, RKO). D: Stuart Heisler. W: Nunnally Johnson from Alan LeMay's novel *Useless Cowboy*. Cast: GARY COOPER, LORETTA YOUNG, Dan DURYEA, William DEMAREST, Ray Teal, Walter Sande, Lane Chandler, Frank Sully, Russell Simpson, Chris-Pin Martin, John Merton, Hank Bell. 89m.

Droll results ensue when a shy mild cowhand (Cooper) who can't shoot straight is mistaken for a notorious gunfighter (Duryea). The bad guy's girl friend (Young) dupes the cowhand into trouble but later relents. Amiably scripted and commendably conceived, but the film often is overrated; it's disappointing because it's so cheaply made. Cooper produced it himself—his first venture into independent operation (it began the trend toward star productions); possibly he ran short of capital; it has the look of an early live-TV drama with flimsy fake sets and phony backlot exteriors and outdoor sequences filmed against such amateurish rear projection that it's obvious the actors never left the sound stages. William Demarest's New York accent makes him a distracting choice as Cooper's saddle partner; and the young Dan Duryea hadn't yet learned to act. Heisler allowed Cooper to get away with too many cute mannerisms and, in his quiet way, he overplayed unforgivably.

ALONG THE GREAT DIVIDE (1950, WB). D: Raoul Walsh. W: Walter Doniger & Lewis Meltzer. Cast: KIRK DOUGLAS, VIRGINIA MAYO, Walter BRENNAN, John AGAR, Ray TEAL, Hugh Sanders, Morris Ankrum, James Anderson, Charles Meredith. 88m.

Of the several film-noir Westerns Walsh directed (*Pursued, Colorado Territory*), this is the weakest. It's well directed but the script— about a tough marshal (Douglas) escorting an accused murderer (Brennan) across the desert to stand trial, fighting off a raging sandstorm and lynch-minded bad guys en route—is tiresome and the two heroes (Douglas, Agar) miscast. The ending is hokey and unbelievable. Douglas, here appearing in his first Western, seems out of place in the saddle; in later films he mastered the Western personality. The film boasts good b&w photography (Sid Hickox) and quite a good score (David Buttolph).

ALVAREZ KELLY (1966, COL). Also titled: THE RICHMOND STORY. D: Edward Dmytryk. W: Franklin Coen. Cast: WILLIAM HOLDEN, RICHARD WIDMARK, JANICE RULE, Victoria SHAW, Patrick O'NEAL, Arthur Franz, Roger C. Carmel, Richard Rust. 116m.

Large-scale Civil War adventure has a Texas cattleman (Holden) delivering a herd to a Yankee army commander (O'Neal); the opposing armies keep rustling the herd from each other. There're hard-fisted disputations and some hokey romances along the way. The climax is a terrific stampede but it's hard to stay awake that long; the pace is slow and the characters are fashionably disagreeable and scruffy so that there's nobody for the audience to like.

AMBUSH (1950, MGM). D: Sam Wood: W: Marguerite Roberts from Luke Short's novel. Cast: ROBERT TAYLOR, ARLENE DAHL, JOHN HODIAK, Don TAYLOR, Jean HAGEN, John McINTYRE, Leon Ames, Bruce Cowling, Chief Thundercloud, Ray Teal, Pat Moriarity. 89m.

Few of the principals are convincing Westerners but despite miscasting this black-and-white oater has sufficient action to provide acceptable entertainment. A civilian scout (Robert Taylor) rides reluctantly for the cavalry; two romantic triangles eat up too much film but the Indian chase sequences that make up the last half of the movie are fairly exciting. This was the last movie of director Sam Wood's long career.

AMBUSH AT CIMARRON PASS (1958, FOX). D: Jodie Copeland. W: Richard G. Taylor, John K. Butler, Robert A. Reeds & Robert W. Woods. Cast: SCOTT BRADY, MARGIA DEANE, Keith Richards, Clint Eastwood, Irving Bacon, Baynes Barron, William Vaughan. 73m.

Clint Eastwood, who has a small part here, has described this contrived yarn about a cavalry patrol riding into an Apache ambush as the low point of his movie career; he has been heard to call it "the worst Western ever made." In any case it's bad.

AMBUSH AT TOMAHAWK GAP (1953, COL). D: Fred F. Sears. W: David Lang. Cast: JOHN HODIAK, JOHN DEREK, David BRIAN, Maria Elena Marques, Ray Teal. 77m.

Four ex-convicts search for a buried cache of stolen loot in territory dominated by Indians who don't want them digging there. Routine; a better film with the same plot is *The Tall Texan.*

AMERICAN EMPIRE (1942, PARA). D: William McGann. W: Robert Bren, Gladys Atwater & Ben Grauman Kohn. Cast: RICHARD DIX, PRESTON FOSTER, FRANCES GIFFORD, Leo CARRILLO, Guinn "Big Boy" WILLIAMS, Robert Barrat, Jack LaRue, Cliff Edwards, Chris-Pin Martin, Hal Taliaferro, Tom London, William Farnum, Guy Rodin. 82m.

Epic in style but medium in budget, this treats of the emergence of the cattle kings of Texas in the decade after the Civil War. It's old-fashioned stuff with juvenile slapstick relief and minimal action; both stars were a bit burly for anything athletic. The plot, reminiscent of *Spawn of the North*, is the one about the good partner and the bad partner, and it brings us to a predictable outcome.

THE AMERICANO (1954, RKO). D: William Castle. W: Guy Trosper from a Leslie T. White novel. Cast: GLENN FORD, FRANK LOVEJOY, Ursula THIESS, Cesar ROMERO, Abbe LANE. 85m.

Transplanted oater, set in Brazil, with a Texas cowboy (Ford) fighting off bandits and women and a Brahma-bull rancher (Lovejoy). Unsteady script, and strictly formula action, but the performers make it fun.

ANDREWS' RAIDERS (1956)—*see* THE GREAT LOCOMOTIVE CHASE.

THE ANGEL AND THE BADMAN (1946, REP). DW: James Edward Grant. Cast: JOHN WAYNE, GAIL RUSSELL, HARRY CAREY, Sr., Bruce CABOT, Irene Rich, Lee Dixon, Tom Powers, Marshall Reed, Paul Hurst. 99m.

Gunslinging outlaw (Wayne) hides out among Quakers and is reformed by the love of a pacifist girl. Despite its old-hat plot the movie is still fresh. The actors are dandy; Grant's direction and Archie J. Stout's photography give it the flavor of one of the better William S. Hart efforts; the script makes the characters intriguing, and second-unit director Yakima Canutt's action sequences are exciting as always. Its main weaknesses are the sometimes slow pace and the dreary score, which is credited to Richard Hageman but seems to consist mainly of passages lifted from stock soundtracks. Wayne produced this (his first; Cooper had showed the way with *Along Came Jones*); Grant was a close associate of Wayne's and it was an association that did not always pay off for audiences—he wrote *The Alamo*, for example.

AN ANGEL FROM TEXAS (1940, WB). D: Ray Enright. W: Fred Niblo, Jr., & Bertram Millhauser from George S. Kaufman's play *The Butter and Egg Man*. Cast: EDDIE ALBERT, ROSEMARY LANE, Wayne MORRIS, Jane WYMAN, Ronald REAGAN. 79m.

Remake of *The Tenderfoot* (1932) and not a bad comedy; Albert is a naive cowboy who gets mixed up with tough guys and Broadway producers.

ANNIE GET YOUR GUN (1950, MGM). D: George Sidney. W: Sidney Sheldon from the play by Herbert & Dorothy Fields, with music & lyrics by Irving Berlin. Cast: BETTY HUTTON, HOWARD KEEL, LOUIS CALHERN, Keenan WYNN, J. Carrol NAISH, Edward ARNOLD, Benay Venuta, John Hamilton, Clinton Sunberg, Edward Earle, Mae Clark, Frank Wilcox. 107m.

The fine Broadway musical comedy was brought to the screen without much disrepair unless you're a stubborn Ethel Merman fan. (Merman had been a hit in the show on Broadway but the producers judged her too hefty and too old to get away with the role on screen; the real Annie Oakley was a teenager when her career began.) Judy Garland was signed but she became ill; Betty Hutton replaced her at the last minute. In effect it's a musical remake of *Annie Oakley* with Howard Keel as sharpshooter Frank Butler and Louis Calhern very good in the role of impresario-star Buffalo Bill Cody, whose Wild West Show provides the setting for the lavish production numbers and the romance between young trick-shot expert Annie and her mentor Butler. Great Irving Berlin tunes, fine performances by everybody—a big solid entertainer. Academy Award to Adolph Deutsch & Roger Edens for the musical scoring. In Technicolor.

ANNIE OAKLEY (1935, RKO). D: George Stevens. W: John Twist, Joel Sayre, Joseph A. Fields & Stewart Adamson. Cast: BARBARA STANWYCK, PRESTON FOSTER, MELVYN DOUGLAS, Moroni OLSEN, Chief THUNDERCLOUD, Andy Clyde, Dick Elliott, Pert Kelton. 87m.

Scruffy frontier gal has a tomboy talent for trick marksmanship and becomes a celebrity sharpshooter with Cody's (Olsen) Wild West Show while romancing crack shot showman (Foster) and dude show manager (Douglas). It has good production, plenty of gusto and Stanwyck at her best. Dated now, and eclipsed by *Annie Get Your Gun*, actually the Stanwyck version is less coy and at least equally enjoyable.

ANOTHER MAN, ANOTHER CHANCE (1977, UA). DW: Claude Lelouch. Cast: JAMES CAAN, GENEVIEVE BUJOLD, Susan TYRRELL, Francis Huster, Diana Douglas, Rossie Harris. 128m.

Curious movie concerns the migration of a young French couple, photographers, to the Wild West, where the husband dies and the widow meets a recently widowed young veterinarian; a romance develops, tentative at first. It's a slow film—some will find it interminable—and it's definitely a Western as seen from a European's viewpoint, but it has quiet charm and warmth. The two stars are excellent in their roles.

APACHE (1954, UA). D: Robert Aldrich. W: James R. Webb from Paul Wellman's novel *Broncho Apache*. Cast: BURT LANCASTER, JEAN PETERS, John McINTIRE, John DEHNER, Charles BUCHINSKY, Paul Guilfoyle, Ian MacDonald, Walter Sande, Morris Ankrum, Monte Blue. 91m.

Muscular Lancaster rushes acrobatically through his role as a renegade Apache warrior who, after Geronimo's (Blue) surrender, carries on a one man war against the whites in Arizona until tamed by love and marriage. Plenty of action. Standout performances by Lancaster and by McIntire as the crusty real-life Chief of Scouts, Al Sieber. Charles Bronson appears under his real name, Buchinsky. Jean Peters is not especially believable as an Apache girl and some of the scripting is too Hollywood-slick. Photography (Ernest Laszlo) is very good, the score (David Raksin) suitable; there are several long dull stretches and the ending (reputedly tacked on by an insensitive front office) is abrupt and implausible, but it's better than most and definitely worth seeing. Lancaster co-produced.

APACHE AGENT (1956)—*see* WALK THE PROUD LAND.

APACHE AMBUSH (1955, COL). D: Fred F. Sears. W: David Lang. Cast: BILL WILLIAMS, Adelle AUGUST, Richard JAECKEL, Tex RITTER, MOVITA, Ray Teal, Kermit Maynard, James Griffith, Buddy Roosevelt, Cactus Peters, Harry Lauter. 69m.

Hero somehow fights his way through the Apache nation, a gang of Mexican bandits and an army of unreconstructed Confederates. It's a tired movie, topheavy with cliches. Williams was put into a lot of low-budget Westerns (these are the next thing to "B" pictures) but he had a thick New York accent and was never convincing in the saddle.

APACHE DRUMS (1951, UNIV). D: Hugo Fregonese. W: David Chandler from a novel by Harry Brown. Cast: STEPHEN McNALLY, COLEEN GRAY, Willard PARKER, James BEST, Arthur Shields, James Griffith, Armando Silvestre, Clarence Muse, Ray Bennett. 75m.

A despised gambler (McNally) proves his mettle by helping the town defend itself against Indian attack. It's the sort of movie that has lines like, "It's when the drums *stop* that you have to start worrying." McNally, sturdy and talented, was wasted in too many oaters of this ilk. This was the last movie produced by famed horror-show veteran Val Lewton.

APACHE RIFLES (1964, FOX). D: William Witney. W: Charles B. Smith, Kenneth Gamet & Richard Schayer. Cast: AUDIE MURPHY, Michael DANTE, Linda LAWSON, L. Q. JONES, John Archer, Ken Lynch, Eugene Iglesias, Joseph A. Vitale, Robert Brubaker, J. Pat O'Malley. 92m.

Baby-faced Murphy is miscast as a tough cavalry captain who tries to restore peace when Indians hit the warpath. Routine oater is a shoestring remake of *Indian Uprising* (1951) and uses stock footage from it.

APACHE TERRITORY (1958, COL). D: Ray Nazarro. W: Charles Marion, George W. George & Frank Moss from Louis L'Amour's novel *Last Stand at Papago Wells*. Cast: RORY CALHOUN, Barbara BATES, John DEHNER, Myron HEALEY, Carolyn Craig, Leo Gordon, Frank DeKova, Reg Parton. 75m.

Shady drifter protects beleaguered pilgrims in hostile ambush country. The dialogue includes such lines as "Awful quiet out there," and "Just a flesh wound." It's speedy enough for the undemanding. Co-produced by Rory Calhoun.

APACHE TRAIL (1942, MGM). D: Samuel Marx & Richard Thorpe. W: Maurice Geraghty & Gordon Kahn from Ernest Haycox's short story "Stage Station." Cast: LLOYD NOLAN, DONNA REED, WILLIAM LUNDIGAN, Chill WILLS, Connie GILCHRIST, Gloria Holden, Trevor Bardette, Grant Withers, Ray Teal, Fuzzy Knight. 79m.

The Writers Guild listings incorrectly give Haycox a screenwriting credit on this one. (He wrote the short story but not the screenplay.) In any case there's little of his touch in evidence; Nolan plays a badman in conflict with his brother who has reformed, with predictable results. Nolan's urban accent militated against his playing a convincing Westerner. Good supporting cast, well-staged action, good score (Sol Kaplan). Fair entertainment. Remade, with some improvement, as *Apache War Smoke*.

APACHE UPRISING (1966, PARA). D: R.G. Springsteen. W: Max Lamb & Harry Sanford from a novel by Sanford & Max Steeber. Cast: RORY CALHOUN, CORINNE CALVET, John RUSSELL, Arthur HUNNICUTT, Jean PARKER, Richard Arlen, Johnny Mack Brown, Lon Chaney, Jr., Gene Evans, DeForest Kelley, Robert H. Harris, George Chandler, Donald Barry, Robert Carricart, Reg Parton, Roy Jensen, Rodd Redwing. 90m.

Complicated "B" plot involves theft and chicanery while Indians are on the warpath. A lot of old-timers are on hand, and Hunnicutt gives one of those emphatic crusty performances, but aside from that, this A.C. Lyles production is a routine oater. Like most of Lyles' films it was filmed very hastily and carelessly (about 12 days was the maximum) but it has its moments; villains Russell and Kelley are especially effective.

APACHE WARRIOR (1957, FOX). D: Elmo Williams. W: Carroll Young, Kurt Neumann, Eric Norden. Cast: Keith LARSEN, Jim DAVIS, Eugenia Paul, Rodolfo Acosta, John Miljan, Lane Bradford. 74m.

Iconoclastic Apache brave's friendship toward a white cavalry scout turns to enmity because of bad guys' machinations. Predictable plot, but it's nicely paced and briskly filmed (in b&w), with Davis very good as the scout. Director Williams was the film editor responsible for cutting *High Noon*—one of the classic editing jobs used as examples in filmmaking classes. This is a shoestring movie but well made and entertaining.

APACHE WAR SMOKE (1952, MGM). D: Harold Kress. W: Jerome L. Davis from Ernest Haycox's short story "Stage Station." Cast: GILBERT ROLAND, ROBERT

HORTON, Glenda FARRELL, Robert BLAKE, Myron HEALEY, Gene Lockhart, Emmett Lynn, Douglas Dumbrille, Hank Worden. 67m.

Remake of *Apache Trail*, with aspects of *Stagecoach* as well. Stage is robbed, passengers take refuge in way station along with outlaws; there's a good-brother bad-brother conflict, and the Indians attack. The movie has two virtues: the characterizations, diluted but drawn from Haycox; and the imposing presence of Gilbert Roland, an electric performer. Static and set-bound but suspenseful low-budget entertainment.

APACHE WOMAN (1955, AI). D: Roger Corman. W: Lou Rusoff. Cast: LLOYD BRIDGES, JOAN TAYLOR, Jean Howell, Chester Conklin, Lance Fuller, Morgan Jones, Paul Birch. 83m.

The Apaches are being framed for predations; a federal snoop (Bridges) is sent to investigate; he falls in love with an Indian girl. It's a tiresomely familiar mini-budget *Broken Arrow*. Yes, that's old-time silent-screen comedian Chester Conklin in a character part. This was the first movie released under the banner of American International, a company that soon became famous for cheap horror movies and beach-party flicks. It also was director Roger Corman's second movie. (His first, also a Western, was *Five Guns West*.)

THE APPALOOSA (1966, UNIV). D: Sidney J. Furie. W: James Bridges & Roland Kibbee from Robert MacLeod's novel. Cast: MARLON BRANDO, ANJANETTE COMER, JOHN SAXON, Emilio FERNANDEZ, Miriam COLON, Rafael Campos, Frank Silvera, Alex Montoya, Larry D. Mann. 99m.

A cowboy's (Brando) prize horse is stolen by a sadistic Mexican bandit (Saxon); the cowboy gives chase, to get his horse back. Like any Brando vehicle this movie has its partisans; I'm not one of them. It has a few excellences: good photography (Russell Metty) and laudable supporting performances by Colon, Fernandez and Montoya. But the arty direction tries to milk suspense from a script that has none; and Brando merely makes faces—indications of rage, fear, stubborn virtue and agonizing thought. In the end it's impossible to believe him. We believed Gary Cooper; all we believe with Brando is that we're watching a celebrity make an exhibition of himself—flexing his thespic muscles in front of our mirror. We see his agonies but we don't see the character he's supposed to portray. That isn't acting; it's emoting. His Method is as mannered and off-

putting as that of a Victorian prima donna. In this film he looks good only when compared with John Saxon, normally a good actor who can be nicely disagreeable in villain roles, but here ridiculous as an overblown psychotic. It is said that Brando's antics on the set cost the producers a fortune; as a result, in an attempt to get their money back, the producers hyped it as a big show, with much ballyhoo; actually it's a slim little oater which, properly cast and directed, could have been quite good; the novel is engaging enough. A similar story handled properly is *Valdez is Coming*.

ARENA (1953, MGM). D: Richard Fleischer. W: Harold Jack Bloom & Arthur M. Loew, Jr. Cast: GIG YOUNG, POLLY BERGEN, JEAN HAGEN, Harry MORGAN, Robert HORTON, Barbara Lawrence, Lee Aaker, Lee Van Cleef, Morris Ankrum, Jim Hayward, George Wallace. 83m.

Originally released in 3-D, this gives us Young as a rodeo star, Bergen as his estranged wife, Lawrence as the woman with whom he's having an affair and Morgan as a washed-up saddle partner gone to seed. Van Cleef stands out, as a fellow rodeo rider. The action sequences are fine (filmed at the Tucson rodeo by cinematographer Paul C. Vogel) but the story is soap opera and suffers by comparison with the previous year's *The Lusty Men*. *Arena* has good performances but it's familiar and lacks spark. It was remade in 1972, without acknowledgment, as *The Honkers*.

ARIZONA (1940, COL). D: Wesley Ruggles. W: Claude Binyon from Clarence Buddington Kelland's novel. Cast: JEAN ARTHUR, WILLIAM HOLDEN, Warren WILLIAM, Edgar BUCHANAN, Porter Hall, Paul Harvey, Byron Foulger, Raymond Hatton, George Chandler, Regis Toomey. 126m.

Heroine (Arthur) wants to own most of Arizona Territory and at the same time land the lighthearted man she loves (Holden). Predictable machinations by villains complicate the plot. Columbia intended this as an empire-building *Cimarron*-style epic; a fortune was spent to build a complete town on location in Arizona (Old Tucson—it is still in use as a set for Westerns). The actors are fine but the movie is leaden and boring.

ARIZONA BUSHWHACKERS (1968, PARA). D: Lesley Selander. W: Steve Fisher & Andrew Craddock. Cast: HOWARD KEEL, YVONNE DeCARLO, JOHN IRELAND, Scott BRADY, Marilyn MAXWELL, Brian DONLEVY, Barton MacLANE, James CRAIG, Monte Montana,

Roy Rogers, Jr., Reg Parton, Eric Cody. Narration by JAMES CAGNEY. 86m.

A.C. Lyles produced this exercise in nostalgia. The veteran players are trapped in a wheezy plot about a gunslinging Galvanized Yankee sheriff (Keel), spying for the Confederacy, who goes up against bad guys (Brady, Craig) who are selling guns to the Apaches. The script is verbose and soporific; Selander's direction (this was the last of his 400-odd films) is listless except for a few lively action sequences. Keel and Ireland perform better than they need to; some of the others are not to be believed—particularly Roy Rogers, Jr., whose career died (not surprisingly) after this one effort. James Craig, fat and looking ill, plays a character called Ike Clanton who's killed off in the opening sequences, whereupon the unfortunate deputy (Ireland) has to haul his body away; buffs will recall that in better days Ireland himself played Ike Clanton in more respectable surroundings. (He appeared in both *Gunfight at the OK Corral* and *My Darling Clementine*.) James Cagney, a friend of Lyles', does not appear but narrates the film—his last movie work prior to *Ragtime*.

THE ARIZONA COWBOY (1950, REP). D: R.G. Springsteen. W: Bradford Ropes. Cast: REX ALLEN, Teale Loring, Gordon Jones, Minerva Urecal, Roy Barcroft, Stanley Andrews, Edmund Cobb, Joseph Crehan, Steve Darrell, Chris-Pin Martin. 73m.

Rex Allen's debut was a "B" oater in which he played himself, proving his father innocent of crimes, impressing the girl, thwarting villains and singing songs. Director, writer and supporting actors all were veterans of thousands of "B" pictures. I include it for sentimental reasons and also because it's a quintessentially typical programmer.

THE ARIZONA KID (1930, FOX). D: Alfred Santell. W: Ralph Block & Joseph Wright, based on a character created by O.Henry. Cast: WARNER BAXTER, MONA MARIS, CAROLE LOMBARD, Arthur Stone, Theodore von Eltz.

The second Cisco Kid movie, sequel to *In Old Arizona*—a "B" plot but an "A" budget, and Lombard had a meaty vamp role. Baxter made a comeback in the Cisco Kid pictures, but even in their own day they were silly.

ARIZONA LEGION (1938, RKO). D: Roy Webb. W: Oliver Drake & Bernard McConville. Cast: GEORGE O'BRIEN, LARAINE JOHNSON, Chill WILLS, Edward LeSaint, Harry Cording, Glenn Strange, Thomas Chatterton.

The Bob Steele plot. George O'Brien came to stardom in silent Westerns (*The Iron Horse*) and was a mainstay during the 1930s of a class of oaters somewhere between "A" and "B"—feature budgets but programmer scripts. O'Brien, a burly amiable actor, was somewhat in the image of Broncho Billy Anderson: engaging with the appearance of naive oafishness. His movies often were leavened with light humor—pallid stuff but less abrasive than the crude slapstick of Wallace Beery, and more energetic than the stolid oaters of Richard Dix. O'Brien was popular at the box office out of all proportion to the rudimentary quality of the vehicles in which he appeared; he remained a star with drawing power until he went into the SeaBees in World War II. When he returned he found he'd lost his following; he continued in movies, but only in supporting roles. His co-star in this one, Miss Johnson, soon changed her name to Laraine Day.

ARIZONA MISSION (1956, UA). Also titled: GUN THE MAN DOWN. D: Andrew V. McLaglen. W: Burt Kennedy & Sam C. Freedle. Cast: JAMES ARNESS, ANGIE DICKINSON, Emile MEYER, Robert J. Wilke, Harry Carey, Jr. 78m.

During a holdup the gang leaves a wounded member behind and he swears to get them for it; essentially the same plot as the later *Shoot-Out*. Arness, already starring in TV's *Gunsmoke*, was a John Wayne protégé; so was McLaglen. Wayne's impetus got this one off the ground. The film marks McLaglen's feature directing debut. It's low-budget but well made, with fine photography (William Clothier), and is best approached as a good "B" picture; seen that way it's not bad at all.

ARIZONA RAIDERS (1936, PARA). D: Charles Barton. W: Robert Yost & John Krafft from Zane Grey's *Raiders of Spanish Peaks*. Cast: LARRY "BUSTER" CRABBE, MARSHA HUNT, Grant WITHERS, Raymond HATTON.

Tongue-in-cheek Zane Grey, well played and amusing; the Bob Steele plot and a "B-plus" budget.

ARIZONA RAIDERS (1965, PARA). D: William Witney. W: Alex Gottlieb, Mary & Willard Willingham from the screenplay for *The Texas Rangers* (1950, COL). Cast: AUDIE MURPHY, GLORIA TALBOT, Ben COOPER, Michael Dante, Larry "Buster" Crabbe. 88m.

Remake of *The Texas Rangers* (1950) with Murphy as a Rebel officer who after the Civil War is given the job of rounding up Quantrill's raiders in Arizona. So far as I know, Quantrill never went within a thousand miles of Arizona, and the "Arizona Rangers" which Murphy heads up in this movie weren't formed until 1902 but never mind all that. In the earlier script on which this was based the story was about the Texas Rangers versus Sam Bass—another example of the interchangeability of Hollywood's version of historical figures. The best of the Quantrill movies was *Dark Command*. This Audie Murphy version leaves a lot to be desired. But there's plenty of gunplay.

THE ARIZONA WILDCAT (1938, FOX). D: Herbert I. Leeds. W: Barry Trivers, Jerry Cady, Frances Hyland & Albert Ray. Cast: JANE WITHERS, LEO CARRILLO, Pauline MOORE, William HENRY, Henry Wilcoxon, Douglas Fowley, Etienne Girardot, Harry Woods. 72m.

Carrillo, a former bandit turned stagecoach driver, adopts a scrappy orphan girl (Withers) in a frontier town. Amusing comedy has a lot of action; well suited to the genial adolescent girl star who nearly supplanted Shirley Temple in the hearts of Fox execs, if not of the public; she grew up to become a good character actress, still seen in commercials.

THE ARIZONIAN (1935, RKO). D: Charles Vidor. W: Dudley Nichols. Cast: RICHARD DIX, LOUIS CALHERN, Margot GRAHAME, Preston FOSTER, Francis Ford, Joe Sawyer, Willie Best. 81m.

Early Earps-in-Tombstone sort of yarn has Calhern as villain and Dix as the marshal who cleans up the town. Vidor's direction drags in spots but the script is first-rate and the actors perform solidly; film is one of the few Westerns of the mid-1930s that can still appeal to an audience.

AROUND THE WORLD IN 80 DAYS (1956, UA). D: Michael Anderson. W: S.J. Perelman, James Poe & John Farrow from Jules Verne's novel. Cast (Western segment): DAVID NIVEN, SHIRLEY MacLAINE, ROBERT NEWTON, CANTINFLAS, FRANK SINATRA, TIM McCOY, MARLENE DIETRICH, GILBERT ROLAND. 167m.

A long Wild West segment of this blockbuster all-star movie has Indians raiding a train and kidnaping Passepartout (Cantinflas) while Phileas Fogg (Niven) is trying to win a bet by living up to the title. Thoroughly amusing. The Michael Todd production won five Oscars, including that for best film.

ARROWHEAD (1952, PARA). DW: Charles Marquis Warren, from W.R. Burnett's novel *Adobe Walls*. Cast: CHARLTON HESTON, JACK PALANCE, KATY JURADO, BRIAN KEITH, Mary Sinclair, Milburn Stone, Robert J. Wilke, John Pickard, James Anderson, William Shannon. 105m.

Unfortunate Nat Holt production has a misanthropic racist "hero" (Heston) who, having been raised among the Indians, sneers at the army's attempts to sign a peace treaty with the Apaches and tries to convince everybody that you can't trust any Indian until he's dead. Heston plays the entire picture with his teeth gritted. By the end he's fighting hand-to-hand with Apache chief Palance. Good scenic photography (Ray Rennahan) and speedy action scenes, a serviceable score (Paul Sawtell), a fine performance by Milburn Stone as Heston's long-suffering sidekick and a believable performance as a cavalryman by Brian Keith (in his feature film debut) do not make up for the low caliber of the script or the tastelessness of the premise. It was movies like this one that provoked so many American Indians into despising Hollywood.

ARROW IN THE DUST (1954, AA). D: Lesley Selander. W: Don Martin from an L.L. Foreman novel. Cast: STERLING HAYDEN, Coleen GRAY, Keith LARSEN, Tom TULLY, Jimmy Wakely, Lee Van Cleef, Carleton Young, Tudor Owen, John Pickard, Sheb Wooley. 79m.

Routine oater wastes Hayden as a hardbitten army deserter impelled by conscience to masquerade as a cavalry officer to get a wagon train through hostile Pawnee country. Good cast but no surprises.

AT GUNPOINT (1955, REP). D: Alfred L. Werker. W: Daniel B. Ullman. Cast: FRED MacMURRAY, DOROTHY MALONE, WALTER BRENNAN, Skip HOMEIER, Tommy Rettig, Frank Ferguson, John Qualen, Jack Lambert. 81m.

Pretty good town-bound Western concerns a shopkeeper who does his duty as a citizen by shooting an escaping outlaw and then is stalked by the outlaw's partners, with the town imitating *High Noon*'s Hadleyville by refusing to help him. It generates suspense, although the plot gimmick is shopworn.

THE AVENGERS (1950, REP). D: John H. Auer. W: Lawrence Kimble & Aeneas MacKenzie from Rex Beach's novel *Don Careless*. Cast: JOHN CARROLL, ADELE MARA, FERNANDO LAMAS, Mona Maris, Roberto Airaldi. 78m.

Good-humored costume hero swashbuckles against a bandit gang that's terrorizing settlers down South America way. Very old-fashioned, even for its time, and Carroll was not a terribly exciting performer; better to stick to the Fairbanks or the Tyrone Power *Mark of Zorro*.

BACKLASH (1956, UNIV). D: John Sturges. W: Borden Chase from a Frank Gruber novel. Cast: RICHARD WIDMARK, DONNA REED, William CAMPBELL, John McINTIRE, Barton MacLane, Harry Morgan, Roy Roberts, Edward C. Platt. 84m.

Despite impressive talents behind and before the cameras, this one is only a dull oater about two disagreeable people (Widmark, Reed) seeking the sole survivor of an Apache massacre who made off with a stolen fortune. The stars spend the whole time chasing gold and each other. At times it gets downright repulsive.

BACK TO GOD'S COUNTRY (1953, UNIV). D: Joseph Pevney. W: Tom Reed, from James Oliver Curwood's story for the 1927 film. Cast: ROCK HUDSON, STEVE COCHRAN, Marcia HENDERSON, Hugh O'Brian. 78m.

Ex-sea captain (Hudson) and his wife settle in the Canadian wilderness and are faced with contrived obstacles and villain Cochran, with all sorts of hokey heroism and adventure and romance and sacrifice before the worthy couple can be free to settle down in last-reel happiness. Cochran makes an appealing bad guy and it's well directed but predictable.

BAD BASCOMB (1945, MGM). D: S. Sylvan Simon. W: William Lipman, Grant Garrett & Marion B. Jackson. Cast: WALLACE BEERY, MARJORIE MAIN, Margaret O'BRIEN, Marshall Thompson, J. Carrol Naish, Frances Rafferty, Frank Darien. 110m.

Typical Beery-Main vehicle has a blustering outlaw tamed by little rascal O'Brien. You have to be a Beery fan to sit through it.

BAD BOY (1949, AA). D: Kurt Neumann. W: Robert D. Andrews, Paul Short & Karl Kamb. Cast: AUDIE MURPHY, JANE WYATT, LLOYD NOLAN, James GLEASON, Martha Vickers. 86m.

Boy's Town-type meller concerns a "hopeless" delinquent who's reformed by the kindly head of a juvenile rehabilitation ranch. Pretty good for its type, less hokey than most; Murphy's film debut.

BAD COMPANY (1972, PARA). D: Robert Benton. W: Benton & David Newman. Cast: JEFF BRIDGES, Barry BROWN, Jim DAVIS, David HUDDLESTON, John SAVAGE, Damon Cofer, Jerry Houser, John Quade, Charles Tyner. 93m.

In 1863, fleeing the Civil War draft, several unappealing youths travel west. They steal chickens, get shot at, and double-cross one another. The film has its partisans but I found it banal and tasteless. Aside from Davis and Huddleston the performers lack magnetism; the gimmicky washed-out color presumably is meant to suggest the sepia of old photographs, and Harvey Schmidt's tinkly piano score is repetitious and excruciatingly annoying. Virtually every "historical" reference is phony or erroneous. The misadventures of the youths are intended to be amusing; unhappily they induce squirms and yawns rather than chuckles.

BAD DAY AT BLACK ROCK (1954, MGM). D: John Sturges. W: Millard Kaufman & Don McGuire from Howard Breslin's short story "Bad Time at Hondo." Cast: SPENCER TRACY, ROBERT RYAN, Anne FRANCIS, Walter BRENNAN, Dean JAGGER, Lee MARVIN, Ernest BORGNINE, John ERICSON, Walter Sande, Russell Collins. 81m.

John J. McReedy (Tracy), a one-armed war veteran, arrives in a dusty desert whistle stop in 1945, looking for a Japanese tenant farmer; at first he doesn't disclose why. From the instant he steps off the train he faces the seething suspicion and hate of a town full of strangers led by a local rancher (Ryan). The script has a few weaknesses—notably a tendency to imitate elements of *High Noon*—but it works; it was nominated for an Oscar. Producer Dore Schary; composer Andre Previn; editor Newell P. Kimlin; cinematographer (CinemaScope, Technicolor) William C. Mellor. One is moved to note that Tracy is not an actor straining to impress us with meaningful facial contortions, visible thought-processes or busy twitchings; Tracy is simply John J. McReedy. And Robert Ryan, as usual, is magnificent; the two were a fine match for each other. Unflaggingly gripping, it's a masterpiece of suspenseful entertainment.

THE BADGE OF MARSHAL BRENNAN (1957, AA). D: Albert C. Gannaway. W: Tom Hubbard. Cast: JIM DAVIS, Arleen WHELAN, Lee VAN CLEEF, Louis Jean Heydt. 76m.

Outlaw (Davis) chances upon a dying marshal and is persuaded by the expiring man to take the marshal's badge and finish his job of rounding up a bandit gang. Davis makes it stronger than it might have been; Van Cleef as usual makes a worthy antagonist; the two actors are amusing, although both have done better work elsewhere, and the plot of this one wheezes with emphysema.

THE BADLANDERS (1958, MGM). D: Delmer Daves. W: Richard Collins from W.R. Burnett's novel *The Asphalt Jungle*.

Cast: ALAN LADD, ERNEST BORG-NINE, KATY JURADO, Claire Kelly, Nehemiah Persoff, Kent Smith, Robert Emhardt, Adam Williams, Anthony Caruso. 83m.

Filmed in Arizona in color, this remake of the classic *Asphalt Jungle* gives us a caper yarn with ex-cons Ladd and Borgnine out to rob a gold mine the owner of which jumped Ladd's claim. There are no surprises. A few strained attempts to get laughs fall dead. Film lacks any reminder of the grit or honesty of the original. Ladd and Borgnine both seem uninterested. Acting is lackluster, script humdrum.

BADLANDS (1939, RKO). D: Lew Landers. W: Clarence U. Young. Cast: ROBERT BARRAT, Noah BEERY, Jr., Guinn "Big Boy" WILLIAMS, Andy Clyde, Addison Richards, Robert Coote, Paul Hurst, Francis Ford, Francis J. McDonald.

Unusual "B" movie has no women in the cast and old character-actor Barrat makes a unique leading man. It's an unacknowledged remake of *The Lost Patrol* with Apaches picking off possemen one by one. Good suspense, quite grim; in some ways a dated programmer, but very interesting.

(Not to be confused with the 1973 Martin Sheen-Sissy Spacek-Warren Oates movie of the same title.)

BADLANDS OF DAKOTA (1941, UNIV). D: Alfred E. Green. W: Gerald Geraghty & Harold Shumate. Cast: ROBERT STACK, RICHARD DIX, ANN RUTHERFORD, FRANCES FARMER, Broderick CRAWFORD, Andy DEVINE, Hugh HERBERT, Lon Chaney, Jr., Fuzzy Knight, Addison Richards, Carleton Young, the Jesters. 73m.

Wild Bill Hickok (Dix), Calamity Jane (Farmer), Jack McCall (Chaney), General Custer (Richards) and other historical characters are featured in this fanciful re-creation of Deadwood in the 1870s. Main story concerns the rivalry between a big-shot tough guy (Crawford) and his young brother (Stack) who grows up from callow smarty-pants to stalwart hero, all of it centering on the question of which brother will win the heart of the beautiful Eastern girl (Rutherford). Guess who wins. The comedy is crude but the pace is quick. Farmer is wonderful. Dated and confused, but fun.

BADLANDS OF MONTANA (1957, FOX). DW: Daniel B. Ullman. Cast: REX REASON, Margia DEAN, Beverly GARLAND, Keith LARSEN, Jack Kruschen. 75m.

Squeaky old plot concerns one-time buddies who are now enemies, with the good guy trying to clean up the town and his ex-partner trying to prevent it. Lacklustre.

THE BAD MAN (1930, WB). D: Clarence Badger. W: Howard Estabrook from a play by P.O. Brown. Cast: WALTER HUSTON, Dorothy REVIER, James RENNIE, Sidney Blackmer, Guinn "Big Boy" Williams. 67m.

Mexican bandit yarn has Huston miscast as a Latin outlaw who sacrifices a whole lot for a friend who's gone straight and fallen in love. Slim yarn had been filmed in 1923 and was remade again in 1937 as the non-Western *West of Shanghai*.

THE BAD MAN (1941, MGM). D: Richard Thorpe. W: Wells Root from the play by P.O. Brown. Cast: WALLACE BEERY, LARAINE DAY, LIONEL BARRYMORE, Ronald REAGAN, Henry Travers, Chill Wills. 70m.

Remake of the 1930 version, with Beery a little better than Huston was as the Mexican outlaw; this one is bolstered by the energetic performance of Barrymore as the old buddy, now reformed, whose fate is riding on the outlaw's loyalty.

BAD MAN OF BRIMSTONE (1938, MGM). D: J. Walter Ruben. W: Ruben, Cyril Hume, Richard Maibaum & Maurice Rapf. Cast: WALLACE BEERY, VIRGINIA BRUCE, DENNIS O'KEEFE, Joseph CALLEIA, Lewis STONE, Bruce CABOT, Guy Kibbee, Noah Beery, Sr., Cliff Edwards. 90m.

Sentimental reform-the-outlaw vehicle has badman Beery learning that a young dude prizefighter (O'Keefe) is his son. You really need to have a taste for Beery's hammy style to sit through these. This one was released originally in sepia tint, later in black-and-white.

BAD MAN OF WYOMING (1940)—see WYOMING.

BADMAN'S COUNTRY (1958, WB). D: Fred F. Sears. W: Orville H. Hampton. Cast: GEORGE MONTGOMERY, NEVILLE BRAND, Larry "Buster" CRABBE, Malcolm Atterbury, Gregory Walcott, Morris Ankrum. 67m.

Lawman Pat Garrett (Montgomery) and pals Wyatt Earp (Crabbe), Bat Masterson (Walcott) and Buffalo Bill (Atterbury) fight it out with a gang led by Butch Cassidy (Brand). Now just for the record, when Cassidy was in his heyday, Garrett was dead, Buffalo Bill was touring his Wild West Show, Earp was prospecting in Alaska and Bat Masterson was newspapering in New York. But never mind. In spite of all that it's still a dreary soporific movie.

BADMAN'S TERRITORY (1946, RKO). D: Tim Whelan. W: Jack Natteford, Luci Ward, Clarence Upson Young and (uncredited) Bess Taffel. Cast: RANDOLPH SCOTT, ANN RICHARDS, Lawrence TIERNEY, Tom TYLER, George "Gabby" HAYES, Steve Brodie, Ray Collins, James Morgan, William Moss, Nestor Paiva, Isobel Jewell, Warren Conway, Virginia Sale, Chief Thundercloud, Andrew Toombes, Kermit Maynard. 97m.

Heroic marshal (Scott) has to fight it out with Jesse and Frank James (Tierney, Tyler), the Daltons (Brodie), Belle Starr (Jewell), Sam Bass (Paiva) and just about every other big-name miscreant who comes to mind. Nat Holt produced this absurdity: history twisted beyond recognition. The "B" antics are actionful, the performances mostly likable, the script bewildering. Poor, but amusing for the kiddies. A 1949 sequel was released as *Return of the Bad Men*.

BAD MEN OF MISSOURI (1941, WB). D: Ray Enright. W: Charles Grayson & Robert E. Kent. Cast: DENNIS MORGAN, JANE WYMAN, ARTHUR KENNEDY, WAYNE MORRIS, Faye EMERSON, Victor JORY, Alan BAXTER, Ricardo CORTEZ, Walter Catlett, Russell Simpson, Howard Da Silva, Roscoe Ates, Willie Best, Robert Winkler, Sam McDaniel. 74m.

Carpetbagging land thieves (Jory, da Silva) drive the Younger Brothers (Morgan, Kennedy, Morris, Baxter) to outlawry in this speedy seventy-four-minute actioner. Unrelated to history, dated and chock-full of familiar set-pieces, still it's fair entertainment, certainly superior to most Warner Brothers Westerns; good b&w photography by Arthur Todd.

BADMEN OF TOMBSTONE (1948, AA). Also titled: LAST OF THE BADMEN. D: Kurt Neuman. W: Philip Yordan & Arthur Strawn from Jay Monaghan's book *Last of the Badmen*. Cast: BARRY SULLIVAN, BRODERICK CRAWFORD, Marjorie REYNOLDS, Fortunio Bonanova, Guinn "Big Boy" Williams, Morris Ankrum, Robert Barrat, Douglas Fowley, Rory Mallinson, Harry Cording. 78m.

Another Wyatt Earp imitation, this one has Sullivan as a town marshal who must contend with outlaws terrorizing old Arizona. It's well done with a strong cast, although Crawford looks hopelessly uncomfortable in the saddle.

BAIT (1954, COL). DW: Hugo Haas, from Samuel W. Taylor's short story "Fever." Cast: HUGO HAAS, CLEO MOORE, JOHN AGAR, Sir Cedric HARDWICKE, Bruno Ve Sota, Emmett Lynn. 79m.

Hugo Haas was a character actor who turned writer-producer-director and made some cheap indies that he managed to distribute through the majors. This one is a naturalistic yarn about an old prospector (Haas) who uses his sexy young blonde wife (Moore) to lure his partner (Agar) into disaster. Wild melodramatics don't manage to make it very interesting.

BAKER'S HAWK (1976, IND). D: Lyman D. Dayton. W: Dan Greer & Hal Harrison, Jr., from a Jack Bickham novel. Cast: CLINT WALKER, BURL IVES, DIANE BAKER, Lee H. MONTGOMERY, Alan YOUNG, Taylor Lacher, Burt Mustin. 98m.

Juvenile wilderness story concerns a kid, his pet bird and some vigilantes. First-rate Utah location photography (Bernie Abramson) helps a bit; performances are mostly adequate, although Ives is good as a gentle crazy hermit who is attacked by a bigoted gang of vigilantes. This is another of the Doty-Dayton "family" productions.

BALLAD OF A GUNFIGHTER (1963). D: Bill Ward. Cast: Marty ROBBINS, Joyce Redd, Michael David.

A couple of happy-go-lucky bandits fight over a girl; strangely, the good guy gets killed. Credits are elusive on this one. I remember seeing it way back when. Robbins, country music star, made two or three movies, all bad; this probably was the worst of them.

THE BALLAD OF CABLE HOGUE (1969, WB). D: Sam Peckinpah. W: John Crawford & Edmund Penney. Cast: JASON RO-BARDS, JR., STELLA STEVENS, Slim PICKENS, Warren OATES, David WARNER, Strother MARTIN. 121m.

A half-mad loner tries to put down roots in mid-desert and build a town on some freshwater springs he has discovered there: they saved his life and he feels compelled to stay with them. Stella Stevens is the whore he lives and fights with; Oates and Martin—surely among the finest of all Western movie villains—are a pair of ne'er-do-wells he must contend with; Warner is an odd itinerant preacher who looms mysteriously. The movie is strange, nearly abstract. It's a very long slow ode to dying values; Peckinpah clearly admires his go-to-hell individualist hero, but the character is so eccentric, the script so elliptical and Robards so mannered and impenetrable that one has trouble staying with this one.

THE BALLAD OF JOSIE (1968, UNIV). Also titled MEANWHILE BACK AT THE RANCH. D: Andrew V. McLaglen. W:

Harold Swanton. Cast: DORIS DAY, PETER GRAVES, George KENNEDY, Andy DEVINE, William Talman, David Hartman, Karen Jensen, Don Stroud, Paul Fix, Harry Carey, Jr., Robert Lowery, Guy Raymond, Audrey Christie. 102m.

Half comedy, half meller is a mild feminist entertainment about a frontier widow who spends more than an hour of screen-time deciding what to do with her life after she's accidentally killed her worthless drunken husband (Lowery) and then spends the last half-hour of the movie importing sheep and raising hell with the Wyoming cattlemen around her, including the one who loves her (Graves). Amiable, but *The Sheepman* was a whole lot funnier.

BANDIDO (1956, UA). D: Richard Fleischer. W: Earl Felton. Cast: ROBERT MITCHUM, URSULA THIESS, ZACHARY SCOTT, GILBERT ROLAND, Henry BRANDON, Rodolfo ACOSTA, Jose Torvay, Douglas Fowley. 91m.

Mitchum is running guns to a Mexican rebel leader (Roland) in 1916; things get muddled up with the heavy-handed villainy of gun-smuggler Scott, smuggler's frustrated wife Thiess, and evil general Brandon. The plot degenerates into a heavy-breathing sequence of double crosses, captures, escapes and chases. But Ernest Laszlo's CinemaScope photography (on Mexican locations) is lovely, the Max Steiner score is good, and one early sequence is marvelous, with a quintessentially insouciant Mitchum tossing casual grenades into the midst of a gun battle.

BANDIT QUEEN (1950, LIP). D: William Berke. W: Victor West & Budd Lesser. Cast: BARBARA BRITTON, Willard PARKER, Barton MacLANE, Philip Reed, Victor Kilian, Thurston Hall, Martin Garralaga, Jack Ingram, Jack Perrin, Margia Dean. 70m.

Female Robin Hood in the Gold Rush days. Grade "Z" and awful.

BANDOLERO! (1968, FOX). D: Andrew V. McLaglen. W: James Lee Barrett & Stanley Hough. Cast: JAMES STEWART, DEAN MARTIN, RAQUEL WELCH, George KENNEDY, Andrew PRINE, Sean McClory, Will Geer, Denver Pyle, Clint Ritchie, Harry Carey, Jr., Donald Barry, Jock Mahoney, Dub Taylor, John Mitchum, Roy Barcroft. 106m.

Stewart has to rescue his brother (Martin) from hanging, gets trapped into flight and outlawry. The hero actually is George Kennedy as a stolid sheriff who pursues the outlaws into Mexico. Nearly everybody ends up at the wrong end of a shootin' iron. Perform-

ances are good, and things move briskly but there's an excess of empty-headed brutality. Good swift directing, Jerry Goldsmith's enjoyable score and William Clothier's nicely lit Panavision photography can't save the film from its hokey screenplay.

BARBAROSA (1981, IND). D: Fred Schepisi. W: Bill Wittliff. Cast: WILLIE NELSON, GARY BUSEY, Isela VEGA, Gilbert ROLAND, Danny De La Paz.

Wilderness adventure about a wild loner (Nelson) and a kid who emulates him (Busey) was not yet released at this book's press time.

THE BARON OF ARIZONA (1949, LIP). DW: Samuel Fuller from an article by Homer Croy. Cast: VINCENT PRICE, ELLEN DREW, Beulah BONDI, Reed Hadley, Vladimir Sokoloff. 90m.

The facts on which it's based are more interesting than the movie itself. James Addison Reavis (Price) was a grand-scale swindling con man of the late nineteenth century who forged documents to prove himself the heir to huge Spanish land grants in the New World. As a result, for a brief time until he was exposed, he took title to half of Arizona. Price turns in a convincing performance; it's a dull movie, melodramatic, but better than the other Westerns that Fuller directed.

BARRICADE (1950, WB). D: Peter Godfrey. W: William Sackheim. Cast: DANE CLARK, RUTH ROMAN, Raymond MASSEY, Robert Douglas. 75m.

Unacknowledged remake of *The Sea Wolf* casts Raymond Massey as the Wolf Larson character (boss of a Western gold-mining camp) and Dane Clark as the innocent who goes against him. It's an interesting movie with its stark symbolic pitting of good against evil—a sort of dry-land *Billy Budd* and fairly well done. Nevertheless Edward G. Robinson and John Garfield did it better in the film of *The Sea Wolf*, which at least had the decency to acknowledge Jack London's novel as its source. In color.

BATTLE AT APACHE PASS (1952, UNIV). D: George Sherman. W: Gerald Drayson Adams. Cast: JOHN LUND, JEFF CHANDLER, Richard EGAN, Beverly TYLER, Hugh O'Brian, Jay Silverheels, Jack Ingram. 85m.

Jeff Chandler was hired to reprise his role of famed Apache leader Cochise here after the box-office success of *Broken Arrow*, but this one's a routine oater with standard cavalry-Indians action sequences. Performances by most of the Universal stock-company starlet school members (Egan, O'Brian, Tyler) were laughably poor, although John Lund made a good leading man.

BATTLE OF ROGUE RIVER (1954, COL). D: William Castle. W: Douglas Heyes. Cast: GEORGE MONTGOMERY, MARTHA HYER, RICHARD DENNING, John CRAWFORD. 71m.

In the 1850s a tough cavalry major (Montgomery) arrives in Oregon to arrange a truce with the Indians so as to pave the way for statehood. Not much action and not much acting. Dull.

BATTLES OF CHIEF PONTIAC (1953, IND). D: Felix Feist. W: Jack DeWitt. Cast: LEX BARKER, Helen WESTCOTT, Lon CHANEY, Jr., Berry Kroeger, Roy Roberts.

Villainous fort commander (Kroeger) sends smallpox-infected blankets to the Indians; a frontiersman (Barker) tries to head off the resulting war. Lon Chaney plays the title character. Whites did, in fact, introduce both smallpox and the practice of scalping to the Indians of North America, but despite that basis in unsavory history this is a "B" meller with "Z" acting.

THE BEAST OF HOLLOW MOUNTAIN (1956, UA). D: Edward Nassour & Ismael Rodriguez. W: Robert Hill & Willis O'Brien. Cast: GUY MADISON, PATRICIA MEDINA, Carlos Rivas, Eduardo Norlega, Mario Navarro. 79m.

Science-fiction Western has a prehistoric monster terrorizing a Mexican village and cowboy Madison trying to vanquish it with lasso and sixgun. There's a gimmicky climax of some interest but it's not worth sitting through the rest of this drivel to see it, unless you are less than nine years of age.

THE BEAUTIFUL BLONDE FROM BASHFUL BEND (1949, FOX). D: Preston Sturges. W: Sturges & Earl Felton. Cast: BETTY GRABLE, CESAR ROMERO, Rudy VALLEE, Olga San Juan, Sterling Holloway, Margaret Hamilton, El Brendel, Chief Thundercloud, Harry Tyler, Porter Hall, J. Farrell MacDonald, Russell Simpson, Chris-Pin Martin, Harry Hayden, Hugh Herbert, Torbin Meyer, Emery Parnell. 77m.

Dance-hall girl gets into trouble when it's discovered she's an expert natural gunslinger. Sturges was famous for his comedies but this wasn't among his better ones. Mostly it's foolish slapstick; a fizzle. In color.

THE BEGUILED (1971, UNIV). D: Don Siegel. W: John E. Sherry & Grimes Grice from a Thomas Cullinan novel. Cast: CLINT EASTWOOD, GERALDINE PAGE, ELIZABETH HARTMAN, Jo Ann

HARRIS, Darleen CARR, Mae Mercer, Pamelyn Ferdin, Melody Thomas. 105m.

Murky gothic Civil War melodrama concerns a wounded Union soldier who hides in a Southern seminary, protected by the girls, into whose insanities (and inanities) he is drawn. Some like it; I find it pretentious. Writers' names are pseudonyms for Albert Maltz and Irene Kamp.

BELLE LE GRAND (1951, REP). D: Allan Dwan. W: D.D. Beauchamp from a Peter B. Kyne story. Cast: VERA HRUBA RALSTON, JOHN CARROLL, Muriel Lawrence, Hope Emerson, Harry Morgan, Stephen Chase, Thurston Hall, John Qualen, William Ching. 91m.

San Francisco gambling queen tries to win back her errant ex-husband. It's a corny soap.

BELLE OF THE NINETIES (1934, PARA). D: Leo McCarey. W: McCarey & Mae West. Cast: MAE WEST, Johnny Mack BROWN, Roger Pryor, Warren Hymer, Katherine De Mille, Duke Ellington, John Miljan, Harry Woods, Wade Boteler, Fuzzy Knight, Mike Mazurki. 73m.

Mae-Western musical comedy has songs by Arthur Johnston and Sam Coslow (including "My Old Flame") performed by West and Duke Ellington's band. Fine for West fans.

BELLE OF THE YUKON (1944, RKO). D: William Seiter. W: James Edward Grant & Houston Branch. Cast: RANDOLPH SCOTT, GYPSY ROSE LEE, DINAH SHORE, Charles Winninger, Guinn "Big Boy" Williams, Bob Burns, Robert Armstrong, Florence Bates, Jack Perrin. 83m.

Meller with music, in color, has the good girl reforming the dance-hall boss. Photography (Ray Rennahan) is good but the movie isn't.

BELLE STARR (1941, FOX). D: Irving Cummings. W: Lamar Trotti, Niven Busch & Cameron Rogers from Rogers' novel. Cast: GENE TIERNEY, RANDOLPH SCOTT, Dana ANDREWS, Chill Wills, John Shepperd, Elizabeth Patterson, Joe Sawyer, Hattie McDaniel, Charles Trowbridge, Olin Howlin. 87m.

Glamorous Tierney is absurdly cast as an outlaw queen. The plot—a female Jesse James reprise—has no connection with reality. The writers were later to become big names, but this script is tiresome; the film has moments of entertaining conflict and drama but mainly it's overblown and hokey. In color, it attempts to imitate aspects of *Gone with the Wind*.

BELLE STARR'S DAUGHTER (1948, FOX). D: Lesley Selander. W: W. R. Burnett. Cast: GEORGE MONTGOMERY, ROD CAMERON, RUTH ROMAN, Henry HULL, Wallace Ford, Isabel Jewell, Jack Lambert. 86m.

Roman, as the title character, comes third in the credits and belongs there; the story—a Bob Steele plot, the girl trying to avenge the murder of her outlaw-queen mother—is an excuse for romantic vying between outlaw Cameron and lawman Montgomery. But acting and action are good.

BEND OF THE RIVER (1952, UNIV). D: Anthony Mann. W: Borden Chase from Bill Gulick's novel *Bend of the Snake*. Cast: JAMES STEWART, ARTHUR KENNEDY, Julia ADAMS, Rock HUDSON, Lori NELSON, J.C. FLIPPEN, Stepin Fetchit, Jack Lambert, Harry Morgan, Chubby Johnson, Royal Dano, Howard Petrie, Frank Ferguson, Ken Curtis, Frances Bavier, Gregg Barton. 91m.

Farmer pioneers migrate to Oregon and encounter opposition from miners, profiteering businessmen and Indians. Stewart is the trail-guide with a shady past, Kennedy the good-natured hedonistic villain, Rock Hudson a gentleman gambler. It's nicely photographed (Irving Glassberg) with a good score (Hans J. Salter); Mann directs excellently and the performances are very good except for Kennedy's: as a Kansas gunslinger he looks, moves and talks too much like a New Yorker. In retrospect, however, the film contains far too many cliches; it's far more dated now than, say, *Ramrod* (made five years earlier). Still, it's good entertainment.

BEST OF THE BAD MEN (1948, RKO). D: William Russell. W: John Twist & Robert E. Andrews. Cast: RANDOLPH SCOTT, ROBERT RYAN, CLAIRE TREVOR, JACK BEUTEL, Robert PRESTON, Barton MacLANE, Carleton Young, Carl Sepulveda. 81m.

There are good plot twists and plenty of actionful sequences in this quick yarn about a manhunt for the Sundance Kid; the stars make it fun, although it's awfully hackneyed.

BEYOND THE PECOS (1945, UNIV). D: Lambert Hillyer. W: Bennett R. Cohen & Jay Karth. Cast: ROD CAMERON, Eddie DEW, Robert Homans, Gene Stutenroth. 63m.

Lone marshal cleans up the territory in predictable fashion. Rod Cameron's movies of the mid-1940s hovered between "A" and "B"; when in doubt I've included them. This one is ambitious for a low-budget feature, but

nothing special, really. Note it was directed by one of William S. Hart's old directors.

THE BIG CAT (1948, EL). D: Phil Karlson. W: Morton Grant & Dorothy Yost. Cast: PRESTON FOSTER, LON McCALLISTER, Forrest TUCKER, Peggy Ann GARNER, Skip HOMEIER, Sara Haden, Irving Bacon. 71m.

Dude kid visits the mountain West and gets involved in the hunt for a killer mountain lion. Plenty of action, and better than average performances, in this juvenile melodrama.

THE BIG COUNTRY (1958, UA). D: William Wyler. W: Wyler, James R. Webb, Sy Bartlett, Robert Wilder and Jessamyn West from Donald Hamilton's novel. Cast: GREGORY PECK, JEAN SIMMONS, BURL IVES, CARROLL BAKER, CHARLTON HESTON, Chuck CONNORS, Charles BICKFORD, Alfonso Bedoya. 166m.

Ex-sea captain (Peck) comes out West to marry Jean Simmons and gets involved in a range war between cattle barons vying for control of the Territory. The plot—from the novelist who started as a Western writer but found later fame with his Matt Helm spy stories—is rather warmed-over Ernest Haycox, but the adaptation by all those big-name writers is first rate and, while it's not profound, it's fun. Produced by William Wyler and Gregory Peck, with spectacular grandeur in the wide-screen photography by Franz Planer, it's a good big-scale all-star Western. Burl Ives won an Academy Award as best supporting actor.

A BIG HAND FOR THE LITTLE LADY (1966, WB). D: Fielder Cook. W: Sidney Carroll. Cast: HENRY FONDA, JOANNE WOODWARD, JASON ROBARDS, Jr., Kevin McCARTHY, Burgess MEREDITH, Charles BICKFORD, Robert Middleton, Paul Ford, John Qualen, Mae Clarke, Gerald Michenaud, James Kenny, James Griffith, Ned Glass, Percy Helton, Allen Collins, Milton Selzer, Virginia Gregg, Chester Conklin. 94m.

The five richest mossyhorns in the territory are holding their annual cutthroat poker game in the back room of a Laredo hotel in 1896. A sorry loser of an ex-gambler (Fonda) and his wife (Woodward) are passing through town, heading to settle on their new homestead down in San Antone, and Fonda—much against the little lady's wishes—gets into the high-stakes game. Then with a fortune on the table he has a heart attack and suddenly it's up to the little lady. . . . It's a funny movie, a handsomely mounted clever yarn filmed, oddly, in the style of an old-fashioned Broadway musical (without the music), with choreographed movement and expansive acting that gives it a stylized and sometimes surreal flavor.

Originally a television play, it's a slim story that depends on its trick-ending gimmick; but much of it is great fun, with a spirited score (David Raskin) and good photography (Lee Garmes), snappily edited (George Rohs) and acted with great gusto and joy by all, particularly McCarthy as a smooth ladies-man lawyer, Robards as a blustery cattle baron, Bickford (who died soon after this, his last film, was completed) as the richest undertaker in the territory, and Middleton as the arbiter of poker rules. There's no shooting or fighting in it, and most of the show takes place indoors, and it's one of the more entertaining Westerns of its era.

BIG JACK (1949, MGM). D: Richard Thorpe. W: Gene Fowler, Marvin Borowsky, Otto Van Eyss & Robert Thoeren. Cast: WALLACE BEERY, MARJORIE MAIN, RICHARD CONTE, Edward ARNOLD, Vanessa Brown, Vince Barnett. 85m.

Beery and Main, bandits in Colonial America, save a young doctor (Conte) from hanging and everybody has a fine time. More engaging for non-Beery fans than most of his movies. This was his last film.

BIG JAKE (1971, NGP). D: George Sherman. W: Harry Julian Fink & Rita M. Fink. Cast: JOHN WAYNE, MAUREEN O'HARA, RICHARD BOONE, Patrick WAYNE, Bobby Vinton, Bruce Cabot, Christopher Mitchum, Glenn Corbett, Harry Carey, Jr., John Doucette, Jim Davis, John Agar, Gregg Palmer, Dean Smith, John Ethan Wayne, Hank Worden, Jerry Gatlin. 110m.

In 1909 Richard Boone's gang of villains perpetrate a gory slaughter on Big Jake's (Wayne's) ranch and kidnap his grandson (John Ethan Wayne, the Duke's real son, named after Wayne's character Ethan Edwards in *The Searchers*). The on-screen relationship between Wayne and O'Hara is a rehash of their roles in *McLintock*. The story of pursuit and retribution is keyed by the opening slaughter and an equally gory carnage at the climax, both sequences unnecessarily grisly; all this was surprising in view of Wayne's usual concern with family-audience films. Photography (William Clothier) and score (Elmer Bernstein) are professional if not terribly inspired, and it's reasonably well directed (this was director Sherman's last

film, of some three hundred, and it was the first Wayne movie he'd directed since they'd worked together in the Three Mesquiteers series in the late 1930s). Batjac production was produced by Wayne's own company.

THE BIG LAND (1957, WB). D: Gordon Douglas. W: David Dortort & Martin Rackin from a Frank Gruber novel. Cast: ALAN LADD, VIRGINIA MAYO, EDMOND O'BRIEN, Julie BISHOP, Anthony CARUSO, John Qualen, Don Castle, John Doucette, David Ladd, George J. Lewis. Narrator: Reed HADLEY. 92m.

A lovely performance by Edmond O'Brien as an alcoholic desperate for a drink enlivens the early portions of this otherwise overblown pulp-formula meller about a drifting Texan (Ladd) who builds a frontier town despite opposition by a villain (Caruso) whose personality and style are reminiscent of the most ludicrous mustache-twisting bad guys of Victorian melodramas. Big budget and lush photography (John Seitz) and a big if routine score (David Buttolph) give the film scope and size, but the characters are familiar, the plot devices purely from stock, the anachronisms typical (saloon girl Mayo sings a 1950s blues in 1860s Kansas) and the acting generally poor. The town and the movie might as well have been called Dullsville.

THE BIG SKY (1952, RKO). D: Howard Hawks. W: Dudley Nichols from A.B. Guthrie, Jr.'s novel. Cast: KIRK DOUGLAS, Dewey MARTIN, Arthur HUNNICUTT, Elizabeth THREATT, Jim DAVIS, Buddy Baer, Steven Geray, Frank DeKova, Hank Worden. 122m.

Pioneer trappers venture up the Missouri River by keelboat through hostile Indian territory to establish a fur-trading post in the 1830s. History is graphically portrayed in this slow black-and-white movie (photographed by Russell Harlan) filmed against the scenery of the Grand Tetons. The story is dramatically big but deliberate. Kirk Douglas plays the happy-go-lucky individualist he soon made his trademark, and the supporting cast—especially Hunnicutt, Martin and Davis—is excellent. Nichols's screenplay retains the grandeur and sweep of the Guthrie novel and it is because of this, more than Howard Hawks's lethargic direction, that the movie works. The original release version (140 minutes long) was cut soon after its release because it was too ponderous. Academy Award nomination to Hunnicutt (best supporting actor).

THE BIG TRAIL (1930, FOX). D: Raoul Walsh. W: Jack Peabody, Marie Boyle,

Florence Postal & Hal G. Evarts. Cast: JOHN WAYNE, MARGUERITE CHURCHILL, Tyrone POWER, Sr., Ward Bond, Chief Thundercloud, El Brendel, Tully Marshall, David Rollins, Ian Keith, Louise Carver. 126m.

Wayne's first significant acting part was the starring role in this epic sequel to *The Oregon Trail*. It's a wagon-train story with a variation of the Bob Steele plot, with Wayne hunting his daddy's killer amid Indian fights, buffalo hunts, river fordings and mountain crossings.

The original version was in 55mm widescreen and in color (photographed by Arthur Edeson), and it ran 158 minutes in length. Surviving prints are mostly in 35mm, in b&w, and just a shade over two hours long. (Some are as short as 109 minutes.)

Raoul Walsh had intended to play the hero himself but he'd lost an eye in an accident while filming *In Old Arizona* so he gave the part, on John Ford's recommendation, to young John Wayne.

Some critics attribute the box-office failure of the movie to Wayne's dreadful acting, while others insist that's a canard; they say Wayne's performance was no worse than those of many contemporary film stars; what probably killed the movie, they say, was its turgid "B" script.

Having seen the movie only in its surviving form I don't know how much has been lost, but on the evidence at hand I would say both schools of criticism are right. The script is poor, but so is Wayne's acting; he is wooden at best, and embarrassingly inept at worst (in the romantic scenes). Today *The Big Trail* is mainly of nostalgic interest. It contains no surprises. Its failure at the box office in 1930 had one important result, however; it relegated Wayne to a decade of hard apprenticeship in dozens of "B" pictures where he learned his craft.

THE BIG TREES (1952, WB). D: Felix Feist. W: John Twist, James R. Webb & Kenneth Earl. Cast: KIRK DOUGLAS, Patrice WYMORE, Eve MILLER, Edgar BUCHANAN, John Archer, Alan Hale, Jr., Charles Meredith, Roy Roberts, Harry Cording, Ellen Corby. 89m.

Brash swindler (Douglas) tries to con landowners out of their giant redwood forests. This was the first ten-gallon-hat flick Douglas made after his uncomfortable Western debut in *Along the Great Divide*. He made this one for no salary in order to get out of his Warner contract; he walks through the part, making the rogue into a bore. Stock footage—despite good original photography (Bert Glennon)—

and a complex and unbelievable plot don't help. The sequoias are magnificent, but the movie isn't.

BILLY THE KID (1930, MGM). D: King Vidor. W: Wanda Tuchack & Laurence Stallings from Walter Noble Burns' book *The Saga of Billy the Kid*. Cast: JOHNNY MACK BROWN, WALLACE BEERY, Kay JOHNSON, Karl Dane, Roscoe Ates, Lucille Powers, Russell Simpson. 96m.

William S. Hart was adviser on this production; it was filmed on locations around the Grand Canyon and in the actual areas of Lincoln County, N.M., where Pat Garrett (Beery) had tracked the Kid (Brown) in 1881. The slow film is rather talky but it recaptures the legend of Billy the Kid very nicely, although of the two endings that were filmed, the one shown in America (romantic hogwash in which Billy survives and Garrett smiles as he watches the Kid and the girl ride into the sunset) was a sorry cop-out; in European release the facts were honored, and Garrett killed the Kid.

The two leading men were not actors of any particular repute. Beery was a mugging ham, Brown an engaging but bland young performer who in a long subsequent career in Westerns (up into the 1960s) never did learn much about acting. But their typecasting in this film was appropriate to the mythology; and the movie conveys an overpowering flavor and sense of history, in terms of time and place, rather than facts. It is seasoned very strongly with the Hart spirit of "authenticity" in its trappings; Hart even gave Brown a revolver that Hart said had belonged to the real Billy the Kid. And the movie was shot on actual locations at a time when they hadn't yet changed perceptibly. These details enhance the film; one feels closer to understanding the folkloric legends.

The movie was filmed originally in two versions: the standard 35mm and a 55mm wide-screen rendition (like that of *The Big Trail*). The latter version is said to have been pictorially magnificent.

BILLY THE KID (1940, MGM). D: David Miller. W: Gene Fowler, H.E. Rogers & Bradbury Foote from Walter Noble Burns's book *The Saga of Billy the Kid*. Cast: ROBERT TAYLOR, BRIAN DONLEVY, Connie GILCHRIST, Ian HUNTER, Mary Howard, Gene Lockhart, Lon Chaney, Jr., Larry "Buster" Crabbe, Chill Wills, Guinn "Big Boy" Williams, Joe Yule, Cy Kendall, Frank Puglia, Henry O'Neill, Tom London, George Chesebro, Ray Teal, Kermit Maynard, Grant Withers, Dick Curtis. 95m.

Sad second-rate remake of the 1930 picture (based, it says, on the same book—a romanticized "history") has little of the story left intact. The scenery is in Technicolor here (good photography by Leonard Smith & William V. Skall), and the cast is big, but the script is a whitewash, divorced not only from history but from the legends and myths of folklore. Herein Billy is a hero who clears the territory of greedy bad guys. Taylor, here in his second oater, was too boudoir-smooth to be convincing as the rugged juvenile Billy (Taylor was only thirty but appeared mature even then). Donlevy, as the hardbitten sheriff, is unconvincing as well (he never made a believable Westerner). Pat Garrett doesn't even appear as a character in this version. The directing is aimless and lethargic. The score (David Snell) is routine. As in Paul Newman's later *The Left-Handed Gun*, Billy is depicted as having been left-handed; he wasn't, but Robert Taylor was. This one was very popular but to view it now is to be disappointed.

BILLY THE KID VS. DRACULA (1966, EMB). D: William Beaudine. W: Carl K. Hittleman. Cast: Chuck COURTNEY, John CARRADINE, Melinda Plowman, Harry Carey, Jr., Roy Barcroft, Olive Carey. 93m.

Carradine at least has the grace to be hammily funny as the vampire in this otherwise dreary "B" nonsense. Courtney, as the hero who decides to reform and settle down but then learns that his girl's kindly old uncle is a midnight bloodsucker, is astonishingly incompetent. So is the film. It's in color, and those who are so retarded as to enjoy it should be sure not to miss the same producers' *Jesse James Meets Frankenstein's Daughter*.

BITE THE BULLET (1975, COL). DW: Richard Brooks: Cast: GENE HACKMAN, JAMES COBURN, CANDICE BERGEN, BEN JOHNSON, IAN BANNEN, JAN-MICHAEL VINCENT, Mario Arteaga, Paul Stewart, Sally Kirkland, Jean Willes, Robert Donner, Dabney Coleman. 131m.

In a long distance horseback endurance race across the Southwest in 1905, a motley collection of characters play out their compulsions and conflicts. Veteran writer-producer-director Brooks (*The Professionals*) can claim far more auteur credit than can most Hollywood filmmakers, but that means he must accept the blame for his misfires, and this is one of them. It's a robust Western with sturdy qualities—big-budget professionalism, a fine score (Alex North), snappy editing (George Granville), admirable Southwest location photography (Harry Stradling, Jr.);

but it's nowhere near as exciting as *The Professionals* nor as significant as Brooks's *In Cold Blood*. It's mechanically contrived and filled with unbelievable incidents; for example, somehow all the characters come together each night in camp along the railroad—hardly likely if they're spread out across many miles of desert in the midst of a marathon race.

It's a better movie than most Westerns of the mid-1970s but unhappily that isn't enough; it deals perfunctorily with a Grand Hotel cast of characters, all of them seemingly lifted out of other movies, most of them not very interesting, some of them too lacking in background and personality; and the movie is curiously lacking in suspense. The actors are good—some (like Ben Johnson) are superb—and some of them manage to hold our interest when they shouldn't, but it is a keen disappointment coming from Brooks.

BITTER CREEK (1954, AA). D: Thomas Carr. W: George Waggner. Cast: WILLIAM ELLIOTT, Beverly GARLAND, Carleton Young, Claude Akins, Forrest Taylor, Earle Hodgins, Holly Bane. 74m.

Nothing new in this Bob Steele plot; but Elliott plays it straight and tough, and there's plenty of "B" action.

BITTER SPRINGS (1950, IND). D: Ralph Smart. W: W.P. Lipscomb & M. Danischewsky. Cast: CHIPS RAFFERTY, Tommy Trinder, Charles Tingwell, Michael Pate, Gordon Jackson, Jean Blue.

Set in Australia and made there by Australians, this pioneer movie concerns a settler whose attempt to build a home is opposed by aborigines. A different and often gripping little movie. Rafferty frequently was described as the Australian John Wayne; the comparison was not far-fetched. And this one's interesting because of the early work of supporting players Gordon Jackson and Michael Pate, both of whom went on to better things—Jackson in such productions as *Upstairs, Downstairs*; Pate—who is Australian—in numerous Hollywood movies like *Hondo*, in most of which he played Indian chiefs.

BLACK BART (1948, UNIV). D: George Sherman. W: Luci Ward, Jack Natteford & William Bowers. Cast: DAN DURYEA, YVONNE De CARLO, Jeffrey LYNN, Percy KILBRIDE, Frank LOVEJOY, Lloyd Gough, John McIntire. 80m.

There was a real Black Bart, a whimsical highwayman who robbed stagecoaches while wearing a black hood, and left pencil-scrawled four-line verses in the empty lockboxes he'd robbed. He was finally tracked down by a Pinkerton detective who traced him through a laundry mark on his handkerchief—an early example of forensic detective work. None of that happens in this movie, however. It's a highly fictionalized version, with Duryea playing the bandit as a Zorro-esque rogue, an outwardly respectable rancher who robs stages for kicks. DeCarlo plays entertainer Lola Montez, and the plot has to do with Black Bart's ambition to destroy the Wells Fargo company. It's all in fun and played that way; the stars are amusing. It's in color. It gets draggy in spots but it's an amiable little entertainment. Remade in 1967 as *The Ride to Hangman's Tree.*

THE BLACK DAKOTAS (1954, COL). D: Ray Nazarro. W: Ray Buffum & DeVallon Scott. Cast: GARY MERRILL, WANDA HENDRIX, John BROMFIELD, Noah Beery, Jr., Jay Silverheels, Frank Wilcox, Peter Whitney. 65m.

Hijacking bandits threaten to disrupt the peace between Sioux and whites; trouble-shooter steps in. It's a standard actioner. But Merrill is an unusual and agreeable hero in a Western.

BLACK HORSE CANYON (1954, UNIV). D: Jesse Hibbs. W: Geoffrey Homes & David Lang from Les Savage, Jr.'s, novel. Cast: JOEL McCREA, Mari BLANCHARD, Race GENTRY, Murvyn Vye. 81m.

A wild stallion is captured, then escapes into the hills; a small group of Westerners attempts to recapture him. It's a gently pastoral film, perfectly in tune with McCrea's leisurely style, although the novel on which it was based was considerably sexier and more hardboiled.

BLACK JACK KETCHUM, DESPERADO (1956, COL). D: Earl Bellamy. W: Luci Ward & Jack Natteford from Louis L'Amour's novel *Kilkenny.* Cast: HOWARD DUFF, Victor JORY, Angela STEVENS, Maggie Mahoney, Ralph Sanford. 82m.

Retired gunslinger tries to tame a town. Not altogether a bad oater; the formula plot is made fresher by a bright script and good acting.

BLACK PATCH (1957, WB). D: Allen H. Miner. W: Leo Gordon. Cast: GEORGE MONTGOMERY, Diane BREWSTER, Sebastian CABOT, Leo Gordon, Strother Martin, Tom Pittman, House Peters, Jr. 83m.

Written by bad-guy actor Gordon, this one features Montgomery as a Civil War veteran, now a sheriff, who's trying to clear his name; it's all about horses and treacly folks and it drips with corn syrup; just awful.

BLACK SPURS (1965, PARA). D: R.G. Springsteen. W: Steve Fisher. Cast: RORY CALHOUN, TERRY MOORE, LINDA DARNELL, SCOTT BRADY, Lon CHANEY, Jr., Bruce Cabot, Richard Arlen. 81m.

An A.C. Lyles production, lawman versus miscreants; creaky old-fashioned hoss-opera fare, with a lot of old-timer actors and Linda Darnell in her last film.

THE BLACK WHIP (1957, FOX). D: Charles Marquis Warren. W: Orville Hampton & Sam Peckinpah. Cast: HUGH MARLOWE, Coleen GRAY, Angie DICKINSON, Paul Richards, Sheb Wooley. 77m.

Bandit gang plots to kidnap the territorial governor; a heroic type (Marlowe) rescues a group of dance-hall girls from the gang's clutches. There are moments of interest; Angie Dickinson is attractive, and Hugh Marlowe always commands attention—he is an excellent actor ill-used by Hollywood, whose commanding voice and rugged good looks might well have been employed to far greater advantage than in the second-rate movies he usually appeared in. (Usually, also, he played bad guys, as in *Rawhide* and *Bugles in the Afternoon.*) The fact that Peckinpah contributed to the screenplay should not cause acceleration in the pulse of any movie buff who has examined the record; Peckinpah's scripts, mostly, range from mediocre to awful.

BLAZING ARROWS *(1931)—See* FIGHTING CARAVANS.

BLAZING SADDLES (1974, WB). D: Mel Brooks. W: Brooks, Norman Steinberg, Andrew Bergman, Richard Pryor & Alan Uger. Cast: CLEAVON LITTLE, GENE WILDER, MADELINE KAHN, MEL BROOKS, Slim PICKENS, Harvey KORMAN, Dom De LUISE, David Huddleston, Claude E. Starrett, Jr. 93m.

Hip black sheriff (Little) and screwball gunslinger (Wilder) save a Western town from something or other. Sprightly farcical parody has a paper-thin story line that serves as an excuse for gags. It's a kid-the-movie movie that makes no attempt to avoid anachronisms; in fact it flaunts them (saddlebags by Gucci, a saloon brawl that ends up on the neighboring set of a top-hat-&-tails musical movie). Characters are called Hedley Lamarr, Buddy Bizarre, Lili Von Shtupp (a wonderful takeoff, by Madeline Kahn, of Marlene Dietrich in *Destry Rides Again*), the Waco Kid (Wilder), Van Johnson, Howard Johnson, Doc Sam Johnson, Olson Johnson, and finally Black Bart (Little). (The movie originally was titled *Black Bart.*)

The subtitle is *Never Give a Saga an Even*

Break; there is a Frankie Laine title ballad that burlesques them all, mercilessly; every effort is made to avoid good taste—the scatology is fierce, and there are endless one-liners like, "Our men are being stampeded and our cattle raped!" It's crude, as plotless and disorganized as a slapstick variety show, and very, very funny. It's easy to nitpick at a movie with a Jewish Indian (Brooks) and a bean-eating scene that draws its humor from the breaking of wind, but it's even easier to sit back and laugh oneself silly. A ridiculous but thoroughly enjoyable movie. The film received three Academy Award nominations including one for best supporting actress (Kahn).

BLOOD ARROW (1958, FOX). **D: Charles Marquis Warren. W: Fred Freiberger. Cast: SCOTT BRADY, PHYLLIS COATES, Paul Richards, Don Haggerty. 75m.**

Mormon gal treks desperately through Indian country trying to get medicine to take back to an ailing town; she encounters villains, Indians and a protector (Brady). Flaccid yarn is unimaginatively filmed.

BLOOD ON THE ARROW (1964, AA). **D: Sidney Salkow. W: Robert E. Kent & Mark Hanna. Cast: DALE ROBERTSON, WENDELL COREY, MARTHA HYER, Paul Mantee, Ted De Corsia, Elisha Cook, Jr., Dandy Curran, Robert Carricart, John Matthews, Tom Reese. 90m.**

A quarrelsome mismatch of characters is besieged in the desert by angry Apaches. Robertson and Hyer are stiff; the banal script leaves even Wendell Corey with nothing plausible to do with his shallow role as a cynical coward. Fairly good Arizona photography (Kenneth Peach) doesn't make up for a two-bit script characterized by very dubious morality, in which cold-blooded murder seems to be accepted as a reasonable problem-solving device, and the double-cross seems a way of life to the heroes.

BLOOD ON THE MOON (1948, RKO). **D: Robert Wise. W: Lillie Hayward, Harold Shumate & Luke Short from Short's novel. Cast: ROBERT MITCHUM, BARBARA BEL GEDDES, ROBERT PRESTON, Walter BRENNAN, Phyllis THAXTER, Tom TULLY, Frank Faylen, Clifton Young, Robert Bray, Charles McGraw, Tom Tyler, Harry Carey, Jr. 88m.**

Mitchum plays a hard drifter caught between opposing sides in a cattlemen-versus-nesters range war. His sympathies lie with the farmers (Brennan, Thaxter) and with ranchers caught in the middle (Tully, Bel Geddes), but the head bad-guy is an old pal (Preston) whom he likes. It's superbly produced, with fine b&w high-country photography (Nicholas Musuraka) and flawless performances; Mitchum, Preston, Bel Geddes and Tully are outstanding. The Roy Webb score is dated and so are some elements of the plot, particularly the last part, which is a let-down because of its trite devices. But the movie is exciting and excellent, widely regarded as a classic Western.

BLUE (1968, PARA). **D: Silvio Narizzano. W: Meade Roberts & Ronald M. Cohen. Cast: TERENCE STAMP, RICARDO MONTALBAN, JOANNA PETTET, KARL MALDEN, Joe De SANTIS, Stathis Giallelis, Anthony Costello, James Westerfield, Peggy Lipton, Jerry Gatlin, Sally Kirkland, Kevin Corcoran, Wes Bishop, Carlos East, Sara Vardi. 113m.**

The title more aptly should be *Blood*. An orphan (Stamp), raised by a Mexican bandit (Montalban), finds himself in a war against his foster father. Stanley Cortez's wide-screen cinematography is very good; little else can be said for this gory mess, with its painfully anachronistic score by Manos Hadjidakis and the lousy dubbing of its international cast. Stamp is British; Narizzano had directed the campy *Georgy Girl*; apparently no one connected with the picture, except second-unit action director Yakima Canutt, knew the first thing about the West or Westerns. The script makes no distinctions between its animalistic villains and its equally animalistic heroes. Stamp had acquitted himself well in other films, notably *Billy Budd*, but here both his phony accent and his performance are dreadful. With the filming of *Blue* the overblown pretentious mod Westerns of the 1960s achieved their nadir.

Oddly, Narizzano simultaneously produced the charming Burt Reynolds movie *Fade In* on the same Utah locations, even using the shooting of *Blue* as a background for the Reynolds romance; the latter, a lovely little film about a rancher who falls in love with a film editor, never went into general distribution and has been seen only on television. Such, sometimes, are the asinine contradictions of Hollywood. *Blue* is unforgivable, a thoroughly disgusting film.

BOBBIE JO AND THE OUTLAW (1976, AIP). **D: Mark L. Lester. W: Vernon Zimmerman. Cast: MARJOE GORTNER, Lynda CARTER, Jesse Vint, Merrie Lynn Ross, Belinda Balaski, Gene Drew, Peggy Stewart. 86m.**

Modern-day quick-draw aficionado in New Mexico fantasizes that he's Billy the Kid; he attracts a following of groupie girls,

BELLE STARR (1941): Gene Tierney, Hattie McDaniel. Entertaining moments but mainly it's hokey, an imitation *Gone with the Wind*. Twentieth Century-Fox

BILLY THE KID (1930): Wallace Beery as Pat Garrett, Johnny Mack Brown as Billy. An overpowering flavor of time and place. MGM

THE BRAVADOS (1958): Gregory Peck. The costume is dudish but it's a grim, hard, pursuit drama. Twentieth Century-Fox

BROKEN LANCE (1954):
Spencer Tracy, Earl Holliman,
Hugh O'Brian, Richard
Widmark, Robert Wagner.
The Brothers Karamazov
go West—with a stunning
performance by Tracy.
Twentieth Century-Fox

BUFFALO BILL (1944): Joel
McCrea, Maureen O'Hara.
Old-fashioned and sudsy,
but a zesty entertainment.
Twentieth Century-Fox

BUTCH CASSIDY AND THE
SUNDANCE KID (1969): Kath-
arine Ross, Paul Newman, Robert
Redford. A slick escapade, hugely
successful at the box office.
Twentieth Century-Fox

CALAMITY JANE
(1953): Doris Day,
Gale Robbins, Howard
Keel. Bouncy amuse-
ment and great fun.
Warner Brothers

CANYON PASSAGE (1946):
Ward Bond, Dana Andrews. Look-
ing on above at left is Lloyd
Bridges (sleeves rolled up). The
only good cinematic adaptation of
the spirit and feeling of Ernest
Haycox's lyrical writing. Universal
Pictures

CARSON CITY (1952). Raymond
Massey, Randolph Scott. A bit of
charm, a bit of humor, plenty of
action. Warner Brothers

CHIEF CRAZY HORSE
(1955): Susan Ball, John
Lund, Victor Mature. As
the Sioux leader Mature is
surprisingly convincing.
Universal Pictures

CIMARRON (1931):
Richard Dix, Irene Dunne.
Yancey Cravat and his bride,
in the only Western ever
to win the Oscar as best picture.
RKO Radio Pictures

COPPER CANYON (1950):
MacDonald Carey, Ray Mil-
land, Hedy Lamarr. Two of
these three people are miscast. Paramount Pictures

COWBOY (1958): Jack
Lemmon, Brian Donlevy.
Good moments in cinematic
water-down of Frank
Harris's racy memoir.
Columbia Pictures

and goes on a killing spree. Exploitive, shabby and cheap.

THE BOLD CABALLERO (1936, REP). DW: Wells Root, from a Johnston McCulley story. Cast: BOB LIVINGSTON, Heather ANGEL, Sig Ruman, Ian Wolfe, Robert Warwick, Charles Stevens.

Spanish governor of Old California is murdered; in steps Zorro (Livingston) to defy the wicked dictator who had the dirty deed done, and to dry the tears of the murdered man's daughter. This programmer was Republic's first Western in color.

BORDER DEVILS (1932, IND). D: William Nigh. W: Murray Leinster & Harry C. Crist (Harry Fraser). Cast: HARRY CAREY, Kathleen COLLINS, George "Gabby" Hayes, Art Mix. 65m.

Fast chase meller with a Bob Steele plot was released shortly after Carey's comeback in *Trader Horn* and tried to capitalize on it.

THE BORDER LEGION (1930, PARA). D: Otto Brower & Edwin H. Knopf. W: Edward E. Paramore, Jr., & Perry Heath from Zane Grey's novel. Cast: RICHARD ARLEN, FAY WRAY, Jack HOLT, Eugene PALLETTE, Stanley Fields, Sid Saylor. 72m.

Remake of oft-filmed Zane Grey yarn, with stock footage from the 1924 version; Federal agent goes undercover to expose the baddies. Remade again in 1938 with George O'Brien and yet again in 1940 with Roy Rogers; those were "B" series entries. It was also filmed in 1934 as *The Last Round-Up* with Randolph Scott. Of them all, the 1930 version probably was the best, with Jack Holt drawing praise as the cheerful outlaw leader who saves the hero's life.

BORDER RANGERS (1950, LIP). D: William Berke. W: Berke & Victor West. Cast: DONALD "RED" BARRY, Robert LOWERY, Judith Allen, Wally Vernon, Barbara Stanley, Bill Kennedy. 62m.

Bob Steele plot; last and probably least of four Lippert Westerns that Barry filmed in 1950; for more information, see *I Shot Billy the Kid*.

BORDER RIVER (1954, UNIV). D: George Sherman. W: William Sackheim & Louis Stevens. Cast: JOEL McCREA, YVONNE De CARLO, Pedro ARMENDARIZ, Alfonso BEDOYA, Nacho Galindo, Howard Petrie, George J. Lewis, Lane Chandler. 80m.

During the Civil War a Rebel officer (McCrea) rides into Mexico to steal gold and use it to buy rifles for the Confederacy. Good work by McCrea and Armendariz but the film adds nothing of much value to the cliches that fill it.

BORN RECKLESS (1930, FOX). D: John Ford. WP: Dudley Nichols from a D.H. Clarke story. Cast: EDMUND LOWE, MARGUERITE CHURCHILL, Catherine Dale OWEN, Warren HYMER, Lee TRACY, Frank Albertson, J. Farrell MacDonald, Jack Pennick, Roy Stewart, Ward Bond. 81m.

Wild girl is tamed by valiant hero. Standard, but big budget for then.

BORN RECKLESS (1958, WB). D: Howard W. Koch. W: Richard Landau & Aubrey Schenck. Cast: MAMIE VAN DOREN, Jeff RICHARDS, Arthur HUNNICUTT, Donald BARRY, Nacho Galindo, Tex Williams. 79m.

Rodeo performers are stirred up to a boil by a blonde sexpot. Hunnicutt—the only thing worth watching in this nauseating mess—essentially repeats the role he played in *The Lusty Men*.

BORN TO THE SADDLE (1952, IND). D: Louis King. W: Adele Buffington. Cast: CHUCK COURTNEY, Leif ERICKSON, Donald Woods, Karen Morley. 73m.

Young racehorse trainer is employed by the man who may have killed his father. Mildewed and tedious.

BORN TO THE WEST (1938, PARA). D: Charles Barton. W: Stuart Anthony and Robert Yost from Zane Grey's novel. Cast: JOHN WAYNE, MARSHA HUNT, JOHNNY MACK BROWN, Alan LADD, James CRAIG, Monte Blue, Lucien Littlefield. 61m.

Cowhands versus rustlers—it's a typical "B" picture of the 1930s but interesting because of its cast. This was the last in a long series of Zane Grey programmers that Paramount cranked out with Randolph Scott, Richard Arlen, George O'Brien and finally Buster Crabbe, who did most of the late-1930s entries previous to this John Wayne clincher.

BOSS NIGGER (1975, IND). D: Jack Arnold. W: Fred Williamson. Cast: FRED WILLIAMSON, D'Urville MARTIN, Carmen Hayworth, H.G. Armstrong, Barbara Lee, William Smith.

Bounty hunter terrorizes a frontier town. Emphasis is on slapstick; blaxploitation movie is funny at times. Unfortunately it never decides whether it's a takeoff of the Eastwood spaghetti shoot-'em-ups or a put-on of the traditional Western; it veers confusingly from one to the other.

THE BOUNTY HUNTER (1954, WB). D: Andre de Toth. W: Winston Miller & Finlay

McDermid. Cast: RANDOLPH SCOTT, Dolores DORN, Marie WINDSOR, Howard Petrie, Harry Antrim, Ernest Borgnine, Paul Picerni, Robert Keys, Phil Chambers, Billy Vincent, Dub Taylor. 79m.

Scott, as the title character, goes after three wanted outlaws. By now this thin plot had contracted anemia; you've got to be a Randolph Scott fanatic to bother with this one. It's one of the least of his pictures.

THE BOUNTY KILLER (1965, EMB). D: Spencer G. Bennett. W: Richard Alexander & Leo Gordon. Cast: DAN DURYEA, ROD CAMERON, Richard ARLEN, Audrey DALTON, Larry "Buster" CRABBE, Johnny Mack BROWN, Bob Steele, Fuzzy Knight, Broncho Billy Anderson, Bob Steele, Grady Sutton, Emory Parnell, I. Stanford Jolley. 92m.

A.C. Lyles didn't produce this one; it was Alex Gordon. He rounded up a passel of old-timers for this oater, in which Duryea plays a dude Easterner who kills an outlaw and becomes a gunslinger, losing his conscience somewhere along the way; there's a downbeat ending. It's more adult and thoughtful than some, but it's pretty terrible, although Duryea is very good: oddly, this little "B" picture features one of the best performances of his career. Dalton is excellent as well, but Rod Cameron (as a bad guy) is given short shrift by the script and does a dull job with it.

THE BOY FROM OKLAHOMA (1954, WB). D: Michael Curtiz. W: Frank Davis, Winston Miller & Michael Fessier. Cast: WILL ROGERS, JR., NANCY OLSEN, Tyler MacDUFF, Lon CHANEY, Jr., Wallace Ford, Merv Griffin, Anthony Caruso, Slim Pickens, Sheb Wooley, James Griffith, Louis Jean Heydt, Clem Bevans.

Rogers is pretty good as the peaceable sheriff of a bandit-dominated town in this comedy-meller. The picture is mild but has charm. Yes, that's TV talk-show host Griffin in a supporting role. A character called Billy the Kid is played herein by Tyler MacDuff.

BOYS' RANCH (1946, MGM). D: Roy Rowland. W: William Ludwig. Cast: JAMES CRAIG, Butch JENKINS, Dorothy PATRICK, Skip HOMEIER, Darryl Hickman, Robert E. O'Connor, Ray Collins, Minor Watson.

Homeless delinquents rise to the challenge of running a Texas ranch. Glutinous, simpering imitation of *Boys' Town* can't hold a candle to it.

BRANDED (1950, PARA). D: Rudolph Mate. W: Sydney Boehm & Cyril Hume

from Evan Evans's novel *Montana Rides*. Cast: ALAN LADD, MONA FREEMAN, CHARLES BICKFORD, Joseph CALLEIA, Robert KEITH, Peter Hanson, Milburn Stone, Tom Tully, Selena Royle, George J. Lewis. 95m.

The plot is the one about the cad (Ladd) who poses as a rich man's (Bickford) long-lost son so he can inherit the wealth. In this case the rich man is a cattle baron, and there's a real son—the one whose place Ladd takes—who's being held captive by a mean Mexican outlaw (Calleia). After the cad falls in love with the rancher's daughter (Freeman) he naturally begins to have second thoughts, and goes off valiantly to rescue the real son. This plot was old in William S. Hart's day. (Author Evan Evans was in fact pulp factory Frederick Faust, best known under his other pen-name "Max Brand.") The melodramatics are abundant but the production is elaborate, the photography (Charles Lang, Jr.) excellent, the cast mostly very good and the direction—by famed cinematographer Rudolph Mate, in his directorial debut—just fine.

THE BRASS LEGEND (1956, UA). D: Gerd Oswald. W: Don Martin, George Zuckerman & Jess Arnold. Cast: HUGH O'BRIAN, NANCY GATES, Raymond BURR, Russell Simpson. 79m.

Lawman pursues villain to the inevitable shoot-out. You've seen it all before. O'Brian is especially wooden in this one, even for him.

THE BRAVADOS (1958, FOX). D: Henry King. W: Philip Yordan from Frank O'Rourke's novel. Cast: GREGORY PECK, JOAN COLLINS, Stephen BOYD, Henry SILVA, Albert SALMI, Lee VAN CLEEF, Kathleen Gallant, Barry Coe, George Voskovec, Herbert Rudley, Andrew Duggan, Ken Scott, Gene Evans. 98m.

Believing them to have murdered his wife, a rancher (Peck) sets out on the trail of four bad guys (Boyd, Salmi, Van Cleef, Silva). It's a grim, hard, pursuit drama, brutal at times, with a pointed message about the futility of revenge. Tough and tight, it has a big look (CinemaScope color photography on Mexican locations by Leon Shamroy) and a heroic stirring score (Lionel Newman); the acting is very good. There are moments when one must wince—the lame tip of the hat to religious faith; the turgid romantic interludes; a tailored and curiously Tom Mix-ish costume worn by the hero—but Henry King, who had previously directed Peck in *The Gunfighter*, always seemed capable of eliciting the actor's best performances. This one is a superior and often quite moving Western.

THE BRAVE ONE (1956, IND). D: Irving Rapper. W: Robert Rich, Harry Franklin & Merrill G. White. Cast: Michel Ray, Elsa Cardenas, Rudolfo Hoyos. 83m.

This is the one about the Mexican boy and his pet bull to which the Academy refused to award the Oscar because "Robert Rich" turned out to be the blacklisted Dalton Trumbo. It's a warm movie but of no great distinction, and it's as hard to understand why it won the Oscar as it is to find excuses for the Academy's withholding the award afterward.

BRAVE WARRIOR (1952, COL). D: Spencer G. Bennett. W: Robert E. Kent. Cast: JON HALL, Christine LARSON, Michael Ansara, Jay Silverheels. 73m.

Set in Indiana in the early 1800s and obviously made under the influence of *Broken Arrow*, this one tries to be fair to the Indian (Shawnee) point of view, but what with the inadequacies of the "B" script, the tedious direction and Hall's thespic inability, it's abysmal.

BREAKHEART PASS (1976, UA). D: Tom Gries. W: Alistair MacLean. Cast: CHARLES BRONSON, BEN JOHNSON, RICHARD CRENNA, Jill IRELAND, Charles DURNING, David HUDDLESTON, Ed Lauter, Bill McKinney, Roy Jenson, Robert Tessier, Rayford Barnes, Joe Kapp, Sally Kirkland, Eddie Little Sky, Casey Tibbs, John Mitchum, Archie Moore. 95m.

Story is set entirely on and near a train traveling through the Rockies. An undercover agent (Bronson) poses as an outlaw to smoke out a gang of gold-stealing gunrunners. Corpses pile up like cordwood and there are some satisfying big-scale crashes and stunts perpetrated by second-unit stunt director Yakima Canutt. The late Tom Gries was a good director (*Will Penny*); Lucien Ballard's color photography is very good except for some studio fakery of process scenery moving past the train windows; Jerry Goldsmith's score is adequate; but the actors wander through their roles without evident interest and the script is a dog. The convoluted story makes no sense; the characters, none of whom is what he seems, are undefined and unabsorbing; it all takes place with virtually no excitement or suspense; the contrived whodunit is lethargic, static and boring.

THE BRIDE COMES TO YELLOW SKY (1952)—*See* FACE TO FACE.

BRIGHAM YOUNG (1940, FOX). D: Henry Hathaway. W: Lamar Trotti & Louis Bromfield. Cast: TYRONE POWER, LINDA DARNELL, DEAN JAGGER, Brian DONLEVY, Mary ASTOR, John CARRADINE, Vincent PRICE, Jean ROGERS, Ann TODD, Moroni Olsen, Jane Darwell, Frank Thomas, Tully Marshall, Marc Lawrence, Stanley Andrews, Chief John Big Tree, Fuzzy Knight, Russell Simpson. 114m.

Twentieth Century-Fox spent a fortune on this sweeping epic about the pioneering trek westward of Mormon leader Brigham Young (Jagger) and his flock to the promised land in Utah, and the founding of the city at the great Salt Lake. The big climactic scene is the storied locust plague and the miracle of the seagulls that saved the Mormons from starvation. Arthur Miller's photography is fine; the scope is vast; but unfortunately the movie is as turgid as molasses, emphasizing pious sentimentality at the expense of entertaining drama. The appealing cast makes it bearable, but only just.

BRIGHTY OF THE GRAND CANYON (1968, IND). DW: Norman Foster from a novel by Marguerite Henry. Cast: JOSEPH COTTEN, Dick FORAN, Pat CONWAY, Karl Swenson, Dandy Curran, Jason Clark. 93m.

Curious little yarn concerns a prospector (Foran) and his pet burro exploring the Grand Canyon in 1906. A claim-jumper (Conway) murders him, after which a neighbor (Cotten) and the burro conspire to track the killer down. Location photography (Ted & Vincent Saizis) emphasizes both the grandeur and the small fauna of the canyon country. It has a certain simpleminded charm; mainly for the kids.

BRIMSTONE (1949, REP). D: Joseph Kane. W: Thames Williamson & Norman S. Hall. Cast: ROD CAMERON, ADRIAN BOOTH, FORREST TUCKER, Walter BRENNAN, Jack HOLT, Jim DAVIS, Jack Lambert, James Brown, Guinn "Big Boy" Williams, Charlita, Hal Taliaferro, Jack Perrin. 90m.

Lawman goes undercover to pose as an outlaw in the attempt to break up an outlaw gang—Walter Brennan and his sons again. (Brennan seemed to have the copyright on that outlaw-patriarch role.) This one hovers somewhere between "A" and "B"—as the former it's undistinguished; as the latter it's good, with an excellent cast.

BROKEN ARROW (1950, FOX). D: Delmer Daves. W: Michael Blankfort from Elliott Arnold's novel *Blood Brother*. Cast: JAMES STEWART, JEFF CHANDLER, DEBRA PAGET, Arthur HUNNICUTT, Basil Ruysdael, Will Geer, Jay Silverheels, Chief

Thundercloud, John Doucette, Iron Eyes Cody, John War Eagle, Nacho Galindo, Trevor Bardette. 93m.

Story concerns white scout Tom Jeffords (Stewart), Apache leader Cochise (Chandler) and the Indian girl (Paget) whom Jeffords marries. Emphasis is on the Apache way of life. *Broken Arrow* received Oscar nominations for best supporting actor (Chandler) and best screenplay; the color photography (Ernest Palmer) is good. Still, it's a slow tearjerker with stilted dialogue and a cop-out ending. Painfully preachy, it overwhelms us in leaden sincerity and patronizing piety. But James Stewart is just dandy (when did he ever give a bad performance?); Hunnicutt, as Chief of Scouts Al Sieber, is delightful; and buffs will note that both Silverheels and Thundercloud were former Tontos from Lone Ranger movies.

Broken Arrow is more important for its influence than for its art. The Western was changed, philosophically, as a result of this picture; seldom thereafter did filmmakers have the nerve to depict Indians as if they were villains simply because they were red men. It would be hard to overstate the effect this movie had; it marked a turning point in America's thinking about the races. Nevertheless, as art and as entertainment it has not stood up with time. It's one of those movies that are better in our memories than they are on re-viewing. Sadly, it's better to let this one sit in the attic of one's mind than to trot it out for another look.

BROKEN LANCE (1954, FOX). D: Edward Dmytryk. W: Richard Murphy & Philip Yordan from a Jerome Weidman novel. Cast: SPENCER TRACY, RICHARD WIDMARK, JEAN PETERS, ROBERT WAGNER, KATY JURADO, Earl HOLLIMAN, Hugh O'BRIAN, Eduard FRANZ, Nacho Galindo, Edmund Cobb, Carl Benton Reid, Russell Simpson, Philip Ober. 97m.

A willful cattle baron (Tracy) angers his Indian wife (Jurado) and his four feuding sons (Widmark, Wagner, Holliman, O'Brian); they all battle one another over money, power, love—anything and everything. The action is plentiful; the complicated rich story builds to a harrowing clifftop climax. But when it's over it is Tracy's remarkable towering performance that one remembers. By far the best of the domineering-father versus sibling-sons Westerns, *Broken Lance* had a complex history. It was a remake of the Edward G. Robinson-Richard Conte movie *House of Strangers*, which was based on a section of the Jerome Weidman novel about Italo-American bankers in New York; but

that story in turn owes a strong apparent debt to Dostoevsky's *The Brothers Karamazov*, which really must be regarded as the initial source of *Broken Lance*. (In turn, *Broken Lance* was later remade into *The Big Show* in 1961— same story in a circus setting. It is obviously an endlessly serviceable plot.) Yordan's screen story won an Oscar, and Katy Jurado—best remembered from *High Noon*— was nominated as best supporting actress. A big and rewarding movie.

THE BROKEN LAND (1962, FOX). D: John Bushelman. W: Edward Lakso. Cast: KENT TAYLOR, Dianna Darrin, Jody McCrea, Jack Nicholson.

Sadistic lawman (Taylor) menaces a girl (Darrin); young Nicholson, a decade before his stardom, is a winning, innocent victim of Taylor's arrogant villainy. Threadbare.

THE BROKEN STAR (1956, UA). D: Lesley Selander. W: John C. Higgins. Cast: HOWARD DUFF, LITA BARON, BILL WILLIAMS, Douglas FOWLEY, Henry Calvin, Addison Richards, Joe Dominguez, John Pickard. 82m.

Lawman (Duff) goes bad and his old pal (Williams) has to go after him. Mediocre.

BRONCO BILLY (1980, WB). D: Clint Eastwood. W: Dennis Hackin. Cast: CLINT EASTWOOD, SONDRA LOCKE, Geoffrey LEWIS, Scatman CROTHERS, Bill McKINNEY Sam BOTTOMS, Dan Vadis, Sierra Pecheur, Walter Barnes, William Prince, Tanya Russell. 96m.

A former shoe salesman from New Jersey has turned himself into a fantasy hero as a trick-shooting Wild West Show star, traveling around the modern West with his shoestring circus in a couple of beat-up trucks accompanied by a tiny troupe of engaging losers (Crothers, McKinney, Bottoms, Vadis). Bronco Billy does a knife-throwing act that involves a lady assistant, and these assistants don't last long on the job; his aim isn't what it ought to be, and the terrified girls soon pack up and quit, so he has to keep recruiting local round-heeled girls for the job. Then along comes a haughty heiress (Locke) trying to escape from her loony husband (Geoffrey Lewis, in a marvelous comic performance); she takes refuge, reluctantly, with the ragtag Wild West Show, and changes take place as a result.

As both actor and director Eastwood displays amusing quiet charm in this movie. It's often quite funny. It was not a tremendous box-office success but then it is a minor movie at best; had it been released a few decades earlier it would have been dismissed as just another imitation of *The Cowboy and the Lady*, which in fact it is.

Beneath its easy laughter and charm, however, the movie has disappointing aspects. Although Bronco Billy realizes he's living out a phony fantasy, nevertheless he lives it out with a bumbling sincerity which turns the character into a somewhat embarrassing caricature of the Western hero. The picture says that the cowboy hero's high moral code is nothing more than a corny joke; and it relies too much on the outdated idea that a man's man can tame an uppity dude woman by beating her up.

There's a wistful sadness about this picture that is out of keeping with its lighthearted comedy. Still, it's unusual and amiable, a small picture but well made, and worth seeing.

BRONCO BUSTER (1952, UNIV). D: Budd Boetticher. W: Horace McCoy & Lillie Hayward from a Peter B. Kyne story. Cast: JOHN LUND, SCOTT BRADY, Joyce HOLDEN, Chill WILLS, Casey Tibbs, Don Haggerty. 81m.

A young novice (Lund) becomes the protégé of a veteran rodeo champ (Wills)— same essential plot as that of *The Lusty Men*, which preceded this one and is still the classic rodeo picture. Well directed.

BUCHANAN RIDES ALONE (1958, COL). D: Budd Boetticher. W: Charles Lang from the Jonas Ward novel. Cast: RANDOLPH SCOTT, Jennifer HOLDEN, Craig STEVENS, Barry Kelley, Tol Avery. 78m.

Drifter Scott tries to prevent the lynching of a young Mexican prisoner by a mob led by sly, smooth baddie Craig Stevens. The paperback "Buchanan" series of novels is mostly tongue-in-cheek, the character a happy-go-lucky wanderer, but this movie version plays it straight, making Buchanan dull by making him serious. Craig Stevens is far too urbane for a Western; Scott seems very tired (this was one of his last pictures); and the movie is set entirely in a town, most of it in the jail. Static, stolid and unexciting.

Jonas Ward was the pen-name of the late William Ard; when he died in the mid-1960s the Buchanan series of novels was continued by other writers who were licensed by the Ard estate. I wrote the first one after Ard's death (*Buchanan's Gun*) and subsequent Buchanan yarns have been written by William R. Cox.

BUCK AND THE PREACHER (1972, COL). D: Sidney Poitier. W: Ernest Kinoy & Drake Walker. Cast: SIDNEY POITIER, HARRY BELAFONTE, RUBY DEE, Cameron MITCHELL, Denny Miller, Nita Talbot, James McEachin, Clarence Muse, John Dierkes, John Kelly. 101m.

Wagonmaster (Poitier) guides ex-slaves to new homesteads in the West, aided by a roguish ex-slave turned Bible-belting con man (Belafonte), and opposed by an ex-Confederate gang leader (Mitchell) who aims to force the black pioneers back to the Louisiana cotton fields where he thinks they belong. There are some noble Indians, some horseback chases, a tongue-in-cheek bank robbery, facedowns and showdowns and a final gundown with villains who never shoot straight while the heroes never miss. The plot is filled with "B" coincidences, unmotivated actions and cardboard characterizations. Poitier's initial directorial effort is mostly competent but unimaginative; the photography (Alex Phillips, Jr.) is serviceable but the score (by jazzman Benny Carter) is frenetic, monotonous and unfeelingly anachronistic. There are times when Poitier ignores the rules and cuts from one shot to another in a bewildering way so that the audience can't tell where the actors are or who's chasing whom. On screen Poitier is no horseman, and if he really fired a sawed-off shotgun from the hip like that he'd be blown into the next county by the recoil. Belafonte's phony teeth cause him to blow many of his lines, and neither star brings the sort of charm to the characters that they evidently intended. The picture can't quite make up its mind whether it's a farce or a lighthearted adventure; it falls awkwardly between the two forms.

BUCK BENNY RIDES AGAIN (1940, PARA). D: Mark Sandrich. W: William Morrow, Edmund Beloin & Z. Myers from a story by Arthur Stringer. Cast: JACK BENNY, PHIL HARRIS, Eddie "Rochester" ANDERSON, Dennis DAY, Ellen DREW, Andy DEVINE, Virginia Dale, Morris Ankrum. 82m.

Movie transfers one of Benny's radio characters to the screen with supporting radio cast intact. Funny in spurts; dated slapstick.

BUCKSKIN (1968, PARA). D: Michael Moore. W: Michael Fisher. Cast: BARRY SULLIVAN, WENDELL COREY, JOAN CAULFIELD, Bill WILLIAMS, Barbara HALE, Lon CHANEY, Jr., John RUSSELL, Barton MacLane, Richard Arlen, Leo Gordon, Emile Meyer. 97m.

Domineering cattle baron (Corey) is opposed by heroic marshal (Sullivan) in this amateurish long-in-the-tooth exercise in familiar-face nostalgia from maverick producer A.C. Lyles. It was Barton MacLane's last movie (he died in 1969) and there are plenty more familiar old-time faces on screen but the kindest word for it all would be overripe.

BUCKSKIN FRONTIER (1943, UA). D: Lesley Selander. W: Norman Houston from a Harry Sinclair Drago novel. Cast: RICH-ARD DIX, JANE WYATT, ALBERT DEKKER, Victor JORY, Lola LANE, Lee J. COBB, Max Baer, Joe Sawyer, Francis McDonald, George Reeves. 71m.

Rivalry between railroader (Dix) and wagon freighter (Dekker) is stirred up by the mustache-twisting villainies of a deliciously devious bad guy (Jory). Like its cast the movie is sturdy, stolid, reliable, but not overly exciting. Same principals as *The Kansan*, made the same year—produced by Harry Sherman, with Russell Harlan's photography and a Victor Young score. These Dix Westerns were "specials," made with a good deal of attention and care, but much of the material is all too familiar and dated.

THE BUCKSKIN LADY (1957, UA). D: Carl K. Hittleman. W: Hittleman, David Lang & Francis Chase, Jr. Cast: PATRICIA MEDINA, RICHARD DENNING, Gerald MOHR, Henry HULL, Hank Worden, Frank Sully. 76m.

Young frontier doctor (Denning) and evil deadly gunslinger (Mohr) are rivals for the affections of the daughter (Medina) of a drunken old sawbones (Hull) whose dissipation and poker losses have led to poverty. It's tedious hokum. Denning couldn't be blander and Mohr was far too citified to make a believable Western gunman.

BUFFALO BILL (1944, FOX). D: William A. Wellman. W: Aeneas MacKenzie, Clements Ripley, Cecile Kramer & Frank Winch. Cast: JOEL McCREA, MAUREEN O'HARA, LINDA DARNELL, THOMAS MITCHELL, Edgar BUCHANAN, Sidney BLACKMER, Anthony QUINN, Chief THUNDERCLOUD, Moroni Olsen, Frank Fenton. Narrator: Reed HADLEY. 89m.

Romantic triangle involves Buffalo Bill Cody (McCrea) with a fiery redhead (O'Hara) and a naive but passionate Sioux Indian girl (Darnell); there are also a lot of cavalry-Indian heroics and some tearjerking had-I-but-known melodramatics, in a very old-fashioned sudsy plot. The Wild West Show, to which Cody devoted most of his life and for which most Americans knew him, is dismissed in a few minutes at the end of the movie. Historically it's pure bunkum. Wellman claimed he'd spent months working up a screenplay with Gene Fowler that limned the real story of William F. Cody—drunk, charlatan, unfaithful husband—but in the end,

he said, the two decided they couldn't destroy a great American legend; they destroyed their screenplay instead. That may have been wise, but this whitewash is sadly disappointing in retrospect, a predictably hokey simplistic biopic that is manufactured out of Hollywood formula and has only the most tenuous basis in real Western myths.

Still, it's a zesty entertainment, big-budget, filmed in Technicolor partly on Utah locations (cinematographer Leon Shamroy; and please note that many prints are in black-and-white because of a subsequent low-budget re-release) with excellent production elements. And Joel McCrea's performance, in an atypical role, is superb; probably his best before *Ride the High Country*.

BUFFALO BILL AND THE INDIANS, OR: SITTING BULL'S HISTORY LESSON (1976, UA). D: Robert Altman. W: Altman & Alan Rudolph, "suggested by" Arthur Kopit's stage play *Indians*. Cast: PAUL NEWMAN, BURT LANCASTER, JOEL GREY, Kevin McCARTHY, Geraldine CHAPLIN, Harvey KEITEL, Will SAMPSON, Denver Pyle, Frank Kaquitts, Robert Doqui, Allan Nichols. 120m.

Rambling episodic movie fitfully concerns a series of confrontations between Buffalo Bill Cody (Newman) and Sioux chief Sitting Bull (Kaquitts) whom Cody has hired as a sideshow star for his Wild West Show. Cody is shown as a drunken phony who yearns for the grit of reality and strives to achieve dramatic power but fails to come to grips with life because he's terrified by the truth; he is comfortable only with fiction, not with fact.

Expensively produced by Dino De Laurentiis and David Susskind, the movie has a static setbound quality because it was shot entirely on a single location in Alberta, Canada that passes for the show's 1885–86 winter encampment near what is now Cody, Wyoming. There isn't much linear story. It's an ambiguous and tenuous yarn, ultimately a failure and a bore because Altman is concerned with polemics rather than people.

The movie isn't a drama; it's an essay. The filmmaker evidently has no affection for any of his characters. His coldness, or rather contempt, toward them creates an indifference in the audience; the film is technically interesting but emotionally bankrupt. None of the characters except Cody's is developed; the other players are mostly anonymous and often interchangeable—they are mouthpieces for positions or cynicisms; they are not human. A few stand out because of the actors: Kevin McCarthy is good as a cynical publicist, Joel Grey as an opportunistic producer, Denver Pyle in a nicely contrasting role as a real lawman, Will Sampson as Sitting Bull's loquacious interpreter. Burt Lancaster, as legend-maker Ned Buntline, is too grave and somber and low-key; Buntline was never an elder statesman—he was the foremost con man of the century, and a flamboyant Barnumesque showman; Lancaster fails to suggest any of that. Geraldine Chaplin plays Annie Oakley with complete lack of personality, but it's more the script's fault than hers. Newman's performance is excellent but the character is false and offensive.

BUFFALO GUN (1962, IND). Cast: MARTY ROBBINS, WAYNE MORRIS, Mary Ellen KAY.

Hijackers raid shipments designated for reservation Indians; a federal agent investigates. A few hillbilly songs are thrown in. It's essentially a throwback to the Gene Autry days. Country singer Robbins made a few mediocre Westerns, of which this one was typical.

BUGLES IN THE AFTERNOON (1952, PARA). D: Roy Rowland. W: Geoffrey Homes & Harry Brown from Ernest Haycox's novel. Cast: RAY MILLAND, HELENA CARTER, FORREST TUCKER, HUGH MARLOWE, Barton MacLANE, Sheb WOOLEY, James Millican, Gertrude Michael, George Reeves. 85m.

Seeking the villain who framed him, an embittered frontiersman (Milland, sadly miscast) enlists in the 7th Cavalry and joins Custer's army on its way to the celebrated debacle at Little Big Horn. Haycox's magnificent novel was turned into a dull, drab movie. Sheb Wooley is colorless as Custer; the milieu is sadly lacking (nearly the whole picture is confined boringly to sound-stage interiors). Tucker shines as a hard-drinking sergeant, but it's Tucker's role, not Haycox's; Barton MacLane, in one of his infrequent sympathetic roles, is acceptable; Hugh Marlowe is marvelous as the villainous Captain Garnett—he alone among the actors captures the Haycox characterization. Other than that it's a listless and shabby insult to a splendid book. Produced by William Cagney.

BULLET FOR A BADMAN (1964, UNIV). D: R.G. Springsteen. W: Mary & Willard Willingham from a novel by Marvin H. Albert. Cast: AUDIE MURPHY, Ruta LEE, Darren McGAVIN, Skip Homeier, Beverley Owen, Alan Hale, Jr., Edward C. Pratt, Mike Kellin, Bob Steele. 80m.

Ex-ranger marries ex-wife of ex-friend, who now robs a bank and then comes after the ex-ranger to get his son back and to exact revenge for the ex-ranger's having stolen his ex-wife. A confused posse chase ensues, complete with Indian fights and gun battles. Old-hat oater sports some superb stunt work; other than that, this tiresome Audiepic is notable only for McGavin's lusty performance as the ex-friend and Joseph F. Biroc's above-average color photography.

BULLWHIP (1958, AA). D: Harmon Jones. W: Adele Buffington. Cast: GUY MADISON, RHONDA FLEMING, James GRIFFITH, Don Beddoe, Dan Sheridan. 80m.

Frontiersman (Madison) is forced to marry shrewish woman (Fleming) in order to avoid being hanged; while he straightens out the muddled affairs of her fur-trading business he tries to humanize her. Very old-fashioned comedy is too cute for its own good.

THE BURNING HILLS (1956, WB). D: Stuart Heisler. W: Irving Wallace from Louis L'Amour's novel. Cast: TAB HUNTER, NATALIE WOOD, Skip HOMEIER, Eduard FRANZ, Ray Teal, Frank Puglia. 93m.

Two young lovers fight off a young psychotic suitor and a gang of unsavory killers in the employ of an evil cattle baron. Eduard Franz, as a wise old half-breed scout, steals what there is to steal of the picture. Hollywood was shooting for the teenage market with it, but the hacked-up Romeo-and-Juliet yarn is a clunker.

BUSH CHRISTMAS (1947, IND). DW: Ralph Smart. Cast: CHIPS RAFFERTY, Helen GRIEVE, Stan Tolhurst, John Fernside.

Five self-reliant kids making their way home through the Australian outback at Christmas time run afoul of horse thieves, and pursue them to get their horses back. It's not altogether unlike John Wayne's later film *The Cowboys*, and Australia's Chips Rafferty had a rough-hewn dignity similar to Wayne's. Superior and charming.

THE BUSHWHACKERS (1951, IND). D: Rod Amateau. W: Amateau & Tom Gries. Cast: JOHN IRELAND, WAYNE MORRIS, DOROTHY MALONE, Lawrence TIERNEY, Lon Chaney, Jr. 70m.

Bitter ex-Confederate (Ireland) has hung up his guns and vowed never to kill again. But circumstances force him to buckle 'em on again. Malone looks pained in her embarrassing rancher's daughter role; Ireland looks bored and Lawrence Tierney—look-alike brother of actor Scott Brady—is lethargically villainous. Routine range-war yarn.

BUTCH AND SUNDANCE: THE EARLY DAYS (1979, FOX). D: Richard Lester. W:

Allan Burns. Cast: WILLIAM KATT, TOM BERENGER, Jill EIKENBERRY, Jeff COREY, Arthur HILL, John SCHUCK, Peter Weller, Brian Dennehy, Michael C. Gwynne, Chris Lloyd. 110m.

Modest "prequel" features young look-alikes for Robert Redford (Katt) and Paul Newman (Berenger) as they set out on their early life of crime in a mutedly madcap West. William Goldman produced it but didn't write it; Jeff Corey repeats his role as a sheriff with elastic principles. Expertly directed. A poorly written minor diversion. The boys' genial immorality is not exactly a heroic example for kids to emulate.

BUTCH CASSIDY AND THE SUNDANCE KID (1969, FOX). D: George Roy Hill. W: William Goldman. Cast: PAUL NEW-MAN, ROBERT REDFORD, KATH-ARINE ROSS, Strother MARTIN, Jeff COREY, Cloris Leachman, Henry Jones, Ted Cassidy, Timothy Scott, George Furth, Kenneth Mars, Donnelly Rhodes, Percy Helton. 112m.

Two luckless outlaws and a good-natured schoolmarm, pursued by a relentless posse after a train robbery, clown their way from Wyoming's Hole-in-the-Wall to South America, encountering amusing characters in their picaresque adventures. The slick escapade alternates slapstick with pathos, leading to a grim ending that doesn't suit the mood of the earlier scenes. Supporting actors like Jeff Corey (as a corrupt sheriff), Strother Martin (as a Bolivian mine manager) and Cloris Leachman (as a hooker) add greatly to the fun, but Newman and Redford are splendidly engaging, and Ross is a fine match for them.

Hugely successful at the box office, this amiable oater won four Oscars (William Goldman for his witty script, Conrad Hall for his wide-screen photography, Burt Bacharach and Hal David for their spry score) and was nominated for two others (best direction, best film; and a subsequent collaboration among Newman, Redford and Hill did win best film—*The Sting*).

Oddly, in some ways the screenplay reads better than it plays. One doesn't notice the anachronisms so much on paper. On screen it doesn't quite convey the feeling that this really is the Old West of fact or of legend or even of tall tales; it seems merely a modern colorful reshaping with a pair of bemused and essentially pathetic characters. The story is actually true, mostly, but the flip banter is in keeping with a Neil Simon play; the fine production values and performances do not quite mitigate an essential sourness, and the

insertion at mid-point of the cute ballad "Raindrops Keep Fallin' on My Head" seems jarringly out of place. Certainly the film is not nearly as sincere or important an effort as the contemporaneous *The Wild Bunch*, but it's grand entertainment.

CAHILL, UNITED STATES MARSHAL (1973, WB). D: Andrew V. McLaglen. W: Harry Julian Fink, Rita M. Fink & Barney Slater. Cast: JOHN WAYNE, GEORGE KENNEDY, Neville BRAND, Gary GRIMES, Clay O'BRIEN, Marie Windsor, Royal Dano, Dan Vadis, Morgan Paull, Jackie Coogan, Denver Pyle, Harry Carey, Jr., Paul Fix, Hank Worden, Scott Walker, Rayford Barnes. 103m.

Upright superhuman old marshal is chagrined when his two sons (Grimes, O'Brien) get involved in a bank robbery. The two kids try to reform but have to fight it out with the rest of the gang (led by meanie George Kennedy). The early portion is the best, with an amusing portrayal by Neville Brand as an irascible half-breed scout; but then it degenerates into bathetic mawkishness and it stretches credulity beyond its limits; quite often it looks like one of those dreary vanity movies that overaged actresses used to make. Part of the picture was shot on locations in Mexico, the rest on studio back-lot exteriors at Burbank, and it's too easy to spot which scenes were shot where. All participants were old hands at this sort of thing and there are a few snappy lines of dialogue; Michael Wayne produced, for John Wayne's Batjac company; McLaglen's directing is, as always, efficient and amiable and appears effortless in its seamless smoothness; the Panavision Technicolor photography is by Joseph Biroc and there's one of Elmer Bernstein's lesser scores; in sum it's not the worst of Wayne's oaters but it's hardly the best.

CALAMITY JANE (1953, WB). D: David Butler. W: James O'Hanlon. Cast: DORIS DAY, HOWARD KEEL, Philip CAREY, Allyn McLERIE, Dick WESSON, Gale Robbins, Paul Harvey, Chubby Johnson, Jack Perrin, Rex Lease. 101m.

Keel is a robust genial Wild Bill Hickok in this frothy musical comedy; Day, a fine entertainer often ridiculed or underrated, is lively and lovely as the strident buckskin frontier gal, and the thin plot is mainly about the feminization of a tomboy. It's bouncy amusement—cute, charming, often funny, very well directed, and great fun. The songs, by Sammy Fain and Paul Francis Webster, include the Oscar-winning hit "Secret Love."

CALAMITY JANE AND SAM BASS (1949, UNIV). D: George Sherman. W: Sherman,

Maurice Geraghty & Melvin Levy. Cast: YVONNE De CARLO, HOWARD DUFF, Willard PARKER, Dorothy HART, Lloyd BRIDGES, Milburn Stone, Norman Lloyd, Clifton Young. 84m.

Outlaw meets lady; predictable results. There's a script with few discernible traces of wit, and De Carlo's overacting is hard to take, and the sophisticated Howard Duff has the decency to look pained. Ridiculous nonsense. In Technicolor.

CALIFORNIA (1947, PARA). D: John Farrow. W: Frank Butler, Theodore Strauss & Boris Ingster. Cast: RAY MILLAND, BARBARA STANWYCK, Barry FITZGERALD, Albert DEKKER, Anthony QUINN, Gavin Muir, Julia Faye, Frank Faylen, George Coulouris, James Burke, Eduardo Ciannelli, Stanley Andrews, Don Beddoe, Roman Bohnen, Ian Wolfe, Francis Ford. 87m.

Gritty wagon-train guide (Milland, miscast) runs afoul of villains who are trying to prevent California from achieving statehood, and falls in with a saloon gal (Stanwyck). With Technicolor photography (Ray Rennahan) and a heroic score (Victor Young) this one seemed to have ambitions to be a panoramic pioneer epic on the Cecil B. De Mille scale. Unfortunately it imitated De Mille's faults (it is turgid and ponderous) without finding any of his virtues. The elephantine drear seems mainly to have been shot on sound-stage sets and in-studio exteriors. Stanwyck, as usual, is better than her material; the others simply walk through.

CALIFORNIA (1963, AIP). D: Hamil Petroff. W: James West, from the screenplay for the 1947 version. Cast: JOCK MAHONEY, FAITH DOMERGUE, Michael PATE, Susan Seaforth, Rudolfo Hoyos. 97m.

Cheapjack remake is smaller, tighter and faster than the original, but it's all done on a shabby "B" level.

CALIFORNIA CONQUEST (1952, COL). D: Lew Landers. W: Robert E. Kent. Cast: CORNEL WILDE, TERESA WRIGHT, John DEHNER, Alfonso Bedoya, George Eldredge. 79m.

The background of this one is the unusual historical conflict between Spanish and Russian settlers on the West Coast of North America in the very early nineteenth century. There's a lot of fast movement but not a great deal of intelligible action. Routine.

THE CALIFORNIAN (1937, FOX). D: Gus Miens. W: Gilbert Wright from a Harold Bell Wright story. Cast: RICARDO COR-

TEZ, Marjorie WEAVER, Katherine De MILLE, Maurice Black, Pierre Watkin. 63m.

Laughing Latin bandit hero gets even with rich land-grabbers on behalf of the poor folks whose lands have been grabbed. The plot is interchangeable with those of the Zorro pictures and especially that of *Robin Hood of El Dorado*. Very dated moviemaking with stilted phony Mexican dialects.

CALIFORNIA PASSAGE (1950, REP). D: Joseph Kane. W: James Edward Grant. Cast: FORREST TUCKER, ADELE MARA, JIM DAVIS, Estelita Rodriguez, Rhys Williams, Peter Miles, Paul Fix, Charles Kemper, Francis J. McDonald, Eddy Waller, Charles Stevens, Alan Bridge, Iron Eyes Cody, Hal Taliaferro, Ruth Brennan. 90m.

The plot is warmed-over *The Covered Wagon* and it's a routine "B-plus" pioneering oater but it comes up as pretty good entertainment, professionally handled all around. Tucker in his infrequent leading-man roles proved both likable and believable; and the late Jim Davis, who died in April 1981 a star at last (he played Jock Ewing in the popular TV series "Dallas"), usually brought conviction and dignity to his Western movie portrayals. The two appeared together in numerous Republic oaters of the early 1950s, and added lustre to even the poorest of them; in the best of them (e.g., *Ride the Man Down*) they could be quite striking.

CALLAWAY WENT THATAWAY (1951, MGM). DW: Norman Panama & Melvin Frank. Cast: FRED MacMURRAY, DOROTHY McGUIRE, HOWARD KEEL, Jesse WHITE. Guest star cameos: CLARK GABLE, ELIZABETH TAYLOR, ROBERT TAYLOR. 81m.

Washed-up "B" cowboy star (Keel) finds his dead career revived by the sudden TV popularity of his old oaters. It's a spoof of the Hopalong Cassidy syndrome, with MacMurray and McGuire very funny as a pair of fast-talking promoters; the satirical burlesque of celebrity, press-agentry and television hype is hilariously right on the button. The film is similar in some ways to *Slim Carter*.

CAMPBELL'S KINGDOM (1957, J. Arthur Rank). D: Ralph Thomas. W: Robin Estridge from Hammond Innes's novel. Cast: DIRK BOGARDE, STANLEY BAKER, Barbara MURRAY, James Robertson JUSTICE, Michael CRAIG, John Laurie. 102m.

Young Englishman goes out to the wilderness of the Canadian Rockies to find out whether his late father's bequest of a possibly oil-bearing mountain is of any real value; he gets embroiled in a tough conflict between oil prospectors and dam builders. Big-scale English movie adheres closely to the Hammond Innes novel, although it was filmed not in Canada but in the European Alps. Excellent performances lead us to a stirring dam-busting climax; it's lusty and literate melodrama with a fine cast.

CANADIAN PACIFIC (1949, FOX). D: Edwin L. Marin. W: Jack DeWitt & Kenneth Gamet. Cast: RANDOLPH SCOTT, JANE WYATT, Victor JORY, J. Carrol NAISH, Nancy Olson, Walter Sande, Robert Barrat, John Hamilton. 94m.

Railroad-building and Indian-fighting Western has surveyor Scott overcoming all obstacles to ram his railroad through the mountains. Hardly up to the standard of *Union Pacific* but it's okay as routine entertainment.

THE CANADIANS (1961, FOX). DW: Burt Kennedy. Cast: ROBERT RYAN, Teresa STRATAS, John DEHNER, Torin THATCHER, Michael Pate, John Sutton, Burt Metcalf, Scott Peters, Richard Alden. 85m.

When six thousand Plains Indians cross over into Canada after wiping out Custer, three Canadian Mounties set out to deal with them (and with assorted baddies). Based loosely on fact, this one was filmed on Saskatchewan locations (in CinemaScope, by superb cinematographer Arthur Ibbetson) and the scenery is lovely but the script is flabby, opera star Stratas is an unconvincing squaw, and even the magnificent Robert Ryan can't save this soporific loser.

CANYON CROSSROADS (1955, UA). D: Alfred Werker. W: Emmett Murphy & Leonard M. Heideman. Cast: RICHARD BASEHART, PHYLLIS KIRK, Russell COLLINS, Stephen Elliott. 83m.

This one's an unusual Western about modern-style claim jumpers harassing prospectors in Utah during the big uranium rush. It's an extremely low-budget film in black-and-white, slow and stagy, but Basehart's strong acting lifts it above the ordinary.

CANYON PASSAGE (1946, UNIV). D: Jacques Tourneur. W: Ernest Pascal from Ernest Haycox's novel. Cast: DANA ANDREWS, SUSAN HAYWARD, BRIAN DONLEVY, HOAGY CARMICHAEL, Ward BOND, Andy DEVINE, Lloyd BRIDGES, Onslow Stevens, Patricia Roc, Fay Holden. 97m.

A ruggedly civilized freighter (Andrews) encounters hazards while building a commercial empire; his ambitions keep being interrupted by his compassion for troubled and afflicted comrades. A richly assorted cast of characters inhabits a complicated and romantically realistic plot, involving early Oregon settlers, displaced Indians, and varieties of plausible chicanery and weakness. There's sufficient action to attract the bust-'em-up aficionado, and Edward Cronjager's understated location color photography is magnificently suited to the story. The ensemble turns in an exquisite gathering of performances—particularly Onslow Stevens as a charmingly cynical gambler dying of consumption, Hoagy Carmichael as a bemused one-man chorus, Ward Bond as a simpleminded Indian-hater, Lloyd Bridges as a tough young hothead and Andy Devine as a good-natured farmer. Brian Donlevy turns in an unusually impressive performance as a weak-willed man with an addiction to poker, and Dana Andrews' work may be the best of his career, as the steady-nerved pipe-smoking Logan Stuart. The only flaw, and it is a slight one, is the casting of Susan Hayward; she is far too strong a personality to be altogether believable as the vacillating heroine torn between Andrews and Donlevy.

Canyon Passage is the only movie to have rendered on the screen a reasonably true reflection of the spirit and feeling of Ernest Haycox's storytelling, right down to his poetic and fascinating dialogue. His prose was lyrical and unique; somehow this film captures it.

CANYON RIVER (1956, AA). D: Harmon Jones. W: Daniel Ullman. Cast: GEORGE MONTGOMERY, MARCIA HENDERSON, Peter GRAVES, Richard Eyer, Francis J. McDonald, Jack Lambert. 80m.

Rancher (Montgomery) faces the obstacles of the cattle-drive trail: outlaws, Indians, so forth. Ullman was a veteran of the rustic cliches, and the movie is numbed and routine.

CAPTAIN JOHN SMITH AND POCAHONTAS (1953, UA). D: Lew Landers. W: Aubrey Wisberg & Jack Pollexsen. Cast: ANTHONY DEXTER, Jody LAWRENCE, Alan Hale, Jr. 74m.

Indian princess saves white settler from execution; you already know the story. Dexter achieved brief stardom because of his resemblance to Rudolph Valentino (he starred in the biopic *Valentino*); unhappily he was a dispirited actor. This one might be described charitably as a "B" movie.

CAPTAIN THUNDER (1931, WB). D: Alan Crosland. W: Gordon Rigby & William K.

Wells from *The Gay Caballero* by Hal Davitt & Pierre Conderc. Cast: VICTOR VAR-CONI, FAY WRAY, Charles Judels, Don Alvarado, Frank Campeau, Robert Elliott, Bert Roach.

Yet another dashing Mexican desperado yarn; poorer than most. Crosland is best remembered as the director of *The Jazz Singer* (1927).

THE CAPTURE (1951, RKO). D: John Sturges. W: Niven Busch. Cast: LEW AYRES, TERESA WRIGHT, Victor JORY, Duncan RENALDO. 81m.

An accidental killing preys on a man's conscience and he becomes a fugitive in Mexico. Thoughtful film is well done by major talents, marred mainly by a pat Hollywood ending.

THE CARIBOO TRAIL (1950, FOX). D: Edwin L. Marin. W: Frank Gruber & John R. Sturdy. Cast: RANDOLPH SCOTT, KAREN BOOTH, BILL WILLIAMS, Dale ROBERTSON, George "Gabby" HAYES, Victor JORY, Douglas KENNEDY, Kansas Moehring, James Griffith. 81m.

Prospectors versus claim-jumpers in the Canadian gold-country West of the 1890s. Fast slick-magazine script and steady performances help, but it's routine.

CARRY ON COWBOY (1966, WB). D: Gerald Thomas. W: Talbot Rothwell. Cast: KENNETH WILLIAMS, SIDNEY JAMES, Angela DOUGLAS, Jim DALE, Peter Butterworth, Alan Gifford, Jon Pertwee, Percy Herbert. 91m.

To clean up Stodge City, a sanitary engineer is sent instead of a marshal, with predictably loony results. Sid James makes an unusual Western outlaw, to say the least. This is hardly the best movie in the wacky British "Carry On" series but it's crudely funny and fast, with lots of enjoyable slapstick of the music-hall kind.

CARSON CITY (1952, WB). D: Andre De Toth. W: Sloan Nibley & Winston Miller. Cast: RANDOLPH SCOTT, RAYMOND MASSEY, Lucille NORMAN, Richard WEBB, James MILLICAN, Larry Keating, George Cleveland, Thurston Hall, Don Beddoe, George Keating, Vince Barnett. 87m.

Fast shoot-'em-up commences with an unusual stagecoach holdup with some coy twists (the road agents lay on a picnic for the passengers) but it's downhill from there as cheerful villain Massey (miscast) tries to prevent construction engineer Scott from building a railroad. Predictable oater has a bit of charm, a bit of humor, some woeful romantics and plenty of action. Dated but compe-

tent. It was the first movie filmed in the studio's new Warnercolor process.

CAST A LONG SHADOW (1959, UA). D: Thomas Carr. W: Martin Goldsmith & John McGreevy from a novel by Wayne D. Overholser. Cast: AUDIE MURPHY, TERRY MOORE, John DEHNER, James BEST, Ann Doran, Denver Pyle, Rita Lynn. 82m.

Drifter returns to the old homestead, and the old feuds are rekindled. Slow but steady formula yarn, slick-magazine style; plenty of plot and action.

THE CAT (1966, EMB). D: Ellis Kadison. W: William Redlin & Laird Koenig. Cast: Roger PERRY, Peggy Ann GARNER, Barry Coe. 83m.

Boy gets lost in the Rockies, makes friends with a mountain lion, is captured by a mean rustler and is rescued from the bad guy's clutches by the mountain lion. Shades of Androcles.

CAT BALLOU (1965, COL). D: Elliott Silverstein. W: Walter Newman & Frank R. Pierson from Roy Chanslor's novel *The Ballad of Cat Ballou*. Cast: JANE FONDA, LEE MARVIN, Michael CALLAN, John MARLEY, Tom NARDINI, Dwayne Hickman, Reginald Denny, Nat "King" Cole, Stubby Kaye, Arthur Hunnicutt, Jay C. Flippen, Bruce Cabot, Nick Cravat. 96m.

When a young woman's father falls ill, human vultures gather, intending to make off with his estate. The young woman hires a gunslinger to defend them, only to learn that her chosen defender is a hopeless drunk and a clumsy stumblebum. That's about the sum of the plot; its developments are fairly absurd. *Cat Ballou* satirizes just about everything and if you blink you may miss a good gag, but it's not overblown like *The Hallelujah Trail* or tasteless like *There Was a Crooked Man* or anachronistic like *Blazing Saddles*; it doesn't strain for laughs—it merely earns them. Tom Nardini is amusing as a sarcastic young Indian but most of the characters are just cutouts; even Jane Fonda has little to do except act wide-eyed and lovable and go along with the absurd plot; the picture stands or falls on Lee Marvin's Oscar-winning dual performance, and it stands, heroically, because Marvin is magnificent (and incredibly funny) as the washed-up drunken ex-gunfighter and his deadly noseless killer brother. He is awesome. And his drunken horse is great, too.

CATLOW (1971, MGM). D: Sam Wanamaker. W: Scot Finch & J.J. Griffith from Louis L'Amour's novel. Cast: YUL BRYNNER, RICHARD CRENNA, Leonard NIMOY, Jo Ann PFLUG, Jeff COREY, Daliah LAVI, David Ladd, Walter Coy, Julian Mateos, Jose Nieto, Bessie Love. 101m.

An ingratiating bandit (Brynner) keeps trying to heist $2 million in gold from a Yankee prison while being pursued, separately, by a good-natured tough lawman (Crenna), a bad-natured mean villain (Nimoy) and the whole Mexican army. Filmed in Spain, produced on a sizable budget, well photographed in color (Ted Scaife), serviceably scored (Roy Budd), briskly edited (John Glen), directed at panic-stricken speed with nonstop action, the picture manages nonetheless to be dreary and listless. Like many Westerns of the 1970s it tries to apologize for its abundant cliches by half-heartedly satirizing itself but, like most spoof Westerns, it fails to decide whether it's burlesque or melodrama or parody. L'Amour's novel was done with straightforward gusto, and had the film emulated that, it might have worked; as it is, the actors seem to have something else on their minds—probably how soon they can finish this rancid nonsense and get on the next plane home.

CATTLE ANNIE AND LITTLE BRITCHES (1981, UNIV). D: Lamont Johnson. W: David Eyre & Robert Ward. Cast: BURT LANCASTER, ROD STEIGER, DIANE LANE, AMANDA PLUMMER, JOHN SAVAGE, John QUADE, Steven Ford, Redmond Gleeson, William Russ, Scott Glenn. 95m.

Based loosely on fact, this one follows a couple of feisty teen-age girls as, enamored of Ned Buntline's heroic dime novels, they ride off to join up with a scruffy gang of Daltin-Doolin outlaws led by crusty Burt Lancaster. The outlaws perpetrate various semi-comic capers and sweepingly chivalrous generosities while pursued by a relentless lawman played in suitably flowery fashion by Rod Steiger. Excellent camera work (Larry Pizer) on Durango locations, and a primitive but fitting score (Sanh Berti, Tom Slocum), help make this comedy-drama one of the more appealing minor Westerns of the early 1980s.

CATTLE DRIVE (1951, UNIV). D: Kurt Neumann. W: Jack Natteford & Lillie Hayward. Cast: JOEL McCREA, Dean STOCKWELL, Leon Ames, Chill Wills. 77m.

Title tells all. Charming, amiable, predictable, forgettable.

CATTLE EMPIRE (1958, FOX). D: Charles Marquis Warren. W: Daniel Ullman, Endre Bohen & Eric Norden. Cast: JOEL McCREA, Gloria TALBOT, Don Haggerty, Phyllis Coates. 82m.

The wheeze about the drifter taken for an outlaw by mistake and forced to clear himself. Competent.

CATTLE KING (1963, MGM). Also titled: GUNS OF WYOMING. D: Tay Garnett. W: Thomas Thompson. Cast: ROBERT TAYLOR, JOAN CAULFIELD, Robert LOGGIA, Robert MIDDLETON, Larry Gates, Ray Teal, Malcolm Atterbury, William Windom. 88m.

Tough rancher (Taylor) is humanized by love, and by the events of a Wyoming range war. Novelist Thompson (not the same one who writes best-selling nonfiction) is a charming Californian/Oregonian who created the *Bonanza* television series; his screen stories tend to feature family relationships, character values and plenty of sentiment. This one was premiered in Odessa, Texas, at the annual convention of the Western Writers of America; I was there, and so was Tommy Thompson, and even though he'd seen it before, the picture brought a tear to Tommy's eye. But then he admits that he cries at supermarket openings.

CATTLE QUEEN (1951, UA). D: Robert Tansey. W: Frances Kavanaugh & Robert Emmett. Cast: Maria HART, John CARPENTER, Drake Smith, William Fawcett, Emile Meyer.

Lady rancher versus bandits and grade Z; this was one of several John Carpenter-produced indies released through United Artists. (He's not the same John Carpenter who made a name for himself directing horror and SF movies starting in the late 1970s.)

CATTLE QUEEN OF MONTANA (1954, RKO). D: Allan Dwan. W: Tom W. Blackburn, Ted Richmond, Robert Blees & Howard Estabrook. Cast: BARBARA STANWYCK, RONALD REAGAN, Gene EVANS, Yvette Dugay, Lance Fuller, Jack Elam, Anthony Caruso, Morris Ankrum, Myron Healey, Chubby Johnson, Rodd Redwing. 88m.

Cattle baron is murdered and his gun-slinging daughter has to fight off the land-grabbing killers as well as a tribe of incensed Indians. Stanwyck gives a far better performance than the movie deserves, but she usually does that. Ronald Reagan gets to play her best friend, but only because Robert Mitchum—originally slated by RKO to co-star in this dog—took one look at the script and went fishing. He was suspended by the studio but he was right to avoid the movie; you'd do well to emulate him.

CATTLE TOWN (1952, WB). D: Noel Smith. W: Tom W. Blackburn. Cast:

DENNIS MORGAN, AMANDA BLAKE, PHILIP CAREY, Rita MORENO, Sheb Wooley, Merv Griffin, Ray Teal, Paul Picerni, Jay Novello, Robert J. Wilke, George O'Hanlon, 71m.

Lawman cleans up tough town. Tenor Morgan had lost none of his charm but he'd gained plenty of weight by the time this was filmed; the movie is equally flabby. Produced by Bryan Foy.

CAUGHT (1931, PARA). D: Edward Sloman. W: Agnes B. Leahy, Keene Thompson, Bella & Sam Spewack. Cast: RICHARD ARLEN, FRANCES DEE, Louise DRESSER, Tom Kennedy, Sid Saylor, Edward Le Saint, James Mason.

Dance-hall madam Calamity Jane (Dresser) complicates the love life of a marshal and his girl friend; mixed into the recipe are the cavalry and some Indians. Forgotten and forgettable. Note that James Mason was an American silent-movie actor who usually portrayed villains and was not related to the English actor of same name of more recent films.

CAVALIER OF THE WEST (1931, IND). DW: J.P. McCarthy. Cast: HARRY CAREY, KANE RICHMOND, Carmen La ROUX, George "Gabby" Hayes, Carlotta Monti. 75m.

This quickie was a programmer that came out prior to Carey's resurgence in *Trader Horn*; the routine hero-versus-landgrabbers flick was of interest mainly because of the presence of Carlotta Monti, who later was to become W. C. Fields's mistress.

CAVALRY COMMAND (1963, IND). D: Lesley Selander. W: Eddie Romero. Cast: JOHN AGAR, Richard ARLEN.

Spanish-American War Western was transplanted to the Philippines and filmed on location there with cowboys-and-Moros action. Haven't seen it.

CAVALRY SCOUT (1951, MONO). D: Lesley Selander. W: Daniel Ullman. Cast: ROD CAMERON, JIM DAVIS, Audrey LONG, James MILLICAN, John Doucette, Cliff Clark, Stephen Chase. 78m.

Heroic scout searches for stolen army property, fights off Indians and finds romance with the sutler's daughter. Familiar and insipid.

CAVE OF OUTLAWS (1952, UNIV). D: William Castle. W: Elizabeth Wilson. Cast: MacDONALD CAREY, ALEXIS SMITH, Victor JORY, Edgar BUCHANAN, Hugh O'Brian, Housely Stevenson, Charles Horvath. 75m.

Most of this movie seems to take place inside Colossal Cave (in southern Arizona) where an unsavory group of rival, greedy characters are hunting for Jesse James's buried treasure. Evidently the actors were able to survive the stench in that cave; as for the film, it doesn't.

THE CHARGE AT FEATHER RIVER (1953, WB). D: Gordon Douglas. W: James R. Webb. Cast: GUY MADISON, FRANK LOVEJOY, VERA MILES, Helen WESTCOTT, Steve BRODIE, Neville BRAND, Ron Hagerthy, Dick Wesson, Onslow Stevens, James Brown, Lane Chandler, Rand Brooks, Dub Taylor. 96m.

Pity the poor compositor-writer who must keep straight the spellings and distinctions among Dan Haggerty, Don Haggerty and Ron Hagerthy.

The story here is the chestnut about the heroic frontiersman (Madison) who leads one tough veteran sergeant (Lovejoy) and a detachment of loafers, prisoners, greenhorns and misfits into Indian territory to rescue two captured girls. Originally released in 3-D, it was intended as a blockbuster and was given a lavish Max Steiner score and high-priced Warnercolor photography by Peverell Marley, complete with the gimmicky 3-D emphasis on a constant hurtling toward the audience's laps of arrows, tomahawks, spears, fists, knives, bodies and even spittle. Guy Madison, fresh from a long-running stint as TV's "Wild Bill Hickok," acts woefully herein; Douglas directs listlessly; Webb's script, arguably his poorest, leaves few cliches unturned. Lovejoy stands out with a taut portrayal of a bitter man, and the film is nearly worth seeing merely for his performance, but the rest of the actors put very little into it and as a result the audience gets very little out.

CHARLEY ONE-EYE (1973, PARA). D: Don Chaffey. W: Keith Leonard. Cast: RICHARD ROUNDTREE, Roy THINNES, Nigel DAVENPORT. 107m.

Black army deserter and his Indian pal encounter assorted hostile individuals whom the two find various bloody ways to kill. Thinnes plays the Indian as if he were born and raised on the streets of Brooklyn; Nigel Davenport, an Englishman, overplays the bounty hunter who's chasing them; Roundtree tries to muster dignity but is defeated by the horrible script. This nauseating and offensive oater was produced by that presumed humanist liberal, television personality David Frost.

CHARRO! (1969, NGP). D: Charles Marquis Warren. W: Warren & Frederic Louis Fox. Cast: ELVIS PRESLEY, INA BALIN, Victor FRENCH, Lynn Kellogg, Barbara Werle, Solomon Sturges, Paul Brinegar, Tony Young, Rodd Redwing. 98m.

Non-musical Western has the star as a tough lawman. You can tell he's supposed to be tough because he hasn't shaved. Non-entertaining as well. A thoroughgoing turkey.

CHATO'S LAND (1972, UA). D: Michael Winner. W: Gerald Wilson. Cast: CHARLES BRONSON, JACK PALANCE, Richard BASEHART, James WHITMORE, Sonia Rangan, Simon Oakland, Ralph Waite, Richard Jordan, Victor French, William Watson, Paul Young, Raul Castro. 110m.

A half-breed Apache (Bronson) is goaded into a fight by a white sheriff and kills him, and is chased by a bigoted posse into Indian country where he picks off his pursuers one by one. When they are all dead the movie is over.

The script attempts to develop its characters but none of it is remotely believable; both writer and director are British, with no evident feeling for the West. You've seen it all before; it's assembled of bits and pieces of *Valdez is Coming, Apache, The Stalking Moon, The Professionals* and *The Searchers.* Bronson's role actually is small and mostly invisible; the protagonist is Major Quincy Whitmore (Palance), an ex-Confederate cavalry officer who leads the posse. Palance's restrained performance is good and one sympathizes with his character; unhappily the "hero" is not nearly as well conceived: Chato is one-dimensional, expressionless, an emotionless killer in the spaghetti-Western mold. The rest of the characters—particularly a warped, vicious, Indian hater (Oakland) and a drunken crackerbarrel philosopher (Basehart)—are measured from the usual old cloth and cut to fit. Director Winner once described the audience for his films to me as "thirteen-year-olds in black leather jackets with zipper pockets. They don't want any of that love stuff. They just want bang-bang." They get plenty of it in cheesy, dreary, phony pictures like this one.

CHEROKEE STRIP (1940, PARA). D: Lesley Selander. W: Norman Houston & Bernard McConville. Cast: RICHARD DIX, FLORENCE RICE, Victor JORY, Andy Clyde, George E. Stone, Douglas Fowley, Morris Ankrum, Tom Tyler, Addison Richards, William Henry. 86m.

Bad guys observe that outlaws use the Strip as a hideout, and use that fact as a pious excuse to steal Indian lands. Upstanding lawman intervenes. It's not up to Dix's usual level but it's better than most "B-plus" oaters of its period.

(Not to be confused with the 1937 *Cherokee Strip*, a Warner Brothers programmer with Dick Foran.)

CHEYENNE (1947)—*See* THE WYOMING KID.

CHEYENNE AUTUMN (1964, WB). D: John Ford. W: James R. Webb from Mari Sandoz's novel. Cast: RICHARD WIDMARK, CARROLL BAKER, JAMES STEWART, EDWARD G. ROBINSON, Karl MALDEN, Sal MINEO, Ricardo MONTALBAN, Arthur KENNEDY, Dolores DEL RIO, Gilbert ROLAND, John CARRADINE, Ben JOHNSON, Elizabeth ALLEN, Patrick WAYNE, Victor JORY, Harry Carey, Jr., Denver Pyle, Mike Mazurki, Ken Curtis, George O'Brien, Shug Fisher, John Qualen, Sean McClory, Carleton Young. 157m.

Cavalry officer (Widmark) does his damnedest to see that the Cheyenne Indians get fair treatment after a peace treaty is signed. The story has a hard time working because it's based on the premise that his efforts will be doomed. It becomes terribly diffuse, with pointless distractions such as a comical poker game featuring James Stewart (as Wyatt Earp) and Arthur Kennedy (as Doc Holliday), both wasted in cameo parts. The statement about the ordeal of the Cheyennes is quite moving, and so long as the movie focuses on that issue it is fine, with good performances (as the Indians) by Del Rio, Roland, Montalban and even Mineo. The William Clothier photography is panoramic, although not quite up to Ford's best standard; Alex North's music is a good complement; Edward G. Robinson has a tiny but outstanding bit as Secretary of the Interior Carl Schurz—a role earmarked for Spencer Tracy, who had to forego it because of illness.

It's a Ford picture (his last Western) and therefore more rewarding than most others, but it's bottom-drawer Ford, flawed by its topheavy casting and its turgid script and by an unusually bad, even for him, performance by Karl Malden in a key role as a Prussian martinet; and such stalwarts as Ben Johnson, Harry Carey, Jr. and Denver Pyle have such fleeting moments on screen that you may not even notice them. It was presented by the *Harvard Lampoon* with a "worst film of the year" award.

THE CHEYENNE SOCIAL CLUB (1970, NGP). D: Gene Kelly. W: James Lee Barrett. Cast: JAMES STEWART, HENRY FONDA, SHIRLEY JONES, Sue Ann

LANGDON, Robert MIDDLETON, Elaine Devry, Arch Johnson, Dabbs Greer. 103m.

Washed-up cowpoke inherits a whorehouse. Trivia buffs can stump their friends ("What Western movie did Gene Kelly direct?") but that's about the only distinction it has to offer. There's a dearth of wit and the comedy falls flat despite heroic efforts on the part of the stars and director. Fonda and Stewart are never *not* worth watching, and Kelly is never without style and grace, but the story is forced and heavy.

CHIEF CRAZY HORSE (1955, UNIV). D: George Sherman. W: Franklin Coen & Gerald D. Adams. Cast: VICTOR MATURE, SUZAN BALL, JOHN LUND, Keith LARSEN, Ray DANTON, David JANSSEN, Robert Warwick, Morris Ankrum, Robert F. Simon, Donald Randolph, James Millican, James Westerfield. 86m.

Friendship between Sioux chief (Mature) and cavalry major (Lund) is eroded by conflicts between the races. It's slow until the big climax but the cast is good (Mature is surprisingly convincing). Suzan Ball, having had a leg amputated against cancer, went ahead and starred in the picture but died soon after its completion; she was twenty-three.

CHISUM (1970, WB). D: Andrew V. McLaglen. W: Andrew J. Fenady. Cast: JOHN WAYNE, FORREST TUCKER, Ben JOHNSON, Patric KNOWLES, Glenn CORBETT, Christopher GEORGE, Geoffrey DEUEL, Bruce Cabot, Andrew Prine, Richard Jaeckel, John Agar, Ray Teal, John Mitchum, Ron Soble, Glenn Langan, Alan Baxter, Pedro Armendariz, Jr., Chris Mitchum. Narrator (unbilled): WILLIAM CONRAD. 111m.

There was a real John Chisum (Wayne)—a Texas cattleman—and there was a real Lincoln County (New Mexico) range war in the early 1880s between the forces of ranchers Tunstall and McSween and featuring the gunplay of Billy the Kid (Deuel) and Pat Garrett (Corbett), but actually the two things had nothing to do with each other except in this movie, in which range baron Wayne mixes it up with rustlers and a rival cattle king (Tucker), with plenty of hard-eyed glaring and threat-slinging and a lot of action coming to a big climax with a glorious and wholly unrealistic Hollywood orgy of shooting and stunt falls, choreographed with the slick hokey professionalism that characterizes many of the McLaglen-Wayne oaters. It's juvenile and trite but as sheer action entertainment for the young-minded it's just fine.

CHUKA (1967, PARA). D: Gordon Douglas. W: Richard Jessup from his novel. Cast: ROD TAYLOR, JOHN MILLS, ERNEST BORGNINE, Luciana PALUZZI, James WHITMORE, Louis HAYWARD, Angela Dorian, Michael Cole. 105m.

An isolated cavalry fort sits out in the middle of nowhere (a plain in Spain) and a horde of Arapahos besiege it, and inside we find an assortment of folks trying to survive. They include Australian actor Taylor as a Western buckskin-jacketed frontiersman, English actor Mills as the cavalry commander, South African actor Hayward as a lecherous drunken officer, Italian actress Paluzzi as a Mexican noblewoman and New York-accented Borgnine as an Irish sergeant. Only James Whitmore manages to be less than ridiculous, as a grizzled hard-drinking civilian scout. The fort, in which the entire action takes place, looks as if it is constructed of balsa and papier mâché; the Indians appear to be "surrounding" it from only one side—all other sides seem wide open but the dialogue keeps telling us that nobody could possibly get out and run for help. Evidently the actors believed it because the writer and director told them to. We wait nearly two hours for the action; when it comes it's flat, unexciting and anticlimactic. The miscasting and amateurishness of performance are matched only by the triteness of the screenplay. Calling this movie bad is like calling a dwarf short.

CIMARRON (1931, RKO). D: Wesley Ruggles. W: Howard Estabrook from Edna Ferber's novel. Cast: RICHARD DIX, IRENE DUNNE, William COLLIER, Jr., Estelle TAYLOR, Edna May Oliver, Nance O'Neil, George E. Stone, Roscoe Ates, Frank Darien, Dennis O'Keeffe. 115m.

Cimarron was the biggest money-maker of 1931 and it won the best picture Oscar, as well as Oscars for best writing adaptation (Estabrook) and best art direction (Max Ree); it was nominated for best direction (Ruggles) and best actress (Dunne). The opening spectacle—the Oklahoma land rush—is tremendous and it's a solid empire-building movie about the conversion of Indian Territory into the state of Oklahoma and the subsequent building of oil feifdoms in the Sooner State; it's soap more than horse opera, spanning forty years in the lives of Yancey Cravat (Dix) and his bride (Dunne, in her film debut), with numerous subplots, imposing photography (Edward Cronjager), a music score of Wagnerian proportion (Max Steiner) and production on a De Mille scale. The picture temporarily rescued RKO

Radio-Pathe from a slide toward bankruptcy. Still, it leaves quite a lot to be desired for modern audiences, and with the climactic land-rush at the beginning rather than the end, it has nowhere to go but downhill. Although just as dated, William S. Hart's *Tumbleweeds* is a more stirring movie about the same time and place.

CIMARRON (1960, MGM). D: Anthony Mann. W: Arnold Schulman from Edna Ferber's novel. Cast: GLENN FORD, MARIA SCHELL, ANNE BAXTER, Arthur O'CONNELL, Edgar BUCHANAN, Aline MacMAHON, Russ TAMBLYN, Robert KEITH, Vic Morrow, Mercedes McCambridge, John Cason, Charles McGraw. 140m.

Flaccid remake of the 1931 film features a good cast but the screenplay is turgid, swollen and not nearly as effective as Estabrook's thirty years earlier; and those who believe in an Anthony Mann oeuvre will have a difficult time finding a place in it for this dispirited elephantine sprawl.

THE CIMARRON KID (1951, UNIV). D: Budd Boetticher. W: Louis Stevens & Kay Lenard. Cast: AUDIE MURPHY, Yvette DUGAY, James BEST, Beverly Tyler, Noah Beery, Jr. 84m.

The Dalton gang (Best, Beery) harasses an ex-gang member (Murphy) who's trying to go straight. Unexceptional oater is nowhere near as solid a job as the movies Boetticher directed with Randolph Scott later in the decade.

THE CISCO KID (1931, MGM). D: Irving Cummings. W: Alfred A. Cohn from an O. Henry story. Cast: WARNER BAXTER, Edmund LOWE, Conchita Montenegro, Willard Robertson, Nora Lane.

Laughing Latin bandit turns himself in for the reward on his own head so he can give the money to a girl in danger of foreclosure.

This was the first movie to use this title but actually it was the third movie about the Cisco Kid, second sequel to *In Old Arizona*, which started the cycle, and *The Arizona Kid*. Budget, production values and cast put all three in the "A" category but they're essentially "B" yarns.

CITY OF BAD MEN (1953, FOX). D: Harmon Jones. W: George W. George & George Slavin. Cast: DALE ROBERTSON, JEANNE CRAIN, Richard BOONE, Lloyd Bridges, Carl Betz. 82m.

A gang of outlaws plans to steal the cash take from the historic Fitzsimmons-Corbett boxing match in Carson City, Nevada, at the turn of the century. Caper yarn is a somewhat

different sort of oater. Fair entertainment, routinely executed.

COLE YOUNGER, GUNFIGHTER (1958, AA). D: R.G. Springsteen. W: Daniel Mainwaring from a Clifton Adams story. Cast: FRANK LOVEJOY, James BEST, Abby DALTON, Jan Merlin, George Keymas. 78m.

Reformed gunslinger has to buckle on his guns again and fight off the outlaw gang that's treeing the town. There's some romance thrown in, and a court trial; a lot of confused subplotting and some tough jaw-jutting. Lovejoy, whose career was at a low ebb when he made this cheapie, makes it bearable, but only just.

COLORADO TERRITORY (1949, WB). D: Raoul Walsh. W: John Twist & Edmund H. North. Cast: JOEL McCREA, VIRGINIA MAYO, Dorothy MALONE, Henry HULL, John ARCHER, Morris ANKRUM, Ian Wolfe, Harry Woods, James Mitchell, Frank Puglia, Houseley Stevenson. 92m.

Ex-convict and his girl set up a caper; it goes sour, and the two end up trapped by a posse in a towering rocky canyon. It's a bald-faced Western remake of Walsh's Bogart gangster classic *High Sierra* and it is not really the "psychological Western" it has been called; it's merely the grim hard ending that has distorted the movie's critical reputation, since its flavor otherwise is more realistic than Gothic. The exciting stunt and action sequences are directed with Walsh's customary great skill. David Buttolph's score is dull, unfortunately, but the performances—particularly by McCrea as the doomed drifter and Ankrum as the marshal who relentlessly hounds him—are outstanding. A very superior Western.

COLT .45 (1950)—*See* THUNDERCLOUD.

COLUMN SOUTH (1953, UNIV). D: Frederick de Cordova. W: William Sackheim. Cast: AUDIE MURPHY, JOAN EVANS, Robert STERLING, Dennis WEAVER, Jack KELLY, Ray Collins, Ralph Moody, Russell Johnson, Bob Steele. 85m.

Young cavalry officer (Murphy) tries to forestall a Navajo uprising in New Mexico during the Civil War. Slow, limp, uninspired.

COMANCHE (1956, UA). D: George Sherman. W: Carl Krueger. Cast: DANA ANDREWS, Linda CRISTAL, Kent SMITH, Reed Sherman, Nestor Paiva, Henry Brandon, Stacy Harris, John Litel, Mike Mazurki. 87m.

After Comanches raid a Mexican town and kidnap several women, a civilian scout (Andrews) tries to expose dastardly renegades and bring peace between Indians and white soldiers. It's lavish with CinemaScope scenery in Mexico (cinematography by Jorge Stahl, Jr.); it looks big; it tries to include some history about Chief Quanah Parker (Smith); and there's plenty of action. But the character intervals are lifeless, the directing drab and the script flaccid; none of the actors seems interested. The score (Herschel Burke Gilbert) is a major detraction.

THE COMANCHEROS (1961, FOX). D: Michael Curtiz. W: James Edward Grant & Clair Huffaker from Paul I. Wellman's novel. Cast: JOHN WAYNE, STUART WHITMAN, INA BALIN, LEE MARVIN, Nehemiah PERSOFF, Bruce CABOT, Michael ANSARA, Edgar Buchanan, Joan O'Brien, Patrick Wayne, Jack Elam, Bob Steele, Richard Devon, John Dierkes, Guinn "Big Boy" Williams. 107m.

A hardbitten Texas Ranger (Wayne) gets mixed up with a roguish gambler (Whitman), a loudmouthed killer (Marvin) and then a gang of Comanchero renegades (Persoff, Ansara) whom the two heroes outfight in their Mexican lair. It's big and lusty, and Lee Marvin is marvelously flamboyant but his role is quite brief. Whitman's overblown performance in the key role of dashing Paul Regret is hard to swallow. The first half of this long rambling film has little to do with the second half; it begins as a tongue-in-cheek farce but turns grim at midpoint with abrupt streaks of meanness and brutality. The huge action scene at the end seems to have been lifted bodily from Wayne's earlier, and far better, *Hondo*. The flip script is characterized by a hokey slickness that is unlike the two screenwriters' usual work; it fails to live up to the virtues of Wellman's panoramic novel.

This was the last film Michael Curtiz directed; he died soon after. Best known for his fast melodramas like *Casablanca*, Curtiz was a Warner Brothers contract director throughout his American career, and like the studio that employed him he never got a handle on Westerns. All his oaters, including several Errol Flynn Westerns, had good pace and superficial gloss but the overall flavor was that of pulp hack work, partly the result of poor screenplays but largely the fact of bad casting, since Curtiz had no feel for the West; three key co-stars in this film (Whitman, Balin, Persoff) are badly out of place in the filmic West. *The Comancheros* is big and lusty, and has its fans, but as cohesive drama it's third rate, and wasn't improved on in its unacknowledged remake, *Rio Conchos*.

COMANCHE STATION (1960, COL). D: Budd Boetticher. W: Burt Kennedy. Cast: RANDOLPH SCOTT, NANCY GATES, Claude AKINS, Skip HOMEIER, Rand Brooks. 74m.

Indians have kidnapped a rancher's wife and when he goes in search of them he tangles with a woman and three hard-bitten bad guys. Very low-budget movie is shot entirely outdoors with a very small cast; it has that peculiar dark-side quality that the best of the Kennedy-Boetticher-Scott oaters had, and it's consistently exciting even though you have to regard Scott's latter-day Westerns as the equivalent of "B" product; in that context they were superbly made.

Except for his emergence from retirement for *Ride the High Country* two years later, this was Randolph Scott's last movie.

COMANCHE TERRITORY (1950, UNIV). D: George Sherman. W: Oscar Brodney & Lewis Meltzer. Cast: MacDONALD CAREY, MAUREEN O'HARA, Charles DRAKE, James BEST, Will Geer, Edmund Cobb, Rick Vallin. 76m.

White villains victimize the Indians; Jim Bowie (Carey) comes to the rescue. Nothing to do with the real Bowie (inventor of the famous knife, and hero of the Alamo) or even the legendary, and despite its upper-case stars it's a lower-case movie. Carey, a good but rather urban and urbane actor who subsequently found a niche as a star of TV soap opera, is not believable as the tough brawling frontiersman; the big knife fight between him and the Comanche chief is laughably bad. In Technicolor.

COMES A HORSEMAN (1978, UA). D: Alan Pakula. W: Dennis Lynton Clark. Cast: JAMES CAAN, JANE FONDA, JASON ROBARDS, JR., George GRIZZARD, Richard FARNSWORTH, Jim Davis. 118m.

In 1945 Colorado a feisty pair of neighbor ranchers (Fonda, Caan) join to fight an evil range baron (Robards) and his dude henchman (Grizzard) who want to drive them off their land. The plot is pure "B" movie, complete with bushwhackings, saloon fistfight, stampede and a perfunctory last-reel gunfight. The wide-screen photography (Gordon Willis) paints lovely scenery but is otherwise misbegotten, inasmuch as the camera is invariably too far from the action or too close to it. The script has no surprises; I found I was silently saying most of the lines before the actors spoke them—it's that predictable. If the filmmakers had known anything at all about Westerns they might have avoided some of the pitfalls into which this creature of numbing cliches stumbles unerringly. It's both pedestrian and lugubriously overblown;

self-consciousness colors every frame. The hero is utterly without personality and the heroine lacks definition: she has many parts but no whole. Farnsworth, as an old cowhand, was mentioned for several acting awards, but his is the only outstanding performance in the film, which is otherwise a bore.

COMIN' AT YA (1981, IND). D: Ferdinando Baldi. W: Lloyd Battista, Wolf Lowenthal, Gene Quintano, Tony Petitto. Cast: TONY ANTHONY, Victoria ABRIL, Gene Quintano, Ricardo Palacios. 97m.

White slavers kidnap a bride at the altar and leave the groom wounded. He goes after them. Many rapes and massacres later, man and wife are reunited. This despicable trash seems designed to exploit the basest fantasies of bloodthirsty savages; it would offend the taste of a halfwit. But it sold tickets, because it was the first major 3-D release in 17 years.

THE COMMAND (1953, WB). D. David Butler. W: Samuel Fuller & Russell Hughes from a James Warner Bellah novel. Cast: GUY MADISON, JOAN WELDON, JAMES WHITMORE, Carl Benton REID, Harvey Lembeck, Ray Teal, Bob Nichols, Don Shelton, Jim Bannon. 88m.

Young army doctor must take command of a cavalry troop in Wyoming, where he faces mutinous soldiers, angry Indians and an epidemic to boot. This was the first Western in CinemaScope (cinematographer Wilfrid M. Cline) and it was given a big production—lots of extras in the battle scenes, sweeping vistas, a towering Dimitri Tiomkin score. But the overplotted story, one of Bellah's poorest, was given short shrift by the screenwriters; the directing is lackadaisical; many of the actors seem uninterested or untalented; and it all simmers into a large but tepid stew.

THE CONQUERORS (1932, RKO). D: William Wellman. W: Howard Estabrook. Cast: RICHARD DIX, ANN HARDING, Edna May Oliver, Donald Cook, Guy Kibbee. 80m.

The arrival of a new railroad takes the place of the land rush in this imitation *Cimarron* that was designed to cash in on the success of the previous year's big hit. There are well-handled dramatics and big production scenes; it's a superior but dated horse opera of the period.

CONQUEST OF COCHISE (1953, COL). D: William Castle. W: Arthur Lewis & DeVallon Scott. Cast: ROBERT STACK, JOHN HODIAK, Joy PAGE, Carol Thurston, Alex Montoya, Fortunio Bonanova, Rodd Redwing, Rico Alaniz. 70m.

Charming love-the-ladies cavalry major (Stack, better than he needs to be) tries to make peace with Apache leader Cochise (Hodiak, ludicrously miscast) despite racial tensions and melodramatic machinations by crude villains.

After the popular success of *Broken Arrow* every hack Hollywood moviemaker tried to capitalize on the romantic celebrity of Cochise. This attempt, by programmer mogul Sam Katzman, is one of the worst—a poor "B" movie with two "A" stars but a "Z" script and an inept supporting cast, a lousy score (Mischa Bakaleinikov) and unimaginative photography (Henry Freulich). The historical anachronisms are absurd: the movie postulates that there are forty thousand ferocious Apache warriors in 1853 Arizona, all on horseback and wearing warbonnets and firing 1894-model repeating rifles. There were in fact a few hundred Chiricahua Apache warriors at most, at any given time, and usually they went to war on foot, armed with Stone Age weapons and never wearing feathered headdresses. But forget history; even on its own never-never-land terms the film is dreary and imbecilic.

COPPER CANYON (1950, PARA). D: John Farrow. W: Jonathan Latimer & Richard English. Cast: RAY MILLAND, HEDY LAMARR, MacDONALD CAREY, MONA FREEMAN, Harry CAREY, Jr., Kent TAYLOR, Hope EMERSON, Frank Faylen, Taylor Holmes, Peggy Knudsen, James Burke, Percy Helton, Phil Van Zandt. 83m.

Gunslinger (Milland) comes to the aid of Civil War veterans who are trying to settle in the West; he finds himself caught between Yankee and Reb veterans who fight their own epilogue to the war.

Of the four principals three are ridiculously miscast; only MacDonald Carey is effective, as a brutal corrupt deputy. Mona Freeman is too treacly to be believed, and as for Milland and Lamarr—about the most absurd parlay in a Western since the Marx Brothers in *Go West*—they allegedly hated each other in person and the enmity comes across on screen. Despite good Technicolor cinematography (Charles B. Lang, Jr.) and a superior score (Daniele Amfitheatrof), this lavish and ludicrous movie is lamentable throughout.

COPPER SKY (1957, FOX). D: Robert Stabler. W: Stabler & Eric Norden. Cast: JEFF MORROW, Coleen GRAY, Paul Brinegar. 74m.

Drunken ex-soldier and Eastern schoolmarm contend with a horde of attacking Indians. Black-&-white "Z" movie.

CORONER CREEK (1948, COL). D: Ray Enright. W: Kenneth Gamet from Luke Short's novel. Cast: RANDOLPH SCOTT, MARGUERITE CHAPMAN, George MACREADY, Edgar BUCHANAN, Sally EILERS, Forrest TUCKER, Wallace Ford, William Bishop, Barbara Read, Joe Sawyer, Russell Simpson, Forrest Taylor. 93m.

A rancher goes after his fiancee's murderer. Revenge yarn is strongly plotted by Luke Short and handled very well by all.

COUNT THREE AND PRAY (1955, COL). D: George Sherman. W: Herb Meadow. Cast: VAN HEFLIN, JOANNE WOODWARD, Raymond BURR, Phil CAREY, Nancy Kulp, Alison Hayes. 102m.

Civil War veteran appoints himself preacher and gathers a flock, but has to pick up his guns again to fight off the minions of the villain (Burr). It's a solid minor film; Woodward, in her first starring part, is excellent, and this was a role to which Heflin brought great power.

COWBOY (1958, COL). D: Delmer Daves. W: Edmund H. North From Frank Harris's *My Reminiscences as a Cowboy*. Cast: GLENN FORD, JACK LEMMON, Brian DONLEVY, Anna KASHFI, Dick York, Richard Jaeckel, Victor Manuel Mendoza, Strother Martin. 91m.

Young dude (Lemmon) goes West, and a leathery trail drover (Ford) teaches him to survive on a cattle drive. The conflicts are more slapstick than dramatic, and it's episodic, and Kashfi (as a Mexican girl) and Donlevy (as a cowboy) are miscast; there are good scenes but it doesn't hang together as well as it might. Credits do not reflect the fact that the blacklisted Dalton Trumbo contributed at least one draft of the script.

THE COWBOY AND THE LADY (1939, UA). D: H.C. Potter. W: S.N. Behrman, Leo McCarey, Sonya Levien & Frank Adams. Cast: GARY COOPER, MERLE OBERON, Walter BRENNAN, Patsy KELLY, Fuzzy Knight, Henry Kolker, Emma Dunn, Harry Davenport, Mabel Todd, Berton Churchill, Charles Richman, Tom London. 91m.

Rodeo cowboy comically romances a rich city girl. Trivial but amiable.

THE COWBOY FROM BROOKLYN (1938, WB). D: Lloyd Bacon. W: Earl Baldwin from a play by Robert Sloane & Louis Pelletier, Jr. Cast: DICK POWELL, PRISCILLA LANE, PAT O'BRIEN, Dick FORAN, Ann SHERIDAN, Ronald REAGAN, Johnnie Davis, Emma Dunn. 80m.

Cowhand who hates cows (Powell) has to prove his credentials as a Westerner in order to get a job on radio. Fragile and silly. Songs by Johnny Mercer, Richard Whiting and Harry Warren. Produced by Hal B. Wallis.

THE COWBOYS (1972, WB). D: Mark Rydell. W: William Dale Jennings, Irving Ravetch & Harriet Frank, Jr., from Jennings's novel. Cast: JOHN WAYNE, Roscoe Lee BROWNE, Bruce DERN, Colleen DEWHURST, Slim PICKENS, Sarah CUNNINGHAM, A. Martinez, Lonny Chapman, Charles Tyner, Robert Carradine, Allyn Ann McLerie, Fred Barker, Jr. 128m.

When his drovers desert him to run off to a gold discovery, a Montana cattleman (Wayne) is reduced to hiring eleven schoolboys to help him drive his herd 400 miles to market. Rustlers take advantage of the situation. Will the rancher make men of the "cowboys" in time?

A few critics panned *The Cowboys* because they felt it glorified the transformation of young boys into vicious killers, but those complaints seemed a bit hypocritical—an attempt to impose the values of the 1970s on the West of the 1870s—and in any case there's nothing mindless about the film and the distinction is made clearly between the heroism of the boys and the viciousness of the bad guys, among whom Bruce Dern stands out. Wayne plays the rough-hewn prairie gentleman to the hilt; it's his best performance between *True Grit* and *The Shootist*. Good photography (Robert Surtees) and an excellent score (John Williams) enhance the film, and the cattle- and horse-working scenes have the flavor of reality. Among the youngsters A. Martinez is especially good in a challenging role. Colleen Dewhurst is good but out of place as an itinerant madam; the role is an unnecessary interruption that annoys. The film is a fairly good drama of justice, morality, responsibility and coming of age; the characters are thinly sketched for the most part, and it's too saccharine, but it's one of the better oaters of its decade.

COW COUNTRY (1953, AA). D: Lesley Selander & Curtis Bishop. W: Adele Buffington & Tom W. Blackburn from Curtis Bishop's novel *Shadow Range*. Cast: EDMOND O'BRIEN, HELEN WESTCOTT, Robert LOWERY, Peggie CASTLE, Raymond Hatton, Jack Ingram, Marshall Reed, Barton MacLane, James Millican, Robert Barrat, Rory Mallinson, George J. Lewis, Sam Flint. 82m.

Mortgaged ranchers are being driven out by villainous foreclosers. Wheezy plot is spiced up with cheap exploitive gimmicks: brutality, leering sexual innuendo, racism. Bilge is a waste of some good performers.

CRIPPLE CREEK (1952, COL). D: Ray Nazarro. W: Richard Schayer. Cast: GEORGE MONTGOMERY, KARIN BOOTH, Jerome COURTLAND, William BISHOP, Richard EGAN, Don PORTER, John DEHNER, Roy Roberts, George Cleveland, Cliff Clark, Byron Foulger. 78m.

Three undercover government agents (Montgomery, Courtland, Egan) infiltrate a boom town to expose a gang of gold-bullion hijackers (Bishop, Porter, Dehner). Much of the action takes place inside a saloon with a charming bar-girl (Booth) at hand. There are night-riding holdups and other such cliches comfortably in place; it all zips along at a good pace, without subtleties or surprises, ty, ical of Montgomery's films—really a "B" picture but in Technicolor.

CRY FOR ME BILLY (1974)—*See* FACE TO THE WIND.

THE CULPEPPER CATTLE COMPANY (1972, FOX). D: Dick Richards. W: Eric Bercovici & Gregory Prentiss. Cast: GARY GRIMES, Billy "Green" BUSH, Luke Askew, Bo Hopkins, Wayne Sutherlin, Royal Dano, Geoffrey Lewis, John McLiam, Matt Clark, Anthony James, Jerry Gatlin, Gregory Sierra, Charlie Martin Smith. 92m.

A sixteen-year-old joins a cattle drive and we are shown the Old West through his wide eyes. No characters are developed at all— even the hero is a callow cipher—except, rudimentarily, that of hard, honest trail boss Frank Culpepper (Bush). A pastiche of predictable trail-drive set pieces and occasional raw jokes and shock-value brutality, the film strives for documentary realism but achieves mainly ennui: it is without suspense, and there isn't any drama in the contrived coming-of-age story. There are gun battles, for example, but since all the characters look alike we have no idea who is shooting at whom.

The movie is set in Texas and Colorado but was filmed in Arizona. It is improved a bit by a good score (Jerry Goldsmith & Tom Scott) but the editing (John Burnett) is uneven, often jerky. The filmic values are arty and glossy (cinematographer Alex Phillips, Jr.) but never very realistic; like the script, they find "authenticity" in 1972 terms rather than 1872 terms and one never becomes unaware that one is watching a hip mod treatment of historical material. The directorial style—this was a first feature by a director of television commercials (his second was the slow stylized *Farewell My Lovely*)—is jazzy, self-conscious and out of kilter with the subject matter. Writer Bercovici has gone on to much better things (TV's *Shogun*, for one).

Keyed by a picaresque story and punched up by intervals of random unmotivated violence, *Culpepper* has interesting touches but is maddeningly pointless and irresolute, as superficial as a cartoon strip.

CURSE OF THE UNDEAD (1959, UNIV). D: Edward Dein. W: Edward & Mildred Dein. Cast: ERIC FLEMING, Michael PATE, Kathleen CROWLEY, John Hoyt, Bruce Gordon, Edward Binns. 76m.

Occult horror melodrama set in the Old West pits a frontier preacher against young girl vampire zombies. Incredibly dreadful and a waste of some good actors.

CURTAIN CALL AT CACTUS CREEK (1950, UNIV). D: Charles Lamont. W: Howard Dimsdale & Stanley Roberts. Cast: DONALD O'CONNOR, GALE STORM, Eve ARDEN, Vincent PRICE, Walter BRENNAN, Harry Shannon, Joe Sawyer. 86m.

An itinerant troupe of actors puts on outrageous melodramas in frontier towns and runs into slapstick troubles when offstage. Broadly played farce is good amusement. In Technicolor.

CUSTER OF THE WEST (1967, ABC). D: Robert Siodmak. W: Bernard Gordon & Julian Halevy. Cast: ROBERT SHAW, MARY URE, JEFFREY HUNTER, TY HARDIN, ROBERT RYAN, Lawrence TIERNEY, Marc Lawrence, Kieron Moore, Fred Kohler, Charles Stalnaker, Robert Hall, John Clark. 140m.

Custer (Shaw) is presented as an intensely angry Rod Steigerish neurotic in this thoroughly international made-in-Spain dirigible. The Indians speak with Italian accents and the sprawling production scenes and expensive, elaborate battle sequences don't make up for the interminable and ponderous between-action scenes. Historical details, and the overall story, are as untrue to reality as they are to legend. The score (Bernard Segall) is poor, and distracting. Philip Yordan produced, and there's good photography (Cecilio Panagua) and the moral questions are treated quite seriously, albeit cynically; but none of it seems real at all. It's not a tenth so entertaining as *They Died with Their Boots On*.

DAKOTA (1945, REP). D: Joseph Kane. W: Lawrence Hazard, Carl Foreman & Howard Estabrook. Cast: JOHN WAYNE, VERA HRUBA RALSTON, Walter BRENNAN, Ward BOND, Mike Mazurki, Ona Munson, Hugo Haas, Grant Withers, George "Gabby" Hayes, Eddy Waller, Jack La Rue, Roy Barcroft, Bobby (Robert) Blake, Robert

Barrat, Sarah Padden, Robert Livingston, George Cleveland. 82m.

Crooked landgrabbers try to swindle the wheat farmers; Duke Wayne rides to the rescue. Republic's boss Herbert J. Yates tended to lavish everything the studio had on these vehicles starring his wife, Vera Ralston, but his was a "B" studio and the flavor of this actioner is that of a programmer stricken with elephantiasis. Dated and predictable.

DAKOTA INCIDENT (1956, REP). D: Lewis Foster. W: Frederick L. Fox. Cast: DALE ROBERTSON, LINDA DARNELL, JOHN LUND, Ward BOND, Regis Toomey, Skip Homeier, William Fawcett, Irving Bacon. 88m.

A stagecoach is ambushed and besieged by Indians; heroes Robertson and Lund protect the other passengers. Brisk.

DAKOTA LIL (1950, FOX). D: Lesley Selander. W: Maurice Geraghty & Frank Gruber. Cast: GEORGE MONTGOMERY, ROD CAMERON, MARIE WINDSOR, Wallace Ford, John Emery, Jack Lambert, Walter Sande, James Flavin, J. Farrell MacDonald, Jack Perrin. 88m.

Secret agent infiltrates an outlaw gang with the aid of a lady forger. Standard hokum.

DALLAS (1950, WB). D: Stuart Heisler. W: John Twist. Cast: GARY COOPER, RUTH ROMAN, STEVE COCHRAN, RAYMOND MASSEY, Leif ERICKSON, Barbara PAYTON, Antonio MORENO, Reed Hadley, Jerome Cowan, Will Wright, Monte Blue, Jose Dominguez, Gene Evans, Buddy Roosevelt, Fred Graham. 94m.

This finds Cooper on a long revenge-search for the three guerrilla killers who wiped out his family and plantation during the Civil War. Reasonably expensive movie has Technicolor, a Max Steiner score, a large cast and plenty of sets. As one of the guerrillas Cochran is especially good and there's a touch of the old William S. Hart flavor to some of the proceedings, and Cooper is in his prime here and a pleasure to see. But the movie isn't; Massey and Roman are stuffy and stiff in their roles as, respectively, villain and lover; and Reed Hadley plays Wild Bill Hickok as if he were a stentorian carney barker. The plot is standard and routine; you can predict every turn of plot. It is, one notes, a Warner Brothers movie and the director was a veteran of those Errol Flynn oaters that Michael Curtiz didn't direct; it has that inept flavor one finds common to the Warner Westerns.

THE DALTON GANG (1949, LIP). DW: Ford Beebe. Cast: DONALD "RED" BARRY, Betty ADAMS, Robert LOWERY, James Millican, Marshall Reed, Byron Foulger. 67m.

Lawman chases outlaws. Not terrible, but not as good as some of the other Lippert Westerns of the period.

THE DALTON GIRLS (1957, UA). D: Reginald Le Borg. W: Maurice Tombragel & Herbert Purdum. Cast: JOHN RUSSELL, MERRY ANDERS, Penny Edwards, Sue George, Lisa Davis. 71m.

Lawman straightens out wild gals. Silly.

THE DALTONS RIDE AGAIN (1945, UNIV). D: Ray Taylor. W: Roy Chanslor & Paul Gangelin. Cast: ALAN CURTIS, KENT TAYLOR, Martha O'DRISCOLL, Lon CHANEY, Jr., Thomas GOMEZ, Noah Beery, Jr., Jess Barker, Douglas Dumbrille, Walter Sande, Milburn Stone, John Litel.

The boys rob a bank, again. Predictable outlaw oater.

DANCE, CHARLIE, DANCE (1937, WB). D: Frank McDonald. W: Crane Wilbur & William Jacobs from George S. Kaufman's play *The Butter and Egg Man*. Cast: STUART ERWIN, Jean MUIR, Glenda FARRELL, Allen Jenkins.

Remake of *The Tenderfoot* (1932) has no verve. Another remake—*An Angel from Texas* (1940)—was much more entertaining.

DANGER ON THE RIVER (1942, UNIV). Also titled: MISSISSIPPI GAMBLER. D: John Rawlins. W: Roy Chanslor, Al Martin & Marion Orth. Cast: KENT TAYLOR, FRANCES LANGFORD, John LITEL, Douglas Fowley, Shemp Howard, Claire Dodd, Wade Boteler. 64m.

Kent Taylor, who looked and sounded like a New Yorker, was among the less believable "Westerners" in films. His presence does not enhance this tired yarn, which is no relation to the later Tyrone Power film *Mississippi Gambler*.

DANIEL BOONE (1936, RKO). D: David Howard. W: Daniel Jarrett & Edgecumb Pinchon. Cast: GEORGE O'BRIEN, John CARRADINE, Heather ANGEL, Ralph Forbes, Clarence Muse, Harry Cording. 81m.

Standard retelling of the Boone legend has Carradine deliciously nasty as the archmeanie Simon Girty. No blockbuster, but good production for a "B-plus" movie.

DANIEL BOONE, TRAIL BLAZER (1956, REP). D: Albert C. Gannaway & Ismael Rodriguez. W: Tom Hubbard & Jack Pat-

rick. Cast: BRUCE BENNETT, Lon CHANEY, Jr., Faron Young. 76m.

A wagon train moves through parlous country, guided by a frontiersman hero. Bennett (onetime Tarzan under his real name, Herman Brix) made a singularly unexciting cowboy hero. Congressman Eugene Siler of Kentucky tried to organize a home-state boycott of this film because it was filmed on locations in Mexico rather than in Kentucky where it was set; that pointless incident was the most interesting thing about the picture—that and the fact that it was the last American movie released in a two-color process (Republic's Cinecolor).

THE DARK COMMAND (1940, REP). D: Raoul Walsh. W: Grover Jones, Lionel Houser, F. Hugh Herbert & Jan Fortune from a novel by W.R. Burnett. Cast: JOHN WAYNE, CLAIRE TREVOR, WALTER PIDGEON, Roy ROGERS, George "Gabby" HAYES, Porter Hall, Marjorie Main, Trevor Bardette. 94m.

Civil War guerrilla captain William Clark Quantrill (Pidgeon) wreaks havoc along the border and threatens to become a dictator with the support of his private army; stalwart heroes (Wayne, Rogers) head him off. With a certain tenuous basis in historical fact, this was Republic's first "epic" in size and budget. It was Duke Wayne's second major Western after *Stagecoach* and the first successful one, *Allegheny Uprising* having proved a dud. It reteamed him with Trevor and provided the added bonus of a towering Walter Pidgeon performance as the mad tyrant Quantrill. Roy Rogers, in a supporting role, comes off surprisingly well as the male ingenue. The music (Victor Young) is fine and Walsh directed with verve. It's essentially big-budget "B" stuff but it's very entertaining.

DAUGHTER OF THE WEST (1951, IND). D: Harold Daniels. W: Raymond L. Schrock from a novel by Robert E. Callahan. Cast: MARTHA VICKERS, Philip REED, Donald WOODS, William Farnum, James Griffith.

In the 1880s a half-breed girl falls in love with an educated Navajo; crisis follows. Sincere, earnest, well-intentioned. But the script is careless and the cheapjack indie production is very poor.

DAVID HARUM (1934, FOX). D: James Cruze. W: Edward N. Westcott. Cast: WILL ROGERS, Louise DRESSER, Evelyn VENABLE, Kent TAYLOR, Noah BEERY, Sr., Stepin Fetchit, Charles Middleton. 83m.

Homespun philosopher-rancher brings together the young lovers (Taylor, Venable). Crackerbarrel nostalgia is strictly for Rogers fans; it's notable mainly as one of the last directorial gasps of *Covered Wagon*'s Cruze.

DAVY CROCKETT, INDIAN SCOUT (1950, UA). Also titled: INDIAN SCOUT. D: Ford Beebe. W: Beebe & Richard Schayer. Cast: GEORGE MONTGOMERY, ELLEN DREW, Noah Beery, Jr., Philip Reed, Chief Thundercloud. 71m.

Civilian scout investigates wagon-train massacres for the army. Crockett just happens to be the name they assigned to the hero. Numbingly routine. In color.

DAWN AT SOCORRO (1954, UNIV). D: George Sherman. W: George Zuckerman. Cast: RORY CALHOUN, PIPER LAURIE, DAVID BRIAN, Alex NICOL, Kathleen HUGHES, Edgar BUCHANAN, Lee Van Cleef, Mara Corday, Skip Homeier, Roy Roberts. 80m.

Gambler-gunfighter (Calhoun) goes against a crooked saloonkeeper (Brian) with lovely Piper Laurie in the middle and a nervous sheriff (Buchanan) gadflying on the fringes. Calhoun and David Brian did several variations on this standard plot; all of them are lively and entertaining.

A DAY OF FURY (1956, UNIV). D: Harmon Jones. W: James Edmiston & Oscar Brodney. Cast: DALE ROBERTSON, MARA CORDAY, JOCK MAHONEY, Carl Benton REID, John DEHNER, Sheila Bromley, Harry Tyler. 78m.

It's the wheeze about the two old buddies, one of whom has become a lawman (Mahoney) and the other of whom has strayed onto the wrong side of the law (Robertson). Robertson is engaging as the charming outlaw but Mahoney—a professional stunt man turned actor—is dull.

DAY OF THE BAD MAN (1958, UNIV). D: Harry Keller. W: Lawrence Roman from a John M. Cunningham story. Cast: FRED MacMURRAY, JOAN WELDON, John ERICSON, Edgar BUCHANAN, Robert MIDDLETON, Marie WINDSOR, Lee Van Cleef, Eduard Franz. 80m.

Frontier circuit judge (MacMurray) is confronted by the four brothers of a convicted murderer: if he sentences the man to death they'll kill him. MacMurray is very good in this one—realistic, steady, torn between fear and duty, much like the hero of *High Noon*, and that's not surprising because Cunningham also wrote the story on which *High Noon* was based. This one is taut and suspenseful, well played.

DAY OF THE EVIL GUN (1968, MGM). D: Jerry Thorpe. W: Charles Marquis Warren & Éric Bercovici. Cast: GLENN FORD, ARTHUR KENNEDY, Dean JAGGER, Nico Minardos, John Anderson, Paul Fix, Royal Dano, Ross Elliott, (Harry) Dean Stanton, James Griffith. 93m.

Good guy and bad guy team up to hunt for women who've been kidnaped by Apaches. It's hard to tell which is the good guy and which is the bad guy, however. Ford and Kennedy swap moral roles partway through the movie. Originally it was made for TV but the studio decided to release it theatrically. Hard to tell why. It's a cheap imitation of *The Searchers* and *Two Rode Together*; the dreary shoot-out at the end is predictable an hour in advance but there's no suspense leading up to it, and anyhow we don't care which of them wins. The acting is mediocre—downright bad on Kennedy's part; the only performer who stands out at all is John Anderson as a sleazy renegade army officer. Anderson has made quite a few bad movies worth looking at—at least for his intermittent appearances in them—and he has enhanced some very good films as well, but in this one his scenes are just about the only good ones. The flick is genuinely tedious.

DAY OF THE OUTLAW (1959, UA). D: Andre De Toth. W: Philip Yordan from a novel by Lee E. Wells. Cast: ROBERT RYAN, BURL IVES, Tina LOUISE, Nehemiah PERSOFF, Jack Lambert, David Nelson, William Schallert, Elisha Cook, Jr., Dabbs Greer, Lance Fuller, Alan Marshall, Helen Westcott. 90m.

Tough self-centered rancher (Ryan) is reluctantly drawn into community problems when a brutal outlaw gang and its wounded leader (Ives) occupy the community. There are cliches, and some of the characters are perfunctory, and a few story-line turnings are rather dated now, but the film's conflict cranks up tight and the climax, involving a long trek into blizzard-slashed mountains, is harrowing. Ryan and Ives are utterly superb. There's a powerful flavor of doomed isolation; it's slow to start but builds a terrific tension. In black-and-white.

THE DEADLY COMPANIONS (1961, PARA). D: Sam Peckinpah. W: Albert S. Fleischman from his novel. Cast: BRIAN KEITH, MAUREEN O'HARA, Steve COCHRAN, Chill WILLS, Strother Martin, Will Wright, Jim O'Hara. 90m.

Trying to atone for the accidental killing of a dance-hall girl's son, a gunslinger (Keith) escorts the woman (O'Hara) across the desert while fighting off Indians and outlaws. The plot and motivations are silly. But the film offers a gritty, fine performance by Brian Keith and a fascinating portrayal, by Chill Wills, of a half-mad killer. O'Hara seems rather too beautiful for the down-on-her-luck character she portrays, but that's a minor cavil; she is, as always, striking and persuasive.

This was the first feature film directed by Sam Peckinpah; in its small-scale action scenes and pedestrian backgrounds it has the same flavor as some of the half-hour episodes of *Have Gun, Will Travel* and *The Westerner* that Peckinpah directed for television. The budget was very small, but the main problem is that the script is amateurish: it sets up a series of hackneyed yet unbelievable premises, then carries forward without suspense. The obligatory multiple gunfight at the end is violent but confused.

THE DEADLY TRACKERS (1973, WB). D: Barry Shear and (unbilled) Samuel Fuller. W: Lukas Heller from a story by Fuller. Cast: RICHARD HARRIS, ROD TAYLOR, Al LETTIERI, Neville BRAND, Paul Benjamin, William Smith, Pedro Armendariz, Jr., Isela Vega, Kelly Jean Peters, William Bryant. 110m.

A gang of outlaw renegades (led by Rod Taylor) murders the wife and son of a peaceable sheriff (Harris); the sheriff tracks the gang to Mexico and turns to violence. *Boy* does he turn to violence!

Samuel Fuller was pulled off the picture and TV director Shear completed it, after which the Warner editors ravaged the footage until Fuller, screenwriter Heller and composer Fred Steiner insisted their names be removed from the credits. Fuller's was removed; Heller's remained; the score is credited to Armando Acosta. (The color photography, by Gabriel Torres on Mexican locations, is quite good.) But it is beyond credibility that they had anything worth saving to start with. The film is a tawdry, unforgivably brutal, obscenely moronic bloodbath. In those respects it is not atypical of Fuller's earlier movies—it's simply more explicitly violent than they were, because the restraints of decency had been abandoned by Hollywood by 1973. The characters are cardboard, the shock effects cheap and the plot puerile. Of the actors only the late Al Lettieri retains any dignity, as a level-headed Mexican lawman, but he's not believably Mexican.

Once again, with this irredeemable trash, the filmmakers of the latter-day Western sold their chance at entertainment for a pot of message: in this case something about those who live by the sword. *The Deadly Trackers* is a deadly bore.

DEADWOOD '76 (1964, IND). Cast: Arch Hall, Jr., Robert Dix.

A youth is mistaken for Billy the Kid. Cheap and very bad.

DEATH OF A GUNFIGHTER (1969, UNIV). D: Robert Totten & Don Siegel. W: Joseph Calvelli from a Lewis B. Patten novel. Cast: RICHARD WIDMARK, LENA HORNE, John SAXON, Carroll O'CONNOR, Kent Smith, Michael McGreevey, Darleen Carr, David Opatoshu, Jacqueline Scott, Jimmy Lydon, Harry Carey, Jr., Morgan Woodward, Mercer Harris, Larry Gates, Dub Taylor. 100m.

Weary washed-up gunslinger-marshal has outlived his usefulness in a town that, now that he's tamed it, turns against him and accuses him of being trigger-happy. Then the outlaws arrive. . . .

You've seen it all before; the fair-sized budget and big cast don't raise it above the level of dull mediocrity. Lena Horne, a grand lady long neglected by filmmakers, is wasted in a thankless role as the marshal's long-suffering mistress, and Widmark plays the hero as if he was tired not only of gunfighting but of acting as well.

That may have had something to do with the fact that Widmark and director Robert Totten allegedly argued throughout the filming until Widmark refused to go on unless Totten was fired from the picture. Don Siegel was hired over the weekend and took over when the picture was approximately half finished; he filmed the remaining half of it in nine working days. This haste was altogether in contrast with Totten's ponderous deliberate pace of shooting, and the discrepancies between the two directors' styles are painfully evident throughout the film. It was shot fairly much out of sequence, so that the two directors' scenes are intermingled throughout the picture; as a result its pace is erratic to say the least. A curious admixture, but not a successful one.

DEATH VALLEY (1946, IND). D: Lew Landers. W: Doris Schroeder. Cast: ROBERT LOWERY, HELEN GILBERT, Nat PENDLETON, Sterling Holloway, Russell Simpson.

Most of the film is devoted to a harrowing chase across Death Valley in merciless heat. Melodramatic grim downbeat "B" picture is not altogether bad but it becomes tedious.

DECISION AT SUNDOWN (1957, COL). D: Budd Boetticher. W: Charles Lang, Jr., from a novel by Vernon L. Flaherty. Cast:

RANDOLPH SCOTT, KAREN STEELE, JOHN CARROLL, Valerie FRENCH, Noah Beery, Jr., John Archer, John Litel. 94m.

Scott plays a hero out for revenge yet again, but this one has a new twist: it turns out the wife whose murder he wants to avenge was a scheming worthless tramp.

A number of cliches are turned inside out; there's a series of unusual twists, and there are gritty suspenseful moments. Boetticher's grim, speedy directing can't be faulted and for a while this one is quite fascinating. It has many adherents among movie buffs—especially among fans of the Boetticher-Scott oaters—but it bogs down, at last, in predictable heroics and in the end it disappoints, partly because almost the entire action is confined to a town set and it rarely ventures outdoors.

THE DEERSLAYER (1943, REP). D: Lew Landers. W: D.S. Harrison, E.D. Derr & John W. Krafft from the novel by James Fenimore Cooper. Cast: BRUCE KELLOGG, YVONNE De CARLO, Larry PARKS, Jean PARKER, Robert Warwick, Addison Richards.

This one was just possibly the worst of all the rotten film versions of Fenimore Cooper's Leatherstocking Tales; but then, as Mark Twain pointed out, Cooper himself was a poor excuse for a writer.

THE DEERSLAYER (1957, FOX). D: Kurt Neumann. W: Neumann & Carroll Young from the James Fenimore Cooper novel. Cast: LEX BARKER, RITA MORENO, FORREST TUCKER, Cathy O'DONNELL, Jay C. Flippen. 78m.

Again the one about the young white man raised by Mohican Indians. Cheapie was filmed on indoor sets with stock rear-projection footage of scenery. It's marginally better than the ludicrous 1943 version but who cares?

DENVER AND RIO GRANDE (1952, PARA). D: Byron Haskin. W: Frank Gruber. Cast: EDMOND O'BRIEN, LAURA ELLIOTT, DEAN JAGGER, STERLING HAYDEN, Lyle BETTGER, J. Carrol NAISH, ZaSu PITTS, Robert Barrat. 87m.

There's a lot of virile action in this railroad-building Western and the plot—the race by two rival Colorado railroads to reach the Royal Gorge—has some basis in history. But several things mar the movie. One is the acting: O'Brien is miscast as a tough frontier character, and Hayden and Bettger chew up all the scenery in sight as they overplay their roles as the head villains, with Bettger so slimy he slides right out of plausibility and Hayden so overblown a ruthless redneck that he might as well be Noah Beery, Sr., in a "Z" Western of the early 1930s. Another problem is the hysterical melodramatics of the script by Gruber, who was a numbed pulp-magazine veteran of every known cliche.

Dean Jagger comes off respectably as the D&RG owner, and ZaSu Pitts has an amusing role as the spunky wife of a railroader, but Laura Elliott is not an appealing heroine. Yet in spite of its weaknesses it's worth seeing—a good action entertainment, jam-packed with fistfights, landslides, gunfights, chases and wrecks. The climactic head-on crash between two recklessly speeding trains was not contrived with special effects or trick photography; two actual full-size trains were demolished, and the wreck is certainly among the most spectacular ever filmed.

THE DESERTER (1971, PARA). D: Burt Kennedy. W: Clair Huffaker from a story by Stuart L. Byrne & William H. James. Cast: BEKIM FEHMIU, JOHN HUSTON, RICHARD CRENNA, CHUCK CONNORS, Ricardo MONTALBAN, Brandon De WILDE, Ian BANNEN, Slim PICKENS, Woody STRODE, Patrick Wayne, Albert Salmi, John Alderson, Fausto Tozzi, Nimmo Palmara, Larry Stewart. 99m.

Deserter hero is pardoned and reinstated in the cavalry so he can lead a band of specialists in a daring assault on an impregnable Apache stronghold.

Filmed in Spain with an international crew and cast, it's a Western *Dirty Dozen* with elements of *The Professionals* and James Bond thrown in. Many will find the genocidal viciousness revolting: the "heroes" plan and execute cold-bloodedly the ambush and annihilation of an entire Indian community. This is the theatre of brutality: unmitigated violence throughout. Much of it is well staged, handled with professional gloss, and most of the actors acquit themselves well enough except for the hero, who is played by a young Israeli actor whose wooden ineptitude boggles the mind.

DESERT GOLD (1936, PARA). D: Charles T. Barton. W: Stuart Anthony & Robert Yost from the Zane Grey novel. Cast: LARRY "BUSTER" CRABBE, MARSHA HUNT, Tom KEENE, Robert CUMMINGS, Raymond Hatton, Monte Blue, Leif Erickson.

Paramount released a very good Zane Grey series in the early 1930s, directed by Henry Hathaway and starring Randolph Scott. Half a decade later the studio trotted out the same stories and remounted them with cheaper productions, using much stock footage from the earlier films, and casting them mainly with "B" actors and up-and-coming ingenues. This one's not altogether bad but it's a programmer, a treasure-hunt yarn with white-hat heroics and black-hat villainy. Still, the hero—unusually but not uniquely—is an Indian.

DESERT PURSUIT (1952, MONO). D: George Blair. W: W. Scott Darling from a novel by Kenneth Perkins. Cast: WAYNE MORRIS, VIRGINIA GREY, Anthony CARUSO, John Doucette, George Tobias, Gloria Talbot, Emmett Lynn. 63m.

Arabs on camels chase a lady gambler and a gun-toting prospector across the West in pursuit of gold. Formula "B" oater.

THE DESPERADO (1954, AA). D: Thomas Carr. W: Geoffrey Homes from a Clifton Adams novel. Cast: WAYNE MORRIS, BEVERLY GARLAND, James LYDON, Rayford Barnes, John Dierkes, Roy Barcroft, Dabbs Greer, Nestor Paiva. 67m.

Youngster goes after the championship mantle of the veteran gunslinger. There are a few good twists on the old plot. Lydon is good as the kid; Morris seems weary.

THE DESPERADOES (1942, COL). D: Charles Vidor. W: Robert Carson from a Max Brand story. Cast: RANDOLPH SCOTT, CLAIRE TREVOR, GLENN FORD, EVELYN KEYES, Edgar BUCHANAN, Guinn "Big Boy" Williams, Raymond Walburn, Porter Hall, Joan Woodbury, Irving Bacon, Glenn Strange. 85m.

Good-natured bandit Ford goes straight and throws in with lawman Scott to bring peace to the territory. Routine, but pleasant performances, and it's in Technicolor.

THE DESPERADOS (1969, COL). D: Henry Levin. W: Walter Brough & Clarke Reynolds. Cast: VINCENT EDWARDS, JACK PALANCE, GEORGE MAHARIS, Sylvia SIMS, Neville BRAND, Christian Roberts, Kate O'Mara, Kenneth Cope, John Paul. 91m.

Reb guerrillas go on plundering after the Civil War. Edwards, Maharis and Roberts play the unlikely sons of Palance in a plot keyed by violent fratricide. Edwards is a wooden and unsympathetic leading man; Palance hams with heavy-breathing silliness; the ending is repulsive.

THE DESPERADOS ARE IN TOWN (1956, FOX). D: Kurt Neumann. W: Neumann & Earle Snell from a Bennett Foster story. Cast: ROBERT ARTHUR, KATHY NOLAN, Rhodes REASON, Dave

O'BRIEN, Rhys Williams, Dorothy Granger, Kelly Thorsden. 72m.

Young Southerner, a bandit, sees his buddy killed and "goes straight" by killing the killers after a lot of menacing, mincing about. Dull.

DESPERATE SIEGE (1951) *See:* RAWHIDE.

DESTRY (1955, UNIV). D: George Marshall. W: Edmund H. North, D.D. Beauchamp & Felix Jackson from Max Brand's novel *Destry Rides Again.* Cast: AUDIE MURPHY, MARI BLANCHARD, Lyle BETTGER, Thomas MITCHELL, Lori NELSON, Edgar BUCHANAN, Wallace Ford, Alan Hale, Jr., Mary Wickes, Ralph Peters. 95m.

Remake can't hold a candle to the 1939 *Destry Rides Again*, which also was directed by George Marshall—suggesting that the quality of script and actors may have as much or more to do with a film's totality than the talent of its director. Murphy is more engaging than you might expect as the soft-spoken, peaceable, easygoing sheriff; but Blanchard has none of the Dietrich magic and the supporting cast—except for Mitchell and Buchanan—is humdrum. Only a few dim reflections of the charm of the older movie manage to glimmer through the trite screenplay.

DESTRY RIDES AGAIN (1932, UNIV). D: Ben Stoloff. W: Robert Keith & Isadore Bernstein from Max Brand's novel. Cast: TOM MIX, Claudia DELL, Andy DEVINE, ZaSu PITTS, Stanley Fields, Francis Ford.

This forgotten movie was the first screen version of *Destry*; it also was Tom Mix's first talkie. It hewed much closer to the original pulp novel than did the later film versions but that was to its detriment, since the novel was hack formula fiction. This one had little of the humor of the later films.

DESTRY RIDES AGAIN (1939, UNIV). D: George Marshall. W: Felix Jackson & Gertrude Purcell from Max Brand's novel. Cast: MARLENE DIETRICH, JAMES STEWART, Brian DONLEVY, Charles WINNINGER, Mischa AUER, Jack CARSON, Una MERKEL, Irene Hervey, Billy Gilbert, Warren Hymer, Allen Jenkins, Tom Fadden, Samuel S. Hinds. 94m.

A peaceable young sheriff (Stewart) is thrown up against some hard-bitten villains in a saloon where Dietrich provides entertainment and lip. (One of her songs is the memorable "See What the Boys in the Back Room Will Have.") Developments, both

comic and dramatic, lead in all directions until the final clinch. (Odd note: this is the first known movie to have an action sequence prior to the opening credits.) Jimmy Stewart was not yet a big star; Marlene Dietrich had appeared in a string of thoroughly bad turkeys in the late 1930s; the novel was uninspired and Marshall's work was unexceptional; yet somehow the combination made magic on the screen—a unique chemistry among the actors, and a willingness—indeed, an eagerness—to play the melodrama for laughs. Delicious entertainment—often imitated, seldom equaled.

DEVIL ON HORSEBACK (1936, IND). DW: Crane Wilbur from his play *The Tiger Smiles.* Cast: Fred KEATING, Lili DAMITA, Tiffany Thayer, Del Campo.

Prima donna movie star (Damita) finds herself up against a dashing Latin bandit in a never-never-land setting. Allegedly a comedy.

DEVIL'S CANYON (1953, RKO). D: Alfred Werker. W: Frederick Hazlitt Brennan, Bennett R. Cohen, Norton S. Parker & Harry Essex. Cast: DALE ROBERTSON, VIRGINIA MAYO, Stephen McNALLY, Arthur HUNNICUTT, Richard Arlen, Morris Ankrum. 91m.

Lawman winds up in prison and reluctantly finds himself involved with mutineers and escapees. It's a static set-bound meller, slow and dreary.

DEVIL'S DOORWAY (1950, MGM). D: Anthony Mann. W: Guy Trosper. Cast: ROBERT TAYLOR, PAULA RAYMOND, LOUIS CALHERN, Marshall THOMPSON, Edgar BUCHANAN, Rhys Williams, James Mitchell, Spring Byington, Chief John Big Tree, Fritz Leiber. 84m.

An Indian (Taylor) who fought in the Civil War returns home to his people in Wyoming, where a crooked lawyer (Calhern) schemes to brew up a war between the tribe and some white sheepmen. Mistreatment by whites and the plight of the Indian are the subjects of this sincere but hackneyed yarn; and Taylor is miscast. It was made contemporaneously with *Broken Arrow* and suffered by comparison. But Mann's direction keeps it moving and the climax has plenty of action.

DIRTY DINGUS MAGEE (1970, MGM). D: Burt Kennedy. W: Joseph Heller, Frank & Tom Waldman, from a David Marboro novel. Cast: FRANK SINATRA, GEORGE KENNEDY, ANNE JACKSON, Lois NETTLETON, Jack ELAM, Michele Carey, John Dehner, Henry Jones, Paul Fix, Harry Carey, Jr., Terry Wilson, Willis Bouchey, Donald Barry, Grady Sutton. 91m.

Scruffy outlaw Sinatra gets mixed up with stupid sheriff Kennedy, greedy madam Jackson, silly Indian chief Fix, pretty Indian girl Carey, dumb soldiers Dehner and Wilson, a stolen strongbox, unfunny shoot-outs and limp gags. It's a lamebrained misfire, a true landmark for chroniclers of horrible movies. Stunts (Jerry Gatlin) and wide-screen photography (Harry Stradling, Jr.) are passable but the score (Jeff Alexander) is frantic and incessant and all other elements—including performances—are tasteless and distasteful. The script (by, among others, author Heller of *Catch 22*) warms over every stale joke in the repertoire of horse-opera spoofs. Two amusing bits—Nettleton's deadly parody, whether intentional or not, of Joanne Woodward, and Jack Elam's lovely cameo as a blustering nasty John Wesley Hardin—do not even begin to redeem it.

DIRTY LITTLE BILLY (1972, COL). D: Stan Dragoti. W: Dragoti & Charles Moss. Cast: MICHAEL J. POLLARD, Lee PURCELL, Charles Aidman, Richard Evans, William Sage, Dean Hamilton. 99m.

Alleged comedy-biography intends to prove, according to ads for the movie, that "Billy the Kid was a Punk." It suggests, indeed, that he was a dull, witless, unwashed punk. Actually it proves mainly that these moviemakers don't have the least idea how to keep an audience awake. Dragoti and Moss were advertising men; on the evidence of this one they should have stayed on Madison Avenue. And Pollard—a singularly unappealing leading man under the best of circumstances—goes through nearly the whole of this film spattered with mud, which doesn't make him any more appetizing. He plays the Kid as a sadistic fool. The monotony of his dreadful performance leaves one hungry for entertainment that offers something other than brainlessness, buffoonery and bloodletting.

DISTANT DRUMS (1951, WB). D: Raoul Walsh. W: Niven Busch & Martin Rackin. Cast: GARY COOPER, MARI ALDON, Arthur HUNNICUTT, Richard WEBB, Robert Barrat, Ray Teal, Sheb Wooley. 101m.

Buckskin-clad Indian fighter leads a small army force into the Everglades to subdue warring Seminoles. This was Cooper's last film prior to his comeback in *High Noon* and it's a poor one. There was something about the story department at Warner Brothers that made it seemingly impossible for that studio to produce a good Western regardless of who wrote it, directed it or starred in it. Busch's story was rewritten to pablum in an attempt

to turn it into a sort of remake of the Walsh-directed *Objective Burma*; Cooper's performance is fine—so is Hunnicutt's, as a coonskin-capped scout—but the supporting cast is woeful; Walsh directs vigorously and Sid Hickox's photography is good but it doesn't matter; Max Steiner's heroic music only emphasizes the poverty of the script, which has that unmistakable Warner Brothers "B" quality. Despite the powerhouse names this one is conventional on all counts: flaccid shoot-'em-up nonsense.

A DISTANT TRUMPET (1964, WB). D: Raoul Walsh. W: John Twist, Richard Fielder & Albert Beich from Paul Horgan's novel. Cast: TROY DONAHUE, SUZANNE PLESHETTE, Diane McBAIN, James GREGORY, William Reynolds, Kent Smith, Claude Akins. 117m.

Cavalry-versus-Indians; heroic young officer bucks the system—you've seen it before. Warners bought a good Paul Horgan novel and lavished huge sums of money on the production in the hope that Walsh would bring off a John Ford sort of movie but the result was a catastrophe because the committee-written script jacks up the title and puts a new story under it, this one containing every known cliche from the previous fifty years of Western filmmaking. The television-name cast adds to the "B" impression despite the hundreds of extras and horses who fill up the colorfully photographed (William H. Clothier) screen. This was Walsh's last film, though he lived on until 1981, when he died at 93.

DOC (1971, UA). D: Frank Perry. W: Pete Hamill. Cast: STACY KEACH, FAYE DUNAWAY, HARRIS YULIN, Mike Whitney, Denver John Collins, Dan Greenburg. 96m.

The critic must always fight the temptation to be snide but films like *Doc* make it hard to be otherwise. Very little in this movie is forgivable. Doc Holliday was frail and sadistic; Keach plays him as though he were a robust, melancholy, tragic hero with a bad toothache. Wyatt Earp was a gambler and an oft-married ladies' man; Harris Yulin plays him as a mincing closet queen. Kate Fisher was Doc's irascible unattractive girl friend; Dunaway portrays her as a snarling but glamorous hysteric. The movie was filmed in Spain, and purports to take place in Tombstone and in heaven. The plot is the sort a demented teenager might dream up after reading (or writing) a superficial debunking article about Earp and Holliday in a flip publication like *New York Magazine*, to which, indeed, author-reporter Hamill was a frequent contributor. It is impossible to be kind to this sort of trash.

DODGE CITY (1939, WB). D: Michael Curtiz. W: Robert H. Buckner. Cast: ERROL FLYNN, OLIVIA De HAVILLAND, ANN SHERIDAN, Bruce CABOT, Alan HALE, Victor JORY, Ward Bond, Frank McHugh, Guinn "Big Boy" Williams, Douglas Fowley, John Litel, Henry Travers, William Lundigan, Russell Simpson, Charles Halton, Henry O'Neill, Gloria Holden, Clem Bevans, Monte Blue, Joseph Crehan, Thurston Hall. 105m.

Swashbuckling hero cleans up wild-and-wicked Dodge City by dealing sixgun justice to baddies Cabot, Jory and Fowley. Flynn's first Western, filmed in Technicolor (Sol Polito and Ray Rennahan), explains his presence as that of an Irish-Australian adventurer, which he was. The production is lavish for Warners; but the screenplay is trite stereotyped junk, and Curtiz never was able to handle Westerns. *Dodge City* is creaky, outdated with its white-hat, black-hat plot and scenery chewing performances by Lundigan, Cabot and Big Boy Williams. The Max Steiner score is rousing enough and considered as a large-scale "B" movie it's actionful enough, but 1939 was the year of *Stagecoach*, *Union Pacific*, *Destry Rides Again* and many other goodies; this one—Warners' entry in the epic oater sweepstakes—ran dead last for quality, although it was a box-office hit.

THE DOMINO KID (1957, COL). D: Ray Nazarro. W: Kenneth Gamet & Hal Biller. Cast: RORY CALHOUN, Kristine MILLER, Andrew DUGGAN, Yvette Dugay, Peter Whitney, Eugene Iglesias, Robert Burton, Roy Barcroft, Denver Pyle. 73m.

Bob Steele plot; revenge in Texas; in black-and-white. Calhoun co-produced this one. It's awkward and routine.

THE DOOLINS OF OKLAHOMA (1949, COL). D: Gordon Douglas. W: Kenneth Gamet. Cast: RANDOLPH SCOTT, JOHN IRELAND, Louise ALLBRITTON, George MACREADY, Noah Beery, Jr., Dick Foran, Jock Mahoney, Al Bridge. 89m.

Misunderstood former outlaw tries to go straight but is prevented by other members of the gang from doing so. The real Bill Doolin was a member of the Dalton gang; after it was wiped out at Coffeyville he formed his own bandit gang in Oklahoma in the 1890s and finally he was brought down by the greatest of the peace marshals, Bill Tilghman. In this mediocre version there's little, if any, similarity to the facts or the legends. This was the first Western to be directed by Gordon Douglas.

THE DRAGOON WELLS MASSACRE (1957, AA). D: Harold Schuster. W: Warren Douglas & Oliver Drake. Cast: BARRY SULLIVAN, DENNIS O'KEEFE, MONA FREEMAN, Katy JURADO, Sebastian CABOT. 88m.

A group of bickering travelers is beleaguered by Apaches in the desert. Old-hat story but very well filmed, with good acting.

DRANGO (1957, UA). D: Hall Bartlett & Jules Bricken. W: Bartlett. Cast: JEFF CHANDLER, JOANNE DRU, Julie LONDON, Donald CRISP, Ronald Howard. 92m.

Union Army officer (Chandler) is sent by carpetbagging officials to restore peace in a Rebel town that his own soldiers plundered during the recent Civil War. Unusual premise dwindles toward routine plotting and leaves one disappointed.

DRUM BEAT (1954, WB). DW: Delmer Daves. Cast: ALAN LADD, Audrey DALTON, Charles BRONSON, Marisa PAVAN, Robert Keith, Rodolfo Acosta, Warner Anderson, Elisha Cook, Jr., Anthony Caruso, Hayden Rorke, Frank Ferguson, Richard Gaines, Frank De Kova, Willis Bouchey. 111m.

President Grant sends an Indian-fighting agent (a lackadaisical Ladd) to the California-Oregon border to straighten out troubles between white settlers and Modoc Indians. Modoc chief Captain Jack is played by Charles Bronson, here enjoying his first major role after having played minor parts as Charles Buchinsky. Filmed in Arizona with towering redrock scenery (in CinemaScope, by J. Peverell Marley & Sid Hickox) that has nothing in common with the Oregon border country, the film has a standard Victor Young score, plenty of shooting, and a literate but unexciting script.

DRUMBEATS OVER WYOMING (1946)—*See* THE PLAINSMAN AND THE LADY.

DRUMS ACROSS THE RIVER (1954, UNIV). D: Nathan Juran. W: John K. Butler & Lawrence Roman. Cast: AUDIE MURPHY, LISA GAYE, Walter BRENNAN, Lyle BETTGER, Hugh O'Brian, Bob Steele, Jay Silverheels, Lane Bradford. 78m.

Greedy for gold, villains invade Indian land. Murphy is one of them but of course he achieves redemption by turning against them and standing up for the Indians. Sufficient commotion to keep action fans awake but there's nothing new in this typical oater.

DRUMS ALONG THE MOHAWK (1939, FOX). D: John Ford. W: Lamar Trotti & Sonya Levien from Walter D. Edmonds' novel. Cast: HENRY FONDA, CLAUDETTE COLBERT, John CARRADINE, Edna May OLIVER, Ward Bond, Robert Lowery, Arthur Shields, Francis Ford, Jessie Ralph, Si Jenks, Chief John Big Tree, Roger Imhof, Mae Marsh, Tom Tyler, Russell Simpson. 103m.

During the Revolutionary War, farmers in the Mohawk Valley contend with Indians, weather, warfare and each other. It's mainly a romance, rambling and episodic, with a typically overpopulated and slow-moving Trotti script. Fine color photography (Bert Glennon) and score (Alfred Newman)—it's dated, and minor Ford, but still solidly entertaining.

DRUMS IN THE DEEP SOUTH (1951, RKO). D: William Cameron Menzies. W: Philip Yordan, Sidney Harmon & Hollister Noble. Cast: JAMES CRAIG, GUY MADISON, BARBARA PAYTON, Barton MacLANE, Craig Stevens. 87m.

Two buddies find themselves on opposite sides when the Civil War breaks out. Director Menzies was best known as a set designer (Tara in *Gone with the Wind*; the sets for *Things to Come*). He does keep the action moving in this one but the actors aren't terrific.

THE DUCHESS AND THE DIRTWATER FOX (1976, FOX). D: Melvin Frank. W: Frank, Jack Ross & Barry Sandler. Cast; GEORGE SEGAL, GOLDIE HAWN, Roy JENSON, Thayer David, Pat Ast, Conrad Janis, Jerry Gatlin, Jennifer Lee, Walter Scott. 103m.

Bumbling gambler (Segal), his funny horse and a devil-may-care hooker (Hawn) get mixed up with a gang of robbers, a group of Mormons, a Jewish wedding, and a lot of chasing around. It's quite engaging, a nice surprise. Joseph Biroc's photography on the Colorado locations is splendid.

DUCK, YOU SUCKER (1972, UA). Also titled: A FISTFUL OF DYNAMITE. D: Sergio Leone. W: Leone, Luciano Vicenzoni & Sergio Donati. Cast: ROD STEIGER, JAMES COBURN, Maria MONTI, Romolo Valil, Rick Battaglia, Franco Graziosi, David Warbeck. 139m.

A trigger-happy Mexican outlaw (Steiger) teams up with an expatriate IRA terrorist (Coburn) to rob a bank. The terrorist, a romantic, tries to politicize the outlaw and turn him into a folk hero against his wishes. Semicomic adventure, set in 1912 Mexico, is less violent than Leone's other Westerns, but that simply makes it duller. It seems to go on forever from one climax to another and finally it simply stops. There are some good gimmicks here and there; one of them—a Pullman-size stagecoach that dominates the early part of the movie—is fascinating. Steiger and Coburn are less than outstanding in their roles; their accents (Mexican and Irish, respectively) are terrible. I know people of taste who find things to like in this interminable picture, but I find it tame and pointless.

THE DUDE GOES WEST (1948, AA). D: Kurt Neumann. W: Richard Sale & Mary Loos. Cast: EDDIE ALBERT, GALE STORM, James GLEASON, Gilbert ROLAND, Binnie Barnes, Barton MacLane, Dick Elliott, Chief Thundercloud, Sarah Padden, Charles Williams. 87m.

Mild gunsmith journeys from New York to a tough Nevada town in the wild 1870s and becomes a gunfighter-hero in spite of himself. It's a gentle comedy, poking fun at Western cliches; pleasantly diverting.

DUDES ARE PRETTY PEOPLE (1942, UA). D: Hal Roach, Jr. W: Louis S. Kaye & Donald Hough. Cast: JIMMY ROGERS, NOAH BEERY, JR., Marjorie WOODWORTH, Marjorie Gateson, Grady Sutton, Paul Hurst, Russell Gleason. 46m.

Short dude-ranch comedy has predictable romances and a couple of songs. Dull.

DUEL AT APACHE WELLS (1957, REP). D: Joseph Kane. W: Robert C. Williams. Cast: BEN COOPER, ANNA MARIA ALBERGHETTI, Harry SHANNON, Jim DAVIS, Bob Steele, Francis J. McDonald. 69m.

Fast-shooting lad tries to save his daddy's ranch from land-grabbers. Juvenile and trite. In black-and-white.

DUEL AT DIABLO (1966, UA). D: Ralph Nelson. W: Marvin H. Albert & Michael M. Grilikhes from Albert's novel *Apache Rising*. Cast: JAMES GARNER, SIDNEY POITIER, BIBI ANDERSSON, Dennis WEAVER, Bill TRAVERS, William REDFIELD, John Hoyt, John Crawford, John Hubbard, Eddie Little Sky, Bill Hart, Alf Elson. 103m.

A gritty civilian scout (Garner) with revenge on his mind, and a Scotsman in uniform (Travers), lead a half-troop of cavalry through hostile territory with two wagonloads of ammunition destined for an isolated fort; they must deal with contentious Apaches, led by chief Chata (Hoyt, suitably inscrutable). There are subplots concerning an ex-sergeant employed to break horses for the army (Poitier) and a storekeeper-freighter

(Weaver) whose relationship is murkily uncertain with his wife (Andersson) who once was kidnapped by Indians and bore a half-breed baby. The plot is very busy and too contrived, full of illogic and coincidence. There is no "duel" in the gunfight sense; the action scenes are Indian battles. Hysterical anachronistic score (Neal Hefti) hurts. Utah photography (Charles F. Wheeler) helps. Pace is slow; there are too many meaningful (i.e., meaningless) pauses. But the acting is good and the characters are interesting. ("Alf Elson" is the director, who likes to play bit parts in his own movies; here he's Colonel Foster.)

THE DUEL AT SILVER CREEK (1952, UNIV). D: Don Siegel. W: Gerald D. Adams & Joseph Hoffman. Cast: AUDIE MURPHY, FAITH DOMERGUE, STEPHEN McNALLY, Susan CABOT, Gerald Mohr, Eugene Iglesias, Lee Marvin, Walter Sande, George Eldredge. 77m.

The Silver Kid (Murphy) joins up with a marshal (McNally) to save peaceable miners from nasty claim-jumpers (Mohr, Marvin). This early directorial effort by Don Siegel is predictable, implausible and dull.

DUEL IN DURANGO (1957, UA). Also titled: GUN DUEL IN DURANGO. D: Sidney Salkow. W: Louis Stevens. Cast: GEORGE MONTGOMERY, Steve BRODIE, Ann Robinson. 73m.

Hero wants to go straight but must contend with his outlaw former pals first. Trite and terrible.

DUEL IN THE SUN (1946, IND). D: King Vidor. W: David O. Selznick & Oliver H.P. Garrett from Niven Busch's novel. Cast: JENNIFER JONES, GREGORY PECK, JOSEPH COTTEN, LIONEL BARRYMORE, WALTER HUSTON, LILLIAN GISH, CHARLES BICKFORD, Herbert MARSHALL, Sidney BLACKMER, Harry CAREY Sr., Joan Tetzel, Butterfly McQueen, Otto Kruger, Lane Chandler, Francis J. McDonald, Victor Kilian, Kermit Maynard, Hank Bell, Si Jenks, Hank Worden, Guy Wilkerson. Narrator (unbilled): ORSON WELLES. 138m.

When her father dies, a voluptuous half-breed tease (Jones) is taken into the home of a cattle baron (Barrymore) who has driven his wife (Gish, and she's exquisite) to drink; the heavy-breathing half-breed girl seduces both the rancher's good dependable son (Cotten) and his flamboyant, wild, bad son (Peck, in a wonderfully stylized performance), and causes wild upheavals in the household and community. This soap-opera plot is grafted onto a standard range-war melodrama that is

mitigated by the scale and scope of the movie, the numerous subplots, the excellence of the production and the marvelous performances by nearly everyone in the cast—notably, in small roles that nearly steal the show, Herbert Marshall as Jones's father; Charles Bickford as a rival cattleman; and Harry Carey as a gritty lawman.

Produced by Selznick with spirited music (Dimitri Tiomkin) and grandiose Technicolor photography (Hal Rosson, Lee Garmes & Ray Rennahan), this extravaganza was years in the filming; at the time of its making it was the most expensive movie ever filmed: it cost $6 million and contained more than 250 hours of film before editing. Uncredited co-directors were Otto Brower, William Dieterle, celebrated designer William Cameron Menzies, Josef von Sternberg and action unit director B. Reaves "Breezy" Eason. The production design (J. McMillan Johnson), art direction (James Basevi) and editing (Hal C. Kern) are splendid. It gave Peck and Jones (Mrs. Selznick) their first big-movie starring roles, and it was Joan Tetzel's debut. Disappointed critics dubbed it "Lust in the Dust" and admittedly it's often awful, especially that final overblown climax on the cliffs. Still, it's lavish with rousing action and big-cast spectacle, and it's one of those thoroughly entertaining bad movies that prove by comparison how turgid De Mille was. Selznick honestly expected *Duel* to top his own *Gone with the Wind*; in that he was sadly mistaken, but nevertheless it's still great fun.

DUEL ON THE MISSISSIPPI (1955, COL). D: William Castle. W: Gerald D. Adams. Cast: LEX BARKER, PATRICIA MEDINA, John DEHNER, Warren Stevens, Craig Stevens. 83m.

The son (Barker) of a bankrupt plantation owner is bonded in service to a low-born Creole girl (Medina), who falls in love with him and helps him overcome the sugar thieves who got his daddy in that fix in the first place. Medina, in this one, seems to be trying out for the mantle of low-budget Yvonne De Carlo; Barker is wooden and soporific; Dehner and the two Stevenses make suitably slippery Louisiana aristocrats. It's a poor film, of note to buffs because its director—who directed several Westerns early in his career—later earned a reputation as a flamboyant showman in the hyping of his horror movies.

THE EAGLE AND THE HAWK (1950, PARA). D: Lewis R. Foster. W: Foster, Jess Arnold & Geoffrey Homes. Cast: JOHN PAYNE, DENNIS O'KEEFE, RHONDA

THE DARK COMMAND (1940): Roy Rogers, John Wayne, George "Gabby" Hayes, and the Republic Studios' posse. The studio's first epic. Republic Pictures

THE DEADLY COMPANIONS (1961): Brian Keith, Chill Wills, Steve Cochran. Sometimes with Peckinpah it's hard to tell where the comedy leaves off and the violence begins. Paramount Pictures

DENVER AND RIO GRANDE (1952): The climactic head-on crash actually demolished two real trains. Paramount Pictures

153

DENVER AND RIO GRANDE (1952): J. Carrol Naish, Laura Elliot, Edmond O'Brien, Dean Jagger. Miscasting mars the movie. Paramount Pictures

THE DESPERADOES (1942): Guinn "Big Boy" Williams (with chair), Irving Bacon (bartender), Glenn Strange and Edgar Buchanan. Every Western had to have its saloon brawl. Columbia Pictures

DESTRY RIDES AGAIN (1939): Marlene Dietrich, James Stewart. Playing the melodrama for laughs. Universal Pictures

DIRTY LITTLE BILLY (1972): Michael J. Pollard illustrating how Billy the Kid was a punk. Columbia Pictures

DISTANT DRUMS (1951): Arthur Hunnicutt, Gary Cooper. A Western remake of *Objective Burma.* Warner Brothers

DOC (1971): Stacy Keach, Harris Yulin. Doc Holliday and Wyatt Earp. Without question the most rancid film version yet. United Artists

DRUM BEAT (1954): Alan Ladd, Charles Bronson. Bronson's first major movie role was as Captain Jack, the Modoc Indian chief. Warner Brothers

DUEL IN THE SUN (1946): Lionel Barrymore (in cape), Joseph Cotten (beside him to the right), Harry Carey (on foot, dark suit), Otto Kruger (on foot, light suit). In its day, the most expensive movie ever filmed. Selznick International

155

THE FAR COUNTRY (1955): John McIntire (in top hat), Jay C. Flippen (battered hat, beard stubble), James Stewart, Walter Brennan; over Stewart's right shoulder can be seen Jack Elam. A fast entertaining movie. Universal Pictures

THE FASTEST GUN ALIVE (1956): Glenn Ford, Broderick Crawford. Carries quick-draw fakery to its logical extreme. MGM

A FISTFUL OF DOLLARS (1966): Clint Eastwood in the first of Sergio Leone's gory, sadistic, spaghetti oaters. United Artists

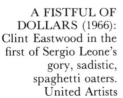

156

FLEMING, Thomas GOMEZ, Fred Clark, Frank Faylen. 104m.

Two mutually distrustful adventurers get involved in the revolution against Maximilian in Mexico in the 1860s. The plot is not dissimilar to the later *Vera Cruz*. Payne seems less innocuous than usual; that's because he's playing straight man to O'Keefe's spirited, if hammy, performance as the cheerful roguish ne'er-do-well. Among the other performers Fleming is merely along for the ride, though her red hair is nice in Technicolor, and Faylen is particularly poor as a sadistic villain. Settle for *Vera Cruz* instead; it's not great but it's better than this one.

EAGLE'S WING (1979, IND). D: Anthony Harvey. W: John Briley & Michael Syson. Cast: MARTIN SHEEN, SAM WATERSTON, HARVEY KEITEL, Stephane Audran, John Castle, Caroline Langrishe.

British-made movie of a pursuit across the Plains in the early nineteenth century received excellent reviews in Britain but had not yet been released in America at this book's press time.

EDGE OF ETERNITY (1960, COL). D: Don Siegel. W: Richard Collins, Knut Swenson & Ben Markson. Cast: CORNEL WILDE, VICTORIA SHAW, Mickey SHAUGHNESSY, Edgar BUCHANAN, Jack Elam, Rian Garrick, Alexander Lockwood. 80m.

Shrewd tough deputy (Wilde) pursues a murderer around the Grand Canyon National Park in this mystery-chase thriller; fine location photography (Burnett Guffey) and a climactic duel in mining buckets suspended on cables above the canyon make it worth seeing, but only just.

EL CONDOR (1970, NGP). D: John Guillermin. W: Larry Cohen & Steve Carabatsos. Cast: JIM BROWN, LEE VAN CLEEF, Patrick O'NEAL, Mariana HILL, Elisha COOK, Jr., Iron Eyes Cody, Imogen Hassall, Gustavo Rojo, John Clark. 102m.

Two superhuman adventurers raid an impregnable Mexican fortress to steal a golden treasure. Simple-minded nonsense was produced by Andre de Toth and filmed in Spain with lavish battle scenes, excellent photography (Henri Persin), an enjoyable score (Maurice Jarre) and the likable-rogue presence of Van Cleef.

EL DORADO (1967, PARA). D: Howard Hawks. W: Leigh Brackett from Harry Brown's novel *The Stars in Their Courses*. Cast: JOHN WAYNE, ROBERT MITCHUM, Arthur HUNNICUTT, James CAAN, Christopher GEORGE, Michele CAREY, Charlene Holt, R.G. Armstrong,

Edward Asner, Paul Fix, Johnny Crawford. 127m.

A fast tough gunfighter (Wayne) helps a liquor-soaked sheriff (Mitchum) rediscover his courage and fight off a gang of town-treeing bad guys (Asner, George) who are trying to bust a prisoner out of the jail; they are helped by a cackling old deputy and a cocky quick-on-the-draw kid.

If that sounds familiar it's because that was exactly the plot of the earlier Hawks-directed film *Rio Bravo*. In this one Wayne plays Wayne, Mitchum is wasted in the role Dean Martin was adequate for, Hunnicutt plays Walter Brennan very well, nearly stealing the show, and James Caan is quite good as "Mississippi"—far better than Ricky Nelson was as an identical character in the earlier film—and Christopher George stands out as the villainous gunslinger (John Russell in the first version). The action scenes in the saloon are carbon copies of the shoot-outs in *Rio Bravo*.

Wayne looks fat, tired and saddlesore. It's impossible to believe him as the lightning-swift gunslinger the script makes him out to be. This is a remarkably un-entertaining and interminable long movie, a geriatric actioner with lousy directing and a very poor script, numbingly predictable. Its running-time is about an hour too long for the story, and I found it a real challenge staying awake to the end. I don't know if it's the worst of Howard Hawks's Westerns (that distinction may belong to *Rio Lobo*) but in any case it's poor.

THE ELECTRIC HORSEMAN (1979, COL). D: Sydney Pollack. W: Robert Garland & Paul Gaer from a story by Shelly Burton. Cast: ROBERT REDFORD, JANE FONDA, Valerie PERRINE, Willie NELSON, John SAXON, Nicolas Coster, Allan Arbus, Timothy Scott. 120m.

A former rodeo champion (Redford) has lost his bearings, been corrupted by commercialism and turned alcoholic. In an effort to redeem himself and recapture the old values, he tries to save a horse that is destined for doom by the commercial promoters. He is abetted in the attempt by a woman reporter (Fonda); they are pursued across the Nevada desert by cops and bad guys (Saxon).

Country singer Willie Nelson, in his film debut, is just fine in his brief scenes as Redford's cynical manager; Perrine is thrown away as his simple-minded ex-wife; Saxon is oily and very good as the villain. But it's essentially a two-character story and it's much too thin to carry such a big movie; it's at least a half hour too long. The editing (Sheldon Kahn) is without zest; the design and art direction (Stephen Grimes, J. Dennis Washington) are unimpressive except for the electrically lit cowboy costume Redford wears early in the film (it was designed by Bernie Pollack). Photography (Owen Roizman) is good but the score (Dave Grusin) only perks up when Willie Nelson sings a couple of soundtrack numbers. The main problem, however, is that *The Electric Horseman* is a "message picture" that insists on slapping the audience across the face with its too-obvious didacticisms about freedom and corruption. It's very talky and unwieldy. The same theme was handled vastly better in *Lonely Are the Brave*. This one is pleasant but minor.

EL PASO (1949, PARA). D: Lewis R. Foster. W: Foster, Robert J. Bren & Gladys Atwater. Cast: JOHN PAYNE, GAIL RUSSELL, Sterling HAYDEN, George "Gabby" HAYES, Dick FORAN, Henry Hull, Eddy Waller, Eduardo Noriega, Mary Beth Hughes, H.B. Warner, Steven Geray. 91m.

The one about the lawyer who reluctantly learns to strap on a gun. Flabby and wheezy with dull slapstick relief.

THE EMIGRANTS (1972, WB). D: Jan Troell. W: Troell & Bengt Forslund from a series of novels by Vilhelm Moberg. Cast: MAX VON SYDOW, LIV ULLMANN, Eddie Axberg, Svenolof Bern. 148m.

The Emigrants is the first half of a long movie about Swedish farmers who uproot themselves during hard times, voyage to the New World in the mid-nineteenth century, and attempt to build new homes and new lives in the American Midwest. The original Swedish version, 191 minutes in length, was cut by 43 minutes for the American market. Nominations for Academy Awards went to *The Emigrants* (best film), Jan Troell (best director) and Liv Ullmann (best actress). Since the two films were made as one, I'll save my comments for the second half; *see* THE NEW LAND.

END OF THE TRAIL (1933, COL). D: D.Ross Lederman. W: Stuart Anthony from a Zane Grey story. Cast: TIM McCOY, Luana WALTERS, Wheeler OAKMAN, Lafe McKee, Chief White Eagle, Wade Boteler.

Message movie was a clumsy but passionate plea for belated justice to the Indians. This was the biggest-budget movie of "B" star McCoy's career; it was photographed (Benjamin Kline) on Wyoming locations with an enormous cast, mostly Arapaho. The film was stilted, larded with endless pontifications documenting the Anglos' despicable history of malfeasance toward red men, but it was sincere, earnest, and unquestionably a landmark.

END OF THE TRAIL (1936, COL). D: Erle C. Kenton. W: Harold Shumate from a Zane Grey story. Cast: JACK HOLT, Louise HENRY, Guinn "Big Boy" WILLIAMS, Douglas Dumbrille, Erle Kenton, Edward LeSaint, Hank Bell, Art Mix, John McGuire, Frank Shannon, Edgar Dearing. 70m.

This had not much to do with the Indian story of the earlier film. Two buddies, Spanish-American War veterans, find themselves on opposite sides of the law in turn-of-the-century Texas; it's a tired old plot but it's handled maturely without much sentimentality and the ending is tough. Oddly, this lesser version hews much more closely to Grey's story than McCoy's film did.

ESCAPE FROM FORT BRAVO (1953, MGM). D: John Sturges. W: Frank Fenton, Philip Rock & Michael Pate. Cast: WILLIAM HOLDEN, ELEANOR PARKER, JOHN FORSYTHE, Polly BERGEN, William DEMAREST, William CAMPBELL, Carl Benton Reid, Richard Anderson, John Lupton, Glenn Strange. 98m.

A complicated plot begins with a romantic triangle—a sharp-tempered Yankee cavalry officer (Holden), a gentlemanly Rebel prisoner (Forsythe) and Parker as the woman torn between them—and leads to the besieging of a handful of Anglos by angry Indians. The outcome is highly unusual. It's photographed excellently (Robert L. Surtees) and there's plenty of commotion in the action scenes and the script is reasonably intelligent. Holden too often is taken for granted; he's a good actor and his presence enhances this film. It was made on location in Death Valley, where the sense of dust-dry heat is effectively captured. It's somewhat glamorized and quite melodramatic and hardly Sturges's best, but it's much better than average.

ESCAPE FROM RED ROCK (1958, FOX). DW: Edward Bernds. Cast: BRIAN DONLEVY, Eilene JANSSEN, Jay C. FLIPPEN, Gary Murray, Rick Vallin, William Phipps. 75m.

Posse pursues a rancher and his girl into Indian territory. Miscast low-budget black-and-white programmer is unappealing.

ESCORT WEST (1959, UA). D. Francis D. Lyon. W: Leo Gordon, Fred Hartshook & Steven Hayes. Cast: VICTOR MATURE, ELAINE STEWART, Faith DOMERGUE, Reba WATERS, Rex INGRAM, Noah BEERY, Jr., William Ching, John Hubbard,

Leo Gordon, Slim Pickens, Harry Carey, Jr., Roy Barcroft, Ken Curtis. 73m.

Heading west through Nevada in 1865 after the end of the Civil War, an ex-Confederate officer and his young daughter encounter some Yankee soldiers, two brunette sisters and a band of renegade Modoc Indians who are determined to wipe out the little party. Formula oater has routine plot and stock characters but is capably handled, enhanced by fine black-and-white CinemaScope outdoor photography (William H. Clothier) and by good performances, especially from Beery as a trail-wise cavalry lieutenant and Ingram as a muleskinner.

AN EYE FOR AN EYE (1966, EMB). D: Michael Moore. W: Bing Russell & Sumner Williams. Cast: ROBERT LANSING, PATRICK WAYNE, Gloria TALBOT, Slim PICKENS, Paul Fix, Strother Martin, Henry Wills, Clint Howard, Rance Howard, Jerry Gatlin. 92m.

A bad guy (Pickens) and his gang kill the wife and child of an ex-gunslinger (Lansing) against whom the bad guys have some kind of unexplained grudge. Naturally the gunslinger tracks them down. En route he teams up with a brash young bounty hunter (Wayne, son of the Duke). These cliches, plus a limp script, a ten-cent budget and poor directing, cripple the film beyond repair. But the scenic photography is fine (Lucien Ballard) and there's a plot twist that is interesting. In an early shoot-out the heroes dispatch Pickens's partners but Pickens, before getting away, wounds both men, blinding the young bounty hunter and crippling the gunslinger's right hand. In an unbelievable but unusual development, the two disabled men continue their quest, each relying on the other to provide the faculty he lacks. It's a strained laughable contrivance but the symbiosis between the two prickly characters is intriguing, largely because of the quality of Lansing's strong performance as the brooding embittered gunslinger.

FABULOUS TEXAN (1947, REP). D: Edward Ludwig. W: Lawrence Hazard, Horace McCoy & Hal Long. Cast: WILLIAM ELLIOTT, CATHERINE McLEOD, JOHN CARROLL, Albert DEKKER, Andy DEVINE, James BROWN, Jim Davis, Robert Barrat, Russell Simpson. 81m.

Carpetbagging totalitarian state police take over Texas after the Civil War; our heroes fight off the tyranny—Texas Rangers versus state police. And of course there's rivalry between Elliott and Carroll over the leading lady. This is a "B"-style melodrama but a big-scale one, and superior to most of Republic's products from the late 1940s.

FACE OF A FUGITIVE (1959, COL). D: Paul Wendkos. W: David Chantler & Daniel Ullman from a Peter Dawson story. Cast: FRED MacMURRAY, Dorothy GREEN, Lin McCarthy, James Coburn, Alan Baxter. 81m.

Accused of murder, an innocent man (MacMurray) runs away and settles in a new town under a new identity; but of course his past catches up with him; trouble dogs his trail. The turns of plot and elaborations of character are quite good. "Peter Dawson" was the brother of "Luke Short" and wrote after a similar fashion. This is distinctly above average, as were most of MacMurray's Westerns.

FACE TO FACE (1952, RKO). Segment: *The Bride Comes to Yellow Sky*. D: Bretaigne Windust. W: James Agee from Stephen Crane's novella. Cast: ROBERT PRESTON, Marjorie STEELE, Minor WATSON, Dan Seymour, Olive Carey. 136m. (Segment: 62m.)

A sheriff's bride-to-be is arriving on the train but first he must deal with the town drunk who's terrorizing the community; only then can he marry the girl. On film, in black-and-white, it comes out as a sort of reverse twist on *High Noon*. It's droll but it turns bitter.

Two famous short stories were packaged by producer Huntington Hartford into this excellent production. The first half of the bill, Joseph Conrad's *The Secret Sharer*, starred James Mason and Michael Pate in a *doppelganger* drama and was directed by John Brahm from a screenplay by Aeneas MacKenzie. Each of the two stories runs about an hour in length. *Bride* is an early example of American black humor, written by the author of *The Red Badge of Courage*. The film is strikingly well done.

FACE TO THE WIND (1974, WB). Also titled: CRY FOR ME, BILLY. D: William A. Graham. W: David Markson. Cast: CLIFF POTTS, Harry Dean STANTON, Xochitl, Don Wilbanks, Woodrow Chambliss. 93m.

Brutal mini-budget ghost-town oater features Stanton as a nicely vile villain and good photography by Jordan Cronenweth; and Potts' performance is fine; but it's a time-waster.

FADE IN (1968, PARA). D: Allen Smithee. W: Jerry Ludwig. Cast: BURT REYNOLDS, BARBARA LODEN, Patricia Casey, James Hampton, Noah Pitlik, Joseph Perry,

George Savalas. Cameos (unbilled): TERENCE STAMP, RICARDO MONTALBAN, JOANNA PETTET. 93m.

A Utah rancher (Reynolds) rents his place out as a location for a shoot-'em-up Western movie; he falls for an assistant film editor (Loden). Small-town milieu (Moab, Utah) and quiet romance are depicted with simple charm. There's gorgeous scenery (cinematographer William Fraker) and a good inobtrusive score (Ken Lauber); editors Aaron Stell and John H. Wheeler do it justice. The film was produced by Silvio Narizzano, who was directing the horrible *Blue* (the filming of which provides the background for this one; its stars play unbilled cameos). *Fade In* was never released to theatres and has been seen in the United States only on television.

FAIR WARNING (1931, FOX). D: Alfred E. Werker. Cast: GEORGE O'BRIEN, George BRENT.

I haven't been able to track down much information about this Western pursuit melodrama.

THE FAR COUNTRY (1955, UNIV). D: Anthony Mann. W: Borden Chase. Cast: JAMES STEWART, RUTH ROMAN, Walter BRENNAN, Corinne CALVET, John McINTIRE, Jay C. FLIPPEN, Steve Brodie, Harry Morgan, John Doucette, Royal Dano, Jack Elam, Robert J. Wilke, Chubby Johnson. 97m.

A self-centered cattleman (Stewart), driving a herd from Oregon to Alaska during the 1896 Klondike gold rush, is opposed by an arrogant woman (Roman), a murder charge, and the self-appointed "law" of the Chilkoot country (McIntire). Eventually he's forced to choose between profit and humanity. Juvenile claptrap here and there but it's a fast yarn with lovely Rocky Mountain scenery; a fine entertaining movie.

FARGO (1952, MONO). D: Lewis D. Collins. W: Jack DeWitt & Joseph Poland. Cast: WILLIAM ELLIOTT, PHYLLIS COATES, Myron HEALEY, Jack Ingram, Robert J. Wilke, Denver Pyle, Stanley Andrews, Tim Ryan, Robert Bray, I. Stanford Jolley.

By this point Elliott's budgets and scripts had sagged; with the move from Republic to Monogram he'd been consigned to low-calibre programmers. This one still gives us a strong William S. Hart-ish reformed-outlaw performance but the plot is a routine combination of the Bob Steele formula and the save-the-girl's-mortgaged-ranch number.

THE FAR HORIZONS (1955, PARA). D: Rudolph Mate. W: Winston Miller & Edmund H. North from Della Gould Emmon's novel *Sacajawea of the Shoshones*. Cast: CHARLTON HESTON, FRED MacMURRAY, DONNA REED, William DEMAREST, Barbara HALE, Alan Reed, Herbert Heyes. 108m.

Nathaniel Hawthorne once complained bitterly about "that damned mob of scribbling women with three names" who seem to have sprung forever out of the American woodwork with their hokey romantic-historical "women's" novels. The story here is a case in point—a treacly lush romanticization of the Lewis (MacMurray) and Clark (Heston) expedition in 1805 to explore the Louisiana Purchase territory as far as Oregon. Adventure and historical drama are sacrificed to the cardboard romance between Heston and Donna Reed as the Indian Sacajawea who guided the explorers across the wilderness continent. MacMurray's performance is more than competent but the other actors leave much to be desired.

THE FASTEST GUITAR ALIVE (1967, MGM). D. Michael Moore. W: Robert E. Kent. Cast: ROY ORBISON, Sammy JACKSON, Maggie PIERCE, Joan FREEMAN, Lyle Bettger, John Doucette, Ben Cooper, Douglas Kennedy, Iron Eyes Cody. 87m.

Two lighthearted saloon-singing Confederate spies pose as entertainers so they can steal Union treasure; then they're forced to return it in secret to the San Francisco Mint. Same plot was used to slightly better advantage in *Sam Whiskey*. Orbison, a country-rock singer, is no actor; at one point herein his sidekick (Jackson) says to him, "You better stick to your singing—you don't have much future in the spy business." Nor in the movie business, evidently. Musical nonsense is limp, lamebrained and listless.

THE FASTEST GUN ALIVE (1956, MGM). D: Russell Rouse. W: Rouse & Frank D. Gilroy from Gilroy's story and TV play. Cast: GLENN FORD, BRODERICK CRAWFORD, JEANNE CRAIN, Leif ERICKSON, Russ TAMBLYN, Rhys Williams, Noah Beery, Jr., Chubby Johnson, J.M. Kerrigan, Allyn Joslyn. 92m.

A storekeeper (Ford) develops a reputation as a fast gun and has to face challenges by various quick-draw champions until finally he must go up against the fastest bad guy of them all (Crawford).

It was filmed as a low-budget black-and-white quickie. But something about it—perhaps merely the title—caught on with the public; it made a box-office fortune and is remembered as a milestone in Hollywood mythology. In retrospect, however, it's a silly, bad movie for a number of reasons, not least among them the miscasting of middle-aged, overweight, citified Broderick Crawford as a lightning-fast gunslinger. The movie carries quick-draw fakery to its illogical extreme. Look closely and you'll see Crawford "fanning" his double-action revolvers (a physical impossibility); look closely again in the final facedown scene just before the draw and you'll see that Ford's Colt is cocked while still in its holster—a sure-fire guarantee he'd blow his foot off if he had real bullets in the gun. Characterizations are somewhat above that level of ineptitude but not sufficiently to justify the reverence in which this mediocre film is held in some quarters.

THE FIEND WHO WALKED THE WEST (1958, FOX). D: Gordon Douglas. W: Harry Brown & Philip Yordan from a Ben Hecht-Charles Lederer screenplay and a story by Eleazar Lipsky. Cast: HUGH O'BRIAN, ROBERT EVANS, Dolores MICHAELS, Linda Cristal, Stephen McNally, Edward Andrews, Emile Meyer, June Blair, Ron Ely. 101m.

An ex-con (O'Brian) sets a trap to nail a crazed killer (Evans) who used to be his cellmate. Photographed (Joseph Macdonald) in black-and-white CinemaScope, this is a cheap Western remake of *Kiss of Death*, the gangster movie in which psychotic killer Richard Widmark achieved stardom by pushing a little old lady down a flight of stairs in her wheelchair. Robert Evans plays the Widmark character (the title role here) and the quality of his acting is such that this role impelled him not to stardom but to retirement from the acting profession; he became a big-time Hollywood producer. The film is full of stupid dialogue badly delivered by both actors in their distracting New York accents. Nauseating flapdoodle.

THE FIERCEST HEART (1961, FOX). D: George Sherman. W: Edmund H. North from a Stuart Cloete novel. Cast: STUART WHITMAN, JULIET PROWSE, RAYMOND MASSEY, Geraldine FITZGERALD, Ken Scott. 91m.

Pioneering wagon train of Boer settlers fights it out with Zulus in this Western-style melodrama re-set in South Africa. It inspires ennui.

FIGHTING CARAVANS (1931, PARA). Also titled: BLAZING ARROWS. D: Otto Brower & David Burton. W: Edward G. Paramore, Jr., Keene Thompson & Agnes B. Leahy from Zane Grey's novel. Cast: GARY COOPER, LILY DAMITA, Ernest TOR-

RENCE, Tully MARSHALL, Eugene Pallette, Fred Kohler, Roy Stewart, Charles Winninger, Chief John Big Tree, Jane Darwell, Iron Eyes Cody. 91m.

Another *Covered Wagon* imitator has Cooper as the intrepid wagon-train scout, boyish in buckskin. Dated.

THE FIGHTING KENTUCKIAN (1949, REP). DW: George Waggner. Cast: JOHN WAYNE, VERA HRUBA RALSTON, Philip DORN, Oliver HARDY, Marie WINDSOR, John HOWARD, Hugo Haas, Grant Withers, Odette Myrtil, Paul Fix, Mae Marsh, Jack Pennick. 100m.

During the War of 1812 a frontiersman (Wayne) comes to the rescue of victimized French settlers in Alabama, protecting them from land-grabbers and romancing an aristocrat's daughter (Ralston). Items of interest are the presences of Oliver Hardy (it's one of his rare appearances without Stan Laurel) and Odette Myrtil, Broadway's "Bloody Mary." John Wayne produced this one to finish out his Republic contract; after this he allegedly refused to appear in any more pictures with Ralston.

FIGHTING MAN OF THE PLAINS (1949, FOX). D: Edwin L. Marin. W: Frank Gruber from his novel. Cast: RANDOLPH SCOTT, JANE NIGH, Bill WILLIAMS, Victor JORY, George "Gabby" HAYES, Douglas Kennedy, James Griffith, Paul Fix, Dale Robertson. 93m.

Frank James (Scott) scours the West for Jesse's murderer. Poor-to-fair oater marked Dale Robertson's film debut.

THE FIREBRAND (1962, FOX). D: Maury Dexter. W: Harry Spalding. Cast: KENT TAYLOR, Valentin de VARGAS, Lisa Montell, Chubby Johnson, Joe Raciti.

Another one about the 1840-ish California bandit Joaquin Murieta (Vargas, in a scenery-chewing performance) and his nemesis the ranger (Taylor, who always played cowboys as if they were Boston Blackie). Trite Zorroesque yarn is strictly for eight-year-olds.

FIRECREEK (1968, WB). D: Vincent McEveety. W: Calvin Clements, Sr. Cast: JAMES STEWART, HENRY FONDA, INGER STEVENS, Dean JAGGER, Ed BEGLEY, Gary Lockwood, Jack Elam, Jay C. Flippen, Barbara Luna, Jacqueline Scott, James Best, Brooke Bundy, Morgan Woodward, John Qualen, Louise Latham, J. Robert Porter. 104m.

A farmer (Stewart) has been elected sheriff but he isn't really a lawman or a gunfighter. Then his town is invaded by a gang of bad guys led by Henry Fonda; now the timid inexperienced sheriff has to defend the town against the five ruthless killers.

The score is good (Alfred Newman) and the two stars make it worthwhile but it's long, slow and pretty dull, a decent script betrayed by lacklustre production and directing.

THE FIRST TEXAN (1956, AA). D: Byron Haskin. W: Daniel Ullman. Cast: JOEL McCREA, FELICIA FARR, Jeff MORROW, Wallace Ford, James Griffith, Chubby Johnson. 82m.

Sam Houston (McCrea) leads the Texas revolt against Mexico's tyranny. Adventurized history is big, actionful and solid. Simpleminded but nice entertainment.

THE FIRST TRAVELING SALESLADY (1956, RKO). D: Arthur Lubin. W: Devery Freeman & Stephen Longstreet. Cast: GINGER ROGERS, CAROL CHANNING, Barry NELSON, David BRIAN, James Arness, Clint Eastwood, Robert Simon, Lane Chandler, Clarence Muse, John Eldridge. 92m.

Two spirited gals go out west to peddle corsets at the turn of the century and get caught up in a misunderstanding about barbed wire. The performances are superior to the script in this labored slapstick comedy; most of its gags tend to collapse under their own excessive weight. Eastwood's first Western role, and RKO's last production.

FISH HAWK (1979, IND). D: Donald Shebib. W: Blanche Hanalis from a novel by Mitchell Jayne. Cast: WILL SAMPSON, Charles Field.

A solitary Indian takes a white kid under his wing. Low-budget wilderness adventure movie is humdrum, although Sampson is imposing.

A FISTFUL OF DOLLARS (1966, UA). D: Sergio Leone. W: Leone & Duccio Tessari. Cast: CLINT EASTWOOD, Marianne KOCH, John Welles, Wolfgang Lukschy. 98m.

Filmed in 1964 but not released in America until two years later, this milestone box-office success elevated minor TV actor Eastwood to stardom, began Leone's fast climb toward big-budget directorial freedom, and created the trend in gory sadistic Italian Westerns. The plot, such as it is, was lifted from Kurosawa's samurai film *Yojimbo* (1961). There are interesting cinematic effects—contrived vulture-like silhouette shots, an excess of looming, gritty close-ups, Ennio Morricone's jangly soundtrack music score, a to-hell-with-it comic-book mindlessness of flippant offhand violence. I confess I cannot remember much of this film although I've seen

it three times; it does not stick to the mind. One's overall reaction may be revulsion or simply boredom, but the film has its importance as a turning point: in it, Leone and Tessari created a new brutal West that had not existed in previous mythology. Certainly it has been a dreadful debasement of the old myths but its uniqueness must be credited. The hero is without personality (unless squinting, shooting and smoking cheroots are taken to be profound marks of character); he's merely a cold killing-machine bent on annihilating armies of enemies who mostly don't seem to have done anything to deserve such harsh punishment. Everything is done at the level of infantile murderous fantasy; its comedy is crude and without even the slyness of a Roadrunner cartoon; there is no dramatic conflict because there are no characters. This film and its successors are historically important but aesthetically lamentable.

A FISTFUL OF DYNAMITE (1972)—*See* DUCK, YOU SUCKER.

FIVE BOLD WOMEN (1959, IND). D: Jorge Lopez-Portillo. W: Mortimer Braus & Jack Pollexfen. Cast: Merry ANDERS, Jeff MORROW, Irish McCalla, Jim Ross, Guinn "Big Boy" Williams.

Marshal (Morrow) is escorting five female miscreants to prison when they're attacked by Indians and by a gang led by the outlaw husband of one of his prisoners. Morrow, a character actor whose main asset was his air of unflappable if overripe dignity, was useless in action roles like this. The movie is flaccid and predictable.

FIVE CARD STUD (1969, PARA). D: Henry Hathaway. W: Marguerite Roberts from Ray Gaulden's novel. Cast: ROBERT MITCHUM, DEAN MARTIN, INGER STEVENS, RODDY McDOWALL, Katherine JUSTICE, John Anderson, Denver Pyle, Whit Bissell, Yaphet Kotto, Ruth Springford, Ted de Corsia. 103m.

There was this poker game. A player got caught cheating. The other players lynched him. Now somebody is avenging the dead man by picking off the members of the poker game, one by one. A professional gambler turned detective (Martin) suspects a fundamentalist brimstone preacher (Mitchum, sleepwalking through the part), a loony young rancher (McDowall, mugging atrociously) and several others. It's obvious and transparent. Hal Wallis produced; the producer-writer-director team also made *True Grit*. And Maurice Jarre wrote the score. And plenty of good actors are on hand. But it's an irritatingly boring movie.

FIVE GUNS TO TOMBSTONE (1960, UA). D: Edward L. Cahn. W: Richard Schayer, Arthur Orloff & Jack De Witt. Cast: James BROWN, Della SHARMAN, Walter Coy, John Wilder.

Young man is forced into his brother's stage-robbing gang. Standard cheap oater.

FIVE GUNS WEST (1955, IND). D: Roger Corman. W: Robert W. Campbell. Cast: JOHN LUND, DOROTHY MALONE, Mike CONNORS, Jack Ingram. 78m.

Confederate ex-cons plunder the West, hunting for a hidden cache of stolen loot. Director Corman's first movie, this was a standard outlaw Western, made on the cheap, but bolstered by good acting.

FIVE MAN ARMY (1970, MGM). D: Don Taylor. W: Dario Argento. Cast: PETER GRAVES, JAMES DALY, Tetsuro TAMBA, Bud SPENCER, Nino Castelnuovo, Marc Lawrence. 105m.

A group of skilled professionals prepares and executes a train heist during the 1914 Mexican Revolution. Filmed in Spain with the usual spaghetti supporting players, this low-budget caper movie easily could have been just another dud; the bonus of excitement is a pleasing surprise: the last one-third of the film depicts a tingling suspenseful train-robbery sequence with a surprising number of tense twists. The dialogue is typical of European Westerns (inexcusably moronic) but the caper itself takes place virtually without dialogue. Taylor directs the action very well.

FLAME OF THE BARBARY COAST (1945, REP). D: Joseph Kane. W: Borden Chase from a story by Prescott Chaplin. Cast: JOHN WAYNE, ANN DVORAK, Joseph SCHILDKRAUT, William Frawley, Virginia Grey, Paul Fix, Butterfly McQueen, Russell Hicks, Rex Lease, Hank Bell. 91m.

A cattleman from Montana (Wayne) comes to San Francisco at the turn of the century and falls in love with a saloon singer (Dvorak), so he buys a gambling hall on the Barbary Coast as a showcase for her. Very little action in this one, although it has the obligatory earthquake-fire climax. Routine.

FLAMING FEATHER (1951, PARA). D: Ray Enright. W: Gerald D. Adams & Frank Gruber. Cast: STERLING HAYDEN, BARBARA RUSH, FORREST TUCKER, Arleen WHELAN, Edgar BUCHANAN, Victor JORY, Richard Arlen, Carol Thurston. 77m.

Renegade bad guy (Jory) is the brains behind Apache pillaging; heroes have to nab him and rescue a white woman who's been kidnapped by the Indians. Hokey.

FLAMING FRONTIER (1958, FOX). D: Sam Newfeld. W: Louis Stevens. Cast: Paisley Maxwell, Cecil Linder, Ben Lennick, Peter Humphreys. 70m.

Half-breed cavalry officer heads off war with the Indians. Dreadful.

FLAMING GUNS (1932, UNIV). D: Arthur Rosson. W: Jack Cunningham from a Peter B. Kyne story. Cast: TOM MIX, Ruth HALL, William FARNUM, George Hackathorne, Clarence Wilson, Bud Osborne. 57m.

Routine Mixture involves an imperiled rancher's daughter; "B" fare.

FLAMING STAR (1960, FOX). D: Don Siegel. W: Nunnally Johnson & Clair Huffaker from Huffaker's novel *Flaming Lance*. Cast: ELVIS PRESLEY, BARBARA EDEN, Dolores DEL RIO, Steve FORREST, John McINTIRE, Rodolfo Acosta, Tom Reese, Karl Swenson. 101m.

The dramatic conflicts center on the efforts by the principals to avert bloodshed between Kiowas and white settlers. It offers a subdued and nonmusical Elvis as the half-breed son of Del Rio and McIntire, both of whom turn in powerful performances. The script is intelligent and thoughtful, though at times its sombre grimness is too heavily emphasized by Siegel's surprisingly deliberate direction and Cyril Mockridge's heavy portentous music. But there's a good deal of action. It's one of Presley's best movies. In CinemaScope.

FLAP! (1969, WB). Also titled: NOBODY LOVES FLAPPING EAGLE and NOBODY LOVES A DRUNKEN INDIAN. D: Carol Reed. W: Clair Huffaker from his novel *Nobody Loves a Drunken Indian*. Cast: ANTHONY QUINN, SHELLEY WINTERS, Claude AKINS, Tony BILL, Victor Jory, Rodolfo Acosta, Anthony Caruso. 106m.

Flapping Eagle (Quinn) is an indignant modern-day Paiute Indian who sets out to arm his poverty-stricken Arizona tribe with modern public relations techniques and draw attention to their troubles. The comedy escalates through the theft of a train, a freewheeling battle with cops, and finally an invasion of the modern city of Phoenix by the Paiutes in what the author-screenwriter describes as the Last Great Indian Uprising.

When I reviewed Huffaker's novel in *The Saturday Review* I observed, "The book is fun but the movie will be a lot better." I was wrong. The film disappeared with curious totality soon after its release; it isn't listed in many of the usual source books, and rarely if ever turns up on TV. The title underwent two changes during initial release. The reason for those changes appears to be the same reason that makes it a rotten movie: the unwillingness to "offend" anybody at all. The book was more screenplay than novel and was therefore unsatisfying as literature but at least it was funny and had the grace not to wallow in propaganda; the movie, on the other hand, is labored and heavy-handed. Nobody involved in it seems to have any comic aptitudes. The result is a thick viscous message picture that seems to go on forever.

FLESH AND THE SPUR (1957, AI). D: Edward L. Cahn. W: Charles B. Griffith, Mark Hanna, Lou Rusoff & Edward L. Cahn. Cast: JOHN AGAR, Marla ENGLISH, Touch (Mike) CONNORS, Raymond Hatton, Joyce Meadows, Bud Osborne.

The Bob Steele plot tinged with sexual innuendo. Very poor.

FOR A FEW DOLLARS MORE (1967, UA). D: Sergio Leone. W: Leone, Fulvio Morsella & Luciano Vincenzoni. Cast: CLINT EASTWOOD, LEE VAN CLEEF, Gian Maria VOLANTE, Mara Krupp, Luigi Pistilli, Klaus Kinski, Robert Camardial, Aldo Sanbrell, Jose Egger, Mario Brega. 130m.

Made quickly in 1965 to cash in on the success in Italy of its predecessor *A Fistful of Dollars*, this one steals its plot from Kurosawa's samurai film *Sanjuro*. Eastwood and Van Cleef play rival bounty killers in pursuit of a gang of bank robbers, vying for the reward money. Eastwood, as the wooden one-track tough guy, is amusingly juxtaposed with Van Cleef as the older, more sophisticated, wily, devious manhunter. The film has more personality than its predecessor (mostly because of Van Cleef, who obviously is having lots of fun) and less stomach-turning viciousness than its successor (*The Good, the Bad and the Ugly*); it's the least unpalatable of the three. But it goes on forever. The score unhappily is inferior to other Ennio Morricone compositions. Massimo Dellamano's Technicolor photography gives the film, like Leone's other spaghetti oaters, some odd pictorial effects—slaughter, gore, cruel silhouettes. Childish, contrived, morally offensive, but fitfully entertaining.

FOR BETTER, FOR WORSE (1974)—*See* ZANDY'S BRIDE.

FORT APACHE (1948, RKO). D: John Ford. W: Frank Nugent from James Warner Bellah's short story "Massacre." Cast: HENRY FONDA, JOHN WAYNE, Shirley TEMPLE, Victor McLAGLEN, Pedro ARMENDARIZ, John AGAR, Ward Bond, Dick Foran, George O'Brien, Grant Withers, Anna Lee, Mae Marsh, Irene Rich, Francis Ford, Jack Pennick, Miguel Inclan, Guy Kibbee, Frank Ferguson. 127m.

A hidebound Custerish by-the-book colonel (Fonda) arrives embittered at a frontier outpost he regards as Siberian exile; his stubborn refusal to learn the peculiarities of Indian warfare causes a near catastrophe. A veteran frontier-wise subordinate (Wayne) tries to set things right but risks his career and life to do it. The plot twists are often unexpected and the characters never as simple as one expects. Photography (Archie J. Stout) is top-drawer. John Agar, recently married to Shirley Temple and making his much-ballyhooed film debut here as the suitor of Fonda's daughter (Temple), is a weak link in the cast. The film's ending makes an interesting statement—later echoed in Ford's *The Man Who Shot Liberty Valance*—about the importance of preserving heroic myths even when they are contradicted by facts. *Rio Grande* is lustier and *She Wore a Yellow Ribbon* more mature but *Fort Apache*, the first of Ford's cavalry trilogy, is grand entertainment, justly regarded as a classic Western.

FORT BOWIE (1958, UA). D: Howard W. Koch. W: Maurice Tombragel. Cast: BEN JOHNSON, Barbara PARRY, Kent TAYLOR, Jim DAVIS, Jan Harrison, Ed Hinton. 79m.

At the last minute the cavalry saves the fort but not the movie. Poor, despite the presences of Johnson and Davis.

FORT COURAGEOUS (1965, FOX). D: Lesley Selander. W: Richard Landau. Cast: DONALD BARRY, Fred Beir, Hanna Landy, Harry Lauter, Walter Reed.

A rape accusation gets a trooper drummed out of the cavalry but then of course he saves the day against the Indians. Forget it.

FORT DEFIANCE (1951, UA). D: John Rawlins. W: Louis Lentz. Cast: BEN JOHNSON, DANE CLARK, Peter GRAVES, Tracie Roberts, Dick Elliott, Iron Eyes Cody, George Cleveland. 81m.

To get revenge a Texan (Johnson) pursues a Civil War deserter (Clark) across hostile Indian country. Low-budget, but Johnson is terrific.

FORT DOBBS (1958, WB). D: Gordon Douglas. W: Burt Kennedy & George W. George. Cast: CLINT WALKER, VIRGINIA MAYO, BRIAN KEITH, Richard EYER, Russ CONWAY, Michael Dante. 90m.

A fugitive from a murder charge (Walker) helps a widow (Mayo) and her young son

(Eyer) escape marauding Comanches. They meet a drifter (Keith) who may be running rifles to the Indians. A lot of action climaxes in a big Indian battle with our hero riding to the rescue, clearing up the misunderstandings about his past and winning the fair damsel.

So much for the plot; it's routine. The budget was small; it's filmed in black-and-white (William Clothier); by all standards it's an unambitious programmer. But this minor movie exemplifies the best that pure unpretentious "B" fare can offer. It's honest; it's superbly made within its limitations. Max Steiner's score is ideal. Second-unit action by assistant director William Kissel is rousing. Clint Walker (in his movie debut, after achieving TV stardom as "Cheyenne") looms like a tree but he's perfectly cast in the laconic role. Virginia Mayo by now had matured into an unglamorous but appealing actress. Brian Keith, in a brief but mercurial contrapuntal role, is brilliant. Russ Conway as the compassionate sheriff is urbane but very good. Gordon Douglas, too many of whose productions have been flabby and oversized, whips this taut story right along, keying the tense conflicts, making it gritty and fast. The script is entirely according to formula but it works; there are fine vignettes and—with occasional lapses into deadly cliche—terse dialogue. The characters are sharply drawn. Historical anachronisms abound but the "B" West is timeless anyhow. Armed with 20–20 hindsight one may quarrel with the number of Indians who bite the dust, but those were the conventions of the genre and ought to be taken on face value for their own time. *Fort Dobbs*, a wholly predictable little programmer, turns out to be a fine gripping vest-pocket sleeper that shows how entertaining a little Western really can be.

FOR THE LOVE OF MIKE (1960, FOX). D: George Sherman. W: D.D. Beauchamp. Cast: RICHARD BASEHART, Stuart ERWIN, Armando Silvestre, Arthur Shields. 84m.

Indian boy (Silvestre) trains his horse in hopes of winning prize money he can use to provide his village with a shrine. Sincere but treacly.

FORT MASSACRE (1958, UA). D: Joseph M. Newman. W: Martin M. Goldsmith. Cast: JOEL McCREA, SUSAN CABOT, Forrest TUCKER, John RUSSELL, George W. Neise, Francis J. McDonald, Denver Pyle, Irving Bacon, Anthony Caruso, Rayford Barnes. 80m.

McCrea plays a bitter Indian-hating cavalry troop leader who tries to lead the remnants of his detachment back to the fort through what seem to be 10,000 hostile Apaches. It's another *Lost Patrol* derivation with men getting picked off one by one but the acting is first-rate and some of the plot twists are surprising. The McCrea character is unusually complicated and it is fascinating to watch the changes in him. Slow, but interesting.

FORT OSAGE (1952, AA). D: Lesley Selander. W: Daniel Ullman. Cast: ROD CAMERON, JANE NIGH, Douglas KENNEDY, Myron Healey, Morris Ankrum, Iron Eyes Cody, Francis J. McDonald. 71m.

Indian uprising again. Ullman wrote dozens of oaters. A few of them were fair-to-good. This is not one of those.

FORT TI (1953, COL). D: William Castle. W: Robert E. Kent. Cast: GEORGE MONTGOMERY, JOAN VOHS, Irving BACON, Lester MATHEWS, James Seay, Ben Aster, Phyllis Fowler, Howard Petrie. 73m.

Set in the Adirondack outpost of Fort Ticonderoga during the French and Indian War, this one has a civilian scout (Montgomery) joining up with Rogers' Rangers to attack the French-held fort after he learns the French are holding his sister and a couple of children captive. If the people on the screen always seem to be aiming arrows, knives, rifles and cannons straight at you it's because the movie was released originally in 3-D—a process that, in this case, only made the picture even more silly than it otherwise would have been. Fair diversion for children.

FORT UTAH (1964, PARA). D: Lesley Selander. W: Steve Fisher & Andrew Craddock. Cast: JOHN IRELAND, VIRGINIA MAYO, Scott BRADY, John RUSSELL, Robert STRAUSS, Jim DAVIS, Don DeFORE, Richard ARLEN, James CRAIG, Donald BARRY, Jim DAVIS, Harry Lauter, Reg Parton, Read Morgan, Eric Cody. 83m.

A hero named Tom Horn (Ireland) helps a pilgrim wagon train through Indian country while fighting off renegade whites (Brady, Davis) and the arrogant wagon-train boss (Russell). The script of this A.C. Lyles production is abominable and the film dreadful on all counts except for a few performances— Ireland is always creditable; Russell seems ill, or distracted, but even so he's powerful; Davis, in a small part, is a fine cowardly villain. Good wide-screen photography (Lothrop Worth) but a silly score (Jimmie Haskell).

FORT VENGEANCE (1953, AA). D: Lesley Selander. W: Daniel Ullman. Cast: JAMES

CRAIG, RITA MORENO, Keith LARSEN, Reginald Denny, Emory Parnell. 75m.

It's Canadian Mounties versus fur pirates and Indians in this turkey, with added conflict between two Mountie brothers (Craig, Larsen).

FORT WORTH (1951, WB). D: Edwin L. Marin. W: John Twist. Cast: RANDOLPH SCOTT, PHYLLIS THAXTER, David BRIAN, Helena CARTER, Dick Jones, Walter Sande, Chubby Johnson, Paul Picerni. 81m.

Once again the ex-gunslinger hangs up his guns and turns to a peaceable trade (editing a newspaper) only to be forced reluctantly to buckle on his six-shooter and fight it out with the lawless guys who've taken over the town. One of Scott's more enervating efforts.

FORTY GUNS (1957, FOX). DW: Samuel Fuller. Cast: BARBARA STANWYCK, BARRY SULLIVAN, Gene BARRY, Dean JAGGER, John Ericson, Jidge Carroll, Eve Brent, Robert Dix, Hank Worden. 80m.

U.S. Marshal brothers (Sullivan and Barry) are pitted against a Clanton-style gang in a Tombstone sort of town; the leader of the bad guys is, ludicrously, Barbara Stanwyck, whose kid brother (Ericson) is a brutal lout who keeps killing people and thereby getting into trouble from which she has to extract him, usually by sending her army of forty gunmen into town to wreak havoc. The black-and-white CinemaScope photography (Joseph Biroc) is acceptable, and a few of the actors acquit themselve well (Sullivan, Barry, Worden), but those are the only competences of this banal, brutal and dehumanizing trash.

Forty Guns is probably the most rancidly vicious Western of the 1950s. It reeks of sexual sadism and moral perversion. The ridiculously portentous soundtrack score (Harry Sukman) sets the tone for this Fuller-produced offense, which apparently served as an inspiration for the witless violence of the Leone-style spaghetti shoot-'em-ups of the 1960s. Fuller has his fans, but in my opinion this picture is an abomination.

FORTY GUNS TO APACHE PASS (1967, COL). D: William Witney. W: Willard & Mary Willingham. Cast: AUDIE MURPHY, Laraine STEPHENS, Kenneth TOBEY, Robert Brubaker, Michael Burns, Michael Blodgett, Michael Keep. Narrator: Maurice Hart. 95m.

Cochise is a villain in this cheapie about a heroic cavalry captain (Murphy) contending with rampaging Apaches, green troopers, beleaguered settlers, desert hardships and a treacherous corporal (Tobey). Like Murphy's other oaters of the 1960s this doesn't measure up to his Universal Westerns of the previous decade.

THE FORTY-NINERS (1954, AA). D: Thomas Carr. W: Daniel Ullman. Cast: WILLIAM ELLIOTT, VIRGINIA GREY, Harry MORGAN, John Doucette, Lane Bradford, Harry Lauter, Earl Hodgins, I. Stanford Jolley, Ralph Sanford. 71m.

One of the last of the "B" Westerns and not a bad one, although it has a cluttered plot. Set in the gold-rush days in California it has Elliott as an avenging peace officer tracking down three murder suspects with the help of a suspicious-looking gambler. In black-and-white.

FORT YUMA (1955, UA). D: Lesley Selander. W: Danny Arnold. Cast: PETER GRAVES, Joan VOHS, Joan Taylor, John Hudson, Addison Richards. 78m.

Apaches and cavalry, set in Arizona but filmed in Utah; nice scenery but dull plot.

FOUR FACES WEST (1948, UA). D: Alfred E. Green. W: Graham Baker, Teddi Sherman, William & Milarde Brent from Eugene Manlove Rhodes's short novel *Paso Por Aqui*. Cast: JOEL McCREA, FRANCES DEE, CHARLES BICKFORD, JOSEPH CALLEIA, William CONRAD, Martin Garralaga, Houseley Stevenson, Forrest Taylor, Glenn Strange, Raymond Largey. 90m.

The story apparently began in Rhodes's mind as a fantasized twist on the legends about Pat Garrett's pursuit of Billy the Kid; Rhodes lived in the town where Billy was killed. McCrea is the beleaguered outlaw, torn between the need for flight and compassion for a helpless invalid; Bickford is powerful as Garrett, Dee is a lovely nurse with whom the fugitive falls in love, Calleia is a sympathetic innkeeper both sinister and magnetic in a complex, devious role. The film has stretches of lyrical beauty. Rhodes was a rancher who knew the people and the atmosphere; the screenwriters conveyed the flavor with justice. The fine photography is by Russell Harlan; the good spare score by Paul Sawtell. It's a splendid example of what a low-budget Western can be: its excellence is such that it can make you feel as if you've never seen a Western before.

FOUR FAST GUNS (1959, UNIV). D: William J. Hole, Jr. W: James Edmiston & Dallas Gaultois. Cast: JAMES CRAIG, MARTHA VICKERS, Brett HALSEY, Richard Martin, Edgar Buchanan, Paul Richards. 72m.

Two gunfighter brothers have a falling out. Tiresome and predictable.

FOUR FOR TEXAS (1963, WB). D: Robert Aldrich. W: Aldrich & Teddi Sherman. Cast: FRANK SINATRA, DEAN MARTIN, ANITA EKBERG, URSULA ANDRESS, Charles BRONSON, Victor BUONO, Richard Jaeckel, Mike Mazurki, Jack Lambert, the Three Stooges, Edric Connor. 124m.

Friendly enemies in 1870ish Galveston (Sinatra, Martin) each try to take over the town's gambling operation. Mammary marvels Ekberg and Andress loom in skimpy costumes. (Scenes were shot in the nude, but edited out before release, for fear of censorship.) Director Aldrich has made great movies and terrible ones. This one is among the worst. The contempt in which all concerned must have held their audience should not be encouraged by willingly viewing this drivel.

FOUR GUNS TO THE BORDER (1954, UNIV). D: Richard Carlson. W: George Van Marter & Franklin Coen from a Louis L'Amour story. Cast: RORY CALHOUN, COLLEEN MILLER, George NADER, Walter BRENNAN, Nina FOCH, John McINTIRE, Jay Silverheels. 82m.

Down-at-the-heels cowpoke (Calhoun) joins his buddies in a bank robbery and then they're off for the border but they have to fight it out with lawmen and Apaches and so forth. Not bad, but not very good.

THE FOURTH HORSEMAN (1932, UNIV). D: Hamilton MacFadden. W: Jack Cunningham & Nina Putnam. Cast: TOM MIX, Margaret LINDSAY, Fred KOHLER, Buddy Roosevelt, Edmund Cobb, Richard Cramer, Raymond Hatton, Rosita Marstini, Walter Brennan. 63m.

Drifting hero foils land-grab by villains Kohler and Cramer. Creaky, but it was one of Mix's few talkies and it's amusing.

FRANKIE AND JOHNNY (1966, UA). D: Frederick de Cordova. W: Alex Gottlieb & Nat Perrin. Cast: ELVIS PRESLEY, DONNA DOUGLAS, Harry MORGAN, Sue Ann LANGDON, Nancy KOVACK, Audrey Christie, Jerome Cowan, Robert Strauss. 87m.

Presley is a not very convincing riverboat gambler who spends most of his time singing songs (high spot is "When the Saints Go Marching In") in this pedestrian attempt to wring a musical movie out of the old folk song and legend about the gal who shot her lover after he done her wrong.

FRENCHIE (1950, UNIV). D: Louis King. W: Oscar Brodney. Cast: JOEL McCREA, SHELLEY WINTERS, John RUSSELL, Elsa LANCHESTER, Marie WINDSOR, John Emery, Paul Kelly, George Cleveland. 81m.

Frenchie is a real fast girl. The town threw her out but now she's back to settle old scores; she's lording it over the boys in the saloon. The easygoing sheriff is played by Joel McCrea. Shelley Winters is as Western as Tugboat Annie. It's a clumsy imitation of *Destry Rides Again*, which in any version—even the least of them—was better than this bomb.

FRIENDLY PERSUASION (1956, AA). D: William Wyler. W: (unbilled) Michael Wilson from Jessamyn West's novel *The Friendly Persuasion*. Cast: GARY COOPER, DOROTHY McGUIRE, ANTHONY PERKINS, Marjorie MAIN, Robert MIDDLETON, Richard EYER, Mark Richman, Phyllis Love, John Smith, Walter Catlett, Russell Simpson, James Seay, William Schallert. 140m.

During the Civil War a family of pacifist Quakers who live on an Indiana farm must face the conflict that erupts within the family when a son (Perkins) feels he has a duty to fight for the Union. The ending was something of a shocker in its day. There is some slapstick concerning Marjorie Main and her man-eating daughters, and the score is not Dimitri Tiomkin's best, and there's a dreadful Pat Boone title song, and the theme is a bit trite and rustic, and it's thick with near-naive nostalgia; but the movie is marvelously scripted, directed and acted—warm and funny. Cooper is delightfully amusing in it.

Michael Wilson wrote the screenplay for Cooper in 1946 but it had to be shelved because of the actor's other commitments. By the time it was filmed a decade later Wilson had been blacklisted by the McCarthy witch hunt; as a result Allied Artists refused to put his name on the credits.

THE FRISCO KID (1979, WB). D: Robert Aldrich. W: Michael Elias & Frank Shaw. Cast: GENE WILDER, HARRISON FORD, Penny PEYSER, Ramon BIERI, Val Bisoglio, George Ralph DiCenzo, William Smith. 122m.

Trekking from Russia across the American frontier to San Francisco, a bumbling rabbi (Wilder) comes under the grudging protection of a gunslinger (Ford); together they suffer misadventures—robberies, Indian attacks, comic chases. I think Gene Wilder is an acquired taste; I haven't acquired it, although I found him amusing enough in *Blaz-*

ing Saddles. This one is heavy-handed farce, all too predictable, leaden.

FROM HELL TO TEXAS **(1958, FOX).** Also titled: THE HELL-BENT KID. D: Henry Hathaway. W: Robert H. Buckner & Wendell Mayes from Charles O. Locke's novel ***The Road to Socorro.*** Cast: DON MURRAY, DIANE VARSI, Chill WILLS, R.G. Armstrong, Jay C. Flippen, Dennis Hopper, Margo, Harry Carey, Jr. 99m.

Saddle tramp (Murray) finds himself being shot at and pursued across the dusty wastes of New Mexico by the minions of a cruel cattle baron (Armstrong). Stark film is masterfully photographed (Wilfrid M. Cline), taut and relentless, fusing a Kafkaesque flavor and a Eugene Manlove Rhodes spirit into a gritty tough drama, superbly played.

FROM NOON TILL THREE **(1976, UA).** DW: Frank D. Gilroy. Cast: CHARLES BRONSON, JILL IRELAND, Douglas V. Fowley, Betty Cole, Davis Roberts, Stan Haze, Hector Morales, Donald Barry. 108m.

When a hapless two-bit outlaw (Bronson) is believed to have died, the woman (Ireland) with whom he had a three-hour affair builds their romance into a worldwide legend through books, plays and songs; then the "dead" outlaw returns to try and reap the benefits of his legend, but nobody believes he's the outlaw because the girl has described him as tall and handsome (Bronson is neither). Even the girl, believing her own lies by now, fails to recognize him.

It's a cute satirical idea for a comedy about the difference between legend and reality. But the execution, and the miscasting of Bronson (he's no light comedian), make it fall flat. The pace is deadly slow.

FRONTIER BADMEN **(1943, UNIV).** D: Ford Beebe. W: Morgan R. Cox & Gerald Geraghty. Cast: ROBERT PAIGE, DIANA BARRYMORE, Anne GWYNNE, Noah BEERY, Jr., Leo CARRILLO, Andy Devine, Lon Chaney, Jr., Tex Ritter, William Farnum, Thomas Gomez, Tom Fadden, Eddy Waller, Kermit Maynard.

Big cast of "B" stars and former stars, and some good trail-drive action scenes (especially a rousing stampede), don't rescue this from its programmer trappings of plot and characterization.

FRONTIER GAL **(1945, UNIV).** D: Charles Lamont. W: Michael Fessier & Ernest Pagano. Cast: YVONNE De CARLO, ROD CAMERON, Andy DEVINE, Fuzzy Knight, Sheldon Leonard, George Eldredge. 84m.

Saloon gal marries a fugitive from the law; together they outwit and outfight the bad guys. Simple trite sex comedy is funny in spots and speedy with brawling "B"-style action. In Technicolor. Subsequently the two stars, both Canadian, made two other features together: *River Lady* and *Salome Where She Danced.*

FRONTIER GUN **(1958, FOX).** D: Paul Landres. W: Stephen Kandel. Cast: JOHN AGAR, Holly BANE, Barton MacLANE, Robert Strauss, Morris Ankrum. 70m.

Put-upon honest sheriff finally has to go out and face the bad guys over gunsights. Cheap tired imitation of *High Noon.*

FRONTIER MARSHAL **(1934, FOX).** D: Lewis Seiler. W: William Counselman & Stuart Anthony from Stuart N. Lake's book *Wyatt Earp, Frontier Marshal.* Cast: GEORGE O'BRIEN, IRENE BENTLEY, George E. STONE, Alan Edwards, Ruth Gillette, Berton Churchill.

First adaptation of Lake's book (followed later by another *Frontier Marshal,* then by *My Darling Clementine,* and later by *Powder River,* 1953) is a capable ordinary oater about the town-taming Earp brothers. Fox gave it a fair budget but it was inferior to the earlier, and similar, *Law and Order.* It wasn't really until the 1940s and 1950s that Earp became a well-known character of Western movie folklore. (By the 1980s he had faded from awareness again; most children born after the early 1960s have never heard of Wyatt Earp.)

FRONTIER MARSHAL **(1939, FOX).** D: Allan Dwan. W: Sam Hellman from Stuart N. Lake's book *Wyatt Earp, Frontier Marshal.* Cast: RANDOLPH SCOTT, CESAR ROMERO, NANCY KELLY, John CARRADINE, Jon HALL, Binnie Barnes, Ward Bond, Chris-Pin Martin, Joe Sawyer, Lon Chaney, Jr., Russell Simpson, Tom Tyler, Edward Norris, Eddie Foy, Jr. 91m.

Here's the story of Wyatt (Scott) and Virgil (Hall) Earp, their dubious friendship with Doc Holliday (Romero) and their conflicts in Tombstone that lead to the gunfight at the OK Corral. This one, filmed on the tenth anniversary of Wyatt's death, began the movies' love affair with the Earps, and it's still highly satisfactory with all the traditional myths solidly in place. At the time of its release it suffered from competition with the slew of blockbuster Westerns that brought the genre out of the doldrums in 1939: *Union Pacific, Man of Conquest, Destry Rides Again, Jesse James* and of course *Stagecoach.* But in retrospect *Frontier Marshall* stands up well against all of them. It's still heartily entertaining.

FRONTIER UPRISING (1961, UA). D: Edward L. Kahn. W: Owen Harris from a George Bruce story. Cast: JIM DAVIS, Nancy HADLEY, Nestor Paiva, Ken Mayer, Addison Richards. 68m.

Black-and-white remake of *Kit Carson* (1940) uses a lot of stock footage from the earlier film. Scout (Davis) leads a wagon train to California in the 1840s through hostile Indian territory. Some of the performers are good but as a whole the film is poor.

THE FURIES (1950, PARA). D: Anthony Mann. W: Charles Schnee from Niven Busch's novel. Cast: BARBARA STANWYCK, WALTER HUSTON, WENDELL COREY, Judith ANDERSON, Gilbert ROLAND, Thomas GOMEZ, Blanche Yurka, Beulah Bondi, Albert Dekker, John Bromfield, Wallace Ford, Louis Jean Heydt, Frank Ferguson, Movita Castaneda, Arthur Hunnicutt. 109m.

This cattle-empire story builds a conflict between a stubborn vital old rancher (Huston) and his determined ambitious daughter (Stanwyck), played out mostly in New Mexico in the 1870s (filmed, of course, in Arizona) but also partly in San Francisco (filmed in Los Angeles).

At one time this sort of scenery-chewing soap-opera Western was called "adult" (because it dealt more with sexual conflicts than with shoot-'em-up ones) and "psychological" (because the characters often were driven by neurotic compulsions); and apparently one requisite of such movies was that Judith Anderson appear in them (compare *Pursued*). The plot is wild and implausible—there are heavy hints of incest and miscegenation—but it's played with great gusto by a fine cast and lives up to its title: it's romantic melodrama of a very high order. It's abetted by robust black-and-white cinematography (Victor Milner). Huston, in his last film, is wonderful. Stanwyck is terrific. The movie is larger than life, and completely absorbing. But on reviewing it out of its time one is reminded of the joke, current in the 1950s, about the difference between the old-fashioned Tom Mix sort of oater and the then-new "adult Western": in the adult Western, the cowboy still loves his horse—but he *worries* about it.

FURY AT FURNACE CREEK (1948, FOX). D: H.Bruce Humberstone. W: Charles G. Booth & Winston Miller from a David Garth novel. Cast: VICTOR MATURE, COLEEN GRAY, Glenn LANGAN, Albert DEKKER, Reginald Gardiner, Robert Warwick, Fred Clark, Jay Silverheels, J.Farrell MacDonald. 88m.

Fast and heavily plotted, this one has two brothers (Mature, Langan) trying to clear the name of their father who was a general accused of having engineered a massacre of unsuspecting Apaches. Albert Dekker is the land-grabbing villain, as usual, and he concocts plenty of chicanery and violence against the good guys. There aren't many surprises but it's pretty well done.

FURY AT GUNSIGHT PASS (1956, COL). D: Fred F. Sears. W: David Lang. Cast: DAVID BRIAN, Lisa DAVIS, Neville BRAND, Richard Long, Addison Richards, Morris Ankrum. 68m.

The usual outlaws-take-over-the-town oater; actionful but routine.

FURY AT SHOWDOWN (1957, UA). D: Gerd Oswald. W: Jason James from a Lucas Todd novel. Cast: JOHN DEREK, Carolyn CRAIG, Nick Adams, John Smith. 75m.

Reformed gunfighter (Derek) has to prove himself to the contemptuous folks of his home town. Slow, talky, dreary and woeful.

THE GALLANT LEGION (1948, REP). D: Joseph Kane. W: Gerald D. Adams, John K. Butler & Gerald Geraghty. Cast: WILLIAM ELLIOTT, ADRIAN BOOTH, Joseph SCHILDKRAUT, Bruce CABOT, Andy DEVINE, Jack Holt, Grant Withers, Adele Mara, James Brown, Hal Taliaferro, Russell Hicks, Harry Woods, Roy Barcroft, Hank Bell, Jack Ingram, George Chesebro, Rex Lease, John Hamilton, Trevor Bardette, Iron Eyes Cody, Kermit Maynard, Cactus Mack, Fred Kohler, Glenn Strange, Joseph Crehan, Marshall Reed, Tex Terry. 87m.

Texas Ranger (Elliott) fights off a gang of political opportunists who want to split Texas up into five pieces (a plot based on an actual provision in the articles under which Texas was absorbed into the United States).

Kane was probably the best "B" director at Republic; the three writers were established pros; the actors were veterans of countless programmers, and in this film practically every Western supporting player who wasn't nailed down to a studio contract was employed—the cast is virtually a "who's who" of the Republic stock company. Officially Elliott was a "B" star and his Republic features never ran in prestige cinemas but many of them, like this one, were every bit as good as other studios' "A" product. Exciting and entertaining.

THE GAL WHO TOOK THE WEST (1949, UNIV). D: Frederick de Cordova. W: William Bowers & Oscar Brodney. Cast: YVONNE De CARLO, CHARLES COBURN, SCOTT BRADY, John RUSSELL,

Russell Simpson, Clem Bevans, James Millican. 84m.

You can tell from the title that it's an Yvonne De Carlo oater. There was always a good deal of comedy in De Carlo's Westerns and this is no exception. As usual she's a songbird entertainer bowling the boys over in frontier Arizona. The good guy versus bad guy plot is the usual thing. It's typical of its kind—no better, no worse. A timekiller, in Technicolor.

THE GAMBLER FROM NATCHEZ (1954, FOX). D: Henry Levin. W: Irving Wallace & Gerald D. Adams. Cast: DALE ROBERTSON, DEBRA PAGET, Thomas GOMEZ, Kevin McCARTHY, Lisa Daniels, Douglas Dick. 88m.

Bob Steele plot is enhanced by colorful riverboat gambling scenes, starlet belles in off-the-shoulder costumes and plenty of duels with blade and bullet. Nothing new but it's cheerfully handled.

THE GAMBLER WORE A GUN (1961, UA). D: Edward L. Cahn. W: Owen Harris from L.L. Foreman's screen story for the 1954 film *The Lone Gun*. Cast: JIM DAVIS, MERRY ANDERS, Mark Allen, Addison Richards, Keith Richards, Joe McGuinn.

Gambler (Davis) buys ranch, must raise orphans and fight off the previous owner's killers. Emphasis on kid stuff. Remake, and improvement, of a George Montgomery oater.

GARDEN OF EVIL (1954, FOX). D: Henry Hathaway. W: Frank Fenton, Fred Freiberger & William Tunberg. Cast: GARY COOPER, SUSAN HAYWARD, RICHARD WIDMARK, Hugh MARLOWE, Cameron MITCHELL, Victor Emanuel Mendoza, Rita Moreno. 99m.

A steamship headed for California is stranded off the Mexican coast with engine trouble. Three of its hardbitten passengers— the monosyllabic Hooker (Cooper), the talkative cynical gambler (Widmark) and the kid who's as fast with his lip as he is on the draw (Mitchell)—together with a tough big vaquero (Mendoza), are recruited by a hardboiled lady prospector (Hayward) to journey into the wilderness mountains with her to rescue her husband (Marlowe) who's had his leg crushed in a mine-tunnel cave-in where he's still trapped under the debris. To get in, rescue the miner and get out, they must run a gamut of bandits and hostile Indians; and the conflict is heightened by jealousies and greed arising within the group. The party gets pared down and the denouement is hard to swallow but the movie is exciting with fast action and fabulously scenic Mexican vistas (photographed in CinemaScope by Milton Krasner and Jorge Stahl, Jr.) and a thrilling score (Bernard Hermann). The soft-spoken adventurer Hooker is in a number of ways the quintessential Gary Cooper screen character.

This one was filmed back-to-back with *Vera Cruz*, which is a much better remembered movie, but I prefer *Garden of Evil*.

THE GATLING GUN (1971, IND). D: Robert Gordon. W: Joseph Van Winkle & Mark Hanna. Cast: GUY STOCKWELL, Barbara LUNA, Robert FULLER, Woody STRODE, Patrick Wayne, Phil Harris, John Carradine, Pat Buttram, Carlos Rivas.

On a patrol through hostile country a gold-hungry soldier (Fuller) tries to steal the army's Gatling gun and sell it to an Apache chief (Rivas). Stockwell is the patrol leader, Strode his scout, the others assorted soldiers and civilians under his protection. They bicker among themselves until they've been picked off one by one and only a few are left. You won't care which few. This is the cheap kind of witless nonsense that's given Westerns a bad name for decades. Stupid dialogue, cardboard characters, atrocious acting, amateurish home-movie directing and badly filmed violence make this one of the worst movies of any kind and any year. The only surprise is the presence of so many reasonably well-known performers, some of whom have done very well elsewhere. Under this director none of them except Strode acquits himself acceptably. Nobody has a right to make a movie this bad for public consumption. (Admittedly it's not quite as silly as *Heaven's Gate* and not quite as offensive as *Forty Guns* but it comes perilously close.)

THE GAY CABALLERO (1932, FOX). D: Alfred Werker. W: Tom Gill. Cast: VICTOR McLAGLEN, GEORGE O'BRIEN, Conchita MONTENEGRO, C. Henry Gordon, Willard Robertson.

Not to be confused with the 1940 film of the same title—a routine Cisco Kid programmer with Cesar Romero—this one had O'Brien as a football star whose ranch was stolen. I know; don't ask. McLaglen is laughable as the title character.

THE GAY DESPERADO (1936, UA). D: Rouben Mamoulian. W: Wallace Smith & Leo Birinski. Cast: NINO MARTINI, IDA LUPINO, Leo CARRILLO, Mischa Auer, Harold Huber, Chris-Pin Martin, James Blakeley, Stanley Fields. 85m.

Charming young lady (Lupino, in her first important screen role) is captured by a gang of Hollywood-style Latin bandits led by popular crooner Martini. There are more songs than plot. Mary Pickford produced this musical; its best features were Lupino's sparkling performance and Lucien Andriot's excellent photography. This was in the days when such titles didn't have the overtone of the double entendre.

GENTLE ANNIE (1944, MGM). **D:** Andrew Marton. **W:** Lawrence Hazard from a MacKinlay Kantor story. **Cast:** JAMES CRAIG, MARJORIE MAIN, Donna REED, Barton MacLane, Harry Morgan, Noah Beery, Sr., Paul Langton, Morris Ankrum, Tom London. 77m.

In 1900 Oklahoma a female outlaw gang leader (Main) and her wild sons (Morgan, Langton) are pursued—very slowly—by a lawman (Craig). The focus is on Main; she is an acquired taste; if you have acquired it you may find this a passable movie but it's dated and very verbose.

THE GENTLEMAN FROM TEXAS (1946, MONO). **D:** Lambert Hillyer. **W:** J.Benton Cheney. **Cast:** JOHNNY MACK BROWN, Claudia DRAKE, Raymond HATTON, Tristram Coffin, Marshall Reed.

Coffin's bad guys have run preceding lawmen out of town; hero Brown, the new marshal, arrives to even the score. Typical of the "B" genre but this is one of the better ones, with a superior script and better acting and directing (by William S. Hart's old director) than most.

GERONIMO (1939, PARA). **DW:** Paul H. Sloane. **Cast:** PRESTON FOSTER, Ellen DREW, Andy DEVINE, William HENRY, Gene Lockhart, Akim Tamiroff, Chief Thundercloud, Monte Blue, Marjorie Gateson, Ralph Morgan, Pierre Watkin, Addison Richards, Francis J. McDonald. 89m.

Subtitled *The Story of a Great Enemy*, this quickie was ballyhooed as if it were a big-budget epic; actually it was simply a peg on which to hang dull exposition, "B" dialogue, bad acting, and stock process footage from half a dozen films, some of them dating back as far as 1912. In plot it's virtually a scene-by-scene remake of *Lives of a Bengal Lancer* (1935), about a trio of soldiers trying to unmask the bad guy who's been selling guns to the Indians. Ellen Drew has one or two lines and spends the rest of the film unconscious; the movie, shot on back-lot sound stages, seems as comatose as the heroine.

GERONIMO (1962, UA). **D:** Arnold Laven. **W:** Laven & Pat Fielder. **Cast:** CHUCK CONNORS, Kamala DAVI, Ross MARTIN, Pat CONWAY, Adam West, Denver Pyle, John Anderson, Larry Dobkin, Armando Silvestre, Enid Jaynes. **Narrator:** WILLIAM CONRAD. 101m.

Not a remake of the 1939 film; this is one of those cultural-message movies that are compounded of one part history, one part two-cent sociology and ninety-eight parts melodramatic hokum. To avoid starvation or massacre of his people, Geronimo (Connors, blue eyes and all) surrenders his band and tries to settle down on the reservation but the evildoing of a scenery-chewing, Indian-hating army captain (Conway) drives him back to the warpath for the predictable shoot-'em-up action. The cast ranges unevenly from ludicrous (Davi as an Apache girl, West as a green lieutenant) to overblown (Conway, all but foaming at the mouth, and Martin as a sage Apache co-chieftain) to downright excellent in the case of John Anderson, here portraying a venal Bible-pounding Indian agent. Filmed on location at Durango, Mexico (Panavision cinematography by Alex Phillips) and sporting a lush score (Hugo Friedhoffer), it has the production attributes of a big movie but the script and thespics of a very, very small one.

GHOST OF ZORRO (1959, REP). **D:** Fred C. Brannon. **W:** Royal Cole, William Lively & Sol Shor. **Cast:** CLAYTON MOORE, Pamela BLAKE, Roy Barcroft, George J. Lewis, Eugene Roth. 68m.

I include this only because it was released as a feature in 1959. Actually it's an abbreviated version of a 1949 Republic serial about a latter-day descendant of Don Diego's who brings "Zorro" back to life to do battle with bad guys who are menacing the completion of the telegraph line in the far West. Bad editing makes the story, such as it is, almost impossible to follow. This is "B" fare at its worst. Moore was much more convincing as the Lone Ranger than he is as Zorro.

GHOST TOWN (1936, IND). **D:** Harry Fraser. **W:** Monroe Talbot. **Cast:** HARRY CAREY, Jane NOVAK, Ruth Findlay, David Sharpe, Earl Dwire. 61m.

This is the sort of picture where tumbleweeds roll across the dusty street. Carey plays a drifter entrapped by outlaws on the run.

GHOST TOWN (1955, UA). **D:** Allen H. Miner. **W:** Jameson Brewer. **Cast:** KENT TAYLOR, Marian CARR, John SMITH, John Doucette, William Phillips.

This one is a Western poverty-row version of *Key Largo*, set in an abandoned town of the Old West with Taylor in the Edward G. Robinson role of snarling villain, Smith in the Bogart role of slow-to-rile good guy, and some Indians taking the place of Anderson's hurricane. The principals do a poor job; it's a dull movie.

GIANT (1956, WB). D: George Stevens. W: Fred Guiol & Ivan Moffat from Edna Ferber's novel. Cast: ROCK HUDSON, ELIZABETH TAYLOR, JAMES DEAN, Carroll BAKER, Chill WILLS, Mercedes McCAMBRIDGE, Jane WITHERS, Earl HOLLIMAN, Dennis HOPPER, Fran Bennett, Sal Mineo, Elsa Cardenas, Sheb Wooley, Monte Hale, Paul Fix, Rod Taylor, Alexander Scourby, Charles Watts, Robert Nichols. 201m.

Empire-building saga spans the years from cattle empires to oil tycoons in Texas, with Hudson and Dean the rival tycoons and Taylor the Eastern girl who marries Hudson and befriends Dean. Hudson isn't a convincing Texan but the rest of the cast is first-rate and Dean's performance as Jett Rink (a role originally slated for Alan Ladd) is electric. The script tries to give equal weight to too many characters and too many years of events; there are soggy elements of soap opera; at nearly three and a half hours it's long for the attention spans of many audiences; but it's good sprawling entertainment, glossy Hollywood at its best. It was filmed in Arizona because the producers couldn't find any place in Texas that they thought looked like Texas. Stevens directed with his usual meticulous professionalism and was abetted by first-class jobs from cinematographer William C. Mellor, composer Dimitri Tiomkin and designer Boris Leven. *Giant* won a best director Oscar for Stevens, and nominations went to Hudson and Dean—both as best actor—and to McCambridge, as best supporting actress.

THE GIRL FROM GOD'S COUNTRY (1940, REP). D: Joseph Kane. W: Elizabeth Meehan & Robert L. Johnson from a Ray Millholland story. Cast: CHESTER MORRIS, JANE WYATT, CHARLES BICKFORD.

In the far North a cop (Bickford) chases a doctor (Morris) who's been accused of a mercy killing. A nurse (Wyatt) provides romance and mediation. There's much rear-projected stock footage of the snowy wilderness through which the pursuit takes us. Routine actioner.

GIRL OF THE GOLDEN WEST (1930, WB). D: John F. Dillon. W: Waldemar Young from David Belasco's play. Cast: ANN HARDING, James RENNIE, Harry Bannister, J. Farrell MacDonald, Arthur Stone.

The first sound version of the Belasco chestnut about the naive girl who falls in love with a dashing outlaw, and the lawman who loves the girl but gallantly gives her up. This one was maudlin and confined to the sound stage with only three sets.

THE GIRL OF THE GOLDEN WEST (1937, MGM). D: Robert Z. Leonard. W: Isabel Dawn & Boyce DeGaw from David Belasco's play; songs & lyrics by Sigmund Romberg & Gus Kahn. Cast: JEANETTE MacDONALD, NELSON EDDY, WALTER PIDGEON, Leo CARRILLO, Buddy EBSEN, Leonard Penn, Priscilla Lawson, Billy Bevan, Noah Beery, Sr., Monty Wooley, Bob Murphy, Francis Ford, Charley Grapewin, Cliff Edwards, Joe Dominguez, Russell Simpson, Chief John Big Tree, Olin Howlin, H. B. Warner. 120m.

The Belasco wheeze was set to music this time, tailored as an operetta for Eddy and MacDonald. Pidgeon plays the lawman. Eddy, as the dashing Latin, is atrocious; and folks in the trade didn't call MacDonald "the cast-iron canary" for nothing. You have to be a real fan of these warbling melodramas to sit through this one.

GIRL OF THE LIMBERLOST (1934, MONO). D: Christy Cabanne. W: Adele Comandini from the Gene Stratton Porter novel. Cast: LOUISE DRESSER, RALPH MORGAN, Marian MARSH, H.B. Walthall, Eric Linden.

Unwanted mother-dominated daughter, evil mother and kindly young fellow; all of it set in rustic backwoods country. This tearjerker, often filmed (sometimes as *Romance of the Limberlost*), was dull the first time around, and the second, and the third and the fourth....

THE GIRL OF THE LIMBERLOST (1945, COL). D: Melchor G. Gerrer. W: Erna Lazarus from Gene Stratton Porter's novel. Cast: Ruth NELSON, James BELL, Dorinda Clifton, Ernest Cossart, Vanessa Brown.

Remake is no improvement.

THE GLORY GUYS (1965, UA). D: Arnold Laven. W: Sam Peckinpah from a Hoffman Birney novel. Cast: TOM TRYON, SENTA BERGER, HARVE PRESNELL, Michael ANDERSON, Jr., James CAAN, Slim Pickens, Andrew Duggan, Adam Williams. 111m.

Cavalry officer (Tryon) and civilian scout (Presnell) vie for the affections of a girl (Berger) during a campaign against the Indians. It's inept, an amateurish imitation of a John Ford oater, long, boring to the point of tears. The acting by the principals, except

FLAMING STAR (1960):
John McIntire, Elvis Presley.
Intelligent and thoughtful;
one of Elvis's best. Twentieth
Century-Fox

FORT DOBBS (1958): Clint
Walker, Brian Keith. A fine
gripping vest-pocket sleeper.
Warner Brothers

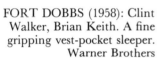

FORTY GUNS (1957):
Barry Sullivan, Barbara
Stanwyck. Reeks of sexual
sadism. Twentieth
Century-Fox

FOUR FACES WEST (1948): Joel McCrea. This one can make you feel as if you've never seen a Western before. United Artists

FOUR FOR TEXAS (1963): Anita Ekberg, Frank Sinatra, Dean Martin, Ursula Andress. Holds its audience in contempt. Warner Brothers

FRENCHIE (1950): Shelley Winters, Joel McCrea, Paul Kelly. Winters is as Western as Tugboat Annie in this unacknowledged remake of *Destry Rides Again.* Universal Pictures

FROM NOON TILL THREE (1976): Jill Ireland, Charles Bronson. A wonderful comic idea gone awry. United Artists

THE FURIES (1950):
Wendell Corey, Barbara
Stanwyck, Walter Huston.
Great gusto and a fine cast;
romantic melodrama of a
high order. Paramount Pictures

GARDEN OF EVIL (1954):
Richard Widmark, Victor
Emanuel Mendoza. The vast
CinemaScope landscape
often dwarfs its travelers in
this good but often under-
rated adventure. Twentieth
Century-Fox

GO WEST (1940): Harpo,
Groucho, Chico Marx,
Diana Lewis, John Carroll.
Wild train-chase is the high
spot of this zany spoof.
MGM

175

THE GREAT SIOUX MASSACRE (1965):
Philip Carey (as Custer), John Matthews, Darren
McGavin. Slapdash and one of the worst,
written by "Fred C. Dobbs." Columbia Pictures

GUN BATTLE AT MON-
TEREY (1957): Ted de Cor-
sia, Sterling Hayden. A "B"
movie overwhelmed by the
natural expressiveness of its
landscape. Allied Artists

Presnell who is satisfactory, is terrible, and Peckinpah's script is very poor.

GOD'S COUNTRY (1946, SG). D: Robert E. Tansey. W: Tansey from a James Oliver Curwood novel. Cast: BUSTER KEATON, Robert LOWERY, Helen GILBERT, William Farnum. 62m.

Keaton relives some of his pantomime routines from silent movie days in this short north-country romantic comedy. Keaton's bits are fun; the rest—"B" plot with romance—is eminently forgettable.

GOIN' SOUTH (1978, PARA). D: Jack Nicholson. W: John H. Shaner, Al Ramrus, Charles Chyer & Alan Mandel. Cast: JACK NICHOLSON, MARY STEENBURGEN, John BELUSHI, Christopher Lloyd, Veronica Cartwright, Richard Bradford, Luana Anders. 109m.

Scruffy horse thief (Nicholson, reprising the sort of character he played in *The Missouri Breaks*) marries a prim Texas ranch lady (Steenburgen) to avoid hanging, and a tentative offbeat romance kindles. Steenburgen, in her first important film role, is outstanding, and there's a wildly funny gundown at the end, but neither excellence saves this movie, which is shabby and incoherent. Nicholson's character is petty, venal and boorish; it's impossible to sympathize with him and we spend the whole film wishing Steenburgen would shoot the spaced-out imbecile.

GOLDEN GIRL (1951, FOX). D: Lloyd Bacon. W: Walter Bullock, Charles O'Beal, Gladys Lehman, Albert Lewis, Arthur Lewis & Edward Thompson. Cast: MITZI GAYNOR, DALE ROBERTSON, Dennis DAY, James Barton, Una Merkel. 108m.

Robertson is a Rebel officer; Gaynor is a dancer-spy named Lotta Crabtree; Dennis Day sings some songs. Familiar and routine.

GOLD IS WHERE YOU FIND IT (1937 WB). D: Michael Curtiz. W: Warren Duff & Robert Buckner from a Clements Ripley novel. Cast: GEORGE BRENT, OLIVIA De HAVILLAND, CLAUDE RAINS, Margaret Lindsay, Barton MacLane, Tim Holt, Marcia Ralston, Sidney Toler, Henry O'Neill, Willie Best, George "Gabby" Hayes, Russell Simpson, John Litel, Henry Davenport, Clarence Kolb, Moroni Olsen, Robert Homans, Eddie Chandler. 90m.

Miners feud with ranchers in early California; Rains (his only Western) plays De Havilland's rancher father; Brent is a bachelor mine superintendent; you can guess the rest. Hal Wallis produced. Excellent photography is by Sol Polito, with special effects photography by Byron Haskin, who later became a

director; the music is by Max Steiner. Good cast is wasted in a typically childish Warners meller—the usual crummy script—but it's in color, and Curtiz whips it along briskly.

GOLD OF THE SEVEN SAINTS (1961, WB). D: Gordon Douglas. W: Leigh Brackett & Leonard Freeman from a Steve Frazee novel. Cast: CLINT WALKER, ROGER MOORE, Leticia ROMAN, Chill WILLS, Robert MIDDLETON, Gene Evans, Roberto Contreras. 87m.

Wary partners—the strong silent hero (Walker) and the voluble Irish rascal (Moore)—fight off evildoers trying to steal a hoard of gold. Good Arizona scenery. Plot is a poor imitation of *The Treasure of the Sierra Madre*; Frazee's novel was a whole lot better. Rate this two-karat at best.

GOLD RAIDERS (1951, UA). D: Edward Bernds. W: Elwood Ullman & William Lively. Cast: GEORGE O'BRIEN, THE THREE STOOGES, Sheila RYAN, Lyle Talbot, Clem Bevans. 56m.

O'Brien's last starring movie casts him as a tired foil for the slapstick stupidity of the Three Stooges. In black-and-white, it's mercifully short and grade "Z."

GONE WITH THE WEST (1975, IND). D: Bernard Girard. Cast: JAMES CAAN, STEFANIE POWERS, SAMMY DAVIS, JR., Aldo RAY, Barbara Werle, Robert Walker, Jr.

Indie comedy appeared in drive-ins in the hinterlands but was withheld by its producers from the major "key" markets, possibly out of fear that it would be ridiculed to death by reviewers. I've never seen it.

GOOD DAY FOR A HANGING (1959, COL). D: Nathan Juran. W: Daniel Ullman & Maurice Zimm from a John Carpenter story. Cast: FRED MacMURRAY, MAGGIE HAYES, Robert VAUGHN, Denver Pyle, James Drury, Joan Blackman, Stacy Harris, Emile Meyer, Russell Thorson. 85m.

An ex-lawman witnesses a murder and captures the charming killer (Vaughn) but neither the townsfolk nor the lawman's own daughter (Blackman) can believe him guilty. It's offbeat but flabby; too slow, not enough complexity of character or action. Still, MacMurray is powerful.

THE GOOD GUYS AND THE BAD GUYS (1969, WB). D: Burt Kennedy. W: Ronald M. Cohen & Dennis Shryack. Cast: ROBERT MITCHUM, GEORGE KENNEDY, DAVID CARRADINE, Tina LOUISE, Martin BALSAM, Lois NETTLETON, John CARRADINE, Douglas FOWLEY,

Marie WINDSOR, Dick Peabody, John Davis Chandler. 91m.

Old time good guy (Mitchum) and old time bad guy (Kennedy) are baited by a pack of young bad guys (David Carradine, Chandler et al.) until the two old guys are goaded into proving who the real men are. They team up to sabotage a robbery engineered by the young toughs. They prove their point but by that time it's hard to care. It's played for laughs but deserves few. An artificially staged chase scene goes on far too long and doesn't work; the trite formulas ultimately overwhelm the feeble comedy.

THE GOOD, THE BAD AND THE UGLY (1966, UA). D: Sergio Leone. W: Leone, Luciano Vincenzoni, Agenore Incrocci & Furio Scarpelli. Cast: CLINT EASTWOOD, ELI WALLACH, LEE VAN CLEEF, Aldo Giuffre, Mario Brega, Luigi Pistilli. 163m.

The impossible-to-follow plot has to do with rival thieves (all three stars) who keep double-crossing one another over stolen loot that is buried in a cemetery somewhere. Before they start digging up the corpses to find it, they manage to fight a whole Civil War battle and several bloody skirmishes among themselves. Eyes fall out, faces are beaten to pulps, legs rot with gangrene and blood flows by the gallon. Eastwood never seems to react at all—perhaps that's meant to be funny; there are sporadic twitches of misguided black humor elsewhere too. Wallach rolls his eyes and burlesques his *Magnificent Seven* villain, not very well. Van Cleef is the most palatable of the three but it's hard to see him through the blood-red haze of Tonino Delli Colli's faddish photography; neither that nor Ennio Morricone's unusually lifeless score helps at all. This was Leone's third Eastwood spaghettier and his longest movie before *Once Upon a Time in the West*; this one is more like a lasagner—a mashed-together deadweight mass of pasta, cheese and bloodsauce. Leone is a great believer in the looming, sinister close-up, a vulturish effect he overdoes so frequently it sometimes appears his movies are nothing but eyeballs, teeth and pores. Like the *Dollars* movies this one is simpleminded and absurd; it's also long, slow and boring.

GO WEST (1940, MGM). D: Edward Buzzell. W: Irving Brecher. Cast: GROUCHO, HARPO and CHICO MARX; John CARROLL, Diana LEWIS, Walter Woolf King, Robert Barrat, Edward Buzzell, June McCloy. 81m.

Spoof is still fun but the musical numbers are humdrum; high spot is a wild train chase in which the zany stars pull the whole train apart for wood to fuel the engine. But that can't stack up to Keaton's silent classic *The General*. This one's okay, but not the Marx Brothers' best by a long shot.

GO WEST, YOUNG LADY (1941, COL). D: Frank R. Strayer. W: Richard Flournoy & Karen DeWolf. Cast: PENNY SINGLETON, GLENN FORD, ANN MILLER, CHARLIE RUGGLES, Allen JENKINS, Jed Prouty, Onslow Stevens, Bob Wills, Edith Meiser.

Young gun-totin' dude tomboy (Singleton) vies with dance-hall queen (Miller) for the attentions of easygoing young sheriff (Ford), while he in turn must deal with stage robbers and a villain in a fancy suit (Stevens). It's mostly music and saloon comedy—a flaccid imitator of *Destry Rides Again*; the thin plot is stretched by several song-and-dance numbers to fill out the film's running time. They're Sammy Cahn songs, not bad at all, and there's good scenic photography (Henry Freulich), but it's all very dated.

GO WEST, YOUNG MAN (1936, PARA). D: Henry Hathaway. W: Mae West from a play by Lawrence Riley. Cast: MAE WEST, WARREN WILLIAM, RANDOLPH SCOTT, Isabel JEWELL, Etienne Girardot, Alice Brady, Elizabeth Patterson, Lyle Talbot, Margaret Perry, Maynard Holmes, Jack LaRue, Xavier Cugat and his orchestra. 82m.

Brash movie queen (West) is stranded in a little Western town and amuses herself with rube farmhand Randolph Scott and generally terrorizes the community. Xavier Cugat's orchestra contributes spirited songs. Amusing, but pretty tame for Mae.

GRAND CANYON (1949, LIP). DW: Carl K. Hittleman. Cast: RICHARD ARLEN, MARY BETH HUGHES, Reed HADLEY, James Millican.

The star of a movie company that's shooting a Western at the Grand Canyon proves obstreperous and, after some adventures, is replaced by a local muleskinner (Arlen), who promptly falls in love with his co-star (Hughes). Filmed partly on location but mainly on the Hollywood back lot, this slight minor near-"B" effort is nicely photographed in sepia (Ernest W. Miller) but it's not memorable.

THE GRAPES OF WRATH (1940, FOX). D: John Ford. W: Nunnally Johnson from John Steinbeck's novel. Cast: HENRY FONDA, Jane DARWELL, John CARRADINE, Charley GRAPEWIN, Russell SIMPSON, Zeffie Tilbury, Frank Sully, Dorris Bowdon, John Qualen, O.Z. Whitehead, Eddie Quillan, Grant Mitchell, Darryl Hickman, Ward

Bond, Frank Darien, Shirley Mills, Paul Guilfoyle, Harry Tyler, Irving Bacon, Kitty McHugh, Roger Imhoff, Charles D. Brown, Charles Middleton. 129m.

This classic social protest film concerns the trek of the Joad family, Depression-bankrupted farmers, from the drought-ruined Dust Bowl of 1930s Oklahoma to the migrant labor camps of California. It put the term "Okies" into the American language. Faithful to the essence of Steinbeck's novel, the film is an angry but uplifting statement about the indomitability of heroic embattled "little people." Some of the speechifying is laid on thick, and Ford's heavy-handed emphasis on "message" can be wincingly painful in retrospect, and the story is a relentless structure of proletarian contrivances in which the villains are mostly vicious greedy black-hatted meanies straight out of "B" serial melodramas, but it's still a stirring document, forceful, unforgettable; it isn't really a Western and doesn't merit long analysis here, but its theme—a sort of ironic parody of the hopeful westward migration of the wagon-train pioneers of an earlier age—dictates its inclusion in this book. It's an ensemble piece rather than a star vehicle; Russell Simpson—normally a bit player—has a principal role as Pa Joad; Jane Darwell as Ma Joad won an Oscar, as did John Ford for his directing; there was a nomination for the Academy Award as best picture, and Henry Fonda, as the Joad son who carries the torch of determination into the next generation, was nominated as best actor—his only such nomination to date.

GRAYEAGLE (1977, AIP). DW: Charles B. Pierce. Cast: BEN JOHNSON, Lana WOOD, Jack ELAM, Iron Eyes CODY, Paul Fix, Alex Cord, Charles B. Pierce, Jacob Daniels, Jimmy Clem, Cindy Butler, Blackie Wetzell. 104m.

Frontiersmen chase some Indians who've kidnapped a white girl. Good Montana scenery (cinematography Jim Roberson) is a plus, and a few actors are okay to watch—Johnson, Elam, Fix—but this hackneyed low-budget rip-off of *The Searchers* is an imbecilic clunker with dialogue the ilk of "Me want 'um wampum."

GREASER'S PALACE (1972, IND). DW: Robert Downey. Cast: Albert Henderson, Allan Arbus, Elsie Downey, Michael Sullivan, Luana Anders. 91m.

New Testament parody-parable is set in a sort of Old West ruled by a tyrant who is challenged by a hip character in a zoot suit who practices a kind of faith healing on the afflicted and thereby attracts a following. Surrealist film is sincere, sometimes funny, but usually incoherent.

THE GREAT BANK ROBBERY (1969, WB). D: Hy Averback. W: William Peter Blatty from a Frank O'Rourke novel. Cast: ZERO MOSTEL, KIM NOVAK, CLINT WALKER, Claude AKINS, Akim TAMIROFF, John ANDERSON, Sam JAFFE, Larry Storch, Elisha Cook, Jr., Mako, Grady Sutton, Ruth Warrick, John Fiedler, John Larch. 98m.

A con man (Mostel), masquerading as a preacher, travels with his "daughter" (Novak) to set up an elaborate tunneling caper to break into a fortress-like bank in a tiny Western town where Jesse James and other felons stash their loot. Several other gangs are planning to rob the same bank, by different methods but simultaneously: a comically tough gunslinger (Akins), the sinister stupid boss (Tamiroff) of an enormous gang of Mexican outlaws that keeps trying to storm the bank with suicidal head-on charges, and a Texas Ranger (Walker) employing a tunnel gang of Chinese laborers in order to break into the bank ahead of the others and catch them all red-handed while getting evidence on Jesse and the rest.

John Anderson stands out as an ultra-mean banker. Walker has one priceless line to Kim Novak, delivered in his ponderous deliberate baritone: "Just because I talk slow don't mean I'm peculiar, ma'am." In the context it's a show stopper. Unfortunately the movie gets too overblown toward the end, as big-budget mad-mad-mad-mad comedies are wont to do, with horsemen chasing trains chasing balloonists and so forth. But there's a lot of funny entertainment along the way.

GREAT DAY IN THE MORNING (1956, RKO). D: Jacques Tourneur. W: Lesser Samuels from a novel by Robert Hardy Andrews. Cast: ROBERT STACK, VIRGINIA MAYO, RUTH ROMAN, Alex NICOL, Raymond BURR, Leo Gordon, Regis Toomey, Carleton Young. 92m.

Pre-Civil War Colorado is the setting for this gold-prospecting soaper in which the conflict between Northern and Southern partisans creates a "B" level of contrived melodrama. The photography is good (William Snyder) but the soundtrack is poor on the prints I've seen, so that much of the dialogue is hard to understand, but most of it doesn't seem worth listening to anyway; it's talky, overwrought and soporific.

THE GREAT DIVIDE (1929, WB). D: Reginald Barker. W: Fred Myton & Paul Perez from the play by William Vaughn Moody.

Cast: IAN KEITH, DOROTHY MACK-AILL, Myrna LOY, Gordon ELLIOTT, Lucian Littlefield, George Fawcett, Roy Stewart, Claude Gillingwater, 72m.

Second remake, first talkie version, of the old meller about the outdoor guy who reforms the callow dude girl. With songs. Treacly but fair; well made. Gordon Elliott later became William "Wild Bill" Elliott.

THE GREAT GUNDOWN (1977, IND). D: Paul Hunt. W: Hunt, Steve Fisher & Robert Padilla. Cast: Robert Padilla, Richard Rust, Malila St. Duval.

Wretched low-budget bloodbath is transparently imitative of *The Wild Bunch* and is utterly without any of its class.

THE GREAT JESSE JAMES RAID (1953, LIP). D: Reginald Le Borg. W: Richard Landau. Cast: WILLARD PARKER, BARBARA PAYTON, Tom NEAL, Wallace Ford. 73m.

The James-Younger gang robs that bank in Northfield, Minnesota again. This typical Lippert mixture of history, fiction and "B" action is a notch below normal, mainly because the cast is humdrum.

THE GREAT LOCOMOTIVE CHASE (1956, BV). Also titled: ANDREWS' RAIDERS. D: Francis D. Lyon. W: Lawrence E. Watkin. Cast: FESS PARKER, JEFFREY HUNTER, Jeff YORK, John LUPTON, Kenneth Tobey, Harry Carey, Jr., Slim Pickens, Eddie Firestone, Don Megowan, Claude Jarman, Jr. 85m.

Based on the same historical incident that Buster Keaton used in his classic *The General* (1926), this Disney pic follows the adventures of a volunteer team of Yankee infiltrator-guerrillas led by Major James J. Andrews (Parker), behind Confederate lines, stealing an important munitions train and racing it toward Union-held territory. The first Medals of Honor were awarded to men of this commando team. Unfortunately Fess Parker's acting is poor and the script is at a juvenile simplistic level, very talky with dull exposition. Keaton's version was infinitely better.

THE GREAT MAN'S LADY (1941, PARA). D: William Wellman. W: W. L. River, Adela Rogers St. John and Seena Owen from a story by Vina Delmar. Cast: BARBARA STANWYCK, JOEL McCREA, Brian DONLEVY, Lloyd Corrigan, K.T. Stevens, Thurston Hall, Lucien Littlefield. 90m.

A woman's sacrifices enable a frontiersman to realize his dream of building a city in the wilderness. Told in flashbacks, the frame of this century-spanning saga—a reminis-cence told to a young reporter (Stevens) by a 100-year-old woman (Stanwyck)—presages *Little Big Man* but the story is a tearjerking episodic romance, marred by silly comedy relief and a contrived sudsy triangle melodrama of misunderstandings and secrets. This is a soapy saga of Manifest Destiny edifice complexes with good photography (William C. Mellor) and a lush score (Victor Young). The McCrea-Stanwyck-Donlevy team was popular with moviegoers in the late 1930s (compare *Union Pacific*) and Paramount tried to keep it going with films like this but the combination was beginning to tire. Still, the acting is just fine and in its dated way it's effective. (The two stars were reunited in 1957's *Trooper Hook*.)

THE GREAT MEADOW (1931, MGM). D: Charles Brabin. W: Brabin & Edith Ellis from a novel by Elizabeth Roberts. Cast: JOHNNY MACK BROWN, ELEANORE BOARDMAN, Helen Jerome EDDY, William Bakewell, Guinn "Big Boy" Williams, Lucille LaVerne, Gavin Gordon.

Lavish epic concerned pioneering in Kentucky in the Daniel Boone days. Not a "B" picture, this was a big-budget feature, but painfully dull.

THE GREAT MISSOURI RAID (1950, PARA). D: Gordon Douglas. W: Frank Gruber from his novel *Broken Lance*. Cast: WENDELL COREY, MacDONALD CAREY, ELLEN DREW, Ward BOND, Anne Revere, Bruce Bennett, Bill Williams, Edgar Buchanan, Jim Bannon, Guy Wilkerson, Paul Fix. 83m.

Another version of the Jesse (Carey) and Frank (Corey) James legend—very well performed by a good cast, but not very fresh any more. In color.

THE GREAT NORTHFIELD MINNESOTA RAID (1972, UNIV). DW: Philip Kaufman. Cast: CLIFF ROBERTSON, ROBERT DUVALL, Luke Askew, R.G. Armstrong, Dana Elcar, Donald Moffat, John Pearce, Elisha Cook, Jr., Royal Dano, Matt Clark, Wayne Sutherlin, Robert H. Harris. 91m.

Cole Younger (Robertson), Jesse James (Duvall) and their gang set out to rob the bank in Northfield, Minnesota. Historically it was their last job. You won't find much history in this movie but there are plenty of sources for it: the Jacksonville, Oregon location photography (Bruce Surtees) and editing (Douglas Stewart) are out of *The Wild Bunch*; the music (Dave Grusin) is derivative of *Bonnie and Clyde*; the comedy—notably a slapstick baseball game—is reminiscent of *Butch Cassidy and the Sundance Kid* and *M*A*S*H*. It's energetic and speedy; I know folks who like it. Several critics lauded it as "authentic" and intelligent. I found it a stupefying example of everything that's gone wrong with Westerns since 1962. There are no characters; only stereotypes and ciphers—you can't tell most of them apart. The acting ranges from good-but-limited (Robertson, a fine actor but straitjacketed by the foolish screenplay so that he really hasn't got a part to play) to Actor's Studio hysterical (Duvall as a viciously psychotic Jesse, part crusader and part Fundamentalist evangelist and part cunning sadist). There are no believable humans anywhere in the film to care about. The production is as jazzy as a TV commercial. It's superficial, phony, empty, characterless, slick, gimmicky, arty, glib, hollow and pretentious. Kaufman has done fine work elsewhere but this early effort is a mess.

THE GREAT SCOUT AND CATHOUSE THURSDAY (1976, AIP). D: Don Taylor. W: Richard Shapiro. Cast: LEE MARVIN, ROBERT CULP, ELIZABETH ASHLEY, OLIVER REED, Sylvia MILES, Strother MARTIN, Kay LENZ, Howard Platt. 102m.

In 1910 an old frontiersman (Marvin), an older crotchety sidekick (Martin) and a Harvard-educated half-breed Indian (Reed) team up to try and retrieve their gold from a smooth operator (Culp) who stole it years ago. Mixed into the episodic comedy are a young whore (Lenz), a tough madam (Miles), the villain's hapless wife (Ashley) and numerous others—there's a large cast, all wasted. The opening heavy-handed gag is a con job involving a rattlesnake in a glass jar; the same gag was handled far better as a throwaway in *McCabe and Mrs. Miller.* The other jokes in this stale farce are equally unoriginal and leaden. Performances are mediocre and the script is inept, but major blame must fall on the director, who has done far better work than this. Filmed in Mexico (it's supposed to pass for Colorado but doesn't succeed) by cinematographer Alex Phillips, Jr., it has a jangly score by John Cameron. It's worse than a time-waster; it bored me to the point of irritation.

THE GREAT SIOUX MASSACRE (1965, COL). D: Sidney Salkow. W: "Fred C. Dobbs" from a story by Salkow & Marvin Cluck. Cast: DARREN McGAVIN, JOSEPH COTTEN, PHILIP CAREY, Julie SOMMARS, Nancy KOVACK, John Matthews, Stacy Harris, Iron Eyes Cody, Michael Pate, Frank Ferguson, Don Haggerty, John Napier, House Peters, Jr. 91m.

The facts of the Custer story are processed into a partly accurate but dramatically bankrupt account of the events leading up to and climaxing with the Seventh Cavalry's debacle at Little Big Horn in 1876. Custer (Carey) is presented interestingly as an officer who at first sympathizes with the Indians but then is turned into a monomaniac by the pressures of overwhelming presidential ambitions. This may be the most balanced film yet made about Custer, but it's also one of the worst; it's slapdash and unprofessional despite the stab at reality and the sweeping Cinema-Scope photography (Irving Lippman) and the big cast and the appearance of big-budget expenditures. Unfortunately the acting is startlingly bad; it's abysmally directed from a stilted talky script. Whoever screenwriter "Dobbs" is, he's not admitting a thing: Fred C. Dobbs is the name of the Bogart character in *The Treasure of the Sierra Madre*—the greedy guy who'll do absolutely anything for gold.

The movie, a textbook example of inept amateurism, was Salkow's last Western.

THE GREAT SIOUX UPRISING (1953, UNIV). D: Lloyd Bacon. W: Gladys Atwater, Frank Gill, Jr., Melvin Levy & Robert J. Bren. Cast: JEFF CHANDLER, FAITH DOMERGUE, Lyle BETTGER, Peter Whitney, Glenn Strange, Walter Sande, Ray Bennett, Stephen Chase. 80m.

A doctor (Chandler), who is a former cavalry officer, tries to prevent war between whites and Indians in Wyoming. Routine and mediocre.

THE GREAT TRAIN ROBBERY (1941, REP). D: Joseph Kane. W: Olive Cooper, Garnett Weston & Robert T. Shannon. Cast: BOB STEELE, Claire CARLETON, Milburn Stone, Si Jenks, Monte Blue.

Not a remake; there's no relation to the Edwin S. Porter original. (You can't copyright a title; *The Great Train Robbery* was also used as the title of a Michael Crichton novel and film of the 1970s about a British robbery.) This is just another programmer about a railroad detective with an amusing plot about a train that disappears.

GUN BATTLE AT MONTEREY (1957, AA). D: Carl K. Hittleman & Sidney A. Franklin. W: Jack Leonard, Lawrence Resner & Frank Fenton. Cast: STERLING HAYDEN, MARY BETH HUGHES, Pamela Duncan, Lee Van Cleef, Ted De Corsia, Byron Foulger. 67m.

The Bob Steele plot. Hayden hated these movies. With good reason.

GUNBELT (1953, UA). D: Ray Nazarro. W: Richard Schayer, Jack De Witt & Arthur Orloff. Cast: GEORGE MONTGOMERY, HELEN WESTCOTT, TAB HUNTER, William BISHOP, Jack Elam. 77m.

The wheeze about the outlaw who tries to go straight but is forced out of his nest by his old buddies. When you come right down to it, George Montgomery made lousy movies, for the most part, even though he's an appealing Western character.

GUN BROTHERS (1956, UA). D: Sidney Salkow. W: Gerald D. Adams & Richard Schayer. Cast: LARRY "BUSTER" CRABBE, NEVILLE BRAND, Ann ROBINSON, Michael Ansara. 79m.

The one about the good brother and the bad brother. Mediocre.

GUN DUEL IN DURANGO (1957)—*See* DUEL IN DURANGO.

GUN FEVER (1958, UA). D: Mark Stevens. W: Stevens, Stanley Silverman, Harry S. Franklin & Julius Evans. Cast: MARK STEVENS, John LUPTON, Jana DAVI, Russell Thorson, Larry Storch, Iron Eyes Cody.

Outlaws slay a rancher's parents and he swears vengeance. Plenty of plot twists, mostly unpleasant ones. The tough grim flavor of this movie is similar to the dark side displayed by Stevens in his disagreeable but compelling *Jack Slade*. A gaunt and powerful actor, Stevens commands attention. I wouldn't call this a good movie but it's interesting.

GUNFIGHT (1961, UA). D: Edward L. Cahn. W: Gerald D. Adams & Richard Schayer. Cast: JAMES BROWN, JOAN STALEY, Gregg PALMER, Ron Soble, Walter Coy, De Forest Kelley. 86m.

Outlaws seek vengeance on a reformed ex-partner. The usual mixture, not very well done.

A GUNFIGHT (1971, PARA). D: Lamont Johnson. W: Harold Jack Bloom. Cast: KIRK DOUGLAS, JOHNNY CASH, KAREN BLACK, RAF VALLONE, JANE ALEXANDER, Eric Douglas, Dana Elcar, Robert J. Wilke. 90m.

Two used-up gunslingers, marking time in their advancing years, decide to shoot it out against each other—after selling high-priced tickets to the show: winner take all.

It's a unique idea: at once fascinating, hard to swallow, dramatic and invalid. (I've only seen it used in one other Western—the forgettable *One Foot in Hell*, 1960.)

Cash is just fine as the dispirited but still dignified Abe Cross, overshadowing Douglas's nicely muted performance as the embittered Will Tenneray. Unfortunately the script doesn't live up to the potential; a lot of it doesn't work, the characters are far too sketchily drawn, and the enigmatic ending—

an attempt at further originality—is merely strained and unsatisfying. It's too low-key and sour, leaning self-consciously on the idea of the Western as tragedy, but it's definitely worth seeing.

The production was financed and capitalized by the Jicarilla Apache tribe but it's not an Indian Western; most of it is confined to a dusty bordertown set and the Mexican bullfight ring where the climactic gunfight takes place.

This one was the logical extreme of the fastest-gun-alive Hollywood mythology (the quick-draw contest being purely an invention of dime novelists and moviemakers) and perhaps it laid that particular myth to rest for good.

GUNFIGHT AT COMANCHE CREEK (1964, AA). D: Frank MacDonald. W: Edward L. Bernds, based on the screenplay for *Last of the Badmen* (1957). Cast: AUDIE MURPHY, BEN COOPER, COLEEN MILLER, John HUBBARD, De Forest Kelley, Jan Merlin. 84m.

A Pinkerton-style operative infiltrates an outlaw gang. Audie Murphy appeared in numerous remakes during the 1960s and this is typical, making use of stock footage from the original (a lacklustre George Montgomery flick) and adding little to it. It's mild entertainment at best.

GUNFIGHT AT DODGE CITY (1959, UA). D: Joseph M. Newman. W: Daniel B. Ullman & Martin M. Goldsmith. Cast: JOEL McCREA, JULIE ADAMS, John McINTIRE, Nancy GATES, Richard Anderson, James Westerfield, Walter Coy, Don Haggerty, Harry Lauter, Wright King. 81m.

Bat Masterson (McCrea) is elected sheriff of Dodge City and cleans up the wild cowtown. It's routine, unfortunately, despite good CinemaScope photography (Carl Guthrie) and typically superior Mirisch Company production values.

This was filmed contemporaneously with Randolph Scott's *Comanche Station*; the two stars then simultaneously retired from screen acting. A few years later they were enticed to come back together in *Ride the High Country*, which to date has been Scott's last film; McCrea narrated one or two movies and then in 1976 emerged from retirement again to star in *Mustang Country*.

GUNFIGHT AT THE OK CORRAL (1957, PARA). D: John Sturges. W: Leon Uris, suggested by an article by George Scullin. Cast: BURT LANCASTER, KIRK DOUGLAS, RHONDA FLEMING, JO VAN FLEET, John IRELAND, Earl HOLLIMAN, Dennis HOPPER, De Forest Kelley, Lee Van Cleef, Lyle Bettger, Ted De Corsia, Whit Bissell, Martin Milner, Kenneth Tobey, Jack Elam, John Camden, Don Castle, Frank Faylen. 122m.

Episodic plot covers the period between the first significant run-in between Wyatt Earp (Lancaster) and Doc Holliday (Douglas) in Fort Griffin, Texas, and the climactic shoot-out between the Earp-Holliday gang and the Clanton-McLowery gang in Tombstone—a period (not suggested in the film) of several years' duration. Because the scene shifts from Texas to Dodge City to Tombstone, the story is necessarily picaresque and unfortunately that makes it suspenseless; the final build-up to the big gundown is fraudulently motivated and perfunctory, so that there's no tension in the movie until the last twenty minutes or so; Ike Clanton (Bettger), leader of the bad guys, doesn't even appear until then. A clumsy effort to tie the story together was made by creating a phony long-standing feud between Doc and Johnny Ringo (Ireland) but it's so overblown with "B" dialogue that it doesn't work. The script is cluttered with truly banal dialogue ("There's a stage for Abilene in the morning. I want you to be on it.") The characters are poorly limned and it's only the actors who make them work. Hollywood convention is honored more faithfully than Western legend; there's a time-consuming, unimaginative romance between Earp and a fictitious lady gambler (Fleming), pointless and dull, filled with simpleminded cliches. Yet the destructive relationship between Doc and Kate Fisher (Van Fleet) is, while overblown, quite effective because of the forcefulness of the actors; Lancaster is very good, and Dennis Hopper, as Billy Clanton, is outstanding. The cinematography (Charles Lang, Jr.) is big and colorful, but the score (Dimitri Tiomkin) is poor, keyed by a silly title song warbled by Frankie Laine.

The film's brawny reputation obscures the fact that it's juvenile and badly written, but despite its faults it's enjoyable a good part of the time. Unhappily the enjoyment ends with the final shoot-out. It's a dull drawn-out battle (contrasted with the real OK Corral fracas, which lasted some thirty seconds), it's anticlimactic and predictable, and the cheap imitation *High Noon* ending with Earp unpinning his badge in disgust and tossing it away is absurd and pointless.

John Ford did it a whole lot better in *My Darling Clementine*.

THE GUNFIGHTER (1950, FOX). D: Henry King. W: William Bowers, Andre de Toth & William Sellers. Cast: GREGORY PECK, Jean PARKER, Millard MITCHELL, Skip HOMEIER, Helen WESTCOTT, Richard JAECKEL, Karl Malden, Anthony Ross, Harry Shannon, B.G. Norman, Verna Felton, Alan Hale, Jr. Tom London, Ellen Corby, James Millican. 84m.

An aging gunfighter (Peck) begins to value peace more highly than reputation He'd like to settle down and hang up his guns, maybe even try to put things back together with his young son and his ex-wife (Parker). But there are too many wild glory-hunting kids (Jaeckel, Homeier) coming after him, constantly challenging him to one more duel.

Peck gives a fine performance (as does Mitchell as his friend the troubled lawman) in this dark brooding psychological Western. It has fine black-and-white photography (Arthur Miller); its action, like that of *High Noon*, observes the Aristotelian unities of pure tragedy, taking place entirely in one place (a dusty town) and in the space of a few tense hours. Nunnally Johnson produced it; De Toth received an Oscar nomination for his screen story.

The yarn has become a cliche because it was imitated so extensively; the film precipitated an entire cycle of gunfighter Westerns. Still, by comparison with its imitators, it remains the towering example.

GUNFIGHTERS (1947, COL). D: George Waggner. W: Alan Le May from Zane Grey's novel *Twin Sombreros*. Cast: RANDOLPH SCOTT, BARBARA BRITTON, Forrest TUCKER, Bruce CABOT, Dorothy Hart, Harry Shannon, James Millican, Charles Kemper. 87m.

A gunfighter who'd prefer to hang up his guns finds himself caught up in the violence of a range war. Good sturdy little actioner has a solid script, well-paced direction and rugged acting. In Technicolor.

GUNFIGHTERS OF ABILENE (1960, UA). D: Edward L. Cahn. W: Orville Hampton. Cast: LARRY "BUSTER" CRABBE, Judith AMES, Barton MacLANE, Russell Thorson, Richard Devon.

Dull old-hat "B" plot concerns villainy and chicanery on the ranch.

GUNFIGHTERS OF CASA GRANDE (1964, MGM). D: Roy Rowland. W: Borden & Patricia Chase & Clarke Reynolds. Cast: ALEX NICOL, Mercedes ALONSO, Jorge MISTRAL, Dick Bentley, Steve Rowland, Phil Posner, Diana Lorys.

Outlaws, led by Alex Nicol, stick up for some Mexican cattle ranchers against predatory raiders who've been rustling their cows.

Dirt-cheap imitation of *The Magnificent Seven* was filmed in Mexico. It's terrible.

GUNFIGHT IN ABILENE (1967, UNIV). D: William Hale. W: John D.F. Black & Berne Giler from Clarence Upson Young's novel *Gun Shy*. Cast: BOBBY DARIN, Emily BANKS, Leslie NIELSEN, Donnelly RHODES, Michael SARRAZIN, Don GALLOWAY, Frank McGrath, Johnny Seven, William Phipps, Barbara Werle, Don Dubbins. 86m.

Ex-rebel soldier (Darin) returns home, is elected sheriff on the strength of his battle-field reputation but finds he's lost his nerve and can't face up to the bad guys who are stirring up violence in a cattlemen-versus-farmers feud. Darin wrote the music for this too. It's a toss-up which is worse: his music or his acting. Routine, predictable meller is an unacknowledged remake of *Showdown at Abilene* (1956), which was neither better nor worse. Michael Sarrazin's screen debut.

GUNFIRE (1950, LIP). D: William Berke. W: Berke & Victor West. Cast: DONALD BARRY, ROBERT LOWERY, Pamela Blake, Wally Vernon. 62m.

Drifter puts his resemblance to Frank James to use by cashing in on it in a series of robberies. Same plot, more or less, as *The Return of Jesse James*. Competent. In black-and-white.

GUNFIRE AT INDIAN GAP (1957, REP). D: Joseph Kane. W: Barry Shipman. Cast: VERA RALSTON, Anthony GEORGE, George Macready, John Doucette, Glenn Strange. 69m.

I never saw this; it disappeared instantaneously on release. It was one of Ralston's last pictures; hubby Herbert J. Yates sold the studio after this one.

GUN FOR A COWARD (1957, UNIV). D: Abner Biberman. W: R. Wright Campbell. Cast: FRED MacMURRAY, JEFFREY HUNTER, JANICE RULE, Dean STOCK-WELL, Chill WILLS, Josephine Hutchinson, Betty Lynn, Iron Eyes Cody, Jane Howard, Robert Hoy, John Larch, Bob Steele. 73m.

The head of a ranching family (MacMurray) has to contend with stampedes, economic problems, rustlers and two feuding younger brothers—the hothead (Stockwell) and the sensitive youth (Hunter) who's been accused of cowardice. It gets hysterical in intensity; it's not so much an actioner as an Oedipal soap opera; but the characters are nicely realized and the slow yarn has a good flavor of the reality of the working West. CinemaScope photography (George Robinson) is first-rate, as is the score (Joseph Gerhenson). The latter part of the film, involving a cattle drive, stampedes and gun battles, tends to bog down in familiar melodrama but the good cast makes it palatable. Superior fare.

GUN FURY (1953, COL). D: Roy Huggins. W: Huggins & Irving Wallace from K.R.G. Granger's novel *Ten Against Caesar*. Cast: ROCK HUDSON, DONNA REED, PHILIP CAREY, Lee MARVIN, Neville Brand, Leo Gordon. 83m.

A Civil War veteran (Hudson) and his bride (Reed) are stagecoaching west to settle down when a psychotic outlaw (Carey) takes a fancy to the bride and abducts her for his own pleasure. Hero gives chase and has to whittle down Carey's sizable gang of vicious screwballs and somehow rescue his wife alive. The raw plot makes it curiously compelling—gripping and tense, with good action. But it's marred by a low-budget style and by woeful acting: we don't feel Hudson's anguish at all, and Carey's performance is possibly the most overblown of his career: he doesn't leave a bit of scenery unchewed. But it'll keep you on the edge of your seat.

GUN GLORY (1957, MGM). D: Roy Rowland. W: William Ludwig from Philip Yordan's novel *Man of the West*. Cast: STEWART GRANGER, RHONDA FLEMING, Chill WILLS, Steve Rowland, James Gregory. 89m.

Reformed gunfighter (Granger) lives with his unhappy son (Rowland) on a little ranch where they are ostracized by the community until the onslaught of bad guys who threaten to drive everybody away gives the hero a chance to prove himself. The writing is first-class; Granger is excellent; it's a formula story but very well handled, very entertaining.

THE GUN HAWK (1963, AA). D: Edward Ludwig. W: Jo Heims, Richard Bernstein & Max Steeber. Cast: RORY CALHOUN, ROD CAMERON, Ruta LEE, Rod LAUREN, John Litel, Morgan Woodward, Lane Bradford, Robert J. Wilke, Rodolfo Hoyos, Greg Barton. 91m.

While the sheriff (Cameron) pursues him, a veteran gunslinger (Calhoun) tries to persuade an ambitious callow kid (Lauren) that there wouldn't be much future in following in his footsteps. In some ways mystical and surreal, the film at times is surprisingly moving despite its minuscule budget, mediocre directing and routine camera work (by Paul Vogel) and a downright terrible score (Jimmie Haskell). Performances are quite good and the script is deft. It's a "B" movie but an interesting one.

GUNMAN'S WALK (1958, COL). D: Phil Karlson. W: Frank Nugent & Ric Hardman. Cast: VAN HEFLIN, TAB HUNTER, Kathryn GRANT, James Darren, Mickey Shaughnessy, Robert F. Simon, Harry Antrim. 97m.

A wild son (Hunter, a fine performance) causes trouble in the life of a rancher with a past (Heflin). Formula stuff is similar in theme to *Gun for a Coward*; it's very well handled with professional polish.

GUNMEN FROM LAREDO (1958, COL). D: Wallace MacDonald. W: Clarke Reynolds. Cast: Robert KNAPP, Jana DAVI, Walter Coy, Paul Birch, Don Harvey. 67m.

Youth, framed for murder, must find the real killer. Cheap and trite.

GUNPOINT (1965, UNIV). D: Earl Bellamy. W: Willard & Mary Willingham. Cast: AUDIE MURPHY, JOAN STALEY, Warren STEVENS, Edgar BUCHANAN, Nick Dennis, Royal Dano, David Macklin, Morgan Woodward, Denver Pyle, John Hoyt, Ford Rainey, Robert Pine, Kelly Thorsden, William Bramley, Roy Barcroft. 87m.

Not to be confused with *At Gunpoint*, this one has Audie as a sheriff who heads a posse trying to rescue a kidnapped girl from a gang of bandits; he is accompanied and hamstrung by a cynical gambler (Stevens), and there are Indian battles, outlaw gunfights, fisticuffs, the works. The script is crammed with foolish exposition; it's ill-staged, with shabby rear projection; it's a less-than-mediocre "B" picture.

THE GUN RIDERS (1969, IND). D: Al Adamson. Cast: Robert DIX, Jim DAVIS, Scott BRADY, John CARRADINE, Paula RAYMOND, Jane Edwards. 98m.

Lawman (Dix) seeks vengeance against Yaqui Indians who killed his wife. He gets involved with gunrunners (Davis), a wagon train led by a preacher (Carradine) and a pimp (Brady), and partakes of a great deal of shooting and talking. None of it makes any sense. Virtually the entire cast ends up dead. The script (uncredited) is replete with lines like, "It's quiet. . . . Too quiet." The terrible score (also uncredited) doesn't help.

GUNS A'BLAZIN' (1932)—*See* LAW AND ORDER.

GUNS FOR SAN SEBASTIAN (1967, MGM). D: Henri Verneuil. W: James R. Webb from a novel by William B. Faherty, S.J. Cast: ANTHONY QUINN, CHARLES BRONSON, ANJANETTE COMER, Sam JAFFE, Silvia Pinal, Pedro Armendariz, Jr., Jorge Martinez de Hoyos. 111m.

An outlaw (Quinn) in Spanish Mexico in the 1750s finds himself masquerading as a priest; circumstances force him to help the villagers fight off marauding Indians and bandits and their mean, nasty leader (Bronson). Quinn plays Zorba the Terrible and it's boring drivel.

GUNSIGHT RIDGE (1957, UA). D: Francis D. Lyon. W: Talbot & Elizabeth Jennings. Cast: JOEL McCREA, MARK STEVENS, Joan WELDON, Slim Pickens, Addison Richards, George Chandler. 85m.

In old Arizona the good guy (McCrea) finally persuades the townsfolk to band together and rout a gang of terrorizing stagecoach bandits whose outlawry has made life unsafe. The "B" plot is handled with professional flair; and it's nicely acted.

GUNSLINGER (1956, IND). D: Roger Corman. W: Charles B. Griffith & Mark Hanna. Cast: JOHN IRELAND, BEVERLY GARLAND, Martin Kingsley, Allison Hayes. 83m.

When a marshal is killed from ambush, his wife (Garland) buckles a six-gun around her shapely hips and takes over his job; she has to contend with a hired gunslinger (Ireland) whom the bad guys import to take care of her. It's laughably amateurish, ordinary "B" hokum, but director Corman in this early shoestring-budget feature added some touches that make it curious and strange. The sets are so flimsily sketched as to be surrealistic—they are almost cartoons—and the blocking and directing of the actors are puzzlingly abstract. It's as if Corman is saying we all know this is a comic-book formula so let's picture it that way.

At times, in its odd way, it works.

GUNSMOKE (1953, UNIV). D: Nathan Juran. W: D.D. Beauchamp from Norman A. Fox's novel *Roughshod.* Cast: AUDIE MURPHY, SUSAN CABOT, Paul KELLY, Charles DRAKE, Jack Kelly, Chubby Johnson. 79m.

Stranger (Murphy) is hired by the bad guys, then turns around and defends the intended victims after he finds out what's really going on. The plot was old-hat at the time of William S. Hart's *Hell's Hinges* but this one's handled quite well—professional and slick but predictable.

GUNSMOKE IN TUCSON (1958, AA). D: Thomas Carr. W: Paul Leslie Pell & Robert Joseph. Cast: MARK STEVENS, FORREST TUCKER, Gale ROBBINS, William Henry, Vaughan Taylor, Richard Reeves, I. Stanford Jolley. 80m.

Outlaw brother (Stevens) vies with lawman brother (Tucker) in a standard tired oater with stupefyingly banal dialogue.

GUNS OF A STRANGER (1973, UNIV). D: Robert Hinkle. W: Charles W. Aldridge. Cast: MARTY ROBBINS, Dovie Beams, Chill Wills.

Drifter (Robbins) sings songs when he's not mopping up bad guys; Dovie Beams, as the lady whose ranch the land-grabbers are after, is a serious candidate for worst actress of the century. Woeful "Z" movie is reminiscent of the singing cowboy junk of the 1930s.

GUNS OF FORT PETTICOAT (1957, COL). D: George Marshall. W: Walter Doniger from a novel by C. William Harrison. Cast: AUDIE MURPHY, KATHRYN GRANT, HOPE EMERSON, Jeff DONNELL, Isobel Elsom, Jeanette Nolan. 80m.

A soldier (Murphy) trains a group of women, whose husbands are away fighting the Civil War, to defend themselves against attack by Indians who are being stirred up by an Indian-hating cavalry colonel. Forced.

GUNS OF THE MAGNIFICENT SEVEN (1968, UA). D: Paul Wendkos. W: Herman Hoffman. Cast: GEORGE KENNEDY, James WHITMORE, Monte MARKHAM, Michael Ansara, Reni Santoni, Joe Don Baker, Frank Silvera, Bernie Casey, Fernando Rey, Scott Thomas, Tony Davis, Jorge Rigaud, Wende Wagner. 106m.

Chris (Kennedy) and the boys rescue a peasant leader from a Mexican prison and help him fend off his village's oppressors. There are a few good lines in the otherwise humdrum script of this made-in-Spain cheapie. To date there have been three sequels to *The Magnificent Seven*; this was the second. No members of the original cast remain, nor the behind the camera crew, except for Elmer Bernstein, whose score as always is reprised.

GUNS OF THE TIMBERLAND (1960, WB). D: Robert D. Webb. W: Aaron Spelling & Joseph Petracca from a Louis L'Amour novel. Cast: ALAN LADD, JEANNE CRAIN, GILBERT ROLAND, Frankie AVALON, Lyle Bettger, Noah Beery, Jr., Alana Ladd, Regis Toomey. 91m.

The ranchers don't want the trees cut down; the lumbermen do. Ladd plays the head lumberman, Roland his partner, Crain a lady rancher. It's slow and ordinary, although the photography (John Seitz) is superior.

GUNS OF WYOMING (1963)—*See* CATTLE KING.

GUN STREET (1961, UA). D: Edward L. Cahn. W: Sam C. Freedle. Cast: JAMES BROWN, Jean WILLES, John Clarke, John Pickard, Peggy Stewart.

Killer busts out of prison and rides to get revenge on those who put him there. Very ordinary.

THE GUN THAT WON THE WEST (1955, COL). D: William Castle. W: James B. Gordon. Cast: DENNIS MORGAN, RICHARD DENNING, Paula RAYMOND, Robert Bice, Ray Gordon. 71m.

During the Civil War two civilian scouts introduce the Springfield rifle to Dakota to help the army fight the Sioux. As history it's nonsense; as entertainment it's every bit as useful as a sleeping pill.

GUN THE MAN DOWN (1956)—*See* ARIZONA MISSION.

THE HALF-BREED (1952, RKO). D: Stuart Gilmore. W: Harold Shumate, Richard Wormser, Robert H. Andrews & Charles Hoffman. Cast: ROBERT YOUNG, JANIS CARTER, JACK BEUTEL, Barton MacLANE, Reed HADLEY, Porter Hall, Connie Gilchrist, Sammy White, Frank Wilcox. 81m.

A silk-smooth gambler (Young) mediates languidly between white bad guys and Indians, and romances a singer (Carter) on the side. The subplot about racial prejudice, focusing around the title character (Beutel), is valid but clumsy. Now and then we get a glimpse of a supposed Apache village dotted with tepees. (Apache Indians never used tepees.) Filmed two years after *Broken Arrow*, this one was ballyhooed as if it were an important serious big-budget movie in the same vein; but it's an amateur effort by comparison, static and slow, most of it confined to saloon interiors. Reed Hadley, as the chief villain, is a comic-strip bad guy, and in style and its black-and-white mannerisms (it's in color, by William V. Skall, but it shouldn't have been) it resembles the pictures of the late 1930s—it's extremely old-fashioned.

THE HALLELUJAH TRAIL (1965, UA). D: John Sturges. W: John Gay from Bill Gulick's novel *The Hallelujah Train*. Cast: BURT LANCASTER, LEE REMICK, BRIAN KEITH, Jim HUTTON, Donald PLEASENCE, Pamela Tiffin, Hope Summers, Martin Landau, Dub Taylor, Robert J. Wilke. Narrator: John DEHNER. 165m.

Cavalrymen (Lancaster, Hutton) escort a wagon train of whiskey to Denver while suffering the predations of thirsty attacking Indians and a drunken loudmouth (marvelously played by Brian Keith) and a gang of crusading temperance ladies led by Lee Remick. Everybody except Keith and Pleasence (who does one of his overwrought frontier characters) looks bored to death. The panoramic photography is pretty (Robert L. Surtees) but would have been far more suitable to a dramatic epic. Maybe United Artists mistook John Sturges for his brother when they signed him to do this one: it was Preston Sturges who had the directorial talent for comedy. This farce is turgid, overblown, overlong, a slapstick dud.

THE HALLIDAY BRAND **(1957, UA). D: Joseph H. Lewis. W: George W. George & George Slavin. Cast: JOSEPH COTTEN, VIVECA LINDFORS, Betsy BLAIR, Ward BOND, Bill WILLIAMS, Jay C. FLIPPEN, Jeanette Nolan, Christopher Dark. 77m.**

Father (Bond), good son (Cotten) and bad son (Williams) are ranchers; you can guess the rest. Director Lewis was an exceptional "B" talent; this one is very well made, intriguingly helmed, with bonuses in Bond's gritty performance and the effective troubled awkwardness of Cotten, who adds dimension to a character scripted on cardboard.

HANG 'EM HIGH **(1968, UA). D: Ted Post. W: Leonard Freeman & Mel Goldberg. Cast: CLINT EASTWOOD, INGER STEVENS, PAT HINGLE, ED BEGLEY, Ruth WHITE, Ben JOHNSON, James MacARTHUR, Charles McGRAW, Bruce DERN, L.Q. Jones, Alan Hale, Jr., Bob Steele, Bert Freed, Arlene Golonka, Dennis Hopper, James Westerfield, Michael O'Sullivan, Russell Thorson, Ned Romero. 114m.**

The survivor of a lynching (Eastwood) makes the lynchers his quarry. He hires on as a deputy marshal to justify his revenge quest. It's overshadowed by the dominating character of Pat Hingle's hanging judge. The film is discussed in detail in Chapter 9. Rate it fair; a good idea gone awry. Pretty good score by Dominic Frontiere and photography by Richard Kline and Leonard South.

THE HANGING OF JAKE ELLIS **(1969, IND). DW: J. Van Hearn. Cast: Charles Napier, Deborah Downey, Bambi Allen, Jim Lemp, Don Derby.**

Cattleman is framed in this bottom-of-the-barrel indie with some topless nude sequences. Tasteless trash.

THE HANGING TREE **(1959, WB). D: Delmer Daves (and Karl Malden). W: Wendell Mayes & Halsted Welles from Dorothy M. Johnson's novel. Cast: GARY COOPER, MARIA SCHELL, Ben PIAZZA, Karl MALDEN, George C. SCOTT, Virginia Gregg, Karl Swenson, King Donovan, John Dierkes, Guy Wilkerson. 106m.**

Cooper's next-to-last Western was an unexpected sleeper: a good minor film with an unusual story about an embittered doctor who holes up in a backwoods mountain mining camp to fight, gamble and drink his way to oblivion until a woman (Schell) arrives in town—the blinded sole survivor of an Indian attack on a stagecoach. The two misfits gravitate toward each other. Newcomer George C. Scott has a small role as a wild-eyed mad preacher; it brought him to stardom. Fine Cascade Mountains location photography (Ted McCord) and a strong score (Max Steiner) contribute to the sometimes moving drama. Delmer Daves became ill during production and Karl Malden took over the directing for a while. The script has holes in it but mostly they're filled by excellent performances.

THE HANGMAN **(1959, PARA). D: Michael Curtiz. W: Dudley Nichols from a Luke Short story. Cast: ROBERT TAYLOR, FESS PARKER, Tina LOUISE, Jack Lord, Mickey Shaughnessy, Gene Evans. 86m.**

A sour unbending lawman (Taylor) won't allow compassion to compromise his fundamentalist eye-for-eye concept of law and justice. Somehow this one misses the mark; the writers and cast are among the best, and the photography (Loyal Griggs) is fine, but the bleak grim yarn is disappointingly routine, despite a very good screenplay and an equally good source. Curtiz simply couldn't direct Westerns.

HANGMAN'S KNOT **(1952, COL). DW: Roy Huggins. Cast: RANDOLPH SCOTT, DONNA REED, Richard DENNING, Lee Marvin, Claude Jarman, Jr., Guinn "Big Boy" Williams, Reed Howes, Glenn Langan, Frank Faylen, Ray Teal, Monte Blue, Clem Bevans. 81m.**

Honest rancher versus bloodthirsty vigilantes. Competent oater has a superior supporting cast of veterans and a satisfactory script.

HANNAH LEE **(1953, IND). Also titled: OUTLAW TERRITORY. D: Gordon Douglas. W: MacKinlay Kantor & Rip von Ronkel from Kantor's novel *Wicked Water*. Cast: MacDONALD CAREY, JOHN IRELAND, JOANNE DRU, Ray Teal, Lane Chandler. 77m.**

Early film about Tom Horn (Called Bus Crow in this version)—a onetime hero who fell on hard times and became a hired killer. Carey plays the killer, Ireland the marshal, Dru the gal between them. (She was, in fact, Ireland's wife.) The movie is something of a misfire, but more interesting than most.

HANNIE CAULDER **(1972, PARA). D: Burt Kennedy. W: Z.X.Jones, Peter Cooper, Ian Quicks & Bob Richards. Cast: RAQUEL**

WELCH, ROBERT CULP, ERNEST BORGNINE, CHRISTOPHER LEE, Jack ELAM, Strother MARTIN, Diana Dors. 85m.

Revenge-obsessed widow (Welch) is taught how to shoot by a drifting bounty hunter (Culp); they hunt a comically inept but vicious trio of bank-robbing brothers (Borgnine, Elam, Martin) who killed her husband and raped her. Filmed in Spain and England, this comedy melodrama is cynical, gruesome, distasteful—and insulting to the intelligence of a halfwit. Culp nicely conveys a kind of doomed darkness about the character he's playing. The rest is rancid.

THE HARD MAN (1957, COL). D: George Sherman. W: Leo Katcher. Cast: GUY MADISON, VALERIE FRENCH, Lorne GREENE, Trevor Bardette, Barry Atwater. 80m.

Willfull cowhand (Madison) opposes the town's tyrannical boss (Greene) and his greedy wife (French); the cowboy appoints himself lawman and sooner or later the action happens but you may be asleep by that time.

THE HARVEY GIRLS (1946, MGM). D: George Sidney. W: Six writers. Songs by Johnny Mercer & Harry Warren. Cast: JUDY GARLAND, JOHN HODIAK, RAY BOLGER, ANGELA LANSBURY, PRESTON FOSTER, Virginia O'BRIEN, Kenny Baker, Marjorie Main, Chill Wills, Jack Lambert, Selena Royle, Morris Ankrum, Horace (Steven) McNally. 101m.

Technicolor musicomedy is a fanciful version of how the Wild West was tamed by waitresses of the Fred Harvey restaurants. Dated but fun. Songs include "The Atchison, Topeka and Santa Fe," which won an Oscar.

HAWMPS (1976, IND). D: Joe Camp. W: William Bickley & Michael Warren. Cast: James HAMPTON, Christopher CONNELLY, Slim PICKENS, Denver Pyle, Jack Elam, Gene Conforti, Mimi Maynard. 125m.

Cornball comedy is loosely based on the army's attempt in 1851 to employ camels in the frontier deserts. Filmed in Arizona by the makers of *Benji*, it's fair family entertainment, although too long. A version of the same history was played straight in *Southwest Passage* (1954).

HEART OF THE NORTH (1938, WB). D: Lewis Seiler. W: Lee Katz & Vincent Sherman from a novel by William B. Mowery. Cast: DICK FORAN, Gloria DICKSON, Patric KNOWLES, Gale Page.

The first Technicolor "B" movie is a hearty actioner about the Canadian Mounties. Dated.

HEARTS OF THE WEST (1975, MGM). D: Howard Zieff. W: Rob Thompson. Cast: JEFF BRIDGES, BLYTHE DANNER, ALAN ARKIN, Andy GRIFFITH, Donald PLEASENCE, Burton Gilliam, Matt Clark, Marie Windsor, Richard B. Shull, Anthony James. 102m.

Naive Iowa farm boy (Bridges) has delusions of being a great writer. His idea of a great writer is Zane Grey. He migrates—mostly accidentally—to the crazy Hollywood of 1933 and tries to get work writing screenplays for oaters. He doesn't get the job, but he does become a stunt man and, briefly, a "B" cowboy star. The movie is fitfully amusing, affectionately recapturing the loony casualness of early programmer filming. It's choppy and doesn't make a lot of sense; at one point our rustic wide-eyed hero suddenly is clever enough to devise a sophisticated con game and bilk a bank—that's atrocious writing. The screenwriter, a young UCLA graduate, had an obvious fondness for old pictures but there are amateurish blunders in the script and in the end the film is dissatisfying because it never decides whether to be comedy, farce or melodrama.

HEAVEN ONLY KNOWS (1947)—See MONTANA MIKE.

HEAVEN'S GATE (1980, UA). DW: Michael Cimino. Cast: KRIS KRISTOFFERSON, ISABELLE HUPPERT, CHRISTOPHER WALKEN, SAM WATERSTON, John HURT, Jeff BRIDGES, Brad Dourif, Joseph Cotten, Geoffrey Lewis, Roseanne Vela, Ronnie Hawkins. 148m. (Originally 219m.)

A Marxist tract about the class struggle, *Heaven's Gate* pits a ludicrously evil cattle baron (Waterston, in black clothes and mustache) against a stalwart but ineffectual lawman (Kristofferson, who seems bewildered) in an incoherent story set against the (utterly spurious) background of Wyoming's Johnson County War. It claims to have a basis in history but it is a compound of lies.

Others in the mess are a heart-of-gold French hooker (Huppert), a saloonkeeper town-boss (Bridges, in the film's least obnoxious performance), a caught-in-the-middle gunslinger (Walken, slight and sensitive and a New Yorker, ridiculously miscast as a tough Westerner) and a Harvard drunk (Hurt, English accent and all) who seems somehow to be on everybody's side at once. Basically it's the one about the evil land-grabbers who want to oust the nesters. The cattlemen have a "death list" of either 125 or 100 names (both figures are given, in different scenes—typical of the film's incoherence) and the nesters—hapless impoverished Eastern Europeans none of whom speak English—band together under Bridges's leadership to fight back; it all comes to a ludicrous bloodbath climax with men and women riding, shooting, throwing dynamite and being blown gorily from their saddles.

Heaven's Gate is the ravings of a lunatic: pathetic trash on an enormous budget (officially $36 million but, with the real costs of borrowed money, more like $50 million all told). Although it is visually stunning (cinematography by Vilmos Zsigmond), virtually every shot is contrived, regardless how impressive; nothing in this film is natural. Everything looks posed. A yellowish-brown wash suffuses the film, and many shots are misted by dust or smoke.

Its flavor is that of a terrible spaghetti Western (yes, the dialogue is that witless) welded to an asinine romantic-triangle picture. Continuity is nonexistent: in one shot, for example, Walken is armed with a rifle and falls back out of frame. He falls into the next shot—armed with a revolver. That's typical of the amateurism of this stupefyingly self-conscious and spectacularly stupid film. It's grossly pretentious. When we first meet Walken we watch him commit a brutal cold-blooded murder; then we are expected to sympathize with his character. That's the sort of putrid morality that suffuses the movie. Naturally a number of French critics have taken it to their bosoms and lauded it unreservedly.

Released in 1980 at 219 minutes, it was so savagely roasted by reviewers that it was withdrawn and re-edited, more than an hour being removed before it was re-released, and died, in the spring of 1981. The cuts made no real improvement. At this book's press time the studio was threatening to release yet another re-cut version with the romance minimized and the bloodshed maximized under the possible title *The Johnson County War*. Silk purse from sow's ear department: I guarantee it will be no improvement. In any version this film just goes to show what Cecil B. De Mille might have been able to do if only he had been a Mongoloid idiot.

HEAVEN WITH A BARBED WIRE FENCE (1939, FOX). **D:** Ricardo Cortez. **W:** Dalton Trumbo, Leonard Hoffman & Ben G. Kohn. **Cast:** GLENN FORD, JEAN ROGERS, Nicholas (Richard) CONTE, Marjorie Rambeau. 62m.

Two drifters (Ford and Conte, both making their screen debuts) try to make a go of it on a ranch; their lives are complicated by the arrival of a refugee girl. The director was bet-

ter known as a silent film star. The picture is talky, actionless and flimsy but pleasant.

HEAVEN WITH A GUN (1969, MGM). **D:** Lee H. Katzin. **W:** Richard Carr. **Cast:** GLENN FORD, CAROLYN JONES, John ANDERSON, David CARRADINE, Barbara HERSHEY, J.D. Cannon, Noah Beery, Jr., Harry Townes, Virginia Gregg, James Griffith, Roger Perry. 100m.

A gunfighter-turned-preacher (Ford) builds his church in an uneasy town and tries to make peace between warring cattlemen and sheepmen. Half-breed girl (Hershey) and tough saloon gal (Jones) vie for the hero's attention. All the actors are good; outstanding are Anderson and Carradine as father and son, and Noah Beery as Anderson's ramrod. The movie shows a real West of working cowhands and the characters are well drawn, although it's preachy (as you might expect) and cornball toward the end. Produced by the brothers Frank and Maurice King, who steadfastly employed blacklisted writers throughout the McCarthy madness.

HELL BENT FOR LEATHER (1960, UNIV). **D:** George Sherman. **W:** Christopher Knopf from Ray Hogan's novel. **Cast:** AUDIE MURPHY, STEPHEN McNALLY, FELICIA FARR, Robert Middleton, Allan Lane. 80m.

Drifter (Murphy) is framed by an unscrupulously ambitious marshal (McNally) for murder. McNally's good performance as the glory-hungry villain lifts it above average.

THE HELL-BENT KID (1958)—*See* FROM HELL TO TEXAS.

HELL CANYON OUTLAWS (1957, REP). **D:** Paul Landres. **W:** Allan Kaufman & Max Glandbard. **Cast:** DALE ROBERTSON, BRIAN KEITH, Rossanna RORY, Dick Kellman, Don Megowan, Buddy Baer. 72m.

Sheriff (Robertson) is too tough for the townsfolk so they install a pacifist in his place. A quartet of meanies takes over the town and soon the hero and his buddy (Keith, very good) are called in to set things right.

HELLDORADO (1934, FOX). **D:** James Cruze. **W:** Frank M. Dazey & Frances Hyland. **Cast:** RICHARD ARLEN, MADGE EVANS, Ralph BELLAMY, James GLEASON, Henry B. Walthall, Helen Jerome Eddy.

Arlen, in a role refused by Spencer Tracy, played a glib promoter involved in a modern-day gold rush to the ghost town of Helldorado. Cruze's direction as usual was lethargic. Produced by Jesse Lasky.

HELLER IN PINK TIGHTS (1960, PARA). D: George Cukor. W: Dudley Nichols & Walter Bernstein from Louis L'Amour's novel. Cast: SOPHIA LOREN, ANTHONY QUINN, Margaret O'BRIEN, Steve FORREST, Eileen HECKART, Ramon Novarro, Frank Silvera, Edmund Lowe, Edward Binns. 100m.

The blonde star (Loren) and manager (Quinn) of a troupe of itinerant hard-luck players try to keep the gang together on a tour through the Wild West. There's some comedy, some romance, some melodrama and some nostalgic glimpses of old-fashioned trouping and backstage life, with a few horse-opera cliches thrown in for good measure. Of his many stories that have been filmed, L'Amour's own favorites are this one and *Hondo*.

HELLER WITH A GUN (1960)—*See* HELLER IN PINK TIGHTS.

HELLFIRE (1949, REP). D: R.G. Springsteen. W: Dorrell & Stuart McGowan. Cast: WILLIAM ELLIOTT, MARIE WINDSOR, FORREST TUCKER, Jim DAVIS, Grant WITHERS, Paul Fix, Denver Pyle, Lane Chandler, Harry Woods, H.B. Warner, Emory Parnell. 79m.

A gambler (Elliott) reforms and pledges to build a church in honor of a roving preacher who's given up his life for the gambler. Windsor plays a ludicrous lady bandit. Saccharine and duller than most Elliott Westerns; but at least it's a slightly offbeat story. In color.

HELLGATE (1953, LIP). D: Charles Marquis Warren. W: Warren & John C. Champion. Cast: STERLING HAYDEN, JOAN LESLIE, Ward BOND, James Arness. 87m.

Wrongfully convicted of spying during the Civil War, a man (Hayden) is sentenced to serve time in New Mexico's brutal Hellgate prison. Fair.

HELL'S CROSSROADS (1957, REP). D: Franklin Adreon. W: John K. Butler & Barry Shipman. Cast: STEPHEN McNALLY, PEGGIE CASTLE, Robert VAUGHN, Barton MacLane, Harry Shannon. 73m.

Jesse and Frank James rob those banks and trains again. Routine.

HELL'S HEROES (1930, UNIV). D: William Wyler. W: Tom Reed from a Peter B. Kyne novel. Cast: CHARLES BICKFORD, Fred KOHLER, Raymond Hatton, Walter James.

Early grim talkie is based on the novel *Three Godfathers*; for a plot summary look under that title. This version was Universal's first all-talking picture to be shot on outdoor locations. Good cast, good director, but it's that same treacly yarn.

HELL'S OUTPOST (1954, REP). D: Joseph Kane. W: Kenneth Gamet from Luke Short's novel *Silver Rock*. Cast: ROD CAMERON, JOAN LESLIE, Chill WILLS, John Russell. 89m.

A modern-day Western mine operator (Cameron) tries to fend off sophisticated claim jumpers; station wagons and pickups replace horses but otherwise it's a familiar slick-magazine Western yarn, well handled.

HE RIDES TALL (1964, UNIV). D: R.G. Springsteen. W: Charles W. Irwin & Robert C. Williams. Cast: DAN DURYEA, MADLYN RHUE, Tony YOUNG, Jo Morrow, Joel Fluellen, R.G. Armstrong. 84 m.

Marshal (Young) retires to get married but first has to face his foster father (Duryea) whose real son he's had to kill. When he reaches Pa's ranch he discovers all sorts of skulduggery. Its potential is dissipated in neurotic gore and bloodthirsty sadism, hot stuff for its time, tame and dull now.

HERITAGE OF THE DESERT (1932, PARA). D: Henry Hathaway. W: Harold Shumate & Frank Partos from Zane Grey's novel. Cast: RANDOLPH SCOTT, SALLY BLANE, Guinn "Big Boy" WILLIAMS, J. Farrell MacDonald, Vince Barnett.

Ranchers, land-grabbers, murders, heroics, romantics—a few yards of the old cloth are measured and cut to fit. But these early Scott-Hathaway-Zane Grey features were capably professional and often very entertaining; some of them hold up very well. This was the first of them, and Hathaway's first directorial credit. Photography was by Archie J. Stout. This was a remake of the 1924 silent film; it was to be remade yet again, as a Republic "B" entry, in 1939.

HIAWATHA (1952, AA). D: Kurt Neumann. W: Arthur Strawn & Daniel Ullman from Longfellow's poem. Cast: VINCENT EDWARDS, Keith LARSEN, Yvette DUGAY, Eugene Iglesias, Morris Ankrum, Michael Tolan. 80m.

You have to see Vince Edwards in a loincloth as an Indian brave to believe it. Our wooden hero tries to head off a war between tribes.

HIGH HELL (1958, PARA). D: Burt Balaban. W: Irve Tunick from a Steve Frazee novel. Cast: JOHN DEREK, ELAINE STEWART, Patrick Allen, Rodney Burke. 87m.

Snowbound triangle is soapy and talky. This was a British production, released in the United States through Paramount Pictures.

HIGH LONESOME (1950, EL). DW: Alan LeMay. Cast: JOHN BARRYMORE, JR., Lois BUTLER, Chill WILLS, John ARCHER, Jack Elam, Clem Fuller, Frank Cordell. 81m.

Neurotic youth (Barrymore) with a mysterious past drifts into a ranch inhabited by killers; violence simmers, then erupts. Barrymore, Jr., also bills himself on occasion as John Drew Barrymore. LeMay's writing was fine (he wrote *The Searchers*) but this directorial effort misfires. In color.

HIGH NOON (1952, UA). D: Fred Zinnemann. W: Carl Foreman from John W. Cunningham's short story "The Tin Star." Cast: GARY COOPER, GRACE KELLY, Thomas MITCHELL, Katy JURADO, Lloyd BRIDGES, Lon CHANEY, Jr., Otto KRUGER, Lee Van Cleef, Sheb Wooley, Ian MacDonald, Jack Elam, Harry Morgan, James Millican, Robert J. Wilke, John Doucette, Tom London, Dick Elliott, Harry Shannon, Eve McVeagh, Ted Stanhope, Cliff Clark. 85m.

High Noon is an exquisite thriller about the ninety minutes before noon on the wedding day of Will Kane, ex-marshal of Hadleyville. Kane learns that Frank Miller (Ian MacDonald), a killer he sent to prison, has been pardoned and will arrive on the noon train to exact revenge. Kane's pacifist Quaker bride (Kelly, her first starring role) tries to persuade him to leave town with her but the middle-aged lawman can't turn his back; he must stay and see it through. Cliche? Of course. But this is the definitive statement. While Kane tries to recruit help from the cowardly hypocritical townsfolk (Mitchell, Chaney, Morgan, Millican), the villain's armed henchmen (Van Cleef, Wilke, Wooley) wait like sinister vultures at the depot. The frightened civilians find their individual excuses for abandoning Kane; only the callow, brash deputy (Bridges, an exceptional performance) shows spunk. The widow Helen Ramirez (Jurado), a lady of dubious reputation who has had affairs with both Kane and the deputy, hovers about the action like a soiled Greek chorus. The clock ticks toward noon; the tension becomes twang-taut; the bride gives the groom an ultimatum: she's leaving with him or without him.

Finally the train arrives. The gundown is still one of the best on film, gripping and fresh, marred only by that disappointing contrivance. But that's one of the film's few flaws, another being the saccharine title song that is warbled incessantly on the soundtrack by Tex Ritter.

The movie has been carped at for its parallels to the then-contemporary McCarthy witch-hunt (Foreman was blacklisted soon after the filming) and for the dubious logic by which a town populated with onetime pioneer frontiersmen turns into a nest of cowards; but movies are myths, not histories, and *High Noon* remains a fine work of dramatic suspense. (The John Wayne-Howard Hawks "retort" to it, *Rio Bravo*, is kid stuff by comparison.)

High Noon won four Academy Awards—best actor (Cooper), best editing (Elmo Williams, Harry Gerstad), best score (Dimitri Tiomkin), best song (Tiomkin & Ned Washington); and was nominated for two more: best picture and best direction. Floyd Crosby's black-and-white photography is excellent without being distracting; the score, despite the treacly song, is powerful; Stanley Kramer produced with a sure hand; directing and performances are all superb and Cooper's is heart-stoppingly splendid, possibly one of the most intense performances by any actor ever to have been filmed.

HIGH PLAINS DRIFTER (1973, UNIV). D: Clint Eastwood. W: Ernest Tidyman. Cast: CLINT EASTWOOD, Verna BLOOM, Jack Ging, Stefan Gierasch, Marianna Hill, Mitchell Ryan, Billy Curtis, Ted Hartley, Scott Walker, Paul Brinegar, John Hillerman, Robert Donner, John Quade, John Mitchum. 105m.

Leather-coated stranger rides into a barren town, proves his virile brutality and is hired to defend the town against the expected arrival of predatory baddies. At the end there's a peculiar surrealist twist of plot. It goes past realism into the abstract, sometimes effectively, and there are interesting ghostly touches, but it's by no means a good movie: it's a sex-and-violence fantasy, faddish and empty, very self-conscious, but in its weird visual structure (the effectively bleak color cinematography is by Bruce Surtees) it's sometimes fascinating.

THE HIRED GUN (1957, MGM). D: Ray Nazarro. W: David Lang & Buckley Angell. Cast: RORY CALHOUN, ANNE FRANCIS, Vincent EDWARDS, Chuck CONNORS, James Craig, John Litel. 65m.

A gunfighter (Calhoun) is hired to kidnap an accused murderess (Francis) and bring her back to Texas to be hanged. Naturally he falls for her and sets out to prove her innocence. Dutiful and ordinary.

THE HIRED HAND (1971, UNIV). D: Peter Fonda. W: Alan Sharp. Cast: PETER FONDA, VERNA BLOOM, WARREN

OATES, Severn DARDEN, Robert Pratt, Ted Markland, Ann Doran, Larry Hagman (uncredited). 93m.

After some years on the drift, a weary cowhand returns to the weatherbeaten wife he deserted in Texas, only to ride out again on a muddled errand of mercy when his saddle partner (Oates) gets in trouble with outlaws. The dismaying ending points up the meaninglessness of this otherwise soporific film about the bleakness of frontier life. The acting is good but no one ever cracks a smile; the film is pretentiously funereal, with self-conscious arty dialogue, drab grubby sets and costumes, and dreadful photography (Vilmos Zsigmond) replete with double exposures, gimmicky shifts of focus, tedious slow motion effects, light-struck whiteouts, repetitious dissolves and montages. The camera does everything possible to draw attention to itself, rather like an infant banging its spoon on the table.

Bruce Langhorne's anachronistic score might have been more appropriate to the soundtrack of a low-budget horror flick.

The movie has interesting moments; Bloom is superb as the beaten-down homestead woman; there's an occasional gritty moment of reality; but mostly the film is bankrupt and boring.

A HOLY TERROR (1931, FOX). D: Irving Cummings. W: Ralph Block, Alfred A.Cohn & Myron Fagan from a Max Brand novel. Cast: GEORGE O'BRIEN, Sally EILERS, Rita La ROY, Humphrey BOGART, Stanley Fields, Robert Warwick, James Kirkwood. 52m.

Dude (O'Brien) comes West to claim his inheritance. Brief tedious "B" oater is notable only because it was Bogart's first appearance in a Western. (He played a shifty ranch foreman who lost his girl to O'Brien.)

HOMBRE (1967, FOX). D: Martin Ritt. W: Irving Ravetch & Harriet Frank, Jr., from Elmore Leonard's novel. Cast: PAUL NEWMAN, FREDRIC MARCH, DIANE CILENTO, RICHARD BOONE, Cameron MITCHELL, Barbara RUSH, Martin BALSAM, Frank Silvera, Peter Lazar, Margaret Blye. 111m.

An Apache-raised white man (Newman) faces the greed and bigotry of a stagecoach load of passengers whose lives he must defend against marauding bandits (Boone, Silvera). Reminiscent of *Stagecoach*, the movie sports very good performances and a taut lean script from the good novel. (Leonard also wrote the gripping *Valdez is Coming*.) It's expertly photographed by James Wong Howe. Unfortunately it tips toward contrived melodramatics

and the ending leaves a bad taste in the mouth.

HOME ON THE RANGE (1935, PARA). D: Arthur Jacobson. W: Ethel Doherty, Grant Garrett & Charles Logue from Zane Grey's *Code of the West*. Cast: RANDOLPH SCOTT, ANN SHERIDAN, Jackie COOGAN, Dean JAGGER, Evelyn Brent, Addison Richards, Fuzzy Knight.

More villainy over the deed to the girl's ranch. Wheezy but swift.

HONDO (1953, WB). D: John Farrow. W: James Edward Grant from a short story by Louis L'Amour. Cast: JOHN WAYNE, GERALDINE PAGE, Ward BOND, Lee AAKER, James ARNESS, Michael PATE, Rodolfo Acosta, Leo Gordon, Paul Fix. 84m.

Hondo Lane (Wayne), a hard-bitten frontiersman riding scout for the army, comes across an isolated rundown ranch occupied by a lonely woman (Page) and her young son (Aaker); her husband (Gordon) has run away out of fear of Vittorio (Pate) and his rampaging band of Apaches but the stubborn woman refuses to leave her home. Complications ensue, leading to a more-or-less predictable outcome; the climax is noisy and filled with large-scale commotion, and somewhat disappointing because it is so predictable while the rest of the film is so fresh. Michael Pate spreads the noble-savage treatment too thick with his Australo-Indian accent, and there are other minor weaknesses, but they are more than overshadowed by the towering excellence of the characterizations.

Hondo is Wayne's most powerful role prior to that of Ethan Edwards in *The Searchers*; he plays the character with grit and grace. Page, in her film debut, is simply splendid; she was nominated for an Oscar as best supporting actress. Both the young boy and Hondo's dog Sam, a scruffy matter-of-fact creature, are key characters without a trace of Hollywood's usual treacly sentimentality. Wayne stock-company regulars Arness and Bond have solid and convincing small parts; Archie J. Stout's photography (originally in 3-D) is sensitive and bears a clear debt to John Ford's tutelage. Grant's screenplay is literate and human. (L'Amour's novel *Hondo* was based on the screenplay, although not credited that way.) Gripping and suspenseful throughout, *Hondo* is a fine example of Western moviemaking.

THE HONKERS (1972, UA). D: Steve Ihnat. W: Ihnat & Stephen Lodge. Cast: JAMES COBURN, LOIS NETTLETON, Slim PICKENS, Jim DAVIS, Anne Archer, Richard Anderson, Mitchell Ryan, Ramon Bieri, Larry Mahan. 102m.

GUNFIGHT AT THE OK CORRAL (1957): Burt Lancaster and Kirk Douglas, as Wyatt Earp and Doc Holliday. Ford did it a lot better. Paramount Pictures

THE GUNFIGHTER (1950): Gregory Peck, Millard Mitchell. The towering example. Twentieth Century-Fox

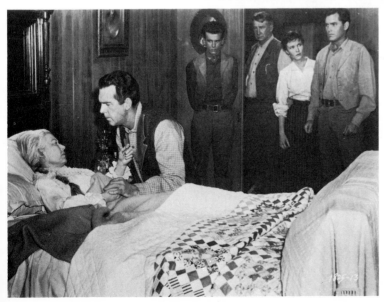

GUN FOR A COWARD (1957): Josephine Hutchinson, Fred MacMurray, Dean Stockwell, Chill Wills, Janice Rule, Jeffrey Hunter. An excellent cast, and a good flavor of the real working West. Universal Pictures

GUN FURY (1953):
Leo Gordon, Philip Carey.
Curiously compelling,
but low-budget style.
Columbia Pictures

GUNSLINGER (1956): John
Ireland, Beverly Garland,
Martin Kingsley. Early surrealistic Roger Corman oater
is comic-book stuff. Ameri-
can-International/ New
World/ Roger Corman

THE HALF-BREED (1952):
Robert Young, Jack Beutel.
Resembles the pictures of the
1930s: extremely old-fashioned. RKO Radio Pictures

HEAVEN'S GATE (1980):
Built for the movie, this
replica of Casper, Wyoming,
complete with vehicles and
hundreds of extras, is
typical of the expenditures
of the overindulged and
undertalented director.
United Artists

HELLFIRE (1949): William Elliott, Marie Windsor. Pious and saccharine, but offbeat. Republic Pictures

HEAVEN WITH A GUN (1969): Barbara Hershey, Glenn Ford. Another parson tames a town with the sixgun and The Word. MGM

HELLER IN PINK TIGHTS (1960): Sophia Loren, Anthony Quinn. Loren's only Western is engaging. Paramount Pictures

HIGH NOON (1952): Lloyd Bridges, Katy Jurado, Gary Cooper, Grace Kelly. An exquisite thriller. United Artists

HOMBRE (1967): Paul Newman, as a white man raised by Indians. Taut and lean. Twentieth Century-Fox

HONDO (1953): John Wayne. His most powerful role prior to *The Searchers*. Warner Brothers

HOW THE WEST WAS WON (1962): Gregory Peck, Thelma Ritter, Robert Preston, Debbie Reynolds. The biggest Western ever filmed. MGM

Rodeo drifter tries to save his marriage without giving up his freedom; it's the same plot as *Arena* (1953). Filmed on location at Carlsbad, New Mexico, this was one of four rodeo movies released in the 1972–1973 season (the others: *Junior Bonner*, *J.W. Coop* and *When the Legends Die*); of the four it was the least ambitious and probably the least profitable. It's an uncertain movie, veering from comedy to melodrama; the characters are only adequately tailored to the slim story. There are touching moments but it owes too much to other films, and Ihnat—an actor whose first directorial outing this was (and his last; he died soon after it was completed)—directed with a regrettable dependence on flashy camera gimmicks. The rodeo action scenes are tame; the movie is genial but unexciting.

HONKY TONK (1941, MGM). D: Jack Conway. W: Marguerite Roberts & John Sanford. Cast: CLARK GABLE, LANA TURNER, CLAIRE TREVOR, Albert DEKKER, Frank MORGAN, Marjorie MAIN, Chill Wills, Henry O'Neill. 105m.

A rakish gambler/con man (Gable) meets a proper Boston maiden in a talky but splashy romance. Big, but not much more than a star vehicle.

HORIZONS WEST (1952, UNIV). D: Budd Boetticher. W: Louis Stevens. Cast: ROBERT RYAN, ROCK HUDSON, JULIA ADAMS, Raymond BURR, John McINTIRE, Judith Braun, James Arness, Hugh O'Brian, Dennis Weaver, Mae Clarke, Tom Powers, Douglas Fowley. 81m.

Ranch romance is a brother-versus-brother oater about empire building in post-Civil War Texas. Ryan's power and excellence are offset by the ineptitude of the young Rock Hudson.

THE HORSE SOLDIERS (1959, UA). D: John Ford. W: John Lee Mahin & Martin Rackin from Harold Sinclair's novel. Cast: JOHN WAYNE, WILLIAM HOLDEN, Constance TOWERS, Hoot Gibson, Althea Gibson, Anna Lee, Russell Simpson, Carleton Young, Basil Ruysdael, Strother Martin, William Henry, Ken Curtis, Stan Jones. 118m.

Loosely based on Colonel Grierson's energetic Union cavalry raid behind Confederate lines in 1863 during the siege of Vicksburg, this devotes most of its running time to a sophomoric conflict between a hard-bitten officer (Wayne) and a peace-loving army doctor (Holden) who has to patch 'em up after Wayne has led them through bloody combat. The dialogue is flat and the melodramatic devices are strained; the cast seem rather wasted but there's commotion enough to please action fans and the photography (William Clothier) is superb. It's vigorous, but far from top-drawer Ford. In dubious distinction, its two stars were paid $750,000 each—the highest fees ever paid to any actor for a single film up to that time.

HOSTILE GUNS (1967, PARA). D: R.G. Springsteen. W: Steve Fisher, Sloane Nibley & James Edward Grant. Cast: GEORGE MONTGOMERY, TAB HUNTER, YVONNE De CARLO, Brian DONLEVY, John RUSSELL, Leo Gordon, Robert Emhardt, Richard Arlen, James Craig, Donald Barry, Pedro Gonzalez-Gonzalez, Emile Meyer, Fuzzy Knight, Roy Jensen, William Fawcett, Reg Parton, Joe Brown. 91m.

Lawman (Montgomery) and deputy (Hunter) escort prisoners across the plains to prison. Terrible script ("Anybody that laughs at Hank Pleasant loses their teeth!" roars Leo Gordon). Unsurprising A.C. Lyles production.

HOUR OF THE GUN (1967, UA). D: John Sturges. W: Edward Anhalt. Cast: JAMES GARNER, JASON ROBARDS, JR., ROBERT RYAN, Steve IHNAT, Albert SALMI, Charles Aidman, Michael Tolan, Frank Converse, Larry Gates, Karl Swensen, Jon Voight, Monte Markham, William Windom, Edward Anhalt, David Perna, Jim Sheppard. 100m.

After the Earp-Clanton shoot-up at the OK Corral in Tombstone, Wyatt Earp (Garner) and the tubercular dying Doc Holliday (Robards) head out on the vendetta trail after Ike Clanton (Ryan) and his cronies. Most of the story is more accurate than most but as it goes along it departs from history; the ending has little basis in reality. (Ike Clanton died a forgotten man long after these events, in actuality.) Lucien Ballard's color cinematography is first-rate; the movie has power—Sturges reassembled his production crew from *Gunfight at the OK Corral* to make this sequel—and it has a pungent flavor of the real Southwest. Robards is excellent as Holliday; Ryan is just fine as the bad guy; in small interesting roles look for Jon Voight (as Curly Bill), screenwriter Anhalt (as a Denver doctor) and David Perna (as Frank McLowery); but Garner, in perhaps his most hardbitten role, steals the show: he is outstanding.

HOW THE WEST WAS WON (1962, MGM). D: John Ford, Henry Hathaway & George Marshall. W: James R. Webb. Cast: DEBBIE REYNOLDS, JAMES

STEWART, JOHN WAYNE, HENRY FONDA, RICHARD WIDMARK, GREGORY PECK, ROBERT PRESTON, RAYMOND MASSEY, LEE J. COBB, CARROLL BAKER, CAROLYN JONES, GEORGE PEPPARD, KARL MALDEN, ELI WALLACH, AGNES MOOREHEAD, Thelma RITTER, Walter BRENNAN, David BRIAN, Andy DEVINE, Harry MORGAN, Russ TAMBLYN, Mickey SHAUGHNESSY, Jay C. FLIPPEN, Lee VAN CLEEF, James Griffith, Joe Sawyer, John Larch, Rodolfo Acosta, Claude Akins, Ken Curtis. Narrator: SPENCER TRACY. 155m.

This episodic epic tried to capture the entire history of the exploration and settlement of the West by following the long life of a woman (Reynolds) from 1830 to 1890; history is encapsulated in vignettes and overlapping sequences through the lives of three generations of the family. There's plenty of action, melodrama, history, music (Alfred Newman), comedy, spectacle. It was filmed in three-camera Cinerama by a number of cinematographers. In the enormous cast Stewart, Reynolds, Peck and Peppard seem to come off best but all the acting is fine, although many of the stars are necessarily limited to cameo appearances. Without question the biggest Western ever filmed, *How the West Was Won* inevitably is overblown and self-conscious and unwieldy—it is a big movie rather than a great movie—but a lot of it is surprisingly entertaining and it's definitely worth seeing. Nominated as best picture, the film won three Academy Awards—best story and screenplay (Webb), best editing (Harold F. Kress) and best sound (Franklin E. Milton).

HUD (1963, PARA). D: Martin Ritt. W: Irving Ravetch & Harriet Frank, Jr., from Larry McMurtry's novel *Horseman, Pass By*. Cast: PAUL NEWMAN, PATRICIA NEAL, MELVYN DOUGLAS, Brandon De WILDE, John Ashley, George Petrie, Whit Bissell, Val Avery. 112m.

More a tableau than a story, *Hud* presents a superb cast in a riveting film about a stern, righteous father (Douglas), his worn threadbare housekeeper (Neal), his orphaned grandson (De Wilde) and his ruthless cynical son (Newman)—all of them twisting emotional knives into one another on a dust-barren Texas ranch. It's gloomy but powerful; a harrowing drama. It won, and earned, Academy Awards for best black-and-white cinematography (James Wong Howe), best actress (Neal) and best supporting actor (Douglas); nominations went to Paul New-

man, Martin Ritt and the screenwriters. Fine Elmer Bernstein score.

HUDSON'S BAY (1940, FOX). D: Irving Pichel. W: Lamar Trotti. Cast: PAUL MUNI, GENE TIERNEY, Laird CREGAR, Vincent PRICE, Nigel BRUCE, Virginia Field, Florence Bates, Ian Wolfe, John Sutton, Chief Thundercloud. 94m.

Talky slow meller depicts the hardships endured by the founders of the fur-trading Hudson's Bay Company in the Canadian wilderness, c. 1670. A big cast, with Laird Cregar notable as a French trapper, doesn't make up for the plotlessness of the script, the woodenness of Pichel's direction or the silliness of Muni's overacting.

THE HUNTING PARTY (1971, UA). D: Don Medford. W: William Norton, Gilbert Alexander & Lou Morheim. Cast: CANDICE BERGEN, OLIVER REED, GENE HACKMAN, Simon OAKLAND, L.Q. Jones, Ronald Howard.

The wife (Bergen) of a powerful sadistic rancher (Hackman) is kidnapped by an outlaw (Reed) and decides she'd rather stay with him, whereupon her husband pursues them with high-powered rifles, intent on slaughtering them both. It's the same plot as that of *The Man Who Loved Cat Dancing* and no better than that one; the script is empty and superficial, abandoning character in favor of cheap effects. Hackman comes off best but it's a stereotyped role. Reed is neither convincingly Western nor sufficiently sympathetic for us to believe Bergen's attachment to him. Bergen seems trapped in a hapless who-cares role. The story loses zing as it goes along, gets very tired about midpoint and never picks up again; the suspense-generating devices don't work at all.

I KILLED GERONIMO (1950, EL). D: Sam Newfield. W: Sam Neuman & Nathaniel Tanchuck. Cast: JAMES ELLISON, Virginia HERRICK, Chief THUNDERCLOUD, Smith Ballew, Myron Healey.

"B" yarn is just what the title suggests—and a neat trick if it were true, given that Geronimo was still around in 1900 selling picture postcards of himself. (He died of natural causes in 1907.) Ellison, a onetime Hopalong Cassidy sidekick, made a brief splash in *The Plainsman* (1936) as Buffalo Bill but then returned to programmers. In the early 1950s he co-starred with Russell Hayden in one of the worst and cheapest of the "B" Western series. Supporting actor Smith Ballew was the onetime Republic singing cowboy who'd dubbed the singing for John Wayne in the Duke's handful of warbling programmers of the early 1930s.

I KILLED WILD BILL HICKOK (1956, IND). D: Richard Talmadge. W: John Carpenter. Cast: John FORBES, Tom BROWN, Helen Westcott. 73m.

This was the last and worst of five oaters that John Carpenter wrote, produced and starred in. (For a discussion of the others, see *Outlaw Treasure*.) As an actor he billed himself sometimes as Carpenter and sometimes as Forbes. This drivel makes Wild Bill Hickok (Brown) out to be a snarling vicious killer; when Johny Rebel's (Forbes) daughter is killed, Johnny goes after Hickok for revenge and kills him. (In fact Hickok was shot in the back by a dull-witted stable boy named Jack McCall.) There are occasional moments of interest in the Carpenter films—they are a bit like the spaghetti oaters of a decade later—but none occurs in this one.

INCIDENT AT PHANTOM HILL (1966, UNIV). D: Earl Bellamy. W: Frank Nugent, Ken Pettus & Barry Tatelman. Cast: ROBERT FULLER, DAN DURYEA, Jocelyn LANE, Claude Akins, Tom Simcox. 88m.

Five Yankee soldiers search the wilds of Texas for a cache of gold that was stolen and hidden some years before. Cheap, but I've seen worse.

INDIAN AGENT (1948, RKO). D: Lesley Selander. W: Norman Houston. Cast: TIM HOLT, GEORGE MONTGOMERY, NAN LESLIE, Richard MARTIN, Noah Beery, Jr., Harry Woods, Iron Eyes Cody. 66m.

Crooked whites scheme to divert Indian food supplies to the black market; our heroes step in on the side of the Indians. One of the better "B" oaters, this has a minimum of cliches.

THE INDIAN FIGHTER (1955, UA). D: Andre de Toth. W: Frank Davis, Ben Hecht & Ben Kadish. Cast: KIRK DOUGLAS, ELSA MARTINELLI, Walter MATTHAU, Diana DOUGLAS, Walter ABEL, Eduard Franz, Alan Hale, Jr., Ray Teal, Lon Chaney, Jr., Elisha Cook, Jr., Hank Worden, Lane Chandler. 88m.

Nothing new in this yarn about a superhuman frontiersman's peace-making efforts among the Sioux in the 1870s, but it's gorgeously filmed on colorful Oregon locations (cinematographer Wilfrid Cline), livened by touches of humor. The Indians are given more depth than was usual at the time. There's a good Franz Waxman score, and Terry Gilkyson warbles soundtrack balladry. Matthau is a fine villain; the supporting cast is excellent. Good adventure. It was the first movie Kirk Douglas produced.

INDIAN LOVE CALL (1954)—See ROSE MARIE.

INDIAN SCOUT (1950)—*See* DAVY CROCKETT, INDIAN SCOUT.

INDIAN UPRISING (1952, COL). D: Ray Nazarro. W: Kenneth Gamet & Richard Schayer. Cast: GEORGE MONTGOMERY, Audrey LONG, Carl Benton REID, Robert SHAYNE, Douglas Kennedy, Joe Sawyer, Hugh Sanders, Eddy Waller. 72m.

Cavalry and frontiersmen versus Geronimo's Apaches. Routine.

INFERNO (1953, FOX). D: Roy Baker. W: Francis Cockrell. Cast: ROBERT RYAN, RHONDA FLEMING, WILLIAM LUNDIGAN, Henry HULL, Carl Betz, Larry Keating, Robert Burton. 83m.

Tyrannical tycoon (Ryan) is left by his spiteful wife (Fleming) and her lover (Lundigan) to die in the desert with a broken leg. He inches his way harrowingly toward survival. It's difficult to summarize without making it sound terrible—and indeed, a television remake, *Ordeal*, is very bad—but it's riveting adventure, focused largely on the solitary isolated struggler; it's strictly a one-man Robert Ryan show, and very powerful. Originally photographed (Lucien Ballard) in 3-D, *Inferno* probably was the best-photographed of all the 3-D efforts of the early 1950s but by the time of its release the fad had died and the movie was released in a flat version.

IN OLD ARIZONA (1929, FOX). D: Raoul Walsh & Irving Cummings. W: Tom Barry from an O.Henry story. Cast: WARNER BAXTER, EDMUND LOWE, DOROTHY BURGESS, Tom SANTSCHI, Chris-Pin Martin, Roy Stewart, Henry Armetta, J. Farrell MacDonald, Frank Campeau. 63m.

This was the first Cisco Kid talkie, the first all-sound Western, Baxter's first talkie of any kind, Burgess's first movie and the first talking picture to be filmed outdoors on location (in California and Utah, not in old or new Arizona, but outdoors nonetheless; cinematography by Arthur Edeson): it is therefore of historical interest. Raoul Walsh, who intended to star in the movie as well as direct it, lost his right eye during the filming; Baxter took over the role and Cummings stepped in to finish the movie; hence the dual directorial credit. Baxter won the Oscar for his performance as the guitar-strumming swashbuckler and the film received Academy Award nominations for best picture and best director. But it was of its time—a romantic triangle melodrama with a gloomy ending. Incidentally, for buffs, the first Cisco Kid on film was Robert Stanley Dunn in the silent *The Caballero's Way* (1923).

IN OLD CALIFORNIA (1942, REP). D: William McGann. W: Gertrude Purcell, Frances Hyland, Robert J. Bren & Gladys Atwater. Cast: JOHN WAYNE, BINNIE BARNES, ALBERT DEKKER, Patsy KELLY, Edgar Kennedy, Harry Shannon, Helen Parrish, Dorothy Granger, Dick Purcell, Charles Halton, Emmett Lynn, Milton Kibbee. 88m.

In the gold rush a Sacramento pharmacist (Wayne) runs afoul of the town boss (Dekker), with predictable results. Wayne made surprisingly few boring "A" Westerns but this one answers that description.

IN OLD SACRAMENTO (1946, REP). D: Joseph Kane. W: Frank Gruber, Frances Hyland & Jerome Odlum. Cast: WILLIAM "WILD BILL" ELLIOTT, CONSTANCE MOORE, Eugene PALLETTE, Lionel STANDER, Ruth Donnelly, Hank Daniels, Jack La Rue, Grant Withers, Bobby Blake, Paul Hurst, Marshall Reed, Hal Taliaferro, Eddy Waller, Lucien Littlefield, Ellen Corby. 73m.

Stage-robber is reformed by love; it's the old William S. Hart plot, a downbeat meller, not as good as Elliott's later Republic miniepics, but the ending may be a surprise to some. This was one of Elliott's first features after his "B" stint as Red Ryder.

IN OLD SANTA FE (1934, REP). D: David Howard. W: Colbert Clark, Wallace MacDonald & John Rathnell. Cast: KEN MAYNARD, GENE AUTRY, Lester "Smiley" BURNETTE, Evalyn KNAPP, George "Gabby" Hayes, H.B. Warner, Kenneth Thomson, Wheeler Oakman. 64m.

This terrible "B" clunker was set on a modern dude ranch with incongruous stagecoach hold-ups and other never-never stuff, but this is the film that started it all: it was Autry's first movie, one of Maynard's last, and the one that launched the singing-cowboy cycle.

INSIDE STRAIGHT (1951, MGM). D: Gerald Mayer. W: Guy Trosper. Cast: DAVID BRIAN, ARLENE DAHL, BARRY SULLIVAN, Mercedes McCAMBRIDGE. 89m.

A ruthlessly ambitious gambler sets out to become a tycoon in San Francisco in the 1870s. The cast lifts it above average but it's pretty much at the "B" level of melodrama.

INVITATION TO A GUNFIGHTER (1964, UA). D: Richard Wilson. W: Richard & Elizabeth Wilson, Alvin Sapinsley, Hal Goodman & Larry Kline. Cast: YUL BRYNNER, JANICE RULE, GEORGE SEGAL, Pat HINGLE, Brad DEXTER, Bert Freed, Alfred Ryder, Clifton James, Mike Kellin, Strother Martin, Clifford Davis. 92m.

A Union town's only Rebel soldier (Segal) has returned from the Civil War to find his farm sold out from under him and Yankees trying to kill him or drive him out. He stubbornly stays to get his farm back, so the town boss (Hingle) hires a gunslinger (Brynner) to get rid of him. From there the plot meanders everywhere, avoiding a confrontation until the end; thick with pretentious talk—the speechmaking is interminable; the directing overdramatizes every throw-away moment; the overwrought score (David Raksin) only emphasizes the poverty of the script. The muted color photography (Joseph MacDonald) is curiously bland by comparison. Segal and Rule play their overwritten roles with dignity and conviction, and the part of Creole gunman Jules Gaspard D'Estaing—a figure of thoughtful if talkative intelligence—is unusual for Yul Brynner; and there are a few curious plot twists that render parts of the story almost abstract. But this static picture always puts me to sleep. I've never managed to endure the whole thing at one sitting.

THE IRON MISTRESS (1952, WB). D: Gordon Douglas. W: James R. Webb from Paul Wellman's novel. Cast: ALAN LADD, VIRGINIA MAYO, Phyllis KIRK, Joseph Calleia, Anthony Caruso, Robert Emhardt. 110m.

Knife inventor and wielder Jim Bowie becomes involved in romances and duels in New Orleans in 1830. Ornate and actionful but hackneyed corn.

THE IRON SHERIFF (1957, UA). D: Sidney Salkow. W: Seeleg Lester. Cast: STERLING HAYDEN, CONSTANCE FORD, John DEHNER, Kent TAYLOR, Darryl Hickman, Will Wright. 73m.

The son (Hickman) of a lawman (Hayden) is accused of murder; the lawman has to prove otherwise. Hayden clearly was bored by the mechanical plot; this was one of his last oaters before he rebelled and fled Hollywood aboard his sailing boat. The movie is worth seeing only for his presence in it.

THE IROQUOIS TRAIL (1950, UA). D: Phil Karlson. W: Richard Schayer. Cast: GEORGE MONTGOMERY, Brenda MARSHALL, Dan O'HERLIHY, Glenn Langan. 85m.

The Bob Steele plot, set against the French and Indian War. Plenty of commotion; plenty of cliches.

I SHOT BILLY THE KID (1950, LIP). D: William Berke. W: Orville Hampton & Ford Beebe. Cast: DONALD BARRY, ROBERT

LOWERY, Barbara WOODALL, Tom NEAL, Judith Allen, John Merton, Jack Perrin, Wally Vernon. 57m.

Pat Garrett (Lowery) chases Billy (Barry) in this low-budget but high-quality programmer. The Lippert movies of the 1949–1952 period, represented by such films as *The Tall Texan* and *Little Big Horn*, were generally superior to the humdrum Westerns of the bigger studios. Executive producer Robert L. Lippert's production teams managed to create a gritty black-and-white atmosphere of Old West authenticity that often was lacking in the glossier productions of the majors. In sets, script, acting and general appearance this movie comes closer than anything since the 1930 *Billy the Kid* to conveying the feeling that this is how things really were. This was the best of a series of four "Donald M. Barry Productions" released by Lippert in 1950; the others were *Gunfire, Train to Tombstone* and *Border Rangers*.

I SHOT JESSE JAMES (1949, SG). D: Samuel Fuller. W: Fuller (and, uncredited, Robert W. Gardner) from a Homer Croy article. Cast: PRESTON FOSTER, BARBARA BRITTON, JOHN IRELAND, Reed HADLEY, Victor KILIAN, J. Edward Bromberg, Tom Tyler, Tom Noonan, Margia Dean, Byron Foulger, Eddie Dunn, Philip Pine. 81m.

Ireland is good as the hapless conscience-stricken Bob Ford (the man who killed Jesse James); Foster plays a sometime lawman who befriends him. Good photography (Ernest Miller) helps, and it's an interesting if rudimentary psychological study of guilt, but it's hammily acted by most of the players, unevenly written and routinely directed by Samuel Fuller, whose directorial debut this was. A Robert L. Lippert production.

I TAKE THIS WOMAN (1931, PARA). D: Marion Gering. W: Vincent Lawrence from a Mary Roberts Rinehart novel. Cast: GARY COOPER, CAROLE LOMBARD, Helen WARE, Lester Vail, Charles Trowbridge, Albert Hart, Sid Saylor, Frank Darien, David Landau. 72m.

Spoiled city-girl visits a Wyoming ranch and gets involved against her better instincts with cowhand Cooper; there's a murder mystery. Weak story was tailored to the two stars.

IT HAPPENED IN HOLLYWOOD (1937, COL). D: Harry Lachman. W: Ethel Hill, Harvey Ferguson, Samuel Fuller & Myles Connolly. Cast: RICHARD DIX, FAY WRAY, Victor KILIAN, Franklin Pangborn, Charlie Arnt, Edgar Dearing.

Cowboy star (Dix) of silent films is washed up by the arrival of talkies. But then he becomes a real-life hero; the publicity propels him back to stardom. It's corny but enjoyable if you're in the mood.

THE JACKALS (1965, FOX). DW: Robert D. Webb. Cast: VINCENT PRICE, Rubert GUNNER, Diana Ivarson, Bob Courtney. 105m.

Remake of *Yellow Sky* is reset in South Africa during its 1883 gold rush. Catch the original. Miss this one.

JACKASS MAIL (1942, MGM). D: Norman Z. McLeod. W: Lawrence Hazard, Lionel Houser & C. Gardner Sullivan. Cast: WALLACE BEERY, MARJORIE MAIN, Darryl HICKMAN, J.Carrol NAISH, Dick Curtis, William Haade. 80m.

Road agent (Beery) shoots a man, then adopts his son (Hickman) and finally fortuitously becomes a hero. It's the customary wheeze; you really have to be a Beery-Main fan.

JACK McCALL, DESPERADO (1953, COL). D: Sidney Salkow. W: David Chandler & John O'Dea. Cast: GEORGE MONTGOMERY, Angela STEVENS, Douglas Kennedy, Jay Silverheels. 75m.

Jack McCall—the retarded lout who killed Wild Bill Hickok—is portrayed herein as a misunderstood good guy who's been framed as a spy and murderer, in a rheumy plot without discernible traces of originality. It's history mangled beyond recognition. It's also a poor movie.

JACK SLADE (1953, AA). D: Mark Stevens & Harold Schuster. W: Warren Douglas. Cast: MARK STEVENS, DOROTHY MALONE, Barton MacLANE, John Litel, Lee Van Cleef, John Harmon, Jim Bannon, Paul Langton, Harry Shannon. 90m.

A troubleshooter (Stevens) for the overland stage outfit is sent to take over a district that's plagued by outlaws. He puts a stop to it but in the course of cleaning up the district he learns to enjoy the killing: it becomes an addiction and he can't stop. Based on historical events, this brooding but compelling movie is a different sort of Western with a feeling of genuine tragedy. It's brutal, grim, downbeat—don't expect light entertainment. In black-and-white.

THE JAYHAWKERS (1959, PARA). D: Melvin Frank. W: Frank, Joseph Petracca, Frank Fenton & A.I. Bezzerides. Cast: FESS PARKER, JEFF CHANDLER, Nicole MAUREY, Henry SILVA, Herbert Rudley, Leo Gordon, Frank De Kova, Don Megowan, Shari Lee Bernatt, Jimmy Carter, Ned Glass, Harry Dean Stanton. 98m.

A distractingly poor score (Jerome Moross) mars the otherwise superior production values of this big-budget, nicely photographed (in wide screen, by Loyal Griggs) Civil War actioner. If you can sit through the slow, dull, opening reels and the wildly implausible premise, it eventually turns into a fairly intriguing yarn about the deadly conflict between a demented brutal Kansas backwoods Napoleon (Chandler) and a vengeful farmer (Parker) who's out to do him in.

JEREMIAH JOHNSON (1973, WB). D: Sydney Pollack. W: John Milius, Edward Anhalt & David Rafiel, based on Vardis Fisher's book *Mountain Man* and the story "Crow Killer" by Raymond Thorp & Robert Bunker. Cast: ROBERT REDFORD, Will GEER, Stephan GIERASCH, Allyn Ann McLERIE, Delle Bolton, Charles Tyner, Joaquin Martinez. 107m.

Fed up with civilization, a young man puts it behind him and ventures into the wilderness circa 1820. There he learns to hunt, fight and survive. He learns mountain-man ways from an old trapper (Geer), marries an Indian woman (McLerie), unintentionally offends some Crow Indians who wipe out his family, and devotes the rest of his life to revenge, entrapping and murdering Indians singly and by twos.

The film is an introspective study of a confused man who proves incapable of coming to terms with anything; ultimately it's a movie about his self-pity, and it leaves a sour taste. In a way, despite its cruel plot, the film is a whitewash; the real "Liver Eating Johnson," who slaughtered hundreds of Crow Indians and did in fact eat their livers, was hardly a Robert Redford type. Redford, curiously cast in such a downbeat part, does not reveal enough to make us care about the character or even to begin to understand him. In any case you need to be in a mood to be bored for long stretches; the action scenes are a long time arriving and are confined briefly to the last quarter of the film. Yet despite its ultra-thin story line *Jeremiah Johnson* is fascinating, simply because its photography (by Duke Callaghan, in wide screen, on locations throughout the American Northwest) is unique: splendid and awesome. Early in this volume I said that movies should be more than mere photography; but *Jeremiah Johnson* is worth seeing simply for the grandeur and beauty of its pictures.

JESSE JAMES (1939, FOX). D: Henry King. W: Nunnally Johnson & Hal Long; Research by Rosalind Shaffer & Jo Frances James. Cast: TYRONE POWER, HENRY FONDA, RANDOLPH SCOTT, Nancy KELLY, Henry HULL, Brian DONLEVY,

Jane Darwell, Slim Summerville, John Russell, John Carradine, Donald Meek, Lon Chaney, Jr., James Flavin, Paul Burns, Eddy Waller, Charles Halton, Harold Goodwin, Harry Tyler, J. Edward Bromberg, Spencer Charters, George Chandler. 105m.

A huge excellent cast bolsters this exciting whitewash of the outlaw James brothers, tracing their lives from Jesse's (Power) youth during the Civil War and the oppressive and brutal events that supposedly radicalized him, through his "growing up" with Quantrill's vicious guerrilla raiders, then to his notorious career as bank and train robber, and finally to his well-known end. Fonda is just fine as his brother Frank. The color photography (George Barnes), partly on Missouri locations, is excellent for its vintage and the director keeps the dense complicated plot moving headlong. King directed three Westerns: this one, *The Gunfighter* and *The Bravados*—they all are excellent. Comparing a full-bodied movie like this to the more recent *Great Northfield Minnesota Raid* or *The Long Riders* is like comparing a long, satisfying, rich novel with a slight novella. (A sequel, with Fonda reprising his role as the surviving brother, was made a year later: *The Return of Frank James*.)

JESSE JAMES MEETS FRANKENSTEIN'S DAUGHTER (1966, EMB). D: William Beaudine. W: Carl K. Hittleman. Cast: JOHN LUPTON, Narda Onyx, Steven Geray, Jim Davis, Estelita, Cal Bolder, Rayford Barnes, William Fawcett, Nestor Paiva. 85m.

Just what the title implies. Companion piece to the same filmmakers' *Billy the Kid vs. Dracula*. This was the last of Beaudine's approximately 250 directorial jobs on "B" movies—it also was just possibly the very worst. Did they really have red plastic helmets in Jesse's day?

JESSE JAMES vs. THE DALTONS (1954, COL). D: William Castle. W: Robert E. Kent, Samuel Newman & Edwin Westrate. Cast: Brett KING, Barbara LAWRENCE, James GRIFFITH, Bill Phipps, Rory Mallinson, John Cliff, Richard Garland, Jack Hendricks, William Tannen, Al Cantor. 65m.

Actually it's Son of Jesse against the Daltons in this 3-D shoot-'em-up.

JESSE JAMES' WOMEN (1954, UA). D: Donald Barry. W: Barry, William R. Cox & D.D. Beauchamp. Cast: DONALD "RED" BARRY, JACK BEUTEL, Peggie CASTLE, Joyce Redd, Lita Baron.

Programmer tries for comedy. Lots of romance, very little action.

JOE DAKOTA (1957, UNIV). D: Richard Bartlett. W: William Talman & Norman D. Jolley. Cast: JOCK MAHONEY, LUANA PATTEN, Lee VAN CLEEF, Charles McGraw, Barbara Lawrence. 79m.

Mystery Western has a tangled plot that includes a missing Indian, feuding oil drillers and murder. Mahoney plays an ex-cavalryman turned amateur detective. Very minor film is competent but dull.

JOE KIDD (1972, UNIV). D: John Sturges. W: Elmore Leonard. Cast: CLINT EASTWOOD, ROBERT DUVALL, John SAXON, Don Stroud, Stella Garcia, Lynne Marta, Clint Ritchie, James Wainwright, Gregory Walcott, Ron Soble. 88m.

Eastwood is hired by an unscrupulous land-grabbing tycoon (Duvall) to kill a Mexican bandit leader (Saxon). Sturges and Leonard have done many good things but this is not among them; the movie is faddishly littered with mindless movement and brutality. Produced by Eastwood's company.

JOHNNY CONCHO (1956, UA). D: Don McGuire. W: McGuire & David Harmon. Cast: FRANK SINATRA, KEENAN WYNN, PHYLLIS KIRK, William CONRAD, Wallace FORD, Christopher Dark, Claude Akins, Willis Bouchey, Howard Petrie, Leo Gordon, Dorothy Adams, John Qualen. 84m.

Disagreeable little bully (Sinatra) tries to come to terms with his own cowardice. There's no way to believe him as a cowboy. Keenan Wynn chews up the scenery as a gun-toting preacher. It's dreadful. Kirk was a replacement for the original leading lady—Gloria Vanderbilt.

JOHNNY GUITAR (1954, REP). D: Nicholas Ray. W: Philip Yordan from a Roy Chanslor novel. Cast: JOAN CRAWFORD, STERLING HAYDEN, MERCEDES McCAMBRIDGE, SCOTT BRADY, Ernest BORGNINE, Ward BOND, Ben COOPER, John CARRADINE, Royal DANO, Paul Fix, Frank Ferguson, Rhys Williams, Ian MacDonald, Trevor Bardette, Denver Pyle, Sheb Wooley, Clem Bevans, Howard Chamberlin, Will Wright, Robert Easton. 111m.

Sexual jealousy pits a lady saloonkeeper (Crawford) against a vicious cattle baroness (McCambridge); each recruits a six-gun crew and they have a war. Hayden, as the title character, plays a hardboiled drifter who doesn't say much but fights well. The crisscrossing relationships and symbolic undercurrents sometimes become too busy to follow. It's fabulously melodramatic, an overwrought fantasy, fierce and Freudian. It contains great suspense, plentiful action, powerful performances and a measure of genuine artistry. Each actor, down to the bit players, has a strong role; some are superb—McCambridge's greedy neurotic bitch is terrifying and brilliant. None of these characters is particularly real—it's really an overblown "B" flick, with none of the humanity of, say, *The Searchers*—but they are fascinating. *Johnny Guitar* defies categorizing; it's far outside any recognizable niche or genre: it's probably a classic, but not of any known school. Frequently it lapses into too-obvious symbolisms, as when Crawford, in a white gown almost virginally bridal, is pursued by a huge posse all of whose members wear black suits because they just came from a funeral. Its pace is uneven, there are wincing cliches throughout and it's all quite implausible, but it's a mesmerizing experience: one of the great good-bad movies. Filmed in Arizona.

JOHNNY RENO (1966, PARA). D: R.G. Springsteen. W: Steve Fisher & Andrew Craddock. Cast: DANA ANDREWS, JANE RUSSELL, Robert LOWERY, Lon CHANEY, Jr., John AGAR, Richard ARLEN, Lyle Bettger, Tom Drake, De Forest Kelley, Tracey Olsen. 83m.

Marshal versus outlaws in the midst of an Indian uprising: yet another A.C. Lyles exercise in casting nostalgia. Creaky shoot-'em-up is at best of wistful interest.

THE JOHNSON COUNTY WAR (1981)— *See* HEAVEN'S GATE.

JOSHUA (1976, IND). D: Larry Spangler. W: Fred Williamson. Cast: FRED WILLIAMSON, Isela VEGA, Calvin Bartlett, Brenda Venus.

Standard revenge plot. Blaxploitation oater apes the Clint Eastwood spaghetti Westerns, even to the cigar in Williamson's mouth. Nothing is explained or motivated; it's just a chase-and-kill movie: idiotic, pointless drivel.

JOURNEY TO SHILOH (1968, UNIV). D: William Hale. W: Gene L.Coon from a Will Henry novel. Cast: JAMES CAAN, MICHAEL SARRAZIN, Brenda SCOTT, Don Stroud, Tisha Sterling, Michael Burns, Paul Petersen, John Doucette, Noah Beery, Jr., Lane Bradford, Rex Ingram, Myron Healey. 101m.

Seven young men decide to ride to Virginia to join the Confederate army; the film follows their encounters, tribulations and maturations on the journey there. It's a good novel and there's plenty of action and the film might have been a good idea but it fizzles because among the cast only Caan has sufficient presence to hold interest; the script is flabby and the production ploddingly directed. This attempt to make a Western with youth appeal (hence the casting of every male ingenue on the lot) has the superficial gloss of one of Universal's factory-made television movies.

JUAREZ (1939, WB). D: William Dieterle. W: John Huston, Aeneas MacKenzie & Wolfgang Reinhardt. Cast: PAUL MUNI, BETTE DAVIS, BRIAN AHERNE, Claude RAINS, Gilbert ROLAND, John GARFIELD, Louis CALHERN, Gale SONDERGAARD, Donald CRISP, Joseph CALLEIA, Grant Mitchell, Pedro de Cordoba, Montagu Love, Robert Warwick, Henry O'Neill, Harry Davenport. 132m.

Muni plays Juarez, the Mexican revolutionary leader of the 1860s, but his role is relatively small and he plays it in subdued fashion as if the thick makeup were caked on his features. The vivid fire in this all-star Warners entry in the bio-pic stakes comes from the stirring performance of Aherne as the Emperor Maximilian, the hapless Hapsburg installed on the puppet throne of Mexico by Napoleon III (Rains) in a cynical effort to evade the consequences of the Monroe Doctrine. Even Bette Davis, who turns in a fine performance as the Empress Carlotta, is very much subordinated to Aherne, who is magnificent as the star-crossed tragic hero whose conscience and life were sacrificed to the Machiavellian machinations of the French court and its on-the-scene general (Crisp). Moving supporting roles are carried expertly by Roland (as one of Aherne's generals) and Garfield (as one of Muni's). It's a fine spectacular movie-movie—huge, lusty, brilliantly written and well directed, with ebullient outsized performances, a handsome score (Erich Wolfgang Korngold) and vivid black-and-white photography (Tony Gaudio). Less of a tract and more of an entertainment than *Viva Zapata*, it comes off better in many respects. Distinguished and exciting biographical adventure.

JUBAL (1956, COL). D: Delmer Daves. W: Daves & Russell S. Hughes from Paul Wellman's novel *Jubal Troop*. Cast: GLENN FORD, ERNEST BORGNINE, ROD STEIGER, Felicia FARR, Valerie FRENCH, Charles BRONSON, Noah Beery, Jr., Jack Elam, John Dierkes, Guy Wilkerson, Basil Ruysdael. 101m.

Rod Steiger as a sadistic gun-toting ranch foreman is amusing—a Method gunslinger—and Borgnine, as a simpleminded Wyoming rancher, and Farr (in her debut) as his sex-ually restless wife, are none too terrific either. When drifting cowhand Ford arrives on the scene, the wife transfers her affections away from hubby's foreman, and this curious double triangle of lust is complicated by the arrival of a sickness-plagued gypsy band of wagon nomads with whom another gunslinging drifter (Bronson) has hooked up. Complexities and contrivances proceed until everybody in the cast seems to be chasing poor Glenn Ford with mayhem in mind. Unfortunately the movie makes use of only a small segment of Wellman's panoramic novel of the opening of the West, and the screenwriters have piled bushels of corn on top of what was originally a vast but speedy yarn that spanned the years from Indian fighting to oil drilling. Anyhow the photography (Charles Lawton, Jr.) is superior, nicely displaying mountainous locations. It's not a bad movie but it does chew up a lot of scenery; you'd do better to look for *The Violent Men*, which does better with similar material.

JUBILEE TRAIL (1953, REP). D: Joseph Kane. W: Bruce Manning from Gwen Bristow's novel. Cast: VERA HRUBA RALSTON, FORREST TUCKER, JOAN LESLIE, JOHN RUSSELL, Jim DAVIS, Pat O'BRIEN, Barton MacLANE, Buddy BAER, Ray Middleton, Richard Webb, James Millican, Martin Garralaga, Nacho Galindo, Don Beddoe, John Holland, Alan Bridge, Rodolfo Hoyos, Marshal Reed, Frank Puglia, Glenn Strange, Jack Elam. 103m.

Heart-of-gold saloon songstress (Ralston) takes an innocent young Eastern bride (Leslie) under her wing to protect her against dastardly cads in the early days of gold-rush California. Oddly, although studio head Herbert J. Yates top-billed his wife (Ralston), her role is peripheral; the main story concerns the romantic conflict over Leslie's affections between the girl's arrogant brother-in-law (Russell) and a frontier trader (Tucker). The novel was to early California what the more recent *Thorn Birds* was to pioneer Australia: a sweeping historical saga with generous helpings of weepy romance. Yates shelled out $100,000 for film rights in the bestseller (a record for Republic) and pulled out all the stops to produce this lavish tearjerking costumer. It might have succeeded at the box office if it had had bigger guns in the cast—say, Joan Crawford and Clark Gable; as it is, it's pictorially impressive—the costumes and sets are extraordinarily elaborate for Republic, and the cast is huge—but the studio's "B" proclivities show through, and in the end it's disappointingly slow.

JUNIOR BONNER (1972, CIN). D: Sam Peckinpah. W: Jeb Rosebrook. Cast: STEVE McQUEEN, ROBERT PRESTON, IDA LUPINO, Joe Don BAKER, Ben JOHNSON, Donald Barry, Barbara Leigh, Mary Murphy, Dub Taylor, Matthew Peckinpah. 101m.

An iconoclastic rodeo rider (McQueen), whose individualism collides with changing times, tries to hang in there. The story is slice-of-life, and very appealing. Peckinpah handles it with unusual restraint; it's a poignant movie with outstanding performances by Lupino and Preston (as McQueen's parents) and by Johnson and Baker. The rodeo action scenes are first-rate, and Lucien Ballard contributes his excellent photography. It's a small movie but very worthwhile.

J.W. COOP (1972, COL). D: Cliff Robertson. W: Robertson, Gary Cartwright & Bud Shrake. Cast: CLIFF ROBERTSON, GERALDINE PAGE, Christina FERRARE, John Crawford, R.G. Armstrong, Marjorie Durant Dye. 112m.

The title character is a rodeo-riding convict who's been in prison for a decade for forgery and resisting arrest. When he's released he decides to hit the professional rodeo circuit because it's what he learned to do in slam. But he discovers the world has changed: rodeo champions devote themselves to stock portfolios now; they fly their private planes from meet to meet, put their pictures and endorsements on ads for lousy products, and generally opt for plastic symbols of success. I don't know if "Coop" is a deliberate reference to Gary Cooper but Robertson's hero reacts to all this just as Cooper would have—with a kind of bemused dismay. At first he tries to make up for lost time; his way is eased by the attachment of a hippie girl (Ferrare, a very good performance). The ending is hard but correct. The supporting cast, many of them nonprofessional rodeo people, is superb, and Robertson as the kid-in-the-poison-candy-store is beyond that; he's damn near perfect.

There is banal self-indulgence here and there, too much fondness for arty effects, an outrageous Method mugging job by Geraldine Page as the hero's crazy old mother, too much editorializing; yet *J.W. Coop* is deeply felt, a moving movie, and a great vehicle for a very talented actor-director.

KANGAROO (1952, FOX). D: Lewis Milestone. W: Harry Kleiner & Martin Berkeley. Cast: PETER LAWFORD, MAUREEN O'HARA, RICHARD BOONE, Finlay CURRIE, Chips RAFFERTY. 84m.

Western, transplanted to Australia, is about a charming con man (Lawford), a hardbitten villain (Boone), a kindly old station (ranch) owner (Currie), his cowpunching ramrod (Rafferty) and an Irish-Australian frontier lass (O'Hara). The plot is the old good-partner, bad-partner wheeze; the only thing worth looking at is the parched Australian location scenery. A good deal of impressive talent was wasted on this one.

THE KANSAN (1943, UA). D: George Archainbaud. W: Harold Shumate from a Frank Gruber novel. Cast: RICHARD DIX, JANE WYATT, ALBERT DEKKER, Victor JORY, Roy ROGERS, Eugene Pallette, Robert Armstrong, Clem Bevans, Francis J. McDonald, Douglas Fowley, Herman Hack. 79m.

Town marshal (Dix) versus villainous town boss (Dekker). Yarn is dressed up with a big budget, a large cast, a more interesting script than most, and a hero modeled on the legends about Earp and Masterson and Hickok. The plot is routine but the ramifications are nicely handled.

KANSAS PACIFIC (1952, AA). D: Ray Nazarro. W: Daniel Ullman. Cast: STERLING HAYDEN, Eve MILLER, Barton MacLANE, Reed Hadley, Douglas Fowley, Irving Bacon, Harry Shannon, Tom Fadden, Myron Healey, James Griffith, Clayton Moore, Jonathan Hale, Lane Chandler, I. Stanford Jolley. 73m.

Railroad builders fight it out with Rebel raiders in black-and-white, with Hayden as an army engineer working undercover to get the line finished so the Western forts can be supplied by the Union forces. The bad guys are Quantrill's (Hadley) Raiders and there's plenty of "B"-style action footage, typical of Allied Artists (formerly Monogram Pictures). Hayden meanders through the part with his mind evidently on something else; the rest of the actors go through their well-worn paces with competence but little spark. Produced by Walter Wanger.

KANSAS RAIDERS (1950, UNIV). D: Ray Enright. W: Robert L. Richards. Cast: AUDIE MURPHY, BRIAN DONLEVY, Marguerite CHAPMAN, Tony CURTIS, Scott BRADY, Dewey MARTIN, Richard LONG, Richard ARLEN, James Best, Richard Egan, John Kellogg, George Chandler. 80m.

Jesse James (Murphy), along with brother Frank James (Long) and friends and relations Kit Dalton (Curtis), Cole and Jim Younger (Best, Martin) and Bloody Bill Anderson (Brady), rides with Quantrill's (Donlevy) Raiders as they become the scourge of Missouri and Kansas during the Civil War. The movie builds to a climax at the burning and sack of Lawrence, Kansas—an event that is not among the more savory episodes of history. For its time this was a brutal and bloody movie. The characterization of Jesse and Frank as kids pushed by circumstances across the law's line, agonizing over the morality of their actions, is a considerable whitewash, at variance with history, but that's forgivable enough. Murphy repeats essentially the same misunderstood-outlaw characterization as his Billy the Kid in *The Kid from Texas*—another example of the interchangeability of Western myth-heroes.

There's a semblance of accuracy in the film's depiction of all these famous outlaws as green kids. They are played mostly by male starlets whom Universal was grooming for bigger things. In actuality the Jameses and Youngers were still in their teens or barely out of them when these events took place. But unfortunately, despite big production values, good action sequences, spectacle and fine Technicolor photography (Irving Glassburg), it's a limp story with silly dialogue and amateurish performances by the apprentice cast. Richard Egan, for example, unbilled in a bit part as a Union lieutenant, is laughably inept. It's fair entertainment for its time, but depressingly dated.

THE KENTUCKIAN (1955, UA). D: Burt Lancaster. W: A. B. Guthrie, Jr., from a Felix Holt novel. Cast: BURT LANCASTER, DIANA LYNN, Walter MATTHAU, John McINTIRE, Una MERKEL, John CARRADINE, Rhys Williams, John Litel, Edward Norris, Diane Foster, Donald MacDonald, Nick Cravat. 103m.

Lancaster's first directorial attempt is a muddled slow yarn about pioneers of the 1820s settling new lands west of the Appalachians. There's lots of action with the spotlight on Lancaster's swashbuckling (he was once a professional circus acrobat with his partner Nick Cravat) but unfortunately there's insufficient story to go with it; the plot is diffuse, jerky and undramatic. That's partly the fault of the script but also partly the fault of the studio which seems to have done a hatchet job of editing prior to release. Lancaster directs his actors with adequate blocking techniques but a decidedly uneven hand, so that some of them come off very well (particularly Matthau, in his movie debut) while others turn in absurd burlesque performances (Lynn, Carradine, Merkel).

KENTUCKY RIFLE (1955, IND). D: Carl K. Hittleman. W: Hittleman, Lee J. Hewitt & Francis Chase, Jr. Cast: CHILL WILLS, CATHY DOWNS, Lance FULLER, Jeanne

CAGNEY, Henry HULL, Jess Barker, Sterling Holloway. 72m.

Wagon pioneers versus Comanches. Nothing very new. It features a supporting cast in search of a star. Okay if you're in an undemanding mood.

KID BLUE (1973, FOX). D: James Frawley. W: Edwin Shrake. Cast: DENNIS HOPPER, WARREN OATES, PETER BOYLE, Ben JOHNSON, Lee PURCELL, Janice RULE, Ralph WAITE, Clifton James, Jose Torvay, Mary Jackson, Claude Ennis Starrett, Jr., Richard Rust, M. Emmet Walsh, Warren Finnerty. 100m.

In 1902 an innocent young train robber (Hopper) decides to go straight, but the world won't let him—especially a mean rednecked sheriff (Johnson). The unfunny comedy has rudimentary characters and is crammed with anachronistic message dialogue. It's tasteless revisionism, and Hopper, at 37, is far too old to play the witless teen-age protagonist.

THE KID FROM TEXAS (1939, MGM). D: S. Sylvan Simon. W: Florence Ryerson, Edgar Woolf, Albert Mannheimer, Milton Merlin & Byron Morgan. Cast: DENNIS O'KEEFFE, FLORENCE RICE, Jack CARSON, Buddy EBSEN, Jessie Ralph, J. M. Kerrigan, Virginia Dale, Iron Eyes Cody, Spencer Charters, Jack Perrin.

A cowboy forms a polo team of Indians and cowhands; they set out to challenge the high society set. Light comedy was fairly amusing in its day.

THE KID FROM TEXAS (1950, UNIV). D: Kurt Neumann. W: Robert H. Andrews & Karl Kamb. Cast: AUDIE MURPHY, GALE STORM, ALBERT DEKKER, Shepperd STRUDWICK, William Talman, Walter Sande, Ray Teal. 78m.

Murphy is Billy the Kid and Dekker is Sheriff Pat Garrett in this version. While it bears little comparison with history or historical characters it does an entertaining job of re-creating legends. It was produced back-to-back with *Kansas Raiders* in which Murphy played the young Jesse James; both films are superior examples of the subgenre, but this one takes the edge because of the intriguing relationship it establishes between the lawman and the outlaw. It's not pretentious like the more recent *Dirty Little Billy* or *Pat Garrett and Billy the Kid*; it's mainly for the kids, but it's straightforward; better entertainment in many ways despite the predictability of its cliches.

KID RODELO (1965, PARA). D: Richard Carlson. W: Jack Natteford from a Louis

L'Amour story. Cast: DON MURRAY, JANET LEIGH, BRODERICK CRAWFORD, Richard CARLSON, Jose Nieto, Julio Pena, Miguel Castillo. 91m.

Stalwart drifter (Murray) protects a beleaguered woman (Leigh) against marauding Indians and some unshaven bad guys (Crawford, Carlson) who've busted out of prison to dig up a fortune in hidden gold. This is a cheapjack runaway production, made in Spain with European crews, facilities and supporting actors. It's in black-and-white with "low budget" engraved on every frame. The acting, even by the seasoned pros, is execrable, and actor Carlson's directing is amateurish, and the script is terrible. A complete waste of time.

THE KILLER INSIDE ME (1975, WB). D: Burt Kennedy. W: Edward Mann & Robert Chamblee from a Jim Thompson novel. Cast: STACY KEACH, Susan TYRRELL, Keenan WYNN, Tisha STERLING, John Dehner, Charles McGraw, Royal Dano, Julie Adams, John Carradine, Don Stroud, Pepe Serna. 99m.

Montana lawman goes berserk, wipes out prostitutes and rednecks while suffering traumatic nightmares keyed by Freudian childhood flashbacks. This one is curious, gothic, but repellent.

THE KING AND FOUR QUEENS (1956, UA). D: Raoul Walsh. W: Margaret Fitts & Richard Alan Simmons. Cast: CLARK GABLE, ELEANOR PARKER, JO VAN FLEET, Jean Willes, Jay C. Flippen, Barbara Nichols, Sara Shane, Roy Roberts, Arthur Shields. 84m.

An outlaw (Gable) comes to a desert ghost town inhabited by the mother (Van Fleet) and four widows of the stage-robbing McDade brothers, who are reputedly dead after a shoot-out with the law. Gable and the five women try to find the brothers' hidden loot and to double-cross one another. Raoul Walsh was fond of saying, "There were actors who didn't like to work with me because they said I worked too fast. Twenty days, twenty-two days to shoot a picture. But I believed they were moving pictures so I moved 'em." Unfortunately the haste is evident in movies like this one. Gable is polished but weary; the movie, with its cynical emphasis on sexual innuendo, is shabby and tawdry. There's virtually no action. Van Fleet's theatrical overplaying is sort of fun; otherwise it's dreary.

THE KISSING BANDIT (1948, MGM). D: Laszlo Benedek. W: Isobel Lennart & John B. Harding. Cast: FRANK SINATRA, KATHRYN GRAYSON, ANN MILLER, Ricardo MONTALBAN, Cyd CHARISSE, J. Carrol Naish, Mildred Natwick, Billy Gilbert, Carleton Young, Joe Dominguez, Mikhail Rasumny, Byron Foulger, Julian Rivero. 102m.

Timid Bostonian (Sinatra) arrives in California to take his late father's place as a road agent whose trademark was that he always kissed his lady victims. A considerable budget, miles of color film, several songs and a number of name stars were lavished on this mind-bogglingly awful dog.

KISS OF FIRE (1955, UNIV). D: Joseph M. Newman. W: Franklin Coen & Richard Collins from a Jonreed Lauritzen novel. Cast: JACK PALANCE, BARBARA RUSH, Rex REASON, Martha HYER, Alan Reed, Larry Dobkin, Leslie Bradley. 87m.

In the seventeenth century some Spaniards journey from Mexico into California, fighting among themselves, fighting off bandits and Indians. There's a lot of fighting. It makes little sense but it's harmless enough.

KIT CARSON (1940, UA). D: George B. Seitz. W: George Bruce. Cast: JON HALL, LYNN BARI, Dana ANDREWS, Harold Huber, Ward Bond, William Farnum, Clayton Moore, C. Henry Gordon, Renie Riano. 95m.

Frontier scout (Hall) vies with a young cavalry officer (Andrews) for the affections of a winsome lass. The photography (John Mescall) is good; there are adequate action sequences and a more realistic portrayal of Navajo Indians than many. But it's nothing to do with the real Kit Carson, and Hall is an unsatisfactory performer, and the melodrama is dated.

LADY FROM CHEYENNE (1941, UNIV). D: Frank Lloyd. W: Warren Duff, Kathryn Scola, Jonathan Finn & Theresa Oakes. Cast: LORETTA YOUNG, ROBERT PRESTON, EDWARD ARNOLD, Gladys George, Frank Craven, Jessie Ralph, Samuel S. Hinds, Dorothy Granger, Charles Ray. 87m.

Possibly the first women's lib oater, this has Young as a schoolmarm in old Wyoming who wins the women's right to vote. (Wyoming during the Civil War was the first state to grant suffrage to its female citizens.) The comedy is preachy and dated but Young and Preston are dandy.

LADY FROM TEXAS (1952, UNIV). D: Joseph Pevney. W: Gerald D. Adams, Harold Shumate & Connie Lee Bennett. Cast: JOSEPHINE HULL, HOWARD DUFF, MONA FREEMAN, Gene Lockhart, Craig Stevens, Jay C. Flippen. 77m.

Eccentric old woman's (Hull) shenanigans upset a staid Western town. Whimsical farce is unusual but nothing special.

A LADY TAKES A CHANCE (1943, RKO). D: William Seiter. W: Robert Ardrey & Jo Swerling. Cast: JEAN ARTHUR, JOHN WAYNE, Phil SILVERS, Charles Winninger, Mary Field, Hans Conreid, Grady Sutton, Don Costello, Herman Hack. 86m.

A wacky New York secretary (Arthur) on a bus tour out West (with fast-talking tour guide Phil Silvers) falls for a cowhand (Wayne) and comedy ensues. It's mostly quite funny. Republic lent Wayne out for this one; it's one of the rare movies in which he accepted second billing.

LASCA OF THE RIO GRANDE (1931, UNIV). D: Edward Laemmle. Cast: LEO CARRILLO, DOROTHY BURGESS, Johnny Mack BROWN.

Another laughing Latin bandit meller, with songs.

THE LASH (1930, WB). D: Frank Lloyd. W: Bradley King from a novel by Lanier & Virginia Bartlett. Cast: RICHARD BARTHELMESS, MARY ASTOR, James RENNIE, Marion Nixon, Fred Kohler, Erville Anderson, Robert Edeson.

This was a Zorroesque yarn about the Spanish dons of early California, a biggie of its time, but Barthelmess was miscast as a dashing caballero and even Astor didn't save it from a dullness relieved only by a lavishly filmed stampede.

THE LAST CHALLENGE (1967, MGM). Also titled: PISTOLERO. D: Richard Thorpe. W: John Sherry & Robert E. Ginna from Sherry's novel. Cast: GLENN FORD, ANGIE DICKINSON, CHAD EVERETT, Gary MERRILL, Royal DANO, Jack ELAM, Frank McGrath, Delphi Lawrence. 105m.

A young pistolero (Everett) arrives in town and spends most of the movie debating whether to shoot it out with the gunslinging town marshal (Ford) to prove who's the fastest gun in the West. It's well acted, well directed, well photographed (Ellsworth Fredericks), and the characters and dialogue are good enough to get by; there might have been several good ways to ring a twist on the familiar formula but this one doesn't find any of them; it's a leadenly predictable reprise of *The Gunfighter*.

THE LAST COMMAND (1955, REP). D: Frank Lloyd. W: Warren Duff & Sy Bartlett. Cast: STERLING HAYDEN, ANNA MARIA ALBERGHETTI, Arthur HUNNICUTT, Ernest BORGNINE, Richard CARLSON, John Russell, J. Carrol Naish, Slim Pickens, Ben Cooper, Jim Davis, Otto Kruger, Virginia Grey, Hugh Sanders, Russell Simpson, Eduard Franz, Morris Ankrum. 108m.

Knife-wielding Jim Bowie (Hayden) is a Mexican citizen whose loyalties are divided when Texas opts for independence; patriotism of birth wins out, and he turns against the Mexican general Santa Anna (Naish) and joins the heroic defenders of the Alamo: Davy Crockett (Hunnicutt) and Colonel Travis (Carlson).

Filmed on Texas locations in Trucolor, with a big budget (for Republic) and cast and a lavish orchestral score by Max Steiner, this is a smaller work than John Wayne's subsequent *The Alamo* but it covers the same ground with considerably more verve and drama. It's mostly on a "B" level of melodramatics but then so was Wayne's; the difference here is in the taut, tingling pace, the fine lusty spirit, the fast, hard action sequences. Performances are superior throughout. The climactic battle was filmed on a fraction of the budget that Wayne wasted on his reenactment of it, but dramatically it's more effective here, drawing forth from audiences an honest tear or two for the gallant defenders.

THE LAST DAY (1975, PARA). D: Vincent McEveety. W: Jim Byrnes & Steve Fisher. Cast: RICHARD WIDMARK, BARBARA RUSH, ROBERT CONRAD, Loretta SWIT, Morgan WOODWARD, Richard Jaeckel, Tim Matheson, Gene Evans, Tom Skerritt, Christopher Connelly, John Locke, Rex Holman, Logan Ramsey. Narrator: Harry MORGAN. 97m.

Peaceable old-time gunslinger (Widmark) is trying to go straight and avoid a showdown with his old enemy Bob Dalton (Conrad) but finally, after endless talk, he's persuaded to organize the defenses of the town of Coffeyville, Kansas, against the forthcoming Dalton gang bank robbery attempt. The history, superficially accurate, is overwhelmed by silly cliches, and the pulpy script is ajar with anachronisms: Grat Dalton (Jaeckel) says to his brother Emmet (Matheson), "Hang in there!" There's virtually no action until the climax; it's pointless, dull and saddlesore; much better is *The Last Ride of the Dalton Gang* (1979). A.C. Lyles produced this one; it was never released in theatres but only on TV.

THE LAST FRONTIER (1955, COL). Also titled: THE SAVAGE WILDERNESS. D. Anthony Mann. W: Philip Yordan & Russell S. Hughes from a novel by Richard E. Roberts. Cast: VICTOR MATURE, GUY MADISON, ROBERT PRESTON, ANNE BANCROFT, James WHITMORE, Peter Whitney, Russell Collins. 98m.

A stubborn, stupid, ruthless, by-the-book

cavalry colonel (Preston) dominates a frontier outpost and foments war with the Indians while driving his wife (Bancroft) into the arms of a trapper scout (Mature); it all leads to a climactic battle with the Indians in which you can pretty well predict who'll get killed and who'll survive. This trashy big-budget junk, a waste of a good cast, is proof that a director like Mann, who directed some of the best Westerns of the 1950s, was no better than the material he had (or chose) to work with. Screenwriter Yordan also has done far better movies than this. The acting is acceptable but not wonderful. This is one of those pictures that Bancroft, who made several dreary Westerns, probably would prefer to forget.

THE LAST HARD MEN (1976, FOX). D: Andrew V. McLaglen. W: Guerdon Trueblood from a Brian Garfield novel. Cast: CHARLTON HESTON, JAMES COBURN, Barbara HERSHEY, Jorge RIVERO, Christopher Mitchum, Michael Parks, Morgan Paull, Larry Wilcox, Thalamus Rasulala, Bob Donner, James Bacon, Terry Pinyerd. 96m.

Story is a pursuit yarn set in Arizona in 1910. A discussion of the filming can be found in Chapter 8. Technical credits: photography by Duke Callaghan, score by Jerry Goldsmith, edited by Fred Chulack, art direction by Edward Carfagno, stunts coordinated by Joseph Canutt. I can't very well "review" this film, since it's my own, but perhaps I may be permitted to admit that I enjoyed being on location with the crew.

THE LAST HUNT (1956, MGM). DW: Richard Brooks from Milton Lott's novel. Cast: STEWART GRANGER, ROBERT TAYLOR, Debra PAGET, Lloyd NOLAN, Russ Tamblyn, Constance Ford, Joe De Santis, Roy Barcroft, Ralph Moody, Fred Graham. 108m.

Taylor sinks his teeth into the surly role of a paranoid psychotic who hunts buffalo because he likes to kill; Granger is likeable as his partner, a veteran conscience-stricken hunter. The innate conflict leads to a falling-out between the partners; by the end they are determined to destroy each other. Subplots involving Indian girls, a wayward kid (Tamblyn) and a hard-drinking peglegged old buffalo skinner (Nolan) merely serve to pad out the film; the supporting players are miscast—Nolan too New Yorkish, Tamblyn absurd as a fruity half-breed, Paget only so-so as an Indian lass. Russell Harlan's CinemaScope photography is postcard-panoramic and the hunt scenes, filmed in South Dakota during the annual thinning of the state's pop-

ulous bison herd, are stark, and convey the film's ecological message with no need for the kind of editorializing that mucked up the more recent *Bless the Beasts and Children*.

This one is admittedly clumsy—the screenplay reduces Lott's complex novel to a slender simple yarn; the acting, except for the two leads, is poor; the movie is too slow. But it's strong stuff and the ending is one you are not likely to forget.

LAST OF THE BADMEN (1948)—*See* BADMEN OF TOMBSTONE.

LAST OF THE BADMEN (1957, AA). D: Paul Landres. W: Daniel Ullman & David Chantler. Cast: GEORGE MONTGOMERY, James BEST, Meg Randall, Michael Ansara, Keith Larsen, Frank Thomas. 79m.

When a Pinkerton detective is killed out West, the Chicago home office sends a pair of crack operatives to find the killer. Standard oater was remade in 1964 as *Gunfight at Comanche Creek*.

LAST OF THE COMANCHES (1953, COL). D: Andre de Toth. W: Kenneth Gamet. Cast: BRODERICK CRAWFORD, BARBARA HALE, Lloyd BRIDGES, Mickey Shaughnessy, Johnny Stewart, Martin Milner, Carleton Young, John War Eagle, Hugh Sanders, Chubby Johnson. 85m.

Hard-bitten cavalry sergeant (Crawford) has to lead a stagecoach load of passengers to safety after a brutal Indian raid. It's been described as an unacknowledged remake of *Sahara* (the Bogart movie which in turn was stolen from a segment of a Russian film). As the subgenre of beleaguered-and-pursued Westerns goes, this isn't a bad example. Shaughnessy's debut.

LAST OF THE DESPERADOS (1955, IND). D: Paul Landres. W: Orville Hampton. Cast: JAMES CRAIG, Margia DEAN, Jim Davis, Barton MacLane, Bob Steele, Stanley Clements, Jack Perrin. 70m.

Sheriff Pat Garrett (Craig), having killed Billy the Kid, sets out to track down four members of Billy's outlaw gang. Routine programmer.

LAST OF THE DUANES (1930, FOX). D: Alfred Werker. W: Ernest Pascal from Zane Grey's novel. Cast: GEORGE O'BRIEN, MYRNA LOY, Lucille BROWN, Walter McGrail, James Mason, Nat Pendleton, Willard Robertson.

First talkie version of the oft-remade Zane Grey yarn didn't hew as closely to the novel as the 1941 movie; this was a standard hero-rescues-damsel-in-distress meller, dated even in its own time but well produced with more outdoor movement than most of the sound-stage-confined movies of its time.

LAST OF THE DUANES (1941, FOX). **D: James Tinling. W: Irving Cummings, Jr., & William Counselman, Jr., from Zane Grey's novel. Cast: GEORGE MONTGOMERY, EVE ARDEN, George E. STONE, Lynne Roberts, Francis Ford, William Farnum, Joe Sawyer, Don Costello, Russell Simpson.**

A gunfighter is accused of murder and has to clear himself. This sticks fairly close to the novel but it's an old tired yarn, not nearly as good a story or movie as the contemporaneous *Riders of the Purple Sage*.

LAST OF THE FAST GUNS (1958, UNIV). **D: George Sherman. W: David P. Harmon. Cast: JOCK MAHONEY, LINDA CRISTAL, GILBERT ROLAND, Eduard FRANZ. 82m.**

A range detective (Mahoney) is hired to search Mexico for the missing brother of an industrialist. Mahoney was a better stunt man than actor but it moves along fast enough.

LAST OF THE MOHICANS (1936, UA). **D: George B. Seitz. W: Philip Dunne, John L. Balderston, Paul Perez & Daniel Moore from James Fenimore Cooper's novel. Cast: RANDOLPH SCOTT, BINNIE BARNES, Bruce CABOT, Philip Reed, Henry Wilcoxon, Robert Barrat. 91m.**

It's the one about the noble Indians who support British frontiersmen against their French-led brothers in the 1840s. As film versions of Fenimore Cooper go, this was among the better efforts—a big production with plenty of action. It was produced by Sam Katzman, who dictated the use of an odd color process, like that of a badly tuned color TV set: the faces were mostly green, the sky brown and the leaves purple. The Indians and canoes were obvious phonies but audiences in 1936 loved it.

LAST OF THE PONY RIDERS (1953, COL). **D: George Archainbaud. W: Ruth Woodman. Cast: GENE AUTRY, Smiley BURNETTE, Kathleen CASE, Dick JONES, Buzz Henry, Gregg Barton. 59m.**

Cheesy sepia idiocy is of interest only because it was Autry's last (93rd) movie and was the last film directed by the prolific Archainbaud.

LAST OF THE REDMEN (1946, COL). **D: George Sherman. W: Herbert Dalmas & George Plympton from James Fenimore Cooper's novel *Last of the Mohicans*. Cast: JON HALL, EVELYN ANKERS, Michael O'SHEA, Julie BISHOP, Larry "Buster" Crabbe, Rick Vallin. 77m.**

Hall plays the noble Indian in this version. Its only advantage over the 1936 Randolph Scott version is that this one's in better color.

THE LAST OUTLAW (1936, RKO). **D: Christy Cabanne. W: John Ford, E. Murray Campbell, John Twist & Jack Townley. Cast: HARRY CAREY, HOOT GIBSON, TOM TYLER, Margaret Callahan, Henry B.Walthall, Russell Hopton, Joe Sawyer. 62m.**

An outlaw (Carey) who has served a long prison term emerges into the modern West and has to get used to the changes that have taken place; he ends up fighting racketeers. John Ford wrote the script for an earlier silent version that he directed; this was a remake. Fair but dated.

THE LAST OUTPOST (1951, PARA). **D: Lewis R. Foster. W: Geoffrey Homes, George Worthington Yates & Winston Miller from a David Lang story. Cast: RONALD REAGAN, RHONDA FLEMING, Bruce BENNETT, Bill WILLIAMS, Noah Beery, Jr., Peter Hanson, Hugh Beaumont, Lloyd Corrigan, John Ridgely, Iron Eyes Cody. 87m.**

Reb (Reagan) and Yank (Bennett) brothers squabble for two hours, then join forces to fight off Apaches. It's sometimes humorous, and well photographed (Loyal Griggs) at Old Tucson, but it's contrived kid stuff.

THE LAST POSSE (1953, COL). **D: Alfred Werker. W: Kenneth Gamet, Seymour & Connie Lee Bennett. Cast: JOHN DEREK, BRODERICK CRAWFORD, CHARLES BICKFORD, WANDA HENDRIX, Henry HULL, Warner Anderson, Will Wright, Monte Blue, Tom Powers, Raymond Greenleaf, James Kirkwood, Eddy Waller, Skip Homeier, James Bell, Guy Wilkerson. 73m.**

When $100,000 is stolen from a range tyrant (Bickford) he puts together a posse to get it back. The flashback story deals mainly with the relationship between the arrogant cattle baron and a washed-up alcoholic lawman (Crawford); it's played out against the posse's trek. The two men vie for leadership and for the loyalty of a youth (Derek) who has obligations to them both. The story is grim and sometimes brutal, at times cheapened by lazy resort to cliches but it's a tough speedy yarn with plenty of grit. Superior black-and-white photography (Burnett Guffey) and the look of a fair-size production budget (for Harry Cohn's penny-pinching studio) give it the flavor of an "A" movie, although it is pulled down by oversimplifications and a silly contrived ending where everything comes unglued. The film's best asset is Crawford's outstanding performance;

usually he's not a believable Westerner but here he's splendid.

THE LAST REBEL (1971, COL). D: Denys McCoy. W: Warren Kiefer. Cast: JOE NAMATH, Woody STRODE, Jack ELAM, Ty HARDIN, Victoria George, Marina Coffa, Mike Forrest. 89m.

As the Civil War ends, a Reb (Namath) joins up with two partners to try and win a fortune playing pool in a frontier whorehouse. So much for the plot. The dialogue is replete with windy generalities that pass for philosophical profundities. Filmed in Italy. Namath, quarterback and celebrity, is an unfortunate actor. The movie is asinine and soporific.

THE LAST RIDE OF THE DALTON GANG (1979, IND). D: Dan Curtis. W: Earl W. Wallace. Cast: CLIFF POTTS, JACK PALANCE, DALE ROBERTSON, Larry WILCOX, Randy QUAID, Bo HOPKINS, Sharon FARRELL, Matt Clark, Royal Dano, R. G. Armstrong, Harris Yulin, Harry Townes, Scott Brady, H. M. Wynant, Julie Hill, Buff Brady. 148m.

This one concerns the Dalton brothers—Bob (Potts), Emmet (Wilcox) and Grat (Quaid)—and their on-again, off-again partnership with Billy Doolin (Hopkins) and their various run-ins (mostly fictitious) with Hanging Judge Isaac C. Parker (Robertson) and icy railroad detective Will Smith (Palance). Three-hour made-for-TV movie is far better than most; it provides an engaging rendition of the Dalton saga. Good photography (Frank Stanley) and score (Bob Cobert) accentuate the professionalism. No more historically accurate than most, this movie nonetheless conveys a much stronger *flavor* of reality than one normally expects of TV productions. There are hearty comic episodes as well. It's good entertainment.

THE LAST ROUND-UP (1934, PARA). D: Henry Hathaway. W: Wells Root & Jack Cunningham from Zane Grey's *The Border Legion*. Cast: RANDOLPH SCOTT, Barbara FRITCHIE, Monte Blue, Fred Kohler, Fuzzy Knight, Barton MacLane, Charles Middleton, Jim Corbett, James Mason. 61m.

Monte Blue was dandy as the gang leader in this umpteenth remake of the old yarn about the outlaw gang that cares. See title *The Border Legion* for other remakes. This was the last of the Hathaway-Scott series, with photography by Archie J. Stout.

LAST STAGECOACH WEST (1957, REP). D: Joseph Kane. W: Barry Shipman. Cast: JIM DAVIS, Mary CASTLE, Victor JORY, Lee VAN CLEEF, Roy Barcroft, Grant Withers, Francis J. McDonald. 67m.

When a stagecoach outfit loses its mail contract, it looks as if it's going out of business until our hero steps in. The cast is better than the script; even old pro Kane couldn't save it.

THE LAST SUNSET (1961, UNIV). D: Robert Aldrich. W: Dalton Trumbo from a Howard Rigsby novel. Cast: KIRK DOUGLAS, ROCK HUDSON, DOROTHY MALONE, Joseph COTTEN, Carol LYNLEY, Neville Brand, Jack Elam, Regis Toomey, Adam Williams. 112m.

Kirk Douglas is a drifter dressed in a black outfit so tight it might have been painted on him. The heavy-breathing plot concerns incest, alcoholism and complex conflicts amongst the folks on a cattle drive trying to get Cotten's cows from Mexico to Texas. There are good scenes but Hudson is clumsy, Douglas self-consciously athletic (parodying himself), Malone overwrought, Lynley undercompetent and Cotten wasted in the background. It's a curious grab bag of sentimental cliches and censor-baiting raciness; Trumbo's script is talky; the pace is erratic.

LAST TRAIN FROM GUN HILL (1958, PARA). D: John Sturges. W: James Poe, Edward Lewis & Les Crutchfield. Cast: KIRK DOUGLAS, ANTHONY QUINN, CAROLYN JONES, Earl HOLLIMAN, Brad Dexter, John Anderson, Ziva Rodann, Brian Hutton, Walter Sande. 94m.

A lawman (Douglas) has to take his rancher friend's (Quinn) son (Holliman) in for trial for raping and murdering the lawman's own wife. The father and his crew besiege the lawman—the plot is similar to that of *3:10 to Yuma*. It's well handled with good suspense but it doesn't have much spark; Sturges reassembled his production crew from *Gunfight at the OK Corral* to film this one and it's superior but very slow of pace.

THE LAST WAGON (1956, FOX). D: Delmer Daves. W: Daves, James Edward Grant & Gwen B. Gielgud. Cast: RICHARD WIDMARK, FELICIA FARR, Nick ADAMS, Susan Kohner, Ray Stricklyn, Douglas Kennedy Tommy Rettig, Stephanie Griffin. 99m.

A fugitive (Widmark), wanted for murder, finds himself trapped into protecting the lives of wagon-train pioneers in hostile Apache country. The plot is old-hat with very few fresh notions to offer, and the acting is of markedly uneven quality; but everything clicks properly and it's tough, swift and solid. In CinemaScope.

LAUGHING BOY (1934, MGM). D: W. S. Van Dyke. W: John Lee Mahin & John Colton from Oliver LaFarge's novel. Cast: RAMON NOVARRO, LUPE VELEZ, Chief Thundercloud, William Dickenson. 79m.

LaFarge's book, about a young Indian couple on and off a New Mexico reservation, has become a classic of Southwestern literature but this film version died at the box office; the film apparently is lost now.

THE LAW AND JAKE WADE (1958, MGM). D: John Sturges. W: William Bowers from Marvin H. Albert's novel. Cast: ROBERT TAYLOR, RICHARD WIDMARK, Patricia OWENS, Robert Middleton, Henry Silva, Burt Douglas, De Forest Kelley. 86m.

Lawman (Taylor) trying to forget his outlaw past is plagued by his cheerfully satanic ex-partner (Widmark); the story takes place during a treasure hunt that's menaced by unfriendly Indians on the warpath. The action scenes are excitingly filmed but the script disappoints and the characterizations are ludicrous, especially Widmark's chortling sadistic villain.

LAW AND ORDER (1932, UNIV). Also titled: GUNS A'BLAZIN'. D: Edward L. Cahn. W: John Huston & Tom Reed from a W. R. Burnett novel. Cast: WALTER HUSTON, HARRY CAREY, Walter BRENNAN, Andy Devine, Ralph Ince, Russell Hopton, Raymond Hatton, Russell Simpson, Harry Woods, Andy Devine, Walter Brennan, Dick Alexander. 69m.

The Earps clean up Tombstone, fighting it out with the Clantons at the OK Corral. Carey plays a Doc Holliday type. It's familiar now, but beautifully done, very tense, its atmosphere obviously indebted to William S. Hart (who was a friend of Wyatt Earp's). Seldom exhibited but still in existence, this may well be the definitive Wyatt Earp movie; at least it vies for that honor with *My Darling Clementine*.

LAW AND ORDER (1953, UNIV). D: Nathan Juran. W: D.D. Beauchamp, John & Gwen Bagni and Inez Cocke from W.R. Burnett's novel. Cast: RONALD REAGAN, DOROTHY MALONE, Preston FOSTER, Alex NICOL, Russell Johnson, Dennis Weaver, Jack Kelly, Chubby Johnson, Ruth Hampton, Barry Kelly, Don Gordon. 81m.

Reagan is all right in this remake but it's a tired echo.

THE LAWLESS BREED (1952, UNIV). D: Raoul Walsh. W: Bernard Gordon & William Alland. Cast: ROCK HUDSON, JULIA ADAMS, John McINTIRE, Michael Ansara, Dennis Weaver, Hugh O'Brian,

Glenn Strange, Stephen Chase, Mary Castle, Tom Fadden. 83m.

John Wesley Hardin (Hudson) tries to settle down so that his son can grow up right; most of the picture is flashbacks as Hardin recounts his wayward past for the kid. It's a plodding yarn, mostly talk. Hardin's life remains to be filmed with any vitality; in reality he was a curious figure, probably the deadliest of all the gunmen—he killed at least fifty people between his adolescence in the Civil War and his incarceration in Texas more than a decade later; in his maturity—much of it served in a penitentiary—he studied law and finally hung out his shingle as an attorney in El Paso, only to be gunned down by a glory-hungry constable. Very little of that history is reflected in the movie at hand.

THE LAWLESS EIGHTIES (1957, REP). D: Joseph Kane. W: Olsen Jesse Smith. Cast: LARRY "BUSTER" CRABBE, John SMITH, Marilyn Saris, Ted de Corsia, John Doucette. 70m.

Old-time gunfighter comes to the aid of a preacher who's victimized by nasty brutes. Low-budget drear.

THE LAWLESS RIDER (1954, IND). D: Yakima Canutt. W: John Carpenter. Cast: JOHN CARPENTER, Frankie Darro, Rose Bascom, Douglas Dumbrille, Kenne Duncan, Bud Osborne, Noel Neill.

Marshal disguises himself as an outlaw to join a rustler gang. Carpenter produced this opus; Canutt, Hollywood's top stunt man and second-unit director, couldn't do much with this one—the script was hopeless but, like Carpenter's other films, this cheap backalley indie sometimes was posed with a peculiar tautness. For more on Carpenter see *Outlaw Treasure*.

A LAWLESS STREET (1955, COL). D: Joseph H. Lewis. W: Kenneth Gamet from a Brad Ward story. Cast: RANDOLPH SCOTT, ANGELA LANSBURY, Warner ANDERSON, Jean PARKER, Wallace Ford, John Emery, Michael Pate, James Bell, Ruth Donnelly, Frank Ferguson, Don Megowan, Jeanette Nolan, Harry Tyler, Harry Antrim, Kermit Maynard, Jack Perrin. 78m.

A marshal cleans up Medicine Bend while rekindling an old romance with a saloon songbird; the thin plot is stretched to fill the running time with the use of several honkytonk numbers. Randolph Scott co-produced this one; the budget is bigger than director Lewis usually worked with; it's well done but simpleminded and routine.

LAWMAN (1971, UA). D: Michael Winner. W: Gerald Wilson. Cast: BURT LANCAS-

TER, ROBERT RYAN, LEE J. COBB, ROBERT DUVALL, Sheree NORTH, Joseph Wiseman, J. D. Cannon, Albert Salmi. 98m.

Unbending marshal (Lancaster) goes up against a mean cattle baron (Cobb), a sadistic cowhand (Salmi), a tough gunslinger (Duvall), a pragmatic but cowardly sheriff (Ryan) and a bittersweet old flame (North). Ostensibly an original, the story is an unacknowledged remake of the 1955 Robert Mitchum *Man with the Gun* with only a few changes. Ryan and North are very good (Ryan never turned in a bad performance in his life) but the characterizations are cardboard, the script turgid, and the film neither plausible nor palatable.

When this one was about to be released, according to director Winner, Burt Lancaster's attorney threatened to enjoin the release unless the credits were changed: Lancaster had it in his contract that only four artists' names could appear above the title, and that Lancaster's name had to come first—but the film was billed as "A Michael Winner Film: Burt Lancaster, Robert Ryan, Lee J. Cobb and Robert Duvall in *Lawman*." A serious wrangle ensued and was only abated when Winner called Lancaster and said, "There *are* only four artists' names above the title, and yours does come first. I'm not an artist—and I've got the reviews to prove it." Lancaster reportedly laughed and relented, and the picture was released with the original credits.

They needn't have bothered. Winner was right. The film is terrible.

LAW OF THE LAWLESS (1964, PARA). D: William F. Claxton. W: Steve Fisher. Cast: DALE ROBERTSON, YVONNE De CARLO, William BENDIX, Bruce Cabot, John Agar, Richard Arlen, Kent Taylor, Lon Chaney, Jr., Barton MacLane. 88m.

A former gunfighter becomes a judge, but now has to buckle on his guns again to save the town from the bad guys during a Kansas murder trial. Familiar veterans in an even more familiar yarn; typical A.C. Lyles production (in fact it was his first). Not bad of its kind.

THE LAW vs. BILLY THE KID (1954, COL). D: William Castle. W: John T. Williams. Cast: SCOTT BRADY, Betta ST. JOHN, James Griffith, Paul Cavanagh, Alan Hale, Jr. 73m.

Yet another romanticized whitewash of Billy the Kid (Brady, much too mature for it) and his love-hate relationship with Sheriff Pat Garrett (Griffith). Humdrum.

THE LAW WEST OF TOMBSTONE (1938, RKO). D: Glenn Tryon. W: John Twist &

Clarence U. Young. Cast: HARRY CAREY, TIM HOLT, Evelyn BRENT, Allan Lane, Eddy Waller, Ward Bond, Paul Guilfoyle, Kermit Maynard, George Irving, Esther Muir, Jean Rouverol, Clarence Kolb. 73m.

A tall-tale-spinning former outlaw brings law 'n' order to a frontier town in this comedy actioner. Like many of Carey's movies of the 1930s this one hovered somewhere in the limbo between "A" and "B" filmdom.

THE LEFT-HANDED GUN (1958, WB). D: Arthur Penn. W: Leslie Stevens from Gore Vidal's teleplay. Cast: PAUL NEWMAN, John DEHNER, Lita MILAN, James BEST, Hurd Hatfield, James Congdon, John Dierkes, Colin Keith-Johnston. 100m.

Billy the Kid (Newman), a handsome carefree youth, becomes an outlaw when he sets out to avenge the murder of a kind gentle cattleman who befriended him. That much is part of the standard romantic mythology. But the Vidal story also tries to explain Billy's murderous motivations in superficial Hollywood-Freudian terms, with homosexual overtones, and we are treated to the spectacle of a nose-picking mumbling Method performance from Newman that is among his worst. Producer Fred Coe and the director had been in television—this was their first movie—and this one had worked a bit better as a live TV play; there, its woeful artificialities hadn't seemed quite so out of place. On the big screen the story demonstrates immediately that its makers knew nothing about the history and/or legends of the West. (For one thing Billy wasn't left-handed.) Only Dehner, as Pat Garrett, is more or less believable in this pastiche of arty gimmickry, slow self-conscious scripting and murky mood photography (by J. Peverell Marley, in black-and-white).

THE LEGEND OF NIGGER CHARLEY (1972, PARA). D: Martin Goldman. W: Goldman & Larry G. Spangler. Cast: FRED WILLIAMSON, D'Urville MARTIN, Gertrude Jeanette, Don Pedro Colley, Alan Gifford. 97m.

A Virginia plantation slave (Williamson) runs away to freedom and becomes a gunslinger. Naturally a slew of bigoted whites feel bound to shoot him down. After he and his friends have taken care of those, he turns to being a good Samaritan in protecting a beleaguered farmer and his half-breed Indian wife. The dialogue in this blaxploitation oater is too idiotic to be described; but the performances are zesty.

THE LEGEND OF THE LONE RANGER (1981, UNIV). D: William A. Fraker. W: Ivan Goff, Ben Roberts, Michael Kane &

William Roberts. Cast: KLINTON SPILS-BURY, Michael HORSE, Jason RO-BARDS, JR., Christopher Lloyd, Matt Clark, Richard Farnsworth, Juanin Clay, John Bennett Perry, Lincoln Tate, Ted Flicker, Patrick Montoya. 98m.

Nicely photographed (Laszlo Kovacs) in Monument Valley, this rehash of the old radio show is too violent and gory for tykes and too stupid for grown-ups. It wastes its first half in imitating *Superman: The Movie* by rehashing the hero's childhood; then it rushes into a witless melodrama involving President Grant (Robards), Wild Bill Hickok (Farnsworth), General Custer (Tate) and Buffalo Bill Cody (Flicker). It's utterly asinine. Fledgling actor Spilsbury registers poorly, and evidently his voice was so bad on the soundtrack that the producers decided to re-dub it. The voice you hear is not Spilsbury's; it's James Keach's, and the lips are not too well synched.

THE LEGEND OF TOM DOOLEY (1959, COL). D: Ted Post. W: Stanley Shpetner. Cast: MICHAEL LANDON, Jo MOR-ROW, Richard Rust, Jack Hogan, Ken Lynch, Dee Pollock, Ralph Moody. 79m.

After the Civil War the Yankee victors put a price on the heads of three young ex-Confederate raiders. Eventually there is a hanging; it's based on the then-popular title song, sung on the soundtrack by the Kingston Trio. The film tries for tragedy, achieves only bathos; its flavor is that of a segment of a cheaply produced TV series. In black-and-white.

LEMONADE JOE (1964, AA). DW: Jiri Brdecka. Cast: Carl Flala, Olga Schoberova, Veta Fialova, Miles Kopeck, Rudy Dale. 84m.

Czech movie is a surprisingly funny spoof of the old "B" Western formula: stalwart white-hatted hero, nasty varmints, a heroine pure. A novelty, hilarious in places.

LET FREEDOM RING (1939, MGM). D: Jack Conway. W: Ben Hecht. Cast: NEL-SON EDDY, VIRGINIA BRUCE, LIONEL BARRYMORE, EDWARD ARNOLD, Victor McLAGLEN, George "Gabby" Hayes, Charles Butterworth, Guy Kibbee, H.B. Warner, Raymond Walburn, Trevor Bardette, C. E. Anderson. 100m.

Eddy moralizes the land-grabbers into treating the homesteaders fairly in this preachy, hokey musical; the climax is a warbled duet—Eddy and Bruce singing "My Country 'Tis of Thee." Ben Hecht, you have no shame.

THE LIFE AND TIMES OF GRIZZLY ADAMS (1974, IND). D: Richard Friedenberg. W: Larry Dobkin. Cast: DON HAG-GERTY, Don Shanks, Lisa Jones, Marjorie Harper. 93m.

A frontiersman hides out in the wilderness from a murder charge and becomes the friend of a Rocky Mountain bear. Threadbare budget and stupid script, but the scenery is nice, the bear is a pretty good actor, and the kids seem to like it. This was the basis for a popular TV series.

THE LIFE AND TIMES OF JUDGE ROY BEAN (1972, NGP). D: John Huston. W: John Milius from a book by C.L. Sonnichsen. Cast: PAUL NEWMAN, ANTHONY PERKINS, AVA GARDNER, STACY KEACH, John HUSTON, Jacqueline BIS-SET, Victoria PRINCIPAL, Ned BEATTY, Roddy McDOWALL, Tab Hunter, Anthony Zerbe, Bill McKinney, Jim Burk. 121m.

There are good comic performances in this burlesque biography of Texas's murderous judge, the self-styled "law west of the Pecos" (portrayed powerfully in *The Westerner* by Walter Brennan). Ava Gardner is fun as Lily Langtry; Stacy Keach is amusing as a black-hearted albino gunslinger; director Huston puts in a cameo appearance as a crazed mountain man with a pet bear. In the title role Paul Newman is engaging and sometimes hilariously wry. But uproarious moments do not a movie make, and this one mostly is superficial and in very bad taste; the comedy is mod black humor, with a vicious murderer for a hero and a plot that relies on brutal pratfall violence for many of its laughs. If you think being hanged or shot is lots of fun, then this is the picture for you. In the middle of the movie everything grinds to a halt so that we can listen to a saccharine ballad sung offscreen by Andy Williams; it's a cheap plagiarism from the "Raindrops" sequence in *Butch Cassidy and the Sundance Kid*, this one composed by Maurice Jarre. Fitfully witty film in the end is so sour it turns poisonous.

LIFE IN THE RAW (1933, PARA). D: Louis King. W: Stuart Anthony. Cast: GEORGE O'BRIEN, CLAIRE TREVOR, Francis Ford, Greta Nissen.

A girl busts up with her beau because she thinks he committed a dastardly crime which in fact was committed by his mean brother, and then—never mind. Standard oater was notable only because it marked Claire Trevor's first appearance on the screen.

THE LIGHT IN THE FOREST (1958, BV). D: Herschel Daugherty. W: Lawrence E.

JESSE JAMES (1939):
Nancy Kelly, Tyrone Power,
Henry Hull. Exciting white-
wash is densely plotted, ex-
pertly directed. Twentieth
Century-Fox

INVITATION TO A GUN-
FIGHTER (1964): George
Segal, Pat Hingle, Yul Bryn-
ner. Just about any Western
must have its gunfight.
United Artists

JOHNNY GUITAR (1954): Ward Bond, Mercedes McCambridge; over Bond's right shoulder can be seen Ian MacDonald. There are a few female bad guys in the Western lexicon; McCambridge's is the most striking of all. Republic Pictures

JUBILEE TRAIL (1953): Jim Davis, Vera Hruba Ralston, Joan Leslie. A sweeping historical saga with "B" proclivities. Republic Pictures

THE KANSAN (1943): Victor Jory, Jane Wyatt, Richard Dix, Albert Dekker. A good cast and nicely handled ramifications. United Artists

KANSAS RAIDERS (1950): Dewey Martin, Hugh O'Brian, Audie Murphy, Richard Long, James Best. Jesse and the boys again, portrayed by the Universal stock-company starlets. Universal Pictures

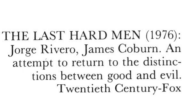

THE LAST HARD MEN (1976): Jorge Rivero, James Coburn. An attempt to return to the distinctions between good and evil. Twentieth Century-Fox

LAST OF THE FAST GUNS (1958): Jock Mahoney, Gilbert Roland. Roland was often better than his material. Universal Pictures

LAW AND ORDER (1932): Raymond Hatton, Walter Huston, Harry Carey. Huston is Wyatt Earp, Carey is the Doc Holliday character: tense and atmospheric. Universal Pictures

LITTLE BIG HORN
(1951): Sheb Wooley, Lloyd
Bridges, John Ireland. The
dusty feel of the real West.
Lippert (Robert L. Lippert
Productions)

LITTLE BIG MAN (1970):
Dustin Hoffman, in a posed
publicity-still as a comical
gunfighter. Arty, pretentious
and self-conscious. National
General Pictures

**LONELY ARE THE
BRAVE** (1962): Kirk
Douglas. The horse is
named Whiskey. It's a classic
about a maverick cowboy
in the changing West.
Universal Pictures

Watkin from a Conrad Richter novel. Cast: JAMES MacARTHUR, CAROL LYNLEY, FESS PARKER, Wendell COREY, Joanne DRU, Jessica TANDY, John McINTIRE, Joseph Calleia, Rafael Campos, Frank Ferguson, Marian Seldes. 92m.

White boy, raised by Indians, must return and live among bigoted white folks. A disappointingly skin-deep and too-pat screenplay was wrung from Richter's thoughtful novel; the Disney movie is slow and preachy. But the strong cast and good photography (Ellsworth Fredericks) help it along. This one was Lynley's screen debut and Fess Parker's last film for Disney.

LIGHT OF THE WESTERN STARS (1930, PARA). D: Otto Brower & Edwin H. Knopf. W: Grover Jones & Mary McHutt from Zane Grey's novel. Cast: RICHARD ARLEN, MARY BRIAN, Fred Kohler, Regis Toomey, Harry Green, George Chandler, Sid Saylor.

Cowhand on a spree marries the first girl he sees, then has to earn her love while tracking his best friend's killer. Comedy-meller was fairly popular in its day.

LIGHT OF THE WESTERN STARS (1940, PARA). D: Lesley Selander. W: Norman Houston from Zane Grey's novel. Cast: RUSSELL HAYDEN, Jo Ann SAYERS, Victor JORY, Eddie DEAN, Tom Tyler, Alan Ladd, Noah Beery, Jr., J. Farrell MacDonald, Morris Ankrum. 64m.

Dude girl comes west to reform her outlaw brother (Jory) and is swept off her feet by a cowhand (Hayden, who usually played "Lucky," Hopalong Cassidy's sidekick). Dated ho-hum meller features an oddball cast. Dean and Tyler were both "B" Western stars; Ladd was working his way up.

THE LION AND THE HORSE (1952, WB). D: Louis King. W: Crane Wilbur. Cast: STEVE COCHRAN, Sherry JACKSON, Ray Teal, Bob Steele, Harry Antrim, George O'Hanlon. 83m.

A modern-day cowhand captures a prize stallion, then loses it to a rodeo promoter and overcomes all kinds of difficulties, including a mountain lion, in getting the horse back. Good Zion National Park locations but silly script and a routine Max Steiner score; it's OK for kids.

LITTLE BIG HORN (1951, LIP). D: Charles Marquis Warren. W: Warren & Harold Shumate. Cast: JOHN IRELAND, LLOYD BRIDGES, MARIE WINDSOR, Reed HADLEY, Jim Davis, Noah Beery, Jr., Hugh O'Brian, Sheb Wooley, Wally Cassel, King Donovan, Rodd Redwing. 86m.

The opening line, honest to Murgatroyd, is, "John, we can't go on seeing each other like this." (Windsor to Ireland.) From there it has nowhere to go but up, and fortunately it does; after the first cornball half hour this settles down into a surprisingly solid little feature about a detachment of cavalrymen discovering that the Sioux and Cheyenne are massing to ambush Custer, and riding desperately across Dakota in an attempt to warn the Seventh Cavalry. Obviously they don't make it in time but that's not the point at issue in the plot; the question is whether any of them will make it at all—they're tracked, sniped at and picked off by Indians all the way. Meanwhile the captain in charge (Bridges) hates his second-in-command (Ireland) because he caught him making a pass at his wife; it's all prickly and very gripping. Here and there it has the look of a low-budget imitation of a John Ford picture, with sky-lined silhouettes of long lines of cavalry (photographed, in black-and-white, by Ernest W. Miller) but one can't object to that. The dusty feel of the real West permeates this one, as it does many of the Lippert Westerns of the early 1950s; it's a tough movie, predictably plotted but formidable of its kind.

LITTLE BIG MAN (1970, NGP). D: Arthur Penn. W: Calder Willingham from Thomas Berger's novel. Cast: DUSTIN HOFFMAN, FAYE DUNAWAY, Martin BALSAM, Jeff COREY, Richard MULLIGAN, Chief Dan GEORGE, Amy Eccles, Cal Bellini, Robert Little Star. 150m.

The frame of this picaresque tale has Hoffman made up to look 115 years old as crabby Jack Crabbe, last of the frontiersmen, telling a modern interviewer the highly colored story of his life and times. A largely farcical satire veering from plausible comedy to simple-minded slapstick idiocy, *Little Big Man* covers numerous Wild West topics from Wild Bill Hickok (Corey) to snake-oil salesmen (Balsam) to Custer (Mulligan) and his Last Stand. The editing is confusingly abrupt (by Dede Allen), the wide-screen photography very good (Harry Stradling, Jr.), the score (John Hammond) anachronistic, consisting as it does of blues tunes played on harmonica and guitar. Ranging from murder to torture, from homosexuality to adultery to incest, it's a mis-aimed comedy that indiscriminately parodies aspects of the real West (Custer et al.) along with purely Hollywood fictions (gunfighter costumes, quick-draw showdowns). Some of the jokes are very 1970-ish, the haircuts very mod, the cast dotted with Westerners and Indians who speak with Hell's Kitchen accents. The characters are cleverly conceived but none of it makes us feel much of anything; it's impossible to care about them because they are caricatures, and because the overacting by most of the performers is more embarrassing than amusing. The best work is provided by Balsam, Corey, and Chief Dan George as an old Cheyenne chief who's seen it all and is surprised by nothing. Arty and pretentious and self-conscious, *Little Big Man* has a large reputation but I find it sloppy, limp and inconclusive, intermittently amusing but mostly offensive; and the cheap, heavy, dishonest references to the war in Vietnam are out of place and vulgar.

THE LITTLEST OUTLAW (1955, BV). D: Roberto Gavaldon. W: Bill Walsh & Larry Lansburgh. Cast: Andres VELASQUEZ, Pedro ARMENDARIZ, Joseph CALLEIA, Rodolfo Acosta, Pepe Ortiz. 75m.

Same plot as *The Electric Horseman* but this time the hero is a little boy (Velasquez) who rescues a horse from slaughter and flees with it through old Mexico, meeting a variety of adventures with bandits, gypsies, bullfighters, a priest and some rugged railroaders. Picaresque and picturesque (good cinematography by Alex Phillips and J. Carlos Carbajal), this Disney effort was filmed twice: once in Spanish, once in English—so that it wouldn't have to be dubbed. It's well made, but all in all a routine juvenile.

LIZA'S PIONEER DIARY (1976, IND). DW: Nell Cox. Cast: Ayn RUYMAN, Katherine Helman, Andra Akers. 87m.

Seen in America only on public television, this low-budget indie concerns a wagon train trek to Oregon in 1848 and the gruelling hazards of everyday trail life faced by a young bride. Pooh-poohed by some critics as a "feminist oater" it is in fact a fresh and gratifyingly realistic pioneer movie, eschewing cliches, bringing the frontier alive with almost painful naturalism. It's rich and moving, warm with passion, beautifully made, superbly acted.

THE LLANO KID (1939, PARA). D: Edward Venturini. W: Wanda Tuchock from a story by O. Henry. Cast: TITO GUIZAR, Jane CLAYTON, Alan MOWBRAY, Gale Sondergaard, Minor Watson, Emma Dunn.

Very loosely based on O.Henry's Cisco Kid, this casts nightclub singer Guizar as a dashing stage robber who, smitten by the beauty of a lady passenger, impulsively removes his mask to kiss her; after that she can identify him and it's a will-she-or-won't-she plot, romantic hokum, dated even in its own time.

THE LONE GUN (1954, UA). D: Ray Nazarro. W: Don Martin & Richard Schayer from an L. L. Foreman story. Cast: GEORGE MONTGOMERY, DOROTHY MALONE, Neville BRAND, Skip Homeier, Frank Faylen. 78m.

Heroic marshal, winsome ranch gal, bad guys trying to tree the town—all the familiar old ingredients are stirred together in a slow-simmering pot. It's talky, and a dud.

LONE HAND (1953, UNIV). D: George Sherman. W: Joseph Hoffman & Irving Ravetch. Cast: JOEL McCREA, BARBARA HALE, Alex NICOL, James Arness, Charles Drake, Tommy Rettig, Roy Roberts. 80m.

Widower father (McCrea) and his son (Rettig) settle on a mountain farm but have to fight it out with bad guys (Nicol et al.). Slightly reminiscent of *Shane* in some ways, the movie has charm but little punch or vigor. Your obedient reviewer, thirteen years old at the time, was an extra in the background in a couple of scenes of this one but when I've seen it on TV those scenes have been edited out. In any case despite its good Colorado location scenery it's pretty slow and predictable.

LONELY ARE THE BRAVE (1962, UNIV). D: David Miller. W: Dalton Trumbo from Edward Abbey's novel *The Brave Cowboy*. Cast: KIRK DOUGLAS, WALTER MATTHAU, Gena ROWLANDS, Carroll O'CONNOR, Michael King, Bill Bixby, George Kennedy, William Schallert, Karl Swensen. 107m.

A maverick cowboy (Douglas, in one of his best roles) who's been smothered by the advance of technological civilization busts out on his horse in search of freedom. Walter Matthau, as the funny gum-chewing sheriff (with Kennedy as his hapless deputy) who pursues the cowboy, all but steals the show. The movie touches a sensitive nerve in us all. It's marred by imagery that's too blatant and simpleminded—a Dalton Trumbo fault—but in spite of that it's a milestone, a small classic, and incidentally a hugely entertaining motion picture. It achieves what *The Electric Horseman* aspires to.

THE LONELY MAN (1957, PARA). D: Henry Levin. W: Harry Essex & Robert Smith. Cast: JACK PALANCE, ANTHONY PERKINS, Elaine AIKEN, Neville BRAND, Robert Middleton, Jack Elam, Elisha Cook, Jr., Lee Van Cleef, Denver Pyle, John Doucette, Claude Akins, Paul Newlan, James Bell, Harry Shannon. 87m.

This one is a psychological Western about the conflict between father (Palance) and son

(Perkins), stemming from the boy's conviction that his no-good pa deserted his ma. A subplot has Palance's former partner (Brand) and his gunmen (Van Cleef, Cook) trying to murder Palance in revenge for an old injury; unfortunately the suspense leading up to the big shoot-out is far superior to the gun battle itself, which includes some last-minute hokum about Palance's failing eyesight—a gimmick probably tacked on as an afterthought to heighten suspense and motivate Perkins's last-reel change of heart. In yet another subplot Aiken (her film debut) attempts to corral wild horses. It's mostly on a near-"B" level but Palance is good. Fine widescreen black-and-white photography (Lionel Linden).

THE LONE RANGER (1956, WB). D: Stuart Heisler. W: Herb Meadow from Fran Striker's radio series. Cast: CLAYTON MOORE, JAY SILVERHEELS, Lyle BETTGER, Bonita GRANVILLE, Beverly Washburn, Robert J. Wilke, John Pickard, Perry Lopez. 86m.

No surprises; creaky old plot; strictly for kiddies, but well made in color for theatrical release and not just a compilation of TV footage.

THE LONE RANGER (1981)—*See* THE LEGEND OF THE LONE RANGER.

THE LONE RANGER AND THE LOST CITY OF GOLD (1958, UA). D: Lesley Selander. W: Robert Schaefer & Eric Freiwald from Fran Striker's radio series. Cast: CLAYTON MOORE, JAY SILVERHEELS, Douglas KENNEDY, William Henry, Charles Watts. 80m.

Masked bad guys and a hidden city of treasure: juvenile stuff but fun.

LONESOME COWBOYS (1968, IND). DW: Andy Warhol. Cast: VIVA (a/k/a Susan Hoffmann), Tom Hompertz, Joe Dallesandro, Eric Emerson.

Vignetted comic depiction of sex on an Arizona dude ranch doesn't make sense, or try to. Pop painter Warhol (remember the giant Campbell's soup cans?) presided over New York's chic pop culture of the mid-1960s—slinky boys, drug freaks, bored sadomasochists who brought new meanings to decadence. Frigid, narcissistic, with a precocious theatricality, the loveless superficial "art" of the Warhol movement created a kind of plastic glamour and popularized "camp." It was Warhol who coined the term *superstar*. This film may be nearly the only Warhol movie in which anything happens at all. He made a day-long film of the Empire State Building; now and then a cloud goes over or a bird flies by. Another is an eight-hour movie of a man sleeping. By comparison with those, *Lonesome Cowboys* is a hotbed of seething excitement.

THE LONESOME TRAIL (1955, LIP). D: Richard Bartlett. W: Bartlett & Ian MacDonald from a Gordon D. Shireffs novel. Cast: JOHN AGAR, Adele JERGENS, Wayne MORRIS, Edgar Buchanan. 72m.

Small rancher has to fight off nasty land grabbers. The gimmick here is that the hero uses a bow and arrow instead of a gun. Tedious drear.

LONE STAR (1952, MGM). D: Vincent Sherman. W: Borden Chase & Howard Estabrook. Cast: CLARK GABLE, AVA GARDNER, Lionel BARRYMORE, Broderick CRAWFORD, Beulah Bondi, Ed Begley, Harry Woods, Nacho Galindo, William Farnum, Chief Nipo Strongheart, Russell Simpson, Moroni Olsen, James Burke, William Conrad, Emmett Lynn. 94m.

Old-time character actor Moroni Olsen plays Sam Houston, and Barrymore is good and crusty as Andrew Jackson, in this old-fashioned formula epic about the struggle to bring Texas into the Union. It's tailored to Gable and Gardner, and comes out more romance than history; Crawford supplies the sneering villainy. Lavish and sprawling but dated.

LONE STAR RANGER (1930, FOX). D: A. F. Erickson. W: John H. Booth & Seton I. Miller. Cast: GEORGE O'BRIEN, Sue CAROL, Walter McGrail, Roy Stewart, Warren Hymer, Richard Alexander, Russell Simpson.

Hero, falsely accused of murder, has to produce the real culprit, who turns out to be the cattle-rustling father of his girl friend. This was billed as "The First Zane Grey All-Talking Picture" but actually the Grey novel was based on the movie, not the other way around.

THE LONE TEXAN (1959, FOX). D: Paul Landres. W: James Landis & Jack Thomas from a novel by Landis. Cast: WILLARD PARKER, AUDREY DALTON, Grant Williams, Douglas Kennedy, June Blair, Tom London. 70m.

Yet another mildewed good-brother-versus-bad-brother oater. It was Tom London's (1883–1963) last movie, with more than 2,000 film appearances behind him starting with *The Great Train Robbery* in 1903; he appeared in more movies than has any other actor to date.

THE LONGHORN (1951, MONO). D: Lewis D. Collins. W: Daniel Ullman.

Cast: WILLIAM ELLIOTT, PHYLLIS COATES, Myron HEALEY, John Hart, William Fawcett, Carol Henry, Marshall Reed, Lee Roberts.

Texas rancher (Elliott) rides to Oregon to buy a herd of Herefords; he's determined to prove they can survive in Texas longhorn country. But now he's got to drive the herd all the way back to Texas; and there are rustlers out thar, not to mention a scheming devious partner (Healey) . . . Old-style meller is one of the better Elliott programmers, with good production values. They don't assemble herds that big for "A" movies nowadays.

THE LONG RIDE HOME (1963, COL). Also titled: A TIME FOR KILLING. **D: Phil Karlson. W: Halsted Welles from a novel by Nelson & Shirley Wolford. Cast: GLENN FORD, GEORGE HAMILTON, INGER STEVENS, Kenneth TOBEY, Timothy CAREY, Emile Meyer, Max Baer, Paul Petersen, Richard X. Slattery, Marshall Reed, Todd Armstrong. 88m.**

Confederate prisoners escape out West; Union officer Ford goes after them. What reduces this from the level of ordinary routine oater to the level of an unwieldy blunder is the inept acting of Hamilton in the key role of the supposedly tough Reb leader. Hamilton has turned in good performances (*Evel Knievel, Home from the Hill, Love at First Bite*) but in this dog he's just dreadful. Other than that the film is unintelligent and excessively violent—exceptionally poor for a Glenn Ford vehicle.

THE LONG RIDERS (1980, UA). **D: Walter Hill. W: James Keach, William Brydan, Stacy Keach & Steven Smith. Cast: DAVID CARRADINE, JAMES KEACH, Keith CARRADINE, Robert CARRADINE, Stacy KEACH, Dennis QUAID, Randy QUAID, Christopher GUEST, Nicholas GUEST, Pamela REED, James WHITMORE, JR., Harry Carey, Jr., Kevin Brophy. 100m.**

Jesse James (James Keach), Cole Younger (David Carradine) and their various brothers and cronies rob banks and trains and come to their inevitable end, as before. The gimmick here is that the historical outlaw brothers are played by actor brothers: The Keaches as Jesse and Frank James; the Carradines as the Youngers; the Quaids as the Miller brothers; the Guests as Bob and Charlie Ford. The facts, as known, are pretty much adhered to, but in skeletal fashion; the movie is a disjointed series of vignettes and no attempt is made to indicate the calendar. (The actual events covered about a dozen years; the film

does not make it clear that all this isn't taking place in a few weeks.) David Carradine is remarkably good, and James Keach makes Jesse James a forceful driven character (you believe he is tough enough to be the leader of these hard men), but the rest of the characters are ciphers with two exceptions, and here again these are badly written roles that are brought to life against the odds by good actors: Whitmore gets great mileage out of his role as a Pinkerton company-man relentlessly hounding the outlaws, and Reed is just marvelous as the hooker Belle Starr. It's humorous and grim by turns, a very stylish film beautifully produced with splendid photography (Ric Waite) and a good unobtrusive score (Ry Cooder). The trouble is, it's very thin; we never get to know who these people are or why they are doing these things, and we don't care about any of them. As an exercise in cinematic technique it is terrific; as a story, a drama or a movie it leaves quite a bit to be desired.

THE LONG ROPE (1961, FOX). **D: William Witney. W: Robert Hamner. Cast: HUGH MARLOWE, BARBARA EDEN, Chris Robinson, Alan Hale, Jr., Robert J. Wilke. 62m.**

Circuit-riding judge (Marlowe) finds a whole town set against him when he has to try a popular citizen for murder. Low-budget black-and-white flick has a fine performance by Marlowe but it's otherwise shabby.

LOVE ME TENDER (1956, FOX). **D: Robert D. Webb. W. Robert H. Buckner & Maurice Geraghty. Cast: RICHARD EGAN, DEBRA PAGET, ELVIS PRESLEY, Mildred DUNNOCK, William CAMPBELL, Neville BRAND, Robert Middleton, Bruce Bennett, James Drury, Russ Conway, Ken Clark, Barry Coe, L. Q. Jones. 89m.**

Romantic conflicts key this dull horse opera with Elvis, in his film debut, as the youngest of several Texas brothers (Egan is the eldest); he's the one who had to stay home during the Civil War; he gets to sing a couple of tunes, including the popular title song. A good deal of money was spent on this CinemaScope feature and it was one of the top-grossing movies of 1956 but it's turgid. Both the title and the casting of Presley were last-minute decisions; originally the role was slated for Cameron Mitchell; it had to be beefed up for Presley, and the imbalance hurts the story.

LOVIN' MOLLY (1973, COL). **D: Sidney Lumet. W: Stephen J.Friedman from Larry McMurtry's novel *Leaving Cheyenne*. Cast:**

ANTHONY PERKINS, BLYTHE DAN-
NER, BEAU BRIDGES, Edward Binns,
Susan Sarandon, Conrad Fowkes. 98m.

For forty years a woman and her two ri-
valrous high-spirited lovers fight, love and
laugh. It's a wistful comedy, or should have
been. McMurtry (*Hud, The Last Picture Show*)
is a fine Texas novelist; Lumet (*Serpico, Network*) is an excellent director; the budget was
big, the cast top drawer (Danner is marvelous), the production lavish. Somehow it
turned out a mess.

McMurtry indicted Lumet in print for
having ruined the film because of a lack of
feeling for the West. Clearly he is right; but
the screenplay is terrible as well. The movie
was first titled *Molly, Gid and Johnny*, then retitled *The Wild and the Sweet*; no title change
could save it, however.

THE LUCK OF ROARING CAMP (1937, MONO). D: Irving Willat. W: Harvey Gates from Bret Harte's story. Cast: Joan WOOD-BURY, Owen Davis, Jr., Robert Kortman, Charles King, Byron Foulger.

Penny-ante cast doesn't help this cheap
version of the treacly yarn about the infant
who brings luck to the mining camp. Corny
and slow.

LUST FOR GOLD (1949, COL). D: S.Sylvan Simon. W: Ted Sherdeman & Richard English from a book by Barry Storm. Cast: GLENN FORD, IDA LUPINO, Gig YOUNG, William PRINCE, Edgar Buchanan, Will Geer, Paul Ford, Eddy Waller, Jay Silverheels, Arthur Hunnicutt, Will Wright, Hayden Rorke, John Doucette, Percy Helton, Trevor Bardette. 90m.

Grim story, extrapolated from fact, concerns the golden treasure of the fabled Lost
Dutchman Mine in Arizona's Superstition
Mountains. Based on a book by the grandson
of Jacob Walz ("the Dutchman"), the movie
recounts the history and legends of the treasure in the form of narrated flashbacks, one of
which occupies most of the film's running
time and concerns the Dutchman (Ford) and
various miscreants who try to jump his claim
in the 1880s. After a shaky start it builds to a
harrowing climax. It's a fine, taut, suspenseful
thriller about the cancerous erosion of greed;
Lupino, in a sense, plays the Bogart part from
The Treasure of the Sierra Madre, and does it
convincingly. Archie J. Stout's black-and-
white photography, on the actual historical
locations, is outstanding. As the bleak, mad,
embattled prospector, Glenn Ford turns in
what may be the finest performance of his
long career. Outside the mainstream, the picture is a curiosity but a fascinating one.

THE LUSTY MEN (1952, RKO). D: Nicholas Ray. W: Horace McCoy, David Dortort & Claude Stamish. Cast: ROBERT MITCHUM, SUSAN HAYWARD, ARTHUR KENNEDY, Arthur HUNNICUTT, Carol Nugent, Walter Coy, Frank Faylen, Maria Hart, Lorna Thayer, Burt Mustin, Jimmy Dodd. 113m.

A beat-up rodeo veteran (Mitchum) lands
a job on a ranch where the young owner
(Kennedy) has stars in his eyes and wants to
be a rodeo champ to escape the humdrum life
of ranching. He enlists Mitchum as his man-
ager-trainer. Against the wishes of his wife
(Hayward) he sells the ranch and sets out on
the rodeo circuit. Success quickly goes to his
head; he becomes arrogant; his wife's affections drift toward the other guy; it all leads to
a downbeat ending. The plot as delineated in
the muddled script verges heavily on soap-op-
eratics; it's dated now, very 1950s Holly-
woodish, and in any case it has been emulated in 'steen imitator movies. Of the three
stars two are notably miscast: New Yorkers
Hayward and Kennedy are not believable as
Westerners.

Those are its faults, and they are grievous;
yet despite all that, the film justly has become
the classic rodeo movie, the one against which
all others must be measured. Why? There are
several reasons. First, Nicholas Ray's masterful direction captures the atmosphere: the
dusty flavor, the nomadic aimlessness of
rodeo life, the finely etched characters hover-
ing in the background. Second is Lee
Garmes's splendid black-and-white photography, which makes it all vivid and real. Third
is a warm and gritty performance by Hunnicutt as a wise, longwinded, hard-drinking old
hand. And finally there is Robert Mitchum's
awesome portrayal of the leathery bronc-
whacked veteran; you can feel every one of
his broken bones and you believe Mitchum's
man of jaded experience and compassionate
wisdom. This is one of the few Westerns I can
think of that transcends its script. It shouldn't
work, but it does.

MACHO CALLAHAN (1970, EMB). D: Bernard L. Kowalski. W: Clifford N. Gould from a Richard Carr story. Cast: DAVID JANSSEN, JEAN SEBERG, LEE J. COBB, James Booth, Pedro Armendariz, Jr., David Carradine, Bo Hopkins, Matt Clark, Richard Anderson, Diane Ladd, Anne Revere, Richard Evans. 97m.

A killer (Janssen) breaks out of a vile Confederate prison and goes after the villains who
put him there. Right away he kills a young
Reb officer (Carradine) over a bottle of
champagne; so the Reb's widow (Seberg)

vows vengeance. With revenge provoking revenge, murder goading murder, the plot winds down through ever more gruesome episodes to a nauseating ending. Few films can claim to make less sense than this one—the story defies reason everywhere and is as impenetrable as it is revolting. Acting is fair, directing is all right, production is big—Joseph E. Levine produced it, in Spain; the photography (Gerry Fisher) is fine and the score (Pat Williams) is heavy but appropriate. Still, with a hero who practices casual murder as a matter of course, this rancid misguided attempt at high tragedy achieves a nadir in Leone-style filmmaking. It's strictly for sadists or those interested in cinematic oddities. (The latter may note that Anne Revere's appearance here is her first in twenty years after she was blacklisted by the McCarthy goons.)

MACKENNA'S GOLD (1969, COL). D: J. Lee Thompson. W: Carl Foreman from Will Henry's novel. Cast: GREGORY PECK, OMAR SHARIF, CAMILLA SPARV, EDWARD G. ROBINSON, Anthony QUAYLE, Eli WALLACH, Lee J. COBB, Telly SAVALAS, Julie NEWMAR, Raymond MASSEY, Keenan WYNN, Burgess MEREDITH, Ted Cassidy, Eduardo Ciannelli, Dick Peabody, John Garfield, Jr., Trevor Bardette. Narrator: Victor JORY. 128m.

A sheriff (Peck) is entrusted by a dying Indian (Ciannelli) with a map of a legendary Valley of Gold. Disbelieving the legend, the sheriff casually destroys the map. But then he's captured by a Mexican bandit (Sharif) who forces him to remember the map and lead him to the gold. A town full of greedy citizens joins the search; both cavalry and Indians chase them for various reasons; most everybody except the three stars gets killed before the sheriff leads the bandit and the woman into the gold-painted canyon where an earthquake sorts things out in one of the worst special-effects scenes ever produced for a major movie.

It was written by fine writers, helmed by a sometimes good (*The Guns of Navarone*) action director, performed by a large cast of otherwise reputable actors (among whom, in this one, Sharif is outstanding for the deadly incompetence of his portrayal), produced by Carl Foreman and Dimitri Tiomkin, photographed by Joseph MacDonald, scored by Quincy Jones—these are all impressive talents; but it hasn't a single redeeming quality. It has got to be the most expensive star-studded two-hour "B" movie ever made: a gargantuan dud of absolutely stunning dreadfulness.

MACKINTOSH AND T.J. (1976, IND). D: Marvin Chomsky. W: Paul Savage. Cast: ROY ROGERS, JOAN HACKETT, Clay O'BRIEN, Billy Green Bush, Luke Askew, Larry Mahan, Andy Robinson, James Hampton, Dennis Fimple, Edith Atwater, Walter Barnes, Dean Smith. 96m.

Roy Rogers' first movie after 1952, this was a simple "inspirational" family movie about a Bible-reading drifter (Rogers) who takes a half-wild kid (O'Brien) under his wing and straightens him out. Set, and filmed, in modern-day Texas, with soundtrack songs by Waylon Jennings, it's a genial enough movie except for an unexpected and gratuitously violent scene. It's undistinguished and predictable fare.

MAD DOG (1976)—*See* MAD DOG MORGAN.

MAD DOG MORGAN (1976, IND). DW: Philippe Mora, from a book by Margaret Carnegie. Cast: DENNIS HOPPER, David GULPILIL, Jack THOMPSON, Frank Thring, Michael Pate. 102m.

Gimmicky Australian movie concerns a bush ranger (outlaw) of the 1850s and his relentless hounding by a detective (Thring) who pursues him and finally, with a posse, runs him down. Hopper plays the highwayman as a twitchy paranoid who looks stoned. There's impressive wide-screen photography (Mike Molloy) on Australian locations. It's based on fact but nevertheless incoherent and empty.

THE MAGNIFICENT SEVEN (1960, UA). D: John Sturges. W: William S. Roberts, based on Akira Kurosawa's 1956 film *The Seven Samurai*. Cast: YUL BRYNNER, STEVE McQUEEN, Eli WALLACH, James COBURN, Charles BRONSON, Robert VAUGHN, Horst BUCHHOLZ, Brad DEXTER, Vladimir Sokoloff, Rosenda Monteros, Whit Bissell, Robert J. Wilke, Jorge Martinez de Hoyos, Val Avery. 126m.

A Mexican village is terrorized by a vicious bandit (Wallach) and his cutthroat gunmen; every season they steal the town's food. The villagers scrape together what paltry goods they have and go north to hire gunfighters to defend them. The only fighting men they can find who'll take the job are a few who can't get gun work elsewhere in a time when the West is going tame. The six gunfighters (Brynner, McQueen, Coburn, Bronson, Vaughn, Dexter) are joined by an eager Mexican youth (Buchholz); they rally the town, prepare its defenses and fight off the bandits. There's a lot of shooting before it's over. The film is faultlessly directed, tunefully scored (Elmer Bernstein; it became a standard), heroically photographed (Charles Lang, Jr.); yet that could be said of many Westerns. *The Magnificent Seven*, to many buffs, has become a minor classic—and perhaps it would have become a major one if it weren't for the obvious obligation to compare it with the Kurosawa film on which it is based; that one was rich with artistry, while the American version is simply a damned engaging diversion, keyed by a taut literate script that invests each character with a strongly individual and empathetic personality. It made stars of theretofore small-time actors Vaughn, Bronson and Coburn, and cemented McQueen as a major star after humdrum parts in a TV series and several unmemorable movies. The action is filmed with edge-of-the-seat excitement and we really *care* about the characters. It's a compelling movie, masterful entertainment. (It spawned three mediocre sequels: *Return of the Seven*, *Guns of the Magnificent Seven* and *The Magnificent Seven Ride*.)

THE MAGNIFICENT SEVEN RIDE (1972, UA). D: George McGowan. W: Arthur Rowe. Cast: LEE VAN CLEEF, STEFANIE POWERS, Michael CALLAN, Mariette HARTLEY, Luke Askew, Allyn Ann McLerie, Pedro Armendariz, Jr., Ed Lauter. 100m.
    A marshal (Van Cleef), a dude writer (Callan) and five convicts protect a passel of widows from Mexican bandits. By this time Hollywood had run out of fresh ideas for sequels to *The Magnificent Seven*; the only thing left here from the (American) original is the Elmer Bernstein score. It's a poor movie with a lot of commotion, signifying nothing.

MAIL ORDER BRIDE (1963, MGM). Also titled: WEST OF MONTANA. DW: Burt Kennedy from a story by Van Cort. Cast: BUDDY EBSEN, KEIR DULLEA, LOIS NETTLETON, Warren OATES, Barbara LUNA, Marie Windsor, Paul Fix, Denver Pyle, Bill Smith. 81m.
    In Montana in the 1890s a young hellion (Dullea) inherits a ranch and a tough old guardian (Ebsen) who picks out a bride (Nettleton) for him in the hope she'll persuade the kid to mend his ways. Pretty good photography (Paul C.Vogel) and score (George Bassman). Comedy is harmless enough.

MAJOR DUNDEE (1965, COL). D: Sam Peckinpah. W: Peckinpah, Harry Fink, Jr., & Oscar Saul. Cast: CHARLTON HESTON, RICHARD HARRIS, Senta BERGER, James COBURN, Jim HUT-TON, Ben Johnson, Warren Oates, L.Q. Jones, Michael Anderson, Jr., R.G. Armstrong, Karl Swenson, Brock Peters, Slim Pickens, Dub Taylor, Michael Pate, Bob Steele, Mario Adorf, John Davis Chandler. 134m.
    A discredited Yankee martinet (Heston), commanding a Civil War prison in the far West and charged with the keeping of Confederate prisoners, Union deserters and civilian felons, leads an expedition out after a tribe of renegade Apaches who've kidnapped some white children and gone on the warpath. All the plot elements are recognizable from other movies (*Two Flags West*, *The Searchers*, so forth) but Peckinpah brings his special energy to this one.
    Producer Jerry Bresler indulged the director by giving him rein to spend a lot of money in Mexico making this, his third feature film. Peckinpah lavished time and gusto on it. Apparently Columbia's executives cut quite a bit of it out in order to bring it down to its present (still overlong) running time. What's left is a tough, jerky, confused melodrama, filmed in a brooding subdued widescreen manner (cinematographer Sam Leavitt) with a serviceable but unoriginal score (Daniele Amphitheatrof); it's a structure of cliches and one finds it very hard to swallow the claims of auteuriste apologists who claim that if Columbia had only left it alone, uncut, it might have been a masterpiece; it hasn't got the heart, the artistry or the originality for that; it's not possible that it ever did, not with such abundant familiar contrivances and such cardboard stereotypes in place of characterizations. Still, it's an interesting precursor to *The Wild Bunch* (some of its sequences are reprised in the later film) and it remains an adequate big-budget Western.

A MAN ALONE (1955, REP). D: Ray Milland. W: Mort Briskin & John Tucker Battle. Cast: RAY MILLAND, MARY MURPHY, Ward BOND, Raymond BURR, Alan Hale, Jr., Lee Van Cleef. 94m.
    A gunfighter (Milland) comes to the aid of an invalided sheriff (Bond), falls in love with the sheriff's daughter (Murphy) and unmasks some baddies who've been robbing stagecoaches and murdering citizens. The acting is all right, although Milland isn't believable as a grizzled tough gunslinger. Most of the movie seems to take place in the sheriff's house; it's static and uninspired. Milland's directorial debut.

MAN AND BOY (1972, IND). D: E. W. Swackhamer. W: Harry Essex & Oscar Saul. Cast: BILL COSBY, Gloria FOSTER, Douglas Turner Ward, Leif Erickson, John

Anderson, Yaphet Kotto, Henry Silva, Dub Taylor. 98m.

Father and son set out to regain their stolen horses; there's some shooting, some villainy, some picaresque episodes and a predictable outcome. The mediocre screenplay touches all the cliche bases, but the film is better than most blaxploitation Westerns, partly because Cosby is so sympathetic.

MAN BEHIND THE GUN (1952, WB). D: Felix Feist. W: Robert Buckner & John Twist. Cast: RANDOLPH SCOTT, PATRICE WYMORE, Philip CAREY, Douglas Fowley, Anthony Caruso, Alan Hale, Jr., Dick Wesson, Lina Romay, Roy Roberts, Morris Ankrum. 81m.

Another undercover-investigator yarn features Randolph Scott as a typically, and tiresomely, upstanding good guy helping California join the Union. Weak script, muddled action and confused pseudohistory; poor.

A MAN CALLED GANNON (1969, UNIV). D: James Goldstone. W: Borden Chase, D. D. Beauchamp & Gene Kearney from the novel *Man Without a Star* by Dee Linford. Cast: ANTHONY FRANCIOSA, Michael SARRAZIN, Susan OLIVER, John ANDERSON, Judi West, James Westerfield, Terry Wilson, Jason Evers, David Sheiner, Eddie Firestone, Gavin MacLeod. 105m.

This is a scene-for-scene remake of *Man Without a Star*; for a plot summary see that title. The remake doesn't measure up, although in a few cases it surpasses it—particularly in the casting of the superb John Anderson in the role previously overacted by heavy-handed Richard Boone. Here the sex is a bit more explicit, the dialogue a bit stronger and the action more brutal, but a number of character-building dialogues have been deleted and Franciosa is no Westerner; he does not bring to the story any of the power or presence of the original (Kirk Douglas). Still, it's not a bad film; it moves right along.

A MAN CALLED HORSE (1969, NGP). D: Elliot Silverstein. Cast: RICHARD HARRIS, Corinna TSOPEI, Judith ANDERSON, Manu Tupou, Jean Gascon, Dub Taylor, Iron Eyes Cody. 114m.

A wealthy English sportsman (Harris) on a well-mounted hunting expedition in the Old West sees his camp overrun by Indians and all his men killed; he survives, and his bravery is so admired by the Sioux that they take him into the tribe; before you know it he's married one of them and virtually taken over. But long before it reached that point I had lost all belief in the hysterically violent proceedings. Judith Anderson is quite effective as a noble Sioux woman, although the role is stereotyped; the rest of the actors are merely there; this film about life among the Indians has its interesting points but its depiction of Indians is almost totally inaccurate—which wouldn't matter if the movie hadn't pretended to be truthful. Basically it's a bad, bloody and overblown melodrama.

THE MAN FROM BITTER RIDGE (1955, UNIV). D: Jack Arnold. W: Teddi Sherman & Laurence Roman from a novel by William MacLeod Raine. Cast: LEX BARKER, MARA CORDAY, Stephen McNALLY, Trevor Bardette. 79m.

Raine's lifetime spanned the real Old West and the early years of the twentieth century. His books have the dusty flavor of authenticity but the plots of old pulp yarns. This cattlemen-versus-homesteaders oater is typical: an extremely dated plot, old-fashioned heroics, strictly "B" material unimproved by the casting of the incapable Lex Barker in the lead.

THE MAN FROM COLORADO (1948, COL). D: King Vidor & Henry Levin. W: Borden Chase, Robert D. Andrews & Ben Maddow. Cast: WILLIAM HOLDEN, GLENN FORD, ELLEN DREW, Edgar BUCHANAN, Jerome Courtland, James Millican, Ray Collins, Jim Bannon, Denver Pyle. 99m.

Nearly a decade earlier the team of Holden and Ford had succeeded at the box office (*Texas*); here the two were paired again in an unusual Technicolor Western about settlers rebelling against the tyrannical behavior of a sadistic hanging judge (played with great relish in a change-of-pace performance by Glenn Ford). It's offbeat, intriguing, a fine colorful action movie. Only a minor part of it was filmed by Vidor before head-of-studio Harry Cohn took him off the picture because Vidor was feuding with Glenn Ford; the actor had taken the studio boss's side in a lawsuit, contradicting Vidor's testimony.

THE MAN FROM DAKOTA (1940, MGM). D: Leslie Fenton. W: Laurence Stallings from a MacKinlay Kantor novel. Cast: WALLACE BEERY, DOLORES DEL RIO, JOHN HOWARD, Donald Meek, Addison Richards, Robert Barrat. 75m.

Union spies (Beery, Howard) cross into the Confederacy with the help of beauteous Del Rio. This one was quite a moneymaker in 1940. It's less overplayed and therefore a bit less dated than most Beery films.

THE MAN FROM DEL RIO (1956, UA). D: Harry Horner. W: Richard Carr. Cast: ANTHONY QUINN, KATY JURADO,

Peter WHITNEY, Douglas Fowley, Whit Bissell, John Larch. 81m.

A scruffy Mexican gunslinger (Quinn) is hired to clean up a town but afterwards he's ostracized by its bigoted citizens. There are formula cliches but it's a good entertainer; the pre-Zorba Quinn is nicely restrained, excellent as the bull-in-a-china-shop hero, and among the supporting cast there are standout jobs by Jurado as a woman of quiet dignity, Fowley as a cynical doctor and Bissell—later a president of the Screen Actors Guild—as the town drunk; but Peter Whitney is miscast as a tough villain with absurd plans of empire. Surprisingly the black-and-white photography by the highly reputed Stanley Cortez is quite unexceptional. But Quinn's steady, sure performance in a complex characterization makes the picture distinctly better than average.

THE MAN FROM GALVESTON (1964, WB). D: William Conrad. W: Dean Riesner & Michael Zagor. Cast: JEFFREY HUNTER, JAMES COBURN, Joanna MOORE, Preston FOSTER, Edward Andrews, Martin West. 56m.

Initially shot as the pilot for the short-lived "Temple Houston" TV series, this black-and-white cheapie was released as a theatrical feature with the characters' names changed—a shift that necessitated some embarrassing last-minute redubbing, so that the voices don't match the lip movements. Warner Brothers needn't have bothered; it's a tedious courtroom meller with a gunslinging lawyer and a soporific mystery plot—you'll guess the outcome long before the lunkheads on camera figure it out. The film of interest only because it marks the directorial debut of producer-actor Conrad (radio's Matt Dillon, TV's Cannon and Nero Wolfe).

THE MAN FROM GOD'S COUNTRY (1958, AA). D: Paul Landres. W: George Waggner. Cast: GEORGE MONTGOMERY, RANDY STUART, Gregg Barton, Susan Cummings, Frank Wilcox. 72m.

Land-grabbers are trying to sew up the area because they know a railroad is going to be built through here. A pair of ex-partners (Montgomery, Barton) find themselves on opposite sides, one of them having become a lawman, the other a hired gunman. The usual formula is played out in the usual way—nothing very interesting.

THE MAN FROM LARAMIE (1955, COL). D: Anthony Mann. W: Philip Yordan & Frank Burt from T.T. Flynn's novel. Cast: JAMES STEWART, CATHY O'DONNELL, ARTHUR KENNEDY, Alex NICOL, Donald CRISP, Aline MacMA-

HON, Wallace FORD, James Millican, Jack Elam, John War Eagle, Gregg Barton, Eddy Waller. 104m.

A horseman (Stewart) undergoes Herculean tests of courage and strength in his covert search for his brother's killers who are supplying the Indians with repeating rifles. He gets embroiled in the violent politics of a range dispute between cattle baron Crisp and cattle baroness MacMahon, with Alex Nicol doltish as Crisp's cowardly bully of a son and Arthur Kennedy slimy as Crisp's ambitious foreman. Stewart gives a tight no-nonsense performance and in some scenes he's truly stunning. MacMahon's work is very strong as well, and there's fine photography (Charles Lang, Jr.) and a pretty good score (George Duning). The film is a darling of the auteurists who've built a cult around Anthony Mann. But I think this is one of his poorer movies; I didn't like it in 1955, and when I looked at it again in 1973 and 1978 I still didn't like it. The script relies too heavily on essential cliches, but the main difficulty is that the film is unforgivably miscast in too many key roles; not for one minute do I ever believe Donald Crisp, Arthur Kennedy or Alex Nicol as Westerners: each of them is about as Western as Buddy Hackett. None of them can sit a horse; none of them moves, talks or *thinks* like a Westerner. Still, for those who may not share my prejudices in that respect, *The Man from Laramie* is fast, suspenseful and well produced.

THE MAN FROM TEXAS (1948, EL). D: Leigh Jason. W: Joseph Fields & Jerome Chodorov from a play by E.B. Ginty. Cast: JAMES CRAIG, LYNN BARI, Wallace Ford, Una Merkel, Johnny Johnston, Harry Davenport, Sara Allgood, Vic Cutler. 63m.

Texas bank robber spends a dull hour debating whether to go straight.

THE MAN FROM THE ALAMO (1953, UNIV). D: Budd Boetticher. W: Niven Busch, Steve Fisher, D.D. Beauchamp & Oliver Crawford. Cast: GLENN FORD, JULIA ADAMS, Victor JORY, Chill WILLS, Hugh O'Brian, George Eldredge, Edward Norris, Jeanne Cooper, Butch Cavell. 79m.

Ford plays a survivor of the wipeout at the Alamo. The townsfolk, convinced he must have fled in cowardly fashion, are suspicious and contemptuous, but Ford keeps his mouth shut, his upper lip stiff and his chin up, suffering all the cliches of outrageously hackneyed dialogue. Toward the end the mystery is solved according to formula. Well directed and well played but it's tedious and virtually without action.

MAN IN THE SADDLE (1951, COL). D: Andre de Toth. W: Kenneth Gamet from Ernest Haycox's novel. Cast: RANDOLPH SCOTT, JOAN LESLIE, ELLEN DREW, Alexander KNOX, George "Gabby" Hayes, Guinn "Big Boy" Williams, Clem Bevans, Frank Sully, Richard Rober. 85m.

Ranch-country yarn has Scott the object of a manhunt ordered by an insanely jealous cattle baron (Knox). Next to *Canyon Passage* this may be the best cinematic adaptation of an Ernest Haycox novel but it's a big jump down and this only gets a slightly-better-than-average rating, mainly because Knox is powerful as the villainous Will Isher, a character modeled more faithfully on the Haycox original than are the rest of the characters in the film.

MAN IN THE WILDERNESS (1971, WB). D: Richard C. Sarafian. W: Jack DeWitt. Cast: RICHARD HARRIS, JOHN HUSTON, Percy HERBERT, Henry Wilcoxon, Prunella Ransome, John Bindon, Manolo Landau, Dennis Waterman, Raul Castro, Ben Carruthers. 105m.

When a mountain man (Harris) is mauled by a bear his companions leave him for dead. The rest is survival, ingenuity, hardship and courage. Often gruesome, sometimes indigestibly pretentious, the film has compelling sequences; the wide-screen photography (Gerry Fisher and Bernie Ford) is gimmicky—too many hazy sun-struck low-angle shots; the score (Johnny Harris) is too lavish. The ending is poor; it relies on contrived coincidences and its details are unconvincing. (In the middle of the wilderness would a man just turn around and start walking toward home, two thousand miles away, without even packing food on his back?) Unnecessary flashbacks try unsuccessfully to illuminate the hero's character; the slow pace leaves room only for a very slim story, and important things seem to have been left out; as a result, the film seems too short. What's missing is characterization. Bass is only half developed as a God-hating, man-hating yet tender natural man right out of Rousseau; Captain William Henry, head of the fur-trapping expedition, is your standard Western movie fundamentalist, somewhat crazy but not very interesting, usually played by Donald Pleasence or John Anderson, here made lively by an arrestingly robust portrayal by John Huston. The movie frustrates because it has the promise of richness but, in the end, only emptiness.

MAN OF CONQUEST (1938, REP). D: George Nichols, Jr. W: Wells Root, Harold Shumate, Jan Fortune & E.E. Paramore, Jr.

Cast: RICHARD DIX, JOAN FONTAINE, Gail PATRICK, Edward Ellis, George "Gabby" Hayes, Victor Jory, Robert Barrat, Ralph Morgan, C. Henry Gordon, Robert Armstrong, Max Terhune, George Letz (George Montgomery), Lane Chandler, Hal Taliaferro, Edmund Cobb, Billy Benedict, Leon Ames, Russell Hicks, Yakima Canutt. 105m.

Sol C. Siegel produced this biopic about Sam Houston, founder of Texas; it was big in scope—Republic's first attempt at an all-out "A" epic—with good acting and big battle scenes expertly filmed by second-unit director B. Reeves "Breezy" Eason; but it was poorly written. The effect was that of an overbuilt programmer.

MAN OF THE FOREST (1933, PARA). D: Henry Hathaway. W: Jack Cunningham & Harold Shumate from Zane Grey's novel. Cast: RANDOLPH SCOTT, HARRY CAREY, NOAH BEERY, Sr., Verna Hillie, Larry "Buster" Crabbe, Barton MacLane, Guinn "Big Boy" Williams, Vince Barnett, Tom Kennedy, Blanche Frederici, Raymond Hatton, Monte Blue, Al Bridge. 59m.

A mysterious woodsman (Scott) finds out that the villains (Beery, MacLane) plan to kidnap the niece (Hillie) of a rancher (Carey) so he kidnaps her himself (to protect her) and of course falls in love with her. There's a nasty lion (!) in the story, too. Paramount invested fair-size budgets in the Hathaway-directed Zane Grey series that ran from 1932 to late 1934, and one hallmark of the series was its quality production. This movie uses extensive stock footage from an earlier silent version, but it's hardly noticeable since Beery and Carey were cast in the same roles they'd played before. The story is very dated but the execution is good; these Paramount Zane Grey oaters are still fairly popular items in the 16mm home-projection movie market.

MAN OF THE WEST (1958, UA). D: Anthony Mann. W: Reginald Rose from a Will C. Brown novel. Cast: GARY COOPER, JULIE LONDON, Lee J. COBB, Arthur O'CONNELL, John Dehner, Jack Lord, Royal Dano, Frank Ferguson, Robert J. Wilke, Joe Dominguez, Guy Wilkerson. 101m.

After a train robbery three passengers (Cooper, O'Connell, London) are stranded and taken captive by an outlaw gang. It turns out the gang boss is Cooper's crazy, mean uncle (Cobb). The outlaws are on the skids but the cackling Uncle has a scheme to rob a bank; he forces Cooper—by agreeing to spare London and O'Connell only if Cooper will play along—to rejoin the outfit and help rob the bank. From there the slow-moving plot has some interesting twists but the picture has a sleazy flavor; it's a distasteful story with mainly dislikeable characters. Cobb, Lord and Dehner all play brutal psychotics, which is overdoing it. (This was Lord's first important screen role; evidently he's still proud of it; God knows why.)

Cooper was miscast, both because he was older than Cobb and looked it so he was not convincing as the nephew, and because there's no way to believe he ever could have been a member of this vicious, brutal, slimy gang of crazy killers. Cobb's acting is wildly overblown; so is Dehner's; and O'Connell's New York flavor militates against the believability of the setting. Cooper hasn't much to do except look pained until near the end, when he mixes into a wild, brutal, hand-to-hand fight; he's far too old for it to be believable.

The film has its partisans but in my opinion it's one of the least of Cooper's movies.

MAN OR GUN (1957, REP). D: Albert Gannaway. W: James Cassidy & Vance Skarstedt. Cast: MacDONALD CAREY, AUDREY TOTTER, James CRAIG, James Gleason. 79m.

Wandering cowpoke (Carey, miscast) decides to overthrow a tyrannical family that runs a town as though it were a feudal fiefdom. Poor script makes for a dud movie.

THE MAN WHO LOVED CAT DANCING (1973, MGM). D: Richard C. Sarafian. W: Eleanor Perry from Marilyn Durham's novel. Cast: BURT REYNOLDS, SARAH MILES, Jack WARDEN, George HAMILTON, Lee J. COBB, Robert Donner, Bo Hopkins, Jay Silverheels, Nancy Malone, Larry Littlebird. 114m.

A discontented wife (Miles) runs away from her stuffed-shirt mining tycoon husband (Hamilton) and falls in with a gang of fleeing outlaws (Reynolds, Warden, Hopkins). Hubby joins a lawman's (Cobb) posse and the chase is on. Jealousies set the outlaws against one another as the posse closes in, and it's all in the midst of Indian country. From there you can plot it yourself. After a while it becomes tedious to keep counting the rapes and attempted rapes. The needlessly downbeat ending doesn't help. Reynolds displays none of his usual gusto. Miles and Hamilton are miscast or inadequate. Cobb, Warden and the others seem dispirited. Harry Stradling's photography, John Williams's spare score and Sarafian's directing all seem competent but it's a cheerless movie. Art director Ed Carfagno discovered some gorgeous Arizona locations, and if you like scenery the movie is worth sitting through for that alone, but little else.

The film's release was overshadowed by two offscreen developments: the mysterious death of Sarah Miles's manager on location, and then screenwriter Perry's much publicized allegations that the movie had been rewritten by producer Martin Poll, playwright Robert Bolt (Miles's husband) and a screenwriter named William Norton, and that the finished movie in no way represents what the late Ms. Perry wrote. In any case, whoever wrote it, it's a lousy picture.

THE MAN WHO SHOT LIBERTY VALANCE (1962, PARA). D: John Ford. W: James Warner Bellah & Willis Goldbeck from the story by Dorothy M. Johnson. Cast: JAMES STEWART, JOHN WAYNE, VERA MILES, Lee MARVIN, Edmond O'BRIEN, Andy DEVINE, Woody STRODE, Ken Murray, Lee Van Cleef, Strother Martin, Jeanette Nolan, John Qualen. 122m.

A young lawyer (Stewart) arrives in a Western town to hang out his shingle. A dude-baiting bully named Liberty Valance (Marvin) beats him up. He's nursed back to health by a mossyhorn rancher (Wayne) and a pretty waitress (Miles) and the rancher's man Friday, called Pompey (Strode). Mixing into things are a drunken editor (O'Brien, a lovely scene-stealing performance) and other citizens who are concerned about the lawless depredations of arrogant gunslingers like Valance. The young lawyer determines to bring law 'n' order to the territory; Valance threatens to kill him if he doesn't lay off; it all leads to a showdown, keyed to the fact that the young lawyer doesn't know how to use a gun. There's a romantic triangle subplot involving Stewart, Wayne and Miles.

A few interesting changes are rung on the old formulas but *Liberty Valance* is confined almost entirely to sound-stage interiors and the occasional studio-set street scene, filmed in simple black-and-white fashion (William Clothier), and very long and slow, with its two leading men rather long in the tooth for their roles. In costumes and a sort of William S. Hart flavor it's a terribly old-fashioned film, rather wistful, lacking in energy. The characterizations are reduced to the simplicities of "B" formulas and I find it a dreary, tired movie.

MAN WITHOUT A STAR (1955, UNIV). D: King Vidor. W: Borden Chase & D. D. Beauchamp from the novel by Dee Linford. Cast: KIRK DOUGLAS, JEANNE CRAIN, CLAIRE TREVOR, Richard BOONE, William CAMPBELL, Jay C. Flippen, Roy Bar-

croft, Sheb Wooley, Eddy Waller, Mara
Corday, Myrna Hansen. 88m.

Wandering cowhand (Douglas) hires on
with a haughty lady rancher (Crain), helps a
kid (Campbell) to grow up, fights it out with
some villains (Boone et al.) and engages in
some humorous scenes with a saloon gal
(Trevor). It's charming, lifelike and adult,
well directed with fine outdoor photography
(Russell Metty) and excellent performances
by everybody except Crain, who's too Hollywood glossy, and Boone, who has too much
Method in his madness. The story, with its
emphasis on the coming of barbed wire and
an end to open-range freedom, has a vaguely
similar theme to that of *Lonely Are the Brave*,
and Kirk Douglas's performance prefigures
that one.

MAN WITH THE GUN (1955, UA). Also ti-
tled: TROUBLE SHOOTER. D: Richard
Wilson. W: Wilson & N. B. Stone. Cast:
ROBERT MITCHUM, JAN STERLING,
Angie DICKINSON, Henry HULL, John
Lupton, Karen Sharpe, Emile Meyer, Ted
De Corsia, Barbara Lawrence. 83m.

A ruthless lonely gunman (Mitchum)
rides into town searching for the wife who
deserted him. He hires on as marshal to get
rid of some bad guys. It's not bad but Mitchum cruises through the role without much
interest; he asserts he does this kind of job
with his eyes shut: "They just paint eyeballs
on my eyelids." Still, even when he's not ex-
erting himself he's got more presence than
most other actors have when they're working
on all eight cylinders. Hull is good as a weak-
kneed sheriff and Sterling as Mitchum's estranged wife (roles later repeated by Robert
Ryan and Sheree North in *Lawman*). There's
good dialogue in the screenplay ("Bo" Stone
also wrote *Ride the High Country*) and the direction builds suspense nicely. This was Samuel Goldwyn, Jr.'s, first production.

MANY RIVERS TO CROSS (1955, MGM).
D: Roy Rowland. W: Harry Brown & Guy
Trosper from a Steve Frazee story.
Cast: ROBERT TAYLOR, ELEANOR
PARKER, Victor McLAGLEN, Rosemary
DeCAMP, Russ TAMBLYN, Jeff Richards,
James Arness, Josephine Hutchinson. 92m.

Tomboyish gal (Parker) sets her sights on
a manly trapper (Taylor), exhausts him to
the point where he agrees to marry her, then
belatedly decides she must earn his love.
Amusing outdoor adventure-comedy is cli-
maxed by some Indian-fighting action.

MARA OF THE WILDERNESS (1965, AA).
D: Frank McDonald. W: Tom W. Blackburn
& Ewing Scott. Cast: Linda SAUNDERS,

Adam WEST, Sean McClory, Denver Pyle.
90m.

Young girl has been raised by Alaskan
wolves. Then she saves the life of an anthropologist (West) and a whole new world opens
up to her. Yup.

THE MARAUDERS (1955, MGM). D:
Gerald Mayer. W: Jack Leonard, Earl Felton
& Alan Marcus. Cast: DAN DURYEA,
Jarma LEWIS, Keenan WYNN, Jeff Rich-
ards, Harry Cording. 81m.

Good rancher versus evil ranchers. Wild
acting, amateur scripting.

MARK OF THE RENEGADE (1951, UNIV).
D: Hugo Fregonese. W: Robert H. Andrews
& Louis Solomon from Johnston McCulley's
novel *The Curse of Capistrano*. Cast:
RICARDO MONTALBAN, CYD CHAR-
ISSE, GILBERT ROLAND, J. Carrol
NAISH, Andrea King, George Tobias, Anto-
nio Moreno, Robert Warwick, Georgia
Backus, Robert Cornthwaite. 81m.

Reprise of *The Mark of Zorro* has its dashing Spanish-American hero (Montalban) engaging in derring-do to bring justice to early
California. Charisse is gorgeous and the
movie is colorful but it's standard stuff.

THE MARK OF ZORRO (1940, FOX). D:
Rouben Mamoulian. W: John T. Foote, Bess
Meredyth & Garrett Fort from Johnston
McCulley's novel *The Curse of Capistrano*.
Cast: TYRONE POWER, LINDA DAR-
NELL, Basil RATHBONE, Pedro de Cor-
doba, Eugene Pallette, Gale Sondergaard, J.
Edward Bromberg, Robert Lowery, Mon-
tagu Love, Victor Kilian, Noah Beery, Jr.,
Janet Beecher, Stanley Andrews, Frank
Puglia. 93m.

The fop, Don Diego (Power), turns out to
be masked avenger Zorro in this dated remake. It's in color, with the hero's sword tip
delicately etching that famous "Z" in his enemies' foreheads; good entertainment for the
kiddies. The big duel between Power and
Rathbone is marvelous.

THE MARKSMAN (1953, AA). D: Lewis D.
Collins. W: Daniel Ullman. Cast: WAYNE
MORRIS, Elena VERDUGO, Rick Vallin,
I. Stanford Jolley, Frank Ferguson. 62m.

Lawman (Morris) rather unsportingly
snipes at his quarry with a high-powered, tel-
escope-sighted rifle. One of the last of the "B"
oaters.

THE MARSHAL'S DAUGHTER (1953,
UA). D: William Berke. W: Robert Duncan.
Cast: KEN MURRAY, PRESTON FOS-
TER, Laurie ANDERS, Hoot GIBSON, Tex
RITTER, Forrest Taylor, Harry Lauter,
Robert Bray, Tom London, Francis Ford.

Guest stars: JOHNNY MACK BROWN, JIMMY WAKELY, BUDDY BAER. 71m.

Comedian Murray tries to look like a Western lawman in this incredibly bad oater. In black-and-white.

MARSHMALLOW MOON (1952, PARA). DW: Claude Binyon from a play by Walter B. Hare. Cast: ALAN YOUNG, DINAH SHORE, ROBERT MERRILL, Guy MITCHELL, Veda Ann BORG, Adele Jergens, Fritz Feld. 95m.

The real title of this movie is *Aaron Slick from Punkin Crick* (it was changed for TV showings). The plot—from a 1919 stage comedy—has a city-slicker con man (Merrill) trying to fleece an innocent widow out of her ranch; a hayseed bumpkin (Young) comes to the rescue. Some mildly diverting duets are sung by Merrill and Shore. It tries to be a nostalgic period piece but succeeds mainly in inspiring ennui.

MASSACRE (1934, WB). D: Alan Crosland. W: Ralph Block & Robert Gessner. Cast: RICHARD BARTHELMESS, ANN DVORAK, Dudley Digges, Claire Dodd, Henry O'Neill, Robert Barrat, Sidney Toler.

College-educated Indian rodeo star (Barthelmess) returns to the reservation to try and ameliorate white men's injustices. Sincere social-protest Western was unusual for its time.

MASSACRE (1956, FOX). D: Louis King. W: D. D. Beauchamp, William Tunberg & Fred Freiberger. Cast: DANE CLARK, James CRAIG, Marta Roth, Jaime Fernandez. 75m.

Western set in Mexico has bad guys selling rifles to Indians so the Indians can massacre folks. Distasteful junk.

MASSACRE CANYON (1954, COL). D: Fred F. Sears. W: David Lang. Cast: PHILIP CAREY, AUDREY TOTTER, Jeff DONNELL, Douglas Kennedy, Guinn "Big Boy" Williams.

Soldiers try to smuggle a wagonload of repeating rifles through Indian territory to a beleaguered fort. Poor.

MASSACRE RIVER (1959, AA). D: John Rawlins. W: Louis Stevens. Cast: GUY MADISON, RORY CALHOUN, Carole MATHEWS, Johnny Sands, Cathy Downs, Steve Brodie, Iron Eyes Cody. 75m.

Romantic rivalries among troopers; slow Indian-fighting oater.

THE MASTER GUNFIGHTER (1975, IND). D: Frank Laughlin. W: Harold Lapland. Cast: TOM LAUGHLIN, Ron O'NEAL, Lincoln KILPATRICK, GeoAnn Sosa, Barbara Carrera, Victor Campos. Narrator: Burgess MEREDITH. 121m.

Amateurish turkey is by the makers of the pop hit *Billy Jack*. The credited director, Frank Laughlin, is producer-star Tom Laughlin's nine-year-old son; it's easy to believe he actually directed it. The hysterical plot is set in the 1830s when not even the revolver, let alone the gunfighter, existed in history; swordfights are intermingled with gunfights; the hero spouts anachronistic liberal anti-violence speeches while viciously wiping out stacks of bad guys; the movie is a rancid example of fascist double-think, incompetent in all respects.

MASTERSON OF KANSAS (1954, COL). D: William Castle. W: Douglas Heyes. Cast: GEORGE MONTGOMERY, NANCY GATES, James GRIFFITH, William HENRY, Jay Silverheels, Bruce Cowling, Jean Willes, David Bruce, Benny Rubin, Gregg Barton, John Maxwell. 73m.

Two-gun sheriff Bat Masterson (Montgomery) deals out comic-book superhero justice to miscreants (Henry, Barton), abetted by Wyatt Earp (Cowling) and hindered by a cynical Doc Holliday (Griffith, whose entertaining depiction of the rogue is the picture's sole asset).

THE MAVERICK (1952, MONO). D: Lewis D. Collins. W: Sidney Theil. Cast: WILLIAM ELLIOTT, PHYLLIS COATES, Myron HEALEY, Russell Hicks, Robert Bray, Florence Lake. 61m.

Cavalrymen fight gunslingers in a war between cattlemen and homestead farmers. Plenty of action keys this superior Elliott programmer.

THE MAVERICK QUEEN (1956, REP). D: Joseph Kane. W: Kenneth Gamet & DeVallon Scott from a Zane Grey novel. Cast: BARBARA STANWYCK, BARRY SULLIVAN, Scott BRADY, Mary MURPHY, Jim Davis, Wallace Ford, Pierre Watkin, Walter Sande, Taylor Holmes. 92m.

Pinkerton cop (Sullivan) goes undercover to get the goods on a gang of outlaws masterminded by ambitious saloonkeeper Stanwyck; naturally they fall in love. Uneven oater is good in places, laughably bad in others. Zane Grey is the most filmed American novelist. To date there have been more than 100 movies based on his works; at press time this was the most recent of them.

McCABE AND MRS. MILLER (1971, WB). D: Robert Altman. W: Altman & Brian McKay from Edmund Naughton's novel *McCabe*. Cast: WARREN BEATTY, JULIE

CHRISTIE, Rene AUBERJONOIS, Hugh MILLAIS, Keith CARRADINE, William Devane, Shelley Duvall, John Schuck, Michael Murphy. 121m.

Near the turn of the century an iconoclastic loser, the drifting gambler John McCabe (Beatty), builds a saloon and whorehouse in a rugged mountain mining camp. He prospers, so a big mining company muscles in to buy or scare him out. During the course of things several jokes are related, both verbal and visual, and McCabe falls in love with the madam of his whorehouse (Christie); there is a gunfight at the end that owes quite a bit to the one in *High Noon*.

McCabe was produced on location in Canada; cast and crew built the town during the filming. It has marvelous touches. Beatty's performance is exquisite: the film is worth seeing if only for his engaging anti-hero. There are quirky historical touches—the faddish kind—that pass for "authenticity" while masking a stereotyped poverty of plot and characterizations. Christie, as the opium-smoking golden-hearted hooker, makes a fair job of a tediously hackneyed part. Remaining characters are ciphers except for Carradine's ill-fated happy drifter and, notably, Hugh Millais's ruthless hired gunman.

The script is more sprightly than this turgid director's handling of it, which tends toward long elegiac caresses of static pictorial compositions. Vilmos Zsigmond's widescreen photography, as usual with him, is annoyingly pretentious—mostly misty, with far too many lightstruck angles and shadow-obscured vagueries. Most of the film takes place in rain or snow; it's a dark movie. Editor Louis Lombardo cut it together at a soporific pace and it is at least half an hour too long. The soundtrack score consists of a few pleasant but hokey folk songs by Leonard Cohen. Altman's most maddening self-indulgence (heard in most of his films) is a penchant for allowing several actors to speak at once so that we can't hear what anyone is saying. The soundtrack as a whole is primitive—scratchy and metallic, like something out of a 1929 talkie.

Critics, in judging this one of the most important Westerns of the 1970s, have called *McCabe* haunting, poetic, glowing, a wonderful ballad. It has such aspects, fitfully; unhappily it's also slow and spiritless—it sneers at mythology but offers nothing in exchange.

McLINTOCK! (1963, UA). D: Andrew V. McLaglen. W: James Edward Grant. Cast: JOHN WAYNE, MAUREEN O'HARA, YVONNE De CARLO, Chill WILLS, Stefanie Powers, Patrick Wayne, Edgar Bu-

chanan, Bruce Cabot, Jerry Van Dyke, Jack Kruschen, Leo Gordon. 124m.

A crusty irascible cattleman (Wayne) tries to win back his estranged wife (O'Hara) with his bellowing voice and his fists in this brawling comedy. There are some very funny sequences; the characters are reminiscent of those played by Wayne and O'Hara in Ford's *The Quiet Man*. It's loud, foolish, broad and enjoyable. It was photographed (William Clothier) in Tucson; I remember hanging around the sets; the actors and crew had great fun making it, and that comes across on the screen.

THE McMASTERS (1970, IND). D: Alf Kjellin. W: Harold J. Smith. Cast: BROCK PETERS, NANCY KWAN, BURL IVES, Jack PALANCE, John Carradine, David Carradine, Dane Clark. 97m.

A black man (Peters) comes home after the Civil War, takes an Indian bride and tries to settle down farming against the bigoted hatred of whites who try to drive him out. It's a tough story but predictable; better than most of the blaxploitation Westerns but encumbered by a dreary script. The acting is excellent. A second version, with a toned-down ending, was released to theatres with about ten minutes chopped out of it.

MEANWHILE BACK AT THE RANCH (1968)—*See* THE BALLAD OF JOSIE.

MEANWHILE BACK AT THE RANCH (1976, IND). DW: Richard Patterson. Cast: GENE AUTRY, DONALD "RED" BARRY, WILLIAM "HOPALONG CASSIDY" BOYD, JOHNNY MACK BROWN, EDDIE DEAN, WILLIAM "WILD BILL" ELLIOTT, HOOT GIBSON, TIM HOLT, BUCK JONES, ALLAN "ROCKY" LANE, LASH LaRUE, BOB LIVINGSTON, KEN MAYNARD, TIM McCOY, TEX RITTER, ROY ROGERS, CHARLES STARRETT, BOB STEELE, JOHN WAYNE, Robert BLAKE, Smiley BURNETTE, Pat BUTTRAM, Yakima CANUTT, George "Gabby" HAYES, Buzz HENRY, Ben JOHNSON, Fuzzy KNIGHT, Richard MARTIN, Dub TAYLOR, many others. Narrator: Pat BUTTRAM.

Produced by Patrick Curtis, this retrospective comedy pastiche combines clips, scenes and stars from the programmers of 1930–1947 into a new plot line overlaid upon the snippets. Absurd, idiotic, nostalgic and funny, it was an official selection of the 1977 Cannes Film Festival and is great fun for those who love old oaters.

MEN OF TEXAS (1942, UNIV). D: Ray Enright. W: Richard Brooks & Harold Shumate. Cast: ROBERT STACK, ANNE

GWYNNE, Broderick CRAWFORD, Ralph BELLAMY, Leo CARRILLO, Jackie Cooper, Jane Darwell, Addison Richards, William Farnum, John Litel.

A Yankee reporter (Stack) in Reconstruction Texas sets out to expose demagogues and carpetbaggers. There's a lot of big-scale action in this heroic patriotic Western; wartime films, regardless of subject matter, often managed to pound away unsubtly at propaganda; but it's well done for its type. A Bill Elliott "B" feature made a few years later, *Fabulous Texan*, covers the same ground on a smaller budget but compares favorably in many respects.

MEN OF THE NORTH (1930, MGM). D: Hal Roach, Sr. W: Willard Mack & Richard Schayer. Cast: GILBERT ROLAND, Nena Quartaro, Arnold Korf, Barbara Leonard.

Mounties pursued bullion thieves in this early routine meller.

THE MICHIGAN KID (1946, UNIV). D: Ray Taylor. W: Roy Chanslor from a Rex Beach novel. Cast: JON HALL, VICTOR McLAGLEN, Rita JOHNSON, Andy DEVINE, Milburn Stone, Stanley Andrews, Byron Foulger, William Ching, William Fawcett. 68m.

Corrupt town bosses take over local properties, including heroine's ranch, so our hero steps in. Poor.

MIRACLE OF THE HILLS (1959, FOX). D: Paul Landres. W: Charles H. Hoffman. Cast: REX REASON, Theona Bryant, Jay North, Eugene Roth, Tracy Stratford, Gilbert Smith. 73m.

A new preacher rides into town and finds himself pitted against the tough lady boss of the community. Feeble cheapie is in black-and-white.

THE MIRACLE RIDER (1935, IND). D: Armand Schaefer & B. Reeves Eason. W: Gerald Geraghty & four others. Cast: TOM MIX, Joan GALE, Charles MIDDLETON, Jason Robards, Sr., Bob Fraser, Niles Welsh, Tom London, Charles King, Wally Wales, Robert Kortman, Chief Standing Bear, Edmund Cobb, George Chesebro, Hank Bell, Lafe McKee, Dick Curtis, Dick Alexander, Chief John Big Tree, Edward Earle, Frank Ellis. 15-chapter serial.

The only serial included in this book, this Mascot oater is listed because it's still being shown frequently and because it was Mix's last movie. The plot almost defies description: it begins with a quick montage of the history of white injustice to Indians from 1777 to 1930, then proceeds into everything from fascism to science fiction: the bad guy (Middle-ton) plans to dominate the world with his remote-control flying buzz-bombs, his revolutionary "X–94" explosives and other marvelous gizmos. It all takes place in that "B" never-never land that mingles the newest (1935) technology with gun-totin' horseback heroics and Indian battles. In one stunt Mix, on his horse Tony, overtakes a speeding tank truck loaded with explosives. He shoots a gun out of the villain's hand (from horseback, at full gallop, at long range), then catches the truck, leaps on board, throws the driver overboard, has a ferocious wrestling match with the remaining bad guy, and is still wrestling on the careening truck when villains on the hilltop shoot at it from ambush: finally we see it blow up spectacularly. That concludes Chapter 1: come back next week to see how Tom survived that one!

THE MISFITS (1961, UA). D: John Huston. W: Arthur Miller. Cast: CLARK GABLE, MARILYN MONROE, MONTGOMERY CLIFT, Eli WALLACH, Thelma RITTER, Kevin McCarthy, Estelle Winwood, James Barton. 124m.

In modern Nevada a frightened divorcee (Monroe) meets an embittered rodeo loser (Clift) and a rootless aging cowboy (Gable) who go into unhappy partnership with a cynic (Wallach) to capture wild mustangs and sell them for dog food. The story draws a too-obvious parallel between the four people and the hapless wild horses they're hunting. Miller tailored the screenplay for Monroe (his wife); it accentuates the poignance of her vulnerability: the warring personalities of over-ripe harlot and terrified little girl. Huston wanted Robert Mitchum to play opposite her but Mitchum didn't like the script; later it was rewritten extensively, but by then Mitchum was working on another picture. One wonders what it would have been like. Gable gives one of his best performances in it, but he never had Mitchum's range or depth. Still, it's a pretty good movie, with fine black-and-white photography (Russell Metty) and a good score (Alex North) and good performances. This was Gable's last picture, and Monroe's, and it was Clift's last significant one; all three died soon after.

MISSISSIPPI GAMBLER (1942)—See DANGER ON THE RIVER.

THE MISSISSIPPI GAMBLER (1953, UNIV). D: Rudolph Maté. W: Seton I.Miller. Cast: TYRONE POWER, PIPER LAURIE, JULIA ADAMS, John McINTIRE, Paul Cavanagh, William Reynolds, John Baer, Ron Randell, Robert Warwick, Ralph Dumke, Guy Williams, Rolfe Sedan, Dennis Weaver. 98m.

Pre-Civil War gentleman gambler (Power) plays for high stakes, woos a spirited aristocrat (Laurie) while being silently adored by another girl (Adams), and gets mixed up in fencing duels, riverboat brawls and gentlemanly matters of honor and repute; in all of which he is cheerfully seconded by his roguish sidekick (McIntire). The trappings are slick and marvelous: fine glossy photography (Irving Glassberg), a spritely score (Frank Skinner), the colorful polish of the Universal style at its best. A sudsy but engaging old-fashioned entertainment, this mini-*Gone with the Wind* is thoroughly professional romantic melodrama, still very enjoyable.

THE MISSOURI BREAKS (1976, UA). D: Arthur Penn. W: Thomas McGuane. Cast: JACK NICHOLSON, MARLON BRANDO, Kathleen LLOYD, Harry Dean STANTON, John McLiam, Randy Quaid, Frederick Forrest, John Ryan, Richard Bradford, Luana Anders, Danny Goldman. 126m.

A tyrannical Montana rancher (McLiam) is losing horses to a gang led by a young rustler (Nicholson) so he hires a weird psychotic killer (Brando) to wipe out the thieves; meanwhile the scruffy rustler is making out with the rancher's sex-starved daughter (Lloyd). That's about the sum of the plot. The film starts with a lynching and veers from comedy to brutality for altogether too long. There are too many vignettes about urination, fly buttoning, outhouses. The killings are repellent, predictable in the manner and style of their shock effects (why must everybody imitate Peckinpah?).

Elliott Kastner produced this one on a big budget; it lost money. It has some virtues. There's a good look and feel of the West, although the photography (Michael Butler) is faddish and irritating; the score (John Williams) is anachronistic but effective. The cast is mostly quite good; in fact Stanton, as Nicholson's rustler partner, virtually steals the movie. Lloyd is too polished for the rustic milieu, and Nicholson is amiably Gary Cooperish as the grubby rustler but Cooper wouldn't have played a horse-thief and that's a problem with this movie: it takes no moral stance, it has no hero. It switches at clockwork intervals from Nicholson to Brando, whose gunslinger "regulator" is contemptible, self-indulgent caricature and belongs in some other movie. Brando, at a gross 250 pounds, looks like a hippo on horseback; his bewildering costume changes (from Buffalo Bill flamboyance to Mother Hubbard drag) are absurd; he speaks alternately with three odd accents (Irish brogue, Plains twang, supercilious English twitter) and one can see his eyes drift toward the off-camera cue cards he uses because he's too lazy to memorize lines. It bothers me that a man with so little respect for his own profession continues to accept enormous sums of money for work that he holds in contempt. This movie should be held that way too.

MOHAWK (1956, FOX). D: Kurt Neumann. W: Maurice Geraghty & Milton Krims. Cast: SCOTT BRADY, RITA GAM, Neville BRAND, Lori NELSON, Allison Hayes, John Hoyt, Rhys Williams, Ted de Corsia, Mae Clarke, Tommy Cook, John Hudson. 79m.

Foppish artist proves his manliness and brings peace between whites and Indians in pre-Revolutionary upper New York. Silly foolishness.

MOLLY AND LAWLESS JOHN (1972, IND). D: Gary Nelson. W: Terry Kingsley-Smith. Cast: VERA MILES, SAM ELLIOTT, Clu GULAGER, John ANDERSON, Cynthia Myers, Charles A. Pinney, Robert Westmoreland. 97m.

The entire opening sequence—a bank robbery—is filmed in slow motion. Other effects are equally gimmicky in this bleak meller about the gentle wife (Miles) of a brutal sheriff (Anderson) who is sweet-talked by a condemned prisoner (Elliott) into helping him break jail, then joins forces with him in a posse-pursued flight across the wilderness. Good New Mexico color photography (Charles Wheeler) enhances this low-budget effort; the pace is slow but it's redeemed by four affecting performances: the actors are terrific.

MONEY, WOMEN AND GUNS (1958, UNIV). D: Richard H. Bartlett. W: Montgomery Pittman. Cast: JOCK MAHONEY, KIM HUNTER, Tim HOVEY, Tom DRAKE, Gene EVANS, Lon Chaney, Jr., William Campbell, James Gleason, Ian MacDonald, Jeffrey Stone, Judy Meredith, Richard Devon, Philip Terry, Don Megowan. 78m.

Oater has a murder-mystery twist: a detective (Mahoney) looks for the four heirs—and the killer—of a murdered prospector. CinemaScope photography (Philip Lathrop) is okay except the camera dolly wobbles here and there. It's rambling, and only for the undemanding; the script is verbose and the acting not terrific, except for Hunter who is always good.

MONTANA (1950, WB). D: Ray Enright. W: James R. Webb, Borden Chase & Charles

THE LONELY MAN
(1957): Robert Middleton,
Jack Palance, Anthony Perkins. Psychological conflict
between father and son.
Paramount Pictures

LONE STAR (1952): Ava
Gardner, Broderick Craw-
ford, Clark Gable. Formula
epic is more romance than
history. MGM

THE LONG RIDERS
(1980): David Carra-
dine, Randy Quaid,
Stacy Keach, James
Keach, Keith Carra-
dine. The historical
outlaw brothers are
played by real
actor-brothers.
United Artists

THE LUSTY MEN (1952):
Arthur Kennedy, Robert
Mitchum. You can feel every
one of Mitchum's broken
bones. RKO Radio Pictures

THE MAGNIFICENT
SEVEN (1960): Yul Brynner,
Charles Bronson, Brad
Dexter. Three of the seven
train the villagers to defend
themselves. United Artists

THE MAN FROM COLORADO
(1948): Glenn Ford, William Holden.
Ford plays the sadistic hanging
judge with great relish.
Columbia Pictures

MAN OF THE WEST (1958):
Lee J. Cobb, Gary Cooper, Julie
London. Cooper is miscast, and
hasn't much to do except look
pained. United Artists

THE MAN WHO SHOT
LIBERTY VALANCE (1962):
Lee Van Cleef, Lee Marvin,
James Stewart, John Wayne.
A terribly old-fashioned film,
rather wistful.
Paramount Pictures

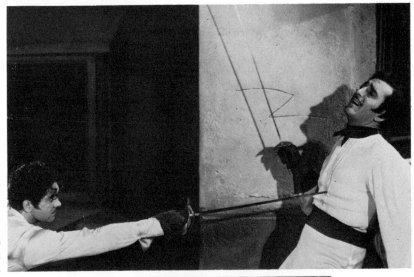

THE MARK OF
ZORRO (1940):
Tyrone Power,
Basil Rathbone.
The big duel is
marvelous. Twentieth
Century-Fox

MASSACRE (1934):
Richard Barthelmess
as a college-educated
rodeo star returns to
the reservation. Sincere,
and unusual for its
time. Warner Brothers

237

THE MAVERICK QUEEN
(1956): Barry Sullivan, Barbara Stanwyck, Scott Brady.
Uneven oater was, to date,
the most recent Zane Grey
movie. Republic Pictures

McCABE AND MRS.
MILLER (1971): Julie Christie, Warren Beatty. The
script is more sprightly than
this turgid director's handling of it. Warner Brothers

THE MISSISSIPPI GAM-
BLER (1953): Piper Laurie,
Tyrone Power, Julia Adams.
Gentleman gambler woos
spirited aristocrat while
being adored by another
girl. The colorful polish
of the Universal style.
Universal Pictures

O'Neal from an Ernest Haycox story. Cast: ERROL FLYNN, ALEXIS SMITH, S.Z. SAKALL, Douglas Kennedy, James Brown, Ian MacDonald, Paul E. Burns, Nacho Galindo, Lane Chandler, Monte Blue, Charles Irwin. 76m.

Two powerful ranchers (Alexis Smith, Douglas Kennedy) are the rulers of the Montana cattle country. In comes Flynn with a huge flock of sheep. A war ensues. The script makes a mess of the Haycox original; the movie is slow, perfunctory, cheap and predictable—possibly the least of all Flynn's Westerns. Karl Freund's Technicolor photography is fine.

MONTANA BELLE (1952, IND). D: Allan Dwan. W: Horace McCoy, Norman S. Hall, M.Coates Webster & Howard Welsch. Cast: JANE RUSSELL, GEORGE BRENT, Scott BRADY, Forrest TUCKER, Andy DEVINE, Dick Elliott, Jack Lambert, Roy Barcroft, Ray Teal. 81m.

Belle Starr throws in with the Daltons. You have to see Jane Russell disguised as a boy to believe it. This silly nonsense was produced in 1948 by Howard Hughes but withheld from distribution for several years.

MONTANA MIKE (1947, UA). D: Albert S. Rogell. W: Art Arthur, Rowland Leigh, Aubrey Wisberg & Ernest Haycox. Cast: ROBERT CUMMINGS, BRIAN DONLEVY, Marjorie REYNOLDS, Bill Goodwin, John Litel, Stu Erwin. 95m.

Fantasy yarn has an angel coming down from Heaven to reform a badman. It's trivial but pleasant; there's some sprightly dialogue that may be traceable to the "additional dialogue" credit given to Haycox.

MONTANA MOON (1930, MGM). D: Malcolm St. Clair. W: Frank Butler & Sylvia Thalberg. Cast: JOHNNY MACK BROWN, JOAN CRAWFORD, RICARDO CORTEZ, Cliff Edwards, Benny Rubin, Dorothy Sebastian, Karl Dane.

Ranch cowboy reforms a jazz girl's wildness. It was deservedly a box-office dud despite big names and sizable budget.

MONTANA TERRITORY (1952, COL). D: Ray Nazarro. W: Barry Shipman. Cast: LON McCALLISTER, WANDA HENDRIX, Preston FOSTER, Clayton Moore, Jack Elam, Myron Healey, Eddy Waller, Trevor Bardette, Hugh Sanders, George Chesebro. 64m.

A young deputy sets out to round up a passel of outlaws. Routine.

MONTE WALSH (1970, NGP). D: William A. Fraker. W: David Zelag Goodman & Lukas Heller from Jack Schaefer's novel.

Cast: LEE MARVIN, JACK PALANCE, JEANNE MOREAU, Mitchell RYAN, Jim DAVIS, Matt Clark, Allyn Ann McLerie, Billy "Green" Bush, G. D. Spradlin, John McLiam, Bo Hopkins, Charles Tyner, Eric Christmas, John Carter, Tom Heaton, John R. McKee. 106m.

While corporations take over the ranches, two aging cowhands try to survive in the dying days of the open-range West. Jeanne Moreau is very moving as an aging whore waiting for Marvin to marry her, and Jim Davis is excellent as the ranch straw-boss who hires the cowboys; Mitchell Ryan stands out as a cowhand driven to outlawry, and Palance is extraordinarily sympathetic in an atypical gentle role. The movie is a long and expensive ($5 million) elegy to the passing of the old days; it's nicely directed and photographed (wide screen, by David M. Walsh) and has something of the look of Remington paintings. The score (John Barry) is fine except for a tacky over-the-credits song; the story is picaresque and meandering but not trite; the acting is all-around excellent. Generally underrated, *Monte Walsh* is a fine film in its elegiac depiction of the humor and hardship of real cowboy life; it's better and more honest, for example, than the similar *Will Penny*.

THE MOONLIGHTER (1953, WB). D: Roy Rowland. W: Niven Busch. Cast: FRED MacMURRAY, BARBARA STANWYCK, Ward BOND, John Dierkes, Morris Ankrum, Jack Elam, William Ching, Charles Halton. 75m.

In the old West the term "moonlighter" referred to a thief who rustled cattle by night. MacMurray plays the embittered title character and Stanwyck is the girl he once loved. Black-and-white pic was released in 3-D. It's a poor story for Niven Busch; the cast makes it palatable, but only just.

MOONLIGHT ON THE PRAIRIE (1936, WB). D: D. Ross Lederman. Cast: DICK FORAN, Sheila MANNORS, George E. Stone, Joe Sawyer, Gordon Elliott, Robert Barrat, Glenn Strange, Dick Jones. 67m.

Bad guys try to steal a defenseless widow's ranch; a rodeo star (Foran) arrives to prove the bad guys are wrong when they claim he's the one who made her a widow. You take it from there. It's "B" fare. Foran sings a couple of songs. This was the first film in his 1936–1937 series of nine Warner programmers. Glenn Strange's screen debut.

MORE DEAD THAN ALIVE (1968, UA). D: Robert Sparr. W: George Schenck. Cast: CLINT WALKER, VINCENT PRICE,

ANNE FRANCIS, Beverly Powers, Paul Hampton, Craig Littler, Mike Henry, Harry Lauter, Emile Meyer, Arvo Ojala. 101m.

After eighteen years in Yuma Prison, Killer Cain (Walker) is released and makes heroic efforts to stay away from the guns and violence that got him in trouble long ago. Fresh twists keep the plot perking sporadically. The uneven script maunders and meanders but the story is different from most: Cain hooks up with a traveling carnival as a trick-shot artist but trouble dogs him. Unfortunately the directing is poor, the production lackadaisical, the photography (Jack Marquette) mediocre and the score (Philip Springer) dreadful. The good moments are unsustained, the script is on a "B" level and the ending is quite disgusting.

MOUNTAIN FAMILY ROBINSON (1979, IND). D: John Cotter. W: Arthur R. Dubs. Cast: Robert F. LOGAN, Susan Damante Shaw, William Bryant, Heather Rattray, Ham Larsen, George "Buck" Flower. 100m.

Modern family returns to nature by homesteading in the Colorado Rockies. It's an unacknowledged remake, with the same cast, of Dubs's *The Wilderness Family* and its various sequels. Beautiful photography (James Roberson) and some cute animals are the only assets; the script is trash.

THE MOUNTAIN MEN (1980, COL). D: Richard Lang. W: Fraser Clarke Heston. Cast: CHARLTON HESTON, BRIAN KEITH, Victoria RACIMO, Stephen Macht, John Glover, Seymour Cassel, David Ackroyd, Cal Bellini, Victor Jory. 102m.

An Indian woman (Racimo) runs away from her brutal husband (Macht); two trappers (Heston, Keith) protect her against the assaults of whole armies of nasty Indians. Heston is earnest; Keith attempts to be funny; both are disagreeable as unwashed, bearded, profane rednecks, and the bloody violence in the numerous Indian fights is excessive and pointless. It's rather like an "R"-rated version of *The Life and Times of Grizzly Adams*, but this one is hardly for family audiences; it's far too brutal. The film marks Lang's directorial debut. Screenwriter is the star's son. It's slow and boring, with a poor distracting score (Michel Legrand).

MRS. MIKE (1949, UA). D: Louis King. W: Alfred L. Levitt & DeWitt Bodeen from a novel by Benedict & Nancy Freedman. Cast: DICK POWELL, EVELYN KEYES, Angela CLARKE, J.M. Kerrigan, John Miljan, Will Wright, Nan Boardman. 99m.

When a city girl marries a Canadian Mountie and they're posted out to the far Northwest at the turn of the century, she learns what frontier life is like. It's pleasant leisurely entertainment, very well acted, the sort they used to call "heartwarming" and "earthy."

MURIETA (1965, WB). Also titled: VENDETTA. D: George Sherman. W: James O'Hanlon. Cast: JEFFREY HUNTER, ARTHUR KENNEDY, Diana LORYS, Robert Camardiel, Sara Lezana.

Joaquin Murieta was a bandit who developed quite a legend in the days when California was still part of Mexico. According to some he was a Robin Hood, a precursor of the *Zorro* fictions; according to others he was a vicious murdering lunatic. Ultimately he was ambushed by a posse, after which his head was pickled in a jar and put on display by the authorities as a warning to would-be imitators. This movie version, filmed in Spain, strays considerably from history; it's low-budget and the script is not very good but the grim yarn holds the attention.

MUSTANG (1960, UA). D: Peter Stevens. W: Tom Gries from a Rutherford Montgomery novel. Cast: JACK BEUTEL, Madalyn Frahey, Steve Keyes, Milt Swift, Robert Gilbert.

A down-at-the-heels rodeo cowboy tames a wild horse. Beutel, the one-shot "star" of the much ballyhooed *The Outlaw*, hung around for a couple of decades, appearing in the occasional cheapie like this one, but he never caught on with audiences; it's no wonder, given how tame these low-budget efforts were.

MUSTANG COUNTRY (1976, UNIV). DW: John Champion. Cast: JOEL McCREA, Nika MINA, Robert FULLER, Patrick Wayne. 79m.

Set in 1925 and filmed in Canada, this has to do with the pursuit of a wild horse by an Indian youth and an ex-rodeoing rancher; the horse-action footage is good nature-adventure stuff but the plot is too slender to keep adults awake; it's mainly for the kiddies, although well handled, and it's of note because it marks the emergence from retirement of Joel McCrea whose last previous screen appearance had been fourteen years earlier. Flashbacks use footage from his old pictures. At seventy, he doesn't appear to have aged much at all, and his great serene personal appeal serves very well. Remarkable scenic vistas are photographed by J. Barry Herron, but awkwardly interpolated wildlife footage distracts and slows the already leisurely pace.

MY DARLING CLEMENTINE (1946, FOX). D: John Ford; W: Samuel C. Engle,

Winston Miller & Sam Hellman from Stuart N. Lake's book *Wyatt Earp, Frontier Marshal*. Cast: HENRY FONDA, LINDA DARNELL, VICTOR MATURE, CATHY DOWNS, Walter BRENNAN, Tim HOLT, John IRELAND, Ward Bond, Grant Withers, Jane Darwell, Alan Mowbray, Russell Simpson, J. Farrell MacDonald, Roy Roberts, Francis Ford, Harry Woods. 97m.

Set in Tombstone and ignoring the Dodge City background of the Earps, this classic features Wyatt (Fonda), Virgil (Holt) and Morgan (Bond) Earp, with Doc Holliday (Mature), arrayed against Old Man Clanton (Brennan), Ike (Withers) and Billy (Ireland) Clanton, and various other miscreants. Francis Ford plays the town drunk, Darnell is Holliday's possessive girl friend, and Downs—as the title character—is very fetching as the girl Wyatt loves.

There's only the flimsiest relationship between this yarn (or its predecessors—it was the second remake of the 1934 *Frontier Marshal*) and history or biographical accuracy, but no matter. It's a great legendary myth. Fonda quietly imbues the Earp character with stunning power. And Ford's visual images (realized via cinematographer Joseph MacDonald), while not spectacularly scenic—most of *Clementine* takes place in town or indoors—could be hung as fine paintings.

MY LITTLE CHICKADEE (1940, UNIV). D: Edward Cline. W: W. C. Fields & Mae West. Cast: W. C. FIELDS, MAE WEST, Dick FORAN, Joseph CALLEIA, Donald Meek, Anne Nagel, Margaret Hamilton. 83m.

The excuse for a plot involves a con man-sheriff (Fields) with a bawdy lady (West), a dapper Mexican bandit (Calleia), an earnest cowpoke (Foran), Indian attack, poker game, train, goat, and whatever else the two zany author-stars thought up as they went along. Absurd, outrageous and hilarious, this comedy is great fun. Foran, who was being paid by the week, kept goading Fields and West by telling each that the other was rewriting lines in order to steal scenes; in this manner Foran provoked endless rewrites of the script that kept the film in production for several months—and kept him working. When you see the twinkle in Foran's eyes on screen you'll understand why it's there.

MY OUTLAW BROTHER (1950, EL). D: Elliott Nugent. W: Gene Fowler & Alfred L. Levitt from a Max Brand novel. Cast: MICKEY ROONEY, ROBERT PRESTON, Robert STACK, Wanda HENDRIX. 80m.

Dude kid comes west, learns his brother is an outlaw, and joins the Texas Rangers. Feeble flick was produced by Rooney in an effort to escape his chronic financial troubles; it didn't help. In black-and-white.

MY PAL THE KING (1932, UNIV). D: Kurt Neumann. W: Richard Schayer. Cast: TOM MIX, MICKEY ROONEY, Paul Hurst, Noel Francis, Jim Thorpe.

Cowboy star Mix teaches boy-king Rooney the rudiments of democracy in this Ruritanian juvenalia; he also disposes of felonious noblemen. Fun.

THE MYSTERIOUS RIDER (1938, PARA). D: George Sherman. W: Maurice Geraghty. Cast: DOUGLAS DUMBRILLE, Marsha HUNT, Sidney Toler.

Masked-savior yarn was a slow never-never-land programmer notable for "B" villain Dumbrille's portrayal of the good guy for a change.

THE NAKED DAWN (1955, UNIV). D: Edgar G. Ulmer. W: Nina & Herman Schneider. Cast: ARTHUR KENNEDY, Betta ST. JOHN, Eugene IGLESIAS, Roy Engel, Charita. 81m.

Romantic triangle involves a young outlaw (Iglesias) and his wife (St. John) with an older outlaw (Kennedy). Except for a few pseudonymously directed "B" series oaters of the 1930s this is the only Western to have been directed by the legendary Edgar G. Ulmer, whose talent sometimes transcended the threadbare scripts and budgets of his back-street productions. This one, for example, was shot in about six days. But those buffs who extol Ulmer tend to see only his excellences; they forget that he was hamstrung by limitations of time and money. Like most of his films, this one is slow and trite, ragged, hasty, poorly acted and badly written. Nevertheless it's worth looking at for its eccentric directorial technique.

THE NAKED GUN (1958, IND). D: Jack Lewis. W: Lewis & Ron Ormond. Cast: WILLARD PARKER, MARA CORDAY, Veda Ann Borg, Barton MacLane, Tom Brown, Chick Chandler.

Hidden Aztec treasure has a curse on it; all these poor folks are getting murdered by somebody who wants the treasure; enter our stalwart investigator. Anemic.

THE NAKED HILLS (1956, AA). D: Josef Shaftel. W: Shaftel & Helen S. Bilkie. Cast: DAVID WAYNE, MARCIA HENDERSON, KEENAN WYNN, James BARTON, Jim BACKUS, Denver Pyle, Frank Fenton, Fuzzy Knight, Myrna Dell, Lewis Russell, Jim Hayward, Steve Terrell. Narrator: Denver PYLE. 73m.

From the 1849 California gold rush to the

1890s this mini-epic covers Western history from the viewpoint of an unlucky prospector (Wayne) who deserts his partner and family in a soul-crushing hard-luck search for gold. It's an oversimplified vest-pocket movie—a saga on a "B" budget—and the greed-for-gold theme is threadbare; but there's uniformly superior quality in the direction, the photography (Frederick Gately), the quiet score (Herschel Burke Gilbert) and the economical editing (Gene Fowler, Jr.). Performances are understated but exemplary; the characters are often surprisingly fresh. But there's too much low-grade melodrama in the machinations of the villains (Backus, Wynn) so the movie adds up to less than its potential.

NAKED IN THE SUN (1957, AA). D: R. John Hugh. W: Hugh & Frank G. Slaughter. Cast: JAMES CRAIG, LITA MILAN, Barton MacLANE, Tony Hunter. 79m.

Colonial-period hero battles slave traders in behalf of the Indians. Slow and dreary.

THE NAKED SPUR (1953, MGM). D: Anthony Mann. W: Sam Rolfe & Harold Jack Bloom. Cast: JAMES STEWART, JANET LEIGH, ROBERT RYAN, Millard MITCHELL, Ralph MEEKER, Michael Pate. 91m.

Three bounty hunters track and capture a fugitive killer (Ryan) and his feisty girl friend (Leigh). The killer and the girl then begin to whittle away at their captors' psychologies, turning them against one another, whipping up greed and suspicion while the bounty hunters try to take them back to civilization through Indian country. The suspense is enhanced by the sinister threat of half-seen Indians (Pate and extras) who keep menacing their movements. The film was shot entirely outdoors, on spectacular Rocky Mountain locations (cinematographer William C. Mellor). The screenplay received an Academy Award nomination. There's an unobtrusive but fine score (Bronislau Kaper) and peerless editing (George White) and splendidly effective acting by the small superb cast; if anyone stands out it is Ryan but they all are stunning.

NAUGHTY MARIETTA (1935, MGM). D: W.S. Van Dyke II. W: John Lee Mahin, Albert Hackett & Frances Goodrich from Victor Herbert's operetta. Cast: JEANETTE MacDONALD, NELSON EDDY, Elsa LANCHESTER, Akim TAMIROFF, Frank Morgan, Dorothy Granger, Cecilia Parker, Douglas Dumbrille. 80m.

French princess (MacDonald) meets Indian scout (Eddy) in this cornball operetta. This was the first MacDonald-Eddy movie. Personally I can't stand the things but if they're your cup of tea, enjoy. It was nominated for the Oscar as best picture.

NAVAJO RUN (1966, AI). D: Johnny Seven. W: Jo Heims. Cast: Johnny Seven, Virginia Vincent, Warren Kemmerling, Ron Soble.

Injured Navajo seeks succour at an isolated ranch peopled by three Indian-haters. Grim cheapie has rattlesnakes and a vicious climax. Distasteful junk.

THE NEBRASKAN (1953, COL). D: Fred F. Sears. W: David Lang & Martin Berkeley. Cast: PHILIP CAREY, Roberta HAYNES, Wallace FORD, Lee Van Cleef, Jay Silverheels, Regis Toomey. 68m.

Yet another half-baked *Broken Arrow* imitator, this has Carey as a civilian army scout who makes friends with a Sioux chief and averts war.

NED KELLY (1970, UA). D: Tony Richardson. W: Richardson & Ian Jones. Cast: MICK JAGGER, Joanne Wolmsley, Allen Bickford, Frank Thring, Clarissa Kaye, Geoffrey Gilmour, Nigel Lovell. 100m.

Kelly was a legendary Australian road agent in the period that coincided with America's Wild West. This one is rambling, slow, disagreeably arty. Jagger, the chief Rolling Stone, is an acquired taste.

NEVADA (1944, RKO). D: Edward Killy. W: Norman Houston from Zane Grey's novel. Cast; ROBERT MITCHUM, ANNE JEFFREYS, Guinn "Big Boy" WILLIAMS, Nancy GATES, Richard MARTIN, Craig Reynolds, Harry Woods, Emmet Lynn. 62m.

Drifter (Mitchum) mixes it up with baddies who are jumping innocent people's mining claims. Remake of a 1935 Buster Crabbe programmer is fast but predictable, with all the standard earmarks right down to the guitar-strumming comic sidekick (Richard Martin as "Chito Rafferty"). Mitchum had played bits in about twenty "B" Westerns with William (Hopalong Cassidy) Boyd or Eddie Dew or Johnny Mack Brown; RKO groomed him as a "B" star and put him in two of these programmer oaters. This was the first (followed by *West of the Pecos*) but Mitchum then went on to "A" stardom and was replaced in this series by Tim Holt.

THE NEVADAN (1950, COL). D: Gordon Douglas. W: George W. George & George F. Slavin. Cast: RANDOLPH SCOTT, DOROTHY MALONE, Forrest TUCKER, George Macready, Jock Mahoney, Frank Faylen. 81m.

Marshal (Scott) chases crooks in this undistinguished black-and-white oater but it's keyed by good stunt work, mostly doubled by Mahoney.

NEVADA SMITH (1966, PARA). D: Henry Hathaway. W: John Michael Hayes from sequences in Harold Robbins's novel *The Carpetbaggers*. Cast: STEVE McQUEEN, SUZANNE PLESHETTE, Karl MALDEN, Brian KEITH, Arthur KENNEDY, Pat HINGLE, Raf VALLONE, Janet Margolin, Martin Landau, Josephine Hutchinson, John Doucette, Ted De Corsia, Howard da Silva, Lyle Bettger. 135m.

Revenge yarn concerns a half-breed (McQueen) who spends several years tracking down the nasty varmints who killed his parents: the Bob Steele plot on an elephantine budget and scale. Good photography (Lucien Ballard) and a ponderous score (Alfred Newman) help some but the picture has no suspense, a fragmented dreary script and extremely poor acting by key performers Malden and Kennedy. McQueen is simply there, in a role that has very little character, and the only bright spot is a short sequence right at the beginning in which Brian Keith brings things to life. Story is based on a lengthy subplot from the bestselling Robbins novel, a role played in the movie *The Carpetbaggers* by Alan Ladd, who was scheduled to star in this one too but he died before it was filmed.

THE NEW LAND (1973, WB). D: Jan Troell. W: Troell & Bengt Forslund from a series of novels by Vilhelm Moberg. Cast: MAX VON SYDOW, LIV ULLMANN, Eddie Axberg, Hans Alfredson, Monica Zetterlund, Halvar Bjork. 161m.

This is the second half of a very long movie, the first half of which is *The Emigrants*. Taken together, as they should be, the two films—based on a series of four novels—concern a group of Swedes who uproot themselves in the mid-nineteenth century and journey from Scandinavia to North America, enduring hardships and adventures, finally settling on a homestead on a Minnesota lake. *The New Land* carries the immigrants through the first twelve years in Minnesota as they push their roots down into the soil. Less drama than saga, less story than history, the two films are a sincere interpretation, and a good insight, into the settlement of the American frontier and the "melting pot" so glibly assumed by historians. Troell's photography (he is his own cinematographer and editor) is delicate and fine. The bleak grandeur of these films is powerful, and Troell is a master of the dramatic use of silence, but the films are seriously unsatisfying. The characters, regardless how subtly they are interpreted by the good actors, are stolid, cheerless and finally boring. The emotional center of

things seems missing. Particularly in *The New Land* segment, the development of events is unrelievedly bleak. Troell's pioneers never prevail; they merely endure, and there are no peaks of triumph, no moments of excitement. The films simply bog down in misery and endless defeats, which the characters barely survive. This has its validity, particularly in the context of the dour Scandinavian character Troell wants to depict, but valid or not it's too reserved, too sad, too grim in its pessimism and despair. Combined, the two films run more than five hours in length; nearly all of it is tearful tedium. It's impressive, no doubt, but sitting through the whole epic requires great fortitude and a tremendous resistance to boredom.

NEW MEXICO (1951, UA). D: Irving Reis. W: Max Trell. Cast: LEW AYRES, MARILYN MAXWELL, Robert HUTTON, Raymond Burr, Andy Devine, Verna Felton, John Hoyt, Jeff Corey, Ted De Corsia. 76m.

Cavalry versus Indians again; good cast, mediocre script.

NIGHT OF THE GRIZZLY (1966, PARA). D: Joseph Pevney. W: Warren Douglas. Cast: CLINT WALKER, MARTHA HYER, Keenan WYNN, Nancy Kulp, Kevin Brodie, Ellen Corby, Jack Elam, Ron Ely, Leo Gordon, Med Flory, Don Haggerty, Sammy Jackson, Regis Toomey. 102m.

A Wyoming homestead family is beset by hardships including a marauding bear. Cornball rustic dialogue weakens the thin story, which is padded with lame comedy and bucolic subplots, but it's well acted.

NIGHT OF THE TIGER (1966)—*See* RIDE BEYOND VENGEANCE.

NIGHT PASSAGE (1957, UNIV). D: James Neilson. W: Borden Chase from a Norman A. Fox novel. Cast: JAMES STEWART, AUDIE MURPHY, Diane FOSTER, Dan DURYEA, Elaine STEWART, Brandon De WILDE, Jay C. Flippen, Robert J. Wilke, Olive Carey, Hugh Beaumont, Jack Elam, Herbert Anderson, Ellen Corby, James Flavin, Paul Fix, Ted Mapes. 90m.

It's brother-versus-brother (Stewart and Murphy) in a fast overplotted yarn about a stolen payroll; the disgraced railroad detective (Stewart) has to try and recover it in order to restore his good name and self-respect, but his kid brother is one of the outlaws. An excellent supporting cast, fine widescreen Rocky Mountain photography (William Daniels) and an excellent Dimitri Tiomkin-Ned Washington score, including a few songs warbled engagingly by Jimmy Stewart himself, make it worth seeing. Anthony Mann had been asked to direct this one but had begged off, largely because he didn't think much of Audie Murphy.

NOBODY LOVES A DRUNKEN INDIAN (1969)—*See* FLAP!

NOBODY LOVES FLAPPING EAGLE (1969)—*See* FLAP!

NO DEFENSE (1929, WB). D: Lloyd Bacon. W: Robert Lord from a story by J. Raleigh Davis. Cast: MONTE BLUE, Kathryn CARVER, William DESMOND, Lee Moran, May McAvoy, William Tooker. 53m.

Silly bridge-building melodrama has engineer protecting his girl friend, whose brother caused a bridge disaster. Transitional part-talkie had both dialogue and title cards.

NO NAME ON THE BULLET (1959, UNIV). D: Jack Arnold. W: Gene L. Coon from a story by Howard Amacker. Cast: AUDIE MURPHY, JOAN EVANS, Charles DRAKE, R. G. Armstrong, Virginia Grey, Warren Stevens, Karl Swensen. 77m.

A drifter (Murphy), known to be a hired killer, rides into town and won't say who his intended target is. As a result all the skeletons come out of the closets; the citizens begin to come apart at their seams, each convinced the hired gunman is after him or her. It's the customary slick Universal treatment on a minuscule budget but the unusual morality tale aspect and above-average acting make it far more interesting than most, and Murphy, much less boyish than usual in a droopy mustache, is fine.

NOOSE FOR A GUNMAN (1960, UA). D: Edward L. Cahn. W: Steve Fisher & Robert B. Gordon. Cast: JIM DAVIS, Barton MacLANE, Lyn Thomas, Harry Carey, Jr., Ted De Corsia, Lane Chandler, John Hart, Leo Gordon, Walter Sande.

Honest gunslinger in suspicious town. Low-budget film generates fair suspense; Davis is very good in it.

NORTH TO ALASKA (1960, FOX). D: Henry Hathaway. W: John Lee Mahin, Martin Rackin & Claude Binyon from a play by Laszlo Fodor. Cast: JOHN WAYNE, STEWART GRANGER, CAPUCINE, FABIAN, ERNIE KOVACS, Mickey SHAUGHNESSY, Karl Swensen, Joe Sawyer, Kathleen Freeman, John Qualen, Douglas Dick, Frank Faylen, Kermit Maynard, James Griffith, Richard Deacon. 122m.

Lusty, bawdy, sock-it-to-'em frontier comedy has lots of free-for-all slug fests. Never mind the plot. Capucine, no Maureen O'Hara, is only adequate for the role of a somewhat befuddled temptress who's fought over by prospector partners Wayne and

Granger in turn-of-the-century Alaska. Fabian (Forte), as the junior partner, is inept, but these flaws are more than made up for by a hilariously villainous performance by Ernie Kovacs. The gags and action are dandy. The music is by Lionel Newman—remember the dreadful title song?—but fortunately the movie is better than that. Wayne is great fun in it.

NORTH TO THE KLONDIKE (1942, UNIV). D: Erle C. Kenton. W: William Castle, Clarence Young, Lou Sarecky & George Bricker from a Jack London story. Cast: BRODERICK CRAWFORD, EVELYN ANKERS, Andy DEVINE, Lon Chaney, Jr., Lloyd Corrigan, Dorothy Granger, Keye Luke. 58m.

Two beefy heroes clean up the outlaws of the Far North so that the settlers can farm in peace. The brawl between Crawford and villain Chaney is sort of fun but the rest of this quickie is very dull.

NORTHWEST MOUNTED POLICE (1940, PARA). D: Cecil B. De Mille. W: Alan LeMay, Jesse Lasky, Jr., & C. Gardner Sullivan. Cast: GARY COOPER, MADELEINE CARROLL, PAULETTE GODDARD, PRESTON FOSTER, Lynne OVERMAN, Robert PRESTON, Robert RYAN, Lon Chaney, Jr., Richard Denning, Akim Tamiroff, Rod Cameron, Regis Toomey, Douglas Kennedy, Monte Blue, Nestor Paiva, George Bancroft, Chief Thundercloud, Lane Chandler, James Seay, Jack Pennick, Montagu Love, Francis J. McDonald, George E. Stone. 125m.

A Texas Ranger (Cooper) pursues a fugitive to Canada; beyond that, the plot is impossible to summarize because it's impossible to follow. Advance PR reached new highs, or lows, in hyping this dirigible: a contest was held, the prizewinner to have the glory of being escorted to the Chicago premiere of the film by Gary Cooper. Twelve thousand women competed.

De Mille's first Technicolor epic is worth seeing mainly for the Mounties' red coats that brighten the screen. That and some of the performances by members of the huge cast, and Victor Young's heroic score, are the only virtues of this overblown dud. Nearly all the "outdoor" filming was done all too obviously on De Mille's indoor sound stages. It's his worst Western, much flabbier and phonier than *The Plainsman*.

An Oscar went to Anne Bauchens for best editing (she edited all De Mille's pictures). It was the beautiful Madeleine Carroll's only Western. Paulette Goddard is wasted in a flamboyant but small role as a gypsy girl.

Cooper is fine, as usual, but there are no surprises in his character or the movie.

NORTHWEST OUTPOST (1947, REP). D: Allan Dwan. W: Richard Sale, Elizabeth Meehan, Angela Stuart & Laird Doyle from the Rudolf Friml operetta. Cast: NELSON EDDY, ILONA MASSEY, Elsa LANCHESTER, Hugo Haas, Lenore Ulric. 91m.

Musical romance is set in early California with cavalry officer Eddy mixing it up with Russian settlers. Eddy, here without Jeanette MacDonald (it is said she'd refused to work with him any more; they hated each other) is just as terrible as usual and the movie seems to reflect his wooden personality.

NORTHWEST PASSAGE (1940, MGM). D: King Vidor (& Jack Conway). W: Laurence Stallings & Talbot Jennings from Kenneth Roberts's novel. Cast: SPENCER TRACY, ROBERT YOUNG, Walter BRENNAN, Ruth HUSSEY, Nat Pendleton, Robert Barrat, Addison Richards, Louis Hector, Truman Bradley, Isabell Jewell, Hank Worden, Ray Teal, Montagu Love, Hugh Sothern. 125m.

Early Technicolor epic (cinematographers Sidney Wagner & William V. Skall) is pseudohistory about Roberts's (Tracy) Rangers and their 1760s expedition into Canada during the French and Indian War. Robert Young took over the second lead, as a young artist who learns outdoor ways, after Robert Taylor refused the part. Despite spectacular scenery and action, and Tracy's reliable performance as the tough guerrilla leader, the movie really is little more than a series of distasteful action scenes in which the white "heroes" massacre, torture, maim and even cannibalize Indians, who are painted as cowardly bad guys all. It's an excessively racist picture. For adults who can recognize its dated mores for what they are, it's a fairly good action-adventure picture, but children should be informed of its historical and moral inaccuracies. Vidor said Conway directed the last scene of the picture.

NORTHWEST RANGERS (1942, MGM). D: Joseph M. Newman. W: David Lang, Gordon Kahn & Arthur Caesar. Cast: JAMES CRAIG, Patricia DANE, William Lundigan, John Carradine, Keenan Wynn, Jack Holt, Grant Withers, Darryl Hickman. 64m.

Bald unacknowledged remake of *Manhattan Melodrama* (the film Dillinger saw just before his death) is re-set in the north woods with Mountie heroics and plenty of stock footage.

NORTHWEST STAMPEDE (1948, EL). D: Albert S. Rogell. W: Art Arthur & Lillie Hayward from a Jean Muir article. Cast: JAMES CRAIG, JOAN LESLIE, JACK OAKIE, Chill WILLS, Victor Kilian, Stanley Andrews. 79m.

Horse yarn is about rivalry between Craig and Leslie and their prizewinning mounts. Humdrum.

OH! SUSANNA (1951, REP). D: Joseph Kane. W: Charles Marquis Warren. Cast: ROD CAMERON, ADRIAN BOOTH, FORREST TUCKER, Chill WILLS, Jim Davis, Douglas Kennedy, William Ching, James Flavin. 90m.

Whites strike gold in the Black Hills. The Indians take offense when white prospectors swarm into the area. The action is complicated by a feud between an up-from-the-ranks officer (Cameron) and his stiff-backed West Point subordinate (Tucker). Familiar fare is well handled by pros.

OKLAHOMA ANNIE (1952, REP). D: R. G. Springsteen. W: Jack Townley & Charles Roberts. Cast: JOHN RUSSELL, JUDY CANOVA, Allen JENKINS, Grant Withers, Roy Barcroft, Housely Stevenson, Minerva Urecal. 90m.

Hillbilly girl cleans up Western town. Awful clunker.

THE OKLAHOMA KID (1939, WB). D: Lloyd Bacon. W: Robert H. Buckner, Warren Duff, Edward Paramore & Wally Klein. Cast: JAMES CAGNEY, HUMPHREY BOGART, Rosemary LANE, Donald CRISP, Ward Bond, Trevor Bardette, Harvey Stephens, Charles Middleton, John Miljan, Irving Bacon, Wade Boteler. 85m.

This has to do with Sooners in the Oklahoma land rush: Cagney as a good badman—a brash young outlaw who's really on the side of the good folks—and Bogart, dressed in black, as a sinister meanie. This one has the trademarked Warner pace—lightning fast action, high-speed staccato dialogue delivered very loudly, rapid cutting, accelerated movement—but in a Western it simply doesn't work. This movie has its partisans among film buffs because there are so many Cagney and Bogart fans; for Warners it was a fairly ambitious movie with a Max Steiner score and James Wong Howe's photography; Al Jennings, the old-time Oklahoma outlaw, was employed as technical adviser. The film was released in sepia and later in black-and-white. But it's terrible.

It's not that *The Oklahoma Kid* has become dated. It never was any good. Cagney and Bogart were, to say the least, unconvincing as Westerners. On its March 1939 release, *Variety* observed that the movie had "all the unbelievable hoke of a small-time Western," and they were quite right. The script, chiefly by Buckner (who also was responsible for many of the studio's thoroughly bad Errol Flynn oaters) is weak and amateurish, and so's the movie.

THE OKLAHOMAN (1956, IND). D: Francis D. Lyon. W: Daniel Ullman. Cast: JOEL McCREA, BARBARA HALE, Brad Dexter, Gloria Talbot, Douglas Dick. 80m.

A doctor settles in a small cattle town and makes enemies of tough guys when he protects an Indian. Standard oater is fairly well done.

OKLAHOMA TERRITORY (1960, UA). D: Edward L. Cahn. W: Orville Hampton. Cast: BILL WILLIAMS, Gloria TALBOT, Ted De Corsia, Walter Sande, Grant Richards. 67m.

Bad guys frame an Indian chief (De Corsia, laughably unconvincing) as a ruse to create warfare and get the Indians thrown off their lands. Williams, complete with New York accent, is not very convincing as the historical Texas prosecutor Temple Houston, who sets things right. Poor.

THE OKLAHOMA WOMAN (1956, IND). D: Roger Corman. W: Lou Rusoff. Cast: PEGGIE CASTLE, RICHARD DENNING, Cathy DOWNS, Touch (Mike) Connors, Martin Kingsley, Edmund Cobb. 72m.

Reformed ex-con, shunned by his neighbors, has to fight it out alone with an outlaw gang led by his ex-girl friend. Lots of coy sexual innuendo. It's rancid.

THE OMAHA TRAIL (1942, MGM). D: Edward Buzzell. W: Jesse Lasky, Jr., & Hugo Butler. Cast: JAMES CRAIG, RUTH HUSSEY, Dean JAGGER, Howard DA SILVA, Chill Wills, Harry Morgan, Edward Ellis, Donald Meek, Edward Buzzell. 60m.

Villain Jagger tries to keep the railroad from coming into his feudal fiefdom. Sophomoric and soporific.

ONCE UPON A HORSE (1958, UNIV). DW: Hal Kanter from a Henry G. Felsen novel. Cast: DAN ROWAN, DICK MARTIN, MARTHA HYER, Leif ERICKSON, Nita Talbot, John McGiver, James Gleason, David Burns, Kermit Maynard, Bob Steele, Tom Keene, Bob Livingston. 85m.

Two lunkhead rustlers steal a herd of cattle and then discover they need money to feed the cattle so they rob a bank. . . . The intervals between laughs are too long in this dull farce. Rowan and Martin, a decade before their TV success in *Laugh-In*, were being groomed as replacements for Dean Martin and Jerry Lewis but it didn't click.

ONCE UPON A TIME IN THE WEST (1969, PARA). D: Sergio Leone. W: Leone, Sergio Donati, Dario Argento & Bernardo Bertolucci. Cast: CHARLES BRONSON, HENRY FONDA, JASON ROBARDS, JR., CLAUDIA CARDINALE, Keenan WYNN, Frank WOLFF, Jack Elam, Woody Strode, Lionel Stander, Gabriele Ferzetti, Paulo Stoppa. 164m.

There are several parallel plots involving a mysterious harmonica-playing hero (Bronson), his on-again, off-again outlaw sidekick (Robards), a beautiful widow (Cardinale), an evil railroad boss (Wolff) and the railroad's vicious trouble shooter (Fonda, in an astonishingly villainous performance). Much of it centers around the relentless advance of the railroad, keyed to the dying tycoon who stubbornly insists on staying alive until his rails bring him to a point from which he can look upon the Pacific Ocean. Then there's a revenge plot, of course—Bronson avenging the murders of his parents many years ago.

This curiosity was the result of Hollywood's granting financial carte blanche to the Italian filmmaker whose "Dollars" movies had been so successful at the box office. Leone brought his crew (including cinematographer Tonino Delli Colli and composer Ennio Morricone) to Monument Valley to shoot much of the footage for the first made-in-America spaghetti Western; it's an enormous ponderous thing that moves, if at all, at an elephantine gait, the camera lingering endlessly on studied tableaux and sinister silhouettes and gritty oily-pore close-ups. Leone apparently has attempted in this film to distill, and completely to abstract, his conception of the basic mythology of the Western away from the reality of the West. Regarded literally the movie is mawkish, absurd, viscous and infuriating; but regarded as a surreal abstraction it can be intriguing—one man's Italianesque view, however distorted, of the essence of all the old Westerns about the epic-scale opening of the far West. There are echoes in this of Zane Grey, Rex Beach, Edna Ferber, even John Ford; but it lacks their moral spirit. This was Leone's attempt to make the definitive Western. In that aim it fails abysmally because the filmmaker clearly has no understanding at all of the fundamental morality of the Western myth. But it's an interesting failure.

ONE DESIRE (1955, UNIV). D: Jerry Hopper. W: Lawrence Roman & Robert Blees from Conrad Richter's novel *Tacey Cromwell*. Cast: ANNE BAXTER, ROCK HUDSON, Julie ADAMS, Natalie Wood, William Hopper, Betty Garde. 94m.

Lady gambler (Baxter) tries to turn respectable but finds her social ambitions in conflict with her love for a gamblin' man (Hudson). Baxter overacts, Hudson underacts; humdrum soap-opera costumer.

ONE-EYED JACKS (1960, PARA). D: George Cukor & Marlon Brando. W: Calder Willingham, Guy Trosper and (uncredited) Sam Peckinpah from a novel by Charles Neider. Cast: MARLON BRANDO, KARL MALDEN, Katy JURADO, Ben JOHNSON, Pina PELLICER, Slim Pickens, Joe Dominguez, Miriam Colon, Elisha Cook, Jr., Rodolfo Acosta, Hank Worden, Larry Duran, Ray Teal, John Dierkes. 141m.

Two bank-robbing sidekicks (Brando, Malden) split up after being pursued by a posse. Malden gets away with the swag, leaving Brando to his fate. Brando survives and ultimately goes after his ex-partner. The chase carries us across the Southwest and Old Mexico and finally California, consuming years. Brando finds his quarry, now a sheriff in Monterey on the coast. A lot of talk, romance, self-conscious posing, meaningful pauses and ferocious grimaces precede the predictable showdown.

Two bright spots of acting are Ben Johnson's greasy villain and newcomer Pina Pellicer's refreshingly different heroine. Much of the movie is photographed lushly (Charles Lang, Jr.) against the unusual scenery of the Carmel-Monterey coast. The music (Hugo Friedhofer) is acceptable. Writing, directing and acting, with few exceptions, are distressingly bad.

The movie began as an idea of Peckinpah's: he wanted to make "the definitive Billy the Kid movie," and later claimed to have done so with his *Pat Garrett and Billy the Kid*; whatever its faults, that one is vastly better than *One-Eyed Jacks*. Veteran director Cukor walked away early because the Star wouldn't take direction. Brando insisted on adding huge scenes that weren't in the script, like an enormous fiesta sequence that cost $600,000 and added nothing but tedium to the overlong movie. In skintight costumery Brando is never for a moment remotely believable as a saddle-born Westerner. Malden is equally unconvincing.

Brando's initial cut of the movie ran five hours in length; the released version, half that long, remains infuriatingly turgid. It tries to be realistic and romantic at once—the contradiction of Brando himself—and succeeds only in being an impenetrable mess. It has its partisans but the basis for their admiration eludes me.

ONE FOOT IN HELL (1960, FOX). D: James B. Clark. W: Aaron Spelling & Sydney Boehm from Spelling's "Playhouse 90" teleplay. Cast: ALAN LADD, DON MURRAY, Dan O'HERLIHY, Dolores MICHAELS, Larry Gates, Barry Coe, Karl Swenson, John Alexander. 90m.

Obsessed with hate for an Arizona town he blames for his pregnant wife's death, a Civil War veteran (Ladd) schemes to destroy the unsuspecting town; he is joined by an embittered drifter (Murray) and a fast-talking English rogue (O'Herlihy). These misfits—plus a harlot (Michaels) and a gunfighter (Coe)—join forces in what soon trails off into a standard perfunctory doomed-caper plot, but not before presenting one new gimmick: a $500 winner-take-all shoot-out in public, later used to better advantage in *A Gunfight*. The role of psycopath is unusual for Ladd; unfortunately the wooden performance is not. He looks tired in this one. Production quality is a bit better than standard, with CinemaScope photography by William C. Mellor and a score by Dominic Frontiere, but the film carries over from its TV origins a reliance on static indoor talk scenes. It's a bit offbeat, but mediocre nonetheless.

100 RIFLES (1969, FOX). D: Tom Gries. W: Gries & Clair Huffaker from a Robert MacLeod novel. Cast: JIM BROWN, RAQUEL WELCH, BURT REYNOLDS, Fernando LAMAS, Dan O'HERLIHY, Hans Gudegast (Eric Braeden), Michael Forrest, Aldo Sanbrell, Soledad Miranda. 110m.

A half-breed Yaqui from the States (Reynolds), who's robbed a bank, and an Arizona lawman (Brown), who's chasing him, come to the aid of a downtrodden tribe of Yaqui Indians (Welch, Forrest et al.) in Mexico circa 1910; the villains are the Mexican army (Lamas) and its German adviser (Gudegast) and the American boss (O'Herlihy) of the Mexican railroad. Turns out Reynolds robbed that bank to get the money to buy 100 rifles to arm the Indians in their revolt against the despotic army. Everything is stirred into a *Magnificent Seven* sort of plot but on a very teenage level, neither very original nor very believable, but Gries directed it with such lusty heroic zest that it's an entertaining, if sometimes overly brutal, example of hardboiled action adventure. It's helped by expert editing (Robert Simpson), good cinematography (Cecilio Panagua) and a fine score (Jerry Goldsmith, reprised in *The Last Hard Men*). The acting is silly in some cases, particularly Lamas and Brown, but the picture moves at such speed that such things hardly seem to matter. Raquel Welch is okay in her tough-Indian role; Reynolds is lots of fun.

ONE MORE TRAIN TO ROB (1971, UNIV). D: Andrew V. McLaglen. W: Don Tait, Dick Nelson & William Roberts. Cast: GEORGE PEPPARD, DIANA MULDAUR, John VERNON, France NUYEN, Ben Cooper, Merlin Olsen, Phil Olsen, Pamela McMyler, Steve Sandor, Richard Loo, John Doucette, Robert Donner, Marie Windsor, Harry Carey, Jr., George Chandler, Donald Barry, Hal Needham. 108m.

Train robber (Peppard) gets good-natured revenge against the ex-partner (Vernon) who framed him into prison; Chinese miners figure in the action and a good bantering relationship between Peppard and Muldaur is deftly developed. The story is slow but cleverly plotted. Nothing profound but good light amusement, nicely directed.

ONLY THE VALIANT (1951, WB). D: Gordon Douglas. W: Edmund H. North & Harry Brown from a Charles Marquis Warren novel. Cast: GREGORY PECK, Ward BOND, Gig YOUNG, Barbara Payton, Neville Brand, Warner Anderson, Lon Chaney, Jr., Jeff Corey, Michael Ansara, Steve Brodie, Hugh Sanders, Herbert Heyes. 105m.

A cavalry troop commander (Peck) tries to defend the ruins of a frontier post against Apache attack with a troop of soldiers who despise him because they think he lost his nerve in a previous battle. There's a lot of action and the grim violence is well handled. But the script is humdrum; Peck's sturdy, strong performance, and those of Bond and a few others, make it worthwhile, but this is the sort of small-scale black-and-white beleaguered outpost Western that Lippert would have handled with far more finesse than Warners. Produced by William Cagney.

OREGON PASSAGE (1957, AA). D: Paul Landres. W: Jack DeWitt from a Gordon D. Shirreffs novel. Cast: JOHN ERICSON, LOLA ALBRIGHT, Edward Platt, John Shepodd, Toni Gerry. 82m.

Cheapie concerns a well-intentioned army officer's inept interference with the lives of Indians in the Northwest. Dull.

THE OREGON TRAIL (1959, FOX). D: Gene Fowler Jr. W: Fowler & Louis Vittes. Cast: FRED MacMURRAY, GLORIA TALBOT, William BISHOP, Nina SHIPMAN, Henry Hull, John Carradine, Elizabeth Patterson, Raymond Hatton, Addison Richards. 86m.

A newspaper correspondent (MacMurray) in the early Oregon Territory tries to get to the bottom of settler-versus-Indian con-flicts. Disappointingly poor CinemaScope movie has a cast that deserves a better vehicle.

THE OUTCAST (1954, REP). D: William Witney. W: John K. Butler & Richard Wormser from a novel by (Willis) Todhunter Ballard. Cast: JOHN DEREK, JOAN EVANS, Jim DAVIS, Catherine McLeod, Ben Cooper, Slim Pickens, Harry Carey, Jr., Bob Steele. 90m.

A youth (Derek) returns to Colorado to fight his evil uncle over the question of rightful ownership of his late father's ranch. Fast-paced yarn has perky direction and good action, marred by Derek's thespic incapacities and a few too many screenplay cliches.

OUTCASTS OF POKER FLAT (1937, RKO). D: Christy Cabanne. W: John Twist & Harry Segall from the Bret Harte story. Cast: PRESTON FOSTER, JEAN MUIR, Van HEFLIN, Virginia WEIDLER, Billy Gilbert, Dick Elliott, Margaret Irving, Frank M. Thomas.

Four people are run out of a California mining camp after some mysterious murders; they take shelter from a blizzard in an isolated cabin in the Sierras, and conflicts erupt among them. This version was stagy and static and dated by the time the 1952 remake came out but the young Van Heflin turned in a strong performance here.

THE OUTCASTS OF POKER FLAT (1952, FOX). D: Joseph M. Newman. W: Edmund H. North from the Bret Harte story. Cast: DALE ROBERTSON, ANNE BAXTER, Cameron MITCHELL, Miriam HOPKINS, Craig Hill, Barbara Bates, Richard Lane, Al St. John, Si Jenks, John Ridgely. 81m.

Cameron Mitchell is good as the bad guy in this stuporous remake.

THE OUTLAW (1943, UA). D: Howard Hughes and (uncredited) Howard Hawks. W: Jules Furthman. Cast: WALTER HUSTON, JANE RUSSELL, JACK BEUTEL, THOMAS MITCHELL, Joe Sawyer, Mimi Aguglia, Lee "Lasses" White, Emery Parnell. 116m.

Fanciful rendition of the Billy the Kid (Beutel) legend introduces not only Pat Garrett (Mitchell) but also Doc Holliday (Huston), with the emphasis on heavy-breathing sex by innuendo when the wounded Billy is nursed back to health by Jane Russell. Producer-director Hughes designed a cantilevered brassiere to enhance Russell's already ample bust, and Hughes said at the time—referring to Russell—there were two good reasons why every American male wanted to see *The Outlaw*. One of the few movies that the adjective "notorious" describes accurately, it was filmed in 1940, released in 1943, but a clamor for censorship withheld its general distribution until 1950, by which time it was no longer clear what the fuss had been about: its appearance, or more specifically Russell's, seemed tame by then. Both releases were accompanied by enormous crude publicity, so there was inevitable critical overreaction. Actually, compared with other oaters of the early 1940s it's not a bad Western, merely a mediocre one. The plot is cornball, but no more so than that of, say, *Billy the Kid*. The acting by Huston is superb, by Mitchell excellent; of Beutel and Russell—well, the less said, the better. It's a spirited movie, helped by Gregg Toland's black-and-white cinematography and Victor Young's score. In his zeal, Hughes shot 470,000 feet of film (about five times the normal amount), of which 10,450 feet were used in the final release version. Amusingly, when it was reissued to theatres in 1976 this once-notorious movie was given a "G" rating ("suitable for general family audiences") by the Motion Picture Association.

THE OUTLAW JOSEY WALES (1976, WB). D: Clint Eastwood and (uncredited) Philip Kaufman. W: Kaufman & Sonya Chernus from a Forrest Carter novel. Cast: CLINT EASTWOOD, Sondra LOCKE, Chief Dan GEORGE, John VERNON, Bill McKINNEY, Paula Trueman, Will Sampson, Sam Bottoms, Joyce Jameson, Royal Dano, John Russell, John Quade. 135m.

A revenge oater, this opens with a rudimentary motivational scene in which a Missouri farmer (Eastwood) watches helplessly while Yankee Redlegs (led by McKinney) pillage his farm and murder his wife and son. He then joins up with Reb guerrillas led by Bloody Bill Anderson (Russell) in order to chase the Redlegs. After the Civil War ends he refuses to surrender, determined to carry out his vendetta. Pursued by enemies he flees from one adventure to another—with Indians, settlers, Comanchero slavers, so forth. Episodic rambling tale tries for epic stature; at the end there's a predictable shoot-out. The film is very long and lavishly produced with high-class arty photography (Bruce Surtees) some of which is too dark and makes it hard to see what's going on. Opening action montage of battle scenes is excellently filmed, but Wales slaughters so many opponents in the first reel that all suspense is lost because we know he's invincible and we don't worry about him thereafter. Eastwood's concept of characterization is to give Wales the trait of spitting tobacco juice on anything or anyone

he doesn't like (usually just before killing them). The rest of the characterizations are equally rudimentary.

Eastwood produced this one and fired its original director (Kaufman) after a few days' shooting. He directed the rest of it quite well, but it's curiously childish in some ways—a kiddie show for the bloodthirsty. It has too much residual spaghetti-oater style, but it tries; it's entertaining.

OUTLAW QUEEN (1957, IND). D: Herbert Greene. W: Pete LaRoche. Cast: ANDREA KING, ROBERT CLARKE, HARRY JAMES, Kenne Duncan, I. Stanford Jolley, Vince Barnett, Jack Perrin. 70m.

Cheap stupid indie has one surprise: presence of bandleader Harry James.

THE OUTLAW'S DAUGHTER (1954, FOX). D: Wesley Barry. W: Samuel Roeca. Cast: BILL WILLIAMS, JIM DAVIS, Kelly RYAN, Elisha Cook, Jr., Guinn "Big Boy" Williams, Sara Haden, George Cleveland. 75m.

A stagecoach is robbed; the daughter of an old outlaw is implicated; enter our hero to straighten things out. Poor.

THE OUTLAWS IS COMING (1965, COL). D: Norman Maurer. W: Maurer & Elwood Ullman. Cast: THE THREE STOOGES (Moe Howard, Larry Howard, Joe De Rita), Adam WEST, Nancy KOVACK, Henry Gibson, Mort Mills. 89m.

The Stooges are teamed with a timid Adam ("Batman") West and a gal called Annie Oakley (Kovack) against ferocious but stupid outlaws. There are moments of amusing satire but most of it is the usual head batting, nose twisting, yelling sort of low comedy for which the Stooges were known; they were in their sixties when this, one of the last of their films, was made, and were far too long in the tooth for this kind of shenanigans. It's in black-and-white.

THE OUTLAW'S SON (1957, UA). D: Lesley Selander. W: Richard A. Simmons from a Clifton Adams novel. Cast: DANE CLARK, Lori NELSON, Ben COOPER, Ellen DREW, Eddie Foy III. 87m.

Reunion of a gunfighter (Clark) and the son he deserted long ago (Cooper) is tame and woefully predictable. In black-and-white.

OUTLAW TERRITORY (1953)—*See* HANNAH LEE.

OUTLAW TREASURE (1955, UA). D: Oliver Drake. W: John Carpenter. Cast: JOHN FORBES, Adele JERGENS, Glenn LANGAN, Michael Whalen, Harry Lauter, Frank Jenks, Hal Baylor. 83m.

This serves up an army troubleshooter and the James brothers looking for a lost federal gold shipment—a familiar mixture, badly stirred.

In this film and in *I Killed Wild Bill Hickok* (1956), writer-producer Carpenter billed himself as "Forbes" in the cast credits. Previously he had starred as "Carpenter" in *Badman's Gold, Son of the Renegade* and *The Lawless Rider*. (It should be noted that this is not the same John Carpenter who made a name for himself as a director of thrillers in the late 1970s.) Carpenter's shoestring indie production company was called Royal West Productions; most of his ten-cent movies were independent releases that rarely turned up anywhere except at the bottom of quadruple bills in drive-in cinemas; this one, however, was released through a major company and therefore is a bit more accessible than the others.

Carpenter's often hysterical movies are not nearly as bad as the legendary films of Edward D. Wood, Jr. (*Glen or Glenda, Plan 9 From Outer Space*) but they can be pretty awful. Now and then they surprise you with an oddball camera angle, a sudden cute line of dialogue or a ludicrously posed tableau; some of the choreography in Carpenter's gunfight scenes is astonishing, and the grimacing and grunting seems inspired by the war games of nine-year-olds. Carpenter's oaters created a fantasy world all their own. Like the Westerns of producer A.C. Lyles they add an interesting footnote to the history of the genre.

OUTLAW WOMEN (1952, LIP). D: Sam Newfield. W: Orville H. Hampton. Cast: MARIE WINDSOR, Richard Rober, Jacqueline Fontaine, Allan Nixon, Jackie Coogan.

Tough lady gamblers fight outlaws to see who gets to run the town. You won't care; it's a totally incompetent movie.

THE OUTRAGE (1964, MGM). D: Martin Ritt. W: Fay & Michael Kanin, based on the *Rashomon* stories by Ryunosuke Akutagawa and the Japanese film *Rashomon*. Cast: PAUL NEWMAN, LAURENCE HARVEY, CLAIRE BLOOM, EDWARD G. ROBINSON, William SHATNER, Howard DA SILVA, Albert Salmi, Thomas Chalmers, Paul Fix. 97m.

Rashomon is a classic Japanese play and film about three people in the wilderness: a husband and wife and the bandit who kidnaps them, then rapes the wife and murders the husband. The story is told four times: by each of the participants and by an observer. In the Japanese movie this four-times-telling illustrates the elusiveness and illusiveness of truth. In this Hollywood Western version it merely provides four boring recitations of the same badly acted nonsense. Despite the big names the directing is very poor, the screenplay sophomoric. In black-and-white.

THE OUTRIDERS (1950, MGM). D: Roy Rowland. W: Irving Ravetch. Cast: JOEL McCREA, ARLENE DAHL, BARRY SULLIVAN, James WHITMORE, Claude JARMAN, Jr., Ramon Novarro, Jeff Corey, Ted De Corsia, Martin Garralaga, Russell Simpson, Dorothy Adams. 93m.

Three Civil War outlaws join a gold-laden wagon train destined for ambush. The action includes stampedes, battles with Apaches and Pawnees, a final showdown between good-partner McCrea and bad-partner Sullivan, and the big Rebel ambush; the action is well staged and frequent, photographed nicely in color by Charles Shoenbaum and accompanied by an Andre Previn score; the acting is not notable—Dahl, Jarman and Novarro are pretty bad, although Whitmore is funny. Fairly big effort, with hundreds of extras, is okay as a time-killer but not much more.

OUT WEST WITH THE HARDYS (1938, MGM). D: George B. Seitz. W: Kay Van Riper, Agnes C. Johnson & Wiliam Ludwig, based on characters created by Aurania Rouverol. Cast: LEWIS STONE, MICKEY ROONEY, Cecilia PARKER, Fay HOLDEN, Ann Rutherford, Tom Neal, Sara Haden, Don Castle, Virginia Weidler, Gordon Jones, Ralph Morgan. 84m.

The series featuring Andy and Judge Hardy (Rooney, Stone) contained fourteen movies that in ten years grossed $75 million back in the days when the dollar was still worth fifty cents. This, the Hardys' Western adventure, was the biggest grosser of them all. The plot is creaky—land-grabbers try to force an old buddy of the judge's off his ranch—and Rooney seems in danger of disappearing altogether inside his huge hat and voluminous sheepskin chaps, but if you like the Andy Hardy pix it's a good one.

THE OVERLANDERS (1946, IND). D: Harry Watt. W: Watt & Dora Birtles. Cast: CHIPS RAFFERTY, Daphne CAMPBELL, Peter Pagan, John Fernside, John Nugent Hayward, Jean Blue, Helen Grieve, Frank Ransome.

Stirring docu-drama relates the true story of a 1,600-mile cattle drive across Australia in 1942—a bold group of Aussies driving their herd across half the continent to get away from a threatened Japanese invasion. Rafferty is dandy as Dan McAlpine, rugged trail

THE MISSOURI BREAKS
(1976): Marlon Brando, Jack
Nicholson. Contemptible
self-indulgent caricature.
United Artists

MONTE WALSH (1970):
Lee Marvin, Jack Palance.
An elegiac depiction with
the look of Remington
paintings. National General
Pictures

MY DARLING CLEM-
ENTINE (1946): Henry
Fonda, Victor Mature.
Wyatt Earp and Doc Holli-
day. A great legendary myth
of stunning power.
Twentieth Century-Fox

MY LITTLE CHICKADEE
(1940): Joseph Calleia, Mae
West, W. C. Fields. Absurd,
outrageous and hilarious.
Universal Pictures

THE NAKED SPUR (1953):
James Stewart, Robert Ryan,
Janet Leigh, Ralph Meeker,
Millard Mitchell. Photo shows
the entire speaking cast and
this splendidly effective
suspense movie was shot
entirely outdoors. MGM

NEVADA (1944): Richard Martin
(on horse with guitar), Guinn
"Big Boy" Williams (on horse with
rope), Robert Mitchum (rope
around neck). Grooming Mitchum
as a "B" oater star. RKO Radio
Pictures

NEVADA SMITH (1966):
Steven McQueen, Brian
Keith. Keith's brief appearance is the only bright spot
in this elephantine adventure. Paramount Pictures

NIGHT PASSAGE (1957):
Audie Murphy, James
Stewart. They play brothers
named "Grant" and "Lee,"
on opposite sides of the law.
Universal Pictures

NOOSE FOR A GUNMAN
(1960): Jim Davis as an honest
gunslinger in a suspicious town. As
usual he's better than the picture
deserves. United Artists

NORTHWEST MOUNTED
POLICE (1940): Preston Foster,
Robert Preston. The director's
first Technicolor epic is run of
De Mille. Paramount Pictures

THE OKLAHOMA KID
(1939): Humphrey Bogart,
James Cagney. The two
were, to say the least, unconvincing as Westerners.
Warner Brothers

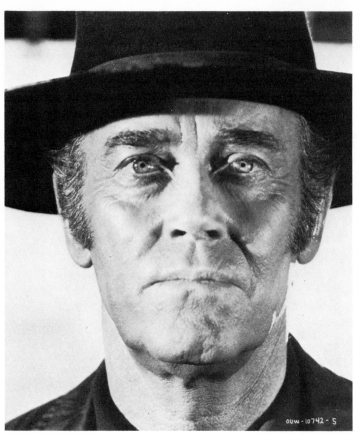

ONCE UPON A TIME IN
THE WEST (1969): Henry
Fonda in an astonishingly
villainous performance.
Studied tableaux, sinister
silhouettes and gritty
oily-pore close-ups.
Paramount Pictures

THE OUTLAW (1943):
Jane Russell, Jack Beutel.
One of the few movies that
the adjective "notorious"
describes accurately.
United Artists

THE OUTLAW JOSEY WALES
(1976): Clint Eastwood slaughters
so many opponents in the first reel
that all suspense is lost because we
know he's invincible. Warner
Brothers

boss who nurses a thousand half-wild cattle and a mismatched crew of men and women across some of the harshest country in the world. Australia's first major international film since silent days, it made for a first-rate debut. Fine black-and-white photography (Sigmund Borradale) and score (John Ireland). A few interiors were shot at Ealing Studios in England but all the outdoor footage (most of the movie) was done on the spot in Australia, filmed with spare economy and unembellished honesty.

OVERLAND PACIFIC (1954, UA). **D: Fred F. Sears. W: J. Robert Bren, Gladys Atwater, Martin Goldsmith & Frederic L. Fox. Cast: JOCK MAHONEY, PEGGIE CASTLE, Adele JERGENS, William BISHOP, Chubby Johnson, Walter Sande, George Eldredge. 73m.**

The railroad sends an undercover agent to find out who's inciting the Indians to obstruct the construction of the line. Juvenile tripe.

THE OX-BOW INCIDENT (1943, FOX). **D: William Wellman. W: Lamar Trotti from Walter Van Tilburg Clark's novel. Cast: HENRY FONDA, Mary Beth HUGHES, Dana ANDREWS, Anthony QUINN, William Eythe, Jane Darwell, Frank Conroy, Francis Ford, Harry Morgan, Harry Davenport, Tom London, Billy Benedict, Marc Lawrence, Rondo Hatton, Victor Kilian, Paul Hurst, Chris-Pin Martin, Stanley Andrews, George Chandler, Hank Bell. 75m.**

Three men (Andrews, Quinn, Ford) are accused of a crime. A lynch mob led by an ex-Civil War general (Conroy) and a ranch matriarch (Darwell) listens coldly to the three men's protestations of innocence. A pair of young drifting cowhands, strangers (Fonda, Eythe), are caught up in it, uncertain what to believe. They remain observers: outsiders, skeptics. They do not intervene. Finally the three men are lynched. Afterward the mob learns that its victims were innocent.

That's the sum of the story; but the telling of it is devastating. A strong, grim, uncompromising movie, *The Ox-Bow Incident* is oft respected but seldom enjoyed by audiences: it lost money at the box office and does not draw big ratings when shown on TV. It has proved too deterministic for most casual moviegoers, and in truth, in dramatic terms it's a lousy story: the protagonists do very little except watch and comment. The story is what the title implies—an incident, depicted in a short quick movie—and it's rather preachy and talky, somewhat dated now, but it retains the ability to clout you between the eyes. Photographed with great artistry in black-and-white by Arthur Miller, *The Ox-Bow Incident* was nominated for the Academy Award as best picture. It is a classic film but, I think, not a classic Western; although it is set in the West of 1885 it is essentially a thematic film on the subject of lynch-mob violence: it has no hero and does not reflect the traditional mythology.

THE PAINTED DESERT (1930, RKO). **D: Howard Higgin. W: Higgin & Tom Buckingham. Cast: WILLIAM BOYD, HELEN TWELVETREES, William FARNUM, Clark GABLE, J. Farrell MacDonald, Richard Cramer, James Mason, Charles Sellon.**

A villain (Gable) stirs up the hatreds of two old-time feudists (Farnum, MacDonald) so he can get his hands on their properties; an engineer (Boyd) reveals his dastardly plottings and reconciles the old boys. This was one of the first "A" Westerns to be filmed outdoors on location after the advent of talkies; the location photography (Ed Snyder) was very good for its time. Of interest to film buffs because it marked one of William Boyd's few appearances in a Western prior to his monopolizing the Hopalong Cassidy image, and it marked Clark Gable's first featured movie role.

THE PAINTED DESERT (1938, RKO). **D: David Howard. W: Jack Cunningham, Oliver Drake & John Rathmell. Cast: GEORGE O'BRIEN, RAY WHITLEY, Laraine JOHNSON (DAY), Fred Kohler, Harry Cording, Lloyd Ingraham.**

Villain (Kohler) tries to block tungsten-ore shipments to get the mine for himself; our hero (O'Brien) steps in to save the day. Routine.

PAINT YOUR WAGON (1969, PARA). **D: Joshua Logan. W: Alan Jay Lerner & Paddy Chayevsky from the Broadway musical comedy by Lerner & Loewe. Cast: LEE MARVIN, CLINT EASTWOOD, JEAN SEBERG, Harve PRESNELL, Ray WALSTON, Tom Ligon, Alan Baxter, John Mitchum, Sue Casey. 166m.**

Disastrous adaptation of the 1948 Broadway musical about a ménage-à-trois amid the whorehouses of a California boom camp in gold-rush days ranks among the more costly movie failures (it cost $20 million in 1969 dollars) but nowhere does one see much evidence of the lavish expenditures. The choreography seems to consist exclusively of boots trampling in mud; the production numbers seem peopled by eight miners and four whores. The miscasting is outrageous—of the principals only Presnell has a singing voice, and only Marvin is comfortable in a comedic role—he simply repeats his bawdy drunk from *Cat Ballou* but this time he overdoes it and doesn't recapture its engaging madness. Eastwood is simply wooden. A few critics seemed surprised that he could carry a tune at all, and praised him for it, but his singing voice is lousy—not that it matters; the music is mediocre, one of Loewe's poorest efforts, and the banal plot is a new one laid on top of the Broadway original; it's purely and simply bad—bad drama and bad taste, stupefyingly crude.

THE PALEFACE (1948, PARA). D: Norman Z. McLeod. W: Edmund Hartman, Frank Tashlin & Jack Rose. Cast: BOB HOPE, JANE RUSSELL, Jeff YORK, Iris Adrian, Jack Searle, Robert Armstrong, Henry Brandon, Clem Bevans, Dick Elliott, Robert Watson, Lane Chandler, Iron Eyes Cody, Stanley Andrews, Olin Howlin, Francis J. McDonald, Nestor Paiva, Earl Hodgins, Dorothy Granger, George Chandler, Harry Harvey. 91m.

A cowardly dentist (Hope) keeps blundering into jeopardy; the sharpshooting Calamity Jane (Russell) keeps saving his skin. Score (Victor Young) is bolstered by songs (Jay Livingston) including the Academy Award-winning "Buttons and Bows"; Ray Rennahan's color photography is fine. Big cast, and it's a fair-to-middling frontier farce that burlesques the cliches amusingly; at times engaging. But, unusually, the sequel was better: see *Son of Paleface*. This one was remade as *The Shakiest Gun in the West*.

PANHANDLE (1948, AA). D: Lesley Selander. W: John C. Champion & Blake Edwards. Cast: ROD CAMERON, CATHY DOWNS, Reed HADLEY, Anne Gwynne, Rory Mallinson, Blake Edwards, Alex Gerry.

Hero cleans up outlaw territory, again, but it's a sturdy little "A-minus" oater with good production, fast direction, snappy script.

PARDNERS (1956, PARA). D: Norman Taurog. W: Jerry Lewis, Jr., Sidney Sheldon & Mervin J. Houser. Songs by Sammy Cahn & Jimmy Van Heusen. Cast: DEAN MARTIN, JERRY LEWIS, Lori NELSON, Agnes MOOREHEAD, Jackie Loughery, Jeff Morrow, Lon Chaney, Jr., John Baragrey. 90m.

A zany tenderfoot (Lewis) and an easygoing cowhand (Martin) manage to blunder their way to cleaning up a frontier town. Unacknowledged remake of *Rhythm on the Range* adds little to the original except an agreeable supporting cast, notably Moorehead as Lewis's wealthy imperious mother. This was the twelfth Martin & Lewis cinecomedy; the formula was getting stale.

THE PARSON AND THE OUTLAW (1957, COL). D: Oliver Drake. W: Drake & John Mantley. Cast: ANTHONY DEXTER, MARIE WINDSOR, SONNY TUFTS, Buddy ROGERS, Jean PARKER, Bob Steele. 71m.

Yet another Billy the Kid movie has the Kid (Dexter) trying to retire and hang up his guns but of course he has to fight it out with baddies. Dexter made his film debut in the title role of the bio-pic *Valentino*, the result of his close physical resemblance to the silent-film star; after that one, every one of Dexter's half-dozen movies was a "comeback" but he never made it.

THE PARSON OF PANAMINT (1941, PARA). D: William McGann. W: Harold Shumate & Adrian Scott from a Peter B. Kyne novel. Cast: CHARLES RUGGLES, ELLEN DREW, Joseph SCHILDKRAUT, Philip Terry, Porter Hall. 84m.

A preacher (Terry) is nearly lynched in a wild Western gold camp. Oddball yarn was gentle but fairly well handled; not bad for its time.

PASSAGE WEST (1951, PARA). D: Lewis R. Foster. W: Foster & Nedrick Young. Cast: JOHN PAYNE, DENNIS O'KEEFE, Arleen WHELAN, Mary Beth Hughes, Dooley Wilson, Frank Faylen, Richard Travis. 80m.

A pair of fugitive outlaws join up with a wagon train in Indian country; you can guess the rest. Payne and O'Keefe worked well together (compare *Eagle and the Hawk*) but the script was nothing special.

PASSION (1954, RKO). D: Allan Dwan. W: Beatrice A. Dresher, Josef Leytes, Miguel Padilla & Howard Estabrook. Cast: CORNEL WILDE, YVONNE De CARLO, Raymond BURR, Lon Chaney, Jr., John Qualen, Rodolfo Acosta, Anthony Caruso. 84m.

Costumer set in early California has a good deal of heavy breathing and a Bob Steele plot.

PAT GARRETT AND BILLY THE KID (1973, MGM). D: Sam Peckinpah. W: Rudolph Wurlitzer. Cast: JAMES COBURN, KRIS KRISTOFFERSON, Bob DYLAN, Jason ROBARDS, Jr., Barry SULLIVAN, Katy JURADO, Richard Jaeckel, Rita Coolidge, L.Q. Jones, Chill Wills, Slim Pickens, Jack Elam, Gene Evans, R.G. Armstrong, Paul Fix, Luke Askew, Matt Clark, John Chandler Davis, John Beck, Harry Dean Stanton, Sam Peckinpah. 105m.

The opening sequence is a wonderful example of excessive redundancy: first we see

Billy the Kid (Kristofferson) and some of his wild buddies shooting the heads off chickens that have been buried up to the necks in sand. It's a very bloody scene. *Then* the credits say, "Directed by Sam Peckinpah."

Pictorially, Peckinpah is John Ford's heir; his camera compositions here, abetted by cinematographer John Coquillon, are wonderful. The story is Peckinpah's as well, even though he didn't take a writing credit; he'd been trying to make this picture for years. (His first attempt, which was taken out of his hands and went awry, ended up as *One-Eyed Jacks*.) Here he uses the Billy the Kid legend as a peg on which to hang his pet theme of the dying of the old ways and their replacement by impersonal evil; his Garrett (Coburn) is almost identical to the character played by Robert Ryan in *The Wild Bunch*—the survivor who's willing to compromise and is corrupted by faceless tycoons and goes out to kill his old comrade. Peckinpah's theme is summed up in one terse exchange. Garrett: "Times are changing, Bill." The Kid: "Times, maybe. Not me." And elsewhere it's pointed out that the Kid will die because "he's got too much play in him" while Garrett doesn't have enough. Billy is depicted as a mercurially engaging killer who enjoys murder as if it were sexual ritual; the corpses pile up like cattle in a slaughterhouse. Garrett, going through Freudian agonizing, keeps avoiding the final confrontation while the Kid's body count keeps soaring; the killings develop a metronomic regularity.

The movie's morality is distorted and there are other poverties as well. Kristofferson, thirty-six at the time, is hardly a kid. Cameos by stars Robards (as Governor Lew Wallace) and Sullivan (as rancher John Chisum, a role virtually eliminated from the theatrical release print but restored in part to the television version) add nothing, and all the good veteran character-actors are wasted in pointless one-shot appearances, many of them (Elam, Jones, Pickens, Armstrong) only appearing long enough to get shot to death in gory slow-motion. There is unforgivable pretentiousness in such awful script devices as the character "Alias" (Bob Dylan, in his movie debut) and the heavy-handed overuse of painfully obvious symbols (Billy on a crucifix, for example).

Dylan's soundtrack score is anachronistic; the lyrics are unusually poor and his voice, as always, is off-key—Dylan seems tone-deaf; there are people who can stand his singing but I'm not one of them. Peckinpah insisted the pervasive use of Dylan's rancid songs wasn't his idea; he also said MGM had cut

about fifteen minutes from his print, butchering the motivations and sense of the story. That may be, but he made the same self-excusing claim for *Major Dundee* and it didn't hold water there. Six film editors are credited in the titles; the result is a rambling, brutal shambles of a movie, very self-conscious and self-indulgent, but sometimes fascinating and always pictorially beautiful.

THE PATHFINDER (1952, COL). D: Sidney Salkow. W: Robert E. Kent from James Fenimore Cooper's novel. Cast: GEORGE MONTGOMERY, HELENA CARTER, Jay SILVERHEELS, Elena Verdugo, Walter Kingsford, Stephen Bekassy, Rodd Redwing, Chief Yowlachie. 78m.

There's plenty of action but not much of a script in this cheap adaptation of the yarn about frontier skirmishes on the Great Lakes during the French and Indian War.

PAWNEE (1957, REP). D: George Waggner. W: Waggner, Louis Vittes & Endre Bohem. Cast: GEORGE MONTGOMERY, LOLA ALBRIGHT, Bill WILLIAMS, Raymond Hatton, Francis J. McDonald. 80m.

The one about the white man who was raised by Indians and faces a conflict of allegiances. Much better done in *Hombre*. This one's trite.

THE PEACEMAKER (1956, UA). D: Ted Post. W: Hal Richards & Jay Ingram from a Richard Poole novel. Cast: James MITCHELL, Rosemarie BOWE, Jess Barker, Dorothy Patrick, Robert Armstrong, Jan Merlin, Hugh Sanders. 81m.

Gunslinger-turned-preacher buckles on his guns and cleans up a wild town. Again. Dirt-cheap.

A PERILOUS JOURNEY (1953, REP). D: R. G. Springsteen. W: Richard Wormser from a novel by Vingie Roe. Cast: VERA HRUBA RALSTON, SCOTT BRADY, DAVID BRIAN, Virginia GREY, Ben Cooper, Hope Emerson, Veda Ann Borg, Leif Erickson. 90m.

A gang of women ship out to California. They journey by wagon train up to the gold fields to find husbands during the 'forty-niner rush. A sort of warm-up for *Jubilee Trail*, this was well produced with a big (for Republic) budget that studio owner Herbert J. Yates lavished on his wife, the ever-tearful ex-skating star Ralston.

THE PERSUADER (1957, AA). D: Dick Ross. W: Curtis Kenyon. Cast: JAMES CRAIG, Kristine MILLER, William TALMAN, Darryl Hickman, Joyce Compton. 71m.

Yet again the one about the parson who straps on his guns to clean up the town. Very dull.

THE PHANTOM STAGECOACH (1957, COL). D: Ray Nazarro. W: David Lang. Cast: WILLIAM BISHOP, Kathleen CROWLEY, Hugh Sanders, Richard Webb, Lane Bradford, Frank Ferguson. 69m.

Competition between stagecoach companies provides the conflict for this routine oater with a lower-case cast of competent but unexciting players.

PIERRE OF THE PLAINS (1942, MGM). D: George B. Seitz. W: Lawrence Kimble & Bertram Millhauser from Edgar Selwyn's play. Cast: JOHN CARROLL, RUTH HUSSEY, Bruce CABOT, Evelyn Ankers, Reginald Owen, Sheldon Leonard, Henry Travers.

Lackluster comedy features Carroll, absurdly, as a French-Canadian frontiersman-scalawag who guides dudes west. You have to hear his phony French accent to believe it.

PILLARS OF THE SKY (1956, UNIV). D: George Marshall. W: Sam Rolfe from Will Henry's novel. Cast: JEFF CHANDLER, DOROTHY MALONE, Ward BOND, Keith ANDES, Lee Marvin. 96m.

A hard-drinking crude womanizing sergeant (Chandler, in an offbeat role) ends up commanding a cavalry unit charged with building a fort and a road in Indian country. Good scenery and plenty of hard-boiled action; it's a pretty good adaptation of the gritty novel.

PIRATES OF MONTEREY (1947, UNIV). D: Alfred L. Werker. W: Sam Hellman, Margaret B. Wilder, Edward T. Lowe & Bradford Ropes. Cast: ROD CAMERON, MARIA MONTEZ, Gilbert ROLAND, Gale Sondergaard, Mikhail Rasumny, Tamara Shayne, Philip Reed. 77m.

Mexicans and gringos vie for control of California in the 1840s; it's a big historical subject but the presence of Cameron and Montez (The "Queen of the B's" who usually played jungle princesses) indicates its level of sophistication. It's in color, a routine programmer with ambitions.

PISTOLERO (1967)—*See* THE LAST CHALLENGE.

THE PLAINSMAN (1936, PARA). D: Cecil B. De Mille. W: Waldemar Young, Harold Lamb, Courtney R. Cooper, Lynn Riggs, Grover Jones & Jeanie Macpherson from a book by Frank Wilstach. Cast: GARY COOPER, JEAN ARTHUR, James ELLISON, Helen BURGESS, Charles BICKFORD, Anthony Quinn, Porter Hall, George "Gabby" Hayes, Chief Thundercloud, John Miljan, Fuzzy Knight, Francis J. McDonald, Paul Harvey, Victor Varconi, Frank McGlynn, Fred Kohler, Harry Woods. 115m.

Wild Bill Hickok (Cooper), Buffalo Bill Cody (Ellison), Calamity Jane (Arthur) and Louisa Cody (Burgess) mix it up with a gunrunning villain (Bickford) and a lot of Indians and killer Jack McCall (Hall) in this heap big De Mille melodrama. The action is plentiful and the performances by most of the players are spirited. But it's juvenile, an overblown programmer.

De Mille hated working outdoors; virtually the entire movie was shot on the Paramount lot with painted backdrops, cycloramas and rear projection. It shows, even though most of the photography (Victor Milner & George Robinson) is expert and the action sequences (by second-unit director Arthur Rosson) are rousing.

Burgess was being groomed for major stardom but died of pneumonia in 1937. James "Shamrock" Ellison soon returned to his sidekick niche in the Hopalong Cassidy "B" series because this wasn't the kind of movie that made a star of anybody; it was entirely De Mille's and Cooper's show, although Arthur's Calamity Jane is funny and sometimes touching. The movie is loosely based on Wilstach's *Prince of Pistoleers*, a whitewashed "biography" of Hickok, but by the time all those screenwriters got done messing with it there wasn't much history or even pseudohistory left. (William S. Hart's silent *Wild Bill Hickok*, which emphasized Hickok's failing eyesight toward the end, was a more poignant treatment of the subject.) At least it is to De Mille's credit that he did not listen to the advisers who wanted to tack on a happy ending. Hickok dies in *The Plainsman*, and the importance of that fact is in its obvious effect on Cooper's performance: knowing the ending, Cooper evidently decided to play Hickok as a doomed tragic hero, and the deliberate dignified grandeur with which he plays the role presages his performances in *The Westerner* and *High Noon*; it is this towering portrayal that makes *The Plainsman* interesting in spite of its poor script and lurching pace and humorless turgid length. Cooper doesn't do much with Hickok as a character, but he somehow magnifies his very presence on the screen into a vaster-than-life portentousness; one leaves the film remembering virtually nothing except Cooper. *The Plainsman* isn't much of a movie but it did establish Cooper permanently as the archetypal Western hero.

THE PLAINSMAN (1966, UNIV). D: David Lowell Rich. W: Michael Blankfort from the screenplay for the 1936 film. Cast: DON MURRAY, Abby DALTON, Guy STOCK-WELL, Bradford DILLMAN, Leslie NIEL-SEN, Emily Banks, Lane Chandler, Henry Silva, Simon Oakland, Edward Burns. 92m.

The original wasn't great but at least it had spectacle and larger-than-life stars. Murray is pleasant, and a good actor, but none of the principals here looks real on horseback; the story hasn't improved any in thirty years; it's a cheap TV-style remake.

THE PLAINSMAN AND THE LADY (1946, REP). Also titled: DRUMBEATS OVER WYOMING. D: Joseph Kane. W: Richard Wormser, Michael Uris & Ralph Spence. Cast: WILLIAM ELLIOTT, VERA HRUBA RALSTON, Gail PATRICK, Joseph SCHILDKRAUT, Andy Clyde, Donald "Red" Barry, Hal Taliaferro, Byron Foulger. 87m.

The plot is about getting the Pony Express through, with the emphasis on cornball romancing. Longwinded "B" drivel was earmarked for John Wayne but the Duke had made two Republic features with Ralston and both of them had laid eggs and he refused to touch this one with a rake. It's one of Elliott's least enjoyable films, though pictorially impressive.

THE PLUNDERERS (1948, REP). D: Joseph Kane. W: Gerald Geraghty, Gerald D. Adams & James Edward Grant. Cast: ROD CAMERON, Ilona MASSEY, Forrest TUCKER, Adrian Booth. 87m.

Outlaw (Tucker) joins cavalry officer (Cameron) to fight Indians. Plenty of cliches but it's a good cast for this kind of picture and it zips right along. In color.

THE PLUNDERERS (1960, AA). D: Joseph Pevney. W: Bob Barbash. Cast: JEFF CHANDLER, JOHN SAXON, Marsha HUNT, Dolores HART, Jay C. Flippen, Ray Stricklyn, Roger Torrey, James Westerfield. 93m.

Four young hoodlums terrorize a cowardly town; it befalls a frightened, reluctant one-armed rancher (Chandler) to deal with the delinquents. In black-and-white (photography by Eugene Polito) with a good score (Leonard Rosenman), it's well directed but the script is predictable.

PLUNDERERS OF PAINTED FLATS (1959, REP). D: Albert C. Gannaway. W: John Green & Phil Shuken. Cast: JOHN CARROLL, CORINNE CALVET, Skip HOMEIER, George MACREADY, Edmund Lowe, Bea Benaderet, Madge Kennedy. 77m.

A gunfighter (Carroll) joins up with a kid (Homeier) who's trailing his pa's killer (Macready). Feeble routine oater was in black-and-white; it was Republic's last release. The company folded, the lot was sold to CBS television, the name and the eagle logo were sold to strangers and the most important of the "B" Western studios was gone.

POCKET MONEY (1972, NGP). D: Stuart Rosenberg. W: Terence Malick & John Gay from J. P. S. Brown's novel *Jim Kane*. Cast: PAUL NEWMAN, LEE MARVIN, Strother MARTIN, Wayne ROGERS, Christine BELFORD, Matt Clark, Hector Elizondo, Kelly Jean Peters, Fred Graham. 102m.

A conniving crook (Marvin) joins a stupid gullible cowhand (Newman) to do a shady cattle-buying job in modern Mexico for a leering chiseler (Martin). The only way one can figure out what the story is about is to read Brown's novel; the movie makes no sense whatever. It's slow, dull and genuinely stupid, a dreary waste of good actors.

The two stars appear bored and half-drunk throughout. Filmed partly in Tucson (cinematographer Laszlo Kovacs) with a "cute" score (Alex North) and a witless Carol King title song, this was the first film produced by the Paul Newman-Sidney Poitier-Barbra Streisand-Steve McQueen company "First Artists" (an emulation of United Artists, which had been formed in the 1920s by Charlie Chaplin, Douglas Fairbanks, Mary Pickford and D.W. Griffith). It didn't bode well for the fledgling corporation. Much of the blame for this turkey probably must be laid against its director and its editor (Bob Wyman); it's ragged, disjointed and pointless.

PONY EXPRESS (1953, PARA). D: Jerry Hopper. W: Charles Marquis Warren & Frank Gruber. Cast: CHARLTON HESTON, FORREST TUCKER, RHONDA FLEMING, JAN STERLING, Michael Moore, Henry Brandon, Porter Hall. 101m.

Buffalo Bill Cody (Heston) and Wild Bill Hickok (Tucker) fight off Indians and outlaws to protect the Pony Express mail service and open the route to California. In an attempt to emulate De Mille, producer Nat Holt hired De Mille's star Heston and a big production team to make this large-scale oater but the result is a juvenile "B" movie gone rampant. Both stars overact. Some of the dialogue is funny but it's hard to tell whether that was intentional.

PONY EXPRESS RIDER (1976, IND). D: Robert Totten. W: Totten, Hal Harrison & Dan Greer. Cast: STEWART PETERSON, Ken CURTIS, Joan CAULFIELD, Slim

Pickens, Jack Elam, Henry Wilcoxon, Buck Taylor, Maureen McCormick, Dub Taylor, Ace Reid, Larry D. Mann, Scott Petersen. 100m.

Title tells all. Made for the kiddies, this is nicely photographed (Bernie Abramson); a pretty good family picture.

PONY SOLDIER (1952, FOX). D: Joseph M. Newman. W: John C. Higgins from a Garnett Weston novel. Cast: TYRONE POWER, Penny EDWARDS, Cameron MITCHELL, Thomas GOMEZ, Robert Horton, Adeline Reynolds, Earl Holliman, Chief Nipo Strongheart. 82m.

Discredited Canadian Mountie (Power) tries to put down a Cree Indian rebellion on the Northwest frontier. Best acting comes from Holliman (his movie debut) and Gomez, in an overblown comic role. Scenery and the red coats are more colorful than the script or direction.

POSSE (1975, PARA). D: Kirk Douglas. W: William Roberts & Christopher Knopf. Cast: KIRK DOUGLAS, BRUCE DERN, James STACY, Bo HOPKINS, Luke Askew, David Canary, Alfonso Arau, Katherine Woodville, Mark Roberts. 92m.

A lawman (Douglas) campaigns for the Senate on a right-wing platform based mainly on his reputation as a heroic law-and-order man. As the excessively contrived and utterly implausible "message" plot develops, his election hinges on the outcome of his pursuit of a notorious outlaw (Dern). An amateurish and anachronistic parable script and a confusion of morality are at the root of the film's weakness: we are meant to sympathize with the outlaw—a despicable killer—while we are supposed to hope the arrogant lawman will lose simply because he is politically ambitious and works for "the railroad" which is supposed to be evil simply because it's a railroad (we never see it commit any evil acts). There's plenty of action (even though it doesn't make much sense), excellent performances, a bad score (Maurice Jarre), serviceable photography (Fred J. Koenekamp); it's better than Douglas's previous directorial effort (*Scalawag*), but one emerges from it bewildered by the comic-book writing, and its tortuous confusion of good and evil.

POSSE FROM HELL (1961, UNIV). D: Herbert Coleman. W: Clair Huffaker from his novel. Cast: AUDIE MURPHY, ZOHRA LAMPERT, JOHN SAXON, Vic MORROW, Robert KEITH, Royal Dano, Lee Van Cleef, Ray Teal, Ward Ramsey, Harry Lauter. 89m.

A good supporting cast—particularly Lampert, a fine comedienne with great charm—is wasted in this run of the mill oater about a posse that goes after four convicts who took over the town, kidnapped a girl and killed the hero's lawman friend.

POTATO FRITZ (1976, IND). D: Peter Schamoni. W: Paul Hengge. Cast: HARDY KRUGER, STEPHEN BOYD, Anton DIFFRING, Christianne Goett, Arthur Brauss, Friedrich von Ledeben, Malachy McCourt, David Hess.

The plot is the wheeze about the supposed Indian villains who turn out to be disguised white men. But the hero—a potato farmer with a sense of humor—is an intriguing character, played nicely by Kruger, and the costumes are accurate for a change in this sauerkraut oater. It was filmed in English.

POWDER RIVER (1953, FOX). D: Louis King. W: Geoffrey Homes & Sam Hellman from Stuart N. Lake's book *Wyatt Earp, Frontier Marshal*. Cast: RORY CALHOUN, CORINNE CALVET, Cameron MITCHELL, Jack OAKIE, Carl Betz, Robert J. Wilke. 78m.

Wyatt Earp again, in yet another movie adaptation—looser than most—of Lake's biography. Cliches, standard character types, uninspired script and direction add up to a routine horse opera with an adequate cast.

POWDERSMOKE RANGE (1936, RKO). D: Wallace Fox. W: Adele Buffington, based on the "Three Mesquiteers" characters created in pulp fiction by William Colt MacDonald. Cast: HARRY CAREY, HOOT GIBSON, BOB STEELE, TOM TYLER, Guinn "Big Boy" WILLIAMS, William FARNUM, William DESMOND, "Boots" MALLORY, Art Mix, Wally Wales, Buzz Barton, Buffalo Bill, Jr., Franklyn Farnum, Buddy Roosevelt.

This was the king of the "B" pictures, advertised as "The Greatest Roundup of Western Stars in History" and "The Barnum and Bailey of Westerns." It also was a tiresomely ordinary programmer. It began the "Three Mesquiteers" series and, with it, the popularity of cowboy trios. In this one Carey, Gibson and Williams are the trio; throughout the series there were numerous personnel changes—the longest-running star was Bob Livingston, but John Wayne took over the Carey part in one series of eight movies. If you're looking for the girl, she was Patricia "Boots" Mallory, real-life wife of actor Herbert Marshall. Today *Powdersmoke Range* is strictly for "B" buffs and curious film historians.

PRAIRIE CHICKENS (1943, UA). D: Hal Roach, Jr. W: Arnold Belgard, Earle Snell &

Donald Hough. Cast: Noah BEERY, Jr., Jimmie ROGERS, Jack Norten. 46m.

A rich drunk inherits a ranch and is bamboozled by two happy-go-lucky cowpokes. Mild short Roach comedy was really a featurette.

PRAIRIE SCHOONERS (1940, COL). D: Sam Nelson. W: Robert L. Johnson & Fred Myton from a George C. Franklin story. Cast: WILLIAM ELLIOTT, Evelyn YOUNG, Bob BURNS, Dub Taylor, Ray Teal, Edmund Cobb, Jim Thorpe.

What the title implies. Early Elliott programmer had a fair budget.

PRAIRIE THUNDER (1937, WB). D: B. Reeves Eason. W: Ed Earl Repp. Cast: DICK FORAN, Ellen CLANCY, Yakima Canutt, Glenn Strange. 67m.

The last of Foran's 1936–1937 series of Warner Brothers singing Westerns (there were nine in all) is one of the better ones— "Breezy" Eason was famous as a second-unit action director and here he had the connivance of Yakima Canutt; as you might expect, the action sequences are first-rate. Foran was the only cowboy star regularly employed at Warners during this period; the studio didn't understand Westerns and its staccato style didn't lend itself to outdoor movies but this one wasn't too bad for a programmer.

THE PROFESSIONALS (1966, COL). DW: Richard Brooks from Frank O'Rourke's novel *A Mule for the Marquesa*. Cast: BURT LANCASTER, LEE MARVIN, ROBERT RYAN, JACK PALANCE, CLAUDIA CARDINALE, WOODY STRODE, Ralph BELLAMY, Joe DeSantis, Elsa Cardenas. 117m.

A ruthless tycoon (Bellamy) recruits four action specialists, one at a time, each for his own expertise (Lancaster's is explosives, Strode's is tracking and bow-and-arrow, Ryan's is horses, Marvin's is weapons and leadership and tactics), to go down into Mexico and invade the impregnable stronghold of a Mexican bandit leader (Palance) and rescue Bellamy's kidnapped wife (Cardinale).

The story is implausible but rousing; this noisy actioner is all commotion and splendidly entertaining, a "caper" movie with dandy players and direction. The photography (Conrad Hall) is lavish in scope; the score (Maurice Jarre) is excellent punctuation. As a ripsnorting yarn of suspense and action *The Professionals* lives up to its title; where it leaves something to be desired is in the occasional pretentious intervals where the characters start talking philosophically about the meaning and nature of life and revolutions and

such. There's too much of that and it's sophomoric, but it's worth putting up with for the rest. Brooks was nominated for an Oscar as best director.

THE PROUD AND THE DAMNED (1972, IND). DW: Ferde Grofe, Jr. Cast: CHUCK CONNORS, Cesar ROMERO, Aron KINCAID, Jose GRECO, Anita Quinn, Maria Grimm, Smokey Roberds, Henry Capps. 94m.

Five Confederate veterans, adrift in South America, get embroiled in a revolution in the Andes. After that the story becomes hard to follow. The hero is killed off halfway through the movie for no ostensible reason. Jose Greco as a nasty Gypsy does a flamenco dance. The photography (Remegio Young) is of the home-movie variety; the acting, except for Connors, is of the high-school dramatics variety; the screenwriting skills of Grofe are on a par with, say, Smiley Burnette's Shakespearean acting abilities. Co-produced by George Montgomery, the film was shot in Spain, and is unforgivable trash.

THE PROUD ONES (1956, FOX). D: Robert D. Webb. W: Edmund H. North & Joseph Petracca from Verne Athanas's novel. Cast: ROBERT RYAN, JEFFREY HUNTER, VIRGINIA MAYO, Walter BRENNAN, Robert Middleton. 93m.

Hardboiled town marshal (Ryan) contends with lawless forces and a youth (Hunter) who has cogent reasons to want to kill him, but becomes his deputy. The story stands or falls on the delicacy with which the relationship between the two men is handled; unfortunately Hunter doesn't measure up to Ryan's level of performance, and the imbalance makes it an uneven movie. But Ryan is great and it's worth seeing.

THE PROUD REBEL (1958, BV). D: Michael Curtiz. W: Joseph Petracca, Lillie Hayward & James Edward Grant. Cast: ALAN LADD, OLIVIA DE HAVILLAND, David LADD, Dean JAGGER, Cecil Kellaway, Henry Hull, Dean Stanton, John Carradine, James Westerfield, Percy Helton. 103m.

The son of a former Confederate soldier has been struck dumb by the trauma of the war; father and son set out on a pilgrimage in search of a doctor who may cure the affliction. On their journey they encounter a spinster rancher (de Havilland) and become involved in her troubles with a rustic land-grabbing patriarch (Jagger) and his nasty sons. The force-the-woman-off-her-land machinations are woefully trite and there are too many obvious echoes of *Shane* in both the script and the casting, and there's the obligatory last-reel shoot-out, but the movie is superior fare. De Havilland came out of self-imposed retirement to appear in it and she gives a moving performance. Disney released this one but it was produced by Sam Goldwyn, Jr., and has more punch than most Buena Vista releases; the photography (Ted McCord) and score (Jerome Moross) are quite good.

THE PURPLE HILLS (1961, IND). D: Maury Dexter. W: Russ Bender & Edith C. Pearl. Cast: GENE NELSON, Joanne BARNES, Kent TAYLOR. 61m.

Two Westerners compete to claim the reward on a dead outlaw while Indians menace them. Cheap and limp.

PURSUED (1947, WB). D: Raoul Walsh. W: Niven Busch. Cast: ROBERT MITCHUM, TERESA WRIGHT, JUDITH ANDERSON, Dean JAGGER, Clifton Young, Alan Hale, Sr., John Rodney, Harry Carey, Jr., Lane Chandler. 101m.

A Western farm family is ruled by a matriarch (Anderson) and menaced by a shadowy villain (Jagger); the focus is on the eldest son (Mitchum) and on a deterministic, relentless tragedy that looms over them all. The basic plot is the old find-your-father's-killer wheeze but it's handled with such a different approach that you probably won't notice the cliche of it. The acting by all four principals is splendid; script and direction are flawless; my main reservation has to do with the inherent disturbing phoniness of this school of filmmaking—this is probably the best example of the brooding, arty "psychological Western" school of movies filled with Freudian symbolism and portentous compositions and dark, stark black-and-white film noir photography.

QUANTEZ (1957, UNIV). D: Harry Keller. W: Anne Edwards & Robert W. Campbell. Cast: FRED MacMURRAY, DOROTHY MALONE, John GAVIN, James Barton, Sydney Chaplin. 80m.

Talky meller concerns thieves who take refuge in a deserted Mexican ghost town after a bank robbery and fall to quarreling among themselves. It's slow and feeble, though the cast is good.

QUANTRILL'S RAIDERS (1958, AA). D: Edward Bernds. W: Polly James. Cast: STEVE COCHRAN, Diane BREWSTER, Leo Gordon, Gale Robbins, Will Wright, Lane Chandler. 68m.

An undercover agent (Cochran) infiltrates the vicious gang of Civil War outlaw leader William Clark Quantrill (Gordon) with predictable shoot-'em-up results. Routine.

THE QUICK GUN (1964, COL). D: Sidney Salkow. W: Robert E. Kent & Steve Fisher. Cast: AUDIE MURPHY, MERRY ANDERS, James BEST, Ted de Corsia, Raymond Hatton, William Fawcett. 86m.

Drifting gunfighter (Murphy) helps a young sheriff (Best) defend his town against marauding outlaws. Typical Murphy fare is nothing special.

THE QUIET GUN (1957, IND). D: William F. Claxton. W: Eric Norden & Earle Lyon from a novel by Lauran Paine. Cast: FORREST TUCKER, JIM DAVIS, Mara CORDAY, Kathleen Crowley, Lee Van Cleef, Tom Brown, Hank Worden, Lewis Martin, Vince Barnett. 72m.

Ordinary sheriff-versus-landgrabbers programmer is made nearly palatable by fine performances by Tucker (as the sheriff) and Davis (as his friend and rival; the villain is Brown, and Van Cleef plays his sadistic gunslinger henchman). Photographed in black-and-white (John Mescall) on studio back lots, it is scored unexceptionally by Paul Dunlap. You have to be a real fan to put up with the hackneyed plot, which builds to the sheriff's defying the town by arresting a whole lynch mob and exposing the town's *High Noon*-style guilt. It bogs down in silly villainy and cheap plot twists that seem left over from a 1946 "B" oater, but the cast performs much better than it needs to, with the result that it can be fun if you're not in a demanding mood.

QUINCANNON, FRONTIER SCOUT (1956, UA). D: Lesley Selander. W: John C. Higgins & Don Martin from a Will Cook novel. Cast: TONY MARTIN, Peggie CASTLE, John Smith, John Bromfield, Ron Randell. 83m.

Nightclub crooner Martin is laughably miscast as a frontiersman in this Grade "Z" Indian-fighting drivel.

RACHEL AND THE STRANGER (1948, RKO). D: Norman Foster. W: Waldo Salt from a Howard Fast story. Cast: LORETTA YOUNG, WILLIAM HOLDEN, ROBERT MITCHUM, Tom TULLY, Sara Haden, Gary Gray, Sara Jackson, Frank Ferguson. 93m.

A laconic pioneer farmer (Holden) buys a bondswoman (Young) and marries her but treats her like a slave until a stranger (Mitchum) arrives and arouses his jealousy and then his love for her. Romantic triangle comedy–melodrama is the usual Hollywood hoke but it's well served up, with lovely performances by the three stars.

RAGE AT DAWN (1955, RKO). D: Tim Whelan. W: Horace McCoy & Frank

Gruber. Cast: RANDOLPH SCOTT, FOR-REST TUCKER, Mala POWERS, J. Carrol Naish, Edgar Buchanan, Myron Healey, Kenneth Tobey, Holly Bane, Howard Petrie. 87m.

Range detective (Scott) is sent to round up the marauding Reno brothers (Tucker, Healey). Very old-fashioned "B" plot is quite well acted but has the look and feel of a creaky 1930s oater.

THE RAID (1954, FOX). D: Hugo Fregonese. W: Sydney Boehm & Francis Cockrell from an article by Herbert R. Sass. Cast: VAN HEFLIN, ANNE BANCROFT, Richard BOONE, Lee Marvin, Tommy Rettig, Peter Graves, Will Wright. 83m.

Based on a true incident, this has Heflin as the leader of a group of Confederate prisoners who escape from a Yankee prison and journey north via Canada into Vermont, where in retaliation for Sherman's destruction of Atlanta they set out to burn and sack the town of St. Albans—the purpose being not only revenge but also an attempt to divert Union troops north away from the beleaguered Confederacy. It starts briskly and moves along pretty well until the plot drags down when Heflin suddenly falls for an attractive widow in the town (Bancroft); from there on it's slush.

THE RAIDERS (1952)—*See* RIDERS OF VENGEANCE.

THE RAIDERS (1963, UNIV). D: Herschel Daugherty W: Gene L. Coon. Cast: ROBERT CULP, BRIAN KEITH, James McMULLAN, Judi MEREDITH, Simon Oakland, Ben Cooper, Alfred Ryder, Trevor Bardette, Harry Carey, Jr., Cliff Osmond, Richard Deacon, Michael Burns. Narrator: BRIAN KEITH. 75m.

During Reconstruction, carpetbaggers force a Texas cattleman (Keith) into a life of crime against the railroad and the army. Trying to bring peace to the situation are Wild Bill Hickok (Culp), Buffalo Bill Cody (McMullan) and Calamity Jane (Meredith). Busy actioner is diluted by poorly intercut stock action footage, several sleazy "B" elements, a blatant score (Morton Stevens), mediocre formula plotting, an excess of exposition, and color photography (Bud Thackery) the processing of which is grainy and uneven. This was devised as a TV pilot but released as a theatrical feature. The actors are well cast and well directed, and there are some deft moments; the moral conflicts sometimes become complicated and intriguing. It's confused but enthusiastic. Keith steals the show.

RAIDERS OF OLD CALIFORNIA (1957, REP). D: Albert C. Gannaway. W: Sam

Roeca & Thomas G. Hubbard. Cast: JIM DAVIS, Arleen WHELAN, Lee Van Cleef, Louis Jean Heydt. 72m.

A heroic frontiersman defends a poor defenseless gal against evil land-grabbers. Humdrum.

RAILS INTO LARAMIE (1954, UNIV). D: Jesse Hibbs. W: D. D. Beauchamp & Joseph Hoffman. Cast: JOHN PAYNE, MARI BLANCHARD, Dan DURYEA, Barton MacLANE, James Griffith, Lee Van Cleef, Joyce MacKenzie, Harry Shannon. 81m.

Army troubleshooter (Payne) helps railroad construction crew get the rails past the vice king (Duryea) of Laramie; nothing new. The plot owes much to Haycox's *Trouble Shooter*, the novel that served as the basis for *Union Pacific*.

THE RAINBOW BOYS (1973, IND). D: Gerald Potterton. Cast: DONALD PLEASENCE, KATE REID, Don CALFA.

Canadian frontier comedy concerns three oddballs trying to find a lost mine in the wilderness; it's squalid, synthetic farce.

RAMONA (1936, FOX). D: Henry King. W: Lamar Trotti from Helen Hunt Jackson's novel. Cast: DON AMECHE, LORETTA YOUNG, Kent TAYLOR, Pauline FREDERICK, John Carradine, Jane Darwell, J. Carrol Naish, Katherine De Mille, Billy Benedict, Russell Simpson, Victor Kilian, Chief Thundercloud, Pedro de Cordoba. 90m.

This was the first (and only) talkie remake of the oft-filmed silent movie about the Indian brave (Ameche) and his squaw (Young) and the mishaps that befall them in old California. (The previous version, in 1928, had starred Warner Baxter and Dolores Del Rio.) This was Fox's (and King's) first full-length Technicolor movie—the budget was big and the score by Alfred Newman suitably imposing. Ameche, in his first starring role, is weak and unsure of himself; Young, as the weepy courageous wife, is drearily distressed and very fragile in appearance—she was ill during the filming and several segments were filmed with doubles. There are songs (by William Kernell) and it's all very hokey, a dated pastoral tragedy, a museum piece now, strictly for cinephiles.

RAMROD (1947, UA). D: Andre de Toth. W: Jack Moffit, Graham Baker & Cecile Kramer from Luke Short's novel. Cast: JOEL McCREA, VERONICA LAKE, Don De FORE, Arleen WHELAN, Preston FOSTER, Charlie RUGGLES, Lloyd Bridges, Ian MacDonald, Jeff Corey, Ray Teal, Nestor Paiva, Housely Stevenson, Hal Taliaferro, Robert Wood, Wally Cassel, Vic Potel, Sarah Haden, Cliff Parkinson. 94m.

Feuding with her range-baron father (Ruggles), a willful, ambitious woman (Lake) stirs up a range war in this tense, complex, fast and excellently plotted little classic. There are numerous subplots, including one reminiscent of *The Virginian* in which foreman McCrea tries to straighten out his wayward pal (De Fore). The film boasts gorgeous black-and-white photography by Russell Harlan and a good score by Adolph Deutsch. It's excellent—and still highly entertaining; it's hardly dated at all. Buffs note that *Ramrod* is one of the silky poker-faced Veronica Lake's only two Westerns (the other was *Stronghold*).

RAMSBOTTOM RIDES AGAIN (1957, RANK). D: John Baxter. Cast: Frankie VAUGHAN, Arthur Askey, Sabrina.

Haven't seen this British comedy-Western set in the mountains of Canada. Am told it's poor.

RANCHO DELUXE (1975, UA). D: Frank Perry. W: Thomas McGuane. Cast: JEFF BRIDGES, SAM WATERSTON, ELIZABETH ASHLEY, Slim PICKENS, Clifton James, Charlene Dallas, Harry Dean Stanton, Richard Bright. 93m.

The heroes in this one are rustlers (compare McGuane's script for *The Missouri Breaks*) and the villain is the rancher (James). It's set in contemporary Montana. Bridges plays a middle-class Eastern youth in rebellion, while Waterston plays his Indian pal; together they try to re-create lost freedoms by stealing cows from the arrogant rancher and seducing the rancher's restless wife (Ashley). They are hunted by a droll, inept detective (Pickens) and they play a lot of practical jokes on folks. The movie is mostly engaging, intermittently funny, a cultish anti-Establishment outlaw comedy. Produced by Elliott Kastner.

RANCHO NOTORIOUS (1952, RKO). D: Fritz Lang. W: Daniel Taradash & Sylvia Richards. Cast: MARLENE DIETRICH, ARTHUR KENNEDY, MEL FERRER, William FRAWLEY, Jack Elam, George Reeves, Lloyd Gough, Frank Ferguson, Francis J. McDonald, Rodd Redwing, John Kellogg, Dan Seymour. 89m.

A cowboy (Kennedy) chases the guy who murdered his girl to a dance-hall that serves as a refuge for fugitives; it is the fiefdom of queen Dietrich. Not much happens. The directing is hard-boiled but exceedingly slow; the going is too turgid for Dietrich, and for the audience. Color and songs try to liven it up but fail. The film has its partisans but it's

implausible and Kennedy is miscast.

RANGE FEUD (1931, COL). D: D. Ross Lederman. W: Milton Krims. Cast: BUCK JONES, John WAYNE, Susan Fleming, Edward LeSaint, Wallace MacDonald, Harry Woods.

John Wayne's father (LeSaint) is falsely accused of murder; the sheriff (Jones) steps in to find the real killer. This one marked Wayne's first appearance in a Western after *The Big Trail*, in which he'd laid such an egg that he was now cast as second fiddle to "B" star Jones.

RANGERS OF FORTUNE (1940, PARA). D: Sam Wood. W: Frank Butler. Cast: FRED MacMURRAY, PATRICIA MORISON, Albert DEKKER, Gilbert ROLAND, Dick Foran, Joseph Schildkraut, Betty Brewer, Minor Watson. 80m.

The plot is imitative of *Three Godfathers*; despite the big-name cast it's confusing, anticlimactic and poor.

THE RARE BREED (1966, UNIV). D: Andrew V. McLaglen. W: Ric Hardman. Cast: JAMES STEWART, MAUREEN O'HARA, BRIAN KEITH, Ben JOHNSON, Juliet MILLS, Don Galloway, Jack Elam, David Brian. 108m.

British mother and daughter (O'Hara, Mills) bring the first Hereford bull to the Wild West to sire a new breed. The movie has a good scenic look to it—McLaglen grew up under John Ford's tutelage and knows how to frame a composition—and there are good action sequences, as when the heavy (Elam) sets off a stampede; it's very well performed by Stewart and Keith (the latter as a comically dour Scot) as two crusty frontiersmen vying for the affections of O'Hara. But the script is predictable.

RATON PASS (1951, WB). D: Edwin L. Marin. W: Tom W. Blackburn & James R. Webb from Blackburn's novel. Cast: DENNIS MORGAN, PATRICIA NEAL, STEVE COCHRAN, Dorothy HART, Scott Forbes, Basil Ruysdael, Louis Jean Heydt. 84m.

Husband and wife fight each other bitterly over a huge ranch; horse/soap-opera is nothing special except for Neal, who makes much more of the villain's part than is written into it.

RAW EDGE (1956, UNIV). D: John Sherwood. W: Harry Essex, Robert Hill, William Kozlenko & James B. Nablo. Cast: RORY CALHOUN, YVONNE De CARLO, Rex REASON, Neville Brand, Mara Corday, Herbert Rudley, Emile Meyer, Robert J. Wilke, Gregg Barton, William Schallert. 76m.

Cattle baron's hired hands plot to murder him so they can fight over his seductive widow. It's set in early (1842) Oregon and Hollywood anachronisms abound (1873 guns, for instance). It's a leering movie, half sexual innuendo and half juvenile "B" plotting, but moderately amusing, with some good gunfight action. Ludicrous title song by Terry Gilkyson.

RAWHIDE (1951, FOX). Also titled: DESPERATE SIEGE. D: Henry Hathaway. W: Dudley Nichols. Cast: TYRONE POWER, SUSAN HAYWARD, HUGH MARLOWE, Dean JAGGER, Edgar BUCHANAN, Jeff Corey, Jack Elam, James Millican, Louis Jean Heydt, George Tobias, Walter Sande, Dick Curtis, Lafe McKee, Si Jenks, Kenneth Tobey, Norman Lloyd. 86m.

A gang of bandits descends on a stage station and holds the people there hostage while waiting to ambush an incoming treasure-laden stage. Among the hostages are Power and Hayward. The story follows predictable lines to an equally predictable shoot-out but the course it takes in getting there is crisp and gripping, thanks to good characterizations and fine black-and-white photography (Milton Krasner) and uniformly good acting plus an outstanding performance by Marlowe as the chief villain. The movie's weakness is its static set-bound plot; the whole film takes place in and around the small stage depot and it has the constricted aura of a one-act play. One may object that Power is a bit too pretty for the grungy role he's playing. But the suspense builds thrillingly and Hayward is very good as the tough lady protecting her infant. Most of all, however, it is Hugh Marlowe's electrifying performance that makes it top-drawer.

THE RAWHIDE TRAIL (1958, AA). D: Robert Gordon. W: Alexander Wells. Cast: REX REASON, NANCY GATES, Ann Doran, Richard Erdman. 67m.

Hero is accused of having sided with Indians in their attacks on settlers; he has to prove his innocence. Black-and-white cheapie is poor.

THE RAWHIDE YEARS (1956, UNIV). D: Rudolph Mate. W: Earl Felton, Robert Presnell, Jr., & D. D. Beauchamp from Norman A. Fox's novel. Cast: TONY CURTIS, COLLEEN MILLER, ARTHUR KENNEDY, William GARGAN, William DEMAREST, Peter VAN EYCK, Minor Watson, Chubby Johnson, Trevor Bardette, Don Beddoe, Robert J. Wilke, Jack Perrin, Kermit Maynard, Rex Lease. 85m.

The plot—about accusations, pursuit, double crosses and romance—is too compli-cated to summarize. Oddball Western emphasizes the racy comic relationship between a quick-witted young riverboat gambler (Curtis, no Westerner but plenty charming) and an engaging villain (Kennedy, even less of a Westerner). It's colorful, actionful and quite funny; the standout performance is that of Van Eyck as a smooth baddie.

REBEL IN TOWN (1956, UA). D: Alfred Werker. W: Danny Arnold. Cast: JOHN PAYNE, RUTH ROMAN, J. Carrol NAISH, Ben Cooper, John Smith, Ben Johnson, James Griffith, Donald Randolph, Leigh Snowden, Kermit Maynard, Bobby Clark, Jack Perrin. 78m.

Ex-Confederate accidentally kills a child after a bank robbery. In black-and-white. Nothing to write home about.

RED CANYON (1949, UNIV). D: George Sherman. W: Maurice Geraghty from Zane Grey's *Wildfire*. Cast: HOWARD DUFF, ANN BLYTH, George BRENT, Edgar Buchanan, Lloyd Bridges, Chill Wills, John McIntire, Jane Darwell, Hank Worden, James Seay, Ray Bennett. 82m.

Drifter (Duff) helps a lady rancher (Blyth) tame her wild horses. A good supporting cast bolsters this ordinary Zane Grey yarn. It's in color.

RED DESERT (1949, LIP). D: Charles Marquis Warren. W: Daniel Ullman. Cast: DONALD "RED" BARRY, Margia DEANE, Tom Neal, Jack Holt, Holly Bane, Byron Foulger, Joseph Crehan, John Cason, Hank Bell, Tom London, George Slocum. 60m.

A foppish gambler (Barry) fights it out with the baddies who run the town. Fair-to-good "B" picture is, of course, not to be confused with the 1965 Antonioni film of the same title.

RED GARTERS (1954, PARA). D: George Marshall. W: Michael Fessier. Songs by Jay Livingston & Ray Evans. Cast: ROSEMARY CLOONEY, JACK CARSON, GUY MITCHELL, Pat CROWLEY, Gene BARRY, Buddy EBSEN, Joanne Gilbert, Reginald Owen, Cass Daley. 90m.

Unwieldy musical spoof is colorful but it's a stagy operetta with Mitchell as a happy-go-lucky cowpoke and Clooney as a saloon songbird.

THE REDHEAD AND THE COWBOY (1950, PARA). D: Leslie Fenton. W: Jonathan Latimer, Liam O'Brien & Charles Marquis Warren. Cast: GLENN FORD, RHONDA FLEMING, EDMOND O'BRIEN, Alan Reed, Ray Teal, Morris Ankrum. 82m.

The redhead, in this black-and-white movie, is a Rebel spy (Fleming); she mistakes an innocent wrangler (Ford) for a fellow spy and the melodrama follows slowly from there. Not very good.

THE REDHEAD FROM WYOMING (1953, UNIV). D: Lee Sholem. W: Polly James & Herb Meadow. Cast: MAUREEN O'HARA, Alex NICOL, William BISHOP, Robert STRAUSS, Dennis Weaver, Jack Kelly, Alexander Scourby, Stacy Harris, Jeanne Cooper, Claudette Thornton, Herman Hack, Palmer Lee, Betty Allen, Jack Perrin. 80m.

Dance-hall canary (O'Hara) presides over a saloon that becomes the battleground for a range war among nesters, rustlers and cattlemen. There's a nice big brawl at the end but other than that it's routine.

RED MOUNTAIN (1951, PARA). D: William Dieterle. W: John L. Meredyth, George F. Slavin & George W. George. Cast: ALAN LADD, LIZABETH SCOTT, JOHN IRELAND, ARTHUR KENNEDY, Jeff COREY, Bert Freed, Jay Silverheels, James Bell. 84m.

A drifting gunslinger (Ladd) escapes a murder frame-up and is recruited into the raiding guerrilla gang of William Clark Quantrill (Ireland). When he finds out what a baddie Quantrill really is, he changes sides and goes after him. Trailing the gang into Colorado he hooks up with a tough lady (Scott) and a vacillating renegade (Kennedy). It gets confused but it's fast, well filmed in black-and-white, and nicely acted for the most part.

RED RIVER (1948, UA). D: Howard Hawks. W: Borden Chase & Charles Schnee from Chase's novel. Cast: JOHN WAYNE, MONTGOMERY CLIFT, Joanne DRU, Walter BRENNAN, John IRELAND, Harry CAREY, Sr., Noah Beery, Jr., Coleen Gray, Harry Carey, Jr., Paul Fix, Shelley Winters, Lane Chandler, Hal Taliaferro, Tom Tyler, Glenn Strange. 125m.

Cattleman Tom Dunson (Wayne) with his toothless comic sidekick (Brennan) rounds up post-Civil War strays in Texas and builds the outfit into an empire during a period of years while he's raising an orphaned youth, Matthew Garth (Clift). The bulk of the story takes place on, and at the end of, a magnificent cattle drive from Texas to Kansas (filmed, naturally, in Arizona). Conflicts erupt between the arrogant Dunson and the maturing Garth, who finally ousts Dunson and assumes leadership of the drive. The two arrive separately in Abilene and events build toward the inevitable showdown—which Hawks, in a compromise, decided to avert at

the last minute. It forces an unbelievable speech on the hapless Joanne Dru, and uses as its action climax a scene Hawks stole from *The Outlaw*. Nevertheless the epic power of *Red River* is immense. It's a classic Western—and an expensive one (rain delays raised the budget from $1.7 million to $3.2 million, in 1948 dollars), with 6,000 cattle on screen.

Red River was conceived as a sort of Western version of *Mutiny on the Bounty*, with Wayne as Captain Bligh and Clift as Fletcher Christian. Actually the relationship between the two men in *Red River* is more moving than that between Bligh and Christian; Hawks obtained from Wayne the best performance he had given up to that time—it still stands as one of his three or four best—and the movie is equally well served by the work of supporting players: Ireland (as a deadly gunslinger), Brennan (in a role similar to that which he played in Hawks's *To Have and Have Not*), Beery (as a cowhand) and Carey, Sr. (as a lawman; it was his last film—he died soon after its completion). Clift, in his starring debut, is stunningly tense and aggressive (as opposed to his usual passive, introspective portrayals). But a large part of the movie's effectiveness is the result of Russell Harlan's black-and-white photography (the scenery is spectacular) and a truly heroic score by Dimitri Tiomkin.

RED SUNDOWN (1956, UNIV). D: Jack Arnold. W: Martin Berkeley from a story by Lewis B. Patten. Cast: RORY CALHOUN, MARTHA HYER, Dean JAGGER, Robert Middleton, James Millican, Trevor Bardette, Leo Gordon, Steve Darrell. 81m.

A gunfighter (Calhoun) reforms, a-la William S. Hart, pins on a deputy's badge and steps in between battling factions in a range war. It's speedy and very well cast.

RED TOMAHAWK (1967, PARA). D: R. G. Springsteen. W: Steve Fisher & Andrew Craddock. Cast: HOWARD KEEL, JOAN CAULFIELD, BRODERICK CRAWFORD, WENDELL COREY, Scott BRADY, Richard Arlen, Tom Drake, Ben Cooper, Donald "Red" Barry, Tracey Olsen. 82m.

Cavalry officer (Keel) tries to ward off a Sioux attack on a Montana town after the Little Big Horn battle. Caulfield plays a character called "Dakota Lil"—a part originally slated for Betty Hutton (she'd played opposite Keel sixteen years earlier in *Annie Get Your Gun*) but she'd had a feud with someone and walked off the movie. You may do the same; it's sodden with cliches, a familiar A. C. Lyles production (last of the series) with old-timers behind and before the cameras.

THE RED, WHITE AND BLACK (1972)— See SOUL SOLDIER.

RELENTLESS (1948, COL). D: George Sherman. W: Winston Miller from a Kenneth Perkins story. Cast: ROBERT YOUNG, MARGUERITE CHAPMAN, Willard PARKER, Akim TAMIROFF, Barton MacLane, Mike Mazurki, Robert Barrat, Clem Bevans, Will Wright, Frank Fenton. 93m.

When his prize pregnant mare, his only possession of value, is stolen by an escaping villain and ridden to death, a single-minded cowboy (Young) tracks the bad guy intending retribution. Mixed into this pursuit is a plot in which the cowboy is framed for murder and chased by a grim lawman (Parker), so that he and his girl must prove his innocence while tracking the real killer. It's a good grim manhunt melodrama with fine Technicolor photography (Edward Cronjager) on Arizona locations, but the plot is episodic, sometimes unconvincing, often hard to follow and sometimes reliant on painful coincidences. Tamiroff plays a scenery-chewing Mexican villain, MacLane overacts as the chief bad guy, and Parker with his New York accent is not believable as a Western sheriff; but Young and Chapman are excellent and the movie holds one's interest throughout.

RELENTLESS (1977, CBS). D: Lee H. Katzin. W: Sam H. Rolfe from Brian Garfield's novel. Cast: WILL SAMPSON, MONTE MARKHAM, John HILLERMAN, Larry WILCOX, Marianna HILL, Ted Markland, Danny Zaplan, Anthony Ponzini, John H. Lawlor. 99m.

A Navajo state trooper pursues a murderous bank-robbing gang of ex-guerrilla soldiers through a blizzard in the Arizona mountains; the film marks Sampson's first top star billing and may be unique in that it casts an American Indian in the role of an American Indian hero. Originally scheduled as a United Artists theatrical release, this had a muddled history and finally was filmed by CBS as a television feature, but it was filmed on a larger-than-usual budget on Arizona locations with a fairly large cast. The photography is by Jack Whitman, the score by John Cacavas. It would hardly be fitting for me to offer a critique.

RENEGADE RANGER (1938, RKO). D: David Howard. W: Oliver Drake & Bennett Cohen. Cast: GEORGE O'BRIEN, RITA HAYWORTH, Tim HOLT, Ray WHITLEY, Robert Kortman. 68m.

Mexicans led by a lady firebrand (Hayworth) try to bring land thieves to justice but they're framed for murder; then in steps Texas Ranger O'Brien. Programmer is chiefly of interest because it marks Hayworth's first appearance in a Western under that name; previously as Rita (or Margarita) Cansino she'd appeared in four "B" horse operas. The change of name also signaled a change in appearance: she shaved her widow's peak hairline back to the now-famous high-forehead Hayworth look.

RENEGADES (1946, COL). D: George Sherman. W: Harold Shumate, Melvin Levy & Francis E. Faragoh. Cast: WILLARD PARKER, EVELYN KEYES, LARRY PARKS, Forrest TUCKER, Edgar BUCHANAN, Ludwig DONATH, Jim Bannon, Francis Ford, C. Henry Gordon, Eddy Waller, Addison Richards, Eddie Acuff, Frank Sully, Willard Robertson. 77m.

When a girl falls in love with an outlaw, our hero shows her the error of her ways. Humdrum actioner, in color.

RENO (1939, RKO). D: John Farrow. W: John Twist & Ellis St. Joseph. Cast: RICHARD DIX, GAIL PATRICK, Anita LOUISE, Paul CAVANAGH, Louis Jean Heydt, Joyce Compton, Hobart Cavanaugh, Laura Hope Crews.

Flashback melodrama was a cornball soap opera about a casino owner who used to be a circuit-riding gambler. Poor work, coming in the big year of 1939 and on the heels of Dix's big *Man of Conquest.*

REPRISAL (1956, COL). D: George Sherman. W: David P. Harmon, Raphael Hayes & David Dortort from Arthur Gordon's novel. Cast: GUY MADISON, FELICIA FARR, KATHRYN GRANT, Michael PATE, Edward PLATT, Otto Hulett, Wayne Mallory, Robert Burton, Ralph Moody, Frank DeKova. 74m.

A half-breed (Madison) tries to pass for white in a bigoted cowtown; the plot is complicated but unconvincing and the pace is slow in this dud attempt to make a statement about racial prejudice; its good intentions can't overcome hackneyed scripting and wooden acting. The photography (by Henry Freulich, on location near Tucson) is marvelous except for some annoying 3-D effects.

REQUIEM FOR A GUNFIGHTER (1965, EMB). D: Spencer G. Bennett. W: R. Alexander, Evans W. Cornell & Guy J. Tedesco. Cast: ROD CAMERON, STEPHEN McNALLY, Olive STURGESS, Tim McCOY, Mike MAZURKI, Johnny Mack BROWN, Bob Steele, Raymond Hatton, Lane Chandler. 90m.

Outlaw gunslinger (Cameron) is mistaken for a deceased judge; posing as the judge he cleans up a lawless town. This looks like one of A. C. Lyles's waxworks Westerns but in fact he didn't produce it. This one is on the wrong side of the borderline of competence; the acting is atrocious, the script and directing are dreadful.

THE RESTLESS BREED (1957, FOX). **D:** Allan Dwan. **W:** Steve Fisher. **Cast:** SCOTT BRADY, ANNE BANCROFT, Jim DAVIS, Scott Marlowe, Jay C. Flippen, Leo Gordon. 81m.

The Bob Steele plot. Bancroft is wasted ludicrously as an Indian lass.

THE RETURN OF A MAN CALLED HORSE (1976, UA). **D:** Irvin Kershner. **W:** Jack DeWitt, suggested by characters from a story by Dorothy M. Johnson. **Cast:** RICHARD HARRIS, Gale SONDERGAARD, Jorge LUKE, Geoffrey LEWIS, Bill Lucking, Claudio Brook, Enrique Lucero, Jorge Russek, Ana De Sade. 129m.

Not for the squeamish, this rehash of *A Man Called Horse* is not so much a sequel as a retread, covering much of the same ground as the original but throwing in a few new ideas (hallucinogenic drugs, for instance) and veering from mysticism to blood and thunder. Story has an English lord (Harris) once again coming to the rescue of a beleaguered little tribe of Sioux Indians who are being victimized by white traders and other Indians; among the former Geoffrey Lewis is fascinating. But he turns in the only interesting performance in the movie, which has no other redeeming features. It has a heavy crashing score (Laurence Rosenthal) that is obtrusive—a sure mark of a lousy movie—and the overly loud sound effects make it a very noisy movie. In a nakedly cynical act of exploitation, the extremely painful test-by-torture scene (hanging a man by the pectorals—a test that probably never took place in real Indian history) that drew so much critical attention to the original *A Man Called Horse* is reprised here with no significant variation. The photography (Owen Roizman) is faddishly misty, and we are asked to believe that the locations around Durango, Mexico, are the landscapes of the Northwest. It's nice to see Sondergaard back on the screen after so many blacklisted years but in her role as an old Indian she's given nothing to do except look long-suffering. A buffalo-hunt sequence, filmed in the United States, stands out for its sad realism, but otherwise the movie is murky, pointless and pretentious.

THE RETURN OF FRANK JAMES (1940, FOX). **D:** Fritz Lang. **W:** Sam Hellman. **Cast:** HENRY FONDA, GENE TIERNEY, Henry HULL, John CARRADINE, Jackie COOPER, Donald Meek, J. Edward Bromberg, George Barbier, George Chandler. 92m.

Beginning with a reprise of the last reel of the Tyrone Power *Jesse James* (which introduced Fonda as brother Frank James), we follow Frank from Jesse's death on a quest for vengeance against the villainous Bob Ford (again played by Carradine); Hull and others also repeat their roles from the earlier film. This sequel is fairly well remembered by movie buffs; it's an elaborate Technicolor production and Gene Tierney is excellent in her movie debut; and in fact it's not a bad picture but it doesn't have the spirited flavor of *Jesse James*. Lang's directorial hand was heavy and humorless, suited to the dark brooding German melodramas he was famous for, rather than outdoor action adventures; there's humor in this one (in the script) but it's laid on with thick unsubtle leadenness, typified by Hull's mannered rantings. A big movie but lamentably dated.

THE RETURN OF JACK SLADE (1955, AA). **D:** Harold Schuster. **W:** Warren Douglas. **Cast:** JOHN ERICSON, MARI BLANCHARD, Neville BRAND, Angie DICKINSON. 77m.

Jack Slade was a complicated murderous character in history, interestingly depicted in the eponymous Mark Stevens movie; this cheapie has the youthful Ericson as the son of Jack Slade, trying to redeem the family's good name by becoming a lawman. Routine.

THE RETURN OF JESSE JAMES (1950, LIP). **D:** Arthur Hilton. **W:** Jack Natteford & Carl K. Hittleman. **Cast:** JOHN IRELAND, ANN DVORAK, Henry HULL, Reed HADLEY, Victor Kilian, Tommy Noonan, Hugh O'Brian, Clifton Young, Margia Dean, Sid Melton, Byron Foulger, Peter Marshall, I. Stanford Jolley. 75m.

A small-time bank robber (Ireland) cashes in on his marked resemblance to the dead Jesse James; he spreads the myth that Jesse's still alive; this offends Frank James (Hadley), who sets out to track down the upstart who's endangering his privacy and security. Ireland plays the bogus Jesse as a blustery fool—an intriguing performance in an interesting movie. There are superior black-and-white photography (Karl Struss) and a good score (Ferde Grofe). Considering the shoestring on which it was filmed this is an astonishingly solid little movie, one of the better examples of the offbeat Lippert productions of its era.

RETURN OF THE BAD MEN (1948, RKO). **D:** Ray Enright. **W:** Jack Natteford, Luci Ward & Charles O'Neal. **Cast:** RANDOLPH SCOTT, ROBERT RYAN, ANNE

JEFFREYS, George "Gabby" HAYES, Robert ARMSTRONG, Steve Brodie, Jason Robards, Sr., Jacqueline White. 90m.

Land rush and outlawry in old Oklahoma: mini-epic with standard cliches is a sequel, of sorts, to the 1946 *Badman's Territory*. Ryan is splendid as the head heavy.

RETURN OF THE CISCO KID (1939, FOX). D: Otto Brower. W: Milton Sperling, based on the O. Henry characters. Cast: WARNER BAXTER, LYNN BARI, Henry HULL, Robert BARRAT, Chris-Pin Martin, C. Henry Gordon, Ward Bond, Cesar Romero, Kane Richmond.

The bandit (Baxter) is reformed and then rejected by the girl in this ho-hum comedy. This was the last of Baxter's Cisco Kid Westerns; Cesar Romero, who plays a bad guy here, later became the Cisco Kid in a "B" series and was in turn succeeded by Gilbert Roland.

RETURN OF THE FRONTIERSMAN (1950, WB). D: Richard Bare. W: Edna Anhalt. Cast: GORDON MacRAE, JULIE LONDON, RORY CALHOUN, Jack HOLT, Fred CLARK, Edwin Rand, Raymond Bond, Britt Wood, Matt McHugh, Richard Egan. 74m.

When sheriff's son (Calhoun) is accused of murder the hero sets out to prove it's a frame. Leisurely but OK; in color. Egan, in a small early role, is unbilled in the credits.

RETURN OF THE GUNFIGHTER (1966, MGM). D: James Neilson. W: Robert H. Buckner & Burt Kennedy. Cast: ROBERT TAYLOR, CHAD EVERETT, Ana MARTIN, Lyle BETTGER, Mort Mills, Michael Pate. 99m.

When a Mexican family is nearly wiped out by baddies (Bettger & co.) the sole survivor, a girl (Martin), appeals to an old family friend, a gunfighter (Taylor); the two are accompanied, in setting out to even the score, by a young man running from a murder charge (Everett). Ordinary yarn is fairly well handled.

RETURN OF THE SEVEN (1966, UA). D: Burt Kennedy. W: Larry Cohen. Cast: YUL BRYNNER, Robert FULLER, Warren OATES, Emilio FERNANDEZ, Julian MATEOS, Claude AKINS, Jordan CHRISTOPHER, Rodolfo ACOSTA. 96m.

This sequel (the first) to *The Magnificent Seven* has one of the seven (Mateos) held captive by bandits who are victimizing peons by using them as slave labor; Chris (Brynner) rounds up his gang of gunslingers to free the captive and the slaves. There is a reprise of the original Elmer Bernstein score but otherwise this is a pallid disappointing sequel— filmed in Spain, perfunctorily acted, mindless and boring.

RETURN OF THE TEXAN (1952, FOX). D: Delmer Daves. W: Dudley Nichols from a Fred Gipson novel. Cast: DALE ROBERTSON, JOANNE DRU, Walter BRENNAN, Richard Boone, Robert Horton, Helen Westcott, Tom Tully. 88m.

A Texas widower and his two sons return to the old homestead and get into a slow talky feud with a nasty rancher. Limp.

RETURN OF WILDFIRE (1948, IND). D: Ray Taylor. W: Carl K. Hittleman & Betty Burbridge. Cast: RICHARD ARLEN, PATRICIA MORISON, Mary Beth HUGHES, James Millican, Reed Hadley. 61m.

Cowboy outwits swindler. Dull "B" pick was one of Arlen's last starring roles before he went to character parts.

RETURN TO WARBOW (1958, COL). D: Ray Nazarro. W: Les Savage, Jr., from his novel. Cast: PHILIP CAREY, CATHERINE McLEOD, Andrew DUGGAN, William Leslie, Jay Silverheels, James Griffith. 67m.

Fleeing outlaws hide the loot in a cache; later they backtrack to recover it; conflicts erupt among them. Fair, compact actioner.

THE REVENGERS (1972, NGP). D: Daniel Mann. W: Wendell Mayes & Steven W. Carabatsos. Cast: WILLIAM HOLDEN, SUSAN HAYWARD, ERNEST BORGNINE, Woody STRODE, Arthur HUNNICUTT, Jorge LUKE, Larry Pennell. 112m.

When Holden's family is wiped out by white-led Indians he rides into Mexico to hunt the evildoers, recruiting gunslingers as he goes; squabbles erupt among his comrades; when he's wounded he's succored by an Irish nurse (Hayward). Toward the end he begins to realize that vengeance is not a fit obsession for a grown man; but things lead to the predictable showdown anyway. The characters are stereotypes—the amoral tough guy (Borgnine), the half-breed kid out to prove himself (Luke), the noble dignified black man (Strode), the preachy moralizing woman (Hayward). It was Hayward's last picture (she died in 1975). Van Heflin, who died just before filming began, was to have played the Borgnine part.

REVOLT AT FORT LARAMIE (1957, UA). D: Lesley Selander. W: Robert C. Dennis. Cast: JOHN DEHNER, Frances HELM, Gregg PALMER, Don Gordon. 72m.

The commandant (Dehner) of a frontier cavalry post is torn between his duty as a

Union officer and his loyalty to the South when the Civil War breaks out. Dehner is very good; it's not a bad picture, though it lacks the spark of real excitement.

THE REWARD (1965, FOX). D: Serge Bourguignon. W: Bourguignon & Oscar Millard from a Michael Barrett novel. Cast: MAX VON SYDOW, YVETTE MIMIEUX, EFREM ZIMBALIST, JR., GILBERT ROLAND, Henry SILVA, Rodolfo ACOSTA, Emilio Fernandez, Nino Castelnuovo, Julian Rivero. 92m.

Bounty hunters fight among themselves for bigger shares of the reward money on a captured fugitive (Zimbalist) in this slow, sombre, morality play set in the present-day Mexican desert but played out on horseback as a timeless wilderness myth. It's an interesting film, reminiscent in flavor of *The Treasure of the Sierra Madre*, and von Sydow is intense (if somewhat boring) as the troubled brooding man of conscience; there are intriguing Malcolm Lowryish twists, and Mimieux is very appealing as the girl hopelessly loyal to the doomed prisoner (an aspect strongly reminiscent of the Janet Leigh character in *The Naked Spur*). Powerfully filmed (Joseph MacDonald, CinemaScope) with a heavy score (Elmer Bernstein), the film has a big expensive look but it lacks the forceful impact to which it aspires; it's leaden, brooding, static and relentlessly cheerless.

RHYTHM ON THE RANGE (1936, PARA). D: Norman Taurog. W: Twelve writers. Cast: BING CROSBY, MARTHA RAYE, FRANCES FARMER, Bob BURNS, Roy ROGERS, Clem Bevans, Sons of the Pioneers, Lucille Gleason, Samuel S. Hinds. 86m.

Rodeo star (Crosby) heads for Arizona on the trail of a runaway heiress (Farmer) and a prize cow. There are frothy tunes but the movie is uneven with too much forced comedy. Martha Raye made her debut in this. It was later remade as *Pardners*.

THE RICHMOND STORY (1966)—See ALVAREZ KELLY.

RICOCHET ROMANCE (1955, UNIV). D: Charles Lamont. W: Kay Lenard. Cast: MARJORIE MAIN, CHILL WILLS, Rudy VALLEE, Pedro Gonzalez-Gonzalez. 80m.

Dull comedy about a rustic old gal running a dude-ranch kitchen.

RIDE A CROOKED TRAIL (1958, UNIV). D: Jesse Hibbs. W: Borden Chase & George Bruce. Cast: AUDIE MURPHY, GIA SCALA, Walter MATTHAU, Henry Silva. 87m.

It's the old wheeze about an outlaw who's mistaken for a dead marshal so he takes the marshal's place and is reformed by wearing the badge. Chase's script is more literate than many but it's routine, interesting mainly for Matthau's lugubrious presence.

RIDE A VIOLENT MILE (1957, FOX). D: Charles Marquis Warren. W: Eric Norden. Cast: JOHN AGAR, Penny EDWARDS, Sheb Wooley, Eva Novak, John Pickard. 80m.

Union spies in the Southwest fight it out with Reb blockade runners. Poor cheapie is badly acted.

THE RIDE BACK (1957, UA). D: Allen H. Miner. W: Anthony Ellis. Cast: WILLIAM CONRAD, ANTHONY QUINN, Lita MILAN, Victor Millan, George Trevino, Ellen Monroe, Joe Dominguez. 79m.

A hard-luck loser (Conrad) is given a badge and sent to Mexico to arrest and bring back a cheerfully ebullient, but dangerous, fugitive killer (Quinn). The grubby, frightened lawman's job is to get the wily outlaw back across the border to jail without being outwitted, outrun or outgunned. Along the way the two are besieged by angry Apache Indians. The script is one of those "psychological" ones, half film noir and half gritty realism. William Conrad produced this engrossing, tense little movie, one of the surprising Western sleepers of its decade. There's a good (for a change) title song, sung by actor Eddie Albert, and a mediocre score (Frank Devol); fine black-and-white photography (Joseph Biroc), and straightforward economical direction. It might be only a slightly better-than-average melodrama were it not for the stirring, even towering, performances by the two stars. Quinn's outlaw is both lovable and terrifying, and Conrad's portly, unglamorous, anxiety-ridden anti-hero is stunningly realized.

RIDE BEYOND VENGEANCE (1966, COL). Also titled: NIGHT OF THE TIGER. D: Bernard McEveety. W: Andrew J. Fenady from an Al Dewlen novel. Cast: CHUCK CONNORS, MICHAEL RENNIE, Kathryn HAYS, Gary MERRILL, Gloria GRAHAME, Claude AKINS, Joan BLONDELL, Bill BIXBY, James MacARTHUR, Arthur O'CONNELL, Paul Fix, Ruth Warwick, Frank Gorshin, Buddy Baer, Robert Q. Lewis, Harry Harvey, Jamie Farr. 100m.

Told in flashback, this tough yarn has a buffalo skinner (Connors) branded with a hot iron by three baddies (Rennie, Akins, Bixby); he sets out to get revenge. Fenady, a good writer-filmmaker (*The Man with Bogart's Face*) somehow missed the boat entirely with this one, possibly the fault of producers and/or the original novel; so did the large and mostly superior cast. It's a relentless one-note movie, wretchedly overacted, and it includes some of the most ludicrously savage brutality this side of the nauseating *Forty Guns*. Filled with sado-masochism and leering sexual innuendo, it nevertheless manages somehow to be utterly boring.

RIDE CLEAR OF DIABLO (1954, UNIV). D: Jesse Hibbs. W: George Zuckerman, Ellis Marcus & D. D. Beauchamp. Cast: AUDIE MURPHY, DAN DURYEA, SUSAN CABOT, Abbe LANE, Denver PYLE, Russell Johnson, Lane Bradford. 80m.

A sort of Bob Steele plot keys one of the better Murphy oaters with Duryea particularly good as a genial villain.

RIDE IN THE WHIRLWIND (1972, IND). D: Monte Hellman. W: Jack Nicholson. Cast: JACK NICHOLSON, CAMERON MITCHELL, MILLIE PERKINS, Katherine SQUIRE, Tom Filer, Brandon Carroll, Rupert Crosse, George Mitchell. 82m.

Young cowboys try to outrun a relentless posse across a bleak landscape after they've been mistaken for members of an outlaw gang. The film has become a cult favorite; it has a deterministic "psychological" aura and a barely coherent plot that hangs thinly on a thread of pursuit and retribution; it attempts to explore the nature of justice and chance, and to some extent it is tense and intriguing, but it's flawed by pretentious artiness; the characters are not developed beyond rudimentary levels, and nihilism alone can't carry a movie.

Nicholson and Hellman co-produced two peanut-budget indie Westerns in 1965 (the other was *The Shooting*) and released them in Europe several years before distributing them in America. They were filmed prior to Nicholson's major acceptance after *Easy Rider* and his subsequent "A" stardom; these two oaters, along with several Lippert and Roger Corman quickies in which Nicholson was featured from 1958 through 1968, were poverty-row pictures filmed on spit, chewing gum and home-movie enthusiasm. They must be given "A" for effort, and the acting in this one, especially by Mitchell, is top-drawer, but it's depressingly morbid and maudlin.

RIDE LONESOME (1959, COL). D: Budd Boetticher. W: Burt Kennedy. Cast: RANDOLPH SCOTT, Karen STEELE, Pernell ROBERTS, James COBURN, James BEST, Lee Van Cleef. 73m.

Ex-sheriff (Scott) captures a young outlaw (Best) and tries to take him to town to claim the reward but the outlaw's buddies gang up to prevent it; meanwhile Indians surround them all.

A little cult has formed around the Westerns that were written by Kennedy, acted by Scott and directed by Boetticher—although most of the members of that cult don't seem aware that the series of pictures is an ensemble effort rather than Boetticher's solo work. Most of the films of this trio were first-rate entertainments; this is one of the best of them—a taut little suspenser with no spare flesh. "Low budget" cries out from every frame but in this case that seems an advantage: the whole movie was shot outdoors (in CinemaScope) and the emphasis is on bleak loneliness, the dwarfing of solitary people against an arid, empty landscape. In his maturity Scott projects a leathery weather-whacked toughness that suits these roles perfectly, and the supporting actors bring more to their stereotyped roles than is often the case. It's nothing profound but it's solid craftsmanship and good, lean, tense suspense all the way. This was James Coburn's motion picture debut.

RIDE OUT FOR REVENGE (1957, UA). D: Bernard Girard. W: Norman Retchin. Cast: RORY CALHOUN, GLORIA GRAHAME, Lloyd BRIDGES, Vincent EDWARDS, Joanne Gilbert. 79m.

Routine plot has lawman-versus-baddies with the complication of Indians being forced off their lands by conniving whites. Brisk brief oater has all the standard cliches but it's reasonably diverting.

THE RIDER OF DEATH VALLEY (1932, UNIV). D: Albert S. Robell. W: Jack Cunningham & Stanley Bergerman. Cast: TOM MIX, LOIS WILSON, Fred KOHLER, Forrest Stanley, Willard Robertson, Mae Busch, Edmund Cobb, Iron Eyes Cody. 77m.

Mix and his horse Tony are chased across the dunes by a huge posse in this stunt-filled actioner.

RIDER ON A DEAD HORSE (1962, AA). D: Herbert L. Strock. W: Stephen Longstreet & James Edmiston. Cast: JOHN VIVYAN, Lisa LU, Bruce GORDON, Kevin Hagen. 72m.

A prospector murders his partner and tries to frame his other partner (Vivyan) for it after leaving him for dead. Plot is the usual revenge chase number in this low-budget black-and-white curiosity; it's done with a certain crude flair.

RIDERS OF DESTINY (1933, MONO). DW: Robert N. Bradbury. Cast: JOHN

WAYNE, George "Gabby" HAYES, Julia PARKER, Forrest Taylor, Yakima Canutt, Al St. John, Lafe McKee. 57m.

Wayne as "Singin' Sandy" (vocals dubbed by Smith Ballew) is hopelessly and uproariously inept in this nonsensical hero-versus-stage robbers programmer, with photography by Archie J. Stout. Wayne wasn't the first singing cowboy (Ken Maynard had that dubious distinction) and he certainly wasn't the best (Dick Foran probably had that distinction), but for horse laughs and speedy action the Duke's "B" pictures, like this one, were fun.

RIDERS OF THE PURPLE SAGE (1931, FOX). D: Hamilton MacFadden. W: John F. Goodrich, Philip Klein & Barry Connors from Zane Grey's novel. Cast: GEORGE O'BRIEN, MARGUERITE CHURCHILL, Noah BEERY, Stanley Fields, James Todd. 63m.

First talkie version (after Tom Mix's celebrated 1925 silent version) had the faithful-to-Grey plot about the gunslinger who exposes the crooked judge and outfights the desperado gang. The "B" sequel, filmed in 1932 with Tom Mix (a remake of a 1918 silent), was titled *The Rainbow Trail*.

RIDERS OF THE PURPLE SAGE (1941, FOX). D: James Tinling. W: William Buckner & Robert Metzler from Zane Grey's novel. Cast: GEORGE MONTGOMERY, Mary HOWARD, Lynn ROBERTS, Kane RICHMOND, Robert Barrat, Leroy Mason, Richard Lane. 58m.

This remake was budgeted and produced as a programmer but it turned out to be a sleeper, due in part to the power of the original novel, an almost medievally heroic yarn that probably was the best of Grey's works. It's dated and juvenile but still entertaining, nearly as good as Tom Mix's 1925 version—the romantic yarn about the drifter Lassiter who cleans up an outlaw territory and at the end, in spectacular and perhaps unintentionally symbolic manner, seals himself and his lady-love off from the rest of the world in an idyllic wilderness fastness. The essence of the fundamental Western myth is captured precisely in this little "B" movie.

RIDERS OF VENGEANCE (1952, UNIV). Also titled: THE RAIDERS. D: Lesley Selander. W: Lyn C. Kennedy, Lillie Hayward & Polly James. Cast: RICHARD CONTE, VIVECA LINDFORS, Barbara BRITTON, Dennis Weaver, Hugh O'Brian, William Reynolds, Richard Martin, Lane Chandler, Trevor Bardette. 80m.

A gentle rancher (Conte) turns avenger after his wife is murdered by vicious claim-jumping land-grabbers in California during the gold rush. The ineptitude of this movie, in view of its fair-size budget and the high-priced cast and the Technicolor locations, boggles the mind. It's just awful: childish "If you don't sign over the deed to your ranch" drivel, with city boy Conte an unconvincing cowboy and the rest of the cast painfully uncomfortable. Buffs will note that the movie marks Dennis Weaver's debut.

RIDE THE HIGH COUNTRY (1962, MGM). D: Sam Peckinpah. W: N. B. "Bo" Stone, Jr. Cast: JOEL McCREA, RANDOLPH SCOTT, Mariette HARTLEY, Edgar BUCHANAN, John ANDERSON, R. G. Armstrong, Warren Oates, James Drury, L. Q. Jones, Ronald Starr. 94m.

A down-at-the-heels ex-lawman (McCrea) in a threadbare frock coat is on the bum. In Denver he meets an old colleague (Scott) who's been reduced to earning a living as a bewigged, buckskin-clad, sharpshooting pitchman in a sleazy sideshow carnival. The two used-up old-timers take a job offered by a banker to ride up into the Rockies and escort a shipment of gold from a mountaintop mining camp down to the bank.

When they pick up the gold one of them is tempted to ride off with it; the other has nothing left except his integrity and he's willing to die to protect that: "All I want is to enter my house justified." This conflict between the two friends keys the action of the movie, which also concerns the liberation of an innocent frontier girl (Hartley, in a stunning debut) from her domineering fundamentalist father (Armstrong), some lusty shenanigans in the mining camp that feature splendid character performances by Anderson, Drury, Oates and Jones and a really outstanding one by Edgar Buchanan as a drunken justice of the peace, and the pursuit of the gold shipment by baddies (Anderson and his family again) who want to steal it from the two scruffy old timers and the kid (Starr) who joins them. The ending is human, poignant, honest and just dandy.

Ride the High Country is, I think, a masterpiece; and it marks an important milestone, because in a way it's both the last of the old Westerns and the first of the new. And actually as well as symbolically it represented a turning point in the history of Western films: it marked the retirement of both McCrea and Scott. (McCrea made a comeback more than a decade later in *Mustang Country* but Scott, at this writing, has not made any more films after *Ride the High Country*.)

RIDE THE MAN DOWN (1952, REP). D: Joseph Kane. W: Mary C. McCall, Jr., from

THE OX-BOW INCIDENT (1943): Anthony Quinn and Dana Andrews (both on horseback) are about to be lynched. A classic film but not a classic Western. Twentieth Century-Fox

PARDNERS (1956): Dean Martin, Jerry Lewis. An easygoing cowhand and a zany tenderfoot blunder their way to cleaning up a frontier town. Paramount Pictures

THE PERSUADER (1957): James Craig, Kristine Miller. Craig is the bad guy in this one. Allied Artists

THE PLAINSMAN (1936): Gary Cooper
as Wild Bill Hickok. A doomed tragic hero,
performed with deliberate dignified grandeur. Paramount Pictures

THE PLAINSMAN AND THE LADY (1946):
Andy Clyde, Vera Hruba Ralston, William Elliott.
The one about getting the Pony Express through;
it's pictorially impressive. Republic Pictures

THE PROFESSIONALS (1966): Woody Strode, Lee Marvin, Robert Ryan,
Burt Lancaster. Four action specialists: a powerhouse cast in a noisy
actioner, all commotion and splendidly entertaining. Columbia Pictures

THE PROUD ONES (1956): Robert Ryan, Jeffrey Hunter. Ryan is great as the hardboiled town marshal. Twentieth Century-Fox

RAMONA (1936): Kent Taylor, Loretta Young, Don Ameche. A weepy triangle, it's all very hokey, a museum piece now. Twentieth Century-Fox

RAMROD (1947): Joel McCrea, Veronica Lake, Don De Fore, Ray Teal, Hal Taliaferro, Wally Cassel. A tense, complex, fast and excellently plotted little classic, still highly entertaining. United Artists

RAWHIDE (1951): Hugh Marlowe, Edgar Buchanan. Marlowe's electrifying performance makes it top-drawer. Twentieth Century-Fox

RIDE THE MAN DOWN (1952): Ella Raines, Forrest Tucker. Right down the line, the actors are ideally cast. Republic Pictures

RIVER OF NO RETURN (1954): Robert Mitchum, Rory Calhoun, Marilyn Monroe, Tommy Rettig. Preminger's only Western has an overproduced watery plot, but performances are good. Twentieth Century-Fox

ROOSTER COGBURN (1975): John Wayne, Katharine Hepburn (under Gatling gun). Warmed over *African Queen* is a vanity showcase for two grey eminences. Universal Pictures

Luke Short's novel. Cast: ROD CA-MERON, ELLA RAINES, BRIAN DON-LEVY, BARBARA BRITTON, Forrest TUCKER, J. Carrol NAISH, Jim DAVIS, Chill WILLS, Jack La Rue, Roy Barcroft, Douglas Kennedy, Paul Fix, Bob Steele. 90m.

A ranch foreman (Cameron) has to fight land-grabbers (Donlevy, Tucker) and rustlers (Davis) to hold together his dead boss's cow outfit for the dead man's daughter (Raines); stirred into the mixture are a vacillating sheriff (Naish) and a romantic conflict for the hero's affections between town girl Britton and ranch girl Raines.

McCall's screenplay is a perfect distillation of the flavor and complication of the novel. Kane's direction is swift and sure. The music (Ned Freeman) is unobtrusive but proper, and the photography (Jack Marta) is thoroughly craftsmanlike. McCall says, "I remember Joe Kane's saying he preferred the picture in black and white. The editing (Fred Allen) was done from a black-and-white print."

It is possibly the casting more than the actors' abilities that makes the performances seem so perfect; right down the line they're ideally cast. *Ride the Man Down* is one of those rare little movies in which everybody does everything right. It's strictly traditional, wholly slick-magazine formula, but originality isn't the only hallmark of excellence and movies like this manage to transcend the formula without departing from it. "From the outset," McCall says, "this was as happy a spell of work as occurs but rarely in a screenwriter's life. Joe Kane is an admirer of Luke Short's work. I loved the novel. In transferring the story to the visual medium we didn't have any problems." There's nothing arty or profound about it, God knows, but *Ride the Man Down* is a fine example of its genre.

RIDE VAQUERO (1953, MGM). D: John Farrow. W: Frank Fenton. Cast: ROBERT TAYLOR, AVA GARDNER, HOWARD KEEL, ANTHONY QUINN, Kurt KASZNAR, Charlita, Ted De Corsia, Rex Lease, Joe Dominguez, Jack Elam, Ben Carter. 90m.

A settler (Keel), his bride (Gardner) and his gunslinging stepbrother (Taylor) mix it up with a bandit (Quinn); the woman's smoldering charms set them all at one another's throats in this heavy-breathing border epic. The emphasis is on sexual innuendo and on rhetorical conversations about the value of revolution. Tedious and silly.

RIDING HIGH (1943, PARA). D: George Marshall. W: Mark Hellinger, Melville Sha-velson, Jack Rose & Robert Riskin. Cast: DICK POWELL, DOROTHY LAMOUR, Victor MOORE, Rod CAMERON, Cass Daley, Ward Bond, Douglas Dumbrille, Max Baer, Gil Lamb, Fritz Feld, Paul Harvey, Milt Britton and his Band. 89m.

Dull dude-ranch musicomedy in color, with Lamour as miner Moore's daughter and Powell as a mining engineer, is not to be confused with the 1956 non-Western Bing Crosby musical.

RIDING SHOTGUN (1953, WB). D: André De Toth. W: Tom W. Blackburn from a Kenneth Perkins story. Cast: RANDOLPH SCOTT, WAYNE MORRIS, Joan WELDON, Joe Sawyer, Charles Buchinsky (Bronson), James Millican, James Bell, Fritz Feld. 74m.

Mistaken for an infamous outlaw, our hero tries to clear his name; to do it he has to wipe out the whole gang. Uninspired.

RIDING WEST (1944, COL). D: William Berke. W: Luci Ward. Cast: CHARLES STARRETT, Shirley PATTERSON, Arthur Hunnicutt, Ernest Tubb, Wheeler Oakman. 53m.

Starrett, best known to "B" audiences as the Durango Kid, here appeared as a Pony Express hero along with Grand Ole Opry singing star Tubb.

RIMFIRE (1949, LIP). D: B. Reeves Eason. W: Arthur St. Claire, Frank Wisbar & Ron Ormond. Cast: JAMES MILLICAN, MARY BETH HUGHES, Henry HULL, Reed HADLEY, Chris-Pin Martin. 67m.

Frontier undercover agent solves ghostly murders. In a rare chance to play a leading role Millican acquits himself well, but it's poor "B" fare.

RIO BRAVO (1959, WB). D: Howard Hawks. W: Jules Furthman, Leigh Brackett & B. H. McCampbell. Cast: JOHN WAYNE, DEAN MARTIN, ANGIE DICKINSON, Ricky NELSON, Walter BRENNAN, John Russell, Ward Bond, Claude Akins, Bob Steele, Pedro Gonzalez-Gonzalez, Harry Carey, Jr., Fred Graham, Myron Healey, Malcolm Atterbury. 140m.

Sheriff John T. Chance (Wayne) jails a murderer (Akins) and then has to hold the jail against the assaults of the murderer's powerful rancher brother (Russell) and his hard-bitten crew. Siding with the sheriff are a cackling old hen of a jailer (Brennan), the town drunk (Martin) and a brash callow kid who's fast with his gun and his lip (Nelson). Mixed into it are a cattleman (Bond), a saloon girl (Dickinson) and a low-comedy hotel clerk (Gonzalez). All these characters are measured from stock and cut to fit, and the plot holds few surprises. Wayne plays his standard leathery hero, spinning his rifle to cock it (an absurdity in practical terms), displaying superhuman bravery. Nelson is wooden. Brennan overplays. The comedy relief is mainly from the Gabby Hayes school. The action climax is a lusty juvenile fantasy, colorful but contrived, choreographed with more artifice than believability. It's overrated, overripe and overlong; it's competent and professional and amusing, yes, but it's also childish, and some of its elements were creaky even in the days of Tom Mix. Hawks and Wayne insisted it was their "answer" to *High Noon* (a picture they disliked because it depicted a town full of American frontiersmen as abject cowards), but that is like answering a serious poem with a nursery-rhyme verse. I remain mystified by the way Howard Hawks's apologists hold this juvenile and predictable movie up as an example of auteuriste genius.

RIO CONCHOS (1964, FOX). D: Gordon Douglas. W: Clair Huffaker & Joseph Landon from Huffaker's novel. Cast: RICHARD BOONE, STUART WHITMAN, TONY FRANCIOSA, Jim BROWN, Edmond O'BRIEN, Wende WAGNER, Warner Anderson, Rodolfo Acosta, Barry Kelly House Peters, Jr., Vito Scotti. 107m.

There's a lot of action in this two-fisted oater. Renegades have stolen a shipment of rifles and plan to sell them to the Apaches; a scruffy gang of adventurers is sent by the army to recover the rifles. Boone plays an ex-Confederate officer with heavy-handed determination. Whitman and Brown (his debut) as Union soldiers are poor. Franciosa is absurd as a conniving Mexican desperado. O'Brien is miscast as the madman who bosses a huge gang of outlaws below the border, hoping to persuade his Apache allies to wipe out the Union army so he can reestablish the Confederacy out west. There's acceptable photography (Joseph MacDonald) and plenty of lusty action; the humor is rough and crude; in sum it's energetic but unbelievable, and it has uncomfortable similarities to *The Comancheros* (1961, also with Stuart Whitman).

RIO GRANDE (1950, REP). D: John Ford. W: James K. McGuinness from a James Warner Bellah novel. Cast: JOHN WAYNE, MAUREEN O'HARA, Victor McLAGLEN, J. Carrol NAISH, Ben Johnson, Harry Carey, Jr., Claude Jarman, Jr., Dick Foran, Grant Withers, Sons of the Pioneers, Chill Wills, Ken Curtis. 105m.

A gritty cavalry officer (Wayne) waits with his command by the Mexican border for orders from General Phil Sheridan (Naish) to cross the river and have it out with Apaches who've been marauding into the United States and then fleeing back into their Mexican rancherias. His estranged wife (O'Hara) shows up when their son (Jarman) enlists in his father's regiment against her wishes. Subplots involve a venal Indian agency sutler (Withers) and various conflicts among the troopers (McLaglen, Foran, Curtis), some of them comic, and a particularly engaging and moving sequence of episodes involving the regiment's subtle protection of Trooper Travis Tyree (Ben Johnson, playing the same character he'd played in *She Wore a Yellow Ribbon*) when a marshal arrives from Texas to extradite him for murder. Harry "Dobie" Carey, Jr., plays Johnson's partner, as he did in other films as well, and early in the picture when the two youngsters put on a Roman-riding display for McLaglen they nearly steal the whole show: a magnificent stunt performed by the actors themselves, it is one of the best equestrian scenes on film.

One or two songs are a bit contrived but not stagy; they fit nicely into the frame of the movie along with Bert Glennon's masterful black-and-white camera work. The Victor Young score is romantic but suitable.

This was the last of Ford's cavalry trilogy; I must point out that all three films (the others were *Fort Apache* and *She Wore a Yellow Ribbon*) were based on the writings of James Warner Bellah, and the fascinating characterizations that set the films apart from the rest of the genre were more Bellah's than Ford's. In any case all the sentiment and rough humor of the Bellah-Ford classics are summed up in this one; it may be the best of the three. It's wildly sentimentalized but that doesn't diminish it for me. I can think of very few Westerns that are much better than *Rio Grande*.

RIO LOBO (1970, NGP). D: Howard Hawks. W: Leigh Brackett & Burton Wohl. Cast: JOHN WAYNE, Jorge RIVERO, Jennifer O'NEILL, Jack ELAM, Christopher Mitchum, George Plimpton, David Huddleston, Jim Davis, Sherry Lansing, Bill Williams, Victor French, Hank Worden, Peter Jason, Mike Henry, Susana Dosamantes. 114m.

A hard-riding Yankee colonel chases train robbers and keeps after them until he catches up, even though the Civil War has ended; thereupon the plot degenerates into land-grabbers and deed-to-the-ranch idiocy and a climax that's a pale carbon copy of that in *Rio Bravo*.

Action stunts (by second-unit director Yakima Canutt), a good score (Jerry Goldsmith), fine photography (William Clothier), a funny performance by Jack Elam (more or less reprising Walter Brennan's part from *Rio Bravo*) and a stalwart job by Latin leading man Rivero as a good guy—these five are the better aspects of this otherwise dreary melodrama. Wayne looks tired and saddlesore; the script is feebleminded. It can't hold a candle to Wayne's better films. This is one of the handful of movies that auteuriste buffs laud as exemplars of the Howard Hawks canon; auteuristes to the contrary, this is virtually an amateur movie.

Buffs will note that the young Mexican girl who saves Wayne's bacon in the last reel, and with whom Wayne more or less goes off into the sunset, is played by Sherry Lansing, who later became head of production at Twentieth Century-Fox.

RIVER LADY (1948, UNIV). D: George Sherman. W: D. D. Beauchamp & William Bowers from a novel by Houston Branch & Frank Waters. Cast: YVONNE De CARLO, ROD CAMERON, Dan DURYEA, Helena Carter, John McIntire, Milton Kibbee, Lloyd Gough, Florence Bates. 77m.

Riverboat gambling queen takes over a logging syndicate and tries to buy the love of an independent lumberman (Cameron). Hokey; in color.

RIVER OF NO RETURN (1954, FOX). D: Otto Preminger. W: Frank Fenton & Louis Lantz. Cast: ROBERT MITCHUM, MARILYN MONROE, RORY CALHOUN, Tommy RETTIG, Murvyn Vye, Douglas Spencer, Ed Hinton. 91m.

Preminger's only Western is an overcooked stew about a widower (Mitchum) and his son (Rettig) who are hired to guide a saloon girl (Monroe) down a rough river on a raft in an attempt to outrun a pack of pursuing Indians. Mixing into it is Monroe's husband (Calhoun), a shiftless gambler who's deserted her but later changes his mind and gets jealous of Mitchum. Performances are good but the watery plot is overproduced. Some of it, particularly the reconstruction of a muddy frontier camp and the marvelous locations, is first-rate moviemaking; but on the whole it disappoints.

THE RIVER'S EDGE (1957, FOX). D: Allan Dwan. W: Harold J. Smith & James Leicester. Cast: ANTHONY QUINN, RAY MILLAND, DEBRA PAGET, Harry Carey, Jr., Chubby Johnson, Byron Foulger, Tom McKee. 87m.

A big-time thief and brutal killer (Milland) forces a hardscrabble rancher (Quinn) to guide him across the desert border into Mexico with his loot; accompanying them are the rancher's unappreciative city-bred jailbird wife (Paget), who happens to be the former girl friend of the killer. This steamy triangle boils over into a bewildering series of illogical developments, most of them absurdly contrived, and a limp *Treasure of Sierra Madre*-type ending. Quinn emerges with dignity intact but Paget is silly and Milland is altogether miscast as the tough ex-Marine killer; he's just awful. This CinemaScope ephemera is set in the modern-day Southwest but was filmed in Mexico.

RIVER'S END (1930, WB). D: Michael Curtiz. W: Charles Kenyon from a James Oliver Curwood story. Cast: CHARLES BICKFORD, EVALYN KNAPP, ZaSu PITTS, J. Farrell MacDONALD, Tom Santschi, David Torrence, Junior Coughlan, Walter MacGrail. 74m.

Canadian pursuit yarn has Bickford, accused of murder, assuming the identity of a presumably dead Mountie who was sent to capture him. Bickford plays both roles. Remake of 1922 silent is dated but fast.

RIVER'S END (1940, WB). D: Ray Enright. W: Barry Trivers & Fred Niblo, Jr., from a James Oliver Curwood story. Cast: DENNIS MORGAN, Elizabeth EARL, Victor JORY, James Stephenson, George Tobias. 68m.

Remake of the 1931 yarn was fairly lively.

ROAD AGENT (1941, UNIV). D: William Nigh. W: Five writers. Cast: LEO CARRILLO, DICK FORAN, Irene HERVEY, Andy Devine. 63m.

Title tells all. Dull fare.

THE ROAD TO DENVER (1955, REP). D: Joseph Kane. W: Horace McCoy & Allen Rivkin from a Bill Gulick novel. Cast: JOHN PAYNE, MONA FREEMAN, Skip HOMEIER, Lee J. COBB, Ray Middleton, Lee Van Cleef, Glenn Strange, Andy Clyde. 90m.

The hotheaded kid brother (Homeier) of a cowhand (Payne) joins an outlaw gang; Payne is tired of getting the kid out of scrapes so he drifts away by himself, ends up running a girl's (Freeman) stagecoach line and then of course the stage is held up by none other than guess who ... It's competent but ordinary.

ROARING FRONTIERS (1941, COL). D: Lambert Hillyer. W: Robert L. Johnson. Cast: WILLIAM ELLIOTT, TEX RITTER, Ruth FORD, Tristram Coffin, Frank Mitchell, George Chesebro, Joe McGuinn, Francis Walker.

Action star Elliott was paired with singing cowboy Ritter in this "B" picture with the usual bust-up-the-outlaw-gang plot. Well done for its period, directed by William S. Hart's old helmsman.

ROBBER'S ROOST (1955, UA). D: Sidney Salkow. W: Salkow, John O'Dea & Maurice Geraghty from Zane Grey's novel. Cast: GEORGE MONTGOMERY, Sylvia FINDLEY, Richard BOONE, Bruce BENNETT, Warren Stevens, Peter Graves, Stanley Clements. 82m.

Marshal sets out to bring down a pair of hard-riding outlaw gangs. Amateurish.

ROBIN HOOD OF EL DORADO (1936, MGM). D: William Wellman. W: Wellman, Walter Noble Burns, Joseph Calleia & Melvin Levy. Cast: WARNER BAXTER, MARGO, Bruce CABOT, Ann LORING, J. Carrol NAISH, Joe Dominguez, Paul Hurst. 86m.

Presumably based on the facts of the life of California bandit Joaquin Murieta, this one has a Zorroesque flavor with Murieta (Baxter) as a reformed outlaw intent on avenging himself on the bad guys who framed him. Dated yarn is expertly directed with a good cast.

ROCK ISLAND TRAIL (1950, REP). D: Joseph Kane. W: James Edward Grant from a novel by Frank J. Nevins. Cast: FORREST TUCKER, ADELE MARA, Bruce CABOT, Adrian BOOTH, Chill WILLS, Jeff Corey, Grant Withers, Barbara Fuller, Roy Barcroft, Pierre Watkin.

Railroad-building mini-epic has lots of action but not much of a script; Kane keeps it moving at a good clip and the performances are OK.

ROCKY MOUNTAIN (1950, WB). D: William Keighley. W: Alan LeMay & Winston Miller. Cast: ERROL FLYNN, PATRICE WYMORE, Scott FORBES, Guinn "Big Boy" WILLIAMS, Slim PICKENS, Dick Jones, Sheb Wooley, Chubby Johnson, Howard Petrie, Yakima Canutt. 83m.

On a mission in the West, a Confederate officer (Flynn) falls in love with a girl (Wymore, Flynn's wife at the time), then relinquishes her to her Yankee boy friend (Forbes) and heroically protects their lives by sacrificing his command in a holding action against attacking Indians. Even the Max Steiner score seems tired in this, Flynn's last Western. It's a trite adventure, a very weak script for LeMay, filmed listlessly outdoors on New Mexico locations (in black-and-white, by Ted McCord) but with a curiously static setbound flavor. In all Flynn had made eight Westerns, all for Warner Brothers, and only one—*They Died with Their Boots On*—was alto-

gether respectable; of the others this one may have been the worst.

Buffs note that Slim Pickens (Louis Lindley) made his movie debut in this one.

RODEO (1952, MONO). D: William Beaudine. W: Charles R. Marion. Cast: John ARCHER, Jane NIGH, Wallace Ford, Frances Rafferty, Frank Ferguson, Jim Bannon. 70m.

Girl takes over an on-the-rocks rodeo and makes it work with the aid of a cowhand. Very cheap picture is pleasant but uninspired.

ROGUE RIVER (1950, EL). D: John Rawlins. W: Louis Lantz. Cast: RORY CALHOUN, PETER GRAVES, Abby DALTON, Frank Fenton, Ralph Sanford. 80m.

Modern-day Western concerns an honest state cop (Graves, his film debut) who becomes embroiled in a bank robbery engineered by his mercurial cousin (Calhoun). Directed with skill and imagination; an ordinary plot, and the acting isn't terrific, but the movie is diverting.

THE ROMANCE OF ROSY RIDGE (1947, MGM). D: Roy Rowland. W: Lester Cole from a MacKinlay Kantor novel. Cast: VAN JOHNSON, JANET LEIGH, Thomas MITCHELL, Marshall Thompson, William Bishop, Elizabeth Risdon, Russell Simpson, Selena Royle. 105m.

The arrival of a mysterious stranger stirs things up in a Missouri valley after the Civil War. It's better than the title might suggest; there's good tension in what's otherwise a standard bucolic yarn with overtones of *Shepherd of the Hills*. Janet Leigh in her debut is excellent. Lester Cole was blacklisted a few years later—one of the "Hollywood Ten"—and did not receive credit for some of his later screenplays, like *Born Free*.

ROMANCE OF THE LIMBERLOST (1938, MONO). D: William Nigh. W: Marion Orth from a Gene Stratton Porter novel. Cast: JEAN PARKER, Eric LINDEN, Marjorie MAIN, Harry Harvey, Edward Pawley.

Yet another version—the second to feature Eric Linden—of the turgid Porter yarn *Girl of the Limberlost* (see listings under that title); strictly for the unsophisticated.

ROMANCE OF THE RIO GRANDE (1929, FOX). D: Alfred Santell. W: Marion Orth from a Katherine F. Gerould novel. Cast: WARNER BAXTER, Mary DUNCAN, Antonio MORENO, Mona MARIS, Robert Edeson. 77m.

Latin lovers and a disputed inheritance. Routine early talkie, with songs.

ROOSTER COGBURN (. . . AND THE LADY) (1975, UNIV). D: Stuart Miller. W: Martin Julien, suggested by the novel *True Grit* by Charles Portis. Cast: JOHN WAYNE, KATHARINE HEPBURN, John McINTIRE, Anthony ZERBE, Richard JORDAN, Strother MARTIN, Richard Romancito, Paul Koslo, Tommy Lee. 107m.

A missionary (Hepburn) joins forces with Marshal Cogburn (Wayne) to track her father's killers. The chase leads through badly plotted, poorly executed adventures, climaxing on a raft floating down the Snake River, with the stars contriving a silly scheme to blow the villains (Jordan, Zerbe) out of the water. The plot, even for a comedy, is so filled with holes that it bears neither analysis nor description. (A sole example: when Cogburn and the lady are surrounded and all seems lost, lo and behold a Gatling gun falls into their hands from nowhere.) Cogburn is depicted as a blustering fool, a hamming and mugging caricature of the lusty vital hero of *True Grit*, and the script (reportedly written pseudonymously by producer Hal Wallis and his wife actress Martha Hyer) is warmed over *African Queen*.

Rooster Cogburn is a vanity showcase for two grey eminences whose careers as top stars began virtually simultaneously in the early 1930s; Hepburn is visibly older than the actor who plays her father; it's a sad movie, empty and silly. Fortunately Wayne redeemed himself after this with *The Shootist*.

ROSE MARIE (1936, MGM). Also titled: INDIAN LOVE CALL. D: W. S. Van Dyke II. W: Frances Goodrich, Albert Hackett & Alice D. Miller from the operetta by Otto A. Harbach, Oscar Hammerstein II, Rudolf Friml & Herbert Stothart. Cast: JEANETTE MacDONALD, NELSON EDDY, Reginald OWEN, James STEWART, Allan JONES, Alan Mowbray, Gilda Gray, Robert Greig, David Niven, Herman Bing, Lucien Littlefield, Russell Hicks, Jack Pennick. 110m.

Lady singer (MacDonald), courted briefly by young David Niven, races against a stalwart Mountie (Eddy) to try to reach her fugitive brother (Stewart) ahead of the law; things get complicated when she falls in love with the lawman. The songs of course include "Indian Love Call." For MacDonald-Eddy operetta lovers only.

ROSE MARIE (1954, MGM). D: Mervyn Leroy. W: Ronald Millar & George Froeschel from the operetta (see above). Cast: ANN BLYTH, HOWARD KEEL, FERNANDO LAMAS, Bert LAHR, Marjorie MAIN, Joan Taylor, Ray Collins, Chief Nipo Strongheart. 115m.

Updated remake returns to the plot of the stage play and has very little left of the pursuit plot of the earlier movie. In this one an orphan tomboy grows up to become the object of romantic vying by a cheerful French-Canadian trapper (Lamas) and a barrel-chested Mountie (Keel). The songs, and the photography (Paul C. Vogel), are pleasant enough but the picture seems far too long.

ROSE OF CIMARRON (1952, FOX). D: Harry Keller. W: Maurice Geraghty. Cast: MALA POWERS, JACK BEUTEL, Bill WILLIAMS, Jim DAVIS, Bob STEELE, William Phipps, Monte Blue, Dick Curtis, Art Smith, Irving Bacon, George Chandler, John Doucette, Tommy Cook, William Schallert, Byron Foulger.

The Bob Steele plot with a girl in place of a boy. Simpleminded black-and-white hack job offers terrible acting but it's speedy and the cast is filled with faces familiar to buffs.

ROSE OF THE RANCHO (1936, PARA). D: Marion Gering. W: Six writers from the play by David Belasco & Richard W. Tully. Cast: JOHN BOLES, GLADYS SWARTHOUT, Charles BICKFORD, H. B. Warner, Pedro de Cordoba, William Howard.

Musical low-comedy oater is about a Jewish cowboy (Willie Howard), lady bandit (Swarthout), vigilantes (Bickford, Warner) and a dull government agent (Boles). It's not so much that it's dated; it was terrible to begin with.

ROSE OF THE RIO GRANDE (1938, MONO). D: William Nigh. W: Dorothy Reid & Ralph Bettinson from a Johnston McCulley story. Cast: JOHN CARROLL, MOVITA (Castaneda), Antonio MORENO, Duncan RENALDO, Don Alvarado, Lina Basquette, George Cleveland. 63m.

Dashing bandido yarn is ludicrous in all respects, particularly inasmuch as Carroll was—to put it kindly—an indifferent horseman at the time; only in later years did he find a firm seat on the saddle. He was regarded in some quarters as Hollywood's vest-pocket answer to Clark Gable; he could act (although his accent is silly here) but he lacked magnetism, and this film had all the hokey stupidity of Monogram's worst serials.

ROUGH NIGHT IN JERICHO (1967, UNIV). D: Arnold Laven. W: Sydney Boehm & Marvin H. Albert from a novel by Albert. Cast: GEORGE PEPPARD, DEAN MARTIN, JEAN SIMMONS, John McINTIRE, Don GALLOWAY, Slim PICKENS, Brad Weston, Richard O'Brien, Carol Anderson, John Napier. 104m.

Evil town boss (Martin) forces his affections on the lady owner of a stagecoach line (Simmons); then a stalwart drifter (Peppard) arrives with his humorous sidekick (McIntire) to stand up for the lady and to outwit and outfight the bad guys (who also include Pickens and Weston). Add to that familiar corn a huge helping of witlessly sadistic mayhem and you get a truly rotten movie; the only performers to salvage their dignity are Simmons and McIntire. Peppard's character is just as disagreeable as Martin's; one entertains the dim hope they may kill each other off, but of course it's more boringly predictable than that.

ROUGH ROMANCE (1930, FOX). D: A. F. Erickson. W: Elliott Lester from a Kenneth B. Clark story. Cast: GEORGE O'BRIEN, HELEN CHANDLER, Antonio MORENO, Harry Cording, Eddie Borden, Roy Stewart. 54m.

Standard low-budget ranch-romance oater is of note to buffs mainly for a brief unbilled appearance by the young John Wayne.

ROUGHSHOD (1949, RKO). D: Mark Robson. W: Geoffrey Homes, Hugo Butler & Peter Viertel. Cast: ROBERT STERLING, GLORIA GRAHAME, Claude JARMAN, Jr., John IRELAND, Jeff Donnell, Martha Hyer, Myrna Dell. 86m.

A homesteader becomes convinced night riders are out to get him. Confused drama is well photographed (Joseph F. Biroc) but muddled.

THE ROUNDERS (1965, MGM). DW: Burt Kennedy from Max Evans's novel. Cast: GLENN FORD, HENRY FONDA, Chill WILLS, Sue Anne LANGDON, Edgar BUCHANAN, Denver Pyle, Joan Freeman, Hope Holliday, Barton MacLane, Peter Fonda. 85m.

Two hard-luck bronc wranglers keep trying to tame an unbreakable horse while they descend from one seedy job to another. The two stars play the not-very-bright cowhands with exquisite aplomb and there is fine support from Chill Wills as a crusty rancher, Langdon and Freeman as the ladies in their lives, and Buchanan as a moonshiner who can't sell his product because he drinks it up too fast. Fine photography (Paul C. Vogel). Buffs note that the young Peter Fonda is not billed in the film's credits.

THE ROUND-UP (1941, PARA). D: Lesley Selander. W: Harold Shumate from a play by Edmund Day. Cast: RICHARD DIX, PATRICIA MORISON, Preston FOSTER, Jerome Cowan, Douglas Kennedy, Lee

"Lasses" White, Don Wilson, Douglas Dumbrille, The King's Men.

Vest-pocket cattle empire epic has Dix as a rancher whose bride's old beau shows up to complicate things. Familiar triangle soapmeller has dated comedy relief and Western trappings.

RUN FOR COVER (1955, PARA). D: Nicholas Ray. W: Winston Miller, Harriet Frank, Jr., & Irving Ravetch. Cast: JAMES CAGNEY, JOHN DEREK, VIVECA LINDFORS, Jean HERSHOLT, Ernest BORGNINE, Jack Lambert, Grant Withers, Ray Teal, Trevor Bardette, Irving Bacon, John Miljan, Gus Schilling, Denver Pyle. 93m.

Aging gunfighter (Cagney) takes a wayward cocky youth (Derek) under his wing, then after a mistaken-identity gunfight is appointed sheriff of a small town where he falls in love with the woman (Lindfors) who nurses him after the shoot-out; conflicts erupt between him and the kid, and between all of them and a gang of outlaws, leading to a long gruelling desert pursuit. It's a well packaged Pine-Thomas production with a good performance by Hersholt, in his last movie, as Lindfors's father. The middle sags but most of it is a good, taut, suspense story: no masterwork by any means but Cagney's presence elevates it and Ray directs with a very sure hand.

RUNNING TARGET (1956, UA). D: Marvin Weinstein. W: Weinstein, Jack C. Couffer & Conrad Hall from a Steve Frazee story. Cast: ARTHUR FRANZ, Doris DOWLING, Myron Healey, James Parnell, Richard Reeves. 83m.

Stolid purposeful sheriff (Franz) leads a posse after four dangerous fugitives. The tense script peoples the movie with exceptionally well drawn characters; directing and acting are quite good; for a low-budget quickie it's remarkably satisfactory.

RUN OF THE ARROW (1956, RKO). DW: Samuel Fuller. Cast: ROD STEIGER, BRIAN KEITH, Sarita MONTIEL, Ralph MEEKER, Jay C. FLIPPEN, Charles BRONSON, Colonel Tim McCOY, Olive Carey, H.M. Wynant, Frank DeKOVA, Neile Morrow. 86m.

A greasy ex-Confederate private (Steiger) hates the Union so much that after the Civil War he joins the Sioux Indians just to have an excuse to carry on his private war against Yankees. Love and events gradually reform him. Brian Keith, as a cavalry officer, steals the show. There's violent action, some of it very vicious for its time, and the photography (Joseph Biroc) is excellent, but it's a very confused melodrama, grim and harsh and filled with hate, and it's curiously ill-structured, lacking balance or rhythm or sense. Steiger's overblown Method makes him stand out like a giraffe in a bathtub: his dialect, veering wildly from phony Southern to phony Irish to simply weird, may remind you of Brando's imbecilic performance in *The Missouri Breaks*, and Steiger's sullen, urban mannerisms are completely out of place here. Jay C. Flippen in a black fright wig is an amusing but altogether unbelievable Sioux Indian; altogether the absurdities are innumerable and stultifying; the film is overdirected nearly to the point of hysteria and overwrought, right down to the all-stops Victor Young score. It has a certain force—that of a blunt instrument—but forceful trash is still trash.

RUN TO THE HIGH COUNTRY (1974, IND). DW: Keith Larsen. Cast: KEITH LARSEN, Karen STEELE, Erik Larsen, Alvin Keeswold, Randy Burt, Lawrence J. Rink.

Competent Utah scenic photography (Herbert Von Theiss) is the only redeeming quality of this badly directed juvenile outdoor adventure about a mountain boy who protects wild animals from hunters and trappers. If a kid emulated such nonsense and tried to befriend untrained wild creatures as happens in these wilderness epics, he'd be inside a cougar's tummy before he could say Grizzly Adams.

RUSTLERS' PARADISE (1935, IND). D: Harry Fraser. W: Weston Edwards & Monroe Talbot. Cast: HARRY CAREY, Gertrude MESSINGER, Edmund COBB, Chuck Morrison, Chief Thundercloud. 60m.

Carey, as usual dressed in black, has it out with cattle thieves in a routine programmer.

RUSTLERS' ROUNDUP (1933, UNIV). D: Henry MacRae. W: Jack Cunningham, Ella O'Neill & Frank Clark. Cast: TOM MIX, Diane SINCLAIR, Douglas DUMBRILLE, Roy Stewart, William Desmond, Noah Beery, Jr., Bud Osborne, Walter Brennan, Gilbert Holmes. 56m.

Just what the title implies. Good stunt work.

THE SACKETTS (1979, NBC). D: Robert Totten. W: Jim Byrnes from two novels by Louis L'Amour. Cast: SAM ELLIOTT, BEN JOHNSON, GLENN FORD, TOM SELLECK, Jeff OSTERHAGE, Jack ELAM, Ruth ROMAN, L.Q. JONES, Marcy HANSON, Slim PICKENS, Mercedes McCAMBRIDGE, John VERNON, Gilbert ROLAND. 184m.

Stylish, well-cast, four-hour TV mini-series interweaves several stories about three brothers (Elliott, Selleck, Osterhage) who get into various scrapes in the old West until, at the end, they are reunited in a big Santa Fe shoot-out. The plot is sometimes bewildering, partly because of the network's churlish decision to cut the film from its original six hours to four. It has the look and flavor of an epic Western of the late 1940s; Totten directs with authority and the characters are well delineated and well portrayed. Douglas Netter's production team, which produced this one, also made *Wild Times*.

SADDLE THE WIND (1958, MGM). D: Robert Parrish. W: Rod Serling & Thomas Thompson. Cast: ROBERT TAYLOR, JULIE LONDON, JOHN CASSAVETES, Donald CRISP, Royal Dano, Charles McGraw, Richard Erdman, Ray Teal, Douglas Spencer. 84m.

A onetime gunfighter (Taylor), who's now a settled-down rancher, has a kid brother (Cassavetes) who's wild and trigger-happy. Things come to a head between them when the kid gets jealous of his brother's interest in his girl friend (London) and when the two brothers quarrel over the right of a family of homesteaders to squat on a corner of the ranch. The homesteaders' patriarch is played by Royal Dano in a relatively brief but stunningly riveting performance of power and magnetism; unfortunately his excellence only emphasizes the poverty of the direction of the other actors. Cassavetes is overblown and miscast as the reckless psychopathic kid, and there's no way to believe he is Taylor's brother. Taylor and London needed strong direction and didn't get it here. Crisp is not believably Western as a neighbor rancher, Taylor's mentor. Despite thoughtful intentions the film is disappointingly stereotyped.

SADDLE TRAMP (1950, UNIV). D: Hugo Fregonese. W: Harold Shumate. Cast: JOEL McCREA, WANDA HENDRIX, Paul PICERNI, John McINTIRE, John RUSSELL, Ed BEGLEY, Jeanette Nolan, John Ridgely, Antonio Moreno, Russell Simpson. 77m.

Charming quiet drifter arrives in the middle of a range war to look after a dead pal's children; he's a "peaceable man" but of course in the end he has to fight it out with the varmints. The characters are cut from stock but well fitted to the story; the dialogue is pretty good; McCrea is exceedingly engaging in his casual way with this sort of role; in short it's unexceptional but satisfactory. It's in Technicolor.

THE SAGA OF HEMP BROWN (1958, UNIV). D: Richard Carlson. W: Stuart

Anthony & Karen DeWolf. Cast: RORY CALHOUN, BEVERLY GARLAND, Russell JOHNSON, John Larch, Allan "Rocky" Lane, Morris Ankrum, Francis J. McDonald. 80m.

Cavalry officer (Calhoun) is framed for a payroll robbery and drummed out of the army; he hooks up with an itinerant medicine show and hunts for the bad guy who framed him. Routine script is poorly directed by actor Carlson.

THE SAGEBRUSH FAMILY TRAILS WEST (1940, IND). D: Peter Stewart. W: William Lively. Cast: Bobby CLARK, Minerva URECAL, Earle Hodgins, Joyce Bryant. 57m.

Even worse than the title suggests, this story about a thirteen-year-old battling bad guys is the sort of movie that gave "B" pictures a bad name. "Peter Stewart" is a nom-de-guerre of prolific hack director Sam Newfield.

SALOME, WHERE SHE DANCED (1945, UNIV). D: Charles Lamont. W: Laurence Stallings from a novel by Michael J. Phillips. Cast: YVONNE DeCARLO, ROD CAMERON, Albert DEKKER, Walter SLEZAK, Marjorie Rambeau, David Bruce, J. Edward Bromberg, John Litel, Arthur Hohl. 90m.

Veil dancer uses her act as a front for her activities as a Civil War spy. It's in Technicolor, with swordfights and songs, but it's a ghastly movie: quite funny but it wasn't intended to be. This was Cameron's first starring role (he was 33) and publicity flacks at the time insisted that it was Yvonne DeCarlo's film debut and that she'd been discovered when she'd submitted her photo in a contest. That canard has found its way into serious filmographies and reference books. Actually she'd been kicking around in "B" pictures for quite a while and even had starred in a few, like *The Deerslayer* (1943). There is, in fact, a whistle-stop town in Arizona west of Gila Bend that calls itself Salome, Where She Danced. Last time I was there it consisted of a one-building combination store, post office and gas station; population three.

SAM WHISKEY (1969, UA). D: Arnold Laven. W: William Norton. Cast: BURT REYNOLDS, ANGIE DICKINSON, CLINT WALKER, OSSIE DAVIS, William SCHALLERT, Rick Davis, Del Reeves, Chubby Johnson. 96m.

A saddle tramp (Reynolds) is lured by a beauty (Dickinson) into trying to smuggle a stolen gold fortune back into the Denver Mint whence it was heisted. The cast is attractive but the comedy falls flat in this farce. Similar plots have been used in such movies as *The Train Robbers* and *The Fastest Guitar Alive*; somehow the premise always seems to lead to a rotten movie; of the three films this is the best but that's saying very little.

SAN ANTONE (1953, REP). D: Joseph Kane. W: Steve Fisher from a Curt Carroll novel. Cast: ROD CAMERON, ARLEEN WHELAN, FORREST TUCKER, KATY JURADO, Douglas KENNEDY, Harry Carey, Jr., Roy Roberts, Rodolfo Acosta, Bob Steele, George Cleveland. 90m.

Manhunt Western has a female villain (Whelan), a confused plot and some preaching about racial intolerance; in black-and-white. Fair.

SAN ANTONIO (1945, WB). D: David Butler & Robert Florey. W: Alan LeMay & W. R. Burnett. Cast: ERROL FLYNN, ALEXIS SMITH, Victor FRANCEN, S. Z. SAKALL, Paul KELLY, Florence Bates, John Litel, Robert Barrat, Robert Shayne, Pedro de Cordoba, Monte Blue, Tom Tyler, Chris-Pin Martin, Harry Cording, Dan Seymour, Normal Willis, Charles Stevens, Francis Ford, Lane Chandler, Hal Taliaferro, Eddy Waller, James Flavin. 111m.

Rancher fights it out with rustlers; the bad guy (Francen) owns the saloon where Flynn's lady-love works, and you can guess the rest. Lavishly assembled with Technicolor photography (Bert Glennon), a heroic score (Max Steiner), this was produced by Robert Buckner—the writer who'd scripted such Flynn oaters as *Santa Fe Trail* and *Dodge City*—and despite all the big names on both ends of the camera it turned out to be dull, unconvincing, mannered and stultifyingly overburdened with formula set pieces (saloon brawls, dance-hall songs, so forth).

THE SAN FRANCISCO STORY (1952, WB). D: Robert Parrish. W: D. D. Beauchamp, Stanley C. Rubin & Edmund L. Hartmann, from a novel by Richard Summers. Cast: JOEL McCREA, YVONNE De CARLO, Sidney BLACKMER, Richard Erdman, Florence Bates, Onslow Stevens, O. Z. Whitehead, Ralph Dumke, Lane Chandler. 80m.

In early muddy San Francisco during the gold rush a miner-turned-vigilante (McCrea) cleans up the tough element. Black-and-white film is well acted but banal.

SANTA FE (1951, COL). D: Irving Pichel. W: Kenneth Gamet & Louis Stevens from a novel by James L. Marshall. Cast: RANDOLPH SCOTT, JANIS CARTER, Jerome COURTLAND, John Archer, Jock Mahoney, Peter Thompson, Chief Thundercloud, Frank Ferguson, Billy House, Irving Pichel. 88m.

Again the one about brothers on opposite sides of the law; in this one Scott is a railroader and his brothers are the train robbers. Briskly directed, in black-and-white.

SANTA FE PASSAGE (1955, REP). D: William Witney. W: Lillie Hayward from the Clay Fisher novel. Cast: JOHN PAYNE, ROD CAMERON, FAITH DOMERGUE, Slim PICKENS, Leo Gordon. 69m.

A scout who hates Indians guides a wagon train from the Missouri River to New Mexico. There's a good deal of color and action but the script emphasizes the cliches, reducing the good novel to a formula oater; acting by the principals is a bit dreary.

SANTA FE TRAIL (1940, WB). D: Michael Curtiz. W: Robert H. Buckner. Cast: ERROL FLYNN, OLIVIA De HAVILLAND, RAYMOND MASSEY, RONALD REAGAN, William LUNDIGAN, Van HEFLIN, Alan Hale, Sr., Guinn "Big Boy" Williams, Ward Bond, Douglas Fowley, Gene Reynolds, Henry O'Neill, John Litel, Moroni Olsen, Alan Baxter, David Bruce, Joe Sawyer, Charles Middleton, Russell Simpson, Russell Hicks, Frank Wilcox, Hobart Cavanaugh, Susan Peters, Spencer Charters, Luis Alberni. 110m.

Six army officers in pre-Civil War Kansas fight battles of words and guns with abolitionist John Brown (Massey, in a role he later repeated in *Seven Angry Men*). The climax is the battle at Harpers Ferry that began the War Between the States. What any of it has to do with the Santa Fe Trail is beyond me. The heroes include Jeb Stuart (Flynn), Robert E. Lee (Olsen) and George Armstrong Custer (played, perhaps fittingly, by Ronald Reagan, although it's an anachronism because at the time of these events Custer was a schoolboy). It's history twisted far beyond recognition: oversimplified theme, overcomplicated plot, hokey slapstick, juvenile nonsense. This was Flynn's third Western; it had the same stock company and crew as the first two, including producer Hal B. Wallis and composer Max Steiner.

SANTEE (1973, IND). D: Gary Nelson. W: Brand Bell. Cast: GLENN FORD, DANA WYNTER, Michael BURNS, Jay SILVERHEELS, Harry TOWNES, Robert J. WILKE, John Larch, Robert Donner, Taylor Lacher, John Bailey, Lindsay Crosby.

An aging horse rancher (Ford) has spent ten years as a bounty hunter searching for the killers of his son. He is thrown together with the greenhorn son (Burns) of an outlaw (Wilke) whom he's been forced to kill. The unexceptional plot misses some good opportunities for suspense; score (Don Randi) is poor and the photography (Donald Morgan) is routine, depicting mostly dull locations on the New Mexico flatlands, and the editing (George W. Brooks) is unusually clumsy—in one early shot a boom microphone seen in several frames should have been cut out, for example. And there's an imbecilic soundtrack ballad, "Jody," sung by rock group Paul Revere and the Raiders. Obviously, then, this movie has its shortcomings. But despite all that, it's a surprisingly satisfying vest-pocket oater, thanks to excellent performances, professionally capable directing and a screenplay that provides believable characters, interesting dialogue and a real flavor of the working West. The movie was distributed independently, did not reach the major markets and was seen by very few people; it deserved a better run for its money.

SASKATCHEWAN (1954, UNIV). D: Raoul Walsh. W: Gil Doud. Cast: ALAN LADD, SHELLEY WINTERS, J. Carrol NAISH, Richard LONG, Hugh O'Brian, Robert Douglas, George J. Lewis, Antonio Moreno, Jay Silverheels, Lowell Gilmore. 87m.

The one about the white man who was raised by Indians. In this case he (Ladd) grows up to be a Canadian Mountie, and his assignment is to persuade the Sioux, who have fled north across the border after the Custer massacre, to return to the States. Winters plays a saloon gal; she's out of place. Filmed on location with magnificent color scenery, near Banff, and plenty of hard-riding action; but it's an insipid screenplay and a largely boring movie.

THE SAVAGE (1952, PARA). D: George Marshall. W: Sydney Boehm from a novel by L. L. Foreman. Cast: CHARLTON HESTON, Susan MORROW, Joan TAYLOR, Peter Hanson, Ted de Corsia, Milburn Stone, Don Porter, Richard Rober. 95m.

Another one about a white man raised by the Sioux. (Compare *Saskatchewan*.) When war between the races breaks out, his loyalties are torn. This one is grimly overacted and the script makes no attempt to probe actual problems, but there's plenty of color and action; it's not as bad as some.

THE SAVAGE HORDE (1950, REP). D: Joseph Kane. W: Kenneth Gamet, Thames Williamson & Gerald Geraghty. Cast: WILLIAM ELLIOTT, ADRIAN BOOTH, Noah BEERY, Jr., Grant WITHERS, Jim Davis, Barbara Fuller, Douglas Dumbrille,

Bob Steele, Will Wright, Roy Barcroft, Hal Taliaferro, Earle Hodgins, Lloyd Ingraham, Charles Stevens, James Flavin, Marshall Reed, Kermit Maynard, George Chesebro, Bud Osborne, Reed Howes. 90m.

Desperado predator gangs versus honest ranchers: the plot is old-hat but it's handled with panache; Beery stands out as small rancher Larrabee; Elliott is the drifting gunman who comes to their aid in classic mythology fashion. Briskly directed, it's one of the best of Elliott's movies, with a powerful cast of fine supporting players, an interesting variation on the same myth that gave us *Shane*.

SAVAGE PAMPAS (1967, IND). D: Hugo Fregonese. W: Fregonese, John Melson, Ulysse de Murat & Homero Manzi. Cast: ROBERT TAYLOR, TY HARDIN, Rosenda MONTEROS, Ron Randell, Marc Lawrence. 99m.

A gang of renegade rebels plunders the Argentine pampas until an officer (Taylor) and his shattered company of soldiers fight them off. Remake of the 1946 Argentine movie *Pampa Barbara* is dull and phony.

THE SAVAGE WILDERNESS (1955)—See THE LAST FRONTIER.

SCALAWAG (1973, PARA). D: Kirk Douglas. W: Albert Maltz & Ben Barzman from Robert Louis Stevenson's novel *Treasure Island*. Cast: KIRK DOUGLAS, Mark LESTER, Neville BRAND, Don Stroud, Lesley Anne Down, George Eastman. 93m.

The action, with songs, is set in the California desert of the 1840s, but this is simply a Western version of *Treasure Island* with Douglas as the peg-legged Long John Silver who shows off his jolly brutal prowess with various weapons to an impressionable boy (Lester) as he tracks a gang of double-crossing pirates who've stolen his treasure of doubloons. Photography (Jack Cardiff) is professionally capable but little else is; the humor is sophomoric, the script silly and the performances poor; it was filmed in Yugoslavia, and looks it. This marked Douglas's directorial debut; he did a better job later with the unfortunate but well-made *Posse*.

THE SCALPHUNTERS (1968, UA). D: Sidney Pollack. W: William W. Norton. Cast: BURT LANCASTER, OSSIE DAVIS, SHELLEY WINTERS, TELLY SAVALAS, Paul PICERNI, Dabney Coleman, Dan Vadis, Armando Silvestre, Nick Cravat. 102m.

Tongue-in-cheek Western latched onto the Black Power theme with Davis as an erudite runaway slave trying to stay free by using his wits; he teams up with a lusty, crude fur-trapper (Lancaster) who's trying to reclaim his stolen pelts from a tribe of Indians and then from the gang of scalphunters who steal the pelts from them. Savalas is the head scalphunter and Winters is his camp-following tart who travels in a wagon that houses her brass bed; the entire picture is on that cornball level of contrivance and forced humor. There's a pretty good score (Elmer Bernstein) but the directing is heavy-handed, the script is too obvious and bogs down in its "meaningful" cliches, and the proceedings are far too predictable to be very entertaining. The film got excellent reviews in some quarters but I suspect that's because its subject matter was fashionable and there were no decent contemporary Westerns with which to compare it; in any case it's clumsy and unwieldy.

THE SEA OF GRASS (1946, MGM). D: Elia Kazan. W: Marguerite Roberts & Vincent Lawrence from Conrad Richter's novel. Cast: SPENCER TRACY, KATHARINE HEPBURN, ROBERT WALKER, MELVYN DOUGLAS, Phyllis THAXTER, Harry CAREY, Edgar BUCHANAN, Robert Armstrong, Douglas Fowley, Robert Barrat, William Challee, Bill Phillips. 131m.

An Eastern bride tries to match strength with her mossyhorn cattleman husband; their marriage has its ups and downs; there are enough plots to keep half a dozen movies busy; the result is confusion; what there is of the show is stolen by the two stars and by Walker as the wastrel son. This is our only opportunity to see the Tracy-Hepburn pairing in a Western; would that it were a better one; unhappily it's a disappointing adaptation of Richter's novel, although it does hold the attention.

THE SEARCHERS (1956, WB). D: John Ford. W: Frank S. Nugent from Alan LeMay's novel. Cast: JOHN WAYNE, JEFFREY HUNTER, VERA MILES, Ward BOND, Ken CURTIS, Natalie Wood, John Qualen, Walter Coy, Hank Worden, Harry Carey, Jr., Antonio Moreno, Patrick Wayne, Henry Brandon, Dorothy Jordan, Olive Carey, Lana Wood, Pippa Scott. 120m.

In essence *The Searchers* tells the straightforward story of a grim ordeal: the relentless five-year hunt by two Texans (Wayne, Hunter) for a young girl (Natalie Wood) who's been kidnapped by a Comanche chief (Brandon). The drama is built on complicated conflicts among the characters and the erosive effects of the events upon their lives; it's too rich to be cheated by any perfunctory summary. Unquestionably *The Searchers* stands as one of the few genuine American film epics. Critic Roger Greenspun (*The New York Times*, September 9, 1973) reckons *The Searchers* to be the greatest American movie of all time. I wouldn't go that far, but it unquestionably is one of the few Westerns that deserve to be regarded as important works of art. In many ways it is the quintessential John Ford movie, although he was getting old and saw things more darkly than before; it is heavier, far less frivolous and romantic than, say, *Rio Grande*.

The movie is perfectly crafted, right down to the photographic framework—a door opening on Monument Valley—which both opens and closes the movie. It is Ford's first wide-screen (VistaVision) movie; he and his cinematographer (Winton C. Hoch) filled every frame with flawlessly splendid composition and subtle imagery. Pictorially it is Ford's masterpiece; for panoramic painter's-eye compositions it has no equal.

One must see the film a dozen times before discovering some of its subtle imagery. The score (Max Steiner) is a trifle dated but suitable, and the editing (Jack Murray) is superb, fitting a vast number of scenes, characters and subplots into the film's two hours. (It must be pointed out that Ford in effect edited his own films in the camera; he rarely shot any scenes that he didn't use.)

Wayne's performance as the bigoted hard Ethan Edwards, a man whose relentlessness is fueled by rage, is one of the finest sustained characterizations I've seen on film. It establishes that Wayne could be a fine actor when he tried, and when he had proper direction. Some of the others in the cast nearly match the quality of his work; particularly notable are Hunter, Miles, Bond, Qualen, Olive Carey, Dobie Carey and Worden.

The film does have weaknesses. The fatuity of some scenes is lamentable. Ford's excesses of bad slapstick comedy, dating right back to his earliest two-reelers, were a failing he never overcame; they are personified in *The Searchers* by Ken Curtis in one of his patented rustic caricatures, by Pat Wayne (John's son) as an improbably inept greenhorn cavalry officer, and by Hunter and Miles in a running-gag love/hate romance that is too cute by far, even though both performers are marvelous. All these are painfully out of place and tend to inspire disbelief, wrenching us out of our deep involvement in the story. The dialogue is abrasively silly now and then; the acting in a few supporting roles is mediocre; these are minor cavils and they don't take away from the fact that *The Searchers* is undeniably, and wonderfully, a masterpiece.

THE SECOND GREATEST SEX (1955, UNIV). D: George Marshall. W: Charles Hoffman. Cast: JEANNE CRAIN, GEORGE NADER, Kitty KALLEN, Bert LAHR, Keith ANDES, Mamie VAN DOREN, Tommy Rall, Paul Gilbert, Jimmy Boyd. 86m.

Musical Western updates *Lysistrata* with ranch women in Kansas banding together to deny sex to their husbands in order to bring an end to a long-term feud. It's mediocre but a curiosity.

THE SECOND TIME AROUND (1961, PARA). D: Vincent Sherman. W: Oscar Saul & Cecil Dan Hansen from a Richard Roberts novel. Cast: DEBBIE REYNOLDS, STEVE FORREST, Andy GRIFFITH, Juliet PROWSE, Thelma RITTER, Isobel Elsom, Ken Scott. 99m.

Comedy concerns a frontier widow who's elected sheriff of a wild cowboy town. Good cast, fair script, snappy directing; nothing new but it's fairly amusing.

THE SECRET OF CONVICT LAKE (1951, FOX). D: Michael Gordon. W: Oscar Saul, Anna Hunger, Jack Pollexfen & Victor Trivas. Cast: GLENN FORD, GENE TIERNEY, ETHEL BARRYMORE, ZACHARY SCOTT, Ann DVORAK, Jeanette Nolan, Richard Hylton. 83m.

A group of escaped convicts take refuge in a storm in a mountain village inhabited only by women. Ford plays the bad guy who reforms and defends the ladies against the other baddies; Barrymore, as the tough matriarch, has great fun in the blustery role. It's trite but very well done. In black-and-white.

THE SECRET OF TREASURE MOUNTAIN (1956, COL). D: Seymour Friedman. W: David Lang. Cast: RAYMOND BURR, Valerie FRENCH, William Prince, Susan Cummings, Lance Fuller. 67m.

The hunt for buried Indian treasure: unimaginative "B" movie.

SECRETS (1933, UA). D: Frank Forzage. W: Frances Marion from the play by Rudolph Besier & May Edington. Cast: MARY PICKFORD, LESLIE HOWARD, C. Aubrey SMITH, Mona MARIS, Blanche Frederici, Herbert Evans, Doris Lloyd, Ned Sparks, Virginia Grey. 85m.

A sort of soap-opera *Covered Wagon*, this has the stars settling a homestead and making a valiant go of it; the movie follows their lives from their first young meeting to old age. This was a remake of a 1924 Norma Talmadge film, also directed by Borzage. Pickford, a great star but not a great actress, is quite terrible in it; it was her last film and one of her few talkies; today it's a period piece.

SEMINOLE (1953, UNIV). D: Budd Boetticher. W: Charles K. Peck. Cast: ROCK HUDSON, BARBARA HALE, Anthony QUINN, Richard CARLSON, Russell Johnson, Lee Marvin, James Best, Hugh O'Brian. 87m.

Army officer (Hudson) fights white villains and warring Seminole Indians in the Deep South—mostly the Everglades—before the Civil War. Standard hokey plot is well directed and has a good supporting cast, but it's nothing more than a time-killer.

SEMINOLE UPRISING (1955, COL). D: Earl Bellamy. W: Robert E. Kent from a Curt Brandon novel. Cast: GEORGE MONTGOMERY, KARIN BOOTH, Ed Hinton, John Pickard, William Fawcett, Rory Mallinson. 74m.

The usual cavalry-versus-Indians formula, this one has less action than most; hapless and mediocre.

SERGEANT RUTLEDGE (1960, WB). D: John Ford. W: James Warner Bellah & Willis Goldbeck from Bellah's novel. Cast: JEFFREY HUNTER, WOODY STRODE, Constance TOWERS, Juano HERNANDEZ, Billie Burke, Jack Pennick, Willis Bouchey, Carleton Young, Walter Reed, Mae Marsh, Hank Worden, Estelle Winwood, Jack Perrin, Bill Henry, Judson Pratt, Chuck Hayward, Fred Libby, Toby Richards, Cliff Lyons. 111m.

A black sergeant (Strode) in the Ninth (Negro) Cavalry Regiment is court-martialed for murder; a white lieutenant (Hunter) tries to prove him innocent. There are action flashbacks to Indian battles and brawls but it's a diffuse yarn; the plot is muddled with confusing elements of rape and bigotry and with a dull romance between Hunter and Towers. Woody Strode's imposing performance is excellent and Bert Glennon's photography is fine but the film is not up to the usual Ford-Bellah standard; it's one of the least of Ford's Westerns. Still, that makes it better than nearly anybody else's.

SERGEANTS THREE (1962, UA). D: John Sturges. W: W.R. Burnett, based on *Gunga Din*. Cast: FRANK SINATRA, DEAN MARTIN, SAMMY DAVIS, Jr., Peter LAWFORD, Joey BISHOP, Ruta LEE, Henry Silva, Gary Crosby. 112m.

The Gunga Din character is Sammy Davis, Jr., as a mascot-like follower of a cavalry troop. It's supposedly an action comedy and the emphasis is on the action with a lot of killing that evidently is supposed to be very funny. This is one of those slapstick rat-pack comedies that Sinatra and his buddies put together for their own amusement; what Bur-

nett and Sturges are doing here is beyond comprehension (as was Robert Aldrich's presence in the similar rat-pack turkey *Four for Texas*). Asinine and nauseating.

SEVEN ALONE (1975, IND). D: Earl Bellamy. W: Eleanor Lamb & Douglas C. Stewart from an Honor Morrow novel. Cast: DEWEY MARTIN, ALDO RAY, Anne COLLINGS, Dean Smith, James Griffith, Stewart Petersen, Bea Morris, Scott Petersen, Dehl Berti. 96m.

In 1843, accompanied by a title song warbled by Pat Boone, seven kids are orphaned and try to make it through to Oregon on their own, two thousand miles by covered wagon; they are variously hindered and assisted along the way by an assortment of frontier types. Very loosely based on fact, this latter-day mini-imitation of *The Covered Wagon* was filmed on Wyoming locations and is representative of the swarm of low-budget independent "family" wilderness movies produced in the mid-1970s for the spillover Walt Disney trade. It's dull, flat, predictable and juvenile; although it was made for theatrical release it has all the flavor of a listless made-for-TV timekiller. The cast, however, is engaging.

SEVEN ANGRY MEN (1955, AA). D: Charles Marquis Warren. W: Daniel B. Ullman. Cast: RAYMOND MASSEY, JEFFREY HUNTER, DEBRA PAGET, Larry PENNELL, James ANDERSON, John SMITH, Guy WILLIAMS, James BEST, Dennis Weaver, Leo Gordon, Dabbs Greer, Ann Tyrrell, James Edwards, John Pickard, Jack Perrin, Robert L. Simon, Dabbs Greer. 90m.

Abolitionist John Brown (Massey, repeating the role he played in *Santa Fe Trail*) ruthlessly dominates his large family of sons (Hunter, Pennell, Anderson, Smith, so forth) in his singleminded attempt to wipe out slavery in the South. Script is superficial with the emphasis on intrafamilial haggling and a Hollywood romance between Hunter and Paget but it hews to the historical line much more closely than most movies of its kind and the solid acting, good directing and rousing climax make it superior to most low-budget oaters. In black-and-white.

SEVEN BRIDES FOR SEVEN BROTHERS (1954, MGM). D: Stanley Donen. W: Albert Hackett, Frances Goodrich & Dorothy Kingsley from Stephen Vincent Benet's short story "Rape of the Sabine Women." Cast: (the brothers): HOWARD KEEL, Russ TAMBLYN, Jeff RICHARDS, Marc Platt, Matt Mattox, Tommy Rall, Jacques d'Amboise. (the brides): JANE POWELL, Julie NEWMEYER (Newmar), Virginia

Gibbs, Ruta Kilmonis (Lee), Virginia Gibson, Nancy Kilgas, Betty Carr, Norma Doggett. **Also featuring Ian Wolfe, Howard Petrie, Russell Simpson, 103m.**

Set in frontier Oregon (circa 1850), this has seven rustic characters looking for wives; it's a delightful, albeit treacly, musicomedy with lusty choreography (Michael Kidd), lively songs (Johnny Mercer, Adolph Deutsch and Saul Chaplin) and plentiful good laughs. An occasional annoying use of painted scenic backdrops for the musical numbers is distracting and the characters are too bucolically simpleminded for belief but it's good fun; nominated for an Academy Award as best picture. Since the 1930s very few successful musicals have been written directly for the screen; this was a signal exception.

SEVEN CITIES OF GOLD (1955, FOX). D: Robert D. Webb. W: Richard L. Breen, John C. Higgins & Joseph Petracca from a novel by Isabelle G. Ziegler. Cast: ANTHONY QUINN, MICHAEL RENNIE, RICHARD EGAN, JEFFREY HUNTER, Rita MORENO, Leslie Bradley, Eduardo Norlega. 103m.

Slow yarn follows pioneer Spanish conquistadors on a trek into what is now the American Southwest, in search of the fabled Seven Cities of Gold, with Quinn very good as the ruthless military leader and Rennie suitably pious as the accompanying priest, Padre Junipero Serra; the yarn is based on history but mucked up with a lot of cornball romancing between Richard Egan and an Indian girl (a part that Moreno plays very well but it's a lousy role) and with the usual contrived conflicts among the cardboard members of the expedition. Rate it fair.

SEVEN GUNS TO MESA (1956, AA). D: Edward Dein. W: Dein, Mildred Dein & Myles Wilder. Cast: Charles QUINLIVAN, Lola ALBRIGHT, James GRIFFITH, Jay Adler, Burt Nelson.

A group of stagecoach passengers is held hostage by baddies waiting to steal a gold shipment. Sleazy imitation of *Rawhide* is a Grade "Z" clunker.

SEVEN MEN FROM NOW (1956, WB). D: Budd Boetticher. W: Burt Kennedy. Cast: RANDOLPH SCOTT, GAIL RUSSELL, Lee MARVIN, John Larch, Walter Reed, Donald "Red" Barry, Fred Graham, Pamela Duncan, John Barradino, Stuart Whitman. 78m.

Outlaws kill the marshal's wife during a robbery; the marshal (Scott) sets out on the vengeance trail. Standard plot makes this one of the lesser Boetticher-Kennedy-Scott oaters

but the supporting cast, particularly Marvin as a bad guy, is very good. Stuart Whitman has a bit part here. Produced by John Wayne's company.

SEVENTH CAVALRY (1956, COL). D: Joseph H. Lewis. W: Peter Packer from a Glendon Swarthout story. Cast: RANDOLPH SCOTT, BARBARA HALE, Jay C. FLIPPEN, Frank Faylen, Jeanette Nolan, Denver Pyle, Leo Gordon, Frank Wilcox, Russell Hicks. 75m.

A cavalry troop returns to the scene of Custer's death seeking his body and the Sioux. Lively film is well acted but routine.

SEVEN WAYS FROM SUNDOWN (1960, UNIV). D: Harry Keller. W: Clair Huffaker from his novel. Cast: AUDIE MURPHY, BARRY SULLIVAN, Venetia STEVENSON, John McINTIRE, Kenneth Tobey, Mary Field. 87m.

A Texas Ranger (Murphy) who goes by the name of Seven Ways From Sundown Jones ("Seven" for short—he was the seventh kid in the family and they all have numbers for names) goes after an engaging gentleman gambler (Sullivan) in a sort of low-key amiable version of the plot of *The Naked Spur*. Huffaker's nice light touch makes this one of the better Audiepix, and it's very well crafted, and Sullivan is excellent.

SHADOW OF CHIKARA (1977, IND). DW: Earl E. Smith. Cast: JOE DON BAKER, SONDRA LOCKE, Slim PICKENS, John Davis CHANDLER, Ted Neeley, Joe Houck, Jr., Linda Dano.

Cheap supernatural indie is about Indians versus demoniac hawks.

THE SHAKIEST GUN IN THE WEST (1967, UNIV). D: Alan Rafkin. W: Jim Fritzell & Everett Greenbaum, based on *The Paleface* (1948). Cast: DON KNOTTS, BARBARA RHOADES, Jackie COOGAN, Donald "Red" BARRY, Ruth McDevitt, Frank McGrath, Hope Summers, Terry Wilson, Dub Taylor, Vaughn Taylor. 101m.

Cowardly Eastern dentist (Knotts) is mistaken for a gunslinger and has to face a gang of baddies, and becomes an unwitting hero, thanks to a sharpshootin' frontier lass (Rhoades). Fatuous remake of Bob Hope's *Paleface* strains for more laughs than it gets.

SHALAKO (1968, CIN). D: Edward Dmytryk. W: J. J. Griffith, Hal Hopper, Scot Finch & Clarke Reynolds from Louis L'Amour's novel. Cast: SEAN CONNERY, BRIGITTE BARDOT, HONOR BLACKMAN, STEPHEN BOYD, JACK HAWKINS, WOODY STRODE, Peter VAN

EYCK, Alexander KNOX, Valerie FRENCH, Eric SYKES, Julian MATEOS, Donald "Red" Barry, Rodd Redwing. 113m.

Bold frontiersman (Connery) gets into trouble with Indians, bad guys and a French countess (Bardot) during a hunting expedition laid on for European VIPs. The pairing of Connery and Bardot was supposed to be explosive at the box office but the picture is a hopeless mess and deservedly laid an egg, demonstrating once again that it takes more than a big budget and a big-name cast to make a bearable movie. This one is a disaster nearly on the scale of *MacKenna's Gold*.

For a Western it had a mind-bogglingly international cast and crew. A rundown: producer Euan Lloyd was Welsh; photographer Ted Moore was South African; Connery was Scots-Irish; Stephen Boyd was Anglo-Irish; Blackman, Sykes, French and the late Jack Hawkins were English; Van Eyck (this was his last film; he died in 1969) was German; Knox was Canadian; Mateos was Mexican; Dmytryk, Strode, Barry and Redwing were Americans; and Bardot, of course, was French. Suffice to say the movie is absurd.

SHAME, SHAME ON THE BIXBY BOYS (1978, IND). D: Anthony Bowers. W: William Bowers. Cast: MONTE MARKHAM, Sammy JACKSON, Donald "Red" Barry.

Cheap indie gunslinger comedy has some laughs.

SHANE (1953, PARA). D: George Stevens. W: A. B. Guthrie, Jr. & Jack Sher from Jack Schaefer's novel. Cast: ALAN LADD, JEAN ARTHUR, VAN HEFLIN, BRANDON De WILDE, Walter Jack PALANCE, Emile MEYER, Edgar BUCHANAN, Elisha COOK, Jr., Ben JOHNSON, John QUALEN, John Dierkes, Ellen Corby, Lee Van Cleef, Douglas Spencer, Paul McVey, John Miller, Edith Evanson, Nancy Kulp, George J. Lewis. 118m.

The half-nameless Shane (Ladd), a buckskinned horseman from nowhere with a mysterious and undoubtedly violent past, arrives in a Wyoming valley in search of refuge or a hiding place or perhaps simply peace. He hires on as a farmhand with an isolated ranch family (Heflin, Arthur, De Wilde) that is being menaced by a powerful anti-sodbuster rancher (Meyer), his tough brother (Dierkes), their arrogant cowhands (Johnson, Van Cleef) and the hired gunslinger (Palance) they've employed to drive the small homesteaders out. Shane becomes attached to the family: manfully to husband and son, romantically but unrequitedly to wife; the relationships are implied more than stated—the film is subtle without being annoyingly

opaque. We are introduced to other settlers (among whom Elisha Cook, Jr., as an unreconstructed childlike ex-Rebel, is outstanding) and to the bemused storekeeper (Buchanan). Range war looms; the range tyrants and homesteaders story is based loosely on the historical Johnson County War which also provided a factual basis for the fictions of such films as *Hannah Lee*, *Tom Horn* and the abysmal *Heaven's Gate*.

In the end, after exhausting every peaceable means, Shane finally confronts the powerful land-grabbing baddies, vanquishes them and their hired hands, and rides away to disappear—wounded, possibly dying, but making the sacrifice because his integrity requires it: riding off, in consummate cowboy hero fashion, into the sunset, alone.

Shane, both in Schaefer's best-selling novel (which was narrated by the little boy) and in the film, is a conscious retelling of the purest elements of the classic Western legend. The plot and Shane's character are in direct line of descent from Zane Grey's Lassiter stories and the films of William S. Hart.

An Academy Award went to Loyal Griggs for best color cinematography; Oscar nominations went to Palance, De Wilde, screenwriter Guthrie and the film itself.

Shane may well be the ultimate expression of the Western legend, but the film does have flaws. It calls attention to itself as self-conscious Myth: one can visualize producer-director Stevens and novelist-screenwriter Guthrie (*The Big Sky*) sitting down together and saying something like, "Now we're going to make the definitive Western." There's something too studied about the panoramic imagery; it's always splendid but sometimes boastful—the calculated contrived perfection militates against its integrity: it lacks the easy grace of, say, the seemingly casual artistry of John Ford, whose camera seemed to just happen upon beautiful compositions. Stevens was capable of spending weeks setting up a single shot, or re-shooting endlessly until he felt he had it right; unfortunately by then a lot of the vitality might have evaporated. *Shane* strives too hard for its effects: the mannered deliberate dignity of pace; the grand epic photography with its seemingly painted, or at least hand-retouched, colors, and the patent symbolism of the lonely, gorgeous Grand Teton locations; the magnificent symphonic score by Victor Young; the measured editing of Tom McAdoo and William Hornbeck; the isolation of the rustic three-building town; the black costume worn by Palance and its contrast with Shane's golden hair and pale buckskins. And Ladd wasn't right for the part, really; he didn't have the charismatic stature for it, although he was far more effective than one might have expected, judging by his previous performances.

Yet despite its pretensions *Shane* codified the essence of the Western, and it remains one of the few altogether towering movies of the genre. One can pick at it, or at any work, but in the end it is a monumentally rewarding film on nearly any level: moving, entertaining, beautiful, even perhaps profound.

SHE CAME TO THE VALLEY **(1981, IND). D: Albert Band. W: Frank Ray Perilli from a Cleo Dawson novel. Cast: RONEE BLAKLEY, DEAN STOCKWELL, Freddy FENDER, Scott Glenn.**

Shoestring indie concerns a family trying to survive along the Rio Grande during the 1915 Mexican revolution. Tex-Mex country singer Fender portrays Pancho Villa in this loud but limp action-romance.

THE SHEEPMAN **(1958, MGM). D: George Marshall. W: William Bowers, James Edward Grant & William Roberts. Cast: GLENN FORD, SHIRLEY MacLAINE, Leslie NIELSEN, Mickey SHAUGHNESSY, Edgar BUCHANAN, Pernell Roberts, Slim Pickens, Willis Bouchey. 85m.**

A stubborn sheepman (Ford) brings a trainload of sheep into cattle country and has to contend with the resistance of his old buddy, cattle baron Nielsen, whose girl friend (MacLaine) falls for the sheepman. Two comic characterizations are played to a tee by Mickey Shaughnessy as a stupid tough guy and Edgar Buchanan as an awesomely ultimate cracker-barrel smartass. As drama it only works fitfully but as comedy it's uproarious, one of the best and funniest of all Western farces.

SHENANDOAH **(1965, UNIV). D: Andrew V. McLaglen. W: James Lee Barrett. Cast: JAMES STEWART, ROSEMARY FORSYTH, KATHARINE ROSS, Glenn CORBETT, Doug McCLURE, Patrick WAYNE, George KENNEDY, Paul Fix, Warren Oates, Charles Robinson, Denver Pyle, James Best, Strother Martin, Tim McIntire, Harry Carey, Jr., Gregg Palmer, Dabbs Greer, Bob Steele, Lane Bradford, Shug Fisher. 105m.**

During the Civil War a fecund farmer (Stewart) tries to keep his several grown children out of the fighting; it's a war with which he wants nothing to do. It's essentially a soap opera more than an action melodrama. The story is heavily influenced by contemporary feelings about the Viet Nam war, of course, and the treatment of that theme is Hollywood-pat; the script leans heavily on contrivance and coincidence as well. But the big cast is first-rate; the photography (William H. Clothier) is excellent as well; it's very well directed—one of McLaglen's best jobs—and quite satisfying as entertainment. In an unusual twist, this film became the basis for the extremely successful Broadway musical of the same title.

THE SHEPHERD OF THE HILLS **(1941, PARA). D: Henry Hathaway. W: Grover Jones & Stuart Anthony from Harold Bell Wright's novel. Cast: JOHN WAYNE, BETTY FIELD, HARRY CAREY, Beulah BONDI, James BARTON, Tom Fadden, Samuel S. Hinds, Marjorie Main, Marc Lawrence, Ward Bond, John Qualen, Fuzzy Knight, Olin Howland, Dorothy Adams. 97m.**

Bucolic romantic melodrama takes place in the Ozarks with Harry Carey as the mysterious peacemaker and Wayne as the rambunctious young feudist who is reformed (and nearly killed). In Technicolor, it has good photography (Charles Lang, Jr.) and good acting, although the overwrought tearjerker plot may make it a bit too soapy for some modern audiences. This was the first talkie remake; there were two earlier silent versions—one in 1927 and, originally, a 1919 version of interest because it was directed by novelist-scenarist Harold Bell Wright.

THE SHERIFF OF FRACTURED JAW **(1958, FOX). D: Raoul Walsh. W: Arthur Dales & Jacob Hay. Cast: KENNETH MORE, JAYNE MANSFIELD, ROBERT MORLEY, William CAMPBELL, Bruce Cabot, Charles Farrell, Ronald Squire, Henry Hull, Sid James. 110m.**

Inept English gunsmith (More) goes West, arrives in a lawless town and somehow becomes sheriff and recruits some friendly Indians to help him keep the peace. Buxom Mansfield looms and leers foolishly throughout the comic proceedings; her songs were dubbed by Connie Francis. It's in CinemaScope. Not bad, but rather foolish.

SHE WORE A YELLOW RIBBON **(1949, RKO). D: John Ford. W: Frank Nugent & Laurence Stallings from two stories by James Warner Bellah. Cast: JOHN WAYNE, JOANNE DRU, Victor McLAGLEN, John AGAR, Ben JOHNSON, Harry CAREY, Jr., Mildred Natwick, George O'Brien, Arthur Shields, Tom Tyler, Harry Woods, Frank McGrath, Jack Pennick, Chief John Big Tree, Fred Graham. 103m.**

Captain Nathan Brittles (Wayne) is being retired by the army; but Indians are on the warpath and the seasoned old fighting man is needed by his regiment. That's the situation in sum but it's handled with exquisite flair. The Oscar-winning photography by Winton C. Hoch is magnificent (it's the only one of Ford's "cavalry trilogy" to have been filmed in color) as is the entire Ford stock company.

In a handful of motion pictures, mostly Westerns, John Wayne brought both power and sensitivity to his roles. *She Wore a Yellow Ribbon* is among those. His performance as the grizzled Captain Brittles—a character considerably older than the actor was at the time—is brilliant, and peerless; it is impossible to think of any other actor bringing Brittles to life so well.

Ford's excessive sentimentality is on hand, particularly as displayed by Victor McLaglen as the burly, loudmouthed, comical Sergeant Quincannon who can burst into tears at the drop of a kepi; so is Ford's weakness for crude slapstick comic relief. But in this film they're all of a piece and every bit works. The movie is filled with action and lusty life and the grand scope of Ford's favorite Monument Valley vistas, painted upon the screen as if by Russell or Remington. *She Wore a Yellow Ribbon* is a marvelously entertaining masterwork: proof that art can be fun.

THE SHOOTING. (1972, IND). D: Monte Hellman. W: Adrien Joyce. Cast: JACK NICHOLSON, MILLIE PERKINS, WARREN OATES, Will HUTCHINS, B.J. Merholz, Charles Eastman. 82m.

A mysterious woman (Perkins) persuades two drifters (Oates, Hutchins) to become bounty hunters and help her in her quest for revenge; she never explains what she wants revenge *for*. The film is a long desert trek, during which a mysterious gunfighter (Nicholson) joins the party and disintegrates it. The identity of the fugitive is never explained; one begins to suspect they are pursuing themselves; much of the movie is abstract to the point of opacity; yet it has compelling moments. Filmed in 1965, this was a companion piece to the Nicholson-Hellman oater *Ride in the Whirlwind*; both films are minor footnotes to the genre and fall into the "B" category but they are imaginative at least, professionally filmed and often interesting. But *The Shooting* is murky and obscure, its point elusive; it can be very frustrating.

SHOOTING HIGH (1940, FOX). D: Alfred E. Green. W: Lou Breslow & Owen Francis. Cast: JANE WITHERS, GENE AUTRY, Robert LOWERY, Marjorie WEAVER, Jack CARSON. 65m.

Young girl (Withers) tries to bring reason to bear on a family feud; she's given an assist by Gene Autry, who—on loan from Repub-

lic—accepted second billing to the child star. He seems more uncomfortable than usual, here; the comedy is lamentably dated.

THE SHOOTIST (1976, PARA). D: Don Siegel. W: Miles Hood Swarthout & Scott Hale from Glendon Swarthout's novel. Cast: JOHN WAYNE, LAUREN BACALL, JAMES STEWART, RON HOWARD, Richard BOONE, Sheree NORTH, Hugh O'BRIAN, Harry MORGAN, John CARRADINE, Scatman CROTHERS, Bill McKINNEY, Richard LENZ, Gregg Palmer, Alfred Dennis, Dick Winslow. 99m.

Aging gunman J. B. Books (Wayne) learns from a gentle doctor (Stewart) that he's dying of cancer. The discovery mellows him; for the first time in his life Books sets aside arrogance and finds compassion for the imperfect beings around him: the parasitical ex-lover (North) and reporter (Lenz) who want to write a lurid book exploiting his legend; the unctuous undertaker (Carradine) who wants to charge admission to view the celebrated corpse; the canny hostler (Crothers) who expects to sell Books's horse and saddle for a fortune to curio hunters; the bitter lawman (Morgan) who shocks the dying man by laughing in his face with relief when he learns Books hasn't come to town to kill him; the semi-delinquent youth (Howard) who jeers at him and then learns to love him; and the boy's timid straitlaced mother (Bacall) who teaches Books about courage. Knowing how his ordained death will take him—with anguished indignity—Books elects the time and method of his own demise: he resolves to go out with dignity intact, and challenges the most murderous gunmen around (Boone, O'Brian, McKinney); the film ends with a shoot-out that has a bit of irony.

The Shootist was the best of the 1976 crowd of oaters, most of the rest of which were bloated and dreadful. It was Wayne's best film in many years, certainly his best performance after *The Searchers*, albeit a restrained one.

Still, it often disappoints. It's slow, low-key, self-conscious; it plods along without feel for nuance, as though it were a respectful but callow dirge. Bad editing (Douglas Stewart) deprives us of those reaction-shots that might have brought power to the scenes; the sets are terribly cluttered with elaborate 1901 Victoriana; and the photography (Bruce Surtees) is dark, sombre, too arty. (I for one am sick to death of natural-light photography in which movies appear to have been filmed in the dark.) The screenplay frequently gravitates toward cheap cliches—notably a pointless scene in which Books gives Howard a shooting lesson; it wasn't in the novel, but seems lifted out of older films like *The Tin Star*, to no advantage; and the ending, as in the otherwise excellent novel, leaves one with the feeling of having been cheated: there should have been something more—some twist, some surprise, some elegance. The acting is uniformly good and the characters are well drawn but the film lacks vitality: it's cold. We keep hoping for a flare-up of the rage that is so justified and that we know Wayne can portray so well but it never happens; Books folds his dignity about him and only allows us an occasional peek at the pain inside, and even as he goes to meet his death he does so with lofty formality. One has the feeling this was not Wayne's fault; the script, and the director, gave him no chance to explode. As a result, the movie lacks passion. But it's a worthy failure and a suitable memorial: it was John Wayne's last movie.

SHOOT OUT (1971, UNIV). D: Henry Hathaway. W: Marguerite Roberts from Will James's novel *The Lone Cowboy*. Cast: GREGORY PECK, Pat QUINN, Susan TYRRELL, James GREGORY, Robert F. LYONS, Jeff COREY, Arthur HUNNICUTT, Paul Fix, Dawn Lyn, Rita Gam. 95m.

A bank robber (Peck) gets out of prison and hunts down the villain (Gregory) who double-crossed him after the robbery, left him for dead and made off with the loot. The bad guy hires a young fast-gun hothead (Lyons, in a very poor performance) to keep tabs on Peck but the brash kid exceeds his orders and things get complicated; they are further muddled when the hero is saddled with a little girl (Quinn) who may or may not be his daughter. Gorgeous landscape photography (Earl Rath), a quietly superior if unoriginal score (Dave Grusin) and a few players in good small roles—Hunnicutt as a bluff rancher, Fix as a railroad conductor and especially Corey as a crippled irascible barkeep—are the only virtues of this dud. The same director, screenwriter and production made *True Grit* but here they had a weak story, and Peck, who looks tired and embarrassed, is miscast; the movie is third rate.

SHOOT-OUT AT MEDICINE BEND (1957, WB). D: Richard L. Bare. W: D. D. Beauchamp & John Tucker Battle. Cast: RANDOLPH SCOTT, ANGIE DICKINSON, JAMES CRAIG, James GARNER, Gordon Jones, Dani Crayne, Trevor Bardette, Don Beddoe, Myron Healey, Guy Wilkerson, Robert Warwick, Lane Bradford. 87m.

Three ex-Indian fighting soldiers (Scott, Garner, Jones) disguise themselves as Quakers while searching for the bad guy (Craig) who sold Randy's brother faulty ammunition, which caused him to die while trying to shoot it out with marauding Sioux. Angie Dickinson is beautiful but has little to do; Garner, in a subordinate part, has little opportunity to be amusing; the black-and-white photography (Carl Guthrie) is uninteresting; the score (Roy Webb) and editing (Clarence Kolster) are sub-competent; the directing is limp; in short this is one of the least of Randolph Scott's oaters.

SHORT GRASS (1951, AA). D: Lesley Selander. W: Tom W. Blackburn from his novel. Cast: ROD CAMERON, CATHY DOWNS, JOHNNY MACK BROWN, Alan HALE, Jr., Jeff YORK, Tristram Coffin, Morris Ankrum, Jack Ingram, Raymond Walburn, Harry Woods, Rory Mallinson.

A wanderer (Cameron) returns to his old ranch to pick up the cudgels against the land-grabbing bad guys. Johnny Mack Brown plays the sheriff. It isn't up there with *Ramrod* or *Ride the Man Down* but it's a pretty good B-plus ranch romance.

SHOTGUN (1953, AA). D: Lesley Selander. W: Clarke Reynolds, Rory Calhoun & John C. Champion. Cast: STERLING HAYDEN, YVONNE De CARLO, ZACHARY SCOTT, Robert J. WILKE, Ralph Sanford, Gay Prescott, John Pickard, Rory Mallinson, Lane Chandler, Angela Greene. 81m.

Gritty unglamorous tough guy (Hayden) sets out to avenge a killing. There's plenty of action. Hayden didn't seem to put much effort into this but his presence is powerful whether he tries or not; this minor oater is a bit better than average for that reason.

THE SHOWDOWN (1950, REP). D: Dorrell & Stuart McGowan. W: The McGowans, Richard Wormser & Don Gordon. Cast: WILLIAM ELLIOTT, MARIE WINDSOR, Walter BRENNAN, Jim DAVIS, Harry MORGAN, Rhys WILLIAMS, William Ching, Leif Erickson, Nacho Galindo, Victor Kilian, Charles Stevens, Henry Rowland. 64m.

An ex-lawman hunts for his brother's murderer; the trail leads him to a gambling den presided over by Marie Windsor. Fairly big budget for an Elliott "B," and a bigger-name cast than usual, make for a solid programmer, routine but well done.

SHOWDOWN (1963, UNIV). D: R. G. Springsteen. W: Bronson Howitzer. Cast: AUDIE MURPHY, KATHLEEN CROWLEY, Charles DRAKE, Harold J. Stone, Nacho Galindo, Skip Homeier, Strother Martin. 79m.

An outlaw gang captures two drifters and steals the stolen bonds they were carrying; the two (Murphy, Drake) go after the gang. Mixed-up plot has a confused morality; production is ordinary; routine Audiepic.

SHOWDOWN (1973, UNIV). D: George Seaton. W: Theodore Taylor & Hank Fine. Cast: ROCK HUDSON, DEAN MARTIN, SUSAN CLARK, Donald MOFFAT, John McLiam, Charles Baca, Jackson Kane. 99m.

Two buddies, both in love with the same girl, find themselves on opposite sides of the law—Hudson as the sheriff, Martin as the train robber. The photography (Ernest Laszlo) is okay but the characters are cardboard, the action listless, the flashbacks interminable and awkward, the acting poor for an "A" production, the plot contrived and predictable.

SHOWDOWN AT ABILENE (1956, UNIV). D: Charles Haas. W: Berne Giler & Clarence U. Young. Cast: JOCK MAHONEY, MARTHA HYER, Lyle BETTGER, David JANSSEN, Grant Williams, Ted de Corsia, Lane Bradford. 80m.

Tired of killing, a Civil War veteran nevertheless pins on a sheriff's badge and comes to the aid of the farmers in their fight against land-grabbers. Uninspired imitator of *Shane* is humdrum fare—mediocre script, poor acting. It was remade in 1967 to no visible advantage as *Gunfight in Abilene*.

SHOWDOWN AT BOOT HILL (1958, FOX). D: Gene Fowler, Jr. W: Louis Vittes. Cast: CHARLES BRONSON, Carole MATHEWS, John CARRADINE, Robert Hutton, Fintan Meyler. 71m.

Bounty hunter (Bronson) runs into resistance from the greedy folks who were supposed to pay him a reward. Small black-and-white oater is of interest mainly because it marks Bronson's first top-billed starring role. Director Fowler is a well known film editor.

SHUT MY BIG MOUTH (1942, COL). D: Charles T. Barton. W: Oliver Drake, Karen DeWolf & Francis J. Martin. Cast: JOE E. BROWN, ADELE MARA, Victor JORY, Forrest TUCKER, Lloyd Bridges, Fritz Feld, Pedro de Cordoba. 69m.

There are some genuine laughs in this one with comedian Brown disguising himself in drag and becoming sheriff and otherwise behaving absurdly as he mops up an outrageously tough outlaw gang. It's fun.

THE SIEGE AT RED RIVER (1954, FOX). D: Rudolph Mate. W: Sydney Boehm, J. Robert Bren, Gladys Atwater & Leo Townsend. Cast: VAN JOHNSON, JOANNE DRU, Richard BOONE, Jeff MORROW,

Craig Hill, Milburn Stone, Robert Burton. 81m.

A Confederate spy (Johnson) tries to steal a Gatling gun from the Union cavalry while a relentless Pinkerton operative (Morrow) closes in on him; there is the inevitable complication when the Reb spy falls in love with a Yankee lass (Dru). Van Johnson's citified accent and mannerisms are out of place; he certainly is no Southerner; that, and the fact that the climax consists of Indian-fighting action footage from Ford's *She Wore a Yellow Ribbon* spliced unconvincingly together with close-ups and rear projection, make it a third-rate "B" picture despite the good cast.

SIERRA (1950, UNIV). D: Alfred E. Green. W: Edna Anhalt & Milton Gunsberg from a Stuart Hardy novel. Cast: WANDA HENDRIX, AUDIE MURPHY, BURL IVES, Dean JAGGER, Sara ALLGOOD, Anthony (Tony) Curtis, Houseley Stevenson, James Arness, Richard Rober, Elliot Reid, Griff Barnett, Elizabeth Risdon, Roy Roberts, John Doucette, I. Stanford Jolley, Jack Ingram. 83m.

Father (Jagger) and son (Murphy), chasing wild mustangs and hiding out in the deep mountains near a crazy hermit (Ives), run afoul of bad guys and an old murder warrant, and suffer various romantic, melodramatic, sentimental and improbable misadventures. Like a few other very early Universal Audie movies, this was given a large budget and good production values. Russell Metty's Technicolor location cinematography is outstanding; the Walter Scharp score is serviceable and there are some good songs sung by Burl Ives. Note that the film was made so early that Murphy was second billed below Hendrix (she soon became his wife) and that the young Tony Curtis was still billing himself as Anthony. Unfortunately the improbabilities of the script—it's a remake of the 1938 melodrama *Forbidden Valley*—and the amateurish acting of the two leads make it a painful movie for modern audiences.

SIERRA BARON (1958, FOX). D: James B. Clark. W: Houston Branch from Tom W. Blackburn's novel. Cast: RICK JASON, BRIAN KEITH, RITA GAM, Mala POWERS, Steve Brodie. 80m.

Unusual treatment of the cattle baron-versus-land grabber yarn has a colorful early-California setting and interesting costumes. The two leading men perform excellently. Unfortunately the climactic gundown is too predictable but it's sturdy entertainment.

SIERRA PASSAGE (1951, MONO). D: Frank McDonald. W: Warren D. Wandberg,

Sam Roeca & Tom W. Blackburn. Cast: WAYNE MORRIS, LOLA ALBRIGHT, Lloyd CORRIGAN, Alan HALE, Jr., Roland WINTERS, George Eldredge. 81m.

Black-and-white programmer has an off-beat premise: an orphan (Morris), raised by a Wild West Show impresario (Corrigan) and his trick-shot artist (Winters), grows up to use the spectacular gun skills he's learned from them to go after the murderer (Hale) of his father. Plot is part romance, part mystery, part pursuit-suspense, and it's quite well conceived but unhappily the dialogue and directing are not up to it. With more care and fewer cliches it might have been an outstanding little vest-pocket oater; as it is, it's curiously compelling despite its disappointments.

SIERRA STRANGER (1957, COL). D: Lee Sholem. W: Richard J. Dorso. Cast: HOWARD DUFF, DICK FORAN, Gloria McGHEE, John HOYT, Barton MacLANE, George E. Stone, Byron Foulger. 74m.

Drifter (Duff) stops a lynching and thereafter finds he's a marked man. Leisurely unsophisticated black-and-white movie is not very well directed.

SILENT BARRIERS (1937, IND). D: Milton Rosner. Cast: RICHARD ARLEN, LILLI PALMER.

Canadian actioner was produced by Gaumont-British. Information about it seems hard to come by.

SILVER CITY (1951, PARA). D: Byron Haskin. W: Frank Gruber from Luke Short's novel *High Vermillion*. Cast: EDMOND O'BRIEN, YVONNE De CARLO, Barry FITZGERALD, Richard ARLEN, Edgar BUCHANAN, Russell HAYDEN, Gladys George, Laura Elliot, Frank Fenton. 90m.

Fugitive engineer-assayer helps a girl and her Irish father defend their mining claim. Fitzgerald is amusing as the father but it's ordinary.

SILVER DOLLAR (1932, WB). D: Alfred E. Green. W: Carl Erickson & Harvey Thew from a biography of H.A.W. Tabor by David Karsner. Cast: EDWARD G. ROBINSON, BEBE DANIELS, Aline MacMAHON, Robert Warwick, Charles Middleton, Leon Ames, Jobyna Howland, Russell Simpson, Bonita Granville. 84m.

Roman à clef is based on the rise of Colorado silver-mining tycoon Horace "Haw" Tabor; it's a hackneyed re-creation of that flamboyant period in Western history, but Robinson is very good and so is Daniels, as his bride (modeled on Baby Doe Tabor, whose story was later made into the opera *The Ballad of Baby Doe*). Not altogether bad entertainment.

SILVER LODE (1954, RKO). D: Allan Dwan. W: Karen DeWolf. Cast: JOHN PAYNE, LIZABETH SCOTT, DAN DURYEA, Dolores MORAN, Hugh Sanders, Harry Carey, Jr., Robert Warwick, Ray Gordon, Frank Sully. 80m.

A fugitive tries to prove he didn't commit the murder they've pinned on him; this was an anti-McCarthyism Western, and topical analogies abound. It's earnest and the directing, by the most prolific of all the old pros, is sure-handed, but it can be skipped.

SILVER QUEEN (1942, UA). D: Lloyd Bacon. W: Bernard Schubert, Cecile Kramer, Forest Halsey & William A. Johnston. Cast: PRISCILLA LANE, GEORGE BRENT, BRUCE CABOT, Lynne OVERMAN, Guinn "Big Boy" Williams, Eugene Pallette. 79m.

Prospector's daughter becomes a professional gambler to pay off her father's grubstake debts, only to have her winnings squandered on a worthless silver mine by her ne'er-do-well husband—and then of course the mine turns out to be not so worthless . . . Dated soap opera.

SILVER RIVER (1948, WB). D: Raoul Walsh. W: Harriet Frank, Jr., & Stephen Longstreet from Longstreet's novel. Cast: ERROL FLYNN, ANN SHERIDAN, Thomas MITCHELL, Bruce BENNETT, Barton MacLANE, Monte Blue, Tom D'Andrea, Joseph Crehan, Jonathan Hale, Alan Bridge. 110m.

A suave gambler (Flynn) gets ambitious; the movie follows his rise, fall and redemption as an empire-building silver baron. He marries the widow of the partner whose death he has caused, then pyramids his empire until the inevitable reversal. Artificial and frequently foolish, the movie is as visibly weary as its star and not nearly on a par with *They Died with Their Boots On*. Barton MacLane plays a silent-movie-style villain who seems to have no reason for his villainy: his every other thought seems to be, "Curses—foiled again!" Still, the photography (Sid Hickox) and music (Max Steiner) are competent and the story is a bit different from most. Warners' lavish expenditures on the budget seem reflected mainly in numerous huge mob scenes that add little to the drama, however, and it's one of the least energetic of Walsh's directorial jobs, confined mainly to back-lot and soundstage sets. Sheridan is tart and lovely but her role is confusing, so that she undergoes several inexplicable changes in attitude toward Flynn, who himself seems uninterested in the whole business. Acting honors go, as usual, to Thomas Mitchell who steals the show as "Plato," the drunken lawyer who is Flynn's vocal conscience.

THE SILVER STAR (1955, LIP). D: Richard Bartlett. W: Bartlett & Ian MacDonald. Cast: EARLE LYON, MARIE WINDSOR, Edgar BUCHANAN, Lon CHANEY, Jr., Barton MacLANE, Richard Bartlett, Morris Ankrum, Steve Rowland. 73m.

A young newly elected sheriff (Lyon) doesn't like the job and is reluctant to throw his weight around and can't see the point in getting shot but proves himself in the crunch. The script relies too much on cliches about the varmints who tree the town, and on conventions from *High Noon*, but it's a thoughtful story about the coming of age of the worried young lawman. Lyon is natural and low-key; Buchanan, as his retired predecessor, is his usual bucolic self; the other players were Poverty Row's resident stock players; it's all blended comfortably and the slow yarn has plentiful charm and a flavor of understated realism that's typical of Lippert's low-budget but not low-class productions. (Robert L. Lippert owned a chain of cinemas and originally began producing his own films to feed them with product; the production company survived about six years.) Actor Lyon produced this black-and-white oater himself, in the dying days of the Lippert filmmaking organization; it doesn't rank with their best (*I Shot Billy the Kid, The Tall Texan, Little Big Horn*) but it's superior fare, much more rewarding than many a far more pretentious movie.

THE SILVER WHIP (1953, FOX). D: Harmon Jones. W: Jesse Lasky, Jr., from Jack Schaefer's novel. Cast: DALE ROBERTSON, KATHLEEN CROWLEY, ROBERT WAGNER, RORY CALHOUN, Lola ALBRIGHT, James Millican, J. M. Kerrigan, John Kellogg, Ian MacDonald. 72m.

A stagecoach guard (Robertson) and his sheriff pal (Calhoun) watch with jaundiced expectations while their energetic young protégé (Wagner) gets himself into a pack of trouble with stage-robbing bad guys; they have to rescue him from the consequences of his misdeeds. Good cast and noisy action. But the directing is lightweight and the script too slow, based on a very short novel by the author of *Shane* that was essentially an extended short story.

THE SINGER NOT THE SONG (1961, WB). D: Roy Baker. W: Nigel Balchin from a novel by Audrey E. Lindop. Cast: DIRK BOGARDE, JOHN MILLS, Mylene DEMONGEOT, Laurence NAISMITH, John BENTLEY, Leslie French, Laurence Payne. 129m.

Mills, garbed in white, plays a priest in Mexico in the 1930s trying to evade the advances of sexy Demongeot; Bogarde, in black, plays a bandit whose relationship to the priest is Graham Greene-ishly ambiguous; the film has curious homosexual aspects. An allegory, it relies more on symbols than on overt action; there's a bloody downbeat climax but it seems incomplete, as if something important were left on the cutting-room floor. But it does have interesting moments, once one gets past the shock of listening to an entire cast of Mexicans with British accents. In CinemaScope. Baker also directed the interesting *Inferno*.

SINGING GUNS (1950, REP). D: R. G. Springsteen. W: Dorrell & Stuart McGowan from Max Brand's novel. Cast: VAUGHN MONROE, ELLA RAINES, Walter BRENNAN, Ward BOND, Ralph Dunn, Billy Gray. 91m.

Gunslinger is chased by baddies in old Arizona; routine low-budget oater in color is of note because of the presence of beauteous Raines and the offbeat casting of singer Monroe in a straight dramatic part. He starred in two Westerns; the other was *The Toughest Man in Arizona*.

SITTING BULL (1954, UA). D: Sidney Salkow. W: Salkow & Jack DeWitt. Cast: DALE ROBERTSON, MARY MURPHY, J. CARROL NAISH, Douglas KENNEDY, Iron Eyes CODY, John Litel, William Hopper, John Hamilton. 105m.

This gives us Custer again (Kennedy) and an army captain (Robertson) sympathetic to the Indians, and the battle at the Little Big Horn and the familiar trappings; Naish is ludicrous in the title role; the Mexican locations were filmed in CinemaScope but that's its only saving grace.

SIX BLACK HORSES (1962, UNIV). D: Harry Keller. W: Burt Kennedy. Cast: AUDIE MURPHY, DAN DURYEA, Joan O'BRIEN, Roy Barcroft, George Wallace, Bob Steele. 80m.

Good guy, bad guy and girl try to survive together amid hostile Apaches. Tiresome standard stuff.

THE SKIN GAME (1971, WB). D: Paul Bogart. W: Peter Stone & Richard Alan Simmons. Cast: JAMES GARNER, LOU GOSSETT, SUSAN CLARK, Edward ASNER, Andrew Duggan, Brenda Sykes. 101m.

Garner and Gossett are magnetically engaging as an itinerant team of swindlers who pose as owner and slave in the South and West; Susan Clark, as a con woman, is delightful; minor comedy is much warmer-hearted than most of the farce Westerns of the 1970s. Quite good.

SKY FULL OF MOON (1952, FOX). DW: Norman Foster. Cast: CARLETON CARPENTER, JAN STERLING, Keenan WYNN, Elaine STEWART, Robert Burton, Emmett Lynn, Sheb Wooley, Douglas Dumbrille. 73m.

Young cowhand arrives in Las Vegas to try and strike it big as a rodeo cowboy; comedy-romance is engaging, mild, well acted.

SLAUGHTER TRAIL (1951, RKO). D: Irving Allen. W: Sid Kuller. Cast: BRIAN DONLEVY, Virginia GREY, Gig YOUNG, Andy DEVINE, Myron Healey, Robert Hutton, Terry Gilkyson, Jim Davis. 78m.

Indian warfare, stagecoach holdups and an unerring proclivity toward hack cliches characterize this dismal vest-pocket *Stagecoach*; Donlevy, as the cavalry commander, is stiff, and the rest of the players are bland except for Gig Young who brings a certain sardonic charm to his portrayal of a bandit rogue. It's accompanied by a hokey soundtrack song vocalized incessantly by a chorus of narrators to the tune, but not the lyrics, of "The Wreck of the Old Ninety-Seven."

SLIM CARTER (1957, UNIV). D: Richard Bartlett. W: Montgomery Pittman, David Bramson & Mary C. McCall, Jr. Cast: JOCK MAHONEY, JULIE ADAMS, Tim HOVEY, Ben Johnson, Barbara Hale, William Hopper. 82m.

Cowboy movie-star heel is reformed by a hero-worshiping little boy (Hovey) and the love of a good woman. It's a bad movie, but like other Hollywood films it didn't start out to be one. Screenwriter McCall, whose husband and collaborator was the late David Bramson, recalls: "We finished our script, left the studio. Several weeks later each of us got a shooting script. We were given story credit, first screenplay credit. Then came the name of the man who rewrote it . . . We didn't like it so much we asked to have our names taken off it." The original script had been based mostly on the career of William Boyd, for whom Bramson had worked in the 1930s; McCall remembers that "it was a case of the man becoming the part—with the passage of time, Bill Boyd and Hopalong Cassidy were indistinguishable one from the other. From that evolved an outline for a picture we wrote together. We called it *A/K/A Slim Carter*." But a producer (Howard Horwitz) and a stu-

dio mucked up the story nicely, as they are wont to do.

SMOKE IN THE WIND (1975, IND). D: Joseph Kane. W: Eric Allen. Cast: JOHN RUSSELL, WALTER BRENNAN, Myron HEALEY, John Ashley, Susan Huston.

Indie was not generally released in the United States and has not been screened for this reviewer. Of interest, at least, because it may have been both Kane's and Brennan's last film; both men died in 1976.

SMOKE SIGNAL (1955, UNIV). D: Jerry Hopper. W: George F. Slavin & George W. George. Cast: DANA ANDREWS, PIPER LAURIE, Rex REASON, William TALMAN, Milburn Stone, Gordon Jones, Robert J. Wilke. 88m.

Survivors of a massacre by Indians journey downriver on rafts on the Colorado through the Grand Canyon to escape the Apaches. Ordinary Indian-fighting plot is very well acted by a good cast and well directed with fine location scenery.

SOLDIER BLUE (1970, EMB). D: Ralph Nelson. W: John Gay from a novel by Theodore V. Olsen. Cast: PETER STRAUSS, CANDICE BERGEN, Donald PLEASENCE, Jorge RIVERO, John Anderson, Dana Elcar. 112m.

An isolated and bewildered young cavalry trooper (Strauss) and a white woman (Bergen) survive a battle with Indians and are thrown together in a fitful story that leads through attempts to head off disaster to a gory massacre of Indians by whites—an overblown cinematic reinterpretation of army-versus-Indian relations inspired largely by Colonel Chivington's historical murder of a village of Indians at Sand Creek, Colorado. This vicious, painful scene is depicted with lip-licking, drooling, voyeuristic explicitness; the film is typically a Joseph E. Levine production—expensive and tasteless.

The real Chivington wasn't an army officer; he was a self-appointed head of militia during the Civil War when the soldiers were away; the massacre he perpetrated was not typical of, or part of, U.S. Army or government policy or even the sentiments of a majority of settlers; but it did happen, as did the wretched madness of Wounded Knee and the dreadful massacre of Indians by white civilians at Camp Grant, Arizona, and these episodes have become the basis for oversimplified polemical movies like *Soldier Blue* just as the Custer debacle, the Powder River ambush, the battle at Apache Pass and other Indian victories provided rationalization for an earlier generation of pictures like *She Wore a Yellow Ribbon* that took the opposite stance.

The trouble with *Soldier Blue* is not that it takes a political stance; the trouble is that the political stance gets in the way of the drama. It's a cure that unhappily manages to be worse than the disease it attempts to treat. The film revels in bloodthirsty brutality; there is only the remotest relationship between the movie and the novel on which it purports to have been based, because Hollywood as usual took a plain-spoken story and used it as a peg on which to hang a sack full of messages and exploitive gore; it is doubtless well intentioned but the effect is disgusting, even though it's very well directed and most of the actors are excellent, excepting Pleasence, whose mugging performance brings new significance to the word "ham."

SOMETHING BIG (1972, NGP). D: Andrew V. McLaglen. W: James Lee Barrett. Cast: DEAN MARTIN, BRIAN KEITH, HONOR BLACKMAN, Ben JOHNSON, Carol WHITE, Albert SALMI, Joyce VAN PATTEN, Denver PYLE, Harry Carey, Jr., David Huddleston, Merlin Olsen, Paul Fix, Bob Steele, Don Knight, Robert Donner. 108m.

A supposedly charming outlaw (Martin, not displaying much charm), attempting to solve all his problems by pulling off a big score, becomes entangled with the blustering colonel's (Keith) inadvertently kidnapped wife (Blackman) as well as a slavering woman-hungry killer (Salmi), sundry other outlaws and idiots, and a confused comedic plot that leaves the cast and the audience equally slack-jawed and agape most of the time. The script has some clever, funny lines but is cluttered with gimmicks—a dog, a skeleton, bagpipes, a wooden leg, a Gatling gun—most of which contribute little or nothing to the story. The Marvin Hamlisch score is all right but the title song, by Burt Bacharach and Hal David, is their poorest imitative reprise yet of "Raindrops Keep Falling on My Head." The photography (Harry Stradling, Jr.) is excellent, as is always the case in McLaglen's movies, and the film is directed with a sure light hand—some of the comedy is reminiscent of his work in *McLintock*. Best scene is a howlingly funny "hommage" to Ford's *She Wore a Yellow Ribbon*, with Keith nicely burlesquing the John Wayne character—the retiring cavalry officer—and Ben Johnson providing Victor McLaglen-ish counterpoint as Keith's numbskull chief of scouts. The movie is neither great nor terrible; much of the comedy falls flat but much of it is entertaining.

SONG OF THE SADDLE (1936, WB). D: Louis King. W: William Jacobs. Cast: DICK

FORAN, Alma LLOYD, Charles Middleton, Glenn Strange. 57m.

Covered-wagon mini-epic is crammed full of action, plot, songs and cliches. But Foran as always is much better than the formula required, and much better than Warner Brothers deserved.

SONG OF THE WEST (1930, WB). D: Ray Enright. W: Harvey Thew from the stage musical *Rainbow* by Oscar Hammerstein II & Laurence Stallings, and the novel by Harold Bell Wright. Cast: JOHN BOLES, VIVIENNE SEGAL, Joe E. BROWN, Maria Wells, Sam Hardy.

Soldier is cashiered for an accidental killing, disguises himself as a preacher to escape jail, becomes a gambler, gets involved in a love affair with the colonel's daughter, and has it out with the bad guys in this dated operetta; it's in color, of sorts.

SON OF BELLE STARR (1953, AA). D: Frank McDonald. W: D. D. Beauchamp, William Raynor & Jack DeWitt. Cast: KEITH LARSEN, Peggie CASTLE, Donna Drake, Myron Healey, Regis Toomey. 70m.

Title tells all. Cheap outlaw oater is in black-and-white.

SON OF PALEFACE (1952, PARA). D: Frank Tashlin. W: Tashlin, Robert L. Welch & Joseph Quillan. Cast: BOB HOPE, JANE RUSSELL, ROY ROGERS, Bill WILLIAMS, Lloyd Corrigan, Jean Willes, Chester Conklin, Harry Von Zell, Iron Eyes Cody, Paul E. Burns, Douglas Dumbrille. Guest cameos: CECIL B. De MILLE, BING CROSBY. 95m.

Harvard dude (Hope) arrives in the Wild West to claim an inheritance left him by his Indian-fighting daddy (the character he played in the original *Paleface*, to which this is a sort of sequel). Naturally he's pursued by baddies wanting the inheritance: chief baddie is gun-toting Jane Russell. Hope is assisted by King of the Cowboys Roy Rogers, and some of the best comedy is performed by Rogers's horse, Trigger. It's probably Hope's funniest Western farce; it's nonsense but it works just right.

SON OF THE RENEGADE (1953, IND). DW: John Carpenter. Cast: JOHN CARPENTER, Lori Irving, Jack Ingram, Joan McKellar, Verne Teters.

A sort of seven-cent *High Noon*, this has corny theatrical acting and wild melodrama and an incredibly cheap production (the sets look ready to topple at any moment) but it has the curiously interesting atmosphere of most of Carpenter's Gower Gulch indies; for more about those, see *Outlaw Treasure*.

ROSE OF THE RIO GRANDE
(1938): Movita Castaneda, John
Carroll. Dashing bandido yarn is
ludicrous in all respects. Monogram Pictures (Allied Artists)

THE ROUNDERS (1965): Glenn
Ford as a hard-luck bronc wrangler who keeps trying to tame an
unbreakable horse. . . . MGM

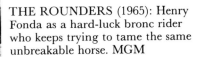

THE ROUNDERS (1965): Henry
Fonda as a hard-luck bronc rider
who keeps trying to tame the same
unbreakable horse. MGM

RUN FOR COVER (1955): James Cagney,
Viveca Lindfors, John Derek. Aging gunfighter and a wayward cocky youth: a good
taut suspense story. Paramount Pictures

RUN OF THE ARROW (1956):
Rod Steiger, Charles Bronson,
Col. Tim McCoy. A very confused
melodrama, filled with hate.
RKO Radio Pictures

SADDLE THE WIND (1958): John Cassavetes, Robert Taylor, Julie London. Heated
but miscast: two brothers quarrel. MGM

THE SAN FRANCISCO
STORY (1952): Yvonne De
Carlo, Joel McCrea. Clean-
ing up the tough element.
Warner Brothers

SANTA FE TRAIL (1940):
Alan Hale, Sr., Guinn "Big
Boy" Williams, Ronald Reagan, Errol Flynn. History
twisted far beyond recognition; Reagan plays Custer.
Warner Brothers

THE SAVAGE HORDE (1950):
William Elliott and Adrian Booth
(embracing), Grant Withers (in
hat), Noah Beery, Jr. (thumb in
pocket). Handled with panache,
briskly directed, with a powerful
cast of fine supporting players.
Republic Pictures

THE SEA OF GRASS (1946):
Katharine Hepburn and Spencer
Tracy in their only Western—
enough plots to keep half a dozen
movies busy. MGM

SECRETS (1933): Leslie Howard, Mary Pickford. Soap-opera *Covered Wagon* is a period piece. United Artists

SEVEN MEN FROM NOW (1956): Lee Marvin, Donald Barry, Randolph Scott. The vengeance trail; the supporting cast is very good. Warner Brothers

THE SHEEPMAN (1958): Glenn Ford, Mickey Shaughnessy, Shirley MacLaine. One of the most uproarious of all Western farces. MGM

THE SONS OF KATIE ELDER (1965, PARA). D: Henry Hathaway. W: William H. Wright, Talbot Jennings, Allan Weiss & Harry Essex. Cast: JOHN WAYNE, DEAN MARTIN, MARTHA HYER, Earl HOLLIMAN, Jeremy SLATE, George KENNEDY, Michael ANDERSON, Jr., James Gregory, Paul Fix, Dennis Hopper, John Litel, Strother Martin, Rhys Williams, John Qualen, Rodolfo Acosta, Percy Kelton, James Westerfield. 112m.

Four brothers (Wayne, Martin, Holliman, Anderson) seek to find out who killed their daddy and swindled their late mother. If you can't guess who done it in the first twenty minutes, you're retarded. There's plenty of brawling and the standard phony choreographed shoot-out beloved of fast-draw buffs and small children. Good photography (Lucien Ballard) and score (Elmer Bernstein)— it's all on a professionally satisfactory plane and if you like to relax with an unsurprising Duke Wayne oater then this should be just your cup of tea. This was Wayne's first film after the operation that successfully removed a cancerous lung; he looks drawn and a bit tentative.

THE SOUL OF NIGGER CHARLEY (1973, PARA). DW: Larry G. Spangler. Cast: FRED WILLIAMSON, D'Urville MARTIN, Denise NICHOLAS, Pedro Armendariz, Jr. 104m.

Sequel to *The Legend of Nigger Charley* has an escaped slave in the Wild West fighting it out with evil slavers, robbing a gold train and joining Mexican revolutionaries—the plot makes no sense. Through it all he's accompanied by a 1930ish sidekick (Martin) who makes Stepin Fetchit look like a genius. Here and there are sparks of needed humor but most of it is inept amateur junk, among the worst films of the blaxploitation fad.

SOUL SOLDIER (1972, IND). Also titled: THE RED, WHITE AND BLACK. D: John Cardos. W: Marlene Weed. Cast: RAFER JOHNSON, CESAR ROMERO, Janee MICHELLE, Lincoln Kilpatrick, Robert DoQui. 84m.

Black troops of the Tenth (Negro) Cavalry Regiment fight it out with Indians. Garrison commander is Cesar Romero. A good deal of stereotyped cheapjack barracks humor and domestic squabblings stretch the thin plot line beyond the point of boredom; sloppy black-power oater is uninspired and soporific.

SOUTH OF ST. LOUIS (1949, WB). D: Ray Enright. W: James R. Webb & Zachary Gold. Cast: JOEL McCREA, ALEXIS SMITH, ZACHARY SCOTT, Dorothy MALONE, Victor Jory, Alan Hale, Jr., Douglas Kennedy, Nacho Galindo, Monte Blue. 88m.

Fast two-fisted oater has two buddies running guns in the Southwest during the Civil War; confused plot has too many cliches but it zips right along and McCrea, as always, brings charm to it. In Technicolor.

SOUTHWEST PASSAGE (1954, UA). D: Ray Nazarro. W: Harry Essex & Geoffrey Homes. Cast: JOHN IRELAND, ROD CAMERON, JOANNE DRU, John DEHNER, Darryl HICKMAN, Guinn "Big Boy" Williams, Mark Hanna. 82m.

In the 1860s the U.S. Cavalry imported Arabian camels to see if they could be used in the American desert in warfare against the Indians. The Southwest proved too stony for the camels' sensitive feet, and the animals were destroyed or turned loose. Decades later some wild ones were still seen wandering in Death Valley.

The assignment of delivering and testing the camels was given to young Lieutenant Edward Beale. In this film version of that history, Beale is played by Rod Cameron; there is some interest generated by his performance as a man obsessed by his stubborn visionary scheme to make the camels succeed. Ireland and Dru spice up the plot as a fugitive outlaw and his lady friend. Although it moves along at a fair clip, it's down near a "B" level. For a comic treatment of the same subject, compare *Hawmps*.

SPENCER'S MOUNTAIN (1963, WB). DW: Delmer Daves from Earl Hamner, Jr.'s novel. Cast: HENRY FONDA, MAUREEN O'HARA, James MacARTHUR, Donald CRISP, Wally COX, Hope Summers, Mimsy Farmer, Virginia Gregg. 120m.

Simpleminded hillbilly father (Fonda) keeps promising to build his family a new home up on the mountain. His wife (O'Hara, gorgeously made up—a bit odd, for a poverty-stricken farmer's wife) is concerned about the romance between their son (MacArthur) and the daughter (Farmer) of a wealthy rancher (Crisp). Filmed on location at Jackson Hole, Wyoming, this attempt at warm homespun romance was written by the author of *The Waltons*; this movie somehow emerges as witless boring treacle.

THE SPIKES GANG (1974, UA). D: Richard Fleischer. W: Irving Ravetch & Harriet Frank, Jr., from Giles Tippette's novel *The Bank Robbers*. Cast: LEE MARVIN, GARY GRIMES, RON HOWARD, Arthur HUNNICUTT, Noah Beery, Jr., Charlie Martin Smith. 96m.

Three Western farm boys are forced—partly by weakness and partly by circumstances—into a life of crime; they come under the wing of an elder desperado (Marvin). Unfortunately neither the dialogue nor the directing conveys any spirit of reality, passion or even interest; even the action scenes are boring. Paper-thin mod Western was filmed in Spain (cinematographer Brian West), and does no justice to Tippette's engaging novel.

THE SPOILERS (1930, PARA). D: Edwin Carewe. W: Bartlett Cormack & Agnes B. Leahy from Rex Beach's novel. Cast: GARY COOPER, KAY JOHNSON, William "Stage" BOYD, Slim SUMMERVILLE, Harry Green. 81m.

Klondike yarn has two gold-greedy "spoilers" vying over a saloon gal; highlight of the story, in all its film versions, has been the monumental hand-to-hand battle that busts up the saloon and then spills out across the whole camp in the deep mud of a wilderness street. Each film version has tried to do this fight more spectacularly than its predecessor. (And aren't we about due for another remake?) This version doesn't measure up to the 1942 one in that respect but it has plentiful action and the young Cooper is well cast. (Note that William "Stage" Boyd is not the same actor who played Hopalong Cassidy. This Boyd was a New York actor whom some of us remember for his stardom in what is undoubtedly the worst movie ever made, the 1935 serial *City of Lost Men*.) This actually was the third screen version, first talkie; the others were in 1913 and 1923.

THE SPOILERS (1942, UNIV). D: Ray Enright. W: Lawrence Hazard & Tom Reed from Rex Beach's novel. Cast: JOHN WAYNE, MARLENE DIETRICH, RANDOLPH SCOTT, Harry CAREY, Richard Barthelmess, William Farnum, George Cleveland, Margaret Lindsay, Samuel S. Hinds, Russell Simpson. 87m.

Fourth of the five film versions was probably the lustiest; the fight between Wayne and Scott is a film classic. Buffs note that William Farnum, who reappears in this one, starred in the 1913 version, and that Barthelmess—playing a bit, here, as a lame bartender—appears here in his last movie.

THE SPOILERS (1955, UNIV). D: Jesse Hibbs. W: Oscar Brodney & Charles Hoffman from Rex Beach's novel. Cast: JEFF CHANDLER, ANNE BAXTER, RORY CALHOUN, Ray DANTON, Barbara BRITTON, John McINTIRE, Wallace Ford, Raymond Walburn, Ruth Donnelly, Roy Barcroft, Carl Benton Reid, Willis Bou-

chey, Jack Perrin, Bob Steele, Lane Bradford, Frank Sully. 84m.

Fifth screen version is the first in color, a Ross Hunter production. The script is flaccid and the actors don't have the clout of those who appeared in the earlier versions, but the fight is big and very muddy.

SPRINGFIELD RIFLE (1952, WB). D: Andre de Toth. W: Charles Marquis Warren, Frank Davis & Sloan Nibley. Cast: GARY COOPER, PHYLLIS THAXTER, DAVID BRIAN, Paul KELLY, Philip CAREY, Guinn "Big Boy" Williams, Lon Chaney, Jr., James Millican, Vince Barnett, Martin Milner, William Fawcett, Alan Hale, Jr., Fess Parker, Ben Corbett, George Eldredge, Rory Mallinson, Holly Bane. 93m.

A Union officer (Cooper) tries to find out who's stealing Yankee horses and how; it's the old programmer gimmick of the agent working undercover in the outlaw gang (in this case the outlaws are Confederates); there's a subplot about the use of the new breech-loading Springfield rifle against Indians. The romance between the leads is perfunctory and the characters are standard, and only sketched in; it's directed without flair, the script is juvenile "B" nonsense, the acting is routine and even Cooper can't lift it above the level of weary silliness. Coming on the heels of *High Noon* this one was a keen disappointment; it's one of Cooper's worst.

THE SQUAW MAN (1931, MGM). D: Cecil B. DeMille. W: Lucien Hubbard, Lenore J. Coffee & Elsie Janis from the play by E. M. Royle. Cast: WARNER BAXTER, LUPE VELEZ, Eleanor BOARDMAN, Charles BICKFORD, Roland Young, Paul Cavanagh, J. Farrell MacDonald, Raymond Hatton.

This was De Mille's third film version of the Royle play; he'd filmed it twice before as a silent; for a plot summary, see the chapter on Silents. Excellent photography on this version was by Harold Rosson but the melodrama was dated even in 1931.

STAGECOACH (1939, UA). D: John Ford. W: Dudley Nichols from Ernest Haycox's short story "Stage to Lordsburg." Cast: JOHN WAYNE, CLAIRE TREVOR, Thomas MITCHELL, Andy DEVINE, John CARRADINE, Louise PLATT, George BANCROFT, Donald MEEK, Berton CHURCHILL, Tim Holt, Francis Ford, Yakima Canutt, Chief John Big Tree, Tom Tyler, Vester Pegg. 99m.

Perhaps the most famous of all Western movies, *Stagecoach* is said to be the film that rescued the genre from its dead-end decline of the 1930s. Actually it was but one of several big 1939 Westerns, some of which were quite good, but it is undeniably a powerful film. An ensemble play rather than a star vehicle, it presents the Ringo Kid (Wayne, in a good-badman role derivative of Hart) as but one of several equals—the stage driver (Devine, cast because he could handle a team), the drunken doctor (Thomas Mitchell—Oscar winner as best supporting actor), the prostitute with a heart of gold (Trevor), the cynical, suave gambler (Carradine), the gentle sheriff (Bancroft), the crooked banker fleeing retribution (Churchill), a nervous whiskey peddler (Meek), a respectable pregnant wife (Platt). Aboard the coach and at the overnight station they play out their romances and conflicts; the cramped coach, and the ceilinged sets (two years before *Citizen Kane*) imbue the movie with a claustrophobic tension; then the stage makes its run through hostile Indian country—a celebrated Yakima Canutt chase, an Indian fight and a well-timed cavalry rescue. With its few survivors it reaches Lordsburg where the avenging Ringo Kid settles an old score.

The black-and-white photography by Bert Glennon is excellent, as one might expect; the score (R. Hageman, F. Harling, J. Leipold & L. Shuken) won an Academy Award.

Stagecoach is an archetype, but it is a period piece. For modern casual audiences it is dated, although as a work of art it probably will hold up as long and as well as *The Virginian* (1929) or *The Searchers* (1956). Plagiarism and imitation have made cliches of the characters and set pieces in *Stagecoach*. The studio exteriors and rear-projection scenery have a cheap look; less than a third of the film was actually shot on the Monument Valley location; and the aura is primitive. There are some great stunts and magnificent action scenes in the picture but there are also moments of very sloppy carelessness, as in the showing of visible rubber-tire tracks (the camera truck) in the chase scene.

One can read in supposedly learned books that *Stagecoach* was John Wayne's first Western (it was approximately his fortieth), that it was the first time Monument Valley had been filmed (it had been in use since before *The Covered Wagon*, but Ford himself hadn't used it in a talkie prior to 1939, mostly because he hadn't made any outdoor talkie Westerns before *Stagecoach*), that the whole picture was shot on location (much of it was shot on the back lot and in the studio) and that it was based on De Maupassant's story "Boule de Suif" (it was not; Haycox, however, was paid $4,000 for the story, outright,

and didn't share in the profits). Myths about *Stagecoach* abound and they're hard to kill. Ford did not produce it; Walter Wanger did. The film did not propel Wayne instantly into superstardom; *Red River* did that. (In the original *Stagecoach* credits, Trevor's name came first.)

Cavils aside, however, *Stagecoach* was highly regarded in its day—it received Oscar nominations as best picture and for best director—and it remains exciting and seminal, justifiably famous, a Western classic.

STAGECOACH (1966, FOX). D: Gordon Douglas. W: Joseph Landon based on the script for the 1939 film. Cast: ALEX CORD, ANN-MARGRET, BING CROSBY, VAN HEFLIN, Michael CONNORS, Robert CUMMINGS, Keenan WYNN, Red BUTTONS, Stefanie POWERS, Slim Pickens. 115m.

To object to movie remakes on principle would be to argue that everything must be frozen forever, that no production of a play should be allowed except for the first one, that one mustn't repaint the Mona Lisa or rewrite *Hamlet*; but such arguments don't really hold water. Great painters often paint the same subject over again; Shakespeare's plots were rarely original with him; composers often write several pieces of music based on the same themes; and in principle filmmakers ought not to be ridiculed for their remakes. Remember that the third version of *The Maltese Falcon* was the film we all remember and love.

But in practice most remakes are failures. This version of *Stagecoach* is not abysmally bad; it's well made, entertaining, colorfully filmed in CinemaScope against lovely Colorado high-country scenery. Heflin and Crosby, reprising the Bancroft and Mitchell roles, are very good, and Alex Cord has no less thespic ability than John Wayne had in 1939, although as a personality Cord lacks Wayne's warmth. The story has been opened out and enlarged—you may never have seen so many Indians bite the dust.

But this version lacks the spark and the genius; at best it's an acceptable oater, unexceptional. It was Crosby's last theatrical film.

STAGECOACH TO DANCER'S ROCK (1962, UNIV). D: Earl Bellamy. W: Kenneth Darling. Cast: WARREN STEVENS, JODY LAWRENCE, Martin LANDAU, Rand Brooks, Judy Dann, Del Moore. 72m.

Passengers on a stagecoach crossing the desert become riled when they begin to suspect one of their number may have smallpox. Low-budget picture tries for suspense, fails; it's dull.

STAGECOACH TO FURY (1956, FOX). D: William F. Claxton. W: Eric Norden & Earle Lyon. Cast: FORREST TUCKER, MARI BLANCHARD, Margia DEANE, Paul Fix, Wallace Ford, Rodolfo Hoyos, Ian Mac-Donald, Rico Alantz, William Phillips, Ellen Corby, Alex Montoya. 75m.

Outlaws, stage robberies, all the usual cliches. In black-and-white.

STAGE TO THUNDER ROCK (1964, PARA). D: William F. Claxton. W: Charles Wallace from his teleplay. Cast BARRY SULLIVAN, MARILYN MAXWELL, KEENAN WYNN, SCOTT BRADY, Lon CHANEY, Jr., John AGAR, Wanda HENDRIX, Anne Seymour, Allan Jones, Robert Strauss, Robert Lowery, Rex Bell, Jr. 78m.

A wounded sheriff (Sullivan) has to contend with a bounty hunter (Brady), a vengeful pursuer (Wynn) and various greedy miscreants in an isolated coach depot. A.C. Lyles produced this misdirected "B" effort that was based on a script for the old *Tales of Wells Fargo* television series; there's pointless brutality, a dearth of tension, a predictable ending, rudimentary action and implausible pulp dialogue. But the photography (W. Wallace Kelley) is very good and the film has an undeservedly excellent performance by Sullivan as the beleaguered lawman.

STAGE TO TUCSON (1950, COL). D: Ralph Murphy. W: Bob Williams, Frank Burt & Robert Libott from a Frank Bonham novel. Cast: ROD CAMERON, WAYNE MORRIS, Sally EILERS, Douglas FOWLEY, Carl Benton Reid, Paul Fix, Kay Buckley, Roy Roberts, Harry Bellaver, Reed Howes.

Plenty of action but juvenile scripting characterize this near-"B" oater about two saddle pals acting as undercover agents who are sent to Tucson to find out who's hijacking stagecoaches; turns out to be Reb sympathizers. Pretty silly stuff, in color.

STAIRS OF SAND (1929, PARA). D: Otto Brower. W: Agnes B. Leahy, Sam Mintz & J. W. Ruben from Zane Grey's novel. Cast: WALLACE BEERY, JEAN ARTHUR, Chester CONKLIN, Phillips R. Holmes, Fred Kohler, Guy Oliver.

Outlaw sacrifices himself for the sake of the pretty girl's boyfriend. Typical sentimental Beery yarn is a museum piece.

THE STALKING MOON (1968, NGP). D: Robert Mulligan. W: Wendell Mayes from Theodore V. Olsen's novel. Cast: GREGORY PECK, EVA MARIE SAINT, Robert FORSTER, Noland CLAY, Frank Silvera, Lonny Chapman, Russell Thorson, Lou Frizzell, Nathaniel Narcisco. 109m.

A civilian scout for the army (Peck) retires, taking with him a white woman (Saint) and her half-Indian son (Clay); they settle in a mountain cabin away from bigoted people but then the boy's father, a Navajo warrior (Narcisco), wants the kid back and shows he's willing to kill to get him. We don't actually see the Navajo until the very end but his presence is felt: a dead animal, a twanging arrow, a young helper (Forster) silently attacked; the final confrontation between Peck and Narcisco is plenty tense but it takes awfully long to get there and the film is lifeless in too many places before that. The grubby, gritty hero of Olsen's novel has been turned into a stalwart Peck hero; the suspense would have worked better with a hero less sure of himself. And there are evidences of sloppiness, for example, in the lack of matching the studio work to the location work: we see Peck unshaven going out of the cabin but when we pick him up outside he's clean-shaven. Such carelessness does not make for great movies.

STAMPEDE (1949, AA). D: Lesley Selander. W: Blake Edwards & John C. Champion from an Edward B. Mann novel. Cast: ROD CAMERON, GALE STORM, Johnny Mack BROWN, Don Castle, Eddy Waller, John Miljan. 78m.

Complex plot concerns a range war between cattlemen; formula theme is fairly well handled.

THE STAND AT APACHE RIVER (1953, UNIV). D: Lee Sholem. W: Arthur Ross from a Robert J. Hogan novel. Cast: STEPHEN McNALLY, JULIA ADAMS, HUGH MARLOWE, Hugh O'BRIAN, Jack Kelly. 77m.

Stranded strangers wait for the Apaches to attack: you know—the one in which the trail-wise hero informs everybody there's no danger until the drums stop.

STAND UP AND FIGHT (1939, MGM). D: W. S. Van Dyke II. W: Forbes Parkhill, James M. Cain, Jane Murfin & Harvey Ferguson. Cast: WALLACE BEERY, FLORENCE RICE, ROBERT TAYLOR, Charles BICKFORD, Selmer Jackson, Charlie Grapewin. 105m.

A young railroad engineer (Taylor, in his first Western) is in constant conflict with a persistent stagecoach-line boss (Beery). A big budget and well known writers were lavished on this one but it was poor.

STAR IN THE DUST (1956, UNIV). D: Charles Haas. W: Oscar Brodney from a novel by Lee Leighton. Cast: JOHN AGAR, RICHARD BOONE, MAMIE VAN DOREN, Coleen GRAY, Leif ERICKSON,

Terry GILKYSON, James GLEASON, Randy Stuart, Paul Fix, Harry Morgan, Stanley Andrews, Clint Eastwood. 90m.

A sheriff (Agar) is caught in a tight spot between cattlemen trying to free a killer who's waiting to be hanged and farmers who insist the hanging go ahead on schedule or they'll lynch him. It's confined to the events of a single day and there are several watered-down *High Noon* cliches, including the title which has nothing to do with this movie but aptly describes the final scene of *High Noon*. Directing is lackadaisical; acting is substandard except for a few stalwart supporting players—Fix and Gleason as weary deputies, and Stuart as a rancher's wife caught in the middle. Van Doren is soporific and Agar, to put it kindly, is no Gary Cooper. The photography (John L. Russell, Jr.) is okay but the soundtrack score (Frank Skinner) is lousy, and the other production values are below Universal's standard.

A curiosity is the device of having Terry Gilkyson and his guitar on hand, visibly, to warble appropriate verses of "Sam Hall," the old English folk song about a hanging. Sam Hall is the name of the movie's condemned jailbird (Boone).

STARS IN MY CROWN (1950, MGM). D: Jacques Tourneur. W: Margaret Scott & Joe David Brown from Brown's novel. Cast: JOEL McCREA, ELLEN DREW, Dean STOCKWELL, Lewis STONE, Amanda Blake, Alan Hale, Jr., Ed Begley, James Arness. 89m.

Another yarn about a gun-toting parson who tames a town with the bullet and the Word. McCrea, and a good script, make it superior.

STATION WEST (1948, RKO). D: Sidney Lanfield. W: Frank Fenton & Winston Miller from Luke Short's novel. Cast: DICK POWELL, JANE GREER, Burl IVES, Agnes MOOREHEAD, Raymond Burr, Steve Brodie, John Doucette, Tom Powers, Guinn "Big Boy" Williams. 92m.

The Luke Short touch is evident in this fast slick actioner about an army officer (Powell) working undercover to expose a killer gang of hijackers in a town dominated by a ruthless woman. This was the only out-and-out Western in which Powell starred, and that's a pity; he's excellent in it. The plot is nothing special but there's fine snappy dialogue and it's solid entertainment.

STAY AWAY, JOE (1968, MGM). D: Peter Tewksbury. W: Michael A. Hoey from Dan Cushman's rodeo novel. Cast: ELVIS PRESLEY, JOAN BLONDELL, Burgess MEREDITH, Katy JURADO, Thomas

GOMEZ, Henry JONES, L. Q. Jones, Quentin Dean, Anne Seymour, Douglas Henderson. 102m.

Stay away, period.

STINGAREE (1934, RKO). D: William A. Wellman. W: Becky Gardiner, Lynn Riggs & Leonard Spigelgass from stories by E. W. Hornung. Cast: RICHARD DIX, IRENE DUNNE, Conway TEARLE, Mary Boland, Andy Devine, Reginald Owen.

Yet another re-teaming of the *Cimarron* stars, this is set in the Australian Outback corner of the RKO back lot with a plot about a beautiful singer and a joking outlaw. Dunne suffers with noble dignity; it's a pretty awful romantic comedy.

THE STORM RIDER (1957, FOX). D: Edward Bernds. W: Bernds & Don Martin from a novel by L. L. Foreman. Cast: SCOTT BRADY, MALA POWERS, Bill WILLIAMS, I. Stanford Jolley. 68m.

Range-war clunker.

STRANGE LADY IN TOWN (1955, WB). D: Mervyn LeRoy. W: Frank Butler. Cast: GREER GARSON, DANA ANDREWS, Cameron MITCHELL, Nick ADAMS, Lois Smith, Douglas Kennedy, Pedro Gonzalez-Gonzalez, Joan Camden, Walter Hampden. 112m.

Lady doctor arrives in Santa Fe in the 1870s and fights masculine bigotry in order to practice medicine; en route she meets famous figures—the names that are dropped include Billy the Kid (Nick Adams), whose sore tooth she pulls, General Lew Wallace (author of *Ben Hur*), Geronimo and anachronistic others. Cameron Mitchell plays her gunslinging wastrel brother—a role he reprised in the later *High Chaparral* TV series. Andrews is a fellow medic who romances her. Because it is set in Santa Fe, New Mexico, naturally it was filmed in Tucson, Arizona. Big budget was lavished on it but if you can stay awake all the way to the end of it you're more insomniac than I am.

STRANGER AT MY DOOR (1956, REP). D: William Witney. W: Barry Shipman. Cast: MacDONALD CAREY, PATRICIA MEDINA, Skip Homeier, Slim Pickens. 83m.

Parson tries to persuade an outlaw to go straight; the crusade brings danger on the parson's family. More soaper than oater, and very slow, this one has a similar theme to *The Singer Not the Song*.

STRANGER ON HORSEBACK (1955, UA). D: Jacques Tourneur. W: Herb Meadow & Don Martin from a Louis L'Amour story. Cast: JOEL McCREA, MIROSLAVA,

Kevin McCARTHY, John CARRADINE, Nancy Gates, Jaclynne Green. 66m.

The one about the gunslinging judge who cleans up a tyrannized territory. Good directing and acting.

STRANGER ON THE RUN (1967, UNIV). D: Don Siegel. W: Dean Reisner & Reginald Rose. Cast: HENRY FONDA, ANNE BAXTER, MICHAEL PARKS, Dan DURYEA, Sal MINEO, Tom Reese, Michael Burns, Lloyd Bochner, Madlyn Rhue, Bernie Hamilton, Zalman King. 97m.

A fugitive (Fonda) is hounded by a sadistic railroad detective (Parks) and his hardbitten gang. Most of the action takes place in a whistle-stop ghost town; there's suspense but it's molasses slow, especially in view of Siegel's presence at the helm. Parks delivers his lines in a peculiar hillbilly accent; most audiences can't understand more than one word in five of his dialogue. Confused, pointless movie was made in Panavision for the big screen but was only released to television.

THE STRANGER WORE A GUN (1953, COL). D: Andre de Toth. W: Kenneth Gamet from a John M. Cunningham story. Cast: RANDOLPH SCOTT, CLAIRE TREVOR, Joan WELDON, George MacREADY, Lee MARVIN, Ernest Borgnine, Alfonso Bedoya, Clem Bevans, Reed Howes, Pierre Watkin, Kansas Moehring. 83m.

Scott gets mixed up with outlaws and involved in their troubles in this confused but interesting oater from a story by the creator of *High Noon*. Excellent cast. This is another of the one-eyed director's pictures originally released in 3-D; it has the irritating earmarks of that film technique (guns and fists pointed at the audience incessantly) but that's easy enough to disregard.

STREETS OF LAREDO (1949, PARA). D: Leslie Fenton. W: Charles Marquis Warren, Louis Stevens & Elizabeth Hill, based on the 1936 film *The Texas Rangers*. Cast: WILLIAM HOLDEN, MacDONALD CAREY, WILLIAM BENDIX, MONA FREEMAN, Stanley RIDGES, Alfonso Bedoya, Robert Kortman, Clem Bevans, Joe Dominguez. 92m.

Two ex-outlaws (Holden, Bendix) reform, join the Rangers and must go after their ex-partner (Carey) who's still an outlaw. Remake of *The Texas Rangers* is a pretty good Technicolor Western for its time; entertaining, although Bendix is out of place in the saddle.

STRONGHOLD (1951, LIP). D: Steve Sekely. W: Wells Root. Cast: ZACHARY SCOTT, VERONICA LAKE, Arturo de Cordova, Rita Macedo. 82m.

At the end of the Civil War a blonde mystery woman (Lake) flees to Mexico and gets involved in Juarez's revolution. Mexican-made film is dull and dated.

SUGARFOOT (1951, WB). Also titled: SWIRL OF GLORY. D: Edwin L. Marin. W: Russell Hughes from a novel by Clarence Buddington Kelland. Cast: RANDOLPH SCOTT, ADELE JERGENS, RAYMOND MASSEY, S.Z. SAKALL, Arthur HUNNICUTT, Robert Warwick, John Hamilton, Hugh Sanders, Hank Worden. 80m.

Ex-Rebel colonel (Scott) in Arizona finds an old enemy (Massey) who rekindles their feud. Actionful movie is not bad; it was retitled for television to distinguish it from the Will Hutchins TV series.

THE SUNDOWNERS (1950, EL). D: George Templeton. W: Alan LeMay from his novel *Thunder in the Dust*. Cast: ROBERT PRESTON, CATHY DOWNS, Robert STERLING, John BARRYMORE, Jr., Chill Wills, Don Haggerty, Jack Elam. 83m.

No relation to the 1960 Robert Mitchum film of the same title, this one—young Barrymore's film debut, and Jack Elam's first Western—is a minor-league *Shane*, well done, with Technicolor and a superior script.

SUNDOWN JIM (1942, FOX). D: James Tinling. W: William Bruckner & Robert F. Metzler from Ernest Haycox's novel. Cast: John KIMBROUGH, Virginia GILMORE, Arleen Whelan, Moroni Olsen, Joseph Sawyer, Lane Chandler, Paul Hurst, Don Costello, LeRoy Mason.

Marshal outwits outlaw killers and exposes a powerful rancher. This "B" clunker, starring a football star unsuccessfully groomed for the screen, has only the most tenuous relationship to Haycox's good novel.

SUNSET PASS (1933, PARA). D: Henry Hathaway. W: Jack Cunningham & Gerald Geraghty from Zane Grey's novel. Cast: RANDOLPH SCOTT, HARRY CAREY, Kathleen BURKE, Tom KEENE, Noah BEERY, Sr., Fuzzy Knight, Kent Taylor, George Barbier, James Mason, Vince Barnett, Charles Middleton, Bob Kortman, Al Bridge. 64m.

The one about the undercover government agent (Scott) who tries to save a kid rustler because he's fallen in love with the kid's sister. Big cattle stampede for a climax. This was one of the lesser Zane Grey oaters of the Hathaway-Scott series; there'd been a silent version in 1929, and there was to be a "B" remake in 1946 with James Warren and Nan Leslie.

SUPPORT YOUR LOCAL GUNFIGHTER (1971, UA). D: Burt Kennedy. W: James Edward Grant. Cast: JAMES GARNER, SUZANNE PLESHETTE, Joan BLONDELL, Jack ELAM, Harry MORGAN, Henry JONES, Chuck CONNORS, Marie Windsor, John Dehner, Gene Evans, Ben Cooper, Terry Wilson, Dub Taylor, Ellen Corby, Grady Sutton, Pedro Gonzalez-Gonzalez. 92m.

Comedy about a cowardly gambler (Garner) who's mistaken for a famous gunslinger owes a great deal of its plot to *Along Came Jones*. It's beautifully cast and Kennedy has a real flair for comedy but it's an old-hat premise and the movie isn't nearly as much fun as its predecessor, *Support Your Local Sheriff.*

SUPPORT YOUR LOCAL SHERIFF (1969, UA). D: Burt Kennedy. W: William Bowers. Cast: JAMES GARNER, JOAN HACKETT, WALTER BRENNAN, Harry MORGAN, Jack ELAM, Henry JONES, Gene Evans, Bruce Dern, Dick Peabody, Willis Bouchey, Walter Burke. 91m.

A heroic stranger (Garner) doesn't want to be sheriff—he's just passing through on his way to Australia—but the folks persuade him to clean up their town before he moves on. So he does so. This movie draws its comedy out of the essence of the Western myth; it's a sidesplitting for-real comic horse opera, splendidly hilarious. The casting, particularly Hackett as an accident-prone girl, Elam as a scruffy deputy and Brennan as an outrageous parody of all the evil patriarchs he'd played, is inspired. It is worth noting that in the 1950s the best comedy Western was *The Sheepman* and that in the 1960s it was this film, and that both pictures were written by William Bowers. (He also wrote *The Gunfighter*—not a comedy, Lord knows, but a good writer is a good writer.) A must-see.

SUSANNAH OF THE MOUNTIES (1939, FOX). D: William A. Seiter. W: Robert Ellis, Helen Logan, Fidel LaBarba & Walter Ferris from a novel by Muriel Denison. Cast: SHIRLEY TEMPLE, RANDOLPH SCOTT, Margaret LOCKWOOD, Victor Jory, Moroni Olsen, J. Farrell MacDonald. 78m.

The one about the little orphan girl adopted by the Canadian Mountie. For Shirley Temple fans only.

SUTTER'S GOLD (1936, UNIV). D: James Cruze. W: Jack Kirkland, Walter Woods, George O'Neil, Howard Hawks, Gene Fowler & Bruno Frank from a novel by Blaise Cendrars. Cast: EDWARD ARNOLD, LEE TRACY, BINNIE BARNES, Harry CAREY, Katherine ALEXANDER, Montague Love, Addison Richards, John Miljan, Robert Warwick, Mitchell Lewis, William Janney, Ronald Cosby, Harry Cording, Jim Thorpe, Billy Gilbert, George Irving. 94m.

Story of the 1848 California gold discovery at John Sutter's (Arnold) mill in the mountains above Sacramento—the strike that began the famous '49ers gold rush—is lush and lavish; it cost a fortune, and lost one. Intended to be the epic to end all epics, it first was offered to Russian master-director Sergei Eisenstein; then Howard Hawks; only then Cruze, because his *The Covered Wagon* was a Western epic that had coined money. The producers neglected to recall it had been a dull movie. So was this one: sluggish, but well acted by a fine cast, and the Franz Waxman score is a distinct plus.

THE SWEET CREEK COUNTY WAR (1978, IND). DW: J. Frank James. Cast: RICHARD EGAN, Albert SALMI, Nita TALBOT, Slim PICKENS, Robert J. Wilke, Joe Orton, Ray Cardi, Tom Jackman.

Small homesteaders (Egan, Salmi) fight back when the evil range baron (Wilke) tries to oust them. It's based more or less on the same bit of history that gave birth to the elephantine *Heaven's Gate*; this one is shabby and cheap, with drab photography (Gregory von Berblinger); the key bad guys (Orton, Cardi) are ineptly acted; but there are a few cute touches and Egan and Salmi are surprisingly sympathetic and charming.

SWIRL OF GLORY (1951)—*See* SUGARFOOT.

TAGGART (1964, UNIV). D: R. G. Springsteen. W: Robert C. Williams from a Louis L'Amour novel. Cast: TONY YOUNG, DAN DURYEA, Jean HALE, David CARRADINE, Harry Carey, Jr., Peter Duryea, Bob Steele, Dick Foran, Anita King, Ray Teal. 85m.

In hostile Indian country, baddies pursue a young vengeance-seeking rider. Muddled but fast.

TAKE ME TO TOWN (1953, UNIV). D: Douglas Sirk. W: Richard Morris. Cast: STERLING HAYDEN, ANN SHERIDAN, Philip Reed, Lane Chandler, Lee Patrick. 81m.

Widowed preacher, with three kids, takes in a fugitive saloon gal. Sentimental nonsense.

A TALENT FOR LOVING (1974, PARA). D: Richard Quine. W: Jack Rose from the Richard Condon novel. Cast: RICHARD WIDMARK, GENEVIEVE PAGE, Cesar

ROMERO, TOPOL, Fran Jeffries, Caroline Munro, Derek Nimmo, Judd Hamilton, Max Showalter. 110m.

Sex-farce tall tale is about a Western family of oversexed boors. The novel tried to make up for its tasteless excesses with an overwhelming gusto; the movie has the excesses but not the gusto. It's leering buffoonery—filmed (in Spain) in 1969 but held in the can for five years, then released to TV only, because there was no way it could survive in the theatres.

TALL IN THE SADDLE (1944, RKO). D: Edwin L. Marin. W: Michael Hogan & Paul Fix from a Gordon R. Young novel. Cast: JOHN WAYNE, ELLA RAINES, George "Gabby" HAYES, Ward BOND, Paul FIX, Raymond Hatton, Audrey Long, Don Douglas, Harry Woods, Elizabeth Risdon, Frank Puglia, Tom London. 87m.

Cowhand can't stand the idea of working for a woman but falls in love with the feisty female owner of an embattled cattle outfit. Unfortunately the plot, while amiable, is strictly programmer stuff, with a lot of static talk leading to a detective-story denouement, unmasking the villains. It's the sort of picture in which just as a character is about to reveal the bad guy's identity he's shot dead by a gunman lurking outside the window. *Tall in the Saddle* has its partisans but it's very dated and small-caliber. Still, Raines is lovely, Hayes is funny, Bond is nicely villainous and Wayne is Wayne.

TALL MAN RIDING (1955,WB). D: Lesley Selander. W: Joseph Hoffman from Norman A. Fox's novel. Cast: RANDOLPH SCOTT, DOROTHY MALONE, Peggie CASTLE, John DEHNER, William Ching, John Baragrey, Robert Barrat, Paul Richards, Lane Chandler. 83m.

A whipped-out rancher (Scott) returns to a Montana valley to get revenge against a tyrannical range boss (Barrat), but the chief bad guy actually is the saloonkeeper (Baragrey) and there's the rancher's daughter (Malone), the golden-hearted saloon songbird (Castle), the shady lawyer (Dehner), the proud dude (Ching), the fast kid gunslinger (Richards), the stagecoach chase, the fistfight, frame-ups and misunderstandings and shoot-outs. Hardly a line and nary a scene is not a cliche. Lackadaisical film is so typical that it could be a textbook of ranch romance formulas.

THE TALL MEN (1955, FOX). D: Raoul Walsh. W: Sydney Boehm & Frank Nugent from Clay Fisher's novel. Cast: CLARK GABLE, JANE RUSSELL, ROBERT RYAN, Cameron MITCHELL, Juan Garcia, Emile Meyer, Steve Darrell, Harry Shannon, Will Wright, Russell Simpson, Mae Marsh. 122m.

Cattle-drive epic has a tough, manly, trail boss (Gable) and the partner (Ryan) with whom he vies for Jane Russell's charms and the kid brother (Mitchell) who's hotheaded and dangerous, and a plot involving natural hazards, Sioux attacks and rustlers. It's virile and lavish in CinemaScope but disappointingly hackneyed and mediocre, bloated far beyond its proper scale: overlong, underscripted, flabbily directed and downright silly. Howard Hawks's brother, William Hawks, produced it, evidently in the hope it would be another *Red River*. It wasn't.

THE TALL STRANGER (1957, AA). D: Thomas Carr. W: Christopher Knopf from a Louis L'Amour novel. Cast: JOEL Mc-CREA, VIRGINIA MAYO, Michael AN-SARA, Leo Gordon, Michael Pate, Whit Bissell. 81m.

Drifter aids a settlers' wagon train when cattle barons challenge them. Not too bad, but predictable.

THE TALL T (1957, COL). D: Budd Boetticher. W: Burt Kennedy from an Elmore Leonard story. Cast: RANDOLPH SCOTT, MAUREEN O'SULLIVAN, RICHARD BOONE, Henry SILVA, Arthur HUNNI-CUTT, Skip HOMEIER, John Hubbard, Robert Burton. 78m.

Arizona rancher (Scott) is captured and beleaguered by baddies (Boone, Silva, Homeier); small actioner was shot mostly on one canyon location, with a siege plot. It starts slow—tedious exposition and lame comedy—and hero Randy is too smilingly goody-two-shoes for belief but once the tension begins it is unrelentingly taut, characteristic of the tense economy of Elmore Leonard's writing (as in his *Hombre* and *Valdez is Coming*). Performances are excellent.

THE TALL TEXAN (1953, LIP). D: Elmo Williams. W: Samuel Roeca & Elizabeth Reinhardt. Cast: LLOYD BRIDGES, MARIE WINDSOR, Lee J. COBB, Luther ADLER, Samuel Herrick, Sid Saylor, George Steele.

Motley, greedy group searches a desert gorge for buried treasure that's hidden on sacred Indian ground; the Indians, annoyed by their trespasses, pick them off one at a time. Story is warmed-over *Treasure of the Sierra Madre* but the character interplay between such marvelously venal characters as Adler and Cobb is great fun. Good black-and-white photography (Joseph F. Biroc). Rate it very high for a low-budget oater.

TAZA, SON OF COCHISE (1954, UNIV). D: Douglas Sirk. W: Gerald D. Adams & George Zuckerman. Cast: ROCK HUDSON, BARBARA RUSH, Gregg PALMER, Joe Sawyer, Morris Ankrum. 79m.

Hudson in the title role is ridiculous and the plot is only slightly less so; cheapjack cavalry-versus-Indians movie is a cynical attempt to cash in on the popularity of *Broken Arrow*.

TELL THEM WILLIE BOY IS HERE (1969, UNIV). DW: Abraham Polonsky from Harry Lawton's novel *Willie Boy*. Cast: ROBERT REDFORD, ROBERT BLAKE, KATHARINE ROSS, SUSAN CLARK, Barry SULLIVAN, John VERNON, Charles McGraw, Shelly Novack, Charles Aidman, Ned Romero, Lou Frizzell. 97m.

In 1909 in the Southern California desert a young Paiute Indian (Blake) gets into trouble, the result of various misunderstandings and bigoted jumpings-to-conclusions. Inevitably there's a murder and the Indian youth runs for it with his Indian girl friend (Ross), pursued by a compassionate but relentless sheriff (Redford) and a not-so compassionate posse. The emphasis is on the contrived deterministic circumstances that bring about the unjust persecution of the youth. Its fashionable Indian-as-tragic-victim theme made it popular, and it was a sentimental favorite at the time because it marked the return to the screen of the long-blacklisted Polonsky, but in fact it's a mediocre movie at best; the characters are either glib stereotypes—the placid, patronizingly liberal white missionary (Clark), the arrogant, ruthless, one-note Indian hater (Sullivan)—or simply undefined and unformed—the insipid and unbelievable Indian girl, the woodenly laconic sheriff. We don't know any of these people except Willie Boy, and we don't even get to know *him* very well, and therefore we cannot give a damn what happens to any of them. We know somebody will get killed at the end but we don't really care who it is. The movie is cluttered with self-contempt and anachronistically modern references; and a sad pretentious emptiness.

TEN DAYS TO TULARA (1958 UA). D: George Sherman. W: Laurence Mascott. Cast: STERLING HAYDEN, Grayce Raynor, Rodolfo Hoyos, Carlos Muzquiz. 77m.

Police pursue Hayden across the Mexican desert in an attempt to recover stolen gold. In black-and-white; inept.

THE TENDERFOOT (1932, WB). D: Ray Enright. W: Earl Baldwin, Monty Banks & Arthur Caesar from a story by Richard Carle and the George S. Kaufman play *The Butter and Egg Man*. Cast: JOE E. BROWN, GINGER ROGERS, Vivian OAKLAND, Allan LANE, Lew Cody, George Chandler, Olin Howlin. 70m.

Naive cowboy gets involved with big city gangsters and Broadway show people. Not much of the wit of the Kaufman play remains; it's a slapstick farce tailored for Brown. It was later remade a couple of times; the best version probably was *An Angel from Texas* (1940).

TENNESSEE'S PARTNER (1955, RKO). D: Allan Dwan. W: Milton Krims, D.D. Beauchamp, Graham Baker & Teddi Sherman from the Bret Harte story. Cast: JOHN PAYNE, RONALD REAGAN, RHONDA FLEMING, COLEEN GRAY, Anthony CARUSO, Morris Ankrum, Chubby Johnson, Angie Dickinson. 86m.

Cowhand (Reagan) takes the side of a nasty gambler (Payne) in a quarrel, after which the two are blamed for the murder of an old prospector. Most of the action takes place in a gold-rush saloon run by "The Duchess" (Fleming). Tame but amiable film reduces the Harte classic to a "B" yarn. Angie Dickinson, unbilled in the title credits, has her first speaking part after her one-line debut in a Doris Day picture.

TENSION AT TABLE ROCK (1956, RKO). D: Charles Marquis Warren. W: Winston Miller from a Frank Gruber novel. Cast: RICHARD EGAN, DOROTHY MALONE, Cameron MITCHELL, Angie DICKINSON, Billy Chapin, Joe DeSantis. 93m.

Gunfighter trying to hide out from his outlaw past is haunted by his old gang when he takes a job in an isolated stagecoach swing station. It's well directed and the cast is fine except for Egan, who is extraordinarily and inexplicably wooden here.

TEN WANTED MEN (1955, COL). D: H. Bruce Humberstone. W: Kenneth Gamet, Irving Ravetch & Harriet Frank, Jr. Cast: RANDOLPH SCOTT, JOCELYN BRANDO, Richard BOONE, Skip HOMEIER, Alfonso BEDOYA, Leo Gordon, Lee Van Cleef, Minor Watson, Francis J. McDonald, Clem Bevans, Donna Martell, Lester Matthews, Tom Powers, Dennis Weaver, Louis Jean Heydt, Kathleen Crowley, Denver Pyle, Jack Perrin, Julian Rivero, Reed Howes, Franklyn Farnum. 80m.

Cattle baron (Scott) versus outlaws—routine oater has a very large cast of veterans.

TEN WHO DARED (1960, BV). D: William Beaudine. W: Lawrence E. Watkin, based on the journals of John Wesley Powell. Cast: BRIAN KEITH, John BEAL, Ben JOHNSON, James DRURY, Dawn Little Sky, L. Q. Jones, R. G. Armstrong, David Stollery, Roy Barcroft. 92m.

Based-on-fact story of an early (1869) exploration of the Grand Canyon is a hopeless mess, stupidly scripted, silly, awkward and embarrassing; the overblown directing verges on hysteria and even Keith mugs and hams unforgivably. Good location cinematography (Gordon Avil).

TERROR IN A TEXAS TOWN (1958, UA). D: Joseph H. Lewis. W: Ben L. Perry. Cast: STERLING HAYDEN, Sebastian CABOT, Carol KELLY, Eugene Martin, Ned Young, Gil Lamb, Victor Millan, Frank Ferguson, Marilee Earle. 80m.

A land-grabber (Cabot) tries to drive out the farmers so he can seize their oil-laden land; the Swedish sailor son of one of the dead farmers tries to fight back but gets little help—the neighbors seem to be fugitives from the cast of *High Noon*. This was the last film directed by Lewis, who achieved a towering reputation among those cineastes who found in such films as this all sorts of fascinating values. I must admit they escape me. There is one clever camera shot—a dollying pan in which the camera moves from interior to exterior, discovering an advancing gunslinger in a window frame—but it's hardly worth sitting through this witless idiocy for that. (Ray Rennahan was cinematographer, in black-and-white; the shot may have been his.) Except for Hayden, who is very good as the Swede, the acting is dreadful, and I would maintain that a director who can't get even basically believable performances out of his actors, no matter what budget limitations he labors under, is—to be kind about it—something less than a genius. The dialogue is hackneyed, the characterizations rudimentary and straight out of 1930s pulp stories, the plot a shade older than Australopithecus, the production similar to a cheap half-hour TV oater of the period, and the overall flavor shabby, predictable, paceless and pallid. It has virtually no action except for the absurd ending, in which Hayden goes into the big gunfight armed only with a harpoon. Even the score (Gerald Fried) is bad.

TERROR TRAIL (1933, UNIV). D: Armand Schaefer. W: Jack Cunningham from a Grant Taylor story. Cast: TOM MIX, Naomi JUDGE, Raymond HATTON, Francis J. McDonald, Robert Kortman, Lafe McKee, Hank Bell, Jay Wilsey (Buffalo Bill, Jr.), Arthur Rankin. 57m.

Programmer about ranch-burning rustlers marked a low point for Mix.

THE TEXAN (1930, PARA). D: John Cromwell. W: Daniel N. Rubin & Oliver Garrett from an O. Henry short story. Cast: GARY COOPER, FAY WRAY, RUSS COLUMBO, Emma DUNN, May ROBSON, James Marcus, Oscar Apfel, Donald Reed. 72m.

The Llano Kid (Cooper) poses as a rich widow's son but then reforms on account of love. Wheezy plot was worn-out even then but the young Cooper is dashing and sincere. Produced by David O. Selznick.

THE TEXAN MEETS CALAMITY JANE (1950, COL). DW: Ande Lamb. Cast: JAMES "Shamrock" ELLISON, Evelyn ANKERS, Jack Ingram, Lee "Lasses" White. 69m.

Calamity Jane fights to claim ownership of a lucrative saloon and a cowhand comes to her assistance. Zilch, in color.

THE TEXANS (1938, PARA). D: James V. Hogan. W: Bertram Millhauser, Paul Sloane & William Wister Haines from Emerson Hough's novel *North of 36*. Cast: RANDOLPH SCOTT, JOAN BENNETT, Walter BRENNAN, May ROBSON, Robert CUMMINGS, Robert BARRAT, Raymond HATTON, Harvey Stephens, Francis Ford, Clarence Wilson, Jack Moore, Chris-Pin Martin, Spencer Charters, William Haade, Irving Bacon, Francis J. McDonald, Jack Perrin, John Qualen, Harry Woods, Wheeler Oakman, Edward LeSaint, Richard Denning. 92m.

Heroic ex-Rebel veterans and a family of ranchers are displaced from their lands by Reconstruction carpetbaggers in post-Civil War Texas; it all leads to a big cattle drive to save the ranch. Remake of the silent *North of 36* uses extensive stock footage from the silent version and from other oldies: it's huge in scale with an enormous cast and zesty Indian fights, cattle drives, riverboats, mob scenes— very well staged and competently photographed (Theodore Sparkuhl) with a big score (Boris Morros), but in plot and characterizations it's overblown "B" fare, quite dated, not very well acted.

TEXAS (1941, COL). D: George Marshall. W: Horace McCoy, Lewis Meltzer & Michael Blankfort. Cast: WILLIAM HOLDEN, GLENN FORD, CLAIRE TREVOR, Edgar BUCHANAN, George BANCROFT, Don Beddoe, Addison Richards, Joseph Crehan, Andrew Toombes, Tom Dugan. 93m.

Two post-Civil War cowpokes set out to strike it rich in freewheeling Texas; one becomes an outlaw (Holden) and the other sticks more or less to the straight and narrow (Ford) and both of them spark the pretty girl (Trevor). It's treated lightly with the emphasis on comedy; as a hilariously villainous frontier dentist Edgar Buchanan shines; he actually was a dentist and this remained his favorite role. Highly superior entertainment.

TEXAS ACROSS THE RIVER (1966, UNIV). **D: Michael Gordon. W: Wells Root, Harold Greene & Ben Starr. Cast: DEAN MARTIN, ALAIN DELON, ROSEMARY FORSYTH, Joey BISHOP, Tina MARQUAND (Aumont), Peter GRAVES, Don Beddoe, Roy Barcroft, Michael Ansara, Andrew Prine. 101m.**

Cowhand (Martin) sets out on a gun-running expedition with a Spanish nobleman on the run (Delon) and an Indian girl (Marquand); they are pursued by a cavalry captain (Graves). Lame comedy has no style and no wit, and features what may be the worst miscasting in the history of Western films: Joey Bishop as an Indian sidekick. To call a picture like this a dog is to give dogs a bad name.

TEXAS BAD MAN (1932, UNIV). **D: Edward Laemmle. W: Jack Cunningham. Cast: TOM MIX, Lucille POWERS, Fred KOHLER, Edward LeSaint, Willard Robertson, Dick Alexander, Franklyn Farnum. 60m.**

Emphasis is on horseback stunts in this near-"B" actioner; fun for Mix fans.

TEXAS BADMAN (1954, MONO). **D: Lewis Collins. W: Joseph F. Poland. Cast: WAYNE MORRIS, ELAINE RILEY, Denver Pyle, Frank Ferguson, Sheb Wooley.**

Mining town sheriff has to go after his own desperado father. Weary.

TEXAS, BROOKLYN AND HEAVEN (1948, UA). **D: William Castle. W: Lewis Meltzer & Earl Baldwin from a novel by Barry Benefield. Cast: GUY MADISON, DIANA LYNN, James DUNN, Audie MURPHY, Florence BATES, Roscoe Karns, Lionel Stander. 76m.**

Dude girl loves horses; cowboy tries to alienate her affections. Dud comedy.

TEXAS CARNIVAL (1951, MGM). **D: Charles Walters. W: Dorothy Kingsley & George Wells. Cast: RED SKELTON, ESTHER WILLIAMS, HOWARD KEEL, ANN MILLER, Keenan WYNN, Paul Raymond, Hans Conried, Tom Tully, Glenn Strange. 77m.**

Mistaken-identity comedy is about a carny tramp taken for a Texas range baron; with music (David Rose). A number of big name stars were shoved into the back seat in this one-man Skelton show. It has very funny moments.

TEXAS LADY (1955, RKO). **D: Tim Whelan. W: Horace McCoy. Cast: CLAUDETTE COLBERT, BARRY SULLIVAN, Horace MacMAHON, Gregory Walcott, Ray Collins, Douglas Fowley, John Litel, Walter Sande, Don Haggerty. 86m.**

Frontier lady newspaper editor and her gambler friend team up against a cattle baron. Predictable, rambling, slow.

THE TEXAS RANGERS (1936, PARA). **D: King Vidor. W: Vidor, Louis Stevens & Elizabeth Hill from a book by Walter Prescott Webb. Cast: FRED MacMURRAY, JACK OAKIE, JEAN PARKER, Lloyd NOLAN, Monte BLUE, Jed Prouty, Edward Ellis, Hank Bell, Bennie Bartlett, Elena Martinez, Frank Shannon. 95m.**

Big episodic Western is presumably based somewhat on real Ranger cases but the main plot is a fiction about two ex-outlaws who join up with the Rangers and then must go after their old partner who's still on the wrong side of the law. MacMurray plays, fairly well, a part originally slated for Gary Cooper. Good photography (Edward Cronjager). It was remade twelve years later as *Streets of Laredo.*

THE TEXAS RANGERS (1950, COL). **D: Phil Karlson. W: Richard Schayer & Frank Gruber. Cast: GEORGE MONTGOMERY, GALE STORM, William BISHOP, Jerome COURTLAND, John DEHNER, Douglas Kennedy, Jock Mahoney, Noah Beery, Jr., Myron Healey, Ian MacDonald, John Litel, John Doucette, Julian Rivero, Trevor Bardette. 68m.**

Ranger hero is pitted against outlaw Sam Bass (Bishop); there's bright-hued Trucolor and a lot of chasing, fighting and shooting; it's simpleminded kid stuff, not very well cast, but okay for the undemanding.

TEXAS RANGERS RIDE AGAIN (1940, PARA). **D: James V. Hogan. W: Horace McCoy & William R. Lipman. Cast: JOHN HOWARD, ELLEN DREW, BRODERICK CRAWFORD, Akim TAMIROFF, May ROBSON, Anthony Quinn, Charlie Grapewin, John Miljan, Tom Tyler, Eddie Acuff, Donald Curtis, Ruth Rogers, Robert Ryan, Monte Blue, Harvey Stephens, Joseph Crehan, Jack Perrin, Gordon Jones. 68m.**

Rangers in patrol cars versus rustlers in trucks. Ellen Drew gets knocked unconscious again in this one (compare *Geronimo*). Despite the big cast it's hackneyed and dreary.

THE TEXICAN (1967, COL). D: Lesley Selander. W: John C. Champion. Cast: AUDIE MURPHY, BRODERICK CRAWFORD, Diana LORYS, Jorge Rigaud, Luz Marquez, Aldo Sanbrell. 91m.

Ex-lawman returns from exile to avenge his brother's murder. As the 1960s wore on, Audie's budgets got smaller and smaller; finally he had to go overseas to make his last few oaters. This tired entry was filmed listlessly in Spain with European supporting actors and crews.

TEX TAKES A HOLIDAY (1932, IND). D: Alvin J. Neitz. W: Robert Walker. Cast: WALLACE MacDONALD, Virginia BROWN FAIRE, Olin Francis, George Chesebro, Ben Corbett. 59m.

Cowboy gets into trouble in saloon; routine comedy.

THERE WAS A CROOKED MAN (1970, WB). D: Joseph L. Mankiewicz. W: David Newman & Robert Benton. Cast: KIRK DOUGLAS, HENRY FONDA, Burgess MEREDITH, Hume CRONYN, Warren OATES, Arthur O'CONNELL, Lee GRANT, John RANDOLPH, Martin GABEL, Claudia McNeil, Alan Hale, Jr., Bert Freed, Victor French, Ann Doran, C. K. Yang. 125m.

A cheerfully amoral outlaw (Douglas in an orange fright wig) is sent to prison and develops an odd relationship with the pious warden (Fonda) who used to be a gunslinging lawman. The relationship is similar to that between Cooper and Lancaster in *Vera Cruz*—humor tinged with suspicion—but this one's shown from the bad guy's rather than the good guy's point of view, and the population of the prison consists faddishly of gallows-humor types: sleazy characters defined by viciousness, stupidity, homosexuality and cowardice. That's not unlike the population of any real prison, but here it's all played for strained, laughs. Pretty soon the prisoner dominates the prison, in a plot twist reminiscent of prisoner-of-war movies like *King Rat*; and there's a final O. Henry trick—an ending that I find nauseating. Benton and Newman have done good things, and Mankiewicz is one of the best of all American filmmakers (*All About Eve*), but this turkey was a dud for all of them. It's not so much a Western as a microcosm; it tries, all too obviously, to make statements. It's long, slow, overacted and monumentally distasteful—an idea gone awry. Neither funny nor illuminating, it is only pretentious trash. It commits the ultimate sin: it is boring.

THESE THOUSAND HILLS (1959, FOX). D: Richard Fleischer. W: Alfred Hayes from the novel by A. B. Guthrie, Jr. Cast: DON MURRAY, LEE REMICK, Richard EGAN, Patricia OWENS, Stuart WHITMAN, Albert DEKKER, Harold J. Stone, Douglas Fowley, Jean Willes, Royal Dano, Fuzzy Knight. 96m.

Overambitious cowhand (Murray) builds a cattle empire but loses the friendship and respect of his old pals. That's the core of this undersized Western with pretensions. It's clumsily scripted to be sure, but the premise was dubious to begin with, because the hero is simply acting out the dream of Manifest Destiny, and it is hard to picture Montana Westerners of the 1880s finding anything wrong with that. The novel made it clear that the hero is on the verge of psychosis; the movie doesn't. Muddled film nonetheless is well made and very well acted.

THEY CAME TO CORDURA (1959, COL). D: Robert Rossen. W: Rossen & Ivan Moffat from Glendon Swarthout's novel. Cast: GARY COOPER, RITA HAYWORTH, VAN HEFLIN, TAB HUNTER, Richard CONTE, Michael CALLAN, Dick YORK, Robert Keith, Jim Bannon, Carlos Romero, Clem Fuller, Edward C. Platt, Maurice Jara. 123m.

In his next-to-last Western Cooper plays an army major being punished for an act of cowardice by having to write up soldiers (in the campaign against Villa's revolutionaries in Mexico, 1915) for the Medal of Honor—a public-relations attempt by the army to give a boost to Washington's pre-World War I recruiting drive. Major Thorne assembles several heroes and leads them, together with a shady fugitive American woman (Hayworth), across the desert toward the military assembly point at Cordura. The trek is menaced by bandits, bad weather and conflicts among the seven travelers. The theme is a man's discovery of the true nature of courage.

It's a good movie; it might have been even better had it not been for the studio's butchery in re-editing it. The journey is graphically bleak and arduously heartbreaking. The acting is uneven but Heflin and Conte are fine and Hayworth is excellent, and Cooper, in his very deliberate interpretation of the role, is shatteringly effective. It's slow, particularly in its early reels, but it's worth staying with.

THEY DIED WITH THEIR BOOTS ON (1942, WB). D: Raoul Walsh. W: Aeneas MacKenzie & Wally Kline. Cast: ERROL FLYNN, OLIVIA De HAVILLAND, Arthur KENNEDY, Gene LOCKHART, Sydney GREENSTREET, Charley GRAPEWIN, Anthony QUINN, Byron Barr (Gig

Young), John Litel, Eleanor Parker, Minor Watson, Stanley Ridges, Walter Hampden, Regis Toomey, Hattie McDaniel, Joe Sawyer, Frank Wilcox, George Eldredge, Joseph Crehan, Eddie Acuff, Irving Bacon, Spencer Charters, Hobart Bosworth, Russell Hicks, Frank Ferguson, John Ridgely. 138m.

Romanticized biography of George Armstrong Custer (Flynn) covers the years from his brash youth at West Point and his service as the youngest general in the Civil War to his violent death at the Little Big Horn in 1876. If you take history seriously this is not for you—any relation between the Flynn character and the real Custer is accidental, and most of the facts have been distorted or ignored in favor of romantic heroics. But it's grand entertainment—Flynn's best Western by far, a lavish movie in the heroic mold, by turns mischievous, sentimental, dramatic, noble and swashbuckling. It has a good screenplay, for a change, as well as energetic spectacle. A Hal Wallis production, it has fine photography (Bert Glennon) and a suitably Wagnerian score (Max Steiner) and plenty of sweep, lusty action and good acting. Its firsts are numerous: it was Eleanor Parker's debut and one of Arthur Kennedy's first films; it was Sydney Greenstreet's first and only Western; it was nearly Gig Young's first picture; gruesomely, it set a new record by killing three stunt riders in the cavalry charge scene (one was impaled on his own sword); and it marked the last screen teaming of Flynn and de Havilland, who evidently knew it would be their last film together at least for a time; the parting scene in the movie may achieve its poignancy because of that: it's superbly played, directed with an understatement that's different from most of the movie's flamboyant scenes. Good stuff.

THEY RODE WEST (1954, COL). D: Phil Karlson. W: DeVallon Scott, Frank Nugent & Leo Katcher. Cast: ROBERT FRANCIS, MAY WYNN, DONNA REED, Philip CAREY, Onslow Stevens. 84m.

Young doctor tries to avert a Kiowa Indian war. Routine plot, good production. Francis and Wynn were a fan-magazine item at the time, having debuted as the young lovers in *The Caine Mutiny*, in which May Wynn was the name of the character played by the starlet.

THIRTEEN FIGHTING MEN (1960, FOX). D: Harry Gerstad. W: Robert Hamner & Jack Thomas. Cast: GRANT WILLIAMS, Carole MATHEWS, Brad DEXTER, Robert Dix, Rayford Barnes, Richard Garland, John Erwin. 69m.

Yanks-versus-Rebs to see who gets the gold shipment. Routine cheap black-and-white oater.

THOMASINE AND BUSHROD (1974, COL). D: Gordon Parks, Jr. W: Marlene Weed. Cast: MAX JULIEN, Vonetta McGEE, George Murdock, Juanita Moore, Glynn Turman. 95m.

Set in 1912 Southwest and filmed in New Mexico, this blaxploitation *Bonnie and Clyde* is confused and mostly silly.

THREE DESPERATE MEN (1951, LIP). D: Sam Newfield. W: Orville Hampton. Cast: PRESTON FOSTER, VIRGINIA GREY, Jim DAVIS, House PETERS, Jr., Ross Latimer, William Haade, Rory Mallinson, Milton Kibbee, Monte Blue, Sid Melton. 71m.

Two brothers try to save a third brother from a frame-up; all three end up on the run. Standard; no surprises.

THREE FACES WEST (1940, REP). D: Bernard Vorhaus. W: F. Hugh Herbert, Joseph M. March & Samuel Ornitz. Cast: JOHN WAYNE, SIGRID GURIE, Charles COBURN, Helen MacKellar, Wade Boteler, Spencer Charters, Trevor Bardette, Russell Simpson. 79m.

Minor Wayne opus is set in the 1930s dust bowl, whence a group of Scandinavian refugees, guided by cowboy Wayne, flees to Oregon with Nazi villains in pursuit. Simple-minded dated flick is anachronistic but could have been worse.

THREE GODFATHERS (1936, MGM). D: Richard Boleslavsky. W: Edward Paramore & Manuel Seff from Peter B. Kyne's novel. Cast: CHESTER MORRIS, LEWIS STONE, Walter BRENNAN, Irene HERVEY, Sidney Toler, Bob Livingston, Roger Imhof, Willard Robertson.

Three outlaws, fleeing through the desert, encounter a woman dying in childbirth. Trying to nurture the infant orphan, they get into various scrapes while fleeing a marshal who's tracking them relentlessly. This oft-filmed tale had been made twice as a silent movie by John Ford (the first time as *Marked Men*, 1919) and would be made yet again by Ford in 1948, and yet again in 1974 as a made-for-TV oater, *The Godchild* (see appendix). This version of the tearjerker was produced by Joseph L. Mankiewicz and it was all right for its time.

THREE GODFATHERS (1948, MGM). D: John Ford. W: Frank S. Nugent & Laurence Stallings from Peter B. Kyne's novel. Cast: JOHN WAYNE, PEDRO ARMENDARIZ, HARRY CAREY, Jr., Ward BOND,

Ben Johnson, Jane Darwell, Mae Marsh, Mildred Natwick, Guy Kibbee, Francis Ford, Hank Worden, Jack Pennick, Victor Potel. 105m.

Same plot as the 1936 version. Sentimental to the point of absurdity, this one has the surviving outlaw stumbling into New Jerusalem, Arizona, lugging the baby into the Last Chance Saloon to the strains of "Holy Night"—on Christmas Eve. It's in color (photographed in Monument Valley by Winton C. Hoch and Charles Boyle) and, like any Ford movie, has its excellences; but it's infected with a case of terminal treacle. Coming as it did after *Fort Apache* this one strikes me as a distinct letdown, a relapse into the dated styles and materials of 1920s melodramas.

THREE HOURS TO KILL (1954, COL). D: Alfred Werker. W: Roy Huggins, Richard Alan Simmons, Alex Gottlieb & Maxwell Shane. Cast: DANA ANDREWS, DONNA REED, Dianne FOSTER, Stephen Elliott, James Westerfield, Laurence Hugo, Richard Coogan, Richard Webb, Carolyn Jones. 77m.

Under a tight time limit a falsely accused stagecoach driver (Andrews), the father of an illegitimate child, tries to clear himself and find the real killer of his former girl friend's brother. Unusual plot twists, adult theme, tough ending, but in the course of things the juvenile script cliches overwhelm it; in the end, despite good acting, it's less than half what the title says it is.

THE THREE OUTLAWS (1957, IND). D: Sam Newfield. W: Orville Hampton. Cast: NEVILLE BRAND, Alan HALE, Jr., Bruce BENNETT, Rodolfo HOYOS, Jose Gonzales.

Bandits steal a big haul, flee to Mexico, settle down in a peon village and deposit the loot in the local bank. Then of course the bank is cleaned out by Mexican robbers. You take it from there. Weary "B" production.

3:10 TO YUMA (1957, COL). D: Delmer Daves. W: Halsted Welles from an Elmore Leonard story. Cast: VAN HEFLIN, GLENN FORD, Felicia FARR, Richard JAECKEL, Henry Jones, Leora Dana, Robert Emhardt, Ford Rainey, George Mitchell. 96m.

Needing money to save his homestead, a stolid farmer (Heflin) takes a bounty job delivering a killer (Ford) to the Yuma penitentiary. Waiting for the train, the farmer holes up with his prisoner in a seedy rail-stop town while the bad guy's gang (Jaeckel, others) lay siege to it. As the train approaches, the farmer knows he's got to emerge into their sights. The suspense builds neatly; it owes a bit to *High Noon* and a bit to *Shane* and the ending, in an attempt to avoid cliches, is strained and implausible; but it's a fine solid movie, one of the last and best of the major Westerns to have been filmed in black-and-white (photography by Charles Lawton, partly on locations in Arizona, where it's set). There's an effective score by George Duning (with a dated theme sung by Frankie Laine). Heflin is dependably sturdy. Ford is outstanding in the unusual part of the charming but deadly killer. Incidentally this is one of the few oaters that are careful to be accurate in the discussions and depictions of geography.

THREE VIOLENT PEOPLE (1956, PARA). D: Rudolph Mate. W: James Edward Grant, Leonard Praskins & Barney Slater. Cast: CHARLTON HESTON, ANNE BAXTER, TOM TRYON, Gilbert ROLAND, Bruce BENNETT, Forrest TUCKER, Elaine Stritch, Robert Blake, Barton MacLane, Peter Hansen, John Harmon. 99m.

Ex-Rebel rancher (Heston), his tarnished bride (Baxter), his one-armed ne'er-do-well brother (Tryon) and his conscience-reminding foreman (Roland) provide the conflicts in this romantic-triangle soap/horse opera; it's set in Texas but filmed in Arizona; there's also a ludicrous plot about fighting off land-grabbers (Bennett, Tucker, MacLane) and the whole thing is on a pulp-magazine level of silliness. The acting is what you'd have to call lusty rather than realistic and the script is characterized by such lines as, "A man must do what a man must do" (Heston actually says that one twice). Mate, best known as a master cinematographer, directed the occasional movie (this was the last Western he helmed) and did so with verve but it's pretty dreadful.

THREE YOUNG TEXANS (1954, FOX). D: Henry Levin. W: Gerald D. Adams from a William McLeod Raine novel. Cast: JEFFREY HUNTER, MITZI GAYNOR, KEEFE BRASSELLE, Michael ANSARA, Harvey Stephens, Dan Riss, Aaron Spelling, Morris Ankrum. 78m.

Two cowpokes and a rancher's daughter rob a train for peculiar reasons; they plan to give the loot back afterwards, but naturally things get fouled up. The dialogue is poor but the complicated plot is often interesting. Film boasts lovely Technicolor photography (Harold Lipstein) and an effective, if overly dramatic, score (Lionel Newman). Brasselle lacks the charm for his part; the rest of the cast is acceptable—Ansara better than that,

THE SHOOTIST (1976):
Lauren Bacall, John Wayne.
The Duke goes out in a
blaze of glory, with dignity
intact, in his last movie.
Paramount Pictures

THE SIEGE AT RED
RIVER (1954): Van Johnson
(light shirt), Joanne Dru.
Johnson, miscast as a Southerner, steals a Gatling gun
from the Union army.
Twentieth Century-Fox

SIERRA BARON (1958):
Rick Jason, Rita Gam, Brian
Keith. Interesting costumes
in an early California setting. Twentieth Century-Fox

SITTING BULL (1954): J. Carrol Naish and Iron Eyes Cody (lower right). Naish is ludicrous in the title role. United Artists

SOUTHWEST PASSAGE (1954): John Ireland makes his getaway on a camel. United Artists

THE SQUAW MAN (1931): Lupe Velez, Warner Baxter. De Mille's third film version of the wheezy chestnut. MGM

THE SPOILERS (1942): John Wayne clips Randolph Scott on the jaw in a posed publicity-still for the climactic fight scene. Universal Pictures

STAGECOACH (1939):
George Bancroft, John
Wayne, Andy Devine,
Vester Pegg. Perhaps the most
famous of all Western
movies—but myths about
it abound. United Artists

STAGECOACH (1966): On top of
the coach: Slim Pickens, Van
Heflin, Alex Cord. In the windows:
Ann-Margret, Stefanie Powers.
Standing: Bing Crosby, Red Buttons, Keenan Wynn, Robert Cummings, Michael Connors. In practice most remakes are failures.
Twentieth Century-Fox

STAGE TO THUNDER ROCK
(1964): Most every Western seems
to have to have its stagecoach.
Photography in these quickie
A. C. Lyles productions often was
quite good. Paramount Pictures

STATION WEST (1948):
Agnes Moorehead, Dick
Powell. Fast slick actioner
was the only out-and-out
Western in which Powell
starred, and that's a pity.
RKO Radio Pictures

THEY CAME TO CORDURA
(1959): Dick York, Michael Callan,
Richard Conte, Gary Cooper, Rita
Hayworth, Van Heflin, Tab
Hunter. Cooper is shatteringly effective in this arduous film about a
journey in search of the true nature of courage. Columbia Pictures

THEY DIED WITH THEIR
BOOTS ON (1942): Errol
Flynn (buckskin jacket) as
George Armstrong Custer
meets his end at Little Big
Horn. Grand entertainment.
Warner Brothers

as a devious Mexican-Indian—but the movie is dated and a bit of a clunker.

THUNDERCLOUD (1950, WB). Also titled: COLT .45. D: Edwin L. Marin. W: Tom W. Blackburn. Cast: RANDOLPH SCOTT, RUTH ROMAN, ZACHARY SCOTT, Lloyd BRIDGES, Alan HALE, Jr., Walter Coy, Chief Thundercloud, Ian MacDonald, Stanley Andrews, Kansas Moehring, Buddy Roosevelt, Hal Taliaferro, Franklyn Farnum, Luther Crockett, Charles Evans, Ben Corbett. 70m.

A salesman (Randolph Scott) for Colt's Patent Firearms Company is the hero; his fancy new six-guns are stolen by villain Zachary Scott and used by the bad guys to kill, rob and maim, so our hero has to try and get 'em back. There are Indian battles galore and wholesale action throughout; it's in Technicolor and very fast, and a lot of old-time cowboy performers appear in it, and it served as the basis for the *Colt .45* TV series with Wayde Preston, but it's dated near-"B" stuff.

THUNDERHOOF (1948, COL). D: Phil Karlson. W: Hal Smith & Kenneth Gamet. Cast: PRESTON FOSTER, Mary STUART, William BISHOP.

Ambitious, hard-breathing three-character yarn concerns a middle-aged rancher (Foster), his young pouty wife, a wild young drifter and their hunt for a wild stallion in the wilderness. Silly plot is filled with coincidence and anti-climax.

THE THUNDERING HERD (1933, PARA). Also titled: BUFFALO STAMPEDE. D. Henry Hathaway. W: Jack Cunningham & Mary Flannery from Zane Grey's novel. Cast: RANDOLPH SCOTT, HARRY CAREY, Judith ALLEN, Barton MacLANE, Larry "Buster" CRABBE, Noah Beery, Sr., Raymond Hatton, Blanche Frederici, Monte Blue, Dick Rush, Frank Rice, Buck Connors, Charles McMurphy, Al Bridge. 59m.

Buffalo hunters fight Indians in this remake of the 1925 silent version which uses a lot of footage, and some of the same actors, from the earlier film. Dated now but excellent for its time; exceptional photography (Ben Reynolds).

THUNDER IN THE SUN (1959, PARA). D: Russell Rouse. W: Rouse & Stewart Stern. Cast: JEFF CHANDLER, SUSAN HAYWARD, Jacques BERGERAC, Blanche Yurka, Carl Esmond, Fortunio Bonanova. 81m.

A wagon train of Basque immigrants is guided through hostile Indian country by trail-scout Chandler on their way to California where they aim to plant vineyards. Set mostly in the Rockies, it has colorful scenery and a hard-breathing plot that has the unfortunate redhead (Hayward) fending off the determined advances of both Chandler and Bergerac. Action scenes include a grass fire and a big Indian fight at the end but the studio edited this one to death and it's jerky and poor as a result.

THUNDER MOUNTAIN (1947, RKO). D: Lew Landers. W: Norman Houston from Zane Grey's novel *To The Last Man*. Cast: TIM HOLT, MARTHA HYER, Richard MARTIN, Steve Brodie, Harry Woods, Jason Robards, Sr. 63m.

Crooked sheriff and saloonkeeper try to grab a ranch that's in the path of a planned irrigation project; they trigger a feud. In step hero Holt and comic sidekick Martin in this "B" version of the strong Zane Grey yarn.

A THUNDER OF DRUMS (1961, MGM). D: Joseph M. Newman. W: James Warner Bellah from his story "Command." Cast: RICHARD BOONE, GEORGE HAMILTON, Luana PATTEN, Richard CHAMBERLAIN, Charles Bronson, Arthur O'Connell, Slim Pickens, James Douglas. 97m.

A hardboiled crude commander (Boone) of a frontier Indian-fighting post resents being burdened with a green lieutenant (Hamilton) from back East who's the son of an important general. Bellah's acceptable yarn (not his best) is defeated by mediocre direction and awful acting; the directing of the on-post scenes seems interminable while the outdoor action sequences are filmed with unimaginative flatness. There have been worse, but this one's no treat.

THUNDER OVER ARIZONA (1956, REP). D: Joseph Kane. W: Sloan Nibley. Cast: SKIP HOMEIER, Kristine MILLER, George MacREADY, Wallace Ford, Nacho Galindo. 75m.

Young cowhand (Homeier) poses as an outlaw in a scheme to protect the girl's ranch from silver-greedy citizens who've been stirred up by the rumor of an ore discovery. Wheezy and cheap.

THUNDER OVER TEXAS (1934, IND). D: John Warner (Edgar G. Ulmer). W: Eddie Craneman & Shirley Castle (Mrs. Edgar G. Ulmer). Cast: GUINN "BIG BOY" WILLIAMS, HELEN WESTCOTT, Robert McKenzie, Marion Shilling. 50m.

Seeking a hidden gold strike, bad guys murder a man and steal his map. His daughter recruits a tough guy to help her get revenge. Plot of this "B" oater is not altogether unlike that of the later *True Grit*. It was shot in three or four days and had the curious bleak flavor often associated with films directed by the legendary Ulmer. (He used a phony name on this one because he was under contract to Universal at the time.)

THUNDER OVER THE PLAINS (1953, WB). D: Andre de Toth. W: Russell Hughes. Cast: RANDOLPH SCOTT, PHYLLIS KIRK, LEX BARKER, Henry HULL, Hugh Sanders, Elisha Cook, Jr., Lane Chandler, Earle Hodgins, Charles McGraw, Fess Parker, James Brown. 82m.

Cavalry officer (Scott) is pitted against carpetbaggers, renegades, his wife's lover (Barker) and a martinet colonel (Hull) in Texas after the Civil War. Standard oater is not helped by Barker's wooden acting.

THUNDER PASS (1954, LIP). D: Frank McDonald. W: Tom Hubbard, Fred Eggers & George Van Marter. Cast: DANE CLARK, Raymond BURR, Dorothy PATRICK, Andy Devine. 76m.

Army officer (Clark) tries to persuade reluctant settlers to come with him to the fort before the rampaging Indians attack them. Routine film is poorly cast; Dane Clark is about as Western as the Bowery.

THUNDER TRAIL (1937, PARA). D: Charles T. Barton. W: Robert Yost & Stuart Anthony from Zane Grey's novel *Arizona Ames*. Cast: GILBERT ROLAND, MARSHA HUNT, Charles BICKFORD, J. Carrol Naish, James Craig, Monte Blue.

Threatened girl, land-grabbers, rustlers, a drifter hero—the story is familiar dated fare but this was one of the best of the low-budget Zane Grey adaptations, with strong script, good production and very good cast. James Craig's debut.

A TICKET TO TOMAHAWK (1950, FOX). D: Richard Sale. W: Sale & Mary Loos. Cast: DAN DAILEY, ANNE BAXTER, RORY CALHOUN, Walter BRENNAN, Arthur HUNNICUTT, Chief Thundercloud, Connie Gilchrist, Will Wright, Paul Harvey, Marilyn Monroe, Charles Kemper, Chief Yowlachie. 90m.

Peaceable traveling salesman (Dailey) is caught in the midst of a rousing race between stagecoach and railroad train across the colorful Colorado Rockies. Things are complicated by such elements as an itinerant theatrical troupe, angry Indians, mean villains, a lady (Baxter) who becomes a deputy marshal, some songs, Marilyn Monroe in a bit part, great Technicolor scenery, excellent cast, bright script, sprightly direction. It's enjoyably confused, a nice spoof.

TIDE OF EMPIRE (1929, MGM). D: Allan Dwan. W: Waldemar Young from Peter B. Kyne's story. Cast: RENEE ADOREE, George DURYEA, Fred Kohler, Paul Hurst, George Fawcett.

Outlaws in old California prey on gold prospectors; rancher hero steps in. Of historical interest, this transitional picture had sound effects but no dialogue.

TIGER ROSE (1929, WB). D: George Fitzmaurice. W: L. G. Rigby & Harvey Thew from a play by David Belasco & Willard Mack. Cast: MONTE BLUE, LUPE VELEZ, RIN TIN TIN, H. B. Warner, Gaston Glass, Slim Summerville, Grant Withers.

Early talkie with a couple of songs was from the stage chestnut about the Irish-accented Mountie (Blue) who is in love with a half-breed girl (Velez) who loves a bad guy (Withers). This may have been the only "A" talkie to feature the wonder dog Rin Tin Tin.

TIMBERJACK (1955, REP). D: Joseph Kane. W: Allen Rivkin from a Dan Cushman novel. Cast: VERA RALSTON, STERLING HAYDEN, David BRIAN, Adolphe MENJOU, Hoagy CARMICHAEL, Chill Wills, Jim Davis, Ian MacDonald, Elisha Cook, Jr., Howard Petrie. 94m.

A bad guy (Brian) is trying to take over the lumber mill; for various reasons he wants to kill the lady (Ralston), and in her flight from him she becomes allied with a man (Hayden) whose father was killed by the same bad guy. Ralston chews up all the scenery in sight; this is a laughably good example of her work—a big-budget Trucolor vehicle, with an excellent supporting cast expertly directed. Republic's stockholders tried to sue the company president, Herbert J. Yates (Ralston's husband), because of the outrageous sum he had to lay out in order to persuade Sterling Hayden to co-star with her in this one.

A TIME FOR KILLING (1963)—See THE LONG RIDE HOME.

THE TIN STAR (1957, PARA). D: Anthony Mann. W: Dudley Nichols, Barney Slater & Joel Kane. Cast: HENRY FONDA, ANTHONY PERKINS, Betsy PALMER, John McINTIRE, Michel Ray, Neville Brand, Mary Webster, Lee Van Cleef, Rodd Redwing. 93m.

Green young sheriff (Perkins) of a wild town is assisted by a veteran bounty-hunting mantracker (Fonda) in cleaning up the town. It isn't mentioned in the credits but this does bear a certain resemblance to the short story

"The Tin Star" by John Cunningham on which the movie *High Noon* was based. It's in black-and-white, with a good Elmer Bernstein score, with Neville Brand effective as the chief bad guy and McIntire in a typically superior performance as a grizzled, sarcastic doctor. It's taut throughout—a good example of Nichols's expert writing—and it's one of the few of Anthony Mann's "outside" Westerns that measured up to his superb Universal pictures with James Stewart (written by Borden Chase). The fancy shooting stunts are performed (mostly off-camera) by trick-shot artist Rodd Redwing. It's pretty good but there are too many treacly hackneyed moments. The plot was used vaguely as a model for the Henry Fonda TV series *The Deputy*.

TOMAHAWK (1951, UNIV). D: George Sherman. W: Silvia Richards, Maurice Geraghty & Daniel Jarrett. Cast: VAN HEFLIN, YVONNE De CARLO, Preston FOSTER, Jack OAKIE, Alex Nicol, Tom Tully, Rock Hudson, John War Eagle. 82m.

Jim Bridger (Heflin) tries to restore peace with the Sioux after a stupid, arrogant army lieutenant (Nicol) murders an Indian boy. It's very talky, with endless gab about enforcing treaties and the plight of Lo, the poor Indian. (American Indians rightly grew tired of hearing about their "plight" in movies that, no matter how well intentioned, made use of the Indians primarily as scenery and as plot devices.) The action scenes are dull in this turkey, and any resemblance between the protagonist and the real historical frontiersman Bridger is accidental.

TOMAHAWK TRAIL (1957, UA). D: Lesley Selander. W: Gerald D. Adams & David Chandler. Cast: CHUCK CONNORS, Susan CUMMINGS, John SMITH, George Neise, Lisa Montiel.

Veteran Indian-fighting sergeant has to wrest command of a cavalry patrol from a psychotic lieutenant. Standard Apache-wars oater; drab.

TOMBSTONE (1942, PARA). Also titled: TOMBSTONE, THE TOWN TOO TOUGH TO DIE. D: William McGann. W: Albert S. LeVino, Edward E. Paramore, Dean Franklin & Charles Beisner from the book by Walter Noble Burns. Cast: RICHARD DIX, FRANCES GIFFORD, Kent TAYLOR, Edgar BUCHANAN, Victor JORY, Don CASTLE, Clem Bevans, Rex Bell, Charles Halton, Harvey Stephens, Chris-Pin Martin, Charles Stevens, Hal Taliaferro, Charles Middleton, Dick Curtis. 79m.

Harry "Pop" Sherman, the Hopalong Cassidy impresario, produced this Wyatt Earp movie and it came too close on the heels of the excellent 1939 *Frontier Marshal*; it suffers by comparison. Burns's book was published in 1928, the year of Earp's death, and gives a romanticized portrait of "The Lion of Tombstone" and his feud with the McLowery-Clanton gang that led to the gunfight at the OK Corral. The usual elements of the story are in place with few surprises. Kent Taylor is inadequate as Doc Holliday; Castle is interesting as Johnny Ringo; Jory (Ike Clanton) and Buchanan (Curly Bill) are okay but unsurprising. Plenty of cliches and very dated. Still, it's a sturdy and fairly spirited Western of the old school.

There seems to be a curious kind of incest in Wyatt Earp movies. Don Castle turned up later in *Gunfight at the OK Corral* as a loud-mouthed drunk; here he plays Ringo, and buffs may recall that Ringo was played in *Gunfight at the OK Corral* by John Ireland—who in turn played Ike Clanton in *My Darling Clementine*.

TOM HORN (1980, WB). D: William Wiard. W: Thomas McGuane & Bud Shrake, based on Tom Horn's autobiography. Cast: STEVE McQUEEN, Linda EVANS, Richard Farnsworth, Billy "Green" Bush, Slim Pickens. 98m.

Historically, Tom Horn was a fascinating character. As a scout he helped run down Geronimo. As a lawman he helped corral the Dalton gang and other miscreants. As a soldier he fought at San Juan Hill with Teddy Roosevelt. Finally, as a "regulator" or "range detective" in the employ of a cattlemen's association in Wyoming, he was commissioned to drive nesters out, and purportedly he did so by murdering several of them from ambush so as to terrorize the others into departing. This took place as a sort of footnote to the Johnson County War, a range war that has provided the basis for such phony films as *Heaven's Gate*; Horn's life itself has provided the material for several films including *Hannah Lee* and the made-for-TV *Mr. Horn*.

Steve McQueen's version—his last Western and next-to-last movie—covers only the aging scout's last days, based on the statements in Horn's jailhouse-written memoir that he was innocent of the murder for which he was tried and convicted; Horn always maintained he'd been framed. The actual story of Horn's last days, involving an abortive jailbreak and an automatic pistol that Horn didn't know how to operate, is quite dramatic, but this film version isn't. It is simply an abysmal mess. There is no plot to speak of; what there is makes no sense. (Horn escapes from jail, then walks right past half a dozen horses, any of which he might ride away on; instead, he walks away, and is soon recaptured. The entire story is on that level of illogic.) There are a couple of bloody, brutal, unnecessary shootings; the rest of the action takes place off-camera.

The movie seems to have been sabotaged by everyone connected with it except John Alonzo, whose panoramic location photography is superb. McQueen's performance is sometimes poignant—partly because we know the actor was to die soon after completing this picture—but I'm told it was largely his meddling that caused the picture to be such a botch: he fired one screenwriter after another (originally the picture was to have been based on Will Henry's superior novel *I, Tom Horn*, and the withdrawal of that source—possibly to avoid paying the author—was an act of cynical churlishness) and one director after another; the credited director, Wiard, has few known credentials and no one seems ever to have heard of him; there is some question how much of the picture was directed by McQueen himself—a man deaf and ill and hardly competent to direct a major film. In any case the result is a picture that is relentlessly downbeat and largely pointless.

TONKA (1958, BV). D: Lewis R. Foster. W: Foster & Lillie Hayward from David Appel's novel *Comanche*. Cast: SAL MINEO, PHILIP CAREY, Joy PAGE, Jerome COURTLAND, Rafael Campos, Slim Pickens, H. M. Wynant, Britt Lomond, Herbert Rudley, John War Eagle. 97m.

Disney picture concerns an Indian youth (Mineo) and his horse which is sold to Custer's (Lomond) cavalry and becomes the only survivor of the fight at the Little Big Horn River. Corny idiocy is hard to swallow even for kiddies, and the low budget cripples the action scenes, but Loyal Griggs's photography is just fine.

TOPEKA (1953, AA). D: Thomas Carr. W: Milton Raison. Cast: WILLIAM ELLIOTT, PHYLLIS COATES, Fuzzy KNIGHT, Denver Pyle, Rick Vallin, Ted Mapes.

Outlaw (Elliott) is offered a job as a lawman; he rounds up his outlaw buddies to help him mop up the bad guys. Black-and-white programmer is nicely done, actionful, with a plot reminiscent of William S. Hart.

TOP GUN (1955, UA). D: Ray Nazarro. W: Richard Schayer & Steve Fisher. Cast: STERLING HAYDEN, Karin BOOTH, William BISHOP, Rod TAYLOR, Regis Toomey, Hugh Sanders, James Millican, Denver Pyle. 73m.

A sheriff with a shadowy past has to fight it out with the bad guys who are trying to dominate the town. Old stuff.

TO THE LAST MAN (1933, PARA). D: Henry Hathaway. W: Jack Cunningham from Zane Grey's novel. Cast: RANDOLPH SCOTT, RICHARD DIX, Esther RALSTON, Noah BEERY, Jack LaRue, Larry "Buster" Crabbe, Shirley Temple, Gail Patrick, Barton MacLane, Fuzzy Knight, Muriel Kirkland, James Mason, Egon Brecher, James Eagles. 61m.

Two feuding clans virtually annihilate each other before young love brings an end to the war. Grey's novel—one of his better ones, if overly flamboyant—was based on the historic Tonto Basin War (also called the Pleasant Valley War) in Arizona in the 1880s and 1890s, a blood feud that made the Hatfield-McCoy squabble look like a barn dance by comparison. A top cast and the winning Hathaway-Cunningham-Randolph Scott combination made this remake of the 1923 silent movie one of the best of Paramount's early 1930s Zane Grey series. Shirley Temple was very small at the time—about four—and has a suitably small part. Remade drably in 1947 as *Thunder Mountain*.

THE TOUGHEST GUN IN TOMBSTONE (1958, UA). D: Earl Bellamy. W: Orville Hampton. Cast: GEORGE MONTGOMERY, BEVERLY TYLER, Jim DAVIS, Lane Bradford, Don Beddoe. 72m.

Routine lawman-versus-outlaws oater.

THE TOUGHEST MAN IN ARIZONA (1952, REP). D: R. G. Springsteen. W: John K. Butler. Cast: VAUGHN MONROE, JOAN LESLIE, Victor JORY, Jean PARKER, Edgar Buchanan, Harry Morgan, Francis Ford. 89m.

Marshal against bandits with a romance on the side; predictable horse opera is a companion piece to *Singing Guns*.

TOWN TAMER (1965, PARA). D: Lesley Selander. W: Frank Gruber from his novel. Cast: DANA ANDREWS, TERRY MOORE, Richard ARLEN, Pat O'BRIEN, Sonny Tufts, Bruce Cabot, Richard Jaeckel, Lyle Bettger, Coleen Gray, Lon Chaney, Jr., Barton MacLane, Jeanne Cagney, Bob Steele. 89m.

Lawyer (Andrews) sets out to find his wife's murderer. It's another A. C. Lyles production with a cast of familiar old-timers and a second-rate pulp story, filmed in no more than a few days.

TRACK OF THE CAT (1954, WB). D: William A. Wellman. W: A. I. Bezzerides from the novel by Walter Van Tilburg Clark.

Cast: ROBERT MITCHUM, TERESA WRIGHT, TAB HUNTER, Diana LYNN, Beulah BONDI, Philip Tonge, Carl Switzer, William Hopper. 102m.

Conflicts within a lunatic mountain family are interrupted by the predations of a mountain lion and the savage hunt for it. Clark's novel was confused but it had a point to make about the nature of humans—a point that gets lost somewhere in the ambitious but muddled script. It becomes an introspective mood piece that misfires; even Mitchum and Wright are lost in the pretentiousness; the star is William Clothier's odd bleached photography: it's in color but starkly restricted to black-and-white subjects (snow, shadows, so forth); Roy Webb's melancholy score doesn't relieve the gloom either. Muted and odd, it's an interesting movie but not very rewarding.

THE TRAIL OF '98 (1929, MGM). D: Clarence Brown. W: Benjamin Glazer from a poem by Robert W. Service. Cast: DOLORES DEL RIO, HARRY CAREY, Tully MARSHALL, Karl Dane, Ralph Forbes, Russell Simpson. 53m.

Traditional set-in-Alaska romantic melodrama had music and sound effects but no dialogue.

TRAIL OF ROBIN HOOD (1950, REP). D: William Witney. W: Gerald Geraghty. Cast: ROY ROGERS, REX ALLEN, ALLAN "ROCKY" LANE, Monte HALE, Penny EDWARDS, Ray CORRIGAN, Tom TYLER, Tom KEENE, Kermit MAYNARD, Jack HOLT, William Farnum, Gordon Jones, Foy Willing and the Riders of the Purple Sage.

Attempt to bolster the fading days of the "B" Western is in color, and every cowboy star on the lot was thrown into it, but it's just another Rogers musicale.

THE TRAIL OF THE LONESOME PINE (1936, PARA). D: Henry Hathaway. W: Grover Jones, Harvey Thew & Horace McCoy from the novel by John Fox, Jr. Cast: FRED MacMURRAY, HENRY FONDA, SYLVIA SIDNEY, Fred STONE, Beulah BONDI, Nigel BRUCE, Robert Barrat, Fuzzy Knight, Spanky MacFarland, Alan Baxter, Samuel S. Hinds, Frank McGlynn, Robert Kortman, Yakima Canutt. 102m.

The coming of the railroad wreaks changes in the lives of Blue Ridge Mountain feudists; a young railroad engineer (MacMurray) helps set things right. Dated hokum is syrupy with sentimentality; it's tedious today, but is generally treated with kind respect—the kind one shows to old folks—because it was a box-office smash and it was the first outdoor epic filmed in the new tri-hued full-color Technicolor. It was Henry Fonda's fourth movie but it was the one that made a star of him: it was the first one in which he created the Fonda character who became familiar in so consistent a string of bucolic roles that Al Capp based his comic-strip character L'il Abner on Fonda as he appeared in this film. Produced by Walter Wanger, who later produced *Stagecoach*, it is a remake of 1916 and 1923 silent versions, the first of them directed by Cecil B. De Mille.

TRAIL OF THE VIGILANTES (1940, UNIV). D: Allan Dwan. W: Harold Shumate. Cast: FRANCHOT TONE, PEGGY MORAN, BRODERICK CRAWFORD, Andy DEVINE, Warren WILLIAM, Mischa Auer, Porter Hall, Charles Trowbridge. 78m.

Eastern crime-buster (Tone) is sent out West to clean up outlaw territory. Fairly big-budget movie kids itself unabashedly and is fun because of the hearty comedy. It was Franchot Tone's only Western.

TRAIL STREET (1946, RKO). D: Ray Enright. W: Norman Houston & Gene Lewis from a William Corcoran novel. Cast: RANDOLPH SCOTT, ROBERT RYAN, Anne JEFFREYS, George "Gabby" Hayes, Steve Brodie, Madge Meredith. 84m.

Bat Masterson (Scott) cleans up Dodge City again. Professionally done, a bit dated now. Ryan, as usual, is a standout, as the chief baddie.

THE TRAIN ROBBERS (1973, WB). DW: Burt Kennedy. Cast: JOHN WAYNE, ANN-MARGRET, ROD TAYLOR, Ben JOHNSON, Christoher GEORGE, Ricardo MONTALBAN, Bobby VINTON, Jerry Gatlin. 92m.

Encouraged by a $50,000 reward, the Duke and his five saddle partners agree to help Ann-Margret get back a half-million-dollar gold treasure originally stolen by her late husband. The search for the gold, and the threat posed by twenty pursuing gunmen, provide the premise for this sloppy sophomoric loser. Filmed on locations around Durango, Mexico (wide screen cinematography by William Clothier), the film is unique in that there are no villainous characters: there are villains to be sure (the twenty gunmen) but they're faceless extras in the background and none of them has any dialogue; they seem to be in the movie solely to give the heroes something to shoot at and throw dynamite at. It's more than an hour into the movie before any of that happens, however. *The*

Train Robbers consists essentially of forty-five minutes of everybody riding from right to left (south) and another forty-five minutes of everybody riding from left to right (north); there's a rudimentary action sequence that passes for a climax, and a cynical surprise ending, but it's a pointless unsophisticated movie, soporific, shallow of story and dreary of conception. The characterizations are paper-thin stereotypes. It's one of the poorest movies associated with any of these people.

TRAIN TO TOMBSTONE (1950, LIP). **D:** Charles F. Reisner. **W:** Victor West, Orville Hampton & Donald Barry. **Cast:** DONALD "RED" BARRY, Judith ALLEN, Robert LOWERY, Tom NEAL, Wally Vernon, Barbara Stanley.

Train robbers and Indian attacks enliven a fair Lippert programmer with a mediocre script but good atmospheric background. Barry, incidentally, did not have red hair and allegedly resented the nickname "Red," which stuck to him after he played Red Ryder in a "B" series in the 1940s.

THE TRAP (1966, RANK). **D:** Sidney Hayes. **W:** David Osborn. **Cast:** OLIVER REED, RITA TUSHINGHAM, Rex Sevenoaks, Barbara Chilcott, Walter Marsh, Linda Goranson. 106m.

Canadian trapper (Reed) buys an orphaned mute girl in pioneer British Columbia; their strange relationship ripens in the Canadian wilderness. Odd British-produced movie is interesting if not gripping; beautifully photographed (Robert Krasker) on location. There are a couple of scenes that aren't suitable for the squeamish. (It is not to be confused with the 1959 Paramount picture of the same title, a gangster pursuit story.)

THE TRAVELING SALESWOMAN (1950, COL). **D:** Charles F. Reisner. **W:** Howard Dimsdale. **Cast:** JOAN DAVIS, Andy DEVINE, Adele JERGENS, Joe Sawyer, Chief Thundercloud. 75m.

Bucolic black-and-white comedy concerns a soap saleslady and her fat, cheerful boyfriend. Predictable corn.

TREACHERY RIDES THE RANGE (1936, WB). **D:** Frank McDonald. **W:** William Jacobs. **Cast:** DICK FORAN, Paula STONE, Monte Blue, Jim Thorpe, Craig Reynolds, Monte Montague, Henry Otho, Don Barclay, Carlyle Moore, Jr., Glenn Strange. 57m.

Buffalo skinners, employed by crooked traders, are victimizing the Cheyenne Indians until our hero steps in. This was one of the better Dick Foran programmers; with songs.

THE TREASURE OF LOST CANYON (1952, UNIV). **D:** Ted Tetzlaff. **W:** Brainerd Duffield & Emerson Crocker from a story by Robert Louis Stevenson. **Cast:** WILLIAM POWELL, JULIE ADAMS, Tommy IVO, Charles Drake, Rosemary De Camp, Henry Hull, John Doucette, Chubby Johnson, Frank Wilcox. 82m.

A lot of lives are changed when an orphan boy (Ivo) comes across a hidden fortune. Unexciting script isn't quite saved by Powell's charming presence as the town doctor.

TREASURE OF PANCHO VILLA (1955, RKO). **D:** George Sherman. **W:** Niven Busch, Robert Bren & Gladys Atwater. **Cast:** RORY CALHOUN, GILBERT ROLAND, SHELLEY WINTERS, Joseph CALLEIA, Carlos Musquiz, Fanny Schiller, Tony Carvajal, Pasquale Pena. 96m.

Adventurer (Calhoun) helps rob a train to get gold for Villa's forces in the 1915 Mexican Revolution; an improbable sequence of double and triple crosses ensues, and the plot is further debased by dull dialogue and an imbecilic romance—Winters, as usual in Westerns, is like a fish out of water. The action sequences are unconvincing, too. But it's excellently photographed (William Snyder) in Morelos, Mexico, and it's worth seeing for Roland's very good performance as a heroic embattled rebel officer.

TREASURE OF THE RUBY HILLS (1955, AA). **D:** Frank McDonald. **W:** Tom Hubbard & Fred Eggers from a Louis L'Amour story. **Cast:** ZACHARY SCOTT, CAROLE MATHEWS, Dick FORAN, Lola ALBRIGHT, Barton MacLane, Raymond Hatton, Stanley Andrews, Steve Darrell, Rick Vallin. 71m.

Range-war Western has a hidden treasure on the side; Scott is a rancher trying to bring peace to squabbling factions. Routine.

THE TREASURE OF THE SIERRA MADRE (1947, WB). **DW:** John Huston from the B. Traven novel. **Cast:** HUMPHREY BOGART, WALTER HUSTON, TIM HOLT, BRUCE BENNETT, Alfonso BEDOYA, Barton MacLane, John Huston, Ann Sheridan, Jack Holt, Clifton Young, Bobby Blake, Ralph Dunn, Jose Torvay, Julian Rivero. 124m.

Four partners prospect for gold in Mexico's harsh mountains. Changes take place in them when they find it. Greed induces paranoia. The plot is old-fashioned, traceable to such novels as Frank Norris's *McTeague*—Traven was a mysterious hermit whose simple Marxist philosophy represented no significant departure from that of the early naturalistic novelists. But the movie is made great by Huston's masterful restructuring of the novel in the screenplay, and its splendidly graphic portrayal in cinematic images, and the work of a superb cast. It is one of the very few genuine works of art in the Western movie genre. Ted McCord's photography and Max Steiner's score are excellent. Academy Awards went to John Huston (best director, best screenplay) and to Walter Huston (best supporting actor)—the only father and son Oscar winners for the same movie. There are choice bits played by various friends of Huston's: Ann Sheridan as a streetwalking whore, Barton MacLane as a loudmouth, young Bobby (Robert) Blake as a talkative Mexican boy, John Huston himself as a tourist. Most of it was filmed under harsh conditions on Sierra Madre locations, but a few scenes—particularly the night-camp sequences—have a dated studio look. Bogart, as Fred C. Dobbs, gives what may be the performance of his career, and Walter Huston is just superb. Alfonso Bedoya, as the sinister grinning bandit ("Badges? Badges? We don't need no stinking badges!") makes his unforgettable screen debut here, and "B" star Tim Holt, together with former Tarzan Bruce Bennett (Herman Brix), are amazingly fine as the third and fourth partners. It's a brilliant movie.

TRIBUTE TO A BAD MAN (1956, MGM). D: Robert Wise. W: Michael Blankfort from a Jack Schaefer story. Cast: JAMES CAGNEY, IRENE PAPAS, Don DUBBINS, Stephen McNALLY, Vic Morrow, Lee Van Cleef, James Griffith, Onslow Stevens, Royal Dano, James Bell, Jeanette Nolan, Chubby Johnson, Tom London, Buddy Roosevelt. 95m.

A young Easterner (Dubbins) makes friends with a tough horse rancher (Cagney) and is drawn into squabbles between rancher and wife (Papas) and gradually is horrified by the rancher's cruel tyranny and arrogant ruthlessness, which rapidly make enemies of everyone around him. There's the inevitable last-reel showdown. It has good photography (Robert L. Surtees), a fine score (Miklos Rozsa), good acting by everybody and a spectacular performance by Cagney, but it's mostly soap-opera stuff. Filming started on it with Spencer Tracy in the lead, but director Wise and MGM fired Tracy for obstreperous conduct; it then became Cagney's—his third and last Western, and certainly his most blazing performance of the three, but the script is poor and it's a shame; Cagney never did make a really good Western.

TROOPER HOOK (1957, UA). D: Charles Marquis Warren. W: Martin Berkeley, David Victor & Herbert Little, Jr., from a Jack Schaefer story. Cast: JOEL McCREA, BARBARA STANWYCK, Earl HOLLIMAN, John DEHNER, Susan Kohner, Royal Dano, Rodolfo Acosta, Edward Andrews, Sheb Wooley. 81m.

A woman, who's scorned by whites because she's lived among Indians, is protected by a gruff but compassionate soldier. Fine performances by the two stars, reunited for the first time in more than a decade, lift this one well above the norm, and it's excellently directed in black-and-white; there's good suspense and action, with Sergeant Hook (McCrea) trying to hold together his band of misfit stragglers in a waterless wasteland imperiled by Apache pursuers.

TRUE GRIT (1969, PARA). D: Henry Hathaway. W: Marguerite Roberts from Charles Portis's novel. Cast: JOHN WAYNE, KIM DARBY, GLEN CAMPBELL, Jeremy SLATE, Robert DUVALL, Strother MARTIN, Jeff COREY, Dennis Hopper, Alfred Ryder, John Doucette, Ron Soble, Donald Woods, Hank Worden, Myron Healey, James Westerfield, John Fiedler, Edith Atwater, Carlos Rivas. 128m.

A fourteen-year-old girl (Darby) hires a curmudgeonly profane old one-eyed manhunter, Rooster Cogburn (Wayne), to find her daddy's killer and avenge the nasty murder. Cogburn, the girl, and a dandified gambler-adventurer (Campbell) set out into the bandit-infested no-man's-land of the Cherokee Strip to sift through all the outlaws there until they find the culprit. There is some doubt, assuming they do find the killer, that the fat drunken old man will be able to outfight or outshoot him, but Cogburn is supremely self-confident, and at the climax there is a genuine thrill when he growls, "Fill your hand you son of a bitch!"

Portis's bestselling novel was a tour de force narrated by the girl as an aged crone, recalling her long-ago frontier adventures as an orphan on the wild frontier. That double frame of narration is lost in the movie and since it provided part of the novel's unique charm it is inevitable that the movie be inferior; but there are other weaknesses in the film as well. Darby is either appealing or appalling as the brat, depending on your taste; and Glen Campbell is a downright poor actor. Still, there are lovely vignettes set in old Fort Smith around Hanging Judge Parker's court, involving various venal characters including a greedy, corrupt horsetrader played marvelously by the late Strother Martin. Wayne's performance is amusing and he won an Academy Award for it, his only Oscar; it was won, perhaps, as much for his recovery from cancer, his out-spoken if simpleminded political honesty and his sheer endurance—*True Grit* marked his fortieth year as a movie star. It's not a great movie but it's quite a good one.

THE TRUE STORY OF JESSE JAMES (1957, FOX). D: Nicholas Ray. W: Walter Newman from Nunnally Johnson's screenplay for the 1939 *Jesse James*. Cast: ROBERT WAGNER, JEFFREY HUNTER, HOPE LANGE, Agnes MOOREHEAD, John CARRADINE, Frank Gorshin, Frank Overton, Marian Seldes, Alan Hale, Jr., Barry Atwater, Rachel Stephens, Alan Baxter, Biff Elliott, Chubby Johnson, Barney Phillips. 92m.

Remake of the Tyrone Power-Henry Fonda *Jesse James* uses essentially the same script—Newman wisely confined his revision to an updating of some of the more obvious archaisms and 1930s period anachronisms. (Sometimes less is more; Newman is a good enough writer to know when not to improve on good work just for the sake of fiddling with it.) I find this remake a good entertainment, nearly equal to the original. Still, the actors don't pack as much conviction, and the flavor is too 1950ish.

TUCSON (1949, FOX). D: William Claxton. W: Arnold Belgard. Cast: JIMMY LYDON, PENNY EDWARDS, Charles Russell, Joe Sawyer, Walter Sande, Harry Lauter.

Rodeo yarn concerns a playboy student who nearly fails his exams because he spends all his time training his quarterhorse for rodeo competitions. Lydon and Edwards have charm but the script is poor.

TUMBLEWEED (1953, UNIV). D: Nathan Juran. W: John M. Lucas from a Kenneth Perkins novel. Cast: AUDIE MURPHY, Lori NELSON, Chill WILLS, K. T. Stevens, Lee Van Cleef, Russell Johnson. 79m.

Accused of deserting a wagon train when Indians attacked it, our young hero sets out to clear his name. Standard formula stuff.

TWENTY-MULE TEAM (1940, MGM). D: Richard Thorpe. W: E. E. Paramore, Cyril Hume, Richard Maibaum, Robert C. DuSoe & Owen Atkinson. Cast: WALLACE BEERY, MARJORIE RAMBEAU, Leo CARRILLO, Anne BAXTER, Douglas Fowley, Clem Bevans. 84m.

Borax miners and freighters are the subject; the plot is the usual Wallace Beery wheeze in which a blustery muleskinner is tamed by a little girl's love. Anne Baxter's debut.

A TWINKLE IN GOD'S EYE (1956, REP). D: George Blair. W: P. J. Wolfson. Cast:

MICKEY ROONEY, Hugh O'BRIAN, Coleen GRAY, Michael CONNORS, Joey Foreman. 73m.

Parson uses humor to tame a tough town. Dull bucolic comedy is in black-and-white.

TWO FLAGS WEST (1950, FOX). D: Robert Wise. W: Casey Robinson, Frank S. Nugent & Curtis Kenyon. Cast: JOSEPH COTTEN, LINDA DARNELL, Jeff CHANDLER, Cornel WILDE, Dale ROBERTSON, Jay C. Flippen, Arthur Hunnicutt, Noah Beery, Jr. 92m.

They called them Galvanized Yankees and there's a historical basis in truth for this yarn about Confederate prisoners of war who are granted freedom from Union prisons in return for their vow to fight Indians on the frontier under command of Yankee officers. (It's been used plenty of times in movies, notably in *Major Dundee*.) In this one Cotten is the heroic Southern commander of the galvanized troops and Chandler, in a relatively early role, plays the psychotic ramrod-stiff Yankee colonel under whose command they must serve. It's slick, in color, trivial but craftsmanlike, with a fine performance by Cotten.

TWO GUN LADY (1956, IND). D: Richard Bartlett. W: Bartlett & Norman Jolley. Cast: PEGGIE CASTLE, ROBERT LOWERY, William TALMAN, Marie WINDSOR, Joe Sawyer. 75m.

Orphaned girl hires lawman to help her track down her daddy's killer; it's the same plot as the later *True Grit* but this one had little style, wit or class.

TWO GUNS AND A BADGE (1953, AA). D: Lewis D. Collins. W: Daniel Ullman. Cast: WAYNE MORRIS, BEVERLY GARLAND, Morris ANKRUM, William Phipps, Roy Barcroft. 69m.

Ex-convict poses as ex-lawman and is hired as deputy sheriff; he proves his mettle and wins the girl. Shabby "B" oater was one of the last of the "B" series programmers.

TWO GUYS FROM TEXAS (1948, WB). D: David Butler. W: I. A. L. Diamond & Allen Boretz from a play by Robert Sloane & Louis Pelletier. Cast: JACK CARSON, DENNIS MORGAN, DOROTHY MALONE, Forrest TUCKER, Gerald MOHR, Penny EDWARDS, Fred CLARK, John Alvin, Monte Blue, The Philharmonic Trio. 86m.

Mild Technicolor musicomedy is a remake of *The Cowboy from Brooklyn*, about a pair of vaudeville entertainers who, stranded on a Texas dude ranch, outwit some bad guys. Amiable performances and songs (by Jule Styne & Sammy Cahn).

TWO MULES FOR SISTER SARA (1970, UNIV). D: Don Siegel. W: Albert Maltz & Budd Boetticher. Cast: CLINT EASTWOOD, SHIRLEY MacLAINE, Manolo Fabregas, Alberto Morin, Armando Silvestre, John Kelly, Enrique Lucero, Jose Torvay. 105m.

A hardscrabble drifter (Eastwood) in Mexico comes across a naked girl (MacLaine) and saves her from being raped. When she puts her clothes on and they turn out to be a nun's habit he's amazed. Then it turns out she's a hooker posing as a nun for nefarious purposes. . . . The villains are French soldiers; it's set in the time of Maximilian and Juarez. There's lots of aimless chasing in this widescreen turkey; I found surprising the incompetence with which the numerous action scenes are filmed, since Siegel and cinematographer Gabriel Figueroa usually are much better than this. The climax is needlessly and offensively bloody. It has charm but mostly it's implausible and silly.

TWO RODE TOGETHER (1961, COL). D: John Ford. W: Frank Nugent from a Will Cook novel. Cast: JAMES STEWART, RICHARD WIDMARK, SHIRLEY JONES, John McINTIRE, Woody STRODE, Linda CRISTAL, Andy Devine, Henry Brandon, Mae Marsh, Anna Lee, Ken Curtis, John Qualen, Harry Carey, Jr., Willis Bouchey, Jeanette Nolan, Paul Birch, Olive Carey, Ford Rainey. 109m.

A Texas lawman (Stewart) and his friend a cavalry officer (Widmark) join forces to seek out the Comanches and barter with them for the return of long-held white women captives. In a sense it's a rehash of *The Searchers*. Stewart gives an excellent performance but the film is a let-down, probably the least of Ford's postwar Westerns despite its big budget. The characters are "B" types; the clumsy slapstick comedy that always threatens to overturn Ford's movies seems particularly out of hand here, and many of the slow, long dialogues are soporific.

ULZANA'S RAID (1972, UNIV). D: Robert Aldrich. W: Alan Sharp. Cast: BURT LANCASTER, Jorge LUKE, Bruce DAVISON, Lloyd Bochner, Richard Jaeckel, Karl Swenson, Joaquin Martinez, Nick Cravat, Douglas Watson, John Pearce. 103m.

A weatherbeaten civilian scout (Lancaster), a green, young dude cavalry lieutenant (Davison), a veteran sergeant (Jaeckel) and a wily Indian scout (Luke) lead a detachment of troopers on an expedition across the Arizona desert to run down renegade war chief Ulzana (Martinez) and his raiding band of reservation-jumping Apaches. By the end virtually everybody is dead. The movie is spare, hard, grim, gruesome, dreary and depressing. It's extremely well plotted and the deliberate pacing suits the story. It's photographed beautifully (Joseph Biroc). Lancaster and Luke are outstanding, Jaeckel and Swenson are quite good, and Davison is quite bad—completely out of place and unconvincing. The screenplay expends too much effort on a faddish attempt to speechify about the poisonousness of bigotry. Lancaster says to Davison, "What bothers you, Lieutenant, is that you don't like to see white men behaving like Indians. Kind of confuses the issue, doesn't it." That's both the strength and the weakness of the film: there's too much message, it's too arty, and the story has to be twisted into awkward contrivances in order to fit the theme. The unsavory ending emphasizes its empty pointlessness; it's an interesting picture, well made, but it leaves a sour taste.

UNCONQUERED (1947, PARA). D: Cecil B. De Mille. W: Charles Bennett, Fredric M. Frank & Jesse Lasky, Jr., from a novel by Neil H. Swanson. Cast: GARY COOPER, PAULETTE GODDARD, Howard DA SILVA, C. Aubrey SMITH, Katherine De MILLE, Ward BOND, Boris Karloff, Cecil Kellaway, Henry Wilcoxen, Virginia Grey, Porter Hall, Lex Barker, Jeff Corey, Mike Mazurki, Robert Warwick, Alan Napier, Jane Nigh, Lloyd Bridges, Jack Pennick, Raymond Hatton, Chief Thundercloud, Iron Eyes Cody, Ray Teal, Byron Foulger, Francis J. McDonald, Lane Chandler, Jay Silverheels, Frank Wilcox, Gavin Muir, Clarence Muse. 146m.

During the Indian wars in pre-Revolutionary War pioneer days, villain Howard Da Silva leches after slave girl Goddard who's rescued by stalwart frontiersman Cooper; Boris Karloff plays an Indian. Color photography (Ray Rennahan) and big score (Victor Young) mark this oversized spectacular which is generally absurd, full of plot and fury but aimless. The acting is mostly awful; Goddard especially chews up the scenery. Viewed uncritically it's undeniable fun here and there but for the most part it's run-of-De Mille.

THE UNDEFEATED (1969, FOX). D: Andrew V. McLaglen. W: James Lee Barrett & Stanley M. Hough. Cast: JOHN WAYNE, ROCK HUDSON, Bruce CABOT, Ben JOHNSON, Antonio AGUILAR, Harry Carey, Jr., Lee Meriwether, Marian McCargo, John Agar, Roman Gabriel, Merlin Olsen, Paul Fix, Royal Dano, Dub Taylor, Pedro Armendariz, Jr., Jan-Michael Vincent, Gregg Palmer. 119m.

Yankee cavalry colonel (Wayne) and Rebel cavalry colonel (Hudson) team up with their respective commands, aiming to sell wild horses to the French army in Mexico during the war between Juarez and Maximilian. Revolutionaries kidnap some women and children, whom they threaten to murder unless the horse herd is delivered to them rather than to the French. There is something that passes for a climax. Story and screenplay are listless and sophomoric; McLaglen is saddled with a silly script, an enormous cast and unwieldy production budget ($6 million) and a hapless co-star: Hudson's ersatz Southern drawl must be heard to be believed. A very disappointing movie to say the least.

UNDER A TEXAS MOON (1930, WB). D: Michael Curtiz. W: Gordon Rigby, Joseph Jackson & Raymond Griffith from a story by Stewart Edward White. Cast: FRANK FAY, MYRNA LOY, Raquel TORRES, ARMIDA, Noah BEERY, Sr., George Stone, Fred Kohler, Tully Marshall, Mona Maris, Betty Boyd, Inez Gomez. 82m.

Musical romance in early Technicolor involves a dashing Mexican desperado (Fay) along the Texas border with various evildoers and lady loves. Spirited; very much of its time.

UNDER THE TONTO RIM (1933, PARA). D: Henry Hathaway. W: Jack Cunningham & Gerald Geraghty from Zane Grey's novel. Cast: STUART ERWIN, Verna HILLIE, Fred KOHLER, Fuzzy Knight, John Lodge, George Barbier. 63m.

One of the duller Zane Grey oaters in Paramount's early talkie series has a foolish cowhand earning love and self-respect by going up against the bad guys in a slow comedy-drama. Photographed by Archie J. Stout. Remake of a 1928 silent film.

UNDER WESTERN SKIES (1945, UNIV). D: Jean Yarbrough. W: Stanley Roberts & Clyde Bruckman. Cast: MARTHA DRISCOLL, Noah BEERY, Jr., Leo CARRILLO, Leon Errol, Irving Bacon, Ian Keith. 83m.

Tribulations of a traveling show in the Old West: plucky troupers, dull songs, silly melodrama, "B" production.

THE UNFORGIVEN (1960, UA). D: John Huston. W: Ben Maddow from Alan LeMay's novel. Cast: BURT LANCASTER, AUDREY HEPBURN, Charles BICKFORD, Audie MURPHY, Lillian GISH, Joseph WISEMAN, John SAXON, Albert Salmi, Doug McClure, Kipp Hamilton. 124m.

Audrey Hepburn, as the foundling adopted daughter of a homestead ranch clan, is the focal point in this story of bigotry and racial conflicts in the Texas Panhandle in the late 1860s. Gish is the mother, Lancaster and Murphy and McClure are the sons. A ghostly shabby apparition in Confederate rags (Wiseman) sets the action off when, motivated by vengeance, he asserts that the orphan girl is in fact an Indian. This sets neighbors (Bickford, Salmi) against the clan and motivates a tribe of Indians to try to get the girl back. The film is heavy and sometimes murky but has moments of beauty and lusty spirit, some bucolic humor and compassion and brutality. It's a huge movie, slow to get started because it has quite a few important characters to introduce, but they're all well drawn and portrayed. Audie Murphy, in the key role of the brother torn between his hatred of Indians and his love for his foster sister, is outstanding—more impressive than anything else he did on screen with the possible exception of *The Red Badge of Courage* (also directed by Huston). Masterful Panavision photography (Franz Planer) and a fine score (Dimitri Tiomkin) pull it together. Too confused and ponderous to be a classic, *The Unforgiven* nevertheless is an excellent psychological Western.

UNION PACIFIC (1939, PARA). D: Cecil B. De Mille. W: Walter DeLeon, C. Gardner Sullivan, Jesse Lasky, Jr., & Jack Cunningham from Ernest Haycox's novel *Trouble Shooter*. Cast: JOEL McCREA, BARBARA STANWYCK, ROBERT PRESTON, BRIAN DONLEVY, Akim TAMIROFF, Evelyn KEYES, Anthony QUINN, Lynne OVERMAN, Fuzzy Knight, J. M. Kerrigan, Robert Barrat, Stanley Ridges, Chief Thundercloud, Henry Kolker, Sid Saylor, Lane Chandler, Lon Chaney, Jr., Regis Toomey, Richard Lane, Frank McGlynn, Francis J. McDonald, Willard Robertson, Harry Woods, Joe Sawyer, Byron Foulger, Stanley Andrews, Elmo Lincoln, Monte Blue, Nestor Paiva, Richard Denning, Harold Goodwin. 135m.

Brawling story of the building of the first transcontinental railroads culminates in the famous meeting of the rails in Utah—the famous driving of the golden spike. There are Indian raids and spectacles aplenty, including of course a tremendous train wreck. The central character conflict revolves around a railroad troubleshooter (McCrea), his Irish girl friend (Stanwyck—her accent is atrocious), a charmingly villainous gambler (Preston) and an equally villainous but uncharming gambler (Donlevy); these characters, thanks to Haycox, are more complicated

THREE VIOLENT PEOPLE (1956): Charlton Heston, Tom Tryon, Gilbert Roland. Actually Roland wasn't the third violent person; that was Anne Baxter, in this loud soap/ horse opera. Paramount Pictures

TRAIL OF THE VIGILANTES (1940): Broderick Crawford, Mischa Auer, Andy Devine, Franchot Tone. This one kids itself unabashedly; the comedy is fun. Franchot Tone's only Western. Universal Pictures

TREASURE OF PANCHO VILLA (1955): Gilbert Roland, Rory Calhoun. As usual, Roland elevates it and makes it worth seeing. RKO Radio Pictures

THE TREASURE
OF THE SIERRA
MADRE (1947):
Humphrey Bogart,
Walter Huston, Tim
Holt. Simply a great
movie. Warner
Brothers

TRUE GRIT (1969):
John Wayne, Glen
Campbell, Kim Darby,
Hank Worden.
Wayne's only Academy
Award, as the cantan-
kerous one-eyed
Marshal Cogburn.
Paramount Pictures

THE TRUE STORY OF JESSE
JAMES (1957): Robert Wagner,
Jeffrey Hunter, Alan Hale, Jr. The
flavor is very 1950ish in this re-
make of the Tyrone Power *Jesse
James.* Twentieth Century-Fox

TWENTY-MULE TEAM (1940):
Wallace Beery, Anne Baxter, Noah
Beery, Jr. (The two actors are
uncle and nephew.) The usual
wheeze; Baxter's debut. Requires
a taste for Beery. MGM

TWO FLAGS WEST (1950): Noah
Beery, Jr., Cornel Wilde, Dale Robertson,
Joseph Cotten. A good cast in a fast
Indian-fighting actioner about Galvanized
Yankees. Twentieth Century-Fox

THE UNFORGIVEN (1960): Doug McClure, Audie
Murphy. Heavy and murky but moments of beauty and
great power. Murphy is outstanding. United Artists

UNION PACIFIC (1939):
Brawling spectacular action in
De Mille's best talkie Western
—a boxoffice blockbuster
in its day and still a grand
example of the Western epic.
Paramount Pictures

VALDEZ IS COM-
ING (1971): Susan
Clark, Burt Lancaster.
A movie about dignity:
not revenge but justice.
Lancaster's one-man-
army performance is
towering. United
Artists

VERA CRUZ (1954): Burt Lancaster, Gary Cooper. Two soldiers of fortune with outrageously superhuman expertise; Lancaster mugs too much, displaying his alligator-toothed grin in every scene. United Artists

THE VIOLENT MEN (1954): Dianne Foster, Barbara Stanwyck, Edward G. Robinson, Brian Keith. Heavy-breathing family conflicts but razor-sharp acting. Robinson hated Westerns: this was his only starring role in one. Columbia Pictures

THE VIRGINIAN (1929): Gary Cooper (white shirt), Eugene Pallette (with bedroll), Richard Arlen (black costume). A timeless classic, still vital and funny and moving by turns; we may not come nearer to the ultimate Western. Paramount Pictures

and interesting than De Mille's usual stalwarts, although there remain De Mille's penchants for leaden exposition and turgid melodramatics; still, some of Haycox's humors and ironies are here, and after a slow start the picture moves briskly (for De Mille) from one climax to another. It copies some scenes almost exactly from Ford's 1924 silent epic *The Iron Horse*, and uses some of Ford's action footage (in very poorly processed rear-projection). *Union Pacific* is De Mille's best talkie Western by a wide margin—a box office blockbuster in its day and still today a good example of the Western epic. Score by Sigmund Krumgold & John Leipold; photography by Victor Milner; edited by Anne Bauchens.

THE UNSINKABLE MOLLY BROWN (1964, MGM). D: Charles Walters. W: Helen Deutsch from Richard Morris's play with music and lyrics by Meredith Willson. Cast: DEBBIE REYNOLDS, HARVE PRESNELL, Jack KRUSCHEN, Ed BEGLEY, Hermione Baddeley, Harvey Lembeck, Vassili Lambrinos, Fred Essler, Lauren Gilbert, Hayden Rorke, Martita Hunt, Vaughn Taylor, Anna Lee. 128m.

Story concerns the ambitions and romances of a pioneer backwoods girl and her energetic rise to success in the gold-mining West. Lavish Western musical, one of the popular successes of its time, was loosely based on fact. It's a good entertainment, with excellent wide-screen photography (Daniel L. Fapp) and a lively score conducted and orchestrated by Robert Armbruster and Calvin Jackson. Academy Award nomination to Debbie Reynolds as best actress.

UNTAMED (1940, RKO). D: George Archainbaud. W: Frederick Hazlitt Brennan & Frank Butler. Cast: RAY MILLAND, PATRICIA MORISON, Akim TAMIROFF, William Frawley, Jane Darwell, Roscoe Ates, Phil Van Zandt, J. Farrell MacDonald, J. M. Kerrigan.

Young doctor braves a blizzard in the Far North to get serum through to an infected community. Dated and pretty bad.

UNTAMED (1955, FOX). D: Henry King. W: Talbot Jennings, Frank Fenton, Michael Blankfort & William A. Bacher from a novel by Helga Moray. Cast: TYRONE POWER, SUSAN HAYWARD, RICHARD EGAN, Agnes MOOREHEAD, Hope EMERSON, Rita MORENO, John Justin, Henry O'Neill. 111m.

A wagon train of Boer settlers fights off Zulus and tries to establish a pioneer settlement in this oater with a South African setting and an actionful Edna Ferber sort of plot with most of the story devoted to romantic rivalries among the various personnel. It's a lavishly junky movie that's totally predictable—the sort that gave Hollywood a bad name among sophisticates who prefer a bit of substance with their corn.

THE UNTAMED BREED (1948, COL). D: Charles Lamont. W: Tom Reed from an Eli Colter story. Cast: SONNY TUFTS, BARBARA BRITTON, William BISHOP, Edgar BUCHANAN, George "Gabby" HAYES, George E. Stone, Joe Sawyer, Gordon Jones, Russell Simpson, Reed Howes, Harry Tyler. 79m.

A top hand gets mixed up with rustlers, ranchers, romance and rattling guns. Photographed in Cinecolor (Charles Lawton Jr.), the film usually is available only in black-and-white prints. Apparently no one connected with it had much respect for it; it's an unintentional parody—a textbook example of hokey lousy horse opera. The acting is terrible—Tufts is howlingly inept with his Brooklyn-sounding speech mannerisms—and the script convoluted, the directing amateurish and the story dull.

UNTAMED FRONTIER (1952, UNIV). D: Hugo Fregonese. W: Gerald D. Adams, John & Gwen Bagni, Houston Branch, Eugenia Night & Polly James. Cast: JOSEPH COTTEN, SHELLEY WINTERS, SCOTT BRADY, Suzan BALL, Minor Watson, Fess Parker, Antonio Moreno, Katherine Emery, John Alexander. 75m.

Overinflated Texas range-war yarn concerns cattle barons versus settlers with "torrid" romances mixed in. It's colorful but confused; not very good. Fess Parker's screen debut.

UTAH BLAINE (1956, COL). D: Fred F. Sears. W: Robert E. Kent & James B. Gordon from Louis L'Amour's novel. Cast: RORY CALHOUN, ANGELA STEVENS, Paul LANGTON, Susan CUMMINGS, Max BAER, Steve Darrell, Ray Teal, Jack Ingram. 75m.

Cowhand against land-grabbers yet again. Minor programmer is well enough made.

THE UTAH KID (1930, TIFFANY). D: Richard Thorpe. W: Frank Howard Clark. Cast: REX LEASE, TOM SANTSCHI, DOROTHY SEBASTIAN, Walter MILLER, Mary Carr, Boris Karloff, Lafe McKee, Bud Osborne.

The one about the outlaw who tries to reform but has to fight it out with his old gang. Tiffany was what its name implies with relation to the rest of the minor "B" studios of the

1930s; this was typical of their product—professional, speedy, slick. Fine then, but not now.

VALDEZ IS COMING (1971, UA). D: Edwin Sherin. W: Roland Kibbee & David Rayfiel from Elmore Leonard's novel. Cast: BURT LANCASTER, SUSAN CLARK, Richard JORDAN, Jon CYPHER, Barton HEYMAN, Frank Silvera, Maria Montez, Nick Cravat. 90m.

This taut drama concerns a Mexican constable (Lancaster) in 1890s Arizona, aging and used up and a figure of ridicule because he's no longer the famous Indian-fighting scout that he used to be. When a ruthless cattleman (Cypher) causes the death of an innocent black man—for sport as much as anything else—the constable tries to persuade the man to provide a little money for the black man's Indian widow. The cattleman laughs at him, spits on him, and finally—when the constable becomes a pest—has him tortured. Thereupon the old scout outfits himself in his old Indian-fighting uniform, loads his antique buffalo rifle and sets out after the cattleman. He has to fight it out with a whole army of the cattleman's henchmen, in a long running chase through spectacular Spanish mountains; he kidnaps the villain's girl friend (Clark) and there are other plot ramifications but mainly it's a straightforward pursuit-and-battle movie from then on. It's not revenge Valdez seeks, but justice: he asks that the Apache widow's existence be acknowledged. It's a movie about dignity—a valid premise but unhappily some scenes are there solely for cheap shock effects, and the subsidiary characters are inadequately defined. Jordan, as a blustery coward, and Heyman, as the cattleman's foreman, fare best; Susan Clark does well with a limited role; the rest are not very good except for the star: Lancaster's towering performance elevates this one-man-army yarn far above most Westerns of the 1970s. Photography (Gaber Pagany) and score (Charles Gross) are superior.

THE VALLEY OF GWANGI (1969 WB). D: James O'Connolly. W: William Bast & Julian More. Cast: JAMES FRANCISCUS, RICHARD CARLSON, Gila GOLAN, Laurence NAISMITH, Curtis Arden, Freda Jackson, Gustavo Rojo. 95m.

Set in 1900 Mexico, this science fiction Western incorporates prehistoric monsters (special effects by Ray Harryhausen—monsters in Dynamation) and dreadful dialogue. It's tyrannosaurus and pterodactyl versus six-gun and lasso. Franciscus and Naismith are capable actors, and money was spent on the

production (cinematography Erwin Hillier, music by Jerome Moross), but the script is dirt-cheap, the directing is poor and the monsters are unconvincing.

VALLEY OF THE SUN (1942, RKO). D: George Marshall. W: Horace McCoy from the novel by Clarence Buddington Kelland. Cast: JAMES CRAIG, LUCILLE BALL, DEAN JAGGER, Cedric HARDWICKE, Antonio Moreno, Peter Whitney, Billy Gilbert, Tom Tyler, Al St. John. 84m.

Frontiersman, sympathetic to the Indians, exposes a dishonest Indian agent. The thin plot has a bad case of anemia but Jagger and Hardwicke are okay and it's well directed with plenty of commotion.

VALLEY OF WANTED MEN (1935, IND). D: Allan James. W: Barry Barringer & Forrest Barnes from a Peter B. Kyne story. Cast: FRANKIE DARRO, LeRoy MASON, Russell Hopton, Grant Withers, Paul Fix.

Tom Swift-type juvenile adventure yarn is dated, strictly for kids.

THE VANISHING AMERICAN (1955, REP). D: Joseph Kane. W: Alan LeMay from Zane Grey's novel. Cast: SCOTT BRADY, AUDREY TOTTER, FORREST TUCKER, Jim DAVIS, Gene LOCKHART, Glenn Strange, Jay Silverheels. 90m.

The one about the frontiersman who helps the Navajos fight off white land-grabbers. In black-and-white. The script and directing are solid enough but Republic stinted on the budget and Brady is miscast.

THE VANQUISHED (1953, PARA). D: Edward Ludwig. W: Winston Miller, Frank L. Moss & Lewis R. Foster from a Karl Brown novel. Cast: JOHN PAYNE, JAN STERLING, Coleen GRAY, Lyle Bettger, Ellen Corby. 84m.

Clean-up-the-town yarn has saloon songs added to stretch the weary plot. Rheumy.

VENDETTA (1965)—*See* MURIETA.

VENGEANCE VALLEY (1951, MGM). D: Richard Thorpe. W: Irving Ravetch from Luke Short's novel. Cast: BURT LANCASTER, ROBERT WALKER, JOANNE DRU, John IRELAND, Sally FORREST, Carleton Carpenter, Hugh O'Brian, Ted De Corsia, Will Wright. 83m.

This one had what was called at the time an "adult" plot—about illegitimate birth and parentage—with a good brother (Lancaster) and a bad brother (Walker) both involved with a cafe waitress (Forrest) who's pregnant. (Sally Forrest seemed for a while to be building a whole career on unwed motherhood: she played a similar role, with some notoriety, in

Not Wanted). The waitress has two angry brothers of her own (Ireland, O'Brian); they come gunning for the man they think got their sister in trouble. All this in ranch country with foreman Lancaster's professional troubles adding problems to his life. This wasn't the best of the Luke Short novels and it's not the best of the movies made from his books but it's not bad, though it's more soap than horse opera.

VERA CRUZ (1954, UA). **D: Robert Aldrich. W: Roland Kibbee, James R. Webb & Borden Chase. Cast: GARY COOPER, BURT LANCASTER, Denise DARCEL, Sarita MONTIEL, Cesar ROMERO, George MACREADY, Henry BRANDON, Ernest Borgnine, Charles Bronson, Jack Elam, Jack Lambert, James Seay, Morris Ankrum. 94m.**

Two soldier-of-fortune adventurers meet, nearly kill each other for trivial reasons, finally join forces and take a job for the emperor Maximilian (Macready) escorting a gold shipment and a lady aristocrat (Darcel) from Mexico City to Vera Cruz, protecting same—with the help of a column of imperial troops led by nasty Henry Brandon—against raids by Juarez's rebels (Romero et al.). Inevitably one partner tries to make off with the gold; the conflict of values leads to a showdown between them. Both heroes are endowed with outrageously superhuman expertise; their exhibitions of marksmanship are terrific and the script builds both of them into larger-than-life men of action. On that level *Vera Cruz* is great fun, but there's also some unnecessary sadistic violence and the picture gets too furious and vicious at times, and Lancaster mugs and hams too much, displaying his alligator-toothed grin in every scene, while Cooper is almost too sober with his glum brooding contrapuntal performance as the laconic tough guy. The supporting cast overacts uniformly so that the movie has a comic-strip quality. The CinemaScope photography (Ernest Laszlo) is vast and lavish. Lancaster's company produced this; Cooper made it in Mexico back-to-back with his *Garden of Evil*, a less well remembered film that I find less dated and more rewarding than *Vera Cruz*.

THE VIGILANTES RETURN (1946, UNIV). **D: Ray Taylor. W: Roy Chanslor. Cast: JON HALL, MARGARET LINDSAY, Andy DEVINE, Paula Drew, Jack Lambert, Robert Wilcox. 67m.**

Another town-taming marshal yarn, it's about as fresh as the title; in color.

VILLA! (1958, FOX). **D: James B. Clark. W: Louis Vittes. Cast: BRIAN KEITH, CESAR ROMERO, Margia DEANE, Rodolfo HOYOS, Ben Wright, Carlos Muzquiz. 72m.**

Hoyos plays the title role in this conventional yarn about a gringo adventurer (Keith) who mixes it up in the 1910–1916 Mexican Revolution. It's pretty dull despite Keith's spirited performance.

THE VILLAIN (1979, COL). **D: Hal Needham. W: Robert G. Kane. Cast: KIRK DOUGLAS, ANN-MARGRET, ARNOLD SCHWARZENEGGER, Paul LYNDE, Foster BROOKS, Ruth BUZZI, Jack ELAM, Strother MARTIN, Mel TILLIS, Robert Tessier. 89m.**

Slapstick "live-action cartoon" feature has characters with such names as Handsome Stranger (Schwarzenegger, former Mr. Universe turned actor), Charming (Ann-Margret) and Cactus Jack Slade (Douglas). Its flavor is akin to that of the old Roadrunner cartoons; it's wild, frenzied, crude, sometimes ridiculous, always unsubtle, totally brainless and occasionally very funny. The energetic pratfalls are well engineered; Douglas is fine as the mean-spirited but incompetent villain who keeps trying, and failing, to steal money; he is foiled in strenuous ways—being smashed into a cliff, flattened by a falling boulder, hit by a speeding train, so forth. It's childish nonsense but, on its level, quite funny.

VILLA RIDES! (1968, PARA). **D: Buzz Kulik. W: Sam Peckinpah & Robert Towne from a book by William D. Lansford. Cast: ROBERT MITCHUM, YUL BRYNNER, CHARLES BRONSON, Grazia BUCCELLA, Herbert LOM, Alexander KNOX, Frank Wolff, Robert Viharo, Jill Ireland, Fernando Rey, Diana Lorys, Antonio Ruiz. 125m.**

Any relation to history is undetectable in this big-budget actioner with Brynner ridiculous in the title role, Bronson expressionless as Villa's right-hand killer and Mitchum wasted as a gringo adventurer-pilot who becomes the one-man air force of the Mexican Revolution. Here and there can be found evidences of Peckinpah's preoccupations with the death of honor and the old values, and their replacement by sneaky villainous politicians (Knox, Lom) to whom the ends justify any means no matter how vicious. There's a lot of pointless mayhem and violence. Uninteresting cinematography (Jack Hildyard) and a jangling misplaced score (Maurice Jarre) don't help, and the directing is befuddled so that it's virtually impossible to follow the plot. The acting by everybody, even including Mitchum, is distressing.

THE VIOLENT MEN (1954, COL). D: Rudolph Mate. W: Harry Kleiner from a Donald Hamilton novel. Cast: GLENN FORD, BARBARA STANWYCK, EDWARD G. ROBINSON, Brian KEITH, Dianne FOSTER, May WYNN, Warner Anderson, Richard Jaeckel, Basil Ruysdael, Lita Milan, James Westerfield, Jack Kelly, Harry Shannon, Edmund Cobb. 96m.

Ingredients of this one are a wheelchair-bound range baron (Robinson), his straying wife (Stanwyck), her foreman-lover (Keith), Robinson's daughter (Foster) and a peaceable neighboring squatter rancher (Ford) who gets mixed up in the family's hard-breathing conflicts. The script is sensationalist and overblown but the acting by the four principals is powerful enough to carry the movie; despite villainy by Robinson, Stanwyck and Keith that's so brutal it's for strong stomachs only, the performances are razor-sharp and it's surprisingly rewarding for such a hard-bitten melodrama; Keith is especially forceful, evil-looking in black moustache and hair dye. Photography (Burnett Guffey & W. Howard Greene) and score (Max Steiner) are first-class. This was Robinson's only starring role in a Western (it was a genre he detested); he had cameos in a few others but no leading roles. Similar in some ways to *Jubal* (also starring Glenn Ford), this probably is the better of the two.

THE VIOLENT ONES (1967, IND). D: Fernando Lamas. W: Douglas Wilson, Charles Davis, Fred Freiberger & Herman Miller. Cast: FERNANDO LAMAS, ALDO RAY, Lisa GAYE, Tommy SANDS, David Carradine, Melinda Marx. 84m.

When three drifters are accused of a girl's murder, a bigoted lynch mob assembles and a Chicano sheriff (Lamas) is caught in the middle. No world-beater but it's a professional job, although the low budget makes it threadbare in spots.

VIRGINIA CITY (1940, WB). D: Michael Curtiz. W: Robert Buckner, Norman Reilly Raine & Howard Koch. Cast: ERROL FLYNN, MIRIAM HOPKINS, RANDOLPH SCOTT, HUMPHREY BOGART, Alan HALE, Guinn "BIG BOY" WILLIAMS, Frank McHugh, Douglas Dumbrille, John Litel, Moroni Olsen, Charles Middleton, Russell Hicks, Paul Fix, Ward Bond, Dick Jones, Frank Wilcox, Victor Kilian, Russell Simpson, Thurston Hall, Charles Halton, Harry Cording, George Reeves, Lane Chandler, Trevor Bardette. 121m.

Three groups try to obtain a big treasure of gold from the Nevada mines during the Civil War: the Union army (Flynn), the Confederate army (Scott) and a gang of Mexican bandits (Bogart). The plot is big and confused. Film was made by the same production team, crew and stock company as the previous year's *Dodge City* (photography by Sol Polito, this time in black-and-white, and music by Max Steiner; produced by Hal Wallis). A few long shots were filmed on Arizona locations and the second-unit stunt work by Yakima Canutt is exciting, but mostly the movie has a static setbound look, confined to interiors and a few soundstage exteriors; this essential phoniness, plus Bogart's pathetic Mexican accent, wooden performances by all and a script that veers from exposition to cliche and back, can't be excused by the handful of stunts and the grandiose scale of the proceedings; it's a hackneyed overbudgeted "B" oater.

THE VIRGINIAN (1929, PARA). D: Victor Fleming. W: Howard Estabrook, Edward E. Paramore, Jr., Grover Jones, Keene Thompson & Joseph L. Mankiewicz from Owen Wister's novel and the play by Wister and Kirk LaShelle. Cast: GARY COOPER, WALTER HUSTON, MARY BRIAN, RICHARD ARLEN, Chester CONKLIN, Eugene PALLETTE, Helen Ware, Jack Pennick, Vince Barnett, James Mason, George Chandler. 90m.

Complicated story concerns the nameless foreman of a ranch—shy, good-humored, finally resolute—and his various relationships with the gentle Eastern schoolmarm (a relationship between West and East that is timelessly reflected in *High Noon*), with his happy-go-lucky pal Steve (Arlen) who steps out of line and forces the Virginian to inflict a harrowing rough justice on him; with the sharply etched denizens of a Wyoming ranching valley; and with the arrogant villain Trampas (Huston).

"If you want to call me that . . . smile!" A half century later, *The Virginian* remains a classic: the essential Western, still vital, still funny and moving by turns. It had been made more than once as a silent picture; this version was Cooper's first talkie and, after *In Old Arizona*, the first smash hit Western talkie. Among its other firsts is Walter Huston's—it was his first film. Assistant director was Henry Hathaway; photography, on Sierra Nevada locations, was by Edward Cronjager and J. Roy Hunt; and uncredited writer Joseph L. Mankiewicz provided the titles and a script polish. Cooper's performance, with a drawling dialect coached by a real Virginian (Randolph Scott), still impresses, but Huston and Arlen aren't far behind. Like many early talkies it has no sound-track score, and to the uninitiated that can make it seem a bit flat at times (hence its lackluster reviews in some film books), but the characterizations are rich and excellent; and the walk-down shoot-out that climaxes the movie has hardly been improved upon. *The Virginian* is fun, and very good; possibly we may never come nearer to the ultimate Western.

THE VIRGINIAN (1946, PARA). D: Stuart Gilmore. W: Frances Goodrich, Albert Hackett & Howard Estabrook from Owen Wister's novel and the play by Wister & Kirk La Shelle. Cast: JOEL McCREA, BRIAN DONLEVY, BARBARA BRITTON, Sonny TUFTS, Tom TULLY, William Frawley, Fay Bainter, Henry O'Neill, Bill Edwards, Paul Guilfoyle, Marc Lawrence, Vince Barnett, Minor Watson. 90m.

Lethargic remake adds little, other than Technicolor, to the earlier version; aside from McCrea and Tully, the cast is inadequate. Studio process photography detracts, and the story is watered down—the humor muted, the characters simplified. It's been reduced to a routine oater.

VIVA VILLA! (1934, MGM). D: Jack Conway (and Howard Hawks). W: Ben Hecht & Howard Hawks from a biography by Edgcombe Pinchon & O.B. Stade. Cast: WALLACE BEERY, FAY WRAY, Leo CARRILLO, Donald COOK, Stuart ERWIN, Joseph SCHILDKRAUT, Katherine De Mille, Arthur Treacher, Henry B. Walthall, Joe Dominguez, Frank Puglia, George E. Stone. 115m.

Covering the years 1910–1916, this sugar-coated biography follows the rise of patriot-bandit Pancho Villa to Robin Hood status in the Mexican Revolution. It's no more faithful to historical fact than are most Hollywood biopics but in its flavor it conveys a spirited sense of time and place. James Wong Howe's cinematography is excellent. The picture was made, somehow, in spite of nearly constant meddling and interference from MGM mogul Louis B. Mayer, who was engaged in a dispute with actor Lee Tracy. Hawks supported Tracy; Mayer yanked both Tracy and Hawks off the picture when it was half completed (Erwin took Tracy's place); Conway was tossed onto the set without preparation, fighting against a budget deadline, and had to try and mesh his style with Hawks's. Hawks had filmed the Mexican location exteriors; Conway directed most of the interiors. Despite all that, the movie works eminently: big, vivid, exciting. It was nominated for an Academy Award as best picture.

VIVA ZAPATA (1952, FOX). D: Elia Kazan. W: John Steinbeck (based—uncredited—on Edgcombe Pinchon's biography). Cast: MARLON BRANDO, JEAN PETERS, ANTHONY QUINN, Mildred DUNNOCK, Joseph WISEMAN, Arnold Moss, Harold Gordon, Margo, Alan Reed, Henry Silva, Lou Gilbert, Frank Silvera, Nina Varela, Frank DeKova. 113m.

Several impressive talents combined to create this movie about the revolutionary life and death of Emiliano Zapata, the illiterate Indian who led a revolution against the tyranny of Mexico's turn-of-the-century regime. Historically it's not terribly accurate, and politically it's simplistic—an idealized treatment of a man who in fact was bloodthirsty and brutal and perhaps more hungry for power than for freeing the poor. But such considerations are rarely the essence of biopics. *Viva Zapata* is both actionful and poetic, an outstanding film. Producer was Darryl Zanuck; black-and-white cinematography is by Joseph MacDonald; the score, by Alex North, has the jangle of Mexican folk music. Kazan studied photographs of the real events and tried to reconstruct the look of the times, but Mexican authorities disapproved the screenplay and the movie ended up being shot in Texas. Quinn received his first Academy Award for his supporting role as Zapata's brother; Brando and Steinbeck were nominated for Oscars; in the title role Brando dominates the film and certainly it's the best performance—indeed, the only good one—he's ever given in a horseback movie. Kazan's self-conscious stylized aura of Eisensteinian classicism makes much of this film too mannered and contrived and studied; the screenplay itself is written at a realistic common-sense level that makes the pretentiousness of the directorial style stick out like a sore thumb; therefore the film is not a stylized whole—rather, it's a plainspoken, honest script upon which the director and leading actor have imposed their own devices. That contradiction of styles weakens the movie, but not enough to destroy it; it's fine work.

THE WACKIEST WAGON TRAIN IN THE WEST (1976, IND). DW: Morrie Parker. Cast: FORREST TUCKER, BOB DENVER.

Cheap indie comedy had not yet been released nationally at press time; possibly it never will be.

WACO (1952, MONO). D: Lewis D. Collins. W: Daniel Ullman. Cast: WILLIAM ELLIOTT, Pamela BLAKE, House Peters, Jr., Rory Mallinson, Paul Fierro, Rand Brooks,

Lane Bradford, Ray Bennett, I. Stanford Jolley.

Outlaw is hired as sheriff to restore order in the titular Texas town. Long-in-the-tooth script and lackadaisical direction make this black-and-white film poorer than most Elliott programmers.

WACO (1966, PARA). D: R. G. Springsteen. W: Steve Fisher from a novel by Harry Stanford & Max Lamb. Cast: HOWARD KEEL, JANE RUSSELL, BRIAN DONLEVY, WENDELL COREY, TERRY MOORE, Richard ARLEN, John AGAR, John SMITH, Robert LOWERY, Willard PARKER, Gene Evans, Ben Cooper, DeForest Kelley, Tracy Olsen, Fuzzy Knight. 85m.

A town, dominated by outlaws, hires a gunslinger (Keel as "Waco") to clean up the saloons. Brightest spot is Corey's good performance as a courageous preacher with a dark past. There's a treacly title song, intoned by Lorne Greene, and most everybody is fairly inept, from the hack pen-work to the acting. A. C. Lyles produced it, of course; his oaters were nearly the only profitable Paramount pictures of the 1960s but his budgets were minimal and the shooting schedules on his movies averaged twelve days or less (versus forty or more for a legitimate "A" film), and some were shot in as little as one week; not even television can work that quickly. But the main weakness, here as in other Lyles pictures, is in the script, which is really quite awful: tired and sleazy. Overripe oaters like this are strictly for nostalgics who are willing to sit through endless sophomoric foolishness to see all those old-timey actors.

THE WAGON MASTER (1929, UNIV). D: Harry Joe Brown. W: Marion Jackson. Cast: KEN MAYNARD, Tom SANTSCHI, Edith ROBERTS, Frank Rice, Jackie Hanlon. 70m.

Maynard produced this early actioner; it was a transitional film, mostly silent footage but with a few talking sequences and songs. Plot is standard covered-wagon hokum.

WAGONMASTER (1950, RKO). D: John Ford. W: Frank Nugent & Patrick Ford. Cast: BEN JOHNSON, HARRY CAREY, JR., WARD BOND, JOANNE DRU, Jane DARWELL, Alan MOWBRAY, Charles Kemper, James Arness, Frances Ford, Ruth Clifford, Jim Thorpe, Russell Simpson, Sons of the Pioneers. 86m.

Two cheerful young drifters (Johnson, Carey) help a wagon train of Mormons, led by Ward Bond as the title character, get across the desert to Utah; the train is menaced by elements, Indians and outlaws. The entire picture takes place outdoors in Monument Valley. It's a leisurely film, in black-and-white, with some "B" elements in script and production. It was Ford's elegy to his old friend Harry Carey, Sr., who had died shortly before filming began. It has been called lyrical, poetic and beautiful; for the most part I fail to find those qualities in much of it, except in Bert Glennon's photography, some of which is stunning. It is an overrated movie by and large—there are cliches of both character and plot; it's a primitive story in many ways, cluttered with melodrama, unconvincing devices, crude humor and treacly sentimentality. It's as good as Ford's *Three Godfathers* and better than his *Two Rode Together* but nonetheless it's vest-pocket Ford. Still, the two leading men have great charm and appeal. The movie served as the basis for the popular long-running TV series "Wagon Train," for which Ford contributed his talents to the filming of the first few Ward Bond episodes.

WAGONS WEST (1952, MONO). D: Ford Beebe. W: Daniel Ullman. Cast: ROD CAMERON, PEGGIE CASTLE, Henry BRANDON, Noah BEERY, Jr., Frank Ferguson, I. Stanford Jolley.

The wheeze about the wagon-boss who exposes bad guys who've been selling rifles to the Cheyenne Indians. Distinctly déjà vu.

WAGONS WESTWARD 1940, REP). D: Lew Landers. W: Harrison Jacobs & Joseph M. Marsh. Cast: CHESTER MORRIS, ANITA LOUISE, BUCK JONES, Ona MUNSON, George "Gabby" HAYES, Guinn "Big Boy" WILLIAMS, Douglas Fowley, Edmund Cobb, Charles Stevens, Trevor Bardette. 70m.

His career as a "B" hero sagging, Buck Jones here plays the villain (although his horse "Silver" is still featured) in a standard ranch romance about land-grabbing rustlers.

WAGON TRAIL (1935, IND). D: Harry Fraser. W: Monroe Talbott. Cast: HARRY CAREY, Gertrude MESSINGER, Edward Norris, Earl Dwire, Chief Thundercloud, Chuck Morrison. 54m.

Wagon freighters fight off ambushers. Carey (Sr.) had appeared in innumerable "B" pictures in silent days, many of them two-reelers; this, like several others in the mid-1930s, was a throwback to those—filmed by a Gower Gulch independent company (Ajax) in a few days on a shoestring budget. Carey, despite his distinctly un-Western Long Island accent, always managed to bring far more dignity to these pictures than they deserved; it was partly personality and partly training—he'd been starring in movies since 1910 and by this time he certainly knew what he was doing. (Amazingly, he looked little different in his last Western, *Red River*, from the way he looked in his first film, Biograph's *Gentleman Joe*, filmed thirty-six years earlier. Carey was born in 1878, died in 1947.)

WAGON WHEELS (1934, PARA). D: Charles T. Barton. W: Jack Cunningham, Charles Logue & Carl A. Buss from Zane Grey's novel *Fighting Caravans*. Cast: RANDOLPH SCOTT, GAIL PATRICK, Monte BLUE, Leila Bennett, Raymond Hatton, Jack Duggan, Olin Howlin.

Wagon scout in buckskins leads the train through Indian country to safety. Another imitation *Covered Wagon*, this one used a great deal of leftover footage from Gary Cooper's *Fighting Caravans* (1931), with Randolph Scott even wearing Cooper's costume so the close-ups would match.

THE WALKING HILLS (1949, COL). D: John Sturges. W: Alan LeMay. Cast: RANDOLPH SCOTT, ELLA RAINES, JOHN IRELAND, Arthur KENNEDY, William BISHOP, Edgar Buchanan, Jerome Courtland. 78m.

Eight men and a beautiful woman seek buried gold in a hostile desert. Good script, directing and cast. Small budget but very good entertainment.

WALK LIKE A DRAGON (1960, PARA). D: James Clavell. W: Clavell & Daniel Mainwaring. Cast: JAMES SHIGETA, NOBU McCARTHY, JACK LORD, MEL TORMÉ, Rodolfo Acosta, Josephine Hutchinson, Michael Pate, Benson Fong, Donald Barry, Tom Kennedy, Tony Young. 95m.

An arrogant bigoted rancher (Lord) rescues a Chinese girl (McCarthy) from the slave market in early San Francisco and takes her back to his small cowtown along with a young Chinese man (Shigeta) who because of racism determines to learn how to be a gunslinger. The acting is mediocre, but black-and-white photography (Loyal Griggs) lends an air of gritty realism. Story is off-trail but not exceptional, and the thinness of the budget is evident, and it's mostly bilge, a simplistic triangle melodrama. As the dressed-in-black gunslinging bad guy, jazz great Mel Tormé is interesting and unusual, but his dialogue is stilted. (Like Glenn Ford, Tormé was in the vanguard of Hollywood's quick-draw vogue of the period; his fancy six-gun work is not faked in this movie.) Acosta, as the sheriff, stands out. Author-director-producer Clavell became better known later on, as screenwriter of *The Great Escape* and author of such novels as *Shogun*.

WALK TALL (1960, FOX). D: Maury Dexter. W: Joseph Fritz. Cast: WILLARD PARKER, JOYCE MEADOWS, Kent TAYLOR, Ron Soble, Alberto Monte. 60m.

Cavalry officer hunts four renegade whites who murdered innocent Shoshone Indians. Limp programmer with over-age stars is in black-and-white.

WALK THE PROUD LAND (1956, UNIV). Also titled: APACHE AGENT. D: Jesse Hibbs. W: Gil Doud & Jack Sher from a biography by Woodworth Clum. Cast: AUDIE MURPHY, ANNE BANCROFT, Pat CROWLEY, Charles DRAKE, Jay SILVERHEELS, Rommy Rall, Robert Warwick, Eugene Mazzola, Anthony Caruso, Victor Millan, Ainsley Pryor, Eugene Iglesias, Morris Ankrum, Addison Richards. 88m.

John P. Clum (Murphy) was, in fact, an important frontier figure—Indian agent during the Apache wars in Arizona, and subsequently mayor of Tombstone and editor of its newspaper the *Epitaph* during the OK Corral era. This lugubrious biopic distorts history in giving Clum a role in the final capture of Geronimo (Silverheels)—an event that occurred a decade after Clum left the Indian agency. The Indian way of life depicted herein never existed outside Hollywood's imagination. But once that has been said, let it be added that the production is colorful and sizable (in CinemaScope) and that Silverheels is excellent in one of his rare major roles. Anne Bancroft is silly as an Apache girl.

WANDERER OF THE WASTELAND (1935, PARA). D: Otto Lovering. W: Stuart Anthony from Zane Grey's novel. Cast: DEAN JAGGER, GAIL PATRICK, Anna Q. NILSSON, Edward Ellis, Larry "Buster" Crabbe, Leif Erickson, Monte Blue, Raymond Hatton, Fuzzy Knight.

This picaresque adventure concerns a youth who goes from riverboat to gold country to Death Valley with loves and tight scrapes along the way. In color, and not bad. Jagger was always low-key but appealing.

WANDERER OF THE WASTELAND (1946, RKO). D: Edward Killy & Wallace Ginsell. W: Norman Houston from Zane Grey's novel. Cast: JAMES WARREN, AUDREY LONG, Richard MARTIN, Al "Fuzzy" St. John, Robert Barrat, Robert Clarke, Harry Woods, Minerva Urecal, Jason Robards, Sr., Tommy Cook. 67m.

The old hero-hunting-his-daddy's-killer wheeze has the two heroes scripted in as hotshot sharpshooters this time. It's actionful but has very little to do with the Zane Grey original. The RKO series of Grey movies in the middle 1940s with scripts by Norman Houston were more polished productions than some of the 1930s Paramount versions but nowhere near as fresh or exciting.

WAR ARROW (1954, UNIV). D: George Sherman. W: John Michael Hayes. Cast: JEFF CHANDLER, MAUREEN O'HARA, Charles DRAKE, Suzan BALL, Dennis Weaver, Jay Silverheels, Noah Beery, Jr., Henry Brandon. 78m.

Cavalry officer (Chandler) is sent to Texas to train "friendly" Seminole Indians for combat against warrior Kiowas. Today the subject matter seems distasteful to say the least, but on its own terms, and for its own time, the picture was reasonably well done, though nothing special.

WAR DRUMS (1957, UA). D: Reginald LeBorg. W: Gerald Drayson Adams. Cast: LEX BARKER, JOAN TAYLOR, Ben JOHNSON, Stuart Whitman. 75m.

Yet another imitation of *Broken Arrow*, this one has Barker ludicrously bad as an Apache chief, Taylor unconvincing as a Mexican girl he marries, and a plot about earnest but doomed efforts on the part of good-hearted people on both sides to bring peace to the frontier. Johnson is the only performer not utterly defeated by the script.

WARLOCK (1959, FOX). D: Edward Dmytryk. W: Robert Alan Aurthur from Oakley Hall's novel. Cast: HENRY FONDA, RICHARD WIDMARK, ANTHONY QUINN, DOROTHY MALONE, Dolores MICHAELS, Tom DRAKE, Wallace Ford, Richard Arlen, Frank Gorshin, Regis Toomey, Donald "Red" Barry, DeForest Kelley. 122m.

Bad guys have the town of Warlock treed until two things happen: first the town dads decide to import a professional town-tamer (Fonda), and second one of the bad guys (Widmark) has a change of heart and hires on as sheriff to protect the town. Into town with the hired gun comes his gambler-killer sidekick (Quinn), who stakes out the biggest saloon in town. For Fonda and Quinn it is possible, without much stretching, to read Earp and Holliday; Oakley Hall's elaborate and excellent story was a fictionalization of the OK Corral legends. Unfortunately, in trying to keep pace with the rich long novel, this CinemaScope movie has to zip from subplot to subplot and in its commendable but only partly successful effort it lurches through thickets of complication so tangled they're very hard to follow. But it's worth trying. It has aspects of everything from homosexuality

to Greek classicism. The cast is powerful, the screenplay much better than the norm, and the directing tough and fast without sacrificing the story's intriguing character development. While *Warlock* does not succeed as well as it might, still it's one of the few instances where Hollywood tried to come to grips with the Western mythology as an epic of archetypal larger-than-life tragedy. Uneven, but fascinating.

WAR PAINT (1953, UA). D: Lesley Selander. W: Richard Alan Simmons, Martin Berkeley, Fred Freiberger & William Tunberg. Cast: ROBERT STACK, JOAN TAYLOR, Peter GRAVES, Keith LARSEN, Jay Silverheels, Charles McGraw. 89m.

Double crosses and dangerous action face a cavalry officer (Stack) and his detachment when they try to reach an Indian hideout to sign a peace treaty. Rugged little black-and-white horse-opera has good script, plentiful action.

WAR PARTY (1965, FOX). D: Lesley Selander. W: George Williams & William Marks. Cast: BEN JOHNSON, DONALD "RED" BARRY, Laurie MOCK, Davey Davison, Michael T. Mikler.

Cavalry patrol against Comanches. Cheapie is grimmer than most, but predictable.

WARPATH (1951, PARA). D: Byron Haskin. W: Frank Gruber from his novel *Broken Lance*. Cast: EDMOND O'BRIEN, POLLY BERGEN, FORREST TUCKER, DEAN JAGGER, Wallace FORD, Harry CAREY, Jr., James Millican, Robert Bray, Paul Fix, Louis Jean Heydt, Frank Ferguson, Monte Blue, Cliff Clark, Walter Sande, Douglas Spencer, Chief Yowlatchie, Paul Burke, Charles Stevens. 95m.

O'Brien enlists in the Seventh Cavalry in 1876 to get the goods on some bad guys; personal conflicts among soldiers are set against the events leading up to Custer's debacle at Little Big Horn. The plot is a bald imitation of that of Haycox's *Bugles in the Afternoon*, even down to Tucker playing the same Irish sergeant he was to play a few years hence in the Haycox movie (Haycox's novel preceded Gruber's by several years; Gruber was a numbed veteran of the hack cliches and a mainstay of lower-case pulp magazines). O'Brien is miscast. But the budget was large, the Montana location photography (Ray Rennahan) excellent, some of the action exciting, and Millican interesting as Custer.

THE WAR WAGON (1967, UNIV). D: Burt Kennedy. W: Clair Huffaker from his novel *The Badman*. Cast: JOHN WAYNE, KIRK DOUGLAS, Howard KEEL, Robert

WALKER, Jr., Keenan WYNN, Bruce CABOT, Valora Noland, Gene Evans, Joanna Barnes, Bruce Dern, Sheb Wooley, Terry Wilson, Frank McGrath. 101m.

An ex-con (Wayne) was framed into prison by a bad guy (Cabot) who then proceeded to take over Wayne's gold claim; now Wayne returns to get his mine—and his gold—back. But the villain is protecting his gold shipments in an armored stagecoach with a steel turret on top in which he has ensconced a Gatling gun. This vehicle is the war wagon of the title. Wayne gathers a little band of misfit helpers (Douglas, Walker, Keel, Wynn) and they set out to bring off an elaborate but childish caper that involves fooling a pack of Indian warriors into helping them attack the armored coach on one of its gold-shipment runs. It's all played for fun with the emphasis on crude jokes; it's silly but energetic. There are those who like the movie and those who don't. I'm one of those who don't; I find it has no more surprises than a bowl of oatmeal—I love comedy-adventure but I want it to surprise me now and then.

WATERHOLE NO. 3 (1967, PARA). D: William Graham. W: Joseph T. Steck & R. R. Young. Cast: JAMES COBURN, CARROLL O'CONNOR, Joan BLONDELL, Claude AKINS, James WHITMORE, Margaret BLYE, Bruce Dern, Timothy Carey, Rupert Crosse. 95m.

A rogue (Coburn) searching for a hidden gold treasure is pestered by a sex-hungry girl (Blye) and her venal sheriff father (O'Connor). There are also bad guys (Akins, Dern) and the madam of a whorehouse (Blondell). In its attempts to turn conventional morality inside out, the film sometimes succeeds hilariously; it's one of the zanier oater spoofs and the cast is outrageously funny, particularly O'Connor, whose role originally was slated for Henry Fonda, who became ill. Robert Burks's slightly warped color photography helps tilt the movie amusingly. Blake Edwards produced. The film has tiresome stretches but in the main it's fun.

WAY OF A GAUCHO (1952, FOX). D: Jacques Tourneur. W: Philip Dunne from a Herbert Childs novel. Cast: RORY CALHOUN, GENE TIERNEY, Hugh MARLOWE, Richard BOONE, Everett Sloane, Jorge Villaldo, Enrique Chalco. 91m.

A young couple settles in the South American wilderness in the 1870s after hero saves heroine from a fate worse than death; but then hero has to turn outlaw to keep his freedom. The villain is Richard Boone in one of his overblown but effective performances. Filmed on location in Argentina, it's a Western in everything but locale and as such it's a notch above average. Good cast helps.

WAY OUT WEST (1930, MGM). D: Fred Niblo. W: Ralph Spence, Byron Morgan, Joseph Farnham & Alfred Block. Cast: WILLIAM HAINES, Polly MORAN, Charles MIDDLETON, Leila Hyams, Cliff Edwards.

Ranch life reforms a gambler. Early effort was very tame. (Laurel and Hardy made a picture with the same title in 1936; see the appendix.)

THE WAY TO THE GOLD (1957, FOX). D: Robert D. Webb. W: Wendell Mayes from a novel by Wilbur D. Steele. Cast: BARRY SULLIVAN, SHEREE NORTH, JEFFREY HUNTER, Walter BRENNAN, Neville Brand, Ruth Donnelly. 94m.

A young ex-convict (Hunter) knows the location of a stolen treasure. Various greedy types—cardboard stereotypes, mostly—make life miserable for him in their attempt to find it. In black-and-white.

THE WAY WEST (1967, UA). D: Andrew V. McLaglen. W: Ben Maddow & Mitch Lindeman from the novel by A. B. Guthrie, Jr. Cast: KIRK DOUGLAS, ROBERT MITCHUM, RICHARD WIDMARK, Lola ALBRIGHT, Jack ELAM, Sally FIELD, Stubby Kaye, Katherine Justice, Michael Witney, John Mitchum, Peggy Stewart, William Lundigan, Ken Murray, Roy Barcroft, Nick Cravat, Harry Carey, Jr. 122m.

Epic-size yarn follows a Missouri-to-Oregon wagon train in 1843 with the focus on the train's visionary but ruthless leader (Douglas), its earnest populist opponent for leadership (Widmark) and a reluctant trail scout who's struggling with the approach of blindness (Mitchum). The wide-screen photography (William H. Clothier) on Oregon locations is excellent and an enormous budget was expended; the novel was to wagon pioneer stories what Guthrie's *The Big Sky* had been to mountain-man yarns—one of the definitive works. Unhappily the screenwriters failed to capture it and the actors show very little feel for it—the over-lush language doesn't work on their lips. Mitchum comes off best but his role is relatively small. McLaglen usually handles brawling action well (cf. *McLintock*) but renders a flaccid quality in this one to scenes that ought to have been grand and thrilling. Main trouble is the script, though; there's far too much plot for the movie's running time, and as a result the characters aren't developed at all. At the boxoffice it was a disaster.

WELCOME TO HARD TIMES (1967, MGM). DW: Burt Kennedy from E. L. Doctorow's novel. Cast: HENRY FONDA, JANICE RULE, Aldo RAY, Keenan WYNN, Janis PAIGE, John Anderson, Fay Spain, Warren Oates, Edgar Buchanan, Denver Pyle, Royal Dano, Elisha Cook, Jr., Alan Baxter, Paul Fix, Lon Chaney, Jr., Michael Shea. 105m.

Peace-loving citizen (Fonda) is reluctant to do violence against the evil gunman (Ray) who's got the town treed, so he's accused of cowardice until finally of course he has to stand and face up. Marvelous cast is wasted in this boring dud. It's molasses-slow, with a trite script and a visible cheapness of production values—the sets look as if they're about to fall down at any moment. Doctorow's novel deserved much better. (He later wrote *Ragtime*.)

WELLS FARGO (1937, PARA). D: Frank Lloyd. W: Paul Schofield, Gerald Geraghty, Frederick Jackson & Stuart N. Lake. Cast: JOEL McCREA, FRANCES DEE, Bob BURNS, Robert CUMMINGS, Mary Nash, Ralph Morgan, Frank Conroy, Lloyd Nolan, Johnny Mack Brown, Porter Hall, Henry O'Neill, Frank McGlynn, Henry Brandon, Harry Davenport, Lucien Littlefield, Chubby Johnson, Clarence Kolb. 115m.

Saga of the stagecoach-express-banking company's development of the Wild West and California, with McCrea playing a troubleshooting trail blazer, is subordinated to a treacly slow romance and a "B" sort of plot larded with mother-in-law villainy and handkerchief-wringing sentimentality. Often associated with De Mille (he had nothing to do with it), *Wells Fargo* is one of the very few big-budget Westerns of the middle 1930s (another was *Sutter's Gold*); it has a continent-spanning story, an excellent Victor Young score and the first appearance of Joel McCrea in a Western (he'd been a comedy and melodrama star for eight years). He proved at home in the saddle here, and hence his selection as the star of *Union Pacific* two years later; and his real-life wife Frances Dee is fetching and charming as the Southern belle; but the film can be a bore unless you are in a tolerant mood. Much later Stuart Lake dusted off his story material from this script for his TV series *Tales of Wells Fargo*.

WESTBOUND (1959, WB). D: Budd Boetticher. W: Berne Giler & Albert S. LeVino. Cast: RANDOLPH SCOTT, VIRGINIA MAYO, Karen STEELE, Michael Pate, Andrew Duggan, Michael Dante, Wally Brown, Walter Barnes, Rory Mallinson, Jack Perrin, Buddy Roosevelt, Kermit Maynard, Walter Reed. 70m.

Yankee cavalry officer (Scott) puts together a stagecoach line while acting as an undercover agent during the Civil War. One cliche after another; it's one of the least, and one of the last, of the Boetticher-Scott oaters, and one notes that the missing ingredient is writer Burt Kennedy.

THE WESTERNER (1940, UA). D: William Wyler. W: Niven Busch, Jo Swerling & Stuart N. Lake. Cast: GARY COOPER, WALTER BRENNAN, Doris DAVENPORT, Dana Andrews, Forrest Tucker, Chill Wills, Paul Hurst, Lillian Bond, Fred Stone, Joe Sawyer, Tom Tyler, Jack Pennick, Trevor Bardette, Art Mix, Hank Bell, Charles Halton. 100m.

A law-abiding cowhand (Cooper) is accused of horse theft and brought before eccentric Judge Roy Bean (Brennan); by an amusing ruse he cons the judge into turning him loose but then he allies himself against Judge Bean with a group of homesteaders when he falls in love with the daughter (Davenport) of one of the farmers. Judge Bean is behind the cattlemen's night-riding efforts to drive the nesters out; inevitably it all leads to a showdown between cowhand and judge, but only after various complications—stampedes, fires and an epic fist fight between Cooper and the young Forrest Tucker in his movie debut. (It's also Dana Andrews's debut.) Yet within the framework of the hackneyed Stuart Lake plot, scenarists Busch and Swerling and the director and crew and cast created a tense and sophisticated masterpiece. The movie concerns itself primarily with the juxtaposition of the conflicting characters portrayed by Cooper and Brennan. The latter won his third Academy Award for the Roy Bean performance; it is pyrotechnic, a scene-stealer, but it wouldn't work if Cooper didn't play against it so perfectly: Cooper's deliberately heroic cowhand is realized with awesome magnitude. The relationship between the two characters, even though it was original with the movie, takes on the giant proportions of an ancient legend steeped in tradition. *The Westerner* tells its simple story with precise and outstanding cinematic artistry.

WESTERN UNION (1941, FOX). D: Fritz Lang. W: Robert Carson. Cast: ROBERT YOUNG, RANDOLPH SCOTT, DEAN JAGGER, Virginia GILMORE, Barton MacLANE, Slim SUMMERVILLE, Chill Wills, John Carradine, Russell Hicks, Irving Bacon, Victor Kilian, Minor Watson, Addison Richards, Chief Thundercloud, Chief John Big Tree, George Chandler. 94m.

In the heroic pattern set by *Wells Fargo* and *Union Pacific* this yarn thrusts the first telegraph line across the West against opposition by bad guys, hostile Indians, and bad guys disguised as hostile Indians. The love story is a triangle with the construction engineer's (Jagger) sister (Gilmore) torn between the heroic tenderfoot (Young) and the trailwise good-badman (Scott). Barton MacLane's dastardly villainy is painfully silent-movie-ish. Despite its dated drawbacks, however, *Western Union* remains a grand entertainment, probably the best of the epics of its period. The spectacle is energetic, exhibited against fine scenic Technicolor photography (Edward Cronjager), and the marvelous action scenes are adroitly edited (Robert Bischoff). Scott's performance as the doomed fiddlefoot is exemplary—possibly his best before *Ride the High Country*—and the usually heavy-handed Lang directs with surprisingly deft levity. There is some dispute as to whether the screenplay followed or preceded the Zane Grey novel; Grey died a few months before the film was completed, and it is alleged that a nameless hack was hired to ghost-write the novel based on Carson's screenplay, but Grey's supporters claim Grey did in fact write the book before he died, and that the screenplay was based on it, rather than the other way round.

WEST OF MONTANA (1963)—*See* MAIL ORDER BRIDE.

WEST OF THE DIVIDE (1933, MONO). DW: Robert N. Bradbury. Cast: JOHN WAYNE, George "Gabby" HAYES, Virginia Brown Faire, Yakima Canutt, Lloyd Whitlock, Earl Dwire, Lafe McKee, Billy O'Brien. 54m.

Typical of Wayne's early-1930s programmers, this fossil (which is still kicking around) has the usual Bob Steele plot wrapped up in a tight little actioner with amusing incidents—particularly a stunt in which from a galloping horse Canutt dives through a (closed) window—and incredible dialogue. Examples:

Villain (Whitlock) to henchman (Canutt): "I've got another plan. Get back to the hideout—I'll see you there later."

Wayne to villain: "You left me for dead, Gentry, but I lived—lived to even up the score! Why, hangin's too good for you, Gentry!"

And, inevitably, Gabby Hayes to Wayne: "Them fellers is shore in a hurry!"

Given lines like that, is it any wonder the acting is atrocious?

Yet there was an actionful zest to these cheap pictures, and an innocence that makes them perennial objects of adoration by generation after generation of fans. By the early 1980s, many of these old programmers were being resurrected on independent television channels and cable systems, and they sometimes are poignant reminders of times when our dreams and our expectations were much more naive but somehow much more pleasurable than they became in the age of cynicism.

WEST OF THE PECOS (1934, RKO). D: Phil Rosen. W: Milton Krims & John Twist from Zane Grey's novel. Cast: RICHARD DIX, Martha SLEEPER, Fred KOHLER, Samuel S. Hinds, Willie Best, Louise Beavers. 56m.

Old Southern gent (Hinds) lost everything except his daughter (Sleeper) in the Civil War. Hero Pecos (Dix) guides them through hostile Indian country to find a new life. Sentimental, heroic and dated.

WEST OF THE PECOS (1945, RKO). D: Edward Killy. W: Norman Houston from Zane Grey's novel. Cast: ROBERT MITCHUM, BARBARA HALE, Richard MARTIN, Rita Corday, Thurston Hall, Bill Williams, Russell Hopton, Harry Woods, Martin Garralaga. 63m.

Drifting cowhand mixes it up with bandits who've abducted a rancher's daughter. The formula contains no surprises and the plot here has little in common with Grey's novel. But Mitchum carries it valiantly. He starred in two of these "B" entries (the other was *Nevada*) before he went on to better things, at which point the series went briefly to James Warren and finally to Tim Holt, who sustained it for several years along with guitar-strumming sidekick Richard "Chito Rafferty" Martin.

WESTWARD HO THE WAGONS! (1956, BV). D: William Beaudine. W: Tom W. Blackburn from a novel by Mary Jane Carr. Cast: FESS PARKER, KATHLEEN CROWLEY, Jeff YORK, Sebastian CABOT, George Reeves, David Stollery, John War Eagle, Iron Eyes Cody, Tommy Cole. 90m.

Title calls it. Disney was trying to cash in on the success of his Davy Crockett promotions by reteaming Parker and York. But aside from an Indian fight sequence, filmed by second-unit director Yakima Canutt, the movie is rambling and aimless.

WESTWARD THE WOMEN (1951, MGM). D: William Wellman. W: Frank Capra & Charles Schnee. Cast: ROBERT TAYLOR, DENISE DARCEL, Hope EMERSON, John McINTIRE, Beverly Dennis, Julie Bishop, Renata Vanni, Chief Nipo Strongheart, Dorothy Granger, Marilyn Erskine. 118m.

A group of California ranchers send two of their kind (Taylor, McIntire) back to Chicago to escort their wagon train of mail-order brides across the country. Diverting, very well directed in black-and-white. Writer Capra was of course better known as the director of meaty comedies like *It's a Wonderful Life*.

WHEELS OF DESTINY (1934, UNIV). D: Albert S. Rogell. W: Nathanial Gazert. Cast: KEN MAYNARD, DOROTHY DIX, Jay WILSEY, Frank Rice, Freddy Sale, Jr., Philip McCullough, Chief John Big Tree, Hank Bell, Wally Wales. 64m.

Covered-wagon pioneer movie has plenty of rootin'-tootin' action, and Maynard warbles a couple of songs—making him, technically, the first singing cowboy hero, and this the first singing cowboy "B" movie. Produced and soundtrack-scored by Ken Maynard, this was the most ambitious movie of his career. It's cumbersome and dated but interesting to diehard buffs and an excellent introduction to Maynard's frantic stunt work. Additionally this one has huge crowd scenes and visual spectacles—some of them borrowed as stock footage from silent pictures but others filmed freshly for this one with a big cast of supporting Indians.

WHEN THE DALTONS RODE (1940, UNIV). D: George Marshall. W: Harold Shumate from a book by Emmett Dalton & Jack Jungmeyer. Cast: RANDOLPH SCOTT, KAY FRANCIS, Brian DONLEVY, Broderick CRAWFORD, Andy DEVINE, Stuart ERWIN, Frank Albertson, George Bancroft, Edgar Buchanan, Mary Gordon, Dorothy Granger. Narrator (unbilled): Edgar BUCHANAN. 80m.

Biopic about the outlaw Dalton brothers (Donlevy, Crawford, Erwin, Albertson) who robbed trains and banks in 1890 Oklahoma is based on Emmett Dalton's book; he also served as technical advisor. One famous element in this film is Yakima Canutt's unique stunt in which the outlaws jump, on horseback, from a fast-moving train; that stunt has never been repeated, although a faked version of it appears in *Posse*. Photography (Jack Otterson) is good; score (Frank Skinner) is dated. The good-humored actioner whitewashes the miscreants, emphasizes comedy and romance; Scott plays a lawyer who tries to keep the boys out of trouble. A more up-to-date version, equally satisfactory, was the 1979 film *The Last Ride of the Dalton Gang*. This was Kay Francis's only Western and it was Edgar Buchanan's first appearance in a Western; he doesn't receive billing in the title credits; his subsequent—credited—debut was in *Texas*.

WHEN THE LEGENDS DIE (1972, FOX). D: Stuart Millar. W: Robert Dozier from Hal Borland's novel. Cast: RICHARD WIDMARK, FREDERIC FORREST, Luana ANDERS, Vito Scotti, John War Eagle, Jack Mullaney, Herbert Nelson. 105m.

A drunken promoter (Widmark) with his eye on the dollar trains a horse-happy Indian youth (Forrest) as a rodeo bronc rider; it becomes clear that the youth has only exchanged the imprisonment of the reservation for the exploitation of his new white mentor. Low-key movie is nicely written and filmed, with superb characterizations and fine acting by the two leads. It's heavy with sociological messages and that makes it less than a great movie but it's well worth seeing.

WHEN THE NORTH WIND BLOWS (1974, IND). DW: Stewart Raffill. Cast: DAN HAGGERTY, Henry BRANDON, Herbert NELSON.

The story in this Sunn Classic production is interchangeable with those of the Frontier Fremont and Grizzly Adams and Wilderness Family oaters; all the right-wing oversimplifications of fact, theme and plot are securely in place. Good color, good scenery; for undemanding "family" audiences.

WHEN THE REDSKINS RODE (1951, COL). D: Lew Landers. W: Robert E. Kent. Cast: JON HALL, MARY CASTLE, Pedro de CORDOBA, James Seay, John Ridgeley. 78m.

Indian-fighting pioneer yarn, set in the 1750s, is cheap and mildewed.

WHISPERING SMITH (1948, PARA). D: Leslie Fenton. W: Frank Butler & Karl Kamb from Frank H. Spearman's novel. Cast: ALAN LADD, ROBERT PRESTON, BRENDA MARSHALL, Donald CRISP, William DEMAREST, Fay Holden, Murvyn Vye, Frank Fenton, Will Wright, Frank Faylen, Ray Teal, Eddy Waller, John Eldridge, Robert Kortman, Frank Butler, J. Farrell MacDonald. 88m.

Tough railroad detective (Ladd) finds himself pitted against a gang of train robbers led by his old saddle partner (Preston, playing a similar role to the one he played in *Blood on the Moon*). Routine yarn has moments of action. It was Ladd's first starring role in a Western and it's a good production with fine Technicolor photography (Ray Rennahan). It's an "A" remake of the earlier "B" picture *Whispering Smith Rides*, a 1936 20th Century-Fox actioner with George O'Brien.

THE WHITE BUFFALO (1976, UA). D: J. Lee Thompson. W: Richard Sale. Cast: CHARLES BRONSON, WILL SAMPSON, Clint WALKER, Kim NOVAK, Jack WARDEN, Stuart WHITMAN, Slim Pickens, John Carradine, Douglas Fowley, Cara Williams, Bert Williams, David Roy Chandler, Shay Duffin, Scott Walker, Dan Vadis, Linda Moon, Chief Tug Smith, Richard Gilliland, Ed Lauter, Scott Walker. 97m.

Oversized Dino De Laurentiis production stars Bronson as Wild Bill Hickok and Sampson as Chief Crazy Horse—two characters who, in real history and all probability, never met—who set out, each for his own muddled symbolic reasons, to hunt a legendary albino buffalo that has inspired a killer mythology identical to that of the shark in Peter Benchley's *Jaws*. The acting is okay but Thompson cannot direct Westerns (compare *MacKenna's Gold*). Paul Lohmann's cinematography, perpetrated at great expense on Colorado locations and involving very difficult snow work in the Rockies including avalanches, Indian battles and a blizzard, is funereally gloomy, the night scenes so dark you can't see a thing; and John Barry's score is hardly his best. The buffalo—a mechanical monster—is a dud; it looks like a stuffed toy, and so does the film, which was withheld from release for more than a year and then dumped unceremoniously onto the general-circulation market. It's truly awful.

WHITE FEATHER (1955, FOX). D: Robert D. Webb. W: Delmer Daves & Leo Townsend from a John Prebble story. Cast: ROBERT WAGNER, JEFFREY HUNTER, DEBRA PAGET, JOHN LUND, Eduard FRANZ, Noah Beery, Jr., Hugh O'Brian, Milburn Stone. 102m.

A powwow at Fort Laramie tries to persuade the Cheyennes (Hunter, Paget, Franz) to move to a new reservation; when they resist the idea, a young surveyor (Wagner) tries to maintain the peace. It's sincere but dull; Prebble, an Englishman, had a warped sense of the West, and mostly the cast is not convincingly Western.

WHITE SQUAW (1956, COL). D: Ray Nazarro. W: Les Savage, Jr., from a novel by Larabie Sutter. Cast: DAVID BRIAN, MAY WYNN, William BISHOP, Grant Withers, Nancy Hale, Myron Healey. 75m.

The government and a white rancher are the antagonists in this dreary yarn about a rancher who doesn't want his land given back to the Indians.

WICHITA (1955, AA). D: Jacques Tourneur. W: Daniel B. Ullman. Cast: JOEL McCREA, VERA MILES, Lloyd BRIDGES, Peter GRAVES, Edgar BUCHANAN, Wallace FORD, Keith LARSEN, Carl Benton Reid, Walter Sande. 81m.

According to Wyatt Earp and his authorized biographer Stuart N. Lake (who served as technical advisor on this one), Earp started out as a buffalo hunter whose first law-officer job was as marshal of the wild and woolly railhead cowtown Wichita, Kansas. Actually Earp was never the marshal of Wichita or of anyplace else for that matter, but forget the facts; the question is whether the movie does a respectable job of reflecting the legends and presenting a drama, and this one does. It's a good minor Western with an excellent cast, very well directed.

THE WILD AND THE INNOCENT (1959, UNIV). D: Jack Sher. W: Sher and Sy Gombert. Cast: AUDIE MURPHY, SANDRA DEE, GILBERT ROLAND, JOANNE DRU, Jim BACKUS, Peter Breck, George Mitchell. 84m.

Oddball yarn concerns a young fur trapper (Murphy), a wild mountain girl (Dee) and their adventures on July Fourth in a frontier town. Lighthearted and lightweight, the comedy is backwoodsy and rustic but very well done. Jack Sher contributed a great deal to the screenplay of *Shane* and this rare directorial attempt was comfortably successful.

WILD BILL HICKOK RIDES (1942, WB). D: Ray Enright. W: Charles Grayson, Paul G. Smith & Raymond Schrock. Cast: BRUCE CABOT, CONSTANCE BENNETT, Warren WILLIAM, Faye EMERSON, Ward Bond, Betty Brewer, Russell Simpson, Howard Da Silva, Frank Wilcox.

Standard land-grabber oater has our hero saving an honest rancher's outfit from the land-grabbers; Constance Bennett, miscast as a dance-hall hostess, was thrown into this cheapie as penance for some infraction of Jack L. Warner's house rules. This near-"B" horse-opera was Warner Brothers's only feature Western of 1942, and there were none at all in 1943 or 1944.

THE WILD BUNCH (1969, WB). D: Sam Peckinpah. W: Peckinpah, Walon Green, Roy N. Sickner and (uncredited) Lee Marvin. Cast: WILLIAM HOLDEN, ERNEST BORGNINE, ROBERT RYAN, Edmond O'BRIEN, Warren OATES, Jaime SANCHEZ, Ben JOHNSON, Strother MARTIN, Albert DEKKER, Emilio FERNANDEZ, L. Q. JONES, Alfonso Arau, Dub Taylor, Elsa Cardenas, John Davis Chandler, Bo Hopkins, Jorge Russek, Chano

Urueta, Sonia Amelio, Aurora Clavel, Fernando Wagner, Paul Harper, Constance White, Lilia Richards, Sam Peckinpah. 144m.

The Wild Bunch concerns a group of aging outlaws in 1912 who are being pursued by a former partner (Ryan) in the employ of a nasty railroad boss (Dekker), and who—having been decimated in an ambush and then fled into Mexico—take a job that is offered by Mapache (Fernandez), a drunken antirevolutionary "general." Angel (Sanchez), the youngest member of the Bunch, is himself a revolutionary, and when Mapache learns this, he tortures the young man. The other outlaws at first attempt to ignore Angel's plight; they try to maintain an every-man-for-himself attitude and to ignore the fact that they are trapped between a distrustful host and the pursuing posse that lurks just outside the encampment (Ryan, Martin, Jones). But it is Angel, with his dedication to "my people, my village—Mexico," who finally reminds Pike and Dutch and Lyle and Tector (Holden, Borgnine, Oates, Johnson) that there is, after all, something still worth fighting for. He reminds them of their moral commitments. Against enormous odds, the four of them set out to rescue him.

In the ending—wildly violent—we see them honor Angel's principles. They **redeem** themselves in a catharsis of blood.

Along the way there are a balletically gory opening battle sequence, a number of lyrical scenes that are by turns tense and funny, a taut, exciting, train robbery sequence, and a face-off between the Wild Bunch and a Mexican army battalion that features a wonderful echo, by Alfonso Arau as lieutenant Herrera, of Alfonso Bedoya's grinning killer in *The Treasure of the Sierra Madre*.

It all is edited together magnificently (film editor Louis Lombardo), although a warning must be issued that the version shown in most theatres is incomplete, lacking not only the army-versus-rebels battle but also several key flashback scenes that serve to illuminate the relationship between Holden and Ryan as well as the rootlessness that Pike (Holden) has felt ever since the woman he loved was shot by her own husband, who also inflicted on Pike the leg injury that now makes him vulnerable to the ridicule of his men. Peckinpah's original cut ran 152 minutes in length; for the sake of pacing, he voluntarily cut it to 144 minutes. (This version apparently is still available from one or two sources in 16mm CinemaScope.) Then the studio and producer Phil Feldman went at it with another set of snips, bringing it down to the 134-minute 35mm wide-screen print that is normally shown. The resulting gaps don't destroy the film but they do delete and dilute several key elements. (Yet another version, shown in Europe, was in 75mm and included one or two scenes never shown in any American version; and in America, still shorter versions—a 123-minute videocassette print that Warners fraudulently proffered as "uncut" and a thoroughly butchered-for-TV one—render the film almost unintelligible.)

The film is discussed in further detail in Chapter 5. The superb, but sometimes gimmicky and attention-demanding, photography is by Lucien Ballard. The Oscar-winning score is by Jerry Fielding. The characters, beautifully portrayed by fine actors, are sometimes rudimentarily drawn and the relationships among them are rather sketchily established because *The Wild Bunch* offers the kind of glimpses one would get in reality, rather than filling up its screen time with expository summaries: most of these characters have known each other for years, and the dialogue among them is the terse kind of shorthand that people use when they know each other so well they can read one another's thoughts. This aspect makes the audience a bit of an outsider, and that exclusion offends some audiences who aren't willing to work a bit in order to achieve an understanding of the film.

Peckinpah undoubtedly contributed a great deal to the precise composition of the film, but he didn't originate the story. It was created by actor Lee Marvin and Walon Green, and refined by associate producer Roy Sickner, before Peckinpah got his hands on it. How much he changed it I can't say, since I have only seen the Peckinpah version of the screenplay, but a comparison of this film with the others that Peckinpah wrote or co-wrote leads to the conclusion that someone other than Peckinpah must have been partly, perhaps chiefly, responsible for the exquisite and elaborate quality of the story and especially the characterizations of this picture. (His only other Western with extraordinarily well-drawn characters is *Ride the High Country*, and he didn't write that one.)

Some critics called *The Wild Bunch* the worst movie of the year; others called it one of the best. Like it or not, it is unquestionably the most powerful Western since *The Searchers*—a landmark film. It especially seems to inspire critical divisiveness between men and women (I have met very few women who liked it, and can recall no female critics who approved of it); those who find fault with it object most strenuously to its lengthy depictions of bloodletting, all of which contain graceful slow-motion intercuts, rendering the violence rhythmic and quite beautiful. To these critics and audiences, the film appears to be simply a childish tantrum on film. I must disagree with that appraisal; it seems to me that *The Wild Bunch* is one of the greatest and most important films of its own time or any other.

THE WILD DAKOTAS (1956, IND). **D: Sam Newfield. W: Tom W. Blackburn. Cast: BILL WILLIAMS, COLEEN GRAY, Jim DAVIS, Dick JONES, Lisa Montell, John Litel.**

Wagon-train boss tries to establish a phony claim to Arapaho land; a heroic surveyor thwarts his scheme and tries to head off an Indian war. Williams is an unconvincing Westerner and the old-hat yarn is weary.

WILD GIRL (1932, FOX). **D: Raoul Walsh. W: Doris Anderson & Edwin J. Mayer** from Bret Harte's story *Salomy Jane*. **Cast: CHARLES FARRELL, JOAN BENNETT, Ralph BELLAMY, Eugene Pallette, Irving Pichel, Minna Gombell, Sarah Padden, Willard Robertson, Louise Beavers. 78m.**

Catching villain seducing his sister, an upright young fellow kills the villain and ends up on the run. He is guided and succored by a wild young girl. Creaky wilderness romance was popular in its day.

WILD HERITAGE (1958, UNIV). **D: Charles Haas. W: Paul King & Joseph Stone** from a Steve Frazee story. **Cast: WILL ROGERS, JR., MAUREEN O'SULLIVAN, TROY DONAHUE, Gigi PERREAU, George "Foghorn" Winslow, Rod McKuen, Casey Tibbs. 77m.**

Leisurely yarn treats the trials and joys experienced by pioneer families trekking westward. It has charm and an engaging cast including poet McKuen and rodeo champ Tibbs and the kid whose voice lives up to his nickname. Mildly adventurous family fare.

WILD HORSE MESA (1932, PARA). **D: Henry Hathaway. W: Harold Shumate & Frank H. Clark** from Zane Grey's novel. **Cast: RANDOLPH SCOTT, SALLY BLANE, Charlie GRAPEWIN, Fred Kohler, George "Gabby" Hayes, Jim Thorpe, Buddy Roosevelt, Lucille LaVerne, James Bush. 61m.**

Bad guys are illegally trapping wild horses in barbed-wire enclosures; hero traps them in the act. Highlight is a stampede. Its professional production values are typical of the Hathaway-Scott Zane Grey Paramounters of the period, of which this was the second. It uses stock footage from the 1925 si-

lent version; and was remade as a "B" entry in 1947.

WILD MUSTANG (1935, IND). **D: Harry Fraser. W: Weston Edwards & Monroe Talbot. Cast: HARRY CAREY, Barbara FRITCHIE, Cathryn Johns, Robert Kortman, George Chesebro, Dell Gordon, Richard Boteler. 57m.**

It's good brother versus bad brother in this horse-taming adventure, a "B" sort of film released by a Poverty Row indie outfit called Ajax.

THE WILD NORTH (1952, MGM). **D: Andrew Marton. W: Frank Fenton from a book by Walter W. Liggett. Cast: STEWART GRANGER, WENDELL COREY, CYD CHARISSE, Morgan Farley, J. M. Kerrigan, Ray Teal, Houseley Stevenson, Howard Petrie, John War Eagle. 97m.**

A dogsled-and-canoe Western, this misses the bull's-eye but hits close to it. Story has a French-Canadian trapper (Granger) pursued and captured in the snowy Far North by a stalwart Mountie (Corey); then the two must brave a tough winter passage back to civilization and keep from being killed by one another. Of the numerous plot twists some are unexpected, and it achieves occasional emotional effectiveness. But there are juvenile contrivances as well, and a slick Hollywood ending. Granger, accent and all, is fine. The music (Bronislau Kaper) and the vast Idaho location photography (Robert Surtees) are very effective. The action is directed with verve and a lively sense of authenticity. And when you watch Wendell Corey perform in his casual way you're forced to realize what a marvelous screen actor he was: in the end it is Corey who overpowers this one and makes it an exceptional adventure film.

WILD ROVERS (1971, MGM). **DW: Blake Edwards. Cast: WILLIAM HOLDEN, RYAN O'NEAL, Karl MALDEN, Lynn CARLIN, Joe Don BAKER, Tom Skerritt, James Olson, Moses Gunn, Rachel Roberts. 109m.**

Frustrated by boredom and poverty an old cowhand (Holden) and a young one (O'Neal) team up to rob a bank so they can live in style. Dubious morality aside, it's a pompous movie afflicted with asinine philosophizing ("Let's you and me rob us a bank," says O'Neal; Holden replies, "That's safer'n gettin' married"). The characters are made of tissue paper and the plot goes nowhere. Photography (Philip Lathrop & Frank Stanley) is fair; score (Jerry Goldsmith) is acceptable. Edwards claims the picture was sabotaged by MGM's James Aubrey but there isn't much evidence that added footage could have saved it. It's boring.

WILD TIMES (1980, IND). D: Richard Compton. W: Don Balluck and (uncredited) Douglas Netter & Jim Byrnes from Brian Garfield's novel. Cast: SAM ELLIOTT, BEN JOHNSON, Pat HINGLE, Penny PEYSER, Timothy SCOTT, Bruce BOXLEITNER, Cameron Mitchell, Leif Erickson, Trish Stewart, Dennis Hopper, L. Q. Jones, Harry Carey, Jr., Gene Evans, Buck Taylor, Geno Silva, Marianne Marks, R. L. Tolbert, Brian Garfield. 200m.

Western about the Western concerns real plains heroes (Elliott, Johnson, Scott) and how they become legends, partly through their own tall-tale-spinning and partly through the exaggerations of a dime novelist (Hingle), who puts them in stage melodramas and then a Wild West Show. The fiction is based loosely on the lives of Doc Carver and Buffalo Bill. Cinematographer John Flinn III shot the picture in wide-screen Panavision for overseas distribution in theatres; in America it was designed, and released, as a television miniseries. Score is by Jerrold Immel. I found it particularly fitting that some of the film was shot on the very Sand Canyon (California) locations where, according to Harry Carey, Jr., his father had chased on-camera rustlers as early as 1912. (Other parts of *Wild Times* were filmed in New Mexico.) I can't very well offer a critique, since it's my own film. Yes, that's me in the "extra" bit as the guy in eyeshade and sleeve garters who sells tickets to the Wild West Show.

THE WILD WEST (1975, IND). Compiled by Laurence Lee Joachim and Barbara Holden.

I didn't get to see this pastiche of film clips featuring, among others, John Wayne, Clint Eastwood, Charles Bronson, Glenn Ford, Henry Fonda, Robert Mitchum, Gregory Peck, Randolph Scott, Richard Widmark, Joel McCrea, Sterling Hayden, Gene Autry, Rod Cameron, William Elliott, Lash LaRue, Tim McCoy, Roy Rogers, Angie Dickinson, Joan Crawford, Grace Kelly, Maureen O'Hara, Barbara Stanwyck, Donald Barry, Robert Blake, Pedro Armendariz, Ernest Borgnine, Lee Van Cleef, John Derek, Buster Crabbe, Fred MacMurray, Ray Milland, Mickey Rooney, Robert Vaughn and Barry Sullivan.

THE WILD WESTERNERS (1962, COL). D: Oscar Rudolph. W: Gerald Drayson Adams. Cast: GUY MITCHELL, James PHILBROOK, Nancy KOVACK, Duane Eddy. 70m.

Confused Civil War "Z" meller concerns a marshal, his bride and a shipment of gold destined for the Union's coffers back East.

WILL PENNY (1968, PARA). DW: Tom Gries. Cast: CHARLTON HESTON, JOAN HACKETT, Donald PLEASENCE, Lee MAJORS, Bruce DERN, Ben JOHNSON, Slim Pickens, Anthony Zerbe, Clifton James, William Schallert, Luke Askew, Lydia Clarke, Quentin Dean. 108m.

Old beat-up cowhand (Heston) finds himself outmoded and useless; the story emphasizes the hardships of frontier life, the harsh challenges of winter survival in the Rockies, the loneliness of a way of life that is anything but glamorous. Still, much of the movie dissipates into a tired, slick-magazine-style romance between Heston and dude widow Hackett, and a hard-to-swallow conflict between Will Penny and a gang of stylized grubby rawhider villains played with scenery-chewing viciousness by Donald Pleasence, Bruce Dern and others: rustic hillbilly psychotics straight out of the television cliche factory. It is this idiocy, evidently perpetrated with an eye toward the action market, that spoils the movie; it is much less than the little masterpiece some critics would have it be. Still, Heston delivers a stirring, stunning performance, and it's quite a good movie, although the similar *Monte Walsh* was superior to it.

WINCHESTER '73 (1950, UNIV). D: Anthony Mann. W: Borden Chase, Robert L. Richards & Stuart N. Lake. Cast: JAMES STEWART, SHELLEY WINTERS, DAN DURYEA, Stephen McNALLY, Millard MITCHELL, John McINTIRE, Charles Drake, Will Geer, Steve Brodie, Jay C. Flippen, James Millican, James Best, Rock Hudson, Tony Curtis. 92m.

A drifter's (Stewart) prize rifle is stolen and he sets out to get it back; the chase covers a lot of territory and involves everything from romance to a cavalry-Indian battle. The long mountain duel between Stewart and Duryea at the finale is a stirring action climax. The screenplay contains a good deal of welcome humor; the characters are sharply drawn and broadly played. Fine photography (William Daniels, noted for his cinematography dating back as far as Erich von Stroheim's *Greed*). Note Tony Curtis and Rock Hudson (the latter as Young Bull, warrior) in small roles—both were young contract players on the lot. Wyatt Earp (Geer) figures as a character in the opening shooting-contest sequence, set in Dodge City. Stewart, in career doldrums, made a comeback in two Westerns that were filmed back-to-back: this one and *Broken Arrow*. Although *Arrow* was the bigger of the two (filmed in color; this one is black-and-

WAGONMASTER (1950):
Ben Johnson, Harry Carey,
Jr. (on fence), Ward Bond,
Russell Simpson, Joanne
Dru. Two cheerful drifters
and a Mormon wagon train:
John Ford's leisurely elegy
to an old friend. RKO
Radio Pictures

WALK TALL (1960):
Willard Parker, Joyce
Meadows, Kent Taylor.
Overage stars in a limp
programmer. Twentieth
Century-Fox

WARLOCK (1959):
Anthony Quinn,
Henry Fonda. Aspects
of homosexuality and
Greek tragedy: one of
the few Hollywood at-
tempts to come to
grips with mythology
as archetypal
tragedy. Twentieth
Century-Fox

WARPATH (1951):
Edmond O'Brien, For-
rest Tucker. Imitation
Haycox and the hero is
miscast. Paramount
Pictures

351

THE WAY WEST
(1967): Robert Mit-
chum, Kirk Douglas.
Leading the wagon
train across an epic
landscape; but the
film is a dud.
United Artists

THE WESTERNER (1940):
Walter Bren-
nan (with holstered
gun), Chill Wills
(black neckerchief),
Gary Cooper (fringed
jacket). A tense and
sophisticated master-
piece with two towering
performances.
United Artists

WESTERN UNION
(1941): Robert Young,
Randolph Scott. In the
heroic pattern; Scott's
performance as the
doomed good-badman
is exemplary. Twen-
tieth Century-Fox

THE WILD BUNCH
(1969): Strother Martin,
L. Q. Jones, Robert Ryan.
Deke Thornton (Ryan) is
bitter because his posse consists of these "chicken-steal-
ing gutter trash." Warner
Brothers

THE WILD BUNCH
(1969): Ben Johnson, Wil-
liam Holden. Trapped be-
tween a distrustful host and
the pursuing posse that lurks
just outside. One of the great
Westerns. Warner Brothers

WILD ROVERS
(1971): William Hol-
den, Ryan O'Neal.
Dubious morality in a
pompous movie, but
Holden, as always, is
just fine. MGM

WILL PENNY (1968): Charlton Heston, as an old beat-up cowhand who finds himself outmoded and useless, delivers a stirring, stunning performance. Paramount Pictures

WINCHESTER '73 (1950): Will Geer (hands clasped), Stephen McNally (with rifle), James Stewart (light hat). A suspenseful and superior film. Universal Pictures

THE WONDERFUL COUNTRY (1959): Robert Mitchum in action as a hard-bitten and rather simple pistolero. The title refers to Mexico. United Artists

white) and received more attention because of its theme, dramatically *Winchester '73* is the superior film.

WINCHESTER '73 (1967, UNIV). D: Herschel Daugherty. W: Daugherty, Robert L. Richards & Richard Reeves from the screenplay for the 1950 version. Cast: TOM TRYON, JOHN SAXON, DAN DURYEA, Joan BLONDELL, John Drew BARRYMORE, Paul Fix, John Dehner, Barbara Luna, John Doucette, Jack Lambert, John Hoyt, Ned Romero. 97m.

Made-for-TV remake is diluted to a sadly juvenile level, with John Saxon taking over the bad-brother role from Duryea, who here assumes an older part, that of the uncle. Blondell is an improvement over Winters but Tryon makes a bland soporific hero. Sluggish, amateurish movie is an incompetent shambles.

WINDWALKER (1981, IND). D: Keith Merrill. W: Ray Goldrup from Blaine M. Yorgason's novel. Cast: TREVOR HOWARD, Nick RAMUS, James Remar, Serene Hedin, Dusty Iron Wing McCrea, Silvana Gallardo, Rudy Diaz. 108m.

A very old Indian relates to his grandchildren the adventures of his bygone youth, when his infant son was kidnapped and he embarked on a long search for him. The film is unique in several respects. For one thing there are no non-Indian characters. Dialogue is in the Crow and Cheyenne tongues; there are subtitles, and some narration, in English. Unhappily Trevor Howard, a fine British actor, is unconvincing and out of place as the dying old Cheyenne warrior. Utah snowscape photography by Reed Smoot is excellent without indulging in hackneyed images, and there is a very good score by Merrill Jensen. This one is far superior to most of the wilderness-family junk genre.

WINGS OF THE HAWK (1953, UNIV). D: Budd Boetticher. W: James E. Moser & Kay Lenard from a novel by Gerald D. Adams. Cast: VAN HEFLIN, JULIA ADAMS, Rodolfo ACOSTA, Abbe LANE, Antonio Moreno, Noah Beery, Jr., George Dolenz, Pedro Gonzalez-Gonzalez. 81m.

A gringo engineer gets caught up in Pancho Villa's 1910 Mexican Revolution. Boetticher keeps it whizzing along and the cast is fine but it's nothing special. Filmed in 3-D.

WINTERHAWK (1976, IND). DW: Charles B. Pierce; narration written by Earl E. Smith. Cast: MICHAEL DANTE, Leif ERICKSON, Woody STRODE, Denver PYLE, L. Q. JONES, Sacheen LITTLEFEATHER, Elisha Cook, Jr., Arthur Hunnicutt, Seaman Glass, Dennis Fimple, Dawn Wells. 98m.

Young white girl is kidnapped by a young Blackfoot Indian (Dante); a pursuit ensues. The title character is depicted as a mystic superhuman cartoon caricature and the other roles are written with similar oversimplification. White villains are shown as dastardly cowards while Indian heroes are improbably virtuous. And the moral basis for the plot is reprehensible—as if kidnapping innocent people were a legitimate solution to grievances. It's draggy, but sometimes overly brutal, with too much slow-motion photography, although the scenery (photographed by Jim Roberson) is rugged and attractive. Good cast is sadly wasted.

WOMAN HUNGRY (1931, WB). D: Clarence Badger. W: Jack Cunningham, Charles Logue & Carl A. Buss from William Vaughn Moody's play *The Great Divide*. Cast: SIDNEY BLACKMER, LILA LEE, Fred KOHLER, Raymond HATTON, Kenneth Thomson, J. Farrell MacDonald.

Very early color Western was a remake of *The Great Divide*, released only a year previously.

WOMAN OF THE NORTH COUNTRY (1952, REP). D: Joseph Kane. W: Norman Reilly Raine, Charles Marquis Warren & Prescott Chaplin. Cast: ROD CAMERON, GALE STORM, Ruth HUSSEY, John AGAR, J. Carrol Naish. 90m.

Meller is set in the Klondike during the gold rush with claim-jumping and ample romancing. It was intended as a vehicle for Vera Ralston but Storm replaced her; it was Storm's last movie to date.

THE WOMAN OF THE TOWN (1943, UA). D: George Archainbaud. W: Aeneas MacKenzie & Norman Houston. Cast: CLAIRE TREVOR, ALBERT DEKKER, BARRY SULLIVAN, Henry HULL, Marion MARTIN, Percy Kilbride, Porter Hall, Dorothy Granger, Clem Bevans, George Cleveland, Beryl Wallace, Teddi Sherman, Russell Hicks, Hal Taliaferro, Glenn Strange, Russell Simpson. 90m.

Honky tonk singer (Trevor) romances Sheriff Bat Masterson (Dekker) in old Dodge City. The cast is fine but there's too much romancing and not enough action for Western fans, and just the reverse for soap-opera fans.

THE WOMAN THEY ALMOST LYNCHED (1953, REP). D: Allan Dwan. W: Steve Fisher from a Michael Fessier story. Cast: JOAN LESLIE, JOHN LUND, Brian DONLEVY, Audrey TOTTER, Ellen Corby, Jim Davis, Minerva Urecal. 90m.

During the Civil War a young Eastern girl learns how to handle roughnecks in a tough Missouri border town. For her efforts she's nearly hanged as a spy. This again has all the stylistic earmarks of a Vera Ralston vehicle, although she wasn't in it: the tear-jerker script, the Trucolor back-lot scenery, the respectable stock-company cast.

THE WONDERFUL COUNTRY (1959, UA). D: Robert Parrish. W: Robert Ardrey from Tom Lea's novel. Cast: ROBERT MITCHUM, JULIE LONDON, PEDRO ARMENDARIZ, Gary MERRILL, Albert DEKKER, Jack OAKIE, Charles McGraw, Anthony Caruso, Mike Kellin, Victor Manuel Mendoza, Satchel Paige, Tom Lea. 96m.

A hard-bitten and rather simple pistolero (Mitchum) crosses the Rio Grande into Texas to buy arms for a Mexican rebel (Armendariz) in the 1870s. He becomes entangled with the wife (London) of a straitlaced army officer (Merrill) and with various gringos, Mexicans and Indians. It's hard and tough but quite slow despite the good story and screenplay; part of the difficulty is that the hero spends much of his time in a cast with a broken leg and as a result the film is, for long stretches, actionless. But it's skillfully filmed with fine photography (Lloyd Crosby, Alex Phillips) and an outstanding score (Alex North). Acting honors go to Mitchum (who produced it), Armendariz and McGraw, the latter as an irascible doctor. The title, incidentally, refers to Mexico.

THE WRATH OF GOD (1973, MGM). DW: Ralph Nelson from a James Graham novel. Cast: ROBERT MITCHUM, FRANK LANGELLA, RITA HAYWORTH, Victor BUONO, Paula Pritchett, Ken Hutchinson, John Colicos, Gregory Sierra, Frank Ramirez. 111m.

In revolution-torn 1920 Mexico a whisky priest (Mitchum) turns gunslinger, joining up with a fugitive IRA terrorist (Hutchinson) and a fat gringo rogue (Buono), fighting it out with the minions of a tinpot despot (Langella) and his lecherous mother (Hayworth). A great deal of machine-gun carnage ensues, both inside and outside churches. Good cinematography (Alex Phillips, Jr., in wide screen) and a good score (Lalo Schifrin) bolster the implausible story, but the three "heroes" are distasteful characters. The story lacks a sympathetic focus. But the mayhem is plentiful. Mitchum seems somnambulistic and the rest of the players chew up the sets; it's a confused movie. Nelson is a director of unarguable talent (*The Lilies of the Field*, *Requiem for a Heavyweight*) but he managed to make three lousy Westerns in a row (the other

two: *Soldier Blue* and *Duel at Diablo*). Note that the novelist "James Graham" is the English thriller-writer Harry Patterson, best known under another pen-name: Jack Higgins.

WYOMING (1940, MGM). Also titled: BAD MAN OF WYOMING. D: Richard Thorpe. W: Jack Jevne & Hugo Butler. Cast: WALLACE BEERY, ANN RUTHERFORD, Marjorie MAIN, Leo CARRILLO, Joseph CALLEIA, Lee Bowman, Bob Watson. 88m.

Yet another reform-the-badman comedy is for those who have acquired a taste for Beery.

WYOMING (1947, REP). D: Joseph Kane. W: Gerald Geraghty & Lawrence Hazard. Cast: WILLIAM ELLIOTT, VERA HRUBA RALSTON, JOHN CARROLL, George "Gabby" HAYES, Albert DEKKER, Virginia GREY, Roy Barcroft, Grant Withers, Dick Curtis, Harry Woods, Maria Ouspenskaya, Francis J. McDonald. 84m.

Hero attempts to resolve a range war instigated by a land baron (Dekker) who wants to drive the nesters out. Ralston's performance is typically emotive but she's less in the foreground than usual. The players are typecast, the script mostly formulaic, the directing typically speedy; it's a pretty good Elliott oater but rather juvenile.

THE WYOMING KID (1947, WB). Also titled: CHEYENNE. D: Raoul Walsh. W: Alan LeMay, Paul I. Wellman & Thames Williamson. Cast: DENNIS MORGAN, JANE WYMAN, ARTHUR KENNEDY, Janis PAIGE, Bruce BENNETT, Alan Hale, Jr., Barton MacLane, Bob Steele, Monte Blue, John Ridgely, Tom Tyler, Tom Fadden, Britt Wood. 100m.

A gambler (Morgan) is hired to track down a notorious outlaw (Kennedy) but falls for the outlaw's wife and of course this complicates everything. Screenplay is okay but Walsh was unable to make any of his five stars believable as a Westerner; the old-fashioned formula picture is pretty laughable as a result.

WYOMING MAIL (1950, UNIV). D: Reginald LeBorg. W: Harry Essex, Leonard Lee & Robert H. Andrews. Cast: STEPHEN McNALLY, ALEXIS SMITH, Howard DA SILVA, Roy Roberts, Dan Riss, Armando Silvestre, Ed Begley, Gene Evans, Whit Bissell, James Arness, Richard Jaeckel, Richard Egan, Roy Wilkerson, Chris-Pin Martin, Frankie Darro, Frank Fenton. 87m.

Undercover agent unmasks a gang of road agents. Again. It's okay, in color, with a supporting cast of up-and-coming players; Begley, as a crooked prison warden, is very good, and so is Arness as a tough member of Da Silva's outlaw band, and the furious plot twists are absurd but sort of fun. McNally, unfortunately, is physically miscast as the hard-bellied bare-knuckle boxer hero.

WYOMING RENEGADES (1955, COL). D: Fred F. Sears. W: David Lang. Cast: PHILIP CAREY, MARTHA HYER, William BISHOP, Gene Evans, Douglas Kennedy, Aaron Spelling, John Cason. 73m.

The one about the outlaw who wants to go straight. Muddled and overacted.

YAQUI DRUMS (1956, AA). D: Jean Yarborough. W: D. D. Beauchamp, Jo Pagano & Paul L. Peil. Cast: ROD CAMERON, MARY CASTLE, Robert HUTTON, J. Carrol NAISH, Denver Pyle, Roy Roberts, Ray Walker. 71m.

Honest rancher comes to blows with a nasty saloonkeeper who has land-grabbing ambitions. Wheezy cheapie is in black-and-white. Incidentally, writer "Bud" Beauchamp pronounced his name "Bo-champ," not "Beechum."

YELLOW DUST (1936, RKO). D: Wallace Fox. W: Cyril Hume, John Twist & Jack Townley from a play by Dan Totheroh & George O'Neil. Cast: RICHARD DIX, LEILA HYAMS, Moroni OLSEN, Jessie Ralph, Andy Clyde, Onslow Stevens.

Prospector (Dix), en route to file his claim, falls in love with a lady singer; flat comic complications ensue, accompanied by songs. Dated burlesque was the third, last and least of the programmers Dix made at RKO in the mid-1930s (the others: *West of the Pecos* and *The Arizonian*). Remake of 1924 silent version.

YELLOW MOUNTAIN (1955, UNIV). D: Jesse Hibbs. W: George Zuckerman, Russell Hughes & Robert Blees from a story by Harold C. Wire. Cast: LEX BARKER, MALA POWERS, HOWARD DUFF, William DEMAREST, John McINTIRE. 78m.

The one about the search for gold under an Indian-infested mountain with bad guys chasing good guys in an attempt to find the gold. Good supporting cast doesn't make up for poor story and wretched acting by Barker.

YELLOW SKY (1948, FOX). D: William Wellman. W: Lamar Trotti & W. R. Burnett. Cast: GREGORY PECK, ANNE BAXTER, RICHARD WIDMARK, Edgar BUCHANAN, John RUSSELL, Harry MORGAN, Robert ARTHUR, James BARTON, Jay Silverheels, Charles Kemper, Victor Kilian, Paul Hurst. 98m.

A hard-bitten gang of outlaws (Peck, Widmark, Russell et al.) rides into a ghost town inhabited only by a stubborn old prospector (Barton) and his comely tomboy granddaughter (Baxter). The outlaws begin to believe the old man has a fortune buried somewhere in town; they mean to get it. Then the outlaw leader (Peck) begins to fall for the girl; it causes a split between him and the rest of the gang. The pressure builds as the outlaws stalk him. It's not a fast action picture but rather a stark and very tense one with carefully developed character conflicts and the kind of hard pictorial imagery Wellman had used before in *The Ox-Bow Incident*, photographed stunningly here by Joseph MacDonald; there's a brooding quiet score by Alfred Newman. It's not a masterpiece—it's quite conventional in plot and development—but it's an excellent, grim, little movie, very taut and involving and suspenseful.

YELLOWSTONE KELLY (1959, WB). D: Gordon Douglas. W: Burt Kennedy from a Clay Fisher novel. Cast: CLINT WALKER, Edward BYRNES, John RUSSELL, Andra MARTIN, Ray Danton, Warren Oates, Claude Akins, Rhodes Reason, Gary Vinson. 91m.

The cast of this one was assembled from the Warners television stock company; the plot has two trappers (Walker, Byrnes) and an Indian girl (Martin) caught up in a Sioux (Russell, Danton) uprising and forced to spy for the army (Reason). Nothing new but it's a competent compact "B" oater with excellent location photography (Carl Guthrie), and Walker—as he often does—brings a surprisingly effective dignity to his role.

THE YELLOW TOMAHAWK (1954, UA). D: Lesley Selander. W: Richard Alan Simmons & Harold Jack Bloom. Cast: RORY CALHOUN, PEGGIE CASTLE, Noah BEERY, Jr., Peter GRAVES, Warner Anderson, Lee Van Cleef, Rita Moreno. 82m.

A scout tries to protect settlers against a Cheyenne uprising. Emphasis is on tame sex; it's dated and dull.

YOUNG BILLY YOUNG (1969, UA). DW: Burt Kennedy from Will Henry's novel *Who Rides with Wyatt*. Cast: ROBERT MITCHUM, ANGIE DICKINSON, ROBERT WALKER, Jr., David CARRADINE, John ANDERSON, Jack KELLY, Paul Fix, Willis Bouchey, Rodolfo Acosta, Deana Martin. 89m.

The novel was about Wyatt Earp and his supposed friendship with Billy Clanton, the outlaw; the screenplay changes the names. Earp becomes Marshal Kane (Mitchum—a steal from the name of the Gary Cooper character in *High Noon*), Clanton becomes Billy Young (Walker), and Jack Kelly plays the villain, John Behan, a saloonkeeper-killer—but in fact John Behan was the real sheriff of Tombstone when the Earps were there fighting the Clantons. This awkward reassembling of names and functions keys the weakness of the film, which has very little in common with the good novel; the plot has been revamped into cliches. Embittered lawman, tracking the man who killed his son, finds him in a hostile town and has to fight off everybody while protecting a wild but well-intentioned juvenile delinquent who reminds him of his dead son. Rory Calhoun appeared in several oaters with similar plots; Mitchum is wasted on it. The music (Shelly Manne) is okay, the title song is sung by Mitchum, and the photography (Harry Stradling) is acceptable, but it's a lacklustre movie.

YOUNG DANIEL BOONE (1950, MONO). D: Reginald LeBorg. W: LeBorg & Clint Johnston. Cast: David BRUCE, Kristine MILLER, Mary Treen, Don Beddoe. 71m.

Pioneers and Indians; customary "B" clunker.

THE YOUNGER BROTHERS (1949, WB). D: Edwin L. Marin. W: Edna Anhalt & Morton Grant. Cast: WAYNE MORRIS, JANIS PAIGE, Bruce BENNETT, Robert HUTTON, James BROWN, Tom Tyler, Alan Hale, Jr., Geraldine Brooks, Fred Clark, Kansas Moehring, Monte Blue. 77m.

If the outlaw Younger brothers (Morris, Hutton, Bennett, Brown), who are on parole, can just stay out of trouble for two more weeks they'll be free. But naturally they are forced into a bank robbery plot by dastardly baddies. It's in Technicolor and can be rated fair-to-good as an oversized "B" effort.

YOUNG FURY (1964, PARA). D: Christian Nyby. W: Steve Fisher & A. C. Lyles. Cast: RORY CALHOUN, VIRGINIA MAYO, Richard ARLEN, William BENDIX, John AGAR, Lon Chaney, Jr., Linda Foster, Preston Pierce, Jody McCrea, Rex Bell, Jr., William Wellman, Jr., Reg Parton. 80m.

A weary middle-aged gunslinger (Calhoun) tames a wild gang of juvenile hellions, one of whom happens to be his son, and then uses them as his army against cutthroat bad guys who invade the town. Nostalgic low-budget picture blends familiar old-time faces with those of the sons of some well known Hollywood figures. An A. C. Lyles production.

THE YOUNG GUNS (1956, AA). D: Albert Band. W: Louis Garfinkle. Cast: RUSS

TAMBLYN, GLORIA TALBOTT, Scott MARLOWE, Walter COY, Myron Healey, Rayford Barnes, I. Stanford Jolley, Chubby Johnson. 84m.

Kid grows up determined to make a name for himself as a gunfighter. Routine hokum is yet another rip-off of *The Gunfighter*.

YOUNG GUNS OF TEXAS (1962, FOX). D: Maury Dexter. W: Henry Cross. Cast: JAMES MITCHUM, Alana LADD, Jody McCREA, Gary Conway, Chill Wills. 78m.

Confederates are chased through Texas at the end of the Civil War by Yankees and by Indians. Feeble actioner features the children of movie stars.

YOUNG JESSE JAMES (1960, FOX). D: William Claxton. W: Orville Hampton & Jerry Sackheim. Cast: RAY STRICKLYN, WILLARD PARKER, MERRY ANDERS, Robert DIX, Emile Meyer, Jacklyn O'Donnell. 73m.

Jesse (Stricklyn), Belle Starr (Anders) Quantrill, the Youngers and others are dragged into this fast but familiar rehash.

THE YOUNG LAND (1959, COL). D: Ted Tetzlaff. W: Norman S. Hall from a John Reese novel. Cast: PATRICK WAYNE, DAN O'HERLIHY, Yvonne CRAIG, Dennis Hopper, Cliff Ketcham. 89m.

Racial issues arise when a gringo in 1840s California goes on trial for murdering a Mexican. Mostly actionless yarn is not too bad. The star is the son of John Wayne.

ZACHARIAH (1971, CIN). D: George Englund. W: Joe Massot, Philip Austin, Peter Bergman, David Ossman & Philip Proctor. Cast: JOHN RUBINSTEIN, Pat QUINN, Dick Van Patten, Don Johnson, Elvin Jones, Country Joe and the Fish. 93m.

Probably the first "gay" Western in general release, this oddity concerns homosexual love between two gunslingers. It's trendy, anachronistic, self-consciously arty and uneven, not deserving of special tolerance or treatment; bad is bad.

ZANDY'S BRIDE (1974, WB). Also titled: FOR BETTER, FOR WORSE. DW: Jan Troell. Cast: GENE HACKMAN, LIV ULLMANN, Eileen HECKART, Susan TYRRELL, Sam BOTTOMS, Joe Santos. 116m.

In California in the 1870s an isolated pioneer rancher sends for a mail-order bride; for the next year the two unhappy people grow unhappier. Dull, pointless movie is another dreary look at the American frontier through the dour eyes of the Scandinavian creator of *The Emigrants* and *The New Land*.

APPENDIX A

DOCUMENTARIES

Gary Cooper's last professional appearance before the camera was as host-narrator of a 1961 one-hour television documentary, "The Real West." Cooper knew he was dying. He put great feeling into the program, which was a brief retelling of the history of the Old West illustrated by montages of tintypes, daguerreotypes, lithographs and photographs.

Of necessity it was superficial, although Cooper's presence made it moving; the program stressed the unromantic hardships of frontier life and, in its zeal to debunk romantic adventurous falsehoods, it failed to mention the fact that in many curious ways our legendary conception of the mythic West is not all that different from the truth.

I worked on cattle ranches when I was a boy. To be sure it is not an easy life and portions of it are dusty and boring. But the cowpuncher often aspires to see himself as men throughout history have seen "the man on horseback"—as a heroic leader (even if all he leads is livestock). That's why, at least up to and including the days when I was a kid, real cowpunchers genuinely enjoyed going to see Western movies at Saturday matinees. They didn't go there to ridicule the anachronisms or mistakes; they went to approve—because, of course, the Western glorified their own existence and enhanced their romantic sense of their own importance. I think Joel McCrea's biggest fans probably were real cattlemen.

(Incidentally, Anglo vaqueros for the past century or more have preferred to be called "cowpunchers," "cowboy" having been a term of disapprobation, dating back to medieval England and carrying over into colonial America—a cowboy was a cattle thief; one "punched" cattle with steel prods to get them aboard railroad trains.)

Cooper's elegiac program was one of surprisingly few documentaries about the West that have been filmed. There are some good wildlife films, from the Disney studios and others, and there have been some rodeo documentaries and such, but the Old West has not been explored very extensively by nonfiction filmmakers. One might think there would be room for, and interest in, filmic explorations of the famous wagon-train, cattle and outlaw trails, including those hundreds of well-preserved ghost towns that still occupy the Western landscape; but such movies remain to be made.

Occasionally as part of a catch-all series of programs the television filmmakers will produce a hoked-up reenactment (a "dramatization") of a celebrated episode of Western history. The shoot-out at the OK Corral has been reenacted several times in pseudodocumentary fashion by programs like *You Are There* and its successors; the Custer debacle, the Chivington massacre at Sand Creek, and the trek across Chilkoot Pass during the Klondike gold rush—I've seen those dramatized, although it has not been feasible to trace those ephemera for this book, since the emphasis herein is on theatrical films rather than television oddities. But significant episodes of Western history remain to be discussed on film and TV—like, for instance, the slaughter at Wounded Knee, or the comical Dodge City War (which involved such characters as the Masterson and Earp brothers, and gambler-gunman Luke Short), or the mapmaking trek of Cooke's "Mormon Battalion" across the Southwestern desert in 1849, or the unsavory massacre of Apaches at Camp Grant, Arizona, or the very large number and variety of Old West town movie sets that have been built, and are permanent fixtures, throughout the United States, or any of a thousand other fascinating topics.

What follows is a brief list of those few documentaries that have appeared and survived.

BEAVER VALLEY (1950, RKO). D: James Algar. W: Lawrence E. Watkins & Ted Sears.

Short (22m) film about the lives of Western wild animals is quite good.

BELLOTA (1969, IND). D: Harry Atwood. W: Philip Spalding.

Half-hour film is subtitled "A Story of Roundup" and provides a stirring glimpse of the modern cowboy's working life and the disappearing traditions of the vaquero. Winner of several awards, the superb film was produced by the University of Arizona and is accompanied by an outstanding soundtrack score by composer Robert Muczynski.

THE BEST OF WALT DISNEY'S TRUE-LIFE ADVENTURES (1975, BV). D: James Algar. W: Algar, Winston Hibler & Ted Sears.

Pastiche combines the highlights of thirteen Disney wildlife documentaries. Released on poor grainy film stock, it's disjointed and hurried.

BLACK RODEO (1972, CIN). D: Jeff Kanew.

Filmed at a Negro rodeo in New York in 1971, this features appearances by Muhammad Ali and Woody Strode (who also narrates). It gives interesting glimpses of black cowboy history.

BORN TO BUCK (1975, IND). D: Casey Tibbs. W: Moelle Carl.

Henry Fonda and Rex Allen narrate this film about a real 400-mile Montana trail drive, a cross-country trek to deliver several hundred wild horses to a new range. Informative, gentle, excellently photographed.

BROKEN TREATY AT BATTLE MOUNTAIN (1975, IND). D: Joel L. Freedman. W: Tom Schachtman.

Robert Redford narrates this one-hour documentary about efforts by a small Shoshone tribe in Nevada to maintain identity in the face of white encroachment. Polemical but moving.

CHANGING WEST—REFLECTIONS ON THE STILLWATER (1981, NBC). DW: Tom Spain.

One-hour TV segment of "NBC Reports" has correspondent Tom Brokaw documenting a six-month study of how small-ranch life in a small Montana community is being changed by encroachments by land developers, economic pressures and mining operations. Exploration of the shifting values of the valley's young people is poignant and distressing.

THE COWBOY (1954, LIP). D: Elmo Williams. W: Lorraine Williams.

Narrated by William Conrad, John Dehner, Larry Dobkin and Tex Ritter, this excellent film limns the lives of working cowboys.

THE GREAT AMERICAN COWBOY (1973, IND). D: Keith Merrill. W: Douglas Kent Hall.

Narrated by Joel McCrea, this rodeo film won the Academy Award as best documentary. It's a filmed study of the rivalry between Phil Lyne and Larry Mahan for the title "World's Champion Cowboy." Very exciting.

THE LAST WAGON (1971, IND). D: Harry Atwood. W: Katie Lee.

Half-hour film offers glimpses of the real

West that accompany authentic old-time American cowboy folk songs by folksinger Lee. Lee is known throughout the Southwest as a wonderful tough eccentric who has spent her life traveling back roads and collecting folk tales and songs. Atwood, whose films (compare *Bellota*) are financed by the University of Arizona, is an extraordinary camera artist and film editor. His movies are more than documentaries; they are works of art.

THE LEGEND OF LOBO (1962, BV). D: James Algar. W: Algar & Dwight Hauser from a book by Ernest Thompson Seton.

Rex Allen narrates this Disney picture about the life of a timber wolf from birth to maturity. Songs by Rex Allen and the Sons of the Pioneers.

THE LIVING DESERT (1953, BV). D: James Algar. W: Algar, Winston Hibler, Ted Sears & Jack Moffitt.

Possibly still the most famous of all wildlife documentaries, this 70m Disney film made a big hit as a theatrical feature and won an Oscar. It explores the wildlife of the Southwestern desert. Numerous photographers contributed footage.

NAVAJO (1952, IND). DW: Norman Foster.

Full-length documentary limns home life and sheepherding in the spectacular Canyon de Chelly country of Arizona's Window Rock Reservation. First rate.

TERRITORY OF OTHERS (1969, IND). D: Dick Robinson. W: Keith Culter.

Treacly but well photographed full-length film surveys the lives of the animals of the Arizona desert.

THE VANISHING PRAIRIE (1954, BV). D: James Algar. W: Algar, Winston Hibler & Ted Sears.

Companion piece to Disney's *The Living Desert*, this 75m film again won an Oscar. It limns wildlife cycles on the Great Plains. Stunning.

VANISHING WILDERNESS (1973, IND). DW: Arthur R. Dubs.

Rex Allen narrates this study of wild fauna in the Rockies. It's poorly organized but the footage is excellent.

APPENDIX B

JUVENILES

An uncharitable and unperceptive critic might suggest that nearly all the films in this book are juvenile. But those that have been relegated to this appendix are films that were made expressly for audiences of children, much as certain books are aimed by their publishers at specific young age groups.

Mostly these films are Western only in the sense that they use the American West as their setting; they seldom embody the qualities of character or theme that mark the Western as a genre. In most of them the problem is not a threat posed by land-grabbers or cattle rustlers or an opposing armed force; rather, it is whether or not the young protagonist's horse will win the big race, or how our zany comedians will survive still more pratfalls into watering troughs.

The films listed herein are Disney comedies, Abbott & Costello farces, child-and-pet movies (boy and his dog, girl and her horse) and even a Bowery Boys and a Henry entry. A few such films—those palatable to adults—have been listed in the main body of the guide.

Credits are listed as they were in the main section but cast lists and commentaries are abridged. Once again, films before 1950 are assumed to be in black-and-white, and those after 1950 in color, unless otherwise described.

ADVENTURES OF BULLWHIP GRIFFIN (1967, BV). D: James Nielson. W: Lowell S. Hawley from a Sid Fleischman novel. Cast: RODDY McDOWALL, SUZANNE PLESHETTE, KARL MALDEN, Harry GUARDINO, Hermione BADDELEY, Cecil Kellaway, Richard Haydn, Liam Redmond, Bryan Russell, Mike Mazurki, James Flavin, Arthur Hunnicutt, Dub Taylor, Pedro Gonzalez-Gonzalez. 110m.

Boston butler (McDowall) in picaresque slapstick adventures in gold rush days. Disney comedy is okay.

ADVENTURES OF GALLANT BESS (1948, EL). D: Lew Landers. W: Matthew Rapf. Cast: CAMERON MITCHELL, AUDREY LONG, Fuzzy Knight, James Millican. 73m.

Rodeo cowboy and wild filly, in color. Routine.

AND NOW MIGUEL (1966, UNIV). D: James Clark. W: Ted Sherdeman & Jane Klove from a Joseph Krumgold novel. Cast: Pat CARDI, Michael ANSARA, Guy STOCKWELL, Clu GULAGER, Pilar del Rey, Joe de Santis. 95m.

Boy on a Mexican sheep farm. Pleasant.

THE APPLE DUMPLING GANG (1975, BV). D: Norman Tokar. W: Don Tait from Jack Bickham's novel. Cast: BILL BIXBY, SUSAN CLARK, DON KNOTTS, TIM CONWAY, David WAYNE, Slim PICKENS, Harry MORGAN, John McGiver. 100m.

Orphans and oafish desperadoes. Disney comedy is goofy but fun.

THE APPLE DUMPLING GANG RIDES AGAIN (1979, BV). D: Vincent McEveety. W: Don Tait suggested by characters from Jack Bickham's novel. Cast: TIM CONWAY, DON KNOTTS, TIM MATHESON, Kenneth MARS, Elyssa DAVALOS, Jack ELAM, Harry MORGAN, Ruth BUZZI, Robert Pine. 88m.

Sequel lacks the spirit of the original. Flaccid.

THE BEARS AND I (1974, BV). D: Bernard McEveety. W: John Whedon from a Robert F. Leslie book. Cast: PATRICK WAYNE, ANDREW DUGGAN, CHIEF DAN GEORGE, Michael ANSARA, Robert Pine. 89m.

Young rancher protects Wyoming bears. Soundtrack song by John Denver. Treacly.

BOWERY BUCKAROOS (1947, MONO). D: William Beaudine. W: Tim Ryan & Edmond Seward. Cast: LEO GORCEY, HUNTZ HALL, Bobby JORDAN, Gabriel DELL, Billy BENEDICT. 66m.

Slapstick Bowery Boys comedy out West.

THE CASTAWAY COWBOY (1974, BV). D: Vincent McEveety. W: Don Tait, Richard Bluel & Hugh Benson. Cast: JAMES GARNER, VERA MILES, ROBERT CULP, Manu TUPOU, Gregory Sierra. 91m.

Disney companion-film to *One Little Indian* is genial old-style "B" oater with Culp as land-grabber trying to grab Miles's land until cowboy hero steps in. Set in Hawaii.

CHARLIE THE LONESOME COUGAR (1968, BV). D: Winston Hibler. W: Jack Speirs. Cast: Ron Brown, Bryan Russell, Linda Wallace. 75m.

Disney kiddie pic is narrated by Rex Allen, about a mountain cat.

CHATTERBOX (1942, REP). D: Joseph Santley. W: George C. Brown & Frank Gill. Cast: JOE E. BROWN, JUDY CANOVA, Rosemary LANE, Anne JEFFREYS, John Hubbard, Gus Schilling. 75m.

Dude-ranch slapstick.

COURAGE OF BLACK BEAUTY (1957, FOX). D: Harold Schuster. W: Steve Fisher from Anna Sewell's novel. Cast: JOHNNY CRAWFORD, Diane BREWSTER. 77m.

A boy, a girl and a horse.

GALLANT BESS (1946, MGM). D: Andrew Marton. W: Jeanne Bartlett & Martin Berkeley from a Marvin Park story. Cast: MARSHALL THOMPSON, George TOBIAS, Clem BEVANS, Jim DAVIS, Chill WILLS. 101m.

Sentimental tearjerker about a youth, his love for his horse, and the troubles brought by war. In color.

GLORY (1956, RKO). D: David Butler. W: Peter Milne from the Gene Markey story. Cast: MARGARET O'BRIEN, WALTER BRENNAN, Charlotte GREENWOOD, John LUPTON. 100m.

Girl and her horse.

GREEN GRASS OF WYOMING (1948, FOX). D: Louis King. W: Martin Berkeley from Mary O'Hara's novel. Cast: PEGGY CUMMINS, CHARLES COBURN, Robert ARTHUR, Burl IVES, Lloyd NOLAN, Preston FOSTER, Geraldine Wall. 1948.

Girl and her horse. In color.

GYPSY COLT (1954, MGM). D: Andrew Marton. W: Martin Berkeley from an Eric Knight novel. Cast: DONNA CORCORAN, WARD BOND, FRANCES DEE, Larry Keating. 72m.

Girl and her horse. It's a remake of *Lassie Come Home*, substituting horse for dog.

HENRY GOES TO ARIZONA (1939, MGM). D: Edwin Marin. W: Florence Ryerson & Milton Merlin from a W. C. Tuttle story. Cast: FRANK MORGAN, Virginia WEIDLER, Gordon JONES, Slim SUMMERVILLE, Porter Hall, Guy Kibbee, Douglas Fowley.

Tenderfoot comedy.

HOT LEAD AND COLD FEET (1978, BV). D: Robert Butler. W: Joe McEveety, Arthur Alsberg & Don Nelson. Cast: JIM DALE, DON KNOTTS, KAREN VALENTINE, Jack ELAM, Darren McGAVIN, Donald "Red" BARRY, John Williams, Gregg Palmer. 90m.

Uproarious Disney slapstick with Dale in three roles; filmed in Oregon.

INDIAN PAINT (1963, IND). DW: Norman Foster from a Glenn Balch novel. Cast: JOHNNY CRAWFORD, JAY SILVERHEELS, Robert CRAWFORD, Jr.

Indian boy and his wild colt.

KING OF THE GRIZZLIES (1970, BV). D: Ron Kelly. W: Jack Spiers from a book by Ernest Thompson Seton. Cast: John Yesno, Chris Wiggins, Hugh Webster, Jack Van Evers. 92m.

Indian and his pet bear.

KING OF THE WILD HORSES (1947, COL). D: George Archainbaud. W: Brenda

Weisberg & Ted Thomas. Cast: GAIL PAT-
RICK, PRESTON FOSTER, Billy SHEF-
FIELD, Guinn "Big Boy" WILLIAMS. 79m.

Boy and his horse.

KING OF THE WILD STALLIONS (1959,
AA). D: R. G. Springsteen. W: Ford Beebe.
Cast: GEORGE MONTGOMERY, DIANE
BREWSTER, Jerry HARTLEBEN, Edgar
BUCHANAN, Emile Meyer, Byron Foulger.
75m.

Widow and her young son, beset by baddies, are protected by a stranger and a wild
stallion.

MISSOURI TRAVELER (1958, BV). D:
Jerry Hopper. W: Norman S. Hall from a
John Burress novel. Cast: BRANDON De
WILDE, GARY MERRILL, Mary HOS-
FORD, Lee MARVIN, Paul FORD. 104m.

Boy and his horse.

MOONLIGHT AND CACTUS (1943,
UNIV). D: Edward Cline. W: Eugene
Conrad & Paul G. Smith. Cast: ANDREWS
SISTERS, LEO CARRILLO, Elyse
KNOX, Eddie Quillan, Minerva Urecal,
Shemp Howard. 60m.

Dude ranch comedy, with songs.

OLD YELLER (1957, BV). D: Robert Ste-
venson. W: Fred Gipson & William Tunberg
from Gipson's novel. Cast: FESS PARKER,
DOROTHY McGUIRE, TOMMY KIRK,
Kevin CORCORAN, Chuck CONNORS,
Jeff YORK, Beverly Washburn. 83m.

Boy and his dog. Fast and warm.

ONE LITTLE INDIAN (1973, BV). D: Ber-
nard McEveety. Cast: JAMES GARNER,
VERA MILES, PAT HINGLE, Jodie FOS-
TER, Clay O'BRIEN, Andrew PRINE. 90m.

Disney comedy is companion piece to
Castaway Cowboy with young Indian boy
(O'Brien) serving as guide to cavalry soldier
(Garner).

THE OUTLAW STALLION (1954, COL).
D: Fred F. Sears. W: David Lang. Cast:
PHILIP CAREY, Dorothy PATRICK, Billy
GRAY, Roy Roberts, Gordon Jones. 64m.

Boy and his horse versus horse thieves.

THE PAINTED HILLS (1951, MGM). D:
Harold Kress. W: True Boardman from an
Alexander Hull novel. Cast: LASSIE, PAUL
KELLY, Bruce COWLING, Gary Gray.
65m.

Lassie goes West: boy and his dog.

THE PALOMINO (1956, COL). D: Ray Na-
zarro. W: Tom Kilpatrick. Cast: JEROME
COURTLAND, Beverly TYLE, Joseph
CALLEIA, Roy Roberts, Gordon Jones,
Trevor Bardette. 72m.

Girl and her horse.

THE RED PONY (1948, REP). D: Lewis
Milestone. W: John Steinbeck from his
story. Cast: ROBERT MITCHUM,
MYRNA LOY, Peter MILES, Louis CAL-
HERN, Shepperd Strudwick, Margaret
Hamilton, Patty King, Robert "Beau"
Bridges. 89m.

Possibly the best of the boy-and-his-horse
movies.

THE RED STALLION (1947, EL). D: Lesley
Selander. W: Robert E. Kent & Crane Wil-
bur. Cast: ROBERT PAIGE, Jane DAR-
WELL, Noreen NASH, Ted DONALD-
SON. 82m.

Boy, horse and ranch; in color.

RED STALLION IN THE ROCKIES (1949,
EL). D: Ralph Murphy. W: Tom Reed
& Francis Rosenwald. Cast: ARTHUR
FRANZ, Jean HEATHER, Jim DAVIS,
Ray COLLINS, Leatrice Joy, Wallace Ford.
85m.

Wild horse hunt. Pretty good; in color.

THE RETURN OF OCTOBER (1948, COL).
D: Joseph H. Lewis. W: Melvin Frank, Nor-
man Panama, Connie Lee & Karen DeWolf.
Cast: GLENN FORD, TERRY MOORE,
James GLEASON. 98m.

"October" is a horse and Moore the teen-
age girl. Okay; in color.

RIDE 'EM COWBOY (1941, UNIV). D:
Arthur Lubin. W: Harold Shumate, John
Grant, True Boardman & Edmund L. Hart-
mann. Cast: BUD ABBOTT, LOU COS-
TELLO, ANNE GWYNNE, DICK
FORAN, Johnny Mack BROWN, Ella
FITZGERALD, Douglas Dumbrille. 86m.

Zany dude-ranch slapstick. Ella sings "A
Tisket, A Tasket."

RIO RITA (1941, MGM). D: S. Sylvan
Simon. W: Richard Connell, Gladys Leh-
man & John Grant, based on the Broadway
musical. Cast: BUD ABBOTT, LOU COS-
TELLO, KATHRYN GRAYSON, JOHN
CARROLL, Tom CONWAY, Barry NEL-
SON. 91m.

Dude-ranch comedy about unmasking
Nazi spies. Limp.

RUN, APPALOOSA, RUN (1966, BV). D:
Larry Lansburgh. W: Larry & Janet Lans-
burgh. Cast: JERRY GATLIN, Adele PA-
LACIOS, Wilbur Plaugher. 71m.

Indian girl rescues horse from mountain
lion. Rodeo scenes follow.

THE SAD HORSE (1959, FOX). D: James B.
Clark. W: Charles Hoffman from a Zoe
Akins novel. Cast: DAVID LADD, PA-
TRICE WYMORE, Chill WILLS, Rex
REASON. 78m.

Boy and his horse.

SAND (1949, FOX). D: Louis King. W: Martin Berkeley & Jerome Cady from Will James's novel. Cast: MARK STEVENS, COLEEN GRAY, RORY CALHOUN, Charlie GRAPEWIN, Jay SILVERHEELS, Iron Eyes CODY. 78m.

Cowboy and his horse. In color. Quite good.

SAVAGE SAM (1962, BV). D: Norman Tokar. W: Fred Gipson & William Tunberg from Gipson's novel. Cast: BRIAN KEITH, Marta KRISTEN, Tommy KIRK, Dewey MARTIN, Kevin CORCORAN, Jeff York, Slim Pickens, Royal Dano, Rodolfo Acosta, Rafael Campos. 103m.

Sequel to *Old Yeller*: boy and his dog, with surprisingly brutal cavalry-Indian conflicts.

SCANDALOUS JOHN (1971, BV). D: Robert Butler. W: Bill Walsh & Don DaGradi from a Richard Gardner novel. Cast: BRIAN KEITH, Michele CAREY, Rick LENZ, Harry MORGAN, Simon Oakland, Bill Williams, Alfonso Arau. 89m.

Unsuccessful Disney slapstick.

SKIPALONG ROSENBLOOM (1951, UA). D: Sam Newfield. W: Dean Reisner & Eddie Forman. Cast: SLAPSIE MAXIE ROSENBLOOM, MAX BAER, Hillary BROOKE, Jackie COOGAN, Fuzzy Knight. 65m.

Slapstick comedy, oafish but funny, starring two heavyweight boxers. In black-and-white.

SMITH! (1969, BV). D: Michael O'Herlihy. W: Louis Pelletier from a book by Paul St. Pierre. Cast: GLENN FORD, NANCY OLSON, Dean JAGGER, Keenan WYNN, Warren OATES, Chief Dan GEORGE, John Randolph, Christopher Shea. 112m.

Stalwart farmer helps persecuted Indian. Uneven Disney comedy.

SMOKY (1934, FOX). D: Eugene Forde. W: Stuart Anthony & Paul Perez from Will James's novel. Cast: VICTOR JORY, IRENE BENTLEY. 61m.

Low-budget dated horse pic. The remakes were better, but Jory was powerful as always.

SMOKY (1946, FOX). D: Louis King. W: Lillie Hayward, Dorothy Yost & Dwight Cummins from Will James's novel. Cast: FRED MacMURRAY, ANNE BAXTER, Bruce CABOT, Burl IVES, Roy Roberts. 87m.

Excellent movie about a man's love for the wild horse he traps and tames. In color. Burl Ives's acting debut (he'd sung in previous films).

SMOKY (1966, FOX). D: George Sherman. W: Harold Medford from the 1946 screenplay. Cast: FESS PARKER, DIANA HYLAND, KATY JURADO, Robert J. WILKE, Hoyt Axton, Chuck Roberson. 102m.

Fair, but not as good as the 1946 version.

SNOWFIRE (1958, AA). DW: Dorrell & Stuart McGowan. Cast: Don MEGOWAN, Molly McGOWAN, Claire Kelly. 81m.

Girl and wild stallion. Tearjerker.

WAY OUT WEST (1937, MGM). D: James V. Horne. W: Charles Rogers, James Parrott, Felix Adler & Jack Jevne. Cast: STAN LAUREL, OLIVER HARDY, Sharon LYNNE, Stanley Fields. 64m.

One of the best of the Laurel & Hardy feature comedies of the sound era.

THE WILD COUNTRY (1971, BV). D: Robert Totten. W: Calvin Clements, Jr., & Paul Savage from Ralph Moody's memoir *Little Britches*. Cast: STEVE FORREST, VERA MILES, RON HOWARD, Jack ELAM, Dub Taylor, Karl Swenson. 100m.

Kiddie rodeo.

WILD STALLION (1952, MONO). D: Lewis D. Collins. W: Daniel Ullman. Cast: BEN JOHNSON, MARTHA HYER, Hugh BEAUMONT, Edgar BUCHANAN, Don Haggerty, Hayden Rorke. 72m.

Man and his horse.

THE WISTFUL WIDOW OF WAGON GAP (1947, UNIV). D: Charles Barton. W: Robert Lees, Frederic I. Rinaldo, John Grant, D. D. Beauchamp & William Bowers. Cast: BUD ABBOTT, LOU COSTELLO, MARJORIE MAIN, Audrey YOUNG, George Cleveland, William Ching. 78m.

Lou Costello as sheriff? Abbott & Costello comedy is tame and routine despite high-powered writing staff.

WOLF DOG (1958, FOX). D: Sam Newfield. W: Louis Stevens. Cast: JIM DAVIS, Allison HAYES, Tony BROWN, Austin Willis. 61m.

Canadian film in black-and-white. Silly nonsense: a dog sorts out a range war.

APPENDIX C
THE MADE-FOR-TV
AND SPAGHETTI
WESTERNS

The main guide discusses some of the more important or more interesting television and European Westerns. The list that follows contains films in both categories that have been shown in the United States but I didn't make Herculean efforts to unearth every ephemeral oater ever filmed on the Spanish plains or sneaked onto a TV screen to fill two hours opposite the World Series.

The spaghetti and sauerkraut Westerns and the filmed-for-TV oaters are not quite the "B" films of the post-1950s era; that description more properly fits the individual episodes of Western television series from *Maverick* to *Gunsmoke* and beyond; some of them were quite good, but in terms of production and organization they were indeed "B" movies. As a rule the European and TV oaters are more like "Z" movies. Most of them are to the Western film what comic books are to the novel.

Made-for-television movies, as defined for inclusion here, are only those that were produced expressly for exhibition on American television. Certain films (e.g., Ferde Grofe's dreadful independent productions like *The Proud and the Damned*, or the big-budget *A Talent for Loving*) were produced as theatrical releases but judged unfit by distributors and seen only on television; properly those can't be called TV movies, and they are covered in the main guide.

Made-for-TV movies are filmed, usually, on very tight shooting schedules (sometimes as tight as twelve days) and limited budgets. Often they employ multiple cameras, which means a scene cannot be lit for a specific camera and therefore the photographic effects are flat, washed-out and uninteresting. In other cases more care is taken, more money spent, more interest invested by the participants; in those cases a good movie can emerge. Some of the better ones (e.g., *The Last Ride of the Dalton Gang*) are discussed in the main body of the guide; those relegated to this appendix are mainly routine ephemera.

The term "spaghetti Western," in its broad sense, can be taken to mean not only Italian-made films but any non-North American Westerns whether shot in Italy, Spain, Yugoslavia, Argentina or Australia. Typically a spaghetti oater may have been filmed from a script written by a French-Italian team of hack writers, directed by a German, produced by an Italian company and filmed in Spain with a cast of English, Italian, American, German, French and/or Spanish performers.

The German subdivision of this category, the "sauerkraut Western," is typified by movies derived from the Fenimore Cooperish pulp novels and stories of the German writer Karl May (who never saw the American West) and his disciples: the tales of Old Shatterhand, Winnetou, Old Surehand, Old Firehand, so forth. These are, if anything, even lower on the ladder of palatability than the spaghetti oaters, but they do point up Germany's continuing love affair with the Wild West. One of Germany's earliest silent-movie hits was Fritz Lang's *The Half Breed* (*Halbblut*) and the Western has always been a particularly favorite Teutonic entertainment. By the 1970s West Germany boasted numerous Western history societies, quick-draw clubs and Wild West saloons—much as it did in the cabaret days of the 1920s. In any case the German Westerns, with one or two exceptions (e.g., *Potato Fritz*—see the main guide for that one), exemplify "Z" moviemaking at its worst (or wurst).

The best known *auteur* in the non-American Western subgenre is, of course, Sergio Leone; his films (*A Fistful of Dollars*, *Once Upon a Time in the West*, so forth) are listed in the main guide. Those of his imitators are listed below.

American action stars who have fallen on hard times sometimes take jobs in cheap European films, including Westerns; their presence is felt to lend an air of authenticity to the spaghetti oaters, both in the international cinema market and on American television broadcasts. One finds the credits of these horse-operas peppered with such names as Joseph Cotten, Farley Granger, Van Heflin, John Ireland, Guy Madison, William Shatner and Eli Wallach. Charles Bronson and Clint Eastwood achieved superstardom in European movies—the latter in Leone's Westerns—and the top Italian Western star of the 1970s was Hollywood emigre Lee Van Cleef, who in previous years had brought sinister distinction to his bad-guy performances in many a genuine American Western, beginning with his forceful debut in *High Noon*.

The spaghetti oater comprises a subgenre quite distinct from the parent form. It may provide pop-culture scholars with material for interesting studies in comparative folklore and values. It exemplifies the distortions that can take place in the course of translation from one culture and language to another. The mythology of the spaghetti Western, such as it is, is a warped, simplistic, childlike variation on the original theme; its morality is twisted beyond recognition and the character of its hero—often a ruthless super-efficient killer with a cruel sense of humor—is a lunatic's cartoon caricature of the Gary Cooper image, combining the superhuman adolescence of our old "B" cowboys with the grubby flip cynicism of modern anti-heroics.

The plot formulas of the spaghetti form are even more rigid and simpleminded than those of our own Ken Maynard and Bob Steele programmers. In the spaghetti formula one finds endless repetitions of two favorite plots:

1) A settlement is beleaguered by a powerful bandit gang until the hero saves the community by butchering every last bad guy.

2) The hero is out to steal an enormous hoard of gold bullion, usually from the Mexican army, but first he has to wipe out several ferocious rivals for the treasure. The cinematic executions of these plots range from the mildly implausible to the wildly ludicrous. There is usually some sort of cavalry-versus-Indians, or Mexican Army-versus-patriotic revolutionaries, or Yanks-versus-Rebs action in the background; nearly always the film is set in the Civil War era or that of the Mexican Revolution, and geographically the spaghetti movies are set in an improbable border region with the action roving back and forth between the United States and Mexico. Most of the films' running times are taken up with double-crosses and gruelling pursuits across hills and deserts, with occasional digressions in saloons, whorehouses, farms and army posts. As for the characters' motivations, they are limited to three: revenge, greed and lechery.

There are variations on these patterns, of course, but seldom do they rise above the most rudimentary levels of plausibility or drama. With very few exceptions the spaghetti Westerns appear to be the crude fantasies of bloodthirsty children. Some of them are comedic, although their humor reflects the mentality of people who laugh when they pull the wings off butterflies. Even the mammoth and admittedly mesmerizing Leone film *Once Upon a Time in the West*, for all its epic size and lush production, assumes a childlike attitude toward violence and morality. For that is what these films are: not so much childish as *childlike* in their total and abysmal disregard for moral sensibilities.

There are no human characters in these films, only crude caricatures. There are no human problems, only melodramatic devices. There are no moral conflicts, only contrived cliches of revenge. There are no evidences of artistry (with a few exceptions), only slavish and unimaginative plagiarisms.

As a body of work the spaghetti films can be dismissed out of hand as the equivalents, or inferiors, of the overblown "B" melodramas of silent-film days.

I find it impossible to take these things seriously, and have sat through very few of them all the way from start to finish, although I've sampled many of them, up to the point where the very idea of looking at another one provoked bile. Therefore this listing is abbreviated, and really is more of a checklist than a guide.

Informational abbreviations include the following:

"**SI**" Spanish/Italian; the spaghetti Western.
"**TV**" made for U. S. television.
"**G**" German (sauerkraut) Western.
"**SP**" series pilot (in most cases the series never eventuated).

In most cases the European Western scripts are credited to five or more writers, many of whom—sensibly—use pen-names. I've eliminated such credits from most of the listings. Cast credits mostly are limited to one or two stars. (Some of them use phony names too. The Italian actor Giuliano Gemma has starred in spaghetti oaters under the names of George Hilton and Montgomery Wood. The actor who calls himself Terence Hill is actually Mario Girotti. The director who bills himself as Anthony Dawson is in fact Antonio Margheriti. Tony Musante, on the other hand, is an American actor.)

I've limited the use of bold typeface to titles only—mostly to save myself a bit of effort. Running times are not given because sources of such information are unreliable, and frankly I doubt anybody would notice much difference anyway if half an hour or so were eliminated from a spaghetti oater.

*

ACE HIGH (1969, PARA—SI). DW: Giuseppe Colizzi. With Eli Wallach, Brock Peters, Kevin McCarthy, Terence Hill, Bud Spencer. Revenge comedy.
ADIOS GRINGO (1965, IND—SI). D: George Finley. From a Harry Whittington novel. With Montgomery Wood, Evelyn Stewart.
ADIOS SABATA (1971, UA—SI). D: Frank Kramer. With Yul Brynner, Pedro Sanchez. Third in the Sabata series, with Brynner replacing Lee Van Cleef.
THE ADVENTURER OF TORTUGA (1964, IND—SI). With Guy Madison.

THE ADVENTURERS (1950, RANK). D: David MacDonald. W: Robert Westerby. With Jack Hawkins, Siobhan MacKenna, Dennis Price, Bernard Lee. Good British movie set in 1902 Transvaal, a sort of *Treasure of Sierra Madre*, quite stark in black-and-white.

AGUIRRE, THE WRATH OF GOD (1972, IND—G). DW: Werner Herzog. With Klaus Kinski, Helena Rojo. True story about conquistadors in Brazil is bloody but beautiful; excellent film.

ALIAS SMITH AND JONES (1971, UNIV—TV, SP). D: Gene Levitt. W: Glen A. Larson & Mathew Howard. With Peter Duel, Ben Murphy, Forrest Tucker, Earl Holliman, Susan Saint James, James Drury. Undisguised plagiarism of *Butch Cassidy and the Sundance Kid*; led to a TV series.

AMONG VULTURES (1964, IND—G). D: Alfred Vohrer. From a Karl May novel. With Stewart Granger, Lex Barker, Elke Sommer, Pierre Brice. Pulpy Shatterhand and Winnetou nonsense.

ANY GUN CAN PLAY (1967, IND—SI). D: Enzo Castellani. W: Enzo Girolami. With Gilbert Roland, Edd Byrnes, George Hilton, Pedro Sanchez.

APACHE FURY (1965, IND—SI). Also titled *Fury of the Apache*. With Frank Latimore. Spaghettimbecility.

APACHE GOLD (1965, IND—G). D: Harald Reinl. From a Karl May story. With Lex Barker, Pierre Brice. Winnetou nonsense.

THE APACHES' LAST BATTLE (1966, IND—G). D: Hugo Fregonese. From a Karl May story. With Lex Barker, Guy Madison, Pierre Brice, Daliah Lavi. Shatterhand nonsense, but Hollywood director.

BACKTRACK (1969, UNIV—TV). D: Earl Bellamy. W: Borden Chase. With James Drury, Ida Lupino, Fernando Lamas, Rhonda Fleming, Philip Carey, Doug McClure, Neville Brand. Culled from *The Virginian* TV series.

BAD MAN'S RIVER (1971, IND—SI). D: Gene Martin. W: Martin & Philip Yordan. With Lee Van Cleef, Gina Lollobrigida, James Mason. Lame comedy.

THE BANDIT (1953)—*See* CANGACIERO.

THE BANDITS (1967, IND). With Robert Conrad, Jan-Michael Vincent, Pedro Armendariz, Jr. Mexican-made movie was shown only on U.S. TV.

THE BANG-BANG KID (1967, IND—SI). D: Stanley Prager. W: Howard Berk. With Guy Madison, Tom Bosley. Foolish comedy about a robot.

BANJO HACKETT (1976, COL—TV, SP). D: Andrew V. McLaglen. W: Ken Trevey. With Don Meredith, Chuck Connors, Jennifer Warren, Dan O'Herlihy, Anne Francis, Slim Pickens, Jeff Corey, Ike Eisenmann, Gloria De Haven, Jan Murray, L. Q. Jones. Kiddie pablum; okay time-killer.

BARNEY (1977, COL). D: David Waddington. Australian kiddie movie.

BARQUERO (1970, UA—SI). D: Gordon Douglas. W: William Marks & George Schenk. With Lee Van Cleef, Forrest Tucker, Warren Oates, Mariette Hartley, Harry Lauter, Armando Silvestre. American runaway production filmed in Spain; drivel.

BEYOND THE LAW (1967, IND—SI). D: Giorgio Stegani. W: Stegani & Fernando di Leo. With Lee Van Cleef, Lionel Stander. Numbskull nonsense.

THE BIG GUNDOWN (1967, COL—SI). D: Sergio Sollima. With Lee Van Cleef, Tomas Milian, Fernando Sancho.

BILLY TWO HATS (1974, UA). D: Ted Kotcheff. W: Alan Sharp. With Gregory Peck, Sian Barbara Allen, Jack Warden, Desi Arnaz, Jr., David Huddleston. Runaway production, filmed in Israel. Routine.

BLACK NOON (1971, COL—TV). D: Bernard L. Kowalski. W: Andrew J. Fenady. With Roy Thinnes, Yvette Mimieux, Ray Milland, Henry Silva, Gloria Grahame, Hank Worden, Lyn Loring. Frontier minister versus occult forces. Creepy and effective.

BOOT HILL (1973, IND—SI). DW: Giuseppe Colizzi. With Terence Hill, Bud Spencer, Woody Strode, Victor Buono, Lionel Stander.

THE BOUNTY KILLER (1967, IND—SI). D: Eugenio Martin. With Tomas Milian. Not to be confused with the 1965 movie of the same title.

THE BOUNTY MAN (1972, IND—TV). D: John L. Moxey. W: Jim Byrnes. With Clint Walker, Richard Basehart, Margot Kidder, John Ericson, Arthur Hunnicutt, Gene Evans. Standard.

THE BRAVOS (1972, UNIV—TV). D: Ted Post. With George Peppard, Pernell Roberts, Belinda Montgomery, L. Q. Jones, Bo Svenson, Vincent Van Patten, Dana Elcar, Randolph Mantooth, George Murdock. Superior Indian-fighting oater.

BRIDGER (1976, UNIV—TV). D: David Lowell Rich. W: Merwin Gerard. With James Wainwright, Sally Field, Ben Murphy, John Anderson, William Windom, Dirk Blocker. Fake history; juvenile pablum.

THE BRUTE AND THE BEAST (1968, AIP—SI). D: Lucio Fulci. W: Fernando Di Leo. With Franco Nero, George Hilton. Yeccch.

BUFFALO BILL (1964, IND—G). D: Mario Costa. With Gordon Scott. Imbecilic.

A BULLET FOR SANDOVAL (1969, UNIV—SI). Also titled: THE DESPERATE MEN. D: Julio Buchs. With Ernest Borgnine, George Hilton.

THE CALL OF THE WILD (1976, IND—TV). D: Jerry Jameson. W: James Dickey from Jack London's novel. With John Beck, John McLiam, Billy "Green" Bush, Johnny Tillotson. Dickey's script can't save listless turgid turkey; the dog gives the best performance.

CANGACIERO (1953, IND). Also titled: THE BANDIT. DW: Lima Barreto. With Marisa Prado, Alberto Ruschel. Fair Brazilian bandit yarn; superb G. Migliori score is haunting.

CANNON FOR CORDOBA (1970, UA—SI). D: Paul Wendkos. W: Stephen Kandel. With George Peppard, Raf Vallone, Peter Duel, John Russell, Don Gordon, Nico Minardos. Better than some; Hollywood supervised.

CAPTAIN APACHE (1971, IND—SI). D: Alexander Singer. W: Philip Yordan & Milton Sperling from S. E. Whitman's novel. With Lee Van Cleef, Carroll Baker, Stuart Whitman. "B" movie with pretensions has good performances but terrible script.

CENTENNIAL (1979, UNIV—TV). D: Virgil Vogel. W: John Wilder from James A. Michener's novel. With David Janssen, Robert Conrad, Richard Chamberlain, Andy Griffith, Michael Ansara, Raymond Burr, Sally Kellerman, dozens of others. Twenty-six-hour miniseries; ambitious and fitfully good.

CHALLENGE TO THE MacKENNAS (1969, IND—SI). D: Leon Klimovsky. With John Ireland.

THE CHARGE OF THE 7TH CAVALRY (1964, IND—SI). D: Alfred DeMartino. W: Eduardo Manzanos. With Edmund Purdom. Lousy dubbing.

CHARLIE COBB: NICE NIGHT FOR A HANGING (1977, UNIV—TV, SP). D: Richard Michaels. W: Peter Fischer. With Clu Gulager, Pernell Roberts, Blair Brown, Chris Connelly, Stella Stevens. Private-eye comedy set in the Old West is mostly unfunny.

CHINO (1973, IND—SI). D: John Sturges. W: Clair Huffaker from Lee Hoffman's novel *The Valdez Horses*. With Charles Bronson, Vincent Van Patten, Jill Ireland. Slow oater about a half-breed horse rancher, filmed in Spain.

THE CHISOLMS (1979, CBS—TV). D: Mel Stuart. W: Evan Hunter from his novel. With Robert Preston, Rosemary Harris, Jimmy Van Patten, Ben Murphy. Six-hour miniseries. Flabby.

THE CHRISTMAS KID (1967, IND—SI). D: Sidney Pink. W: Jim Heneghan. With Jeffrey Hunter, Louis Hayward. Dull lawman meller was produced by Dino De Laurentiis.

COCKEYED COWBOYS OF CALICO COUNTY (1971, UNIV—TV). D: Tony Leader. W: Ranald MacDougall. With Dan Blocker, Nanette Fabray, Mickey Rooney, Jim Backus, Wally Cox, Jack Elam, Jack Cassidy, Noah Beery, Jr., Byron Foulger. Amiable but dull comedy.

COMPANEROS (1973, CIN—SI). D: Sergio Corbucci. With Jack Palance, Franco Nero, Tomas Milian, Fernando Rey. Routine spaghetti clunker has good Ennio Morricone score.

COTTER (1971, UNIV—TV). D: Paul Stanley. W: William D. Gordon. With Don Murray, Carol Lynley, Rip Torn, R. G. Armstrong, Lonny Chapman, Ford Rainey, Sherry Jackson. Slow rodeo meller.

THE CRUEL ONES (1966, IND—SI). D: Sergio Corbucci. With Joseph Cotten, Julian Mateos, Evelyn Stewart. Good Morricone score.

CUTTER'S TRAIL (1970, CBS—TV). With John Gavin, Marisa Pavan, Joseph Cotten, Beverly Garland. Fair chase meller.

THE DANGEROUS DAYS OF KIOWA JONES (1966, MGM—TV). D: Alex March. W: Frank Fenton & Robert Thompson from Clifton Adams's novel. With Robert Horton, Diane Baker, Sal Mineo, Nehemiah Persoff, Gary Merrill, Robert H. Harris. Not bad Plains-trek pioneering oater.

THE DAUGHTERS OF JOSHUA CABE (1972, UNIV—TV). D: Paul Wendkos. W: Paul Savage. With Buddy Ebsen, Jack Elam, Leslie Ann Warren, Don Stroud, Karen Valentine, Henry Jones, Leif Erickson, Ron Soble, Michael Anderson, Jr. First of several unamusing TV flicks.

THE DAUGHTERS OF JOSHUA CABE RETURN (1975, UNIV—TV). D: Paul Wendkos. W: Paul Savage. With Dan Dailey, Carl Betz. Dreary sequel.

DAVY CROCKETT AND THE RIVER PIRATES (1956, BV—TV). D: Norman Foster. W: Foster & Tom W. Blackburn. With Fess Barker, Buddy Ebsen, Jeff York. Culled from the TV series.

DAVY CROCKETT, KING OF THE WILD FRONTIER (1955, BV—TV). D: Norman Foster. W: Tom W. Blackburn. With Fess Parker, Buddy Ebsen, Hans Conreid. Three one-hour TV shows spliced into one 93-minute movie: episodic, ragged, juvenile. But the Disney series was extraordinarily popular and so was Blackburn's title song.

DAY OF ANGER (1970, NGP—SI). D: Tonino Velerii. From a novel by Ron Barker. With Lee Van Cleef, Giuliano Gemma. Trash.

DAY OF FIRE (1968, IND—SI). DW: Paolo Bianchini. With John Ireland. Very dull.

DAY OF THE LANDGRABBERS (1969)—*See* LAND RAIDERS.

DEAD OR ALIVE (1967)—*See* A MINUTE TO PRAY, A SECOND TO DIE.

DEAF SMITH AND JOHNNY EARS (1973, MGM—SI). D: Paulo Cavara. W: Harry Essex & Oscar Saul. With Anthony Quinn, Franco Nero, Pamela Tiffin. Quinn plays a deaf-mute. If he were also blind he would be a suitable audience for this movie.

DEATH RIDES A HORSE (1969, UA—SI). D: Giulio Petroni. W: Luciano Vicenzoni. With Lee Van Cleef, John Phillip Law, Anthony Dawson. Revenge nonsense, but there's a superior Morricone score.

THE DEERSLAYER (1979, NBC—TV). D: Dick Friedenberg. With Steve Forrest, Ned Romero. Clumsy.

THE DESPERADO TRAIL (1965, IND—G). D: Harald Reinl. W: Harald Peterson from a Karl May story. With Lex Parker, Pierre Brice. Sauerkrud.

THE DESPERATE MEN (1969)—*See* A BULLET FOR SANDOVAL.

THE DESPERATE MISSION (1969, FOX—TV). D: Earl Bellamy. W: Richard Collins & Jack Guss. With Ricardo Montalban, Earl Holliman, Slim Pickens, Ina Balin, Roosevelt Grier. Drivel about Joaquin Murieta.

DESPERATE WOMEN (1980, NBC—TV). D: Earl Bellamy. With Susan Saint James, Dan Haggerty, Ronee Blakley. Unfunny comedy.

THE DEVIL AND MISS SARAH (1971, UNIV—TV). D: Michael Caffey. W: Calvin Clements. With James Drury, Gene Barry, Janice Rule, Slim Pickens, Charles McGraw. Occult horror plus gunslinging.

THE DIRTY OUTLAWS (1971, IND—SI). Also titled: EL DESPERADO. D: Franco Rossetti. With Chip Corman. Ludicrous junk.

DJANGO (1965, IND—SI). D: Sergio Corbucci. With Franco Nero.

DJANGO'S GREAT RETURN (1977, IND—SI). DW: Enzo Castellari. With Franco Nero, Woody Strode. Umpteenth sequel is no improvement.

DJANGO SHOOTS FIRST (1966, IND—SI). D: Sergio Corbucci. With Glenn Saxon, Evelyn Stewart, Fernando Sancho. Trash.

DONNER PASS (1979, NBC—TV). D: James L. Conway. With Robert Fuller, Andrew Prine, John Anderson. Pseudohistory; pseudodrama.

DON'T TURN THE OTHER CHEEK (1975, IND—SI). D: Duccio Tessari. From a Lewis B. Patten novel. With Eli Wallach, Lynn Redgrave, Franco Nero. Attempts and fails to be funny.

DUEL AT RIO BRAVO (1965)—*See* GUNMEN OF THE RIO GRANDE.

DUEL AT THE RIO GRANDE (1964, IND—SI). D: Mario Caiano. With Sean Flynn, Gaby Andre. Zorro-type swashbuckler. Moronic.

DYNASTY (1976, IND—TV). D: Lee Phillips. W: Sidney Carroll from a story by James A. Michener. With Sarah Miles, Stacy Keach, Harris Yulin. Fairly good empire-building frontier soap opera, created by Michener expressly for TV. Not to be confused with the later modern-day "Dynasty" series that began in 1981.

EL DESPERADO (1971)—*See* THE DIRTY OUTLAWS.

EVERY MAN FOR HIMSELF (1968)—*See* THE RUTHLESS FOUR.

THE FAR-OUT WEST (1967, UNIV—TV). With Ann Sheridan. Episodes of the "Pistols 'n' Petticoats" TV series strung together.

FEMALE ARTILLERY (1973, UNIV—TV). With Dennis Weaver, Ida Lupino, Nina Foch, Albert Salmi. Allegedly a comedy.

THE FINAL SHOT (1970, IND—SI). D: Sergio Sollima. With Charles Bronson, Telly Savalas, Jill Ireland.

FIND A PLACE TO DIE (1972, IND—SI). D: Hugo Fregonese. W: Ralph Grave. With Jeffrey Hunter; made in 1967 before Hunter's death, but not released in the U. S. until five years later.

FINGER ON THE TRIGGER (1965, AA—SI). D: Sidney Pink. With Rory Calhoun. Especially moronic shoot-'em-up.

FLAMING FRONTIER (1965, WB—G). D: Alfred Vohrer. W: Fred Denger from a Karl May story. With Stewart Granger, Pierre Brice. Even kids wince at the stupidities of these Surehand-Winnetou turkeys.

FOUR RODE OUT (1969, IND—SI). D: John Peyser. With Pernell Roberts, Leslie Nielsen.

FRONTIER HELLCAT (1966, COL—G). D: Alfred Vohrer. From a Karl May story. With Stewart Granger, Elke Sommer, Pierre Brice.

FRONTIER RANGERS (1959, MGM—TV). D: Jacques Tourneur. W: Gerald Drayson Adams. With Keith Larsen, Angie Dickinson, Buddy Ebsen, Lisa Gaye. Woeful oater culled from a defunct series.

FURY OF THE APACHE (1965)—*See* APACHE FURY.

FURY RIVER (1959, MGM—TV). D: George Waggner & Jacques Tourneur. W: Gerald Drayson Adams. With Keith Larsen, Buddy Ebsen. Continuation of *Frontier Rangers*.

GERONIMO'S REVENGE (1960, BV—TV). D: James Neilson. With Tom Tryon, Darryl Hickman, Harry Carey, Jr. Fourth Disney movie culled from the "Tales of Texas John Slaughter" series. Apparently the producers didn't realize the title is a euphemism for borderland amoebic dysentery, but it describes the film.

GET MEAN (1976, IND—SI). D: Ferdinando Baldi. With Tony Anthony.

THE GODCHILD (1974, IND—TV). D: John Badham. With Jack Palance, Keith Carradine, Jack Warden. TV remake of *Three Godfathers*.

GOD'S GUN (1976, IND). DW: Frank Kramer. With Lee Van Cleef, Jack Palance. Matzo-ball Western, filmed in Israel; dreary.

GOD WAS ONCE IN THE WEST (1968, IND—SI). D: Mario Girolami. With Gilbert Roland. Brooding, artificial, sometimes interesting.

GOLDENROD (1977, IND—TV). D: Harvey Hart. W: Lionel Chetwynd from a novel by Herbert Harker. With Tony Lo Bianco, Donald Pleasence, Gloria Carlin. Rodeo soap opera is well written but miscast.

THE GUN AND THE NUN (1971, UNIV—TV). D: Jeffrey Hayden & Barry Shear. W: Stephen Kandel, B. W. Sandefur & John Thomas James. With Ben Murphy, Peter Duel, J. D. Cannon, Jane Wyatt, William Windom. Tedium culled from the "Alias Smith and Jones" series.

THE GUN AND THE PULPIT (1974, UNIV—TV). D: Daniel Petrie. With Marjoe Gortner, Slim Pickens, Pamela Sue Martin, David Huddleston, Karl Swenson, Estelle Parsons. Familiar oater: gunfighter masquerades as a preacher.

GUNFIGHT AT RED SANDS (1965, IND—SI). D: Richard Blasco. W: Albert Band & Alfredo Antonini. Cast: Richard Harrison. "Blasco" is a pseudonym of Albert Band's.

GUNMEN OF THE RIO GRANDE (1965, AA—SI). Also titled: DUEL AT RIO BRAVO. D: Tulio Demicheli. With Guy Madison as "Wyatt Earp."

GUNS OF DIABLO (1964, MGM—TV). D: Boris Sagal. W: Berne Giler from a Robert Lewis Taylor novel. With Charles Bronson, Susan Oliver, Kurt Russell, Douglas Fowley, Jan Merlin. Culled from the "Travels of Jamie McPheeters" series.

GUNS OF NEVADA (1967, IND—SI). With George Martin.

GUNS OF THE REVOLUTION (1972, IND). D: Arthur Lubin. With Ernest Borgnine. Mexican film; ruthless general versus the Church, 1917.

THE HANGED MAN (1974, UNIV—TV). D: Michael Caffey. With Steve Forrest, Cameron Mitchell, Will Geer, Dean Jagger, Rafael Campos, Sharon Acker, Barbara Luna. Odd, and not too terrible; well acted.

HARDCASE (1972, UNIV—TV). D: John L. Moxey. W: Sam Rolfe & Harold Jack Bloom. With Clint Walker, Stefanie Powers, Alex Karras, Pedro Armendariz, Jr. Pursuit in the desert, from the authors of *The Naked Spur*.

HATE FOR HATE (1967, IND—SI). D: Domenico Paolella. With John Ireland, Fernando Sancho.

THE HATFIELDS AND THE McCOYS (1974, IND—TV). DW: Clyde Ware. With Jack Palance, Steve Forrest, James Keach, Morgan Woodward, Karen Lamm, Robert Carradine. Hillbilly feud revisited; excellent performances by the two stars, but a slight movie.

THE HELLBENDERS (1968, EMB—SI). D: Sergio Corbucci. W: Albert Band. With Joseph Cotten, Julian Mateos. Brutal, tasteless, inept.

THE HELLIONS (1962, COL). D: Ken Annakin. From a teleplay by Harold Swanton. With Richard Todd, Anne Aubrey, Lionel Jeffries, James Booth. English movie sets *High Noon* to African drumbeats in the Transvaal, 1890s; terrible movie.

HITCHED (1972, UNIV—TV). D: Boris Sagal. With Tim Matheson, Sally Field, Neville Brand, John Anderson, Slim Pickens, Henry Jones, John Fiedler, Kathleen Freeman. Lamebrained romantic comedy.

HONDO AND THE APACHES (1967, MGM—TV). D: Lee Katzin. W: Andrew Fenady, based on James Edward Grant's screenplay for *Hondo* from Louis L'Amour's short story. With Robert Taylor, Gary Merrill, Michael Rennie, Kathie Browne, Noah Beery, Jr., Jim Davis, Michael Pate, John Smith. Remake of the John Wayne movie has Pate reprising his role as Apache leader Vittorio.

HONKY TONK (1974, MGM—TV). D: Burt Kennedy. W: Douglas Heyes based on the screenplay for the 1941 film. With Richard Crenna, Margot Kidder, Stella Stevens, John Dehner, Will Geer. Hapless remake.

HOW THE WEST WAS WON (1977, MGM—TV, SP). D: Burt Kennedy & Daniel Mann. W: Six credited writers. With James Arness, Eva Marie Saint, Jack Elam, Anthony Zerbe, Bruce Boxleitner. Six-hour marathon film is not so much a remake as a new version; sequel to a previous pilot, *The Macahans*.

THE INTRUDERS (1970, UNIV—TV). D: William Graham. With Don Murray, Anne Francis, John Saxon, Edmond O'Brien, Gene Evans. *High Noon*ish but dull.

INVASION OF JOHNSON COUNTY (1976, UNIV—TV). D: Jerry Jameson. W: Nicholas E. Baehr & Roy Huggins. With Bill Bixby, Bo Hopkins, John Hillerman, Billy "Green" Bush. Purports to be the true story of the Wyoming range war but turns out to be the usual drivel.

IT CAN BE DONE, AMIGO (1971, IND—SI). D: Maurizio Lucidi. W: Raphael Azcona. With Jack Palance, Bud Spencer. Comedy. Not funny.

JOHNNY HAMLET (1972, IND—SI). D: Enzo G. Castellani. W: Castellani, Tito Scardamaglia & Sergio Corbucci, "based on Shakespeare's *Hamlet*." With Gilbert Roland, Chip Gorman, Pedro Sanchez. Yeah, sure.

JOHNNY YUMA (1967, IND—SI). D: Romolo Guerrieri. With Mark Damon. No relation to the old Nick Adams "Rebel" TV series.

JORY (1973, EMB). D: Jorge Fons. W: Gerald Herman & Robert Irving from Milton R. Bass's novel. With Robby Benson, John Marley, B. J. Thomas, Brad Dexter. Routine revenger; made in Mexico.

A KILLING AT SUNDIAL (1967, IND—SI). With Melvyn Douglas, Angie Dickinson.

KILL THEM ALL AND COME BACK ALONE (1970, IND—SI). D: Enzo G. Castellani. With Chuck Connors, Frank Wolff. Seven Rebels set out to steal Yankee gold again. *Very* bad.

KUNG FU (1971, UNIV—TV, SP). With David Carradine, Barry Sullivan. Juvenile tripe; pilot for the popular series.

LAND RAIDERS (1969, COL—SI). Also titled: DAY OF THE LANDGRAB-BERS. D: Nathan Juran. With George Maharis, Telly Savalas, Arlene Dahl, Paul Picerni, Guy Rolfe. Cain and Abel out West. Idiotic.

THE LAST GUN (1964, IND—SI). With Cameron Mitchell, Frank Wolff. Retired gunslinger has to buckle on his guns again.

LAST OF THE RENEGADES (1964, IND—G). D: Harald Reinl. From a Karl May story. With Lex Barker, Pierre Brice, Anthony Steel. Another Shatterhand-Winnetou turkey.

LAST RIDE TO SANTA CRUZ (1964, IND—G). D: Harald Reinl. With Edmund Purdom, Mario Adorf. Revenge and pursuit clunker.

THE LAST TOMAHAWK (1965, IND—G). D: Harald Reinl. From a James Fenimore Cooper novel. With Anthony Steffens, Karin Dor. "Strongheart."

LAW OF THE LAND (1976, IND—TV, SP). D: Virgil Vogel. W: John Wiler & Sam Rolfe. With Jim Davis, Barbara Parkins, Andrew Prine, Darleen Carr. Not bad; pilot for "The Deputies" series.

THE LEGEND OF CUSTER (1967, FOX—TV, SP). D: Norman Foster. W: Four writers. With Wayne Maunder, Slim Pickens, Noah Beery, Jr., Michael Dante, Robert F. Simon, Mary Ann Mobley. Silly pilot for short-lived series was pictorially interesting and actionful.

LEGEND OF THE GOLDEN GUN (1979, NBC—TV). D: Alan J. Levy. With Hal Holbrook, Keir Dullea, Jeff Osterhage. Revenge-obsessed farmer versus Quantrill's raiders; not bad.

LITTLE HOUSE ON THE PRAIRIE (1974, NBC—TV, SP). D: Michael Landon. W: Blanche Hanalis from the novel by Laura Ingalls Wilder. With Michael Landon, Karen Grassle, Victor French. Listless treacly pilot for the successful series.

LOCK, STOCK AND BARREL (1971, UNIV—TV, SP). D: Jerry Thorpe. With Tim Matheson, Belinda Montgomery, Claude Akins. Newlyweds on the frontier. Dumb.

THE LONGEST HUNT (1968, IND—SI). D: Mario Amendola. With Keenan Wynn, Brian Kelly. Rancid.

A LONG RIDE FROM HELL (1970, CIN—SI). D: Alex Burks. W: Steve Reeves & Roberto Natale from a Gordon D. Shirreffs novel. With Steve Reeves, Wayde Preston.

THE MACAHANS (1976, MGM—TV, SP). D: Bernard McEveety. W: Jim Byrnes. With James Arness, Eva Marie Saint, Richard Kiley, Bruce Boxleitner. Pilot for a series based on *How the West Was Won*. Turgid.

MADRON (1971, IND). D: Jerry Hopper. W: Edward Chappel. With Richard Boone, Leslie Caron. Gunfighter helps stranded nun. Israeli film is overacted and tedious.

A MAN CALLED NOON (1973, NGP—SI). D: Peter Collinson. With Richard Crenna, Stephen Boyd, Farley Granger.

A MAN CALLED SLEDGE (1970, COL—SI). D: Vic Morrow. W: Morrow & Frank Kowalski. With James Garner, Dennis Weaver, John Marley, Wayde Preston, Claude Akins, Tony Young. Brainless formula Dino De Laurentiis production is well acted.

A MAN FROM OKLAHOMA (1964, IND—G). D: Harald Reinl. With Rich Horn. Sheriff versus wicked rancher. Trash.

THE MARK OF ZORRO (1974, UNIV—TV). D: Don McDougall. With Frank Langella, Ricardo Montalban, Gilbert Roland, Yvonne De Carlo, Robert Middleton. Soporific swordplay and derring-don't. Reprises the Alfred Newman score from the 1940 version. Buffs note that both Roland and Montalban appeared in another version, *Mark of the Renegade*.

MASSACRE AT FORT HOLMAN (1972, IND—SI). Also titled: A REASON TO LIVE, A REASON TO DIE. D: Tonino Valerii. With James Coburn, Telly Savalas, Bud Spencer. Bad spaghetti imitation of *The Dirty Dozen.*

MASSACRE AT FORT PERDITION (1965, IND—SI). D: Joseph E. Lacy. With Jerry Cobb, Marta May. Bottom of the barrel.

MASSACRE AT SAND CREEK (1956, COL—TV). With John Derek, Everett Sloane, Gene Evans. *Playhouse 90* drama has been shown occasionally as a feature film; it's a grim, conscientious depiction of the unhinged Colonel John Chivington (Sloane) and his terrible raid on helpless Cheyenne women, children and old people in their unsuspecting camp at Sand Creek, Colorado, during the Civil War—well-made pocket historical drama.

THE MERCENARY (1970, UA—SI). D: Sergio Corbucci. W: Luciano Vincenzoni. With Jack Palance, Franco Nero, Tony Musante. Atrociously dubbed.

MINNESOTA CLAY (1964, IND—SI). D: Sergio Corbucci. With Cameron Mitchell, Fernando Sancho. A gunfighter who's going blind cleans up a town. Puerile.

A MINUTE TO PRAY, A SECOND TO DIE (1967, CIN—SI). Also titled: DEAD OR ALIVE. D: Franco Giraldi. W: Albert Band. With Alex Cord, Arthur Kennedy, Robert Ryan. Sickening bloody mess, an insult to good actors.

MISSION OF DANGER (1959, MGM—TV). D: Jacques Tourneur & George Waggner. W: Gerald Drayson Adams. With Keith Larsen, Buddy Ebsen, Patrick MacNee. Flaccid fare culled from a defunct series.

THE MOST WANTED WOMAN (1976, FOX—TV). Also titled: WANTED: THE SUNDANCE WOMAN. D: Lee Philips. With Katharine Ross, Steve Forrest, Stella Stevens. Ross reprises her Etta Place role from *Butch Cassidy and the Sundance Kid* for this sequel, which is several notches better than another sequel, *Mrs. Sundance* (see below).

MR. HORN (1979, CBS—TV). D: Jack Starrett. W: William Goldman. With David Carradine, Richard Widmark, Karen Black. Story of Tom Horn began with a wonderful screenplay but it was ruined by bad casting, lacklustre directing and a constricted budget. Four-hour film is mediocre.

MRS. SUNDANCE (1974, FOX—TV). D: Marvin Chomsky. W: Christopher Knopf. With Elizabeth Montgomery, Robert Foxworth, L. Q. Jones, Arthur Hunnicutt, Robert Donner. Sequel to *Butch Cassidy and the Sundance Kid* follows Etta Place after the heroes' death. Jones and Hunnicutt are very good but the rest is banal TV junk. See also *The Most Wanted Woman*, above.

MUSTANG (1971, BV—TV). D: Roy Edward Disney. W: Calvin Clements, Jr. With Charles Baca; narrated by Ricardo Montalban. Disney pic about a wild stallion was shown on *The Wonderful World of Disney*; for kids.

MUTINY AT FORT SHARP (1965—SI). With Broderick Crawford.

MY NAME IS NOBODY (1974, UNIV—SI). D: Tonino Valerii. With Henry Fonda, Terence Hill. Moronic comedy; sad waste of Fonda.

NAVAJO JOE (1967, UA—SI). D: Sergio Corbucci. With Burt Reynolds, Fernando Rey. Indian (Reynolds) survives a massacre, goes after the white perpetrators one by one. Banal, tedious Dino De Laurentiis production.

NEVADA SMITH (1975, UNIV—TV, SP). With Cliff Potts, Lorne Greene, Adam West. Uses the name of the character but little else; not much relationship to the Harold Robbins character or the Steve McQueen movie. Insipid junk.

THE NEW DAUGHTERS OF JOSHUA CABE (1976, UNIV—TV). D: Bruce Bilson. W: Paul Savage from a story by Margaret Armen. With John McIntire, Jack Elam. Second sequel to *Daughters* and indistinguishable from the others; harmless hokum.

THE NEW MAVERICK (1979, ABC—TV, SP). D: Hy Averback. With James Garner, Jack Kelly, Charles Frank. About "Cousin Ben" (Frank); disappointing. Not related to the subsequent *Bret Maverick* series with Garner.

THE NIGHT RIDER (1979, ABC—TV). D: Hy Averback. W: Stephen J. Cannell. With David Selby, George Grizzard, Pernell Roberts, Harris Yulin. Dreadful Zorro rip-off.

NIGHT RIDERS (1963, IND). With Gaston Santos, Alma Aguirre. Mexican oater, lawman against bandits, humdrum.

THE NINE LIVES OF ELFEGO BACA (1959, BV—TV). D: Norman Foster. With Robert Loggia, James Dunn, Lynn Bari. About a lawyer-sheriff; patched together from segments of a Disney series.

ONE SILVER DOLLAR (1975, IND—SI). D: Giorgio Ferroni. W: George Finley. With Montgomery Wood, Evelyn Stewart. Gory and revolting.

ORDEAL (1973, FOX—TV). D: Lee H. Katzin. W: Francis Cockrell. With Arthur Hill, Diana Muldaur, James Stacy, Michael Ansara, MacDonald Carey. Scene-by-scene remake of *Inferno* is flaccid.

THE OREGON TRAIL (1976, UNIV—TV, SP). D: Boris Sagal. W: Michael Gleason. With Rod Taylor, Blair Brown, David Huddleston, Douglas Fowley, Lina Purl. Wagon train hokum.

OUTLAW OF RED RIVER (1966, IND). With George Montgomery. Mexican film about the outlaw who tries to go straight.

THE OVER THE HILL GANG (1969, UNIV—TV). D: Jean Yarbrough. W: James Brewer from a story by Leonard Goldberg. With Walter Brennan, Edgar Buchanan, Andy Devine, Jack Elam, Ricky Nelson, Gypsy Rose Lee, Pat O'Brien, Chill Wills, Edward Andrews, Myron Healey, Guy Wilkerson. Mediocre comedy features some old-timers having a lot of fun.

THE OVER THE HILL GANG RIDES AGAIN (1970, UNIV—TV). D: George McCowan. W: Richard Carr. With Walter Brennan, Fred Astaire, Edgar Buchanan, Andy Devine, Chill Wills, Paul Richards, Lana Wood. More of the same.

PANCHO VILLA (1971, IND—SI). With Telly Savalas, Clint Walker, Chuck Connors, Anne Francis, Walter Coy. Inept.

THE PATHFINDER AND THE MOHICAN (1956, IND—TV). With Jon Hart, Lon Chaney, Jr. Segments culled from the *Hawkeye* TV series.

PAYMENT IN BLOOD (1968, COL—SI). D: E. G. Rowland. With Guy Madison, Edd Byrnes. Civil War setting and senseless mayhem.

PETER LUNDY AND THE MEDICINE HAT STALLION (1977, UNIV -TV). D: Michael O'Herlihy. With Leif Garrett, Mitchell Ryan, John Anderson. Fair kiddie show is about a teen-age Pony Express rider.

PIONEER WOMAN (1973, UNIV—TV). D: Buzz Kulik. W: Suzanne Clauser. With Joanna Pettet, William Shatner, David Janssen. Young widow on the frontier; quickie is not too terrible—good cast.

PIRATES OF THE MISSISSIPPI (1964, IND—G). D: Harald Reinl. With Horst Frank, Brad Harris.

A PISTOL FOR RINGO (1966, IND—SI). DW: Duccio Tessari. With Montgomery Wood, Fernando Sancho. Nauseating.

A PLACE CALLED GLORY (1966, EMB -G). D: Ralph Gideon. W: Fernando Lamas and two others from a Karl May story. With Lex Barker, Pierre Brice. Shatterhand and Winnetou again.

POWDERKEG (1971, UNIV—TV, SP). DW: Douglas Heyes. With Rod Taylor, Dennis Cole, Fernando Lamas, John McIntire, Michael Ansara. Pilot for the *Bearcats* TV series. Fair.

PURSUIT ACROSS THE DESERT (1961, IND). With Pedro Armendariz. Mexican movie concerns a lawman forced to track an accused killer he knows to be innocent. Armendariz is very good.

THE QUEST (1976, COL—TV, SP). D: Lee H. Katzin. W: Tracy Keenan Wynn. With Kurt Russell, Tim Matheson, Brian Keith, Cameron Mitchell, Neville Brand, Will Hutchins, Keenan Wynn, John Anderson, Morgan Woodward, Terry Pinyerd. Pilot for a short-lived series is better than most, features marvelous performances by Keith and Mitchell, and imaginative sets.

RAMPAGE AT APACHE WELLS (1965, IND—G). D: Harold Phillips. From a Karl May story. With Stewart Granger, Pierre Brice. Shatterhand and Winnetou versus oil swindlers. Drivel.

RANSOM FOR ALICE (1977, IND—TV, SP). D: David Lowell Rich. W: Jim Byrnes. With Yvette Mimieux, Gil Gerard, Gene Barry, Harris Yulin. Fetching lady marshal story is anemic juvenile drivel.

RAW DEAL (1976, IND). D: Russell Hagg. W: Patrick Edgeworth. With Gerard Kennedy, Christopher Pate. Funny Australian oater; okay.

A REASON TO LIVE, A REASON TO DIE (1975)—*See* MASSACRE AT FORT HOLMAN.

THE REDMEN AND THE RENEGADES (1956, IND—TV). With John Hart, Lon Chaney, Jr., John Vernon. Culled from the *Hawkeye* series.

THE RED PONY (1972, UNIV—TV). From John Steinbeck's short novel. With Henry Fonda, Maureen O'Hara. Very good, but not quite as good as the Robert Mitchum version (see *Appendix "A": Juveniles*).

RED SUN (1971, NGP—SI). D: Terence Young. W: Laird Koenig, Denne Bart Petitclerc, William Roberts & Lawrence Roman. With Charles Bronson, Toshiro Mifune, Ursula Andress, Alain Delon, Capucine. Ludicrous, infantile, amoral but sometimes funny movie features gunslinger versus samurai swordsman. Fair Maurice Jarre score.

THE RELENTLESS FOUR (1965, UA—SI). D: Prijo Zeglio. With Adam West, Robert Hundar, Robert Camardial. Junk.

RETURN OF SABATA (1972, UA—SI). D: Frank Kramer. With Lee Van Cleef, Pedro Sanchez. Noisy, sickening bloodbath.

RIDE AND KILL (1965, IND—SI). With Alex Nicol. Amateurish trash.

RIDE A NORTHBOUND HORSE (1969, BV—TV). With Ben Johnson, Carroll O'Connor, Jack Elam, Andy Devine. Engaging minor Disney comedy.

THE RIDE TO HANGMAN'S TREE (1967, UNIV—TV). D: Al Rafkin. With Jack Lord, James Farentino. Terrible remake of *Black Bart*.

RINGO AND HIS GOLDEN PISTOL (1966, IND—SI). D: Sergio Corbucci. With Mark Damon. Atrociously dubbed.

ROBBERY UNDER ARMS (1958, IND). D: Jack Lee. With Peter Finch, Laurence Naismith, David McCallum. Australian outlaw romance.

ROYCE (1976, IND—TV). D: Andrew V. McLaglen. W: Jim Byrnes. With Robert Forster, Michael Parks, Marybeth Hurt. Imitation *Hondo* is not bad.

THE RUTHLESS FOUR (1968, IND—SI). Also titled: EVERY MAN FOR HIMSELF. D: Giorgio Capitani. W: Fernando Di Leo. With Van Heflin, Gilbert Roland, George Hilton, Klaus Kinski. Bad script, but well acted.

SABATA (1970, UA—SI). D: Frank Kramer. W: Renato Izzo & Gianfranco Parolini. With Lee Van Cleef. First in a series (Yul Brynner later replaced Van Cleef). Enough murders to fill Boot Hill.

SAM HILL (1971, UNIV—TV, SP). With Ernest Borgnine, Will Geer, Bruce Dern, J. D. Cannon. Dumb deputy detective. Dumb movie.

SAVAGE GRINGO (1965, IND—SI). With Ken Clark, Yvonne Bastien.

THE SAVAGE GUNS (1961, MGM—SI). D: Don Taylor. With Richard Basehart, Alex Nicol.

SCALPLOCK (1966, COL—TV, SP). D: James Goldstone. With Dale Robertson, Lloyd Bochner, Diana Hyland, John Anderson. Pilot for *The Iron Horse* series. Slow and dispirited.

THE SCAVENGERS (1971, IND—SI). D: R. L. Frost. With Jonathan Bliss. Carrion.

THE SEEKERS (1954, IND). D: Ken Annakin. With Jack Hawkins, Glynis Johns. Pioneers in New Zealand. Not bad.

SEVEN GUNS FOR THE MacGREGORS (1968, COL—SI). D: Frank Grafield. With Robert Wood, Fernando Sancho. The family that robs together.

THE SHADOW OF ZORRO (1962, IND—SI). D: Joaquin Marchent. With Frank Latimore. Same old zilch.

SHAGGY (1948, PARA). D: Robert Tansey. With Robert Shayne, Brenda Joyce. Spanish boy-and-his-dog yarn; fair.

SHATTERHAND (1967, IND—G). D: Hugo Fregonese. From a Karl May story. With Lex Barker, Guy Madison, Pierre Brice, Daliah Lavi. A German-Yugoslav-French-Italian production!

THE SHERIFF WAS A LADY (1964, COL—G). D: Hugo Fregonese. With Mamie Van Doren, Freddy Quinn, Rik Battaglia. Ridiculous garbage.

SHOOT (1964, IND—G). With Lex Barker, Rik Battaglia. Another Karl May oater. Rock bottom.

SHOOTOUT IN A ONE-DOG TOWN (1974, UNIV—TV). D: Burt Kennedy. W: Larry Cohen & Dick Nelson. With Richard Crenna, Richard Egan, Stefanie Powers, Jack Elam, Arthur O'Connell, Michael Ansara, Dub Taylor, Gene Evans. Some comedy, some melodrama; a cut below average, if possible—truly dreadful. Filmed in Mexico.

SIDEKICKS (1974, WB—TV, SP). D: Burt Kennedy. W: William Bowers, based on Richard Alan Simmons's characters. With Lou Gossett, Larry Hagman, Jack Elam, Blythe Danner, Harry Morgan, Gene Evans, Denver Pyle, Noah Beery, Jr., Dick Peabody, John Beck. Pilot based on *The Skin Game* movie is fatuous.

SIGN OF ZORRO (1960, BV—TV). D: Norman Foster & Lewis R. Foster. With Guy Williams, John Dehner, Lisa Gaye. Patchwork of several episodes of Disney's *Zorro* series.

THE SILENT GUN (1969, PARA—TV). D: Michael Caffey. With Lloyd Bridges, Ed Begley, Pernell Roberts, Susan Howard, Edd Byrnes, John Beck. Banal timekiller.

SIX GUN LAW (1961, BV—TV). D: Christian Nyby. W: Maurice Tombragel. With Robert Loggia, James Dunn, James Drury, Kenneth Tobey. Pallid whodunit was culled from segments of the Disney series *The Nine Lives of Elfego Baca.*

SOLDIERS OF PANCHO VILLA (1959, IND). With Pedro Armendariz, Dolores Del Rio, Maria Felix. Mexican film is worthwhile just to see the three great stars.

SOMETHING FOR A LONELY MAN (1968, UNIV—TV). D: Don Taylor. With Dan Blocker, Susan Clark, Warren Oates, John Dehner, Don Stroud. Blacksmith redeems himself after a foolish faux pas. Mildly charming.

SONNY AND JED (1973, IND—SI). D: Sergio Corbucci. With Telly Savalas, Susan George, Tomas Milian. Fair Morricone score.

SON OF A GUNFIGHTER (1964, MGM—SI). D: Paul Landres. W: Clarke Reynolds. With Russ Tamblyn, Fernando Rey. Terrible.

SON OF DJANGO (1967, IND—SI). D: Osvaldo Civirani. With Guy Madison, Fernando Sancho. Spaghettimbecility.

STAMPEDE AT BITTER CREEK (1961, BV—TV). D: Harry Keller. W: Damon P. Harmon. With Tom Tryon, Stephen McNally, Sidney Blackmer, Bill Williams, Harry Carey, Jr., Grant Williams. Disney episodes strung together from the *Tales of Texas John Slaughter* series.

THE STRANGER AND THE GUNFIGHTER (1976, COL—SI). D: Anthony Dawson. W: Barth J. Sussman. With Lee Van Cleef, Lo Lieh. Idiotic karate-Western comedy is asinine.

A STRANGER IN TOWN (1966, MGM—SI). D: Luigi Vanzi. With Tony Anthony, Frank Wolff. About as imaginative as the title.

THE STRANGER RETURNS (1967, MGM—SI). D: Luigi Vanzi. With Tony Anthony, Dan Vadis. As if the first one wasn't bad enough.

STRANGERS AT SUNRISE (1968, IND). D: Percival Rubens. W: Rubens & Lee Marcus. With George Montgomery, Deana Martin, Brian O'Shaughnessy. South African production is set in turn-of-the-century Transvaal—heroes are Boer farmers aided by an American adventurer against vicious British army deserters. Unsophisticated but well made.

SUNSCORCHED (1964, IND—G). With Mark Stevens, Marianne Koch, Mario Adorf. Outlaw clunker was made in Spain by Germans.

TAKE A HARD RIDE (1975, FOX—SI). D: Anthony Dawson. W: Eric Bercovici & Jerry Ludwig. With Lee Van Cleef, Jim Brown, Fred Williamson, Dana Andrews, Barry Sullivan, Jim Kelly, Catherine Spaak, Harry Carey, Jr., Robert Donner. Ersatz *The Professionals* with good cast and great stunts, filmed, of all places, in the Canary Islands.

TALES OF TEXAS JOHN SLAUGHTER (1959, BV—TV). D: Harry Keller. W: Damon P. Harmon. With Tom Tryon, Robert Middleton, Harry Carey, Jr. Disney oater strung together from episodes of the TV series has no resemblance to the real-life Arizona pioneer John Slaughter.

THE TALL WOMEN (1966, AA—SI). D: Sidney Pink. W: Jim Heneghan. With Anne Baxter, Maria Perschy. Seven women cross Indian country. Amateurish.

TENDERFOOT (1964, BV—TV). D: Byron Paul. With Brian Keith, Brandon De Wilde, James Whitmore, Richard Long. Three-part Disney TV comedy is innocuous.

TERROR AT BLACK FALLS (1968, IND—G). With House Peters, Jr., Sandra Knight, I. Stanford Jolley. Seeking revenge for his son's death and the loss of his right hand, a man holds several hostages and murders three of them before the sheriff hero moves in. Irredeemable trash.

THEY CALL ME HALLELUJAH (1972, IND—SI). D: Anthony Ascot. W: Tito Carpi. With George Hilton, Agata Flory, Robert Camardiel.

THEY CALL ME TRINITY (1972, EMB—SI). DW: E. B. Clucher. With Terence Hill, Farley Granger, Bud Spencer. Joseph E. Levine production is played for comedy but it's grubby, perverted, witless, asinine, unfunny and dreadfully dubbed.

THIRTY WINCHESTERS FOR EL DIABLO (1965, IND—SI). D: Frank G. Carrol. With Karl Mohrer, John Heston, Jose Torres. Dead bodies galore. The hero ("Heston") is about as believable in the saddle as Porky pig. Astonishingly imbecilic.

THIS IS THE WEST THAT WAS (1974, UNIV—TV). With Ben Murphy, Kim Darby, Jane Alexander, Matt Clark, Tony Franciosa, Bill McKinney, Stuart Margolin. Sort of comedy version of *The Plainsman* features Hickok, Calamity Jane and Buffalo Bill as youngsters. Inept.

THIS SAVAGE LAND (1969, UNIV—TV, SP). D: Vincent McEveety. W: Richard Fielder. With Barry Sullivan, George C. Scott, John Drew Barrymore, Brenda Scott, Andrew Prine, Glenn Corbett. Pilot for the series *The Road West* features George C. Scott, just prior to his emergence as a major film star, as a Quantrill-type raider leading a crazed gang of cutthroats and harassing a pioneer family in Wyoming. Routine TV flick is poorly written but well cast.

THREE BULLETS FOR A LONG GUN (1970, EMB—SI). D: Peter Henkel. W: Keith Watt & Beau Brummell. With Beau Brummell, Keith Watt. Usual hoard of stolen gold. Beau who?

THREE GUNS FOR TEXAS (1965, UNIV—TV). D: David Lowell Rich, Paul Stanley & Earl Bellamy. W: John Black. With Neville Brand, Philip Carey, Peter Brown, Martin Milner, Albert Salmi, Dub Taylor, Richard Devon. Patchwork of three one-hour episodes of the *Laredo* series is cut down to one 97-minute movie.

THE THREE SWORDS OF ZORRO (1964, IND—SI). With Guy Stockwell. Poor.

THUNDER AT THE BORDER (1966, COL—G). D: Alfred Vohrer. With Rod Cameron, Pierre Brice. Yet another Karl May yarn.

TODAY WE KILL, TOMORROW WE DIE (1972, CIN—SI). D: Tonino Servi. W: Dario Argento. With Bud Spencer, Wayde Preston. Yet another samurai-versus-sixgun asininity.

THE TORCH (1950, IND). D: Emilio Fernandez. With Pedro Armendariz, Paulette Goddard, Gilbert Roland. Mexican remake of *Enamorada* is the wheeze about the outlaw who's reformed by the love of an aristocratic girl. But the stars are very good.

A TOWN CALLED HELL (1971, IND—SI). D: Robert Parrish. W: Richard Aubrey. With Robert Shaw, Telly Savalas, Martin Landau, Stella Stevens, Fernando Rey, Al Lettieri. Sadism and revolution—set in Mexico, filmed in Spain.

THE TRACKERS (1971, PARA—TV). D: Earl Bellamy. W: Gerard Gaiser. With Sammy Davis, Jr., Ernest Borgnine, Jim Davis, Julie Adams. Sassy, black trail-scout aids bigoted rancher. Predictable.

THE TRAMPLERS (1966, EMB—SI). DW: Albert Band from a Will Cook novel. With Joseph Cotten, James Mitchum, Gordon Scott, Franco Nero. A bit less nauseating than most.

THE TREASURE OF SILVER LAKE (1962, COL—G). D: Harald Reinl. W: Harald G. Petersen. With Lex Barker, Rik Battaglia. Juvenile junk.

TRINITY IS STILL MY NAME (1971, IND—SI). DW: E. B. Clucher. With Terence Hill, Bud Spencer, Harry Carey, Jr. Comedy, of sorts, is a sequel to *They Call Me Trinity*.

TWO VIOLENT MEN (1964, IND—SI). With Alan Scott, George Martin.

THE UGLY ONES (1968, UA—SI). D: Eugenio Martin. From a novel by Marvin H. Albert. With Richard Wyler, Tomas Milian. One-man massacre yarn is mind-bogglingly dreadful.

UP THE MacGREGORS! (1968, COL—SI). D: Frank Grafield. With David Bailey, Jorge Rigaud. Up whose?

VENDETTA (1976, IND). D: Joe Manduke. With Jim Brown, Lee Van Cleef, John Marley, Matt Clark. Israeli companion piece to *God's Gun*.

THE VENGEANCE OF PANCHO VILLA (1967, IND—SI). D: Joe Lacy. W: M. Sebares. With John Ericson, James Philbrook, Gustavo Rojo. Dud.

VIVA MARIA (1965, UA). D: Louis Malle. With Brigitte Bardot, Jeanne Moreau, George Hamilton. Action comedy, filmed in Mexico; French production; foolish and dreadful.

VIVA REVOLUTION (1956, IND). With Pedro Armendariz, Maria Felix. Fine Mexican film about the Pancho Villa revolution is a romanticizing whitewash but very entertaining.

WANTED: THE SUNDANCE WOMAN (1976)—*See* THE MOST WANTED WOMAN.

WHITE COMANCHE (1967, IND—SI). D: Gilbert Lee Kay. W: Frank Gruber & Robert Holt. With William Shatner, Joseph Cotten. Shatner as half-breed twins makes a fool of himself in both roles; Cotten is wasted as an old lawman with nerves of rust. Preposterous.

WILD STAMPEDE (1962, IND). With Luis Aguilar, Christiane Martel. Mexican movie about revolution is feebly plotted.

THE WILD WILD WEST REVISITED (1980, CBS—TV). D: Burt Kennedy. With Robert Conrad, Ross Martin, Paul Williams. Campy reprise of an old series was released shortly before Ross Martin's death.

WILD WOMEN (1970, UNIV—TV). D: Don Taylor. With Hugh O'Brian, Anne Francis, Marilyn Maxwell, Marie Windsor, Robert F. Simon. Astonishingly stupid oater.

WINCHESTER FOR HIRE (1967, IND—SI). D: E. G. Rowland. With Guy Madison, Edd Byrnes, Louise Barrett. Brutal.

THE YOUNG COUNTRY (1970, UNIV—TV). With Walter Brennan, Joan Hackett, Roger Davis, Peter Duel, Wally Cox. Unfunny comedy.

YOUNG PIONEERS (1976, IND—TV, SP). D: Michael O'Herlihy. W: Blanche Hanalis from a novel by Rose Wilder Lane. With Roger Kern, Linda Purl. Young marrieds head west; from the writers and producers of *Little House on the Prairie*. Sugary inane juvenile leaves no cliche unturned. Typically, it is set in Dakota and was filmed in Arizona.

YOUNG PIONEERS' CHRISTMAS (1976, IND—TV, SP). Same credits as above. Sequel is no improvement.

YUMA (1971, UNIV—TV). D: Ted Post. With Clint Walker, Barry Sullivan, Edgar Buchanan, Kathryn Hays, Mark Richman, Morgan Woodward. Somebody's out to get the new marshal. Limp.

ZORRO (1961, IND—SI). D: Joaquin Marchent. With Frank Latimore. Same old yarn, badly dubbed.

ZORRO (1975, AA—SI). D: Duccio Tessari. W: Giorgio Arlorio & Richard Walter. With Alain Delon, Stanley Baker. These guys don't even have the decency to credit Johnston McCulley's novel as the source of their wild yarn which changes, but does not improve, the original.

ZORRO THE AVENGER (1963, IND—SI). D: Joaquin Marchent. With Frank Latimore, Maria Luz Galicia, Charles Korvin. Spaghettidiocy.

SELECTIVE BIBLIOGRAPHY

Many books and essays about Westerns are in French. Many of those published in English have been influenced by the French ones.

A great deal of critical writing about films seems to be done by students who are eager to find campy excellences in even the most woeful clunkers. There is only a limited body of work that displays a sensible recognition of the difference, in artistic terms, between, let us say, films directed by Samuel Fuller and films directed by Anthony Mann (the former being warmed-over "B" pictures, the latter being solidly crafted "A" movies that are sometimes of significant dramatic value). It's fine for fanatical programmer buffs to extol the genius of an Edgar G. Ulmer or a Joseph H. Lewis; but when one reads those paeans one has the suspicion that their authors may have suffered an imbalance of judgment and a loss of sensibility: Ulmer may well have been the finest "B" director who ever lived but, judged on the work he turned out, he didn't create anything that is going to be of significance to the arts of the future, and at the same time his films are of limited value as entertainments because they were so shabbily produced and poorly written. It is simply pointless to compare his work with, say, John Ford's; there is no rational basis for real comparison: it's like trying to compare a penny dreadful with a good novel.

The references listed in this bibliography range widely in seriousness, sensibility, usefulness and readability. Where it seems cogent I have appended a few descriptive and perhaps opinionated remarks. Personally I think the best popular book on the subject, both for its information and for its good writing, remains Fenin and Everson's *The Western*. Other works may be better organized or filled with more facts, but none has been written with quite such an enthusiastic and encompassing view of the subject. I tend to quarrel with some of the authors' opinions but those quarrels are what keep criticism alive; their book is excellent.

There is such a vast and ever-growing abundance of short essays about Westerns in periodicals of all kinds that it would be impossible to list them here; this brief compendium is limited to books, and the books are limited with a few exceptions to those that deal primarily or at least partially with "A" Western films. One or two representative books about "B" oaters are included but those listings hardly scratch the surface.

*

AGEL, Henri, ed. **Le Western**. Paris, 1961; revised by Jean Gili, Paris, 1969. One of the pioneer French critical works, this is comprehensive but critically overblown.

BARBOUR, Alan G. **The Thrill of it All**. New York, 1971. Pictorial book about "B" Westerns emphasizes the series programmers of the 1930s and 1940s.

BAZIN, Andre. **What is Cinema?** Berkeley, Calif., 1971. Volume 2 contains translations of three of French critic Bazin's essays on Westerns; very serious, highblown and rather funny if you don't happen to agree with his pompous, preposterous conclusions.

BELLOUR, Raymond, ed. **Le Western**. Paris, 1966; revised, Paris, 1968. French reference guide lists directors, actors, historical sources and the like—similar to, but more scholarly than, Eyles's book (see below).

BOGDANOVICH, Peter. **John Ford**. New York, 1968. Extended monograph by the young critic-director-disciple is good reading.

CAWELTI, John G. **The Six-Gun Mystique**. Bowling Green, Ohio, 1971. Discusses key directors and films, and analyzes the Western myth. Scholarly, thoughtful.

CLAPHAM, Walter C. **Western Movies**. London, 1974. Cheap quickie pictorial book rehashes subject matter of many others, adds nothing and is filled with inaccuracies, but has fairly good pictures.

CORNEAU, Ernest N. **The Hall of Fame of Western Film Stars**. North Quincy, Mass., 1969. This one takes an amateur film buff's approach, lists some 150 Western movie actors (mostly "B" stars) together with their (incomplete) film credits.

EVERSON, William K. **A Pictorial History of the Western Film**. New York, 1969. This illustrated coffee-table book reprises the material in Fenin and Everson's *The Western*, adding numerous photographs in color. Good reading, excellent photos.

EYLES, Allen. **The Western**. New York, 1967; revised, 1975. Reference guide covers some 2,500 films (most of them "B" movies) and is not nearly as complete as it pretends to be; it cross-indexes the films to names, but credits are limited to a few hundred names, and inaccuracies abound. The book contains no story summaries or critiques; it's strictly for the fact buff, no good for browsing and of limited usefulness on account of its lack of comprehensiveness (a fault dictated largely by the problem of publication costs: a comprehensive book would have been prohibitively large and expensive).

FENIN, George N., and Everson, William K. **The Western**. New York, 1962; revised, 1973. Still the best survey in English, this has plentiful superb black-and-white photos and a fine thoughtful text. But it emphasizes William S. Hart too much and takes "B" movies terribly seriously. It's organized chronologically, a historical summary, and only selected films are discussed.

FORD, Charles. **Histoire du Western**. Paris, 1964. Another *auteuriste* polemic in French, this has very little to add to earlier similar works.

FRAYLING, Christopher. **Spaghetti Westerns: Cowboys and Europeans from Karl May to Sergio Leone**. New York, 1981. Badly written dense tome tells us much more than we want to know about the subject, emphasizing—inevitably—the films of Leone.

FRENCH, Philip. **Westerns**. New York, 1974. Scholarly personal-statement monograph treats the Western from a sociopolitical bias; it's interesting but overblown and lacking in perspective, although it's refreshingly sharp-witted.

FRIAR, Ralph, and Friar, Natasha. **The Only Good Indian: The Hollywood Gospel**. New York, 1972. This chronicles the history of Hollywood's maltreatment of Indians; it's a one-sided polemic, quite strident, but interesting and well illustrated, although the authors have not done their homework adequately.

HORWITZ, James. **They Went Thataway**. New York, 1976. Off-trail memoir recounts the author's tracking down and interviewing of numerous old-time "B" stars. It's nostalgic, charmingly written and sometimes quite moving. Peppered with useful and intelligent commentaries on the movies, it emphasizes the 1930–1950 programmers.

KITSES, Jim. **Horizons West**. Bloomington, Indiana, 1969. Monograph appraises the Western films of directors Boetticher, Mann and Peckinpah, with Fuller thrown in for good measure. The structural analysis of the Western is interesting but the rest is rampantly *auteuriste* and therefore I can't buy it.

LENIHAN, John H. **Showdown: Confronting Modern America in the Western Film**. Urbana, Ill., 1980. Sociological analysis studies the way Westerns have reflected changing American attitudes. Interesting but pedantic. It has an excellent comprehensive bibliography.

MANCHEL, Frank. **Cameras West**. New York, 1971. Brief history of Westerns is readable but it's been done better elsewhere.

McCLURE, Arthur F., and Jones, Ken D. **Heroes, Heavies and Sagebrush**. New York, 1972. Illustrated compilation of biographical sketches of "B" movie actors is of interest mainly to programmer fans.

MEYER, William R. **The Making of the Great Westerns**. New Rochelle, N. Y., 1979. Discusses the actual filming of thirty Western movies, chronologically arranged from *Tumbleweeds* to *McCabe and Mrs. Miller*. It's rather unsophisticated—a fan's approach, rather than a critic's.

NACHBAR, Jack, ed. **Focus on The Western**. New York, 1974. Collection of essays is extremely useful; there are fifteen articles, some of which are fascinating, but many of which display the common critical fallacy of attributing to filmmakers intentions they probably never had, or even thought of.

PARKINSON, Michael, and Jeavons, Clyde. **A Pictorial History of Westerns**. New York, 1972. This covers the same ground as Fenin and Everson, and does not cover it nearly so well, but some of the many illustrations are excellent. Both authors are English movie buffs who seem to have seen a lot of movies without understanding some of them.

PARRISH, James Robert, and Pitts, Michael R. **The Great Western Pictures**. Metuchen, N. J., 1976. Lists several hundred movies alphabetically with filmographies, summaries and quotes from contemporaneous reviews. The basis for selection seems murky and quirky, and it's a bit amateurish with its overenthusiasms for mediocre films. Contains numerous black-and-white stills.

PILKINGTON, William T., and Graham, Don, eds. **Western Movies**. Albuquerque, 1979. Catch-all scholarly compendium reprints a dozen essays, some of them interesting, others simply pedantic and pretentious. The book tries to represent all critical schools of thought, and is representative, but for obvious reasons it necessarily lacks focus.

PLACE, J. A. **The Western Films of John Ford**. New York, 1973. Useful, interesting study includes filmographies, plot summaries and illustrations.

RAINEY, Buck. **Saddle Aces of the Cinema**. New York, 1979. A fan's notes on the careers of a miscellany of actors, mostly "B" stars, are accompanied by filmographies and black-and-white photographs from the author's collection. Nostalgic and minor.

RIEUPEYROUT, Jean-Louis. **Le Western**. Paris, 1953; revised and expanded in 1971 as **La Grande Aventure du Western**. This long monograph began the French trend toward overblown *auteuriste* appraisals of Hollywood horse-operas.

ROTHEL, David. **The Singing Cowboys**. New York, 1978. Pictorial compendium is limited to the careers of seven stars (Gene Autry, Tex Ritter, Roy Rogers, Eddie Dean, Jimmy Wakely, Monte Hale, Rex Allen), with an additional chapter that briefly rounds up such warbling cowhands as Dick Foran, Fred Scott, Smith Ballew, Jack Randall, Tex

Fletcher, Dusty King, George Houston, James Newill and Bob Baker. It's mostly for wistful Saturday matinee fans.

SILVER, Charles. **The Western Film**. New York, 1976. Very good, although short and rigid-minded, survey of myth Westerns; well illustrated.

TUSKA, Jon. **The Filming of the West**. New York, 1976. This informal but huge book tries to cover the entire gamut of Western movie history by tying its narrative to an analysis of 100 key movies. Mainly it emphasizes "B" films—Mix, Maynard and their ilk. Disjointed, it suffers from an apparent lack of critical standpoint, but it contains a great deal of fascinating information about the individual films.

WARMAN, Eric, and Vallance, Tom. **Westerns**. London, 1964. Disorganized survey covers ground better mapped by Fenin and Everson.

WRIGHT, Will. **Sixguns and Society: A Structural Study of the Western**. Berkeley, Calif., 1975. Pompous, scholarly study manages, as do many pedantic essays, to discuss oaters as if they were abstractions to be dissected in scientific fashion.

See also the various books in *The Films of . . .* series, published in New York during the 1960s and afterward, covering the cinematic careers of such actors as Gary Cooper, Kirk Douglas, Errol Flynn, Clark Gable, William Holden, Anthony Quinn, James Stewart and John Wayne, and the various books in the *Focus on . . .* and *The Hollywood Professionals* series on the work of such directors as Raoul Walsh, Henry King, Henry Hathaway, Howard Hawks and others.